PSYCHOLOGY AND EDUCATION OF THE GIFTED

Third Edition

Edited by Walter B. Barbe

and Joseph S. Renzulli

115892

Irvington Publishers, Inc., New York

TO
Marilyn W. Barbe
Mary Jo Renzulli

Library of Congress Cataloging in Publication Data

Barbe, Walter Burke, 1926-   ed.
  Psychology and education of the gifted.

    Includes bibliographies and index.
    1. Gifted children--Education--Addresses,
essays, lectures. 2. Gifted children--Psychology
--Addresses, essays, lectures. I. Renzulli,
Joseph S. II. Title.
LC3993.B36   1980   371.95   80-11174
ISBN 0-8290-0234-0

Printed in the United States of America

CONTENTS

iii

Identification of the Gifted and Creative

Part III.
DEVELOPING AND ENCOURAGING GIFTEDNESS

Program Development

Instructional Approaches

ACKNOWLEDGEMENTS

*T*he editors would like to express their appreciation to the many persons who have helped to make this book possible. Our sincere thanks are extended to the authors and publishers of the articles for permission to reprint their material in this book. The field of education in gifted and talented has expanded and matured bacause of the tireless efforts of the researchers and writers who have contributed to the richness of the content in this area of special education. Volumes such as this one would not be possible if these dedicated persons did not make a major commitment to the development of new ideas and concepts.

The editors express their sincere appreciation to the many persons who aided us in the preparation of the manuscript. Elaine Talada was responsible for serving as the genereal manager of all aspects of locating articles and obtaining permissions from authors and publishers. Marcia Balnanosis and Ann Lesser assumed the responsibility for final review and editing of the manuscript. Sally Casinghino prepared the manuscript and helped to organize numerous activities related to the preparation of the final form. Finally we would like to thank our colleagues Jim Cross, Jim Delisle, Jean Gubbins, Sally Reis, and Linda Smith for numerous sugges-tions related to the selection of articles and recommendations that have helped this volume to reflect a variety of topics and points of view.

W.B.B.
J.S.R.

Preface

*D*uring the past decade our nation has experienced a remarkably renewed interest in the psychology and education of gifted and talented children. This interest has been reflected in many ways. First and foremost, there has been a dramatic increase in the number of programs and variety of special services offered to gifted and talented children at the local school level. Increased financial support from both the federal government and numerous state governments has helped to stimulate these increases in programs; however, many school districts are forging ahead with programs through the use of local financial resources. Another area in which the growing interest in gifted and talented education has been readily apparent is in the increased numbers of college and university training programs. Numerous workshops, institutes, and short-term training programs have also been developed by various institutions and agencies throughout the nation.

The growing areas of interest listed above have been stimulated by and in turn are stimulating an ever increasing body of research and professional literature related to all aspects of programming for the gifted and talented. At least five professional journals on the gifted and creative are now available and many of the journals that deal with general education issues are now devoting more and more space to the area of the gifted and talented.

With such a vast amount of material to draw upon, the task of selecting material to include in this third edition of *Psychology and Education of the Gifted* has been a particularly difficult one. In view of the large amount of high quality material available, this edition could easily have escalated to two or three times its present size, however, space limitations have forced us to make many difficult decisions in the selection process. As in the previous edition, we have attempted to include material that deals with philosophical and theoretical issues, significant research findings, and practical suggestions for identifying and providing programs for gifted and talented youngsters. We were guided in our selection procedures by a concern for presenting several points of view and a wide variety of programming ideas. For this reason contradictory points of view are sometimes encountered between and among the material selected, and the results of certain research studies are not always in complete agreement with one another. A conscientious effort has been made to include what the editors believe to be those materials that will be of most value to theorists, researchers, and practitioners in both the fields of psychology and education.

A second concern beyond the selection of material for the book relates to the manner in which the book is organized. An attempt has been made to develop an organizational pattern that is generally consistent with the major topics and issues that might be covered in a graduate level training course dealing with the gifted and talented. The intended purposes of the book are varied, however; as a collection of much of the outstanding literature in this area it can serve as a text in a course on the gifted or as a supplementary set of resource materials for such a course. We also hope that bringing together these many pieces dealing with the theoretical and practical aspects of a particular problem area will make the book a useful resource for both serious scholars and program developers.

The book is divided into three major parts and nine sections. Included are materials on the historical development of the psychology and education of the gifted, characteristics of gifted and creative individuals, and issues related to identifying and providing programs for highly able students. Special attention is given to certain topics such as the arts, underdeveloped talent, and teaching the gifted and talented. We also have attempted to include selections that deal with programs and practices at various age and grade levels.

An overriding concern in the development of this book was to provide a collection that reflects the classic contributions to the field that have endured the "test of time" so far as their usefulness is concerned, while bringing to the attention of the reader some of the more contemporary contributions from literature about the talented and gifted. In spite of the many new developments taking place in this field, a solid foundation based on the accumulated wisdom of the past is considered to be an important ingredient for sound thinking and program development. Thus, one of our goals has been to keep these "classic" contributions under one cover for use by scholars and practitioners in the field.

The editors would like to express their appreciation to the many authors and publishers who granted us permission to reprint their materials in this book. It is their efforts, individual commitments to the field, and creativity that have made this volume possible, and we are greatly in their debt for both the production of such high quality materials and their generosity in allowing us to make use of them.

The editors offer their sincere thanks to those persons who aided us in the preparation of the manuscript. Elaine Talada provided invaluable assistance by locating articles, obtaining permissions from authors and publishers, and generally supervising the overall production of the entire manuscript. Without her able assistance and untiring efforts in tracking down materials, authors, and sources of permission this book would not have been possible. We also would like to acknowledge Sally Casinghino for her assistance in preparing the manuscript. Finally, we would like to express our thanks to graduate students in the area of education for the gifted and talented at the University of Connecticut for completing questionnaires and rating scales that helped to guide us in making decisions about the usefulness and value of various selections.

Walter B. Barbe
Joseph S. Renzulli

PSYCHOLOGY AND EDUCATION OF THE
GIFTED

Third Edition

Part I
Introduction to the
Study of Giftedness

The psychology and education of gifted children has become one of the important concerns of our society. Acceptance of the need for attention to the full development of the potential of each individual is gradually becoming a reality. University research, government support and parental concern are all being directed toward providing better education for children who are different—those with special education needs—whether the special education be for physical or mental handicaps, learning disabilities, or giftedness.

More and more is being learned about the physical characteristics, interests, attitudes, and mental abilities of all children—the retarded, average, and gifted—but far less research has been done on the psychology of gifted children. If psychology is to be defined as the study of man in relation to his environment, there is definitely a need to devote more attention to the psychological problems involved both in the study and education of the gifted individual. The study of the gifted is well underway; an understanding of the gifted will come about only from using what is known in an attempt to aid him in his adjustments.

The misconceptions concerning gifted individuals, widely believed before Terman disproved them, and to some extent still believed by many people today, probably come from the writings in the late nineteenth century of such men as Lombroso and Nisbet. In *The Man of Genius* (Lombroso, 1895), published in London and New York, and widely read throughout the world, Lombroso attempted to show that insanity was closely related to genius. In *The Insanity of Genius* (Nisbet, 1895), Nisbet purports to prove this same theory.

While no intelligent person today believes "genius and insanity go hand in hand," there is evidence that those individuals scoring in the highest ranges of the intelligence test (over 180) are characterized by adjustment problems different from those of the average child. Leta Hollingworth recognizes this in *Gifted Children*, in which she states, "Another generali-

1

zation that can be made about these children (over 180 I.Q.) is that nearly all have been school problems" (Hollingworth, 1926).

Perhaps the very existence of abilities so far superior to those of the average makes for this poorer adjustment. It must be remembered, however, that gifted children in general are better adjusted than the average. This does not mean that they have fewer adjustments to make, but rather that even though they may face more adjustments than do the average, they generally make such adjustments successfully.

Probably no change in the attitude of the American public has been so great as that toward gifted children. At one time the gifted child was thought to be a physical weakling and a social misfit, so parents' determination to have only an average child was to be expected. But long after the bespectacled introvert concept had been completely disproved, parents held on to the popular notion that "average" was really good enough. What they really meant, of course, was that they wanted a child potentially capable of achieving at a higher level than they did, but one who would have none of the negative traits that were supposed to go along with mental superiority. Being very unrealistic about the fact that "average" was not good enough to achieve near the level to which they aspired for their children, parents nevertheless felt that they must maintain the "average" label for their child. Fortunately, this universal worship of the average has changed. Today, for the first time in nearly a century, parents are saying that they hope they have a gifted child. The freedom that allows parents to make this statement is perhaps the greatest change since Terman's original studies which disproved the previously held notions about the eccentricity of giftedness. There is indeed hope for the gifted that was not present even a few years ago.

The beginning of the change in attitudes toward the gifted can be marked at the time Lewis Terman began to study gifted children in California. This was climaxed by the presentation in 1947 of Volume IV of *Genetic Studies of Genius*, entitled *The Gifted Child Grows Up* (Terman and Oden, *op. cit.*). To Lewis Terman must go the credit for having started us on the path toward a new era, one in which all children will be accepted for what they are and will be allowed to develop those innate abilities they possess without fear of ridicule from a society characterized by mediocrity.

The establishment of the American Association for Gifted Children in 1947 is another landmark in the increasing attention to children who are exceptional in a different way. The appearance of *The Gifted Child* (Witty, 1951), gave new impetus to the movement. The Educational Policies Commission booklet, *Education for the Gifted*[1] drew still more attention to the gifted.

In 1953 the National Association for Gifted Children[2] was formed with the purpose of providing an organization for both teachers and parents concerned with the problem of the gifted child. *The Gifted Child Quarterly* is a publication of this organization which provides valuable information to teachers and parents, bibliographies, and reviews of recent books on the gifted. The Association for the Gifted[3], a division of the Council for Exceptional Children, is another organization which has in recent years provided influential leadership in furthering the cause of education for the gifted. This organization has been especially active in sponsoring federal legislation that led to a nationwide study of educational provisions for the gifted and the areas of gifted education that are still in need of further development. The study also led to the establishment of the Office of the Gifted and Talented in the United States Office of Education and to the first National/State Leadership Training Institute for the Gifted and Talented.

In Historical Development, the first section in Part I of this book represents an attempt to provide the reader with an introduction to the development of the study, as well as with an understanding of the gifted. Terman points out that "to discover the internal and external factors that help or hinder the fruition of exceptional talent, and to measure the extent of their influences, are surely among the major problems of our time." The cyclic nature of interest in the gifted, viewed so rationally by Tannenbaum, is of major concern to those working in this area. Tannenbaum's review of the mood of the United States, particularly as it concerns the gifted, from the pre-Sputnik era to the present time provides the background for planning for the gifted in the 1980's. He concludes with the challenging thought that "the presence of the ablest is beginning to make a difference in the total school atmosphere, which demonstrates that they are capable of enhancing all of education if their learning capacities are properly respected."

The last contribution in this section is by Paul A. Witty who lived and contributed professionally to the cause of the gifted from the 1920's through the 1970's. His perspective of not only what has happened, but of the challenges that lie ahead, mark him as one of the soundest and most concerned individuals in the field. That he gave so much offers the base upon which to build, for despite the gains "there continues to be a very great neglect of gifted and creative people."

Concepts and Concerns About Giftedness, the second section in Part I, reflects the present move away from concepts of a single kind of giftedness. While this broader definition may complicate further the identification of giftedness, it increases the likelihood of the realization of the potential of each individual. Torrance's contribution, "Emerging Concepts of Giftedness," reviews the research and thinking concerning giftedness and wisely concludes that emphasis must be placed on potential. As Torrance discusses emerging concepts of giftedness, Renzulli brings into focus the definition of giftedness in a manner which includes ability, task commitment, and creativity. To this, Ward adds a discussion on the nature of giftedness. And from what kinds of families do gifted youngsters come? Barbe presents a study of the family background of a large group of gifted children, and concludes that gifted children come from not just the economic and culturally favored background but from all types of family backgrounds, the disadvantaged as well as the advantaged.

References

Hollingworth, Leta. *Gifted Children*. New York: The Macmillan Company, 1926, 265.

Lombroso, C. *The Man of Genius*. New York: Charles Scribner's Sons, 1895.

Nisbet, J. F. *The Insanity of Genius*. London: DeLaNore Press, 1895.

Terman and Oden. *The Gifted Child Grows Up*.

Witty, Paul, (editor). *The Gifted Child*. Boston: D. C. Health & Company, 1951.

Notes

[1] Educational Policies Commission, *Education of the gifted*. Washington, D.C.: National Education Association, 1950.

[2] National Association for Gifted Children (8080 Springvalley Drive, Cincinnati, Ohio).

[3] The Association for the Gifted, Council for Exceptional Children (1920 Association Drive, Reston, Virginia, 22091).

Lewis M. Terman

The Discovery and Encouragement of Exceptional Talent

I am deeply sensible of the honor of being invited by the American Psychological Association, through its special committee, to give the initial lecture in the Walter V. Bingham Lecturship series.

I am especially happy that Chancellor Kerr and the psychology department of the University of California graciously acceded to my request that the address be given here, where I have many friends and where so much notable research has been done on the mental, physical and personality development of children; where such famous experiments have been made on the purposive behavior of rats, both gifted and dull; where authoritarian minds have been so exhaustively probed; and where the recently established Institute of Personality Assessment is engaged in such promising investigations.

Before beginning my lecture I should like to pay tribute to the life work of the late Walter Van Dyke Bingham, at whose request this lectureship was established by Mrs. Bingham. Born in Iowa in 1880, young Walter early demonstrated his exceptional gifts by skipping both the third and fourth grades and by graduating from high school at the age of 16. As a freshman in college he was the youngest in his class and the only one to make a straight A record. After graduating from Beloit College he taught in high schools for four years, then entered the graduate school of the University of Chicago and in 1908 won his doctorate in psychology with honors. From 1908 to 1910 he was instructor at Teachers College and assistant to Edward L. Thorndike. In 1910 he was appointed assistant professor at Dartmouth to

Reprinted from *American Psychologist,* Vol. 9, No. 6 (June, 1954), pp. 221-230. By permission of the American Psychological Association.

teach all their classes in psychology, but when he left there five years later the staff included an instructor and two full professors, all selected by Dr. Bingham. His rare ability to recognize exceptional talent is indicated by the fact that both of these professors became college presidents.

From 1915 to 1924 Dr. Bingham was professor of psychology and the head of the division of applied psychology at the Carnegie Institute of Technology, and it was here that he found the opportunity he had long wanted to promote large-scale investigations in applied psychology. The faculty he assembled for that purpose was one of the most distinguished ever brought together anywhere in this country. Among them were J.B. Miner, L.L. Thurstone, Walter Dill Scott, Kate Gordon, and E.K. Strong. Three others appointed as consultants were F.L. Wells, G.M. Whipple, and Raymond Dodge. It was this faculty that, under the wise leadership of Dr. Bingham, laid the solid foundation for vocational and industrial psychology in America.

When our country entered the war in 1917, nearly all of the Carnegie group were soon engaged in psychological work either for the Surgeon General or for the War Department or for both. Dr. Bingham was a member of Yerkes' committee of seven that devised the army mental tests, in 1917-1918 was a member of the Committee on Classification of Personnel (the committee charged with devising and administering vocational tests in all the army camps), and in 1918-1919 was Lt. Colonel in the Personnel Branch of the Army General Staff.

During World War II even greater service was rendered by Dr. Bingham as chief psychologist for the Office of Adjutant General from 1940 to 1946. In this capacity he and his committee were responsible not only for the Army General Classification Test that was administered tt the many millions of inductees, but also for advising on the entire program of psychological services in the armed forces. In this capacity too he was in position to influence the selection of men best qualified to head the various branches of military psychology. I have no doubt that the extraordinary success of the work accomplished by psychologists during the war was largely due to his leadership and to his judgment of men.

If time permitted, I should like to tell you about his more than 200 publications, about the great variety of problems they dealt with, and the contributions they made in several fields of psychology, but I am sure that if Dr. Bingham were here he would want me to get on with our scheduled program.

I have often been asked how I happened to become interested in mental tests and gifted children. My first introduction to the scientific problems posed by intellectual differences occurred well over a half-century ago when I was a senior in psychology at Indiana University and was asked to prepare two reports for a seminar, one on mental deficiency and one on genius. Up to that time, despite the fact that I had graduated from a normal college as a Bachelor of Pedagogy and had taught school for five years, I had never so much as heard of a mental test. The reading for those two reports opened up

6

a new world to me, the world of Galton, Binet and their contemporaries. The following year my MA thesis on leadership among children (10) was based in part on tests used by Binet in his studies of suggestibility.

Then I entered Clark University, where I spent considerable time during the first year in reading on mental tests and precocious children. Child prodigies, I soon learned, were in that time in bad repute because of the prevailing belief that they were usually psychotic or otherwise abnormal and almost sure to burn themselves out quickly or to develop postadolescent stupidity. "Early ripe, early rot" was a slogan frequently encountered. By the time I reached my last graduate year, I decided to find out for myself how precocious children differ from the mentally backward, and accordingly chose as my doctoral dissertation an experimental study of the intellectual processes of fourteen boys, seven of them picked as the brightest and seven as the dullest in a large city school (11). These subjects I put through a great variety of intelligence tests, some of them borrowed from Binet, and others, many of them new. The tests were given individually and required a total of 40 or 50 hours for each subject. The experiment contributed little or nothing to science, but it contributed a lot to my future thinking. Besides "selling" me completely on the value of mental tests as a research method, it offered an ideal escape from the kinds of laboratory work which I disliked and in which I was more than ordinarily inept. (Edward Thorndike confessed to me once that *his* lack of mechanical skill was party responsible for turning *him* to mental tests and to the kinds of experiments on learning that required no apparatus.)

However, it was not until I got to Stanford in 1910 that I was able to pick up with mental tests where I had left off at Clark University. By that time Binet's 1905 and 1908 scales had been published, and the first thing I undertook at Stanford was a tentative revision of the 1908 scale. This, after further revisions, was published in 1916. The standardization of the scale was based on tests of a thousand children whose IQ's ranged from 60 to 145. The contrast in intellectual performance between the dullest and the brightest of a given age so intensified my earlier interest in the gifted that I decided to launch an ambitious study of such children at the earliest opportunity.

My dream was realized in the spring of 1921 when I obtained a generous grant from the Commonwealth Fund of New York City for the purpose of locating a thousand subjects of IQ 140 or higher. More than that number were selected by Stanford-Binet tests from the kindergarten through the eighth grade, and a group mental test given in 95 high schools provided nearly 400 additional subjects. The latter, plus those I had located before 1921, brought the number close to 1,500. The average IQ was approximately 150, and 80 were 170 or higher (13).

The twofold purpose of the project was, first of all, to find what traits characterize children of high IQ, and secondly, to follow them for as many years as possible to see what kinds of adults they might become. This meant that it was necessary to select a group representative of high-testing children

7

in general. With the help of four field assistants, we canvassed a school population of nearly a quartermillion in the urban and semi-urban areas of California. Two careful checks on the methods used showed that not more than 10 or 12 per cent of the children who could have qualified for the group in the schools canvassed were missed. A sample of close to 90 per cent insured that whatever traits were typical of these children would be typical of high-testing children in any comparable school population.

Time does not permit me to describe the physical measurements, medical examinations, achievement tests, character and interest tests, or the trait ratings and other supplementary information obtained from parents and teachers. Nor can I here describe the comparative data we obtained for control groups of unselected children. The more important results, however, can be stated briefly: children of IQ of 140 or higher are, in general, appreciably superior to unselected children in physique, health, and social adjustment; markedly superior in moral attitudes as measured either by character tests or by trait ratings; and vastly superior in their mastery of school subjects as shown by a three-hour battery of achievement tests. In fact, the typical child of the group had mastered the school subjects to a point about two grades beyond the one in which he was enrolled, some of them three or four gardes beyond. Moreover, his ability as evidenced by achievement in the different school subjects is so general as to refute completely the traditional belief that gifted children are usually one-sided. I take some pride in the fact that not one of the major conclusions we drew in the early 1920's regarding the traits that are typical of gifted children has been overthrown in the three decades since then.

Results of thirty years' follow-up of these subjects by field studies in 1927-1928, 1939-1940, and 1951-1952, and by mail follow-up at other dates, show that the incidence of mortality, ill health, insanity, and alcoholism is in each case below that for the generality of corresponding age, that the great majority are still well adjusted socially, and that the delinquency rate is but a fraction of what it is in the general population. Two forms of our difficult Concept Mastery Test, devised especially to reach into the stratosphere of adult intelligence, have been administered to all members of the group who could be visited by the field assistants, including some 950 tested in 1939-1940 and more than 1,000 in 1951-1952. On both tests they scored on the average about as far above the generality of adults as they had scored above the generality of children when we selected them. Moreover, as Dr. Bayley and Mrs. Oden have shown, in the twelve-year interval between the two tests, 90 per cent increased their intellectual stature as measured by this test. "Early ripe, early rot" simply does not hold for these subjects. So far, no one has developed postadolescent stupidity!

As for schooling, close to 90 per cent entered college and 70 per cent graduated. Of those graduating, 30 per cent were awarded honors and about two-thirds remained for graduate work. The educational record would have been still better but for the fact that a majority reached college age during the great depression. In their undergraduate years 40 per cent of the men and 20 per cent of the women earned half or more of their college expenses, and the total of undergraduate and graduate expenses earned amounted to $670,000, not counting stipends from scholarships and fellowships, which amounted to $350,000.

The cooperation of the subjects is indicated by the fact that we have been able to keep track of more than 98 per cent of the original group, thanks to the rapport fostered by the incomparable field and office assistants I have had from the beginning of the study to the present. I dislike to think how differently things could have gone with helpers even a little less competent.

The achievement of the group to midlife is best illustrated by the case histories of the 800 men, since only a minority of the women have gone out for professional careers (15). By 1950, when the men had an average age of 40 years, they had published 67 books (including 46 in the fields of science, arts and the humanities, and 21 books of fiction). They had published more than 1,400 scientific, technical, and professional articles; over 200 short stories, novelettes, and plays; and 236 miscellaneous articles on a great variety of subjects. They had also authorized more than 150 patents. The figures on publications do not include the hundreds of publications by journalists that classify as news stories, editorials, or newspaper columns; nor do they include the hundred, if not thousands of radio and TV scripts.

The 800 men include 78 who have taken a PhD degree or its equivalent, 48 with a medical degree, 85 with a law degree, 74 who are teaching or have taught in a four-year college or university, 51 who have done basic research in the physical sciences or engineering, and 104 who are engineers but have done only applied research or none. Of the scientists, 47 are listed in the 1949 edition of *American Men of Science*. Nearly all of these numbers are from 10 to 20 or 30 times as large as would be found for 800 men of corresponding age picked at random in the general population, and are sufficient answer to those who belittle the significance of IQ differences.

The follow-up of these gifted subjects has proved beyond question that tests of "general intelligence," given as early as six, eight, or ten years, tells a great deal about the ability to achieve either presently or 30 years hence. Such tests do not, however, enable us to predict what direction the achievement will take, and least of all do they tell us what personality factors or what accidents of fortune will affect the fruition of exceptional ability. Granting that both interest patterns and special aptitudes play important roles in the making of a gifted scientist, mathematician, mechanic, artist, poet, or musical composer, I am convinced that to achieve greatly in almost any field, the special talents have to be backed up by a lot of Spearman's g, by which is meant the kind of general intelligence that requires ability to form many sharply defined concepts, to manipulate them, and to perceive subtle relationships between them; in other words, the ability to engage in abstract thinking.

The study by Catherine Cox of the childhood traits of historical geniuses gives additional evidence regarding the role of general intelligence in exceptional achievement. That study was part of our original plan to investigate

9

superior ability by two methods of approach: (a) by identifying and following living gifted subjects from childhood onward; and (b) by preceeding in the opposite direction and tracing the mature genius back to his childhood promise. With a second grant from the Commonwealth Fund, the latter approach got under way only a year later than the former and resulted in the magnum opus by Cox entitled *The Early Mental Traits of Three Hundred Geniuses* (1). Her subjects represented an unbiased selection from the top 510 in Cattell's objectively compiled list of the 1,000 most eminent men of history. Cox and two able assistants then scanned some 3,000 biographies in search of information that would throw light on the early mental development of these subjects. The information thus obtained filled more than 6,000 typed pages. Next, three psychologists familiar with mental age norms read the documentary evidence on all the subjects and estimated for each the IQ that presumably would be necessary to account for the intellectual behavior recorded for given chronological ages. Average of the three IQ estimates was used as the index of intelligence. In fact two IQ's were estimated for each subject, one based on the evidence to age 17, and the other on evidence to the mid-twenties. The recorded evidence on development to age 17 varied from very little to an amount that yielded about as valid an IQ as a good intelligence test would give. Examples of the latter are Goethe, John Stuart Mill, and Francis Galton. It was the documentary information on Galton, which I summarized and published in 1917 (12), that decided me to prepare plans for the kind of study that was carried out by Cox. The average of estimated IQ's for her 300 geniuses was 155, with many going as high as 175 and several as high as 200. Estimates below 120 occurred only when there was little biographical evidence about the early years.

It is easy to scoff at these post-mortem IQ's, but as one of the three psychologists who examined the evidence and made the IQ ratings, I think the author's main conclusion is fully warranted; namely, that "the genius who achieves highest eminence is one whom intelligence tests would have identified as gifted in childhood."

Special attention was given the geniuses who had sometime or other been labeled as backward in childhood, and in every one of these cases the facts clearly contradicted the legend. One of them was Oliver Goldsmith, of whom his childhood teacher is said to have said "Never was so dull a boy." The fact is that little Oliver was writing clever verse at 7 years and at 8 was reading Ovid and Horace. Another was Sir Walter Scott, who at 7 not only read widely in poetry but was using correctly in his written prose such words as "melancholy" and "exotic." Other alleged childhood dullards included a number who disliked the usual diet of Latin and Greek but had a natural talent for science. Among these were the celebrated German chemist Justus von Liebig, the great English anatomist John Hunter, and the naturalist Alexander von Humboldt, whose name is scattered so widely over the maps of the world.

In the cases just cited one notes a tendency for the direction of later achievement to be foreshadowed by the interests and preoccupations of

10

childhood. I have tried to determine how frequently this was true of the 100 subjects in Cox's group whose childhood was best documented. Very marked foreshadowing was noted in the case of more than half of the group, none at all in less than a fourth. Macaulay, for example, began his career as historian at the age of 6 with what he called a "Compendium of Universal History " filling a quire of paper before he lost interest in the project. Ben Franklin before the age of 17 had displayed nearly all the traits that characterized him in middle life: scientific curiosity, religious heterodoxy, wit and buffoonery, political and business shrewdness, and ability to write. At 11 Pascal was so interested in mathematics that his father thought it best to deprive him of books on this subject until he had first mastered Latin and Greek. Pascal secretly proceeded to construct a geometry of his own and covered the ground as far as the 32nd proposition of Euclid. His father then relented. At 14 Leibnitz was writing on logic and philosophy and composing what he called "An Alphabet of Human Thought." He relates that at this age he took a walk one afternoon to consider whether he should accept the "doctrine of substantial forms."

Similar foreshadowing is disclosed by the case histories of my gifted subjects. A recent study of the scientists and nonscientists among our 800 gifted men (15) showed many highly significant differences between the early interests and social attitudes of those who became physical scientists and those who majored in the social sciences, law, or the humanities. Those in medical or biological sciences usually rated on such varaibles somewhere between the physical scientists and the nonscientists.

What I especially want to emphasize, however, is that both the evidence on early mental development of historical geniuses and that obtained by follow-up of gifted subjects selected in childhood by mental tests point to the conclusion that capacity to achieve far beyond the average can be detected early in life by a well-constructed ability test that is heavily weighted with the g factor. It remains to be seen how much the prediction of future achievement can be made more specific as to field by getting, in addition, measures of ability factors that are largely independent of g. It would seem that a 20-year follow-up of the thousands of school children who have been given Thurstone's test of seven "primary mental abilities" would help to provide the answer. At present the factor analysts don't agree on how many "primary" mental abilities there are, nor exactly on what they are. The experts in this field are divided into two schools. The British school, represented by Thomson, Vernon, and Burt, usually stop with the identification of at most three or four group factors in addition to g, while some representing the American school feel the scores of 40 or 50 kinds of tests into a hopper and manage to extract from them what they believe to be a dozen or fifteen separate factors. Members of the British school are as a rule very skeptical about the realities underlying the minor group factors. There are also American psychologists, highly skilled in psychometrics, who share this skepticism. It is to be hoped that further research will give us more information that we now have about the predictive value of the group factors. Until such information is available, the scores on group factors can contribute little to vocational guidance beyond what a good test of general intelligence will provide.

I have always stressed the importance of *early* discovery of exceptional abilities. Its importance is now highlighted by the facts Harvey Lehman has disclosed in his monumental studies of the relation between age and creative achievement (8). The striking thing about his age curves is how early in life the period of maximum creativity is reached. In nearly all fields of science, the best work is done between ages 25 and 35, and rarely later than 40. The peak productivity for works of lesser merit is usually reached 5 to 10 years later; this is true in some twenty fields of science, in philosophy, in most kinds of musical composition, in art, and in literature of many varieties. The lesson for us us from Lehman's statistics is that the youth of high achievement potential should be well trained for his life work before too many of his creative years have been passed.

This raises the issue of educational acceleration for the gifted. It seems that the schools are more opposed to acceleration now than they were thirty years ago. The lockstep seems to have become more and more the fashion, notwithstanding the fact that practically everyone who has investigated the subject is against it. Of my gifted group, 29 per cent managed to graduate from high school before the age of 16 ½ years (62 of these before 15 ½), but I doubt if so many would be allowed to do so now. The other 71 per cent graduated between 16 ½ and 18 ½. We have compared the accelerated with the nonaccelerated on numerous case history variables. The two groups differed very little in childhood IQ, their health records are equally good, and as adults they are equally well adjusted socially. More of the accelerates graduated from college, and on the avergae nearly a year and a half earlier than the nonaccelerates; they averaged high in college grades and more often remained for graduate work. Moreover, the accelerates on the average married .7 of a year earlier, have a trifle lower divorce rate, and test just a little higher on a test of marital happiness (14). So far as college records of accelerates and nonaccelerates are concerned, our data closely parallel those obtained by the late Noel Keys (3) at the University of California and those by Pressey (9) and his associates at Ohio State University.

The Ford Fund for the advancement of Education has awarded annually since 1951 some 400 college scholarships to gifted students who are not over 16 ½ years old, are a year or even two years short of high school graduation, but show good evidence of ability to do college work. Three quarters of them are between 15 ½ and 16 ½ at the time of college entrance. A dozen colleges and universities accept these students and are keeping close track of their success. A summary of their records for the first year shows that they not only get higher grades than their classmates, who average about two years older, but that they are also equally well adjusted socially and participate in as many extracurricular activities (17). The main problem the boys have is in finding girls to date who are not too old for them! Some of them have started a campagn to remedy the situation by urging that more of these scholarships be awarded to girls.

The facts I have given do not mean that all gifted children should be rushed through school just as rapidly as possible. If that were done, a majority with IQ of 140 could graduate from high school before the age of 15. I do believe, however, that such children should be promoted rapidly enough to permit college entrance by the age of 17 at least, and that a majority would be better off to enter at 16. The exceptionally bright student who is kept with his age group finds little to challenge his intelligence and all too often develops habits of laziness that later wreck his college career. I could give you some choice examples of this in my gifted group. In the case of a college student who is preparing for a profession in science, medicine, law, or any field of advanced scholarship, graduation at 20 instead of the usual 22 means two years added to his professional career; or the two years saved could be used for additional training beyond the doctorate, if that were deemed preferable.

Learned and Wood (7) have shown by objective achievement tests in some 40 Pennsylvania colleges how little correlation there is between the student's knowledge and the number of months or years of his college attendance. They found some beginning sophomores who had acquired more knowledge than some seniors near their graduation. They found similarly low correlations between the number of course units a student had in a given field and the amount he knew in that field. Some with only one year of Latin had learned more than others with three years. And, believe it or not, they even found boys just graduating from high school who had more knowledge of science and were about to begin teaching science in high schools! The sensible thing to do, it seems, would be to quit crediting the individual high school or the individual college and begin crediting the individual student. That, essentially, is what the Ford Fund scholarships are intended to encourage.

Instruments that permit the identification of gifted subjects are available in great variety and at nearly all levels from the primary grades to the graduate schools in universities. My rough guess is that at the present time tests of achievement in the school subjects are being given in this country to children below high school at a rate of perhaps ten or twelve million a year, and to high school students another million or two. In addition, perhaps two million tests of intelligence are given annually in the elementary and high schools. The testing of college students began in a small way only 30 years ago; now almost every college in the country requires applicants for admission to take some kind of aptitude test. This is usally a test of general aptitude, but subject-matter tests and tests of special aptitudes are sometimes given to supplement the tests of general aptitude.

The testing movement has also spread rapidly in other countries, especialy in Britain and the Commonwealth countries. Godfrey Thomson devised what is now called the Moray House test of intelligence in 1921 to aid in selecting the more gifted 11-year olds in the primary schools for the privilege of free secondary education. This test has been revised and is given annually to about a half million scholarship candidates. The Moray House tests now include tests of English, arithmetic, and history. In 1932 the Scottish Council for Research in Education (18) arranged to give the Moray House test of intelligence (a group test) to all the 90,000 children in Scotland who were born in 1921, and actually tested some 87,000 of them. The Stanford-Binet tests have been translated and adapted for use in nearly all the countries of Europe and in several countries of Asia and Latin America. Behind the Iron Curtain, however, mental tests are now banned.

I have discussed only tests of intelligence and of school achievement. There is time to mention only a few of the many kinds of personality tests that have been developed during the last thirty-five years: personality inventories, projective techniques by the dozen, attitude scales by the hundred, interest tests, tests of psychotic and predelinquent tendencies, tests of leadership, marital aptitude, masculinity-femininity, et cetera. The current output of research on personality tests probably equals or exceeds that on intelligence and achievement tests, and is even more exciting.

Along with the increasing use of tests, and perhaps largely a result of it, there is a growing interest, both here and abroad, in improving educational methods for the gifted. Acceleration of a year or two or three, however desirable, is but a fraction of what is needed to keep the gifted child or youth working at his intellectual best. The method most often advocated is curriculum achievement for the gifted without segregating them from the ordinary class. Under ideal conditions enrichment can accomplish much, but in these days of crowded schools, when so many teachers are overworked, underpaid, and inadequately trained, curriculum enrichment for a few gifted in a large mixed class cannot begin to solve the problem. The best survey of thought and action in this field of education is the book entitled *The Gifted Child*, written by many authors and published in 1951 (16). In planning for and sponsoring this book, The American Association for Gifted Children has rendered a great service to education.

But however efficient our tests may be in discovering exceptional talents, and whatever the school may do to foster those discovered, it is the prevailing *Zeitgeist* that will decide, by the rewards it gives or withholds, what talents will come to flower. In Western Europe of the Middle Ages, the favored talents were those that served the Church by providing its priests, the architects of its cathedrals, and the painters of religious themes. A few centuries later the same countries had a renaissance that included science and literature as well as the arts. Although presumably there are as many potential composers of great music as there ever were, and as many potentially great artists as in the days of Leonardo da Vinci and Michaelangelo, I am reliably informed that in this country today it is almost impossible for a composer of *serious* music to earn a living except by teaching, and that the situation is much the same, though somewhat less critical, with respect to artists.

The talents most favored by the current *Zeitgeist* are those that can contribute to science and technology. If intelligence and achievement tests don't discover the potential scientist, there is a good chance that the annual Science Talent Search will, though not until the high school years. Since

14

Westinghouse inaugurated in 1942 this annual search for the high school seniors most likely to become creative scientists, nearly 4,000 boys and girls have been picked for honors by Science Service out of the many thousands who have competed. As a result, "Science Clubs of America" now number 15,000 with a third of a million members—a twentyfold increase in a dozen years (2). As our need for more and better scientists is real and urgent, one can rejoice at what the talent search and the science clubs are accomplishing. One may regret, however, that the spirit of the times is not equally favorable to the discovery and encouragement of potential poets, prose writers, artists, statesmen, and social leaders.

But in addition to the over-all climates that reflect the *Zeitgeist,* there are localized climates that favor or hinder the encouragement of given talents in particular colleges and universities. I have in mind especially two recent investigations of the differences among colleges in the later achievement of their graduates. One by Knapp and Goodrich (4) dealt with the undergraduate origin of 18,000 scientists who got the bachelor's degree between 1924 and 1934 and were listed in the 1944 edition of *American Men of Science.* The list of 18,000 was composed chiefly of men who had taken a PhD degree, but included a few without a PhD who were starred scientists. The IBM cards for these men were then sorted according to the college from which they obtained the bachelor's degree, and an index of productivity was computed for each college in terms of the proportion of its male graduates who were in the list of 18,000. Some of the results were surprising, not to say sensational. The institutions that were most productive of future scientists between 1924 and 1934 were not the great universities, but the small liberal arts colleges. Reed College topped the list with an index of 132 per thousand male graduates. The California Institute of Technology was second with an index of 70. Kalamazoo College was third with 66, Earlham fourth with 57, and Oberlin fifth with 56. Only a half-dozen of the great universities were in the top fifty with a productivity index of 25 or more.

The second study referred to was by Knapp and Greenbaum (5), who rated educational institutions according to the proportion of their graduates who received certain awards at the graduate level in the six-year period from 1946 to 1951. Three kinds of awards were considered: a PhD degree, a graduate scholarship or fellowship paying at least $400 a year, or a prize at the graduate level won in open competition. The roster of awardees they compiled included 7,000 students who had graduated from 377 colleges and universities. This study differs from the former in three respects: (a) it deals with recent graduates, who had not had time to become distinguished but who could be regarded as good bets for the future; (b) these good bets were classified according to whether the major field was science, social science, or the humanities; and (c) data were obtained for both sexes, though what I shall report here relates only to men. In this study the great universities make a better showing than in the other, but still only a dozen of them are in the top fifty institutions in the production of men who are good bets. In the top ten, the University of Chicago is third, Princeton is eighth, and Harvard is tenth; the other seven in order of rank are Swarthmore 1, Reed 2, Oberlin 4, Haverford 5, California Institue of Technology 6, Carleton 7, and Antioch 9. When the schools were listed separately for production of men who were goods bets in science, social science, and the humanities, there were eight that rated in the top twenty of all three lists. These were Swarthmore, Reed, Chicago, Harvard, Oberlin, Antioch, Carleton, and Princeton.

The causes of these differences are not entirely clear. Scores on aptitude tests show that the intelligence of students in a given institution is by no means the sole factor, though it is an important one. Other important factors are the quality of the school's intellectual climate, the proportion of able and inspiring teachers on its faculty, and the amount of conscious effort that is made not only to discover but also to motivate the most highly gifted. The influence of motivation can hardly be exaggerated.

In this address I have twice alluded to the fact that achievement in school is influenced by many things other than the sum total of intellectual abilities. The same is true of success in life. In closing I will tell you briefly about an attempt we made a dozen years ago to identify some of the nonintellectual factors that have influenced life success among the men in my gifted group. Three judges, working independently, examined the records (to 1940) of the 730 men who were then 25 years old or older, and rated each on life success. The criterion of "success" was the extent to which a subject had made use of his superior intellectual ability, little weight being given to earned income. The 150 men rated highest for success and the 150 rated lowest were then compared on some 200 items of information obtained from childhood onward (14). How did the two groups differ?

During the elementary school years, the A's and C's (as we call them) were almost equally successful. The average grades were about the same, and average scores on achievement tests were only a trifle higher for the A's. Early in high school the groups began to draw apart in scholarship, and by the end of high school the slump of the C's was quite marked. The slump could not be blamed on extracurricular activities, for these were almost twice as common among the A's. Nor was much of it due to difference in intelligence. Although the A's tested on the average a little higher than the C's both in 1922 and 1940, the average score made by the C's in 1940 was high enough to permit brilliant college work, in fact was equaled by only 15 per cent of our highly selected Stanford students. Of the A's, 97 per cent entered college and 90 per cent graduated; of the C's, 68 per cent entered but only 37 per cent graduated. Of those who graduated, 52 per cent of the A's but only 14 per cent of the C's graduated with honors. The A's were also more accelerated in school; on the average they were six months younger on completing the eighth grade, 10 months younger at high school graduation, and 15 months younger at graduation from college.

The differences between the educational histories of the A's and C's reflect to some degree the differences in their family backgrounds. Half of the A fathers but only 15 per cent of the C fathers were college graduates, and twice as many of A siblings as of C siblings graduated. The estimated

16

number of books in the A homes was nearly 50 per cent greater than in the C homes. As of 1928, when the average age of the subjects was about 16 years, more than twice as many of the C parents as of A parents had been divorced.

Interesting differences between the groups were found in the childhood data on emotional stability, social adjustments, and various traits of personality. Of the 25 traits on which each child was rated by parent and teacher in 1922 (18 years before the A and C groups were made up), the only trait on which the C's averaged as high as the A's was general health. The superiority of the A's was especially marked in four volitional traits: prudence, self-confidence, perseverance, and desire to excel. The A's also rated significantly higher in 1922 on leadership, popularity, and sensitiveness to approval or disapproval. By 1940 the difference between the groups in social adjustment and all-round mental stability had greatly increased and showed itself in many ways. By that time four-fifths of the A's had married, but only two-thirds of the C's and the divorce rate for those who had married was twice as high for the C's as for the A's. Moreover, the A's made better marriages; their wives on the average came from better homes, were better educated, and scored higher on intelligence tests.

But the most spectacular differences between the two groups came from three sets of ratings, made in 1940, on a dozen personality traits. Each man rated himself on all the traits, was rated on them by his wife if he had a wife, and by a parent if a parent was still living. Although the three sets of ratings were made independently, they agreed unanimously on the four traits in which the A and C groups differed most widely. These were "persistence in the accomplishment of ends," "integration toward goals, as contrasted with drifting," "self-confidence," and "freedom from inferiority feelings." For each trait three critical ratios were computed showing, respectively, the reliability of the A-C differences in average of self-ratings, ratings by wives, and ratings by parents. The average of the three critical ratios was 5.5 for perseverance, 5.6 for integration toward goals, 3.7 for self-confidence, and 3.1 for freedom from inferiority feelings. These closely parallel the traits that Cox found to be especially characteristic of the 100 leading geniuses in her group whom she rated on many aspects of personality; their three outstanding traits she defined as "persistence of motive and effort," "confidence in their abilities," and "strength or force of character."

There was one trait on which only the parents of our A and C men were asked to rate them; that trait was designated "common sense." As judged by parents, the A's are again reliably superior, the A-C difference in average rating having a critical ratio of 3.9. We are still wondering what self-ratings by the subjects and ratings of them by their wives on common sense would have shown if we had been impudent enough to ask for them!

Everything considered, there is nothing in which our A and C groups present a greater contrast than in drive to achieve and in all-round mental and social adjustment. Our data do not support the theory of Lange-Eichbaum (6) that great achievement usually stems from emotional tensions

17

that border on the abnormal. In our gifted group, success is associated with stability rather than instability, with absence rather than with presence of disturbing conflicts—in short with well balanced temperament and with freedom from excessive frustrations. The Lange-Eichbaum theory may explain a Hitler, but hardly a Churchill; the junior senator from Wisconsin, possibly, but not a Jefferson or a Washington.

At any rate, we have seen that intellect and achievement are far from perfectly correlated. To identify the internal and external factors that help or hinder the fruition of exceptional talent, and to measure the extent of their influences, are surely among the major problems of our time. These problems are not new; their existence has been recognized by countless men from Plato to Francis Galton. What is new is the general awareness of them caused by the manpower shortage of scientists, engineers, moral leaders, statesmen, scholars, and teachers that the country must have if it is to survive in a threatened world. These problems are now being investigated on a scale never before approached, and by a new generation of workers in several related fields. Within a couple of decades vastly more should be known than we know today about our resources of potential genius, the environmental circumstances that favor its expression, the emotional compulsions that give it dynamic quality, and the personality distortions that can make it dangerous.

References

1. Cox, Catharine C., *The Early Mental Traits of Three Hundred Geniuses.* Vol. II of *Genetic Studies of Genius,* Terman, L. M. (ed.). Stanford: Stanford Univer. Press, 1926.

2. Davis, W., Communicating Science. *J. Atomic Scientists,* 1953, 337-340.

3. Keys, N., The Underage Student in High School and College. *Univ. Calif. Publ. Educ.,* 1938, **7,** 145-272.

4. Knapp, R. H., & Goodrich, H. B., *Origins of American Scientists.* Chicago: Univer. of Chicago Press, 1952.

5. Knapp, R. H., & Greenbaum, J. J., *The Younger American Scholar: His Collegiate Origins.* Chicago: Univ. of Chicago Press, 1953.

6. Lange-Eichbaum, W., *The Problem of Genius.* New York: Macmillan, 1932.

7. Learned, W. S., & Wood, B. D., The Student and His Knowledge. *Carnegie Found. Adv. Teaching Bull.,* 1938, No. 29.

8. Lehman, H. C., *Age and Achievement.* Princeton: Princeton Univer. Press, 1953.

9. Pressey, S. L., *Educational Acceleration: Appraisals and Basic Problems.* Columbus: Ohio State Univer. Press, 1949.

10. Terman, L. M., A Preliminary Study in the Psychology and Pedagogy of Leadership. *Pedag. Sem.,* 1904, **11,** 413-451.

11. Terman, L. M., Genius and Stupidity: A Study of Some of the Intellectual Processes of Seven "Bright" and Seven "Dull" Boys. *Pedag. Sem.,* 1906, **13,** 307-373.

12. Terman, L. M., The Intelligence Quotient of Francis Galton in Childhood. *Amer. J. Psychol.,* 1917, **28,** 209-215.

13. Terman, L. M. (ed.), *et al. Mental and Physical Traits of a Thousand Gifted Children.* Vol. I of *Genetic Studies of Genius,* Terman, L. M. (ed.). Stanford: Stanford Univer. Press, 1925.

14. Terman, L. M., & Oden, M. H., *The Gifted Child Grows Up.* Vol. IV of *Genetic Studies of Genius,* Terman, L. M. (ed.).Stanford: Stanford Univer. Press, 1947.

15. Terman, L. M., Scientists and Nonscientists in a Group of 800 Gifted Men. *Psychol. Monogr.,* 1954, **68,** in press.

16. Witty, P. (ed)., *The Gifted Child.* Boston: Heath, 1951.

17. *Bridging the Gap Between School and College.* New York: The Fund for the Advancement of Education, 1953.

18. *The Intelligence of Scottish Children.* Scottish Council for Research in Education. London: Univer. of London Press, 1933.

Abraham J. Tannenbaum

Pre-Sputnik to Post-Watergate Concern about the Gifted

*T*he half-decade following Sputnik in 1957 and the last half-decade of the 1970s may be viewed as twin peak periods of interest in gifted and talented children. Separating the peaks was a deep valley of neglect in which the public fixed its attention more eagerly on the low functioning, poorly motivated, and socially handicapped children in our schools. It was not simply a case of bemoaning the plight of able and then disadvantaged learners, with each population taking turns as the pitied underdog or the victim of unfair play. Rather than *transferring* the same sentiments from one undereducated group to another, the nation found itself *transforming* its mood from intense anxiety to equally profound indignation: anxiety lest our protective shield of brainpower become weaker, rendering us vulnerable to challenge from without, followed by indignation over social injustice in the land, which could tear us apart from within. Now we are experiencing a revival of earlier sensitivities to the needs of the gifted. Judging from these vacillations in national temperament, it seems as if we have not yet succeeded in paying equal attention simultaneously to our most and least successful achievers at school.

The cyclical nature of interest in the gifted is probably unique in American education. No other special group of children has been alternately embraced and repelled with so much vigor by educators and laymen alike. Gardner saw signs of public dilemma rather than fickleness when he commented that "the critical lines of tension in our society are between *emphasis on individual performance and restraints on individual performance*" (Gardner, 1961). Such conflict would arise logically from a failure to reconcile our commitments to excellence and to equality in public education. Fostering excellence means recognizing the right of gifted children to realize their potential, but it also suggests something uncomfortably close to encouraging elitism if the ablest are privy to educational experiences that are denied all other children. On the other hand, promoting egalitarianism will guarantee increased attention to children from lower-status environments who are failing at school. As we concentrate more exclusively on raising the performance levels of these minorities, however, there is danger of discriminating against the minority of gifted students by denying their right to be challenged adequately on grounds that they are advantaged. Perhaps because we cannot live exclusively with excellence or egalitarianism for any length of time and tend to counterpose rather than reconcile them, we seem fated to drift from one to the other indefinitely.

The 1950s: Pre-Sputnik and Post-Sputnik

From the current perspective, the 1950s are viewed as sedate, conservative years, at least in contrast to the convulsive 1960s. But this kind of hindsight is fairly myopic. While it is true that America was spared too much internal dissension, except for McCarthyism and some grumbling about our involvement in Korea, still it was the age of cold warfare at its worst and its threat to the psyche seemed lethal. Two superpowers, determined to undo each other's political systems, possessed the ultimate weapon of destruction, and each feared that the other would use that weapon as a deterrent if it imagined itself about to be attacked.

Unlocking secrets of the atom to produce the bomb represented a scientific as well as a military breakthrough, increasing the dependency of armed power on the innovativeness of the scientist. Americans had grown confident that our country's leadership in science and technology was unchallengeable. We expected ourselves to be always the first in creating new gadgetry to make life and death easier, whether through sophisticated home appliances, computer systems, communications equipment, or explosives with the power of megatons of TNT. Imagine the shock, then, when this illusion was shattered by the successful launching of Sputnik by none other than our arch enemy in the midst of a cold war that at any moment could turn hotter than any conflict in history. Sputnik was not simply a demoralizing technological feat; it had potential military applications as well. Suddenly, the prestige and survival of a nation were jeopardized because the enemy's greatest minds of the day had outperformed ours, and the Russians capitalized on this coup by broadcasting to every nation on earth its success, at long last, in reducing America to a second-class power.

Although the shock of Sputnik in 1957 triggered unprecedented action on behalf of the gifted, educators had already expressed their lament over public indifference to these children much earlier in that decade. In 1950, for example, the Educational Policies Commission decried the school's neglect of mentally superior children and the resulting shrinking of manpower in the sciences, arts, and professions.[1] A year later, the Ohio Commission on Children and Youth revealed that only 2 percent of the schools in that state had special classes for the gifted and a mere 9 percent reported any kind of enrichment in the regular classroom.[2]

Criticism of the elementary and high schools eventually came also from the academic community. In 1953, Bestor, an academician, published a sensational indictment of public education for practicing what he considered its special brand of fraudulence on America's children (Bestor, 1953).

Because of what he regarded as a misplacement of power in the hands of know-nothing "educationists," Bestor was convinced that schools provided meager intellectual nourishment or inspiration, especially for the gifted who often marked time in their studies until graduation released them from boredom and euphoria.

To some extent, the eagerness among educators to increase the nation's talent supply was inspired by politicians and economists who had worried about our diminishing reservoir of high-level manpower in science and technology even before Sputnik dramatized the problem. For example, Wolfle, Director of the Commission on Human Resources and Advanced Training, asserted that the United States failed to prepare enough men and women in the natural sciences, the health fields, teaching, and engineering (Wolfle, 1954). Only six of ten in the top 5 percent and only half of the top 25 percent of high school graduates went on to earn college diplomas. At the more advanced levels, a mere 3 percent of those capable of earning the Ph.D actually did so. What made matters worse were expectations that the shortages would become even more acute in the late 1950s unless the schools succeeded in encouraging gifted students to continue on to advanced studies.

Manpower statistics confirmed the existence of shortages in key professions. Again, the cause of this alarming situation was attributed to the commitment of the schools to deal with mediocrity rather than superiority. Allegedly, teachers were geared to work with average or even below average students, with the result that the ablest were often disregarded. Many dropped out of school before graduation or refused to go on to college after four years of high school.

Aside from the exhortative statements and surveys dramatizing the failure to educate gifted children, there is also evidence of scholarly activity in the early part of the decade. Few people could forecast the impact of Guilford's paper on creativity on the subsequent research pertaining to the nature and measurement of productive thinking (Guilford, 1950). That paper encouraged psychometrists to abandon the assumption that tests of general intelligence, such as those developed in the early part of the century by Lewis Terman, could be used to locate the pool of children out of which virtually all of the gifted would probably emerge. Rather, Guilford's model brought attention to multiple aptitudes, including divergent production or "creativity," as it is sometimes called. His ideas about creativity and its measurement were later adapted by Getzels and Jackson in their comparison of "high creative-low IQ" and "high IQ-low creative" students at the University of Chicago High School (Getzels and Jackson, 1958). This study had a stunning influence on educational researchers because it announced a breakthrough in the use of so-called "creativity" measures to identify a talent resource that would be overlooked by tests of general intelligence. The question of whether instruments for assessing creativity can locate otherwise undiscoverable talent has never been fully settled (Crockenberg, 1972), but protagonists for the use of such tests have inspired the kind of

22

general enthusiasm that today would greet an announcement of new sources of energy.

Much of the work in the early 1950s was codified in *Education for the Gifted*, the fifty-seventh yearbook of the National Society for the Study of Education. Published in 1958, it was the first yearbook of the Society on the topic since 1924.

Despite the work of specialists on the gifted and the portents and premonitions concerning Russia's strides in building its talent reservoir, there was no serious action in America's schools until Sputnik was launched in 1957. At that time, the rhetoric started to become more strident and the research more abundant, and together they either produced or accompanied radical changes in public education. We were convinced that the Russians slipped ahead of us in space technology because we had insufficient manpower to advance the sciences. Predictably, the schools were singled out as scapegoats.

While the nation kept careful watch on scientific developments in the Soviet Union, it also monitored the rate at which Soviet education was producing new scientists and the kind of training they received in the process. Invariably, invidious comparisons were made between the enemy's system and ours. One report claimed that before graduating from a Russian high school, a student had to complete five years of physics, biology, and a foreign language, four years of chemistry, one year of astronomy, and as many as ten years of mathematics.[3] Our own graduates were woefully undereducated by comparison. Worse than that, the young people in American colleges earning science degrees and committing their talents to defense-related professions did not compare in number with their counterparts in the Soviet Union.

It was essential to build up our supply of high-level human resources quickly or else risk seeing a national emergency deteriorate into a national catastrophe. In time, school officials began to acknowledge that something was wrong with public education and that there was much overhauling to be done. It was probably the mounting exposés of malpractice in the schools, capped by Sputnik and its ominous implications, that moved them out of their complacency and made them more reform-minded. Indeed, the reaction to Sputnik might not have been so swift and strong if the critics' cries for change in our schools had not had a cumulative effect.

When the educational community finally took action on behalf of the gifted, it did so with alacrity. Public and private funds became available to assist in the pursuit of excellence, primarily in the fields of science and technology. Academic coursework was telescoped and stiffened to test the brainpower of the gifted. Courses that had been offered only at the college level began to find their way into special enrichment programs in high school and subsequently in elementary school. Even the self-contained classroom, which had been a tradition in elementary education, briefly gave way to limited departmental instruction in a few localities. Attempts were made to introduce foreign languages in the elementary schools, but that too did not last long after an auspicious beginning. Also making short-lived appearances were courses with such attractive titles as the Mathematics of Science, Opera Production, Seminar in the Humanities, Integration of the Arts, World Affairs, Structural Linguistics, and Critical Thinking. There were even special efforts made to locate and nurture giftedness among the socially disadvantaged, most notably through the P.S. 43 Project in New York City, which later became the widely heralded but eventually ill-fated Higher Horizons Program. Interest spread also to school systems in rural areas and to colleges and universities where the gifted were provided with enrichment experiences never before extended to them.

There is no way of knowing precisely what percentage of our schools offered something special to the gifted in the years immediately after Sputnik. Many of the crash programs were never taken seriously enough by their sponsoring institutions to last long. But there were prominent exceptions that started out as enrichment experiences for the gifted only and later changed the curriculum for all children. Much of what is taught today in the mathematics and sciences, for example, is a legacy of post-Sputnik designs in gifted education. Similar influences can be felt in current secondary school programs that are comprehensive enough to accommodate human diversity without shortchanging the gifted. Conant expressed the sentiment of the late 1950s in a report entitled *The American High School Today* (Conant, 1959). He offered a broad, twenty-one step plan for changing secondary education with special emphasis on core courses that were challenging in content and required of all students regardless of their career plans. His proposals took special note of the academically gifted (the upper 15 percent) and the highly gifted (the upper 3 percent). The tougher standards he suggested for them were far more acceptable to school officials than were those recommended by Bestor and his fellow critics.

In addition to the plethora of special enrichment activities initiated in the schools during the late 1950s and early 1960s, there was an upsurge in research activity dealing with the characteristics and education of gifted children. Investigations in vogue at the time focused primarily on such topics as the relative effectiveness of different administrative designs (for example, ability grouping, enrichment in regular classes, and acceleration); the social status of the gifted at school and its effect on their motivation to learn; the causes and treatment of scholastic underachievement among children with high potential; achievement motivation and other non-intellective factors in high-level learning; and the psychosocial correlates of divergent thinking processes. Professional journals were deluged with research reports and with exhortations to do something special for the gifted. So rapid was the buildup of literature in the field that one writer claimed there were more articles published in the three-year period from 1956 to 1959 than in the previous thirty years (French, 1959).

High scholastic standards and standing, academic advancement, studiousness, and career-mindedness were conspicuous themes in our schools. It became virtually unthinkable for a gifted child to bypass the tougher courses in favor of the less demanding ones. It certainly was no time for youth to do their own thing or to enjoy the privilege of doing nothing. Instead, they were brought up in a period of total talent mobilization, requiring the most ableminded to fulfill their potentials and submit their developed abilities for service to the nation.

The 1960s: A Decade of Turmoil

The 1960s opened with John F. Kennedy's election to the presidency amid promises and dreams of a modern utopia. There was excitement in the air as the nation prepared itself to sweep away the stodginess of the 1950s and create a new age of excellence. Kennedy's earliest presidential messages made it clear that brains and loyalty to the flag were among our most precious assets. He announced boldly his intention to put a man on the moon by 1970, a clear sign that we were accepting Russia's challenge for supremacy in space exploration and that the most brilliant scientists would be called upon to make such a feat feasible. This meant encouraging the largest possible number of able students to enroll in science programs that offered them the best possible special education. For who else but the gifted could yield from their ranks a cadre of scientists qualified to honor the President's commitment?

There were other hints of meritocracy in the air. Kennedy gathered around him some of the most precocious men (although few women) of his generation to advise him on governmental matters. Known then as the "Whiz Kids," some had earned their reputations as scholars at leading universities and others as promising idea men in industry. All of them projected an image of braininess with a zest for unraveling the chief executive's knottiest problems. They were gifted children grown up and enjoying the glamor of fame and power rather than living in relative obscurity as so many other gifted people must do, even in their most productive years. At last, able children had their own celebrity role models to emulate, much as budding athletes and entertainers have theirs.

It would, of course, be naive to suggest that we had reached a point in history when the brilliant student was taking his place alongside the sports star as a hero on campus. Far from it. Research by Coleman (1962) and Tannenbaum (1962) demonstrated that acclaim among peers was far more easily achieved on the athletic field than on the honor roll. Still, the Kennedy years were making good on promises of social and economic rewards for those willing to cultivate their superior scholastic abilities despite the lack of enthusiastic cheering from schoolmates.

The bids were high for brains in the early 1960s, but there was a string attached. President Kennedy himself expressed it best in his immortal admonition to his countrymen: "Ask not what your country can do for you—ask what you can do for your country." It was a call for unselfish accomplishment, to dedicate the work of our citizens to the greater glory of the nation. Those with higher abilities had more to contribute and were therefore under pressure not to bury their talents or even to indulge in creative productivity that was impractical. The feeling during that cold war period was that the scientist could better serve the nation than the poet.

Judging from the career plans of gifted children in the late 1950s and early 1960s, they evidently believed that the nation was worth serving. By far the largest number of students with high tested intelligence majored in the sciences, and many of them aspired to enter fields of technology that could somehow help the defense effort. The lure of employment opportunities in these industries and professions was reinforced by the glamorization of science as man's most exciting modern frontier.

Yet, the flurry of activity on behalf of the gifted has left some unfinished business to haunt us. Even the threat of Sputnik and the indulgence of excellence during the Kennedy era were not enough to guarantee that the needs of the gifted would be cared for perpetually at school. Instead, enrichment was considered a curricular ornament to be detached and discarded when the cost of upkeep became prohibitive. Moreover, the fervor with which guidance counselors ushered gifted youths into science programs backfired to some degree as large numbers of these students switched their academic majors by the time they reached their sophomore year in college (Watley, 1968), and many who did stay on to pursue the careers mapped out for them became victims of the shaky fortunes of the aerospace industry. On the other hand, little more than lip service was paid to the needs of a special breed of students not gifted academically but possessing exceptional talent in the arts, mechanics, and social leadership. Also, whatever work was done in defining and measuring divergent productivity remained in the research laboratory. Few people attempted to develop ways of cultivating this kind of intellective functioning and translating it into curriculum sequences. Finally, the national talent hunt failed to penetrate the socially disadvantaged minorities whose records of school achievement were well below national norms and whose children with high potential were much harder to locate because their environments provided too little of the requisite encouragement and opportunity to fulfill whatever promise they might have shown under other circumstances. A notable exception to this general neglect of talent among the underprivileged was the aforementioned P.S. 43 project in New York City, which was then modified to become the Higher Horizons Program (Landers, 1963). But these efforts were shortlived, coming to an end when a subsequent evaluation revealed no special accomplishments of the program, perhaps due to an underestimate of costs, personnel, curriculum planning, and just plain hard work needed to duplicate on a much larger scale the earlier successes at P.S. 43 (Wrightstone, 1964).

Focus on Underprivileged Minorities

The 1954 Supreme Court decision to desegregate public schools set off an inexorable movement toward updating the Constitution and the Bill of Rights. Once again, education became the linchpin of a national priority, this time for social justice, as it had formerly been for the Great Talent Hunt. Separatism and equality were declared an impossible combination and therefore unconstitutional. Educators and social and behavioral scientists placed the cause of disadvantaged children at the top of their priority list, even ahead of the gifted. We were now more concerned with bolstering freedom and equality within our borders than with playing the lead on the world stage despite the unabated pressures of cold warfare that brought confrontations between East and West in Europe, Southeast Asia, and the Middle East.

In addition to diverting interest away from the gifted, the advocacy movement for the socially disadvantaged actually contested at least two features of special programs for the ablest: (a) the use of intelligence tests and other conventional measures of aptitude as a means of determining who deserves to be called gifted; and (b) grouping children in special classes for the gifted on the basis of their performance on these kinds of assessments. The intelligence test, a major instrument for determining academic potential ever since Terman initiated his monumental studies of genius in the early part of the century, came under heavy attack for being biased against some racial minorities and the socioeconomically depressed. It was charged that the problem-solving tasks, which are mostly verbal, favor children with experience in higher-status environments. Consequently, these children obtain higher scores, thus creating the delusion that they are basically more intelligent and perhaps even born with superior intellect. As a result of these charges, some urban centers with large racial minorities, notably New York and Los Angeles, discontinued the use of such tests.

The push toward greater egalitarianism aggravated a mild distrust of intelligence testing that had always existed in this country. Many suspected that it is vaguely antidemocratic to declare, on the basis of a test score, that a child is fated to become an achiever or a failure, economically comfortable or uncomfortable, and a high- or a low-status person, even if such forecasts allowed broad limits of error. Such an idea did not square with our traditional faith in this country that one is given the freedom and opportunity to make of himself what he will. The residual aversion to testing intelligence on grounds that predestines inequality among *individuals* was compounded by charges that the measures discriminate against racial and socioeconomic *groups* as well. It was enough to threaten the use of mainstay instruments for identifying gifted children.

Since racial minorities, such as Hispanics, Blacks, Chicanos, and Native Americans, traditionally performed less well at school than did white majorities, it was logical to regard ability grouping for the gifted as de facto racial segregation. Critics argued that schools were practicing blatant favoritism by creating separate classes for children who rated superior on conventional measures of intellect and also by offering those chosen few a kind of enrichment in their curriculum that was denied everyone else. The objections were not against special ability grouping per se for the gifted, or even the unique educational experience reserved for them because of their ability. What created the furor was the practice of denying enough children from disadvantaged subpopulations their rightful access to these classes. There was an overwhelming sentiment favoring the idea that high potential is equitably distributed among all races, privileged and underprivileged, but that life's circumstances in some groups are oppressive enough to cast a shadow over their innate competencies.

Thus we see that American education was not able to reconcile its interest in the gifted with its concern about the disadvantaged, nor could it design a satisfactory methodology for locating and cultivating giftedness among these minority groups. The dilemma was easy to resolve inasmuch as it reduced itself to a choice between battling for social justice or pursuing excellence, and there was no doubt as to which of the two would better fit the mood of the 1960s.

VIET NAM AND DISSENTING YOUTH

During the brief Kennedy era, the United States faced the communist world in several near-conflicts. In each instance, we emerged with our self-image intact as the champions of the free world against forces of darkness. The subsequent adventure in Viet Nam turned out to be disastrously different, despite the fact that President Johnson justified our entanglement on the same grounds that his predecessor defended his risks of war in Berlin and Cuba. Eventually, the nation grew tired of the war, suspicious of politicians' promises of a quick victory, and increasingly convinced that our country was meddling in affairs of other nations rather than serving as a judge and enforcer of what was morally right in the world.

Among the many casualties of the Viet Nam conflict was our perception of giftedness in political leadership. The Whiz Kids of the Kennedy years, many of whom had stayed on in the Johnson era to help formulate strategy for the war effort, rapidly lost their image as people who could become heroes in public life by virtue of their brainpower alone. In fact, their sad history seemed to prove that being supersmart in the scholastic sense of the term was no guarantee of superunderstanding of man's most serious problems and how to solve them. Gifted youth on campuses throughout the country learned to despise them for their role in the Viet Nam debacle rather than revere them as graduated honors students distinguishing themselves as national leaders (Halberstam, 1972).

A far more serious by-product of Viet Nam was a growing unrest among students in the colleges. Kenneth Keniston, who studied these young people in great detail, made it quite clear that a complex mix of personal attributes, familial influences, peer associations, and school environments set them

28

apart from their more conforming age-mates (Keniston, 1971). It is noteworthy, however, that a disproportionate number of disaffected youth on campus distinguished themselves in their studies at school and were frequently enrolled in some of the more enriched and prestigious programs. Their immediate targets were the colleges they were attending, which represented to them an establishment with archaic standards for success and unreasonable controls over their lives. Yet these same gadflies in centers of learning were themselves described in one study as possessing high degrees of intellectualism (Flacks, 1967).

The unrest on campus underwent some dramatic changes over a relatively short period of time. As one observer remarked, "The key difference between the Berkeley riots of 1964 and the Columbia crisis of May, 1969 is that in the pre-Columbian case the major impetus for unrest stemmed from the perceived abuse or misuse of authority ('Do not bend, fold, or mutilate'), whereas the later protest denied the legitimacy of authority" (Bennis, 1970). The revolt was not only against institutions (educational or otherwise) and their leaders; it was also against a tradition of rationalism that sanctified ivory-tower scholarship. When Columbia rioters willfully destroyed a professor's research files, the act may have carried a message that goes beyond ordinary vandalism. It seemed to imply that all the work invested in accumulating those files was a waste of the professor's talent, which ought to have been dedicated to building a better society rather than dabbling in trivia and esoterica. And to make matters worse, the educational establishment expected its brightest students to follow in the footsteps of professors like him.

Many questions were raised among gifted college students as to whether they ought to funnel their psychic energies into a life of the mind. Many were attracted to the sensitivity training movements, which told them that "talking is usually good for intellectual understanding of personal experience, but it is often not effective for helping a person *to experience*—to feel" (Schutz, 1967). Accordingly, man should not be seen simply, as though he were a machine, but rather as a complex biological, psychological, and social organism who can fulfill himself through all of these dimensions of his being. Every part of the body has to be exercised to its fullest potential, which means building up the strength and stamina of its muscles, its sensory awareness and aesthetic appreciation, its motor control, and the gamut of its emotional and social feelings. Inhibiting other aspects of self for the sake of the intellect amounts to robbing life of its multidimensionality, so the task of the individual is to make something of all his capacities, even if in so doing he cannot make the most of any of them.

Significantly, a new utopia emerged in the form of Consciousness III, depicted by Reich in his best seller, *The Greening of America*. One of the postulates of this new world was described by Reich as follows:

> Consciousness III rejects the whole concept of excellence and comparative merit. . . . It refuses to evaluate people by general standards, it refuses to

classify people, or analyze them. Each person has his own individuality, not to be compared to that of anyone else. Someone may be a brilliant thinker, but he is not "better" at thinking than anyone else, he simply possesses his own excellence. A person who thinks very poorly is still excellent in his own way. Therefore people are in no hurry to find out another person's background, schools, achievements, as a means of knowing him; they regard all of that as secondary, preferring to know him unadorned. Because there are no governing standards, no one is rejected. Everyone is entitled to pride himself, and no one should act in a way that is servile, or feel inferior, or allow himself to be treated as if he were inferior (Reich, 1970).

Thus we see how life for campus dissidents became strangely paradoxical. Many of them espoused the habits of intellectualism generally associated with gifted students. At the same time they rejected excellence and its trappings as violations of democracy and too stultifying to the attainment of total joy and liberation. Even those consenting to live the life of the mind learned an unforgetable lesson from the events in Viet Nam. No longer could they be adjured to cultivate their talents for the sake of their country's prestige and need for survival. The immoral war in Southeast Asia tarnished the nation's image enough to discourage such commitments among many who could potentially be counted among our high-level human resources. Besides, some may have felt it faintly dehumanizing to be treated like natural resources; it simply did not fit well with the new spirit of selfhood and individuality.

THE DEVALUATION OF SCIENCE

For many years, consuming or producing scientific knowledge was regarded as a human virtue, particularly if it helped conquer nature in order to make man's life more comfortable. There was hardly much doubt that gifted children would derive great personal satisfaction and a certain measure of power and freedom if they became highly informed about the secrets of the universe or contributed significantly to unraveling some of these mysteries. In the 1960s, however, serious doubts were raised about the value of scholarship as it had been traditionally transacted in the schools. Significant segments of campus youth began to sour on knowledge factories, and Herbert Marcuse, one of their most influential spokesmen, warned about the mechanizing, denaturalizing, and subjugating impact of knowledge (Marcuse, 1964).

Gifted youth in the age of Sputnik were bombarded with the message that a lifetime devotion to achievement in science was not only in the interests of the state, but of mankind in general. Such pursuits have their own built-in ethic, that any efforts at pushing back the frontiers of theory and research deserve the highest commendation because they attest to man's divine-like power of mastering his environment and creating his own brand of miracles in it. Suddenly the nation was told that man's science is as fallible as he is himself. Among the most vocal critics were the environment-minded scientists who warned that, in our enthusiasm for conquering nature, we may be destroying ourselves in the process unless we impose restraints on such activity (Bereano, 1969). Perhaps the best-known writer to forecast doom if science were to continue on its conventional course was the biologist Commoner, whose book *Science and Survival*, enjoyed wide circulation and influence. Commoner took the ecological point of view that the elements of nature are integrated but our knowledge of these elements is so limited that we do not see their connectedness. Expressing deep concern about the preoccupation of science with the elegance of its methods rather than the danger of its products, he directed much of his fire at the polluting effects of such symbols of technological giantism as nuclear testing and industrial waste. He acknowledged the need for brainpower to enrich scientific thinking, but he also warned that "no scientific principle can tell us how to make the choice, which may sometimes be forced upon us by the insecticide problem, between the shade of the elm tree and the song of the robin" (Commoner, 1966). With such caveats, it became more difficult to convince gifted children that a life dedicated to science is the kind of high calling it once was unless closer links were made between the intellect and the conscience.

Besides being tarnished because they failed to take account of their human consequences, careers in science lost more of their glitter when the job market in various related fields began to tighten. The manpower crisis dramatized by Sputnik gradually calmed down when we began to overtake the Russians in the technology race and achieved a victory of sorts by transporting the first man to the moon in 1969. Manpower shortages in the various fields of science were no longer critical, partly because the flood of graduates in the early 1960s had filled available jobs, and also because the cold war was not considered serious enough to create new jobs through lucrative defense contracts. In fact, by the late 1960s, many Americans were suspicious of the so-called "military-industrial complex" for carving too much out of the tax dollar to support projects that were wasteful in times of peace. The primary need was to solve the problems of social unrest rather than to prop up our defense technology. Many would be scientists and engineers began to realize that these professions attracted neither the prestige nor occupational rewards that would have been guaranteed only a few years earlier. Unfortunately, however, the supply of scientific talent did not slow down in accordance with the reduced demand, and as a result of the imbalance, many highly trained personnel found themselves either unemployed or working at unskilled jobs outside their fields.

The 1970s: A Renewed Interest

The decline of attention to the gifted in the 1960s is evident in the contrasting number of professional publications on that subject at the beginning and end of the decade. The number of entries under "Gifted

Children" in the 1970 volume of *Education Index* was less than half the number in the 1960 volume. Nevertheless, by the outset of the present decade, there were unmistakable signs of a revival of interest. Probably the biggest boost came from a 1970 congressional mandate that added Section 806, "Provisions Related to Gifted and Talented Children," to the Elementary and Secondary Education Amendments of 1969 (Public Law 91-230). This document expressed a legislative interest in the gifted that eventually led to federal support of program initiatives throughout the country.

As a result of federal encouragement and some public and private initiative, the gifted have been exposed to an increasing number of special educational experiences in the 1970s. While as late as 1973 fewer than 4 percent of the nation's gifted children were receiving satisfactory attention at school, and most of the fortunate ones were concentrated in ten states, by 1977 every state in the union demonstrated at least some interest in the ablest.

Leadership at the federal level also grew much stronger in the first half of the decade. After being in existence for a brief three-year period as an understaffed, temporary unit in the U.S. Office of Education, Bureau of the Handicapped, the Office of the Gifted and Talented was given official status by legislation in 1974. The Special Projects Act resulted in a 1976 appropriation of $2.56 million for developing professional and program resources in the field. That allocation was renewed for 1977, and there is every reason to expect that federal support will be sustained at least for the years immediately ahead. There are also proposals for legislation that would change the Bureau of the Handicapped to the Bureau of Exceptional Persons, thus including gifted and talented individuals as eligible for sustained support of their education, along with the handicapped. If passed, such federal legislation will go a long way toward erasing the image of education for the gifted as being only a periodic fad in the schools. It is admittedly a way of forcing attention on the ablest by tying their fortunes to those of the handicapped, for whom funding rarely abates appreciably. The public may never feel equally sympathetic to both groups, but it could be forced to reduce some of its favoritism toward one over the other if they are combined rather than separate recipients of support through legislation.

The thrust of recent activity for the gifted has been mostly programmatic and promotional, with relatively little emphasis on research. Funding at all levels is invested in curriculum enrichment, teacher education, and training for leadership in the field. As part of their work on curriculum, many educators are designing or adapting special instructional systems in order to offer the ablest students experiences that are uniquely appropriate for them, not just promising practices from which all children can derive benefits.

Present-day efforts to design distinctive curricula for the gifted may result in some lasting contributions to the field. Products that have already been developed and distributed in many localities incorporate large numbers of exercises in divergent thinking. This trend reflects the foundational work of several prolific educators whose writings fairly dominated the field during the 1960s. Among the most widely influential persons has been E. Paul Torrance, who alone and with the help of occasional collaborators was responsible for at least seven major books and monographs as well as a large number of professional papers on the subject of creativity from 1960 to 1970. The popularity of research and materials development pertaining to divergent thinking is also having its impact on the classroom more than ever before. "Values clarification" has made its debut in recent years and is gradually spreading in classes for the gifted. It introduced a new dimension in the curriculum by stimulating children to understand themselves better and to develop belief systems and behavior codes that they can justify as bases for some of the most important decisions of their lives.

Again, as in the post-Sputnik period, interest has been expressed in gifted children who have high social intelligence and in those especially talented in the visual and performing arts. It is hard to say whether educators today are paying more attention to the needs of such children than their predecessors did two decades ago. From all indications, it would seem that they are not as yet far beyond the lip-service level of commitment. Even less fortunate are the gifted among underprivileged minority populations who still remain largely neglected, except in the arts, but not deliberately so. There is no doubt that many educators would gladly initiate enrichment experiences for these children and that support could be obtained for such plans if they stood a chance of success. Yet, the profession is still stymied in its efforts to find a way of discerning high-level academic potential that is buried under a thick overlay of social and economic handicaps. In fact, it is no less difficult today than ever before to tease out and inspire the fulfillment of scholarly talent in the nation's underprivileged classes.

Generally, the enrichment programs initiated in the present decade have been impressive in their variety, inventiveness, the extent of their dissemination, and in the spirit and proficiency with which they are being implemented. The same cannot be said for research productivity. A review of the state of research for the years 1969-1974 revealed a fairly bleak picture (Spaulding); only thirty-nine reports on the gifted and talented had been published in that period. Today, these efforts continue to be limited, but there are several major projects now underway that deal with the nature and nurture of talent at all age levels.

What prompted the resurgence of activity in gifted education after nearly a decade of quiescence? A full answer probably will not come until future historians can view the 1970s in a proper time perspective. But the explanation that seems most obvious right now is America's backlash against awareness-oriented youth who turned excessively self-indulgent, and against campus revolutionaries who trashed some sacred scholarly traditions. Geoffrey Wagner has recently published a scathing indictment of universities for compromising academic standards, inflating grades, and diluting degree requirements in order to fend off unrest among students (Wagner, 1976). Perhaps these are signs that the pendulum is inevitably swinging away from extreme egalitarianism in the direction of excellence. It is hard to imagine that there would be a popular acceptance of the Consciousness III notion about brilliant minds not being better at thinking than anyone else and poor thinkers necessarily being excellent in their own ways. This kind of argument is too fantasy-ridden to flourish successfully even in an egalitarian-minded society. There are, however, legacies of the 1960s that are volatile enough today to have prevented the gifted from making a comeback. They include the following realities:

1. Few manpower shortages exist at the high-skill levels. The job market is glutted with Ph.D's who cannot find work in their fields of training. In 1976, the starting salary of college graduates was only 6 percent above that of the average American worker, whereas in 1969, a person with a college diploma could earn 24 percent more than the national mean (*Newsweek*, April 26, 1976).

2. The cold war, while relentless, does not threaten any new surprises to shake our confidence in the nation's talent reservoir. There is even talk of moderating the confrontation between East and West through policies of detente and the SALT talks.

3. It is not much easier today than in the late 1960s to persuade our ablest students that they have to work hard at school in order to serve their country in ways that only they can. National policies in Viet Nam and in the civil rights movement had persuaded too many of them that the country was not worthy of such dedication. When the Viet Nam war came to an end, Watergate emerged to reinforce the cynicism and alienation of youth, including many gifted individuals among them.

4. Quality, integrated education is as much a dream today as it has ever been. A prodigious amount of work yet remains to be done before underprivileged children can begin to derive their rightful benefits from experiences at school. That kind of investment of effort in compensatory programs usually draws attention away from curricular enrichment for the gifted.

5. Science and scientists are still monitored critically for possible moral lapses. The most recent controversy concerning value judgments in the scientific community has revolved around experiments in genetic engineering. Some gifted children may choose to avoid fields of science in order to keep their consciences clear about possibly opening any kind of Pandora's box in scientific discovery.

6. The 1970s have experienced hard times and drastic cutbacks in expenditures for education. Programs for the gifted are usually the most expendable ones when budgetary considerations force cutbacks in services to children.

Despite the aforementioned lingering influences of the 1960s, we are experiencing a drift toward excellence after indulging egalitarianism for awhile. This revival of interest, however, is no more a sign of pure historical inevitability than w.. its decline a decade ago. It is rather, in part at least, a sign of initiatives taken by people who believe in differentiated education at every ability level and who are participating in vigorous campaigns to save the shools.

Attention to individual competencies among the handicapped has dramatized the need to individualize education, with every child receiving a fair share of what is uniquely appropriate for him, regardless of how deficient or proficient he is in mastering curriculum content. It is logical, then, that the gifted also receive special attention to accommodate their unique learning strengths and thereby demonstrate the educator's attention to human differences. Eventually, PL 94-142 may include the gifted, which would take us a long way toward actualizing the belief that democracy in education means recognizing how children are unlike each other, and doing something about it. Protagonists for the gifted argue that the more sophisticated we become in discerning human individuality and the more inventive we are in providing for individual needs of the ablest, the more likely we are to achieve equality in the schools.

THE ROLE OF THE GIFTED IN "RESCUING" PUBLIC EDUCATION

It is no secret that educators are searching desperately for ways to maintain order in thousands of classrooms. This is especially true in big-city schools where more than 10 percent of the nation's pupil population is enrolled. The dismal picture is a familiar one: scholastic achievement levels are three, four, and even five years below norms; drugs, violence, vandalism, and truancy have reached epidemic proportions; and costs are climbing to such a height that there may soon be insufficient funds to pay the bills while maintaining an adequately staffed program (*Ibid.*, 1977). Many middle-class families have fled the inner city or sought help from private schools in order to provide a meaningful educational experience for their children. This has further aggravated the situation in urban centers.

School administrators are aware that one way to bring back the middle classes to the schools is to initiate special programs for the gifted. They are, therefore, opening so-called "magnet schools" that offer enrichment activities in particular subject matter areas and are luring back to their classrooms sizable numbers of children who would otherwise be studying elsewhere. The presence of the ablest is beginning to make a difference in the total school atmosphere, which demonstrates that they are capable of enhancing all of education if their learning capacities are properly respected. This truism may turn out to be the most important lesson learned from our experience with gifted and talented children in the 1970s.

References

Bennis, Warren G. A funny thing happened on the way to the future. *American Psychologist*, 1970, **25**, 595-608.

Bereano, Philip L. The scientific community and the crisis of belief. *American Scientist*, 1959, **57**, 484-501.

Bestor, Arthur E., *Educational wastelands*. Urbana, Ill.: University of Illinois Press, 1953.

Coleman, James S. *The adolescent society*. Glencoe, Ill.: The Free Press, 1962.

Commoner, Barry. *Science and survival*. New York: The Viking Press, 1966, p. 104.

Conant, James B. *The American high school today*. New York: Mc-Graw-Hill, 1959.

Crockenberg, Susan B. Creativity tests: a boon or boondoggle for education? *Review of Educational Research*, 1972, **42**, 27-45.

Flacks, Richard. The liberated generation: an exploration of the roots of student protest. *Journal of Social Issues*, 1967, **23**, no. 3, 52-75.

French, Joseph L., ed. *Educating the gifted*. New York: Henry Holt, 1959.

Gardner, John. *Excellence: Can we be equal and excellent too?* New York: Harper and Row, 1961, p. 33.

Getzels, Jacob W. and Philip W. Jackson. The meaning of 'giftedness': An examination of an expanding concept. *Phi Delta Kappan*, 1958, **40**, 75-77.

Guilford, Joy P. Creativity. *American Psychologist*, 1950, **5**, 444-454.

Halberstam, David. *The best and the brightest*. Westminster, Md.: Random House, 1972.

Keniston, Kenneth. *Youth and dissent: The role of a new opposition*. New York: Harcourt, Brace, Jovanovich, 1971.

Landers, Jacob. *Higher horizons progress report*. New York: Board of Education of the City of New York, 1963.

Marcuse, Herbert. *One-dimensional man*. Boston: Beacon Press, 1964.

Newsweek, April 26, 1976.

Ibid., September 12, 1977.

Reich, Charles A. *The greening of america*. New York: Random House, 1970, pp. 226–227.

Schutz, William C. *Joy: Expanding human awareness*. New York: Grove Press, 1967, p.11.

Spaulding, R. L. Summary report of issues and trends in research on the gifted and talented. (undated manuscript).

Tannenbaum, Abraham J. *Adolescent attitudes toward academic brilliance*. New York: Teachers College Press, 1962.

Wagner, Geoffrey. *The end of education*. South Brunswick, N. J.: A. S. Barnes, 1976.

Watley, Donivan J. *Stability of career choices of talented youth.* Evanston, Ill.: National Merit Scholarship Corp., 1968.

Wolfle, Dael. *America's resources of specialized talent.* New York: Harper and Row, 1954.

Wrightstone, J. Wayne, et al. *Evaluation of the higher horizons program for underprivileged children.* New York: Board of Education of the City of New York, 1964.

Notes

[1] Educational Policies Commission. *Education of the gifted.* Washington, D. C.: National Education Association, 1950.

[2] Ohio Commission on Children and Youth. *The status of the gifted in Ohio.* Columbus: Ohio Department of Education, 1951.

[3] *Soviet commitment to education.* Report of the First U.S. Education Mission to the U. S. S. R., Bulletin 1959, No. 16, Office of Education. U.S. Department of Health, Education and Welfare. Washington, D. C.: U.S. Government Printing Office, 1959.

Paul A. Witty

The Education of the Gifted and the Creative in the U.S.A.

*T*he advent of the intelligence test in America ushered in a period in which most schools recognized the problem of caring for individual differences. There was frequent adaptation of the curriculum to care more adequately for slow-learning and retarded pupils, and occasional attempts were made to enrich and extend the experiences of the rapid-learning and gifted pupil.

The gifted child was typically considered to be a pupil whose IQ was very high, a concept which has persisted over a very long period of time among educators. The practice is traceable, to a large extent, to the work of L. M. Terman and his associates who devised an individual intelligence test and administered it to large numbers of pupils who were assigned to categories according to their ratings. Pupils who earned IQ's of 130 and higher were designated as "gifted" and those of IQ 140 and higher were classified as "genius or near genius." Early studies of elementary school pupils revealed that about one per cent earned IQ's which placed them in the "gifted" group. More recent studies have yielded somewhat higher percentages.

Large scale genetic studies of the gifted were initiated about 1920 and were summarized by L. M. Terman and Melita H. Oden (16a). In a magazine article, Terman concluded that gifted children are:

> ...in general, appreciably superior to unselected children in physique, health, and social adjustment; markedly superior in moral attitudes as measured either by character tests or by trait ratings; and vastly superior in their mastery of school subjects as shown by a three-hour battery of achievement tests. In fact, the typical child of the group had mastered the school subjects to a point about two grades beyond the one in which he was enrolled, some of them three or four grades beyond(15).

In the foregoing investigation, the remarkable academic achievement of the gifted child was revealed. Subsequent study showed that this superiority was generally maintained. Terman wrote:

Witty, Paul A. "The Education of the Gifted and the Creative in the U. S. A." *The Gifted Child Quarterly*, Summer, 1971, Vol. XV, No. 2.

...close to 90 per cent entered college and 70 per cent graduated. Of those graduating, 30 per cent were awarded honors and about two-thirds remained for graduate work(15).

Continued investigation of the gifted as adults, as well as study of proven geniuses, convinced Terman that:

...the genius who achieves the highest eminence is one whom intelligence tests would have identified as gifted in childhood(15).

Although the findings of the writer's early studies of high IQ children corroborated Terman's reports, he differed markedly in his interpretation of the data. He doubted whether one is jusified in asserting that a high IQ may be used to predict attainment that may be regarded as the work of "genius," and stressed the importance of other factors such as unusual opportunity, drive, and interest. However, he recognized the value of intelligence test ratings in selecting pupils of high academic promise. Such ratings seem suitable, when supplemented by other data, for the identification of the verbally gifted pupil.

Administrative Procedures Recommended for the Gifted

Perhaps the most conspicuous finding of the early studies was the demonstration of the rapid learning and educational promise of the gifted pupil. About half of the pupils in the writer's studies learned to read before entering school, almost forty per cent before they were five years of age, and some at ages three and four. Moreover, they mastered academic materials with such rapidity that by the time they had reached the fifth or sixth grade in school, they had, on the average, knowledge and skills of pupils classified two full grades above them. As they grew older, the attainment of many pupils grew less commensurate with their early promise. It became clear that the typical curriculum was unsuitable to offer these pupils sufficient challenge and motive for effective and continuous learning. Accordingly, it was recommended that moderate amounts of acceleration of school progress be employed and that enrichment be provided in special classes and in the regular classroom. In the twenties, special classes were formed in a few cities in various states such as California, Ohio, New York, and Pennsylvania. The practice was not widely employed because of inadequate numbers of gifted pupils in many communities and because of the prevailing attitude which led to a fear of the creation of an intellectually elite group through special attention to the gifted. Moreover, many administrators believed that the gifted pupil could take care of himself. As a result, relatively few efforts were made to enrich opportunities for the gifted during the period 1925-1950.

Increased Provisions After 1950

An increased interest in providing special opportunities for the gifted transpired following the publication of Terman and Oden's *The Gifted Child Grows Up* (16a), and *The Gifted Child* (25) edited by Paul A. Witty for the *American Association for Gifted Children,* an organization formed after World War II to foster interest in the education of the gifted. Impetus was given to efforts to identify and encourage gifted children by widespread dissemination of facts concerning the neglect of our greatest human resource at the time when the need for personnel of outstanding ability in science and related fields was crucial. During the following decade, a large number of books, articles and lengthy bibliographies reflected the expanding interest in the gifted. Special classes, partial segregation, and acceleration (or grade skipping) were used more frequently in the elementary school, and in the secondary school "honors classes" (especially in science) and "honors schools" were organized for the gifted. In some schools, provisions were made for superior high school students to enter college early or to obtain college credit for enriched courses taken in high school(13, 20).

Notable was the provision of scholarships and awards which served to offer further motivation and incentive for gifted high school students. For example, in 1956 the National Merit Scholarship Corporation granted 556 awards. By the end of its fourth year, more than 3,000 superior students had entered college with Merit Scholarships according to the Fourth Annual Report of the National Merit Scholarship Corporation. Magazines addressed to teachers and administrators also indicated steps that might be taken to provide more frequent identification of gifted pupils and ways to make more adequate provisions for them. One such article, addressed to school administrators by the present writer, was distributed widely by the editors of The Nation's Schools (February, 1956) and thousands of reprints were sent on request. Thus, a movement to offer the gifted child greater opportunities gained recognition in schools throughout the United States.

The foregoing educational practices were designed primarily to furnish increased opportunities for verbally gifted pupils in the elementary and the secondary school. These gains were heartening. There were, however, some conspicuous limitations in these commendable efforts. For example, the research studies, on which the selection of the gifted was based, were made when pupils were of school age. Very young children were not included.

During this period, opportunities for intellectual stimulation of young children were seldom found in the typical home, preschool center, and traditional kindergarten. One of the chief obstacles to the provision of such opportunities was the prevailing belief that the IQ was relatively constant, fixed, and unchangeable. It was believed that inborn factors accounted in large measure for the child's intelligence (or IQ) and that by the side of heredity, all other factors were "dwarfed in comparison."

Failure to Recognize the Significance of Early Learning

In the years around 1960, a group of "cognitive" psychologists began to explore the nature and extent of learning in early childhood under varying conditions. The studies showed clearly the child's need for intellectually stimulating experiences during the early "crucial" years. In a recent book entitled *Revolution in Learning: The Years from Birth to Six,* Maya Pines states:

> Millions of children are being irreparably damaged by our failure to stimulate them intellectually during their crucial years ... from birth to six. Millions of others are being held back from their true potential(12).

Maya Pines pointed out further that "The child's intelligence grows as much during the first four years of life as it will grow during the next thirteen."(12). It was indicated, too, that failure to provide stimulation and nurture during the early years would have far-reaching adverse effects. Moreover, it was held that opportunities offered at this time have a marked positive influence in increasing learning ability and heightening intelligence, particularly in areas where "disadvantage" prevails. Thus J. McV. Hunt writes:

> ...it is not unreasonable to entertain the hypothesis that, with a sound scientific educational psychology of early experience, it might become feasible to raise the average level of intelligence — by a substantial degree ... this "substantial degree" might be of the order of 30 points of IQ(11).

The foregoing hypothesis will need to be examined and tested carefully. It is, however, clear that the IQ is no longer looked upon as a product chiefly of hereditary factors. The pendulum has swung to an emphasis on environmental influences. Accordingly, programs in early education have been proposed to improve intelligence(2, 5). Remarkable attainment in reading and language has already been reported for children who have been accorded early learning opportunities(4).

Identification of the Creative Pupil

During the period of increased interest in the gifted pupil, it became evident that intelligence tests would not enable one to identify successfully pupils having a high potential for creative expression. This fact was long ago pointed out by the present writer who indicated that the intelligence test does not usually elicit imaginative, original, or unique response. Repeatedly, it has been found recently that if one were to limit selection of "gifted" pupils to those of IQ 130 and higher, he would fail to include the majority of creative pupils (17, 18). The present writer proposed, therefore, that the definition of the gifted be expanded to include "any child whose performance in a worthwhile type of human endeavor is consistently or repeatedly remarkable."

Efforts have been made in recent years to construct tests of "creativity" without marked success. Critics have emphasized the limitations in certain tests and the desirability of caution in using them. It has become clear that creativity is not a general trait, and that an individual who is creative in one area will not necessarily be creative in another (9).

Techniques for Identifying Creative Pupils

Despite the limitations of tests of creativity, there are a number of practical approaches which are being increasingly used to find children whose creative promise is great. For example, in a study made by the present writer, the remarkable film of the Swedish photographer Arne Sucksdorff, *The Hunter and the Forest,* was shown in many schools in a large number of American cities. There is no commentary for the film, but a musical score and the sounds of animals and birds are employed as accompaniments.

After large numbers of pupils had seen the film, they were asked to write a commentary, a poem, or a story about it. The products of slightly more than ten per cent suggested unique creative ability. If a very high IQ had been used as the criterion for the gifted, a majority of these pupils would not have been included. Moreover, many of the outstanding compositions were written by pupils who had not previously been observed as having unusual aptitude in writing. If additional outstanding performance substantiated the first demonstration of exceptional ability by these pupils, they would be considered potentially gifted in this area.

Because of such findings, the present writer suggested that a search be made, not only for pupils of high verbal ability, but also for those of promise in mathematics and science, writing, art, music, drama, mechanical ability, and social leadership.

Motivated by the research of J. P. Guilford, scholars are increasingly recognizing the prevalence of undiscovered talent, and some are stressing multiple talents in children and youth (9, 10). For example, Calvin W. Taylor points out that there are many kinds of talent and indicates that if a search is limited to one type among seven talent groups, 50 per cent of the pupils would be included since they would be above average. If six types were included, the per cent would be about 90 for children above average in one or more items (14a). Such approaches for selecting talented pupils are promising, but will need to be studied further.

Differences Between the Gifted and the Creative

The writer has already noted some of the characteristics of gifted children identified by intelligence tests. They were found to be well-adjusted socially and congenial with their peers. Creative pupils differ markedly from the verbally gifted in these respects. E. P. Torrance stresses the problem in adjustment displayed by the creative pupil:

> In no group thus far studied have we failed to find relatively clear evidence of the operation of pressures against the most creative members of the group, though they are far more severe in some classes than in others (18).

Support is given to the findings of Torrance by a remarkable study reported by Victor and Mildred G. Goertzel (8). These authors chose 400 persons, acknowledged as "eminent" by the large numbers of biographies recently written about them; in childhood:

> They showed their greatest superiority in reading ability; many read at the age of four. Almost all were early readers of good books. They were original thinkers and had scant patience with drill and routine. They were likely to be rejected by their playmates...(8).

The authors concluded that "Three out of five of the Four Hundred had serious school problems."

> Now as in the days of the Four Hundred, the child who is both intelligent and creative remains society's most valuable resource. When we learn to work with him instead of against him, his talents may reward us in ways beyond our ability to imagine (8).

It is at once clear that reading may be used advantageously in helping to meet the needs of gifted and creative pupils. Not only will wide reading enable a pupil to satisfy and extend his interests, but it may also help him to meet personal and social problems successfully and build an appropriate ideal of self (21, 23, 24).

Promising Trends in the Education of the Gifted

We may note two encouraging trends in the education of the gifted. The first is the adoption of a broader concept of the gifted to include children demonstrating a capacity for high level creative response, and the extension · and development in schools, generally, of programs for identifying and encouraging such pupils. The second is found in the notable efforts of parents and teachers to recognize the problem and to become involved in meeting it more adequately. Already there is evidence that increased involvement is being practiced by parents of young children who are employing helpful suggestions found in books such as Joan Beck's *How to Raise a Brighter Child* (2). They are being aided further by following recommendations included in books such as *Helping the Gifted Child* (22). Kits of materials such as the one developed in association with the television program *Sesame Street,* and the *Adventures in Discovery* program of the Western Publishing Company are also being used successfully.

Teachers, too, are becoming involved in programs for gifted and creative students as is suggested in a Reading Aids Booklet entitled *Reading for the Gifted and the Creative Student.* In Chapter III, Walter B. Barbe and Joseph Renzulli present the results of their recent survey of practices in the education of the gifted and the creative student in various states (1). The teachers participating in these programs are to be commended for their efforts to foster the development of gifted and creative pupils in their classrooms. Many of the programs are designed to encourage creative expression in the form of *divergent* and *evaluative* behavior as well as creative reading in the classroom (17, 18).

Despite the above gains, there continues to be a very great neglect of gifted and creative pupils. In a provocative article entitled "Characteristics of Gifted Children" published in 1967, Stanley Krippner indicates that "... society still allows many of its brightest young people to pass by unnoticed" and that "...most school systems have not reached a stage where creativity is properly cultivated or where giftedness is widely appreciated" (26).

Not only is the regrettable condition found in elementary and secondary schools, but it also persists in colleges where, as Krippner states, "The scope of student protest at colleges and universities demonstrates that professors and administrators — are sometimes inept caretakers of America's most valuable resource, its gifted individuals" (26).

It is to be hoped that the present meager opportunities will be greatly extended in the future, since as Arnold Toynbee has written:

> To give a fair chance to potential creativity is a matter of life and death for any society. This is all-important, because the outstanding creative ability of a fairly small percentage of the population is mankind's ultimate capital asset, and the only one with which only Man has been endowed (19).

References

1. Barbe, Walter B., and Renzulli, Joseph. Chapter III in *Reading for the Gifted and the Creative Student,* Reading Aids Booklet. Newark, Delaware: International Reading Association, 1971.

2. Beck, Joan. *How to Raise a Brighter Child.* New York: Trident Press, 1967.

3. Chall, Jeanne S. *Learning to Read: The Great Debate.* New York: McGraw-Hill, 1967.

4. Durkin, Dolores. *Children Who Read Early.* New York: Teachers College Press, Columbia University, 1966.

5. Engelmann, Siegfried, and Engelmann, Therese. *Give Your Child a Superior Mind.* New York: Simon and Schuster, Inc., 1966.

6. Gallagher, James J. *Teaching the Gifted Child.* Boston: Allyn and Bacon, Inc., 1964.

7. Getzels, J. W., and Jackson, P. W. *Creativity and Intelligence.* New York: John Wiley and Sons, Inc., 1962.

8. Goertzel, Victor, and Goertzel, Mildred G. *Cradles of Eminence.* Boston: Little, Brown and Company, 1962.

9. Guilford, J. P. "Potentiality for Creativity," *Gifted Child Quarterly,* 6 (Autumn, 1962).

10. Guilford, J. P. *Intelligence, Creativity, and Their Educational Implications.* San Diego, California: Robert R. Knapp, Box 234, 1968.

11. Hunt, J. McV. *Intelligence and Experience.* New York: The Ronald Press Company, 1961.

12. Pines, Maya. *Revolution in Learning — The Years from Birth to Six.* New York: Harper and Row Publishers, Inc., 1967.

13. Pressey, S. L. "Educational Acceleration: Appraisals and Basic Problems," *Educational Research Monographs,* No. 31. Columbus, Ohio: The Ohio State University, 1949.

14a. Taylor, Calvin W. "Be Talent Developers," *Today's Educational,* (December, 1968).

14b. Taylor, Calvin W., and Barron, Frank (Editors). *Scientific Creativity: Its Recognition and Development.* New York: John Wiley and Sons, 1963.

15. Terman, Lewis M. "The Discovery and Encouragement of Exceptional Talent," *The American Psychologist,* 9 (June, 1954).

16a. Terman, Lewis M., and Oden, Melita H. *The Gifted Child Grows Up.* Vol. IV of *Genetic Studies of Genius,* edited by Lewis M. Terman. Stanford, California: Stanford University Press, 1947.

16b. Terman, Lewis M., and Oden, Melita H. "The Stanford Studies of the Gifted," Chapter Three in *The Gifted Child,* edited by Paul A. Witty. Boston: D. C. Heath and Company, 1951.

17. Torrance, E. Paul. "Explorations in Creative Thinking," *Education,* 81 (December, 1960).

18. Torrance, E. Paul. "Problems of Highly Creative Children," *Gifted Child Quarterly,* 5 (Summer, 1961).

19. Toynbee, Arnold. "Is America Neglecting Her Creative Minority?" *Accent on Talent,* 2 (January, 1968).

20. Witty, Paul A., and Wilkins, W. L. "The Status of Acceleration or Grade Skipping as an Administrative Device," *Educational Administration and Supervision,* 19 (May, 1933).

21. Witty, Paul A. "The Gifted Pupil and His Reading," *Highlights for Teachers,* No. 7 (February, 1967).

22. Witty, Paul A. *Helping the Gifted Child.* Chicago: Science Research

Associates, 1952. Revised in collaboration with Edith H. Grotberg, 1970.

23. Witty, Paul A. "Reading for the Gifted" (Featured Address) in *Reading and Realism,* Proceedings of the Thirteenth Annual Convention of the International Reading Association, edited by J. Allen Figurel. Newark, Delaware: International Reading Association, 1969.

24. Witty, Paul A., *et. al. Reading for the Gifted and the Creative Student,* Reading Aids Booklet. Newark, Delaware: International Reading Association (forthcoming).

25. Witty, Paul A. (Editor). *The Gifted Child.* Boston: D. C. Heath and Company, 1951.

26. Witty, Paul A. (Guest Editor). *Education* (September—October, 1957). See article by Stanley Krippner entitled "Characteristics of Gifted Children," pp. 15-20. In addition to Stanley Krippner's article, this issue of *Education* (September-October, 1967) contains an excellent annotated bibliography on the gifted and the creative by Edith H. Grotberg, pp. 52-56.

E. Paul Torrance

Emerging Concepts of Giftedness

Many teachers, school administrators, counselors, school psychologists, and parents complain that there is no commonly accepted definition of giftedness, even among national and international authorities. When educational and civic leaders plead for support for programs for educating teachers of gifted children or for appropriate educational programs for gifted children, many legislators oppose such support, arguing that not even the experts know how to identify those who are gifted. They contend that if there is disagreement about identifying the gifted it is futile to attempt to educate teachers especially for the gifted and to provide special kinds of educational opportunities for them.

The problem, strangely, is not that the experts do not know how to identify gifted children, nor even that there is any genuine disagreement among the national and international authorities. The truth is that we have been expanding our concept of giftedness and that we have been learning an increasingly large number of ways of identifying a greater number of different kinds of gifted children.

Another problem is that many of those who have sought support for programs for gifted children have had fixed notions about giftedness. In many cases their ideas have been so patently erroneous that their proposals have not made sense to legislators and other would-be supporters. In some cases these fixed ideas have centered around one type of giftedness, usually the type identified by an intelligence test and represented by the index known as the "IQ." Until recently there has been little support for Paul Witty's (1951) definition of giftedness as "consistently superior performance in

---

Torrance, E. Paul *Gifted Child in the Classroom.* The MacMillan Company, New York, 1965.

any socially useful endeavor." Others have been overconcerned about the degree of giftedness and have argued that the gifted must have IQ's of 180, 150, 140, or some other figure. From arguments around this point there has arisen a great deal of confusing terminology, such as "genius," "highly gifted," "extremely gifted," "moderately gifted," "talented," and the like. Other arguments have centered around the fixity of the intelligence quotient.

Generally, however, serious students of the problem of educating gifted children agree that our expanding knowledge makes it clear that the problem is complex but not necessarily confusing. It is quite clear that there is a variety of kinds of giftedness that should be cultivated and are not ordinarily cultivated without special efforts. It is clear that if we establish a level on some single measure of giftedness, we eliminate many extremely gifted individuals on other measures of giftedness. It is also clear that intelligence may increase or decrease, at least in terms of available methods of assessing it, depending upon a variety of physical and psychological factors both within the individual child and within his environment.

The complexity engendered by our expanding knowledge of the human mind and its functioning should be exciting and challenging rather than confusing. The author hopes that the reader will find it so because this is the nature of things as teachers and parents experience them in trying to educate gifted children. Furthermore this complex view of the nature of giftedness permeates this book. The author hopes that it will help the reader feel more comfortable, yet excited and challenged, in his efforts to teach gifted children in elementary and high-school classrooms.

Challenge of a Complex View of Giftedness

The acceptance of a realistically complex view of the human mind is itself a tremendous advance. In moving from an oversimplified (and patently erroneous) view of giftedness to a more complex one, we have reached a position where we can avoid many of the errors of the past. We should be able to develop a more humane kind of education for gifted children—one in which children will have a better chance to achieve their potentialities.

This more complex view of giftedness is causing us to reevaluate many of the classical experiments upon which we have built educational practices. From this reexamination it is becoming clear that children should be provided opportunities for mastering a variety of learning and thinking skills according to a variety of methods and that the outcomes of these efforts should be evaluated in a variety of ways. It will be one of the purposes of this book to illustrate some of this variety of learning and thinking skills, methods of learning, and evaluation procedures.

It is to be hoped that young teachers, as well as experienced educational leaders, will not be impatient with the complexity or the incompleteness of knowledge about giftedness. We do not yet know the end of the complexity of the functioning of the human mind and personality. This book, however, is inspired by the conviction that it is high time that we begin developing the strategies, methods, and materials that have built into them an acceptance of this complexity. In large part it is derived from the author and his associates' experimental work with gifted children.

In his own studies of creative giftedness the author has continued to be increasingly impressed by the wonderful complexity of this single aspect of man's intellectual functioning. Many fascinating insights concerning the functioning of children's minds occur even when we limit ourselves to the examination of such qualities of thinking as fluency of ideas, spontaneous flexibility, originality, and elaboration. Some children are exceptionally fluent in the production of ideas expressed in words but are unable to express ideas in figural or auditory symbols. Others may be tremendously fluent in expressing ideas in figural form but appear paralyzed mentally when asked to express them in words or sounds. Similar phenomena seem to occur when we consider creative movement or kinesthetic behavior.

A child may not be able to express his ideas verbally, visually, or any other way with a great deal of fluency and yet be quite gifted in other kinds of constructive, creative behavior. He may produce a small number of ideas, but each idea may be quite original or unusual and of high quality. He may be able to take a single idea and do an outstanding job of elaborating or expanding it, or he may produce ideas which show a great deal of flexibility of thinking.

The complexity of children's creative thinking does not end here. A child might respond quite creatively to one task and barely respond to another. For example, some children show tremendous originality and elaboration on the Incomplete Figures Test and respond very poorly to the Circles Test and vice versa (Torrance, 1962a). The Incomplete Figures Test confronts the child with incomplete structures, and this produces tension in most observers, making them want to complete the structures and integrate or synthesize their relatively unrelated elements. The pages of circles of the Circles Test, however, confront the subject with "perfect structures." In order to produce pictures and objects which have as a major part a circle, the child has to disrupt or destroy these "perfect structures," the circles. In the creative process there seems to be an essential tension between the two opposing tendencies symbolized by these two tasks: the tendency toward structuring and synthesizing and the tendency toward disruption and diffusion of energy and attention. Most children seem able to express both tendencies with equal skill, but others seem able to express only one of these tendencies to any great degree.

The author has mentioned here only a few of the ways he has devised for measuring the mental abilities involved in creative thinking, yet he realizes that he has only begun to represent psychometrically the different ways children can express their creative giftedness.

Some of the Scientific Bases of Emerging Concepts

Many educators and psychologists have been struggling for years to tear themselves away from concepts of a single type of giftedness. Undoubtedly this struggle has been motivated by vague anxieties that such concepts lead to errors and inhumane treatment for many children. The difficulty has been in finding a way to conceptualize the various kinds of intellectual giftedness and to develop measures of the different kinds of mental abilities involved. There have been numerous brave but unsuccessful attempts. For example, on the basis of the report of the Norwood Committee in England (Burt, 1968), the Education Act of 1944 in that country gave recognition to the hypothesis that there are different kinds of intellectual giftedness. Burt, in fact, maintains that the Education Act of 1944 assumes that children differ more in quality of ability than in amount. This act recommended a tripartite classification of secondary school, based on the idea that there are three main types of giftedness: a literary or abstract type to be educated at grammar schools, a mechanical or technical type to be educated at technical schools, and a concrete or practical type to be educated at modern schools. Burt argues that this scheme has not worked out as well as had been hoped. This may well be due, however, to still another oversimplification of the problem. Many believe, nevertheless, that this tripartite system in England is much more successful than earlier systems based on a single type of giftedness.

Guilford's structure of intellect (1956, 1959) and research related to the creative thinking or divergent production abilities have been especially effective in directing educators and psychologists away from their dependence upon a single measure of giftedness. Guilford has given what amounts virtually to a periodic table of different kinds of intelligence. His theoretical model of the structure of intellect has three dimensions: operations, content, and products.

In this model the operators are the major kinds of intellectual activities or processes, the things that the organism does with the raw materials of information. The first, *cognition,* includes discovery, awareness, recognition, comprehension, or understanding. The second, *memory,* refers to retention or storage, with some degree of availability, of information. Then there are two types of *productive thinking* in which something is produced from what has been cognized or memorized: *divergent production*, or the generation of information, from given information, where emphasis is upon variety and quantity of output from the same source, and *convergent production,* or the generation of information where emphasis is upon achieving unique or conventionally accepted best outcomes (the given information fully determines

50

the response). The fifth operation is *evaluation*, reaching decisions or making judgments concerning the correctness, suitability, adequacy, desirability, and so forth of information in terms of criteria of identity, consistency, and goal satisfaction.

These five operations act upon each of the kinds of content (figural, symbolic, semantic, and behavioral) and products (units, classes, systems, transformations, and implications). In this book the term *productive thinking* will be used to refer to what Guilford has defined as *convergent production* and *divergent production*. The term *creative thinking* will be used to refer to such abilities as fluency (large number of ideas), flexibility (variety of different approaches or categories of ideas), originality (unusual, off-the-beaten track ideas), elaboration (well developed and detailed ideas), sensitivity to defects and problems, and redefinition (perceiving in a way different from the usual, established, or intended way or use). *Measured creative thinking ability* will be used to refer to test scores which have been devised to assess these abilities.

Guilford and his associates' monumental work remained almost totally neglected by educators until Getzels and Jackson (1962) showed that highly creative or divergent thinking adolescents achieved as well as their highly intelligent peers, in spite of the fact that their average IQ was 23 points lower. Since at least 1898, psychologists had been producing instruments for assessing the creative-thinking abilities, making pleas for using such measures to supplement intelligence tests and recommending educational changes needed to develop creative talent. In the main these earlier efforts to generate interest in creative development and other types of intellectual tests were ignored or soon forgotten. Many of these earlier efforts are receiving attention now.

In selecting materials for this book, a serious effort has been made to provide ideas that can be used in teaching gifted children in both regular and segregated classrooms. The ideas presented have almost infinite possibilities for use with a variety of types of gifted children. It is to be expected that in the hands of some groups of gifted children the line of development from these methods and materials will be quite different from what will ensue in other groups. These materials and methods rarely require that specific questions be answered in a given way. It is to be hoped that teachers will not give severe disapproval when children answer questions or offer solutions to problems in a different way or ask different, more penetrating questions. Such questions and solutions are essential in many kinds of gifted performance.

Single studies such as those of Getzels and Jackson (1962) always leave many questions unanswered. Since the Getzels-Jackson data were obtained from a single school, one with an unusually large number of gifted students, their study did not tell us under what conditions their results could be anticipated. This author and his associates have undertaken fifteen partial replications of the Getzels-Jackson study, hoping to obtain some clues to answer this question. In ten of these studies the results have been essentially

51

the same as in the Getzels-Jackson study. In the other five the high IQ group scored significantly higher than the highly creative group on tests of achievement. In general it has been our impression that the children in these five schools were taught primarily by methods of authority and had very little chance to use their creative-thinking abilities in acquiring educational skills. In most the average IQ was lower than in the schools where the Getzels-Jackson results were confirmed. These observations suggested that the phenomena Getzels and Jackson report may occur only in schools where students are taught in such a way that they have a chance to use their creative thinking abilities in acquiring traditional educational skills or where the average IQ in the entire school is rather high.

It was observed that the highly creative pupils in at least two of the five divergent schools overachieved in the sense that their educational quotients were considerably higher than their intelligent quotients. Thus we thought that an ability gradient might be operating. According to the concept of the ability gradient suggested by J.E. Anderson (1960), ability level can be thought of in terms of thresholds, and questions can be asked about the amount of the ability necessary to accomplish a task. Then consideration can be given to the factors that determine function beyond this threshold. There are cutoff points of levels about which the demonstration of ability in relation to minimum demands is determined by other factors. In other words the creative-thinking abilities might show their differential effects only beyond certain minimal levels of intelligence.

To test this possibility, Yamamoto (1964) in one of the Minnesota studies of creative thinking, reanalyzed the data from six of the partial replications already mentioned. In each case students who scored in the top 20 per cent on the test of creative thinking were divided into three groups according to IQ (above 130, 120 to 129, and below 120). In general the achievement of the first two groups did not differ from each other but was significantly higher than that of the third group (IQ below 120). This finding supports suggestions made previously by several people, including this author (Torrance, 1962a), Roc (1960), and MacKinnon (1961).

Still almost unnoticed by educators is that part of the Getzels-Jackson study (1962) dealing with two kinds of psychosocial excellence or giftedness—that is, high social adjustment and high moral courage. It was found that just as the highly intelligent student is not always highly creative, the highly adjusted student is not always highly moral. Further it was found that although the highly moral students achieved at a higher level than the highly adjusted students, the teachers perceived the highly adjusted students as the leaders rather than the highly moral ones. This is especially significant in a peer-oriented culture such as we have in the United States. It is well to recognize the dangers of giving the greater rewards to those who accept the peer-value system and adjust almost automatically to the immediate group, almost without reference to moral values.

It is the contention of the author that we can do a better job of helping children achieve excellence in both social adjustment and moral courage.

From time to time investigators have assaulted the concept of fixed intelligence. Despite this the view that intelligence is a capacity fixed once and for all by genetic inheritance is still held quite widely. Indeed a great deal of empirical evidence seems at first glance to support the idea of fixed intelligence. Recently, however, Hunt (1961) proposed alternative explanations and summarized evidence which undermines this hypothesis.

It has been shown that performances (scores, not IQ) on the Binet-type intelligence tests improves with age. Age-discrimination, however, was one of the criteria Binet used in selecting items. Although Binet himself (1909) regarded intelligence as "plastic," the fact that performance on tests selected on age-discrimination criteria showed improvement with age has been used to conclude that development is predetermined by genetic inheritance. Another argument has been that individual children show considerable constancy from one intelligence test to another. Since all intelligence tests traditionally have been validated against the Binet-type test, this is to be expected. It has also been shown that there are high intercorrelations among the various Binet-type tests, and this has been presented as evidence in favor of a high "g" (general ability) factor. Another argument of the adherents of fixed intelligence has been based on evidence which shows that intelligence tests are fairly good predictors of school achievement. Since curricula and achievement tests have been based on the intelligence-test concept of the human mind, this too is to be expected.

Studies involving hereditary versus environmental determination also have been used to support the idea of fixed intelligence. The evidence here, however, frequently has not supported the idea of fixed intelligence. Both hereditary and environmental influences interact in determining mental growth and educational achievement.

Hunt (1961) has summarized evidence from studies of identical twins reared apart, from repeated testing of the same children in longitudinal studies, and from studies of the effects of training or guided, planned learning experiences. He believes that studies of the constancy of the IQ within individuals pose the most serious challenge to fixed intelligence. These include studies both of the stability with which individuals maintain their positions within a given group of individuals from one testing to another testing and of the variations of IQ within specific individuals.

Studies of the effects of schooling have been fairly convincing. Out of a group of people tested at some earlier age, those who complete the most schooling show the greatest increases and fewest decreases in IQ. Hunt cites studies by Lorge (1945), Vernon (1948), and deGroot (1948, 1951). In the areas of early environmental influences, Hunt mentions the sustained work of Wellman, Skeels, and their colleagues of the Iowa group. This group continued their studies over many years, demonstrating many of the effects of training at the kindergarten and nursery level. The studies of Spitz (1945, 1946) have been quite influential in convincing psychiatrists and social caseworkers that intelligence is crucial during the early years of life. Children deprived of social interaction or mothering fail to develop naturally either physically or mentally.

Long-standing beliefs in predetermined development have been used frequently to support the concept of fixed intelligence. Much evidence, however, indicates that deprivations of experience make a difference in rates of various kinds of growth. The more severe the deprivations of experience have been, the greater has been the decrease in the rates of development.

Arguments concerning inherited patterns of mental growth have also been placed in doubt by the work of Hunt (1961), Ojemann (1948), Ojemann and Pritchett (1963), and others. The evidence seems to indicate that intellectual development is quite different when chidren are exposed to guided, planned learning experiences from that which occurs when they encounter only what the environment just happens to provide.

This has led to the suggestion that educational programs should be based upon guided, planned experiences which in turn are based upon an analysis of the requirements of the learning task and the condition of the child. Analysis of the task must include a consideration of the structure of the task, possible strategies or processes by which the task can be achieved (alternative ways of learning, kinds of discriminations to be made, and so forth), and the settings or conditions which facilitate or impede achievement of the task (cultural, social, physical, and the like). Analysis of the child's condition should consider the stage of development relevant to the concepts or skills to be learned, the level of relevant abilities, especially the most highly developed ones (memory, logical reasoning, originality, judgments of space, and so forth), and the individual child's preferred ways of learning. The concern is with potentiality rather than norms. Examples of such educational experiences will be outlined in the section on classroom procedures.

Conclusion

In this chapter an effort has been made to show how recent breakthroughs in research concerning the human mind and personality and their functioning have resulted in the emergence of a new and challenging concept of giftedness. This concept stresses the importance of emphasis upon potentiality rather than upon norms and single measures of giftedness. It involves movement away from concepts of a single type of giftedness and fixed intelligence and beliefs in predetermined development. In the following chapters an effort will be made to outline educational goals, identification procedures, strategies of motivation, and methods and materials of instruction appropriate for the education of gifted children.

Joseph S. Renzulli

What Makes Giftedness? Reexamining a Definition

*T*hroughout recorded history and undoubtedly even before records were kept, people have always been interested in men and women who display superior ability. As early as 2200 B.C. the Chinese had developed an elaborate system of competitive examinations to select outstanding persons for government positions (DuBois, 1970), and down through the ages almost every culture has been fascinated by its most able citizens. Although the areas of performance in which one might be recognized as a gifted person are determined by the needs and values of the prevailing culture, scholars and laypersons alike have debated (and continue to debate) the age-old question: What makes giftedness?

The purpose of this article is therefore threefold. First, I shall analyze some past and current definitions of giftedness. Second, I shall review studies that deal with characteristics of gifted individuals. Finally, I shall present a new definition of giftedness that is operational, i.e., useful to school personnel, and defensible in terms of research findings.

The Definition Continuum

Numerous conceptions and countless definitions of giftedness have been put forth over the years. One way of analyzing existing definitions is to view them along a continuum ranging from "conservative" to "liberal," i.e., according to the degree of restrictiveness used in determining who is eligible for special programs and services.

Restrictiveness can be expressed in two ways. First, a definition can limit the number of performance areas that are considered in determining eligibility for special programs. A conservative definition, for example, might limit eligibility to academic performance only and exclude other areas such as music, art, drama, leadership, public speaking, social service,

Reprinted from Phi Delta Kappan, Vol. 60, No. 3 (November 1978), pp. 180–184. By permission of the author and publisher.

55

and creative writing. Second, a definition may specify the degree or level of excellence one must attain to be considered gifted.

At the conservative end of the continuum is Lewis Terman's definition of giftedness, "the top 1% level in general intellectual ability, as measured by the Stanford-Binet Intelligence Scale or a comparable instrument" (Terman et al., 1926).

In this definition restrictiveness is present in terms of both the type of performance specified (i.e., how well one scores on an intelligence test) and the level of performance one must attain to be considered gifted (top 1%). At the other end of the continuum may be found more liberal definitions, such as the following one by Paul Witty:

> There are children whose outstanding potentialities in art, in writing, or in social leadership can be recognized largely by their performance. Hence, we have recommended that the definition of giftedness be expanded and that we consider any child gifted whose performance, in a potentially valuable line of human activity, is consistently remarkable (Witty, 1958).

Although liberal definitions have the obvious advantage of expanding the conception of giftedness, they also open up two "cans of worms" by introducing the values issue (What are the potentially valuable lines of human activity?) and the age-old problem of subjectivity in measurement.

In recent years the values issue has been largely resolved. There are very few educators who cling to a "straight IQ" or purely academic definition of giftedness. "Multiple talent" and "multiple criteria" are almost the bywords of the present-day gifted student movement, and most educators would have little difficulty in accepting a definition that includes almost every area of human activity that manifests itself in a socially useful form.

The problem of subjectivity in measurement is not as easily resolved. As the definition of giftedness is extended beyond those abilities clearly reflected in tests of intelligence, achievement, and academic aptitude, it becomes necessary to put less emphasis on precise estimates of performance and potential and more emphasis on the opinions of qualified human judges in making decisions about admission to special programs. The issue boils down to a simple and yet very important question: How much of a trade-off are we willing to make on the objective/subjective continuum in order to allow recognition of a broader spectrum of human abilities? If some degree of subjectivity cannot be tolerated, then our definition of giftedness and the resulting programs will logically be limited to abilities that can only be measured by objective tests.

The USOE Definition

In recent years the following definition set forth by the U.S. Office of Education (USOE) has grown in popularity, and numerous states and school districts throughout the nation have adopted it for their programs:

56

Gifted and talented children are those . . . who by virtue of outstanding abilities are capable of high performance. These . . . children . . . require differentiated educational programs and/or services beyond those normally provided by the regular school program in order to realize their [potential] contribution to self and society.

Children capable of high performance include those who have demonstrated any of the following abilities or aptitudes, singly or in combination: 1) general intellectual ability, 2) specific academic aptitude, 3) creative or productive thinking, 4) leadership ability, 5) visual and performing arts aptitude, 6) psychomotor ability (Marland, 1972).

The USOE definition has served the very useful purpose of calling attention to a wider variety of abilities that should be included in a definition of giftedness, but at the same time it has presented some major problems. The first lies in its failure to include nonintellective (motivational) factors. That these factors are important is borne out by an overwhelming body of research, which I shall consider later.

A second and equally important problem relates to the nonparallel nature of the six categories included in the definition. Two of the six categories (specific academic aptitude and visual and performing arts aptitude) call attention to fields of human endeavor or general performance areas in which talents and abilities are manifested. The remaining four categories are more nearly processes that may be brought to bear on performance areas. For example, a person may bring the process of creativity to bear on a specific aptitude (e.g., chemistry) or a visual art (e.g., photography). Or the processes of leadership and general intelligence might be applied to a performance area such as choreography or the management of a high school yearbook. In fact, it can be said that processes such as creativity and leadership do not exist apart from a performance area to which they can be applied.

A third problem with the definition is that it tends to be misinterpreted and misused by practitioners. It is not uncommon to find educators developing entire identification systems based on the six USOE categories and in the process treating them as if they were mutually exclusive. What is equally distressing is that many people "talk a good game" about the six categories but continue to use a relatively high intelligence or aptitude score as a minimum requirement for entrance into a special program. Although both of these problems result from misapplication rather than from the definition itself, the definition is not entirely without fault, because it fails to give the kind of guidance necessary for practitioners to avoid such pitfalls.

The Three-Ring Conception

Research on creative/productive people has consistently shown that although no single criterion should be used to identify giftedness, persons who have achieved recognition because of their unique accomplishments and creative contributions possess a relatively well-defined set of three interlocking clusters of traits. These clusters consist of above-average though not necessarily superior general ability, task commitment, and creativity (see Figure 1). It is important to point out that no single cluster "makes giftedness." Rather, it is the interaction among the three clusters that research has shown to be the necessary ingredient for creative/ productive accomplishment. This interaction is represented by the shaded portion of Figure 1. It is also important to point out that each cluster is an "equal partner" in contributing to giftedness. This point is important. One of the major errors that continues to be made in identification procedures is overemphasis on superior abilities at the expense of the other two clusters of traits.

Figure 1. The Ingredients Of Giftedness.

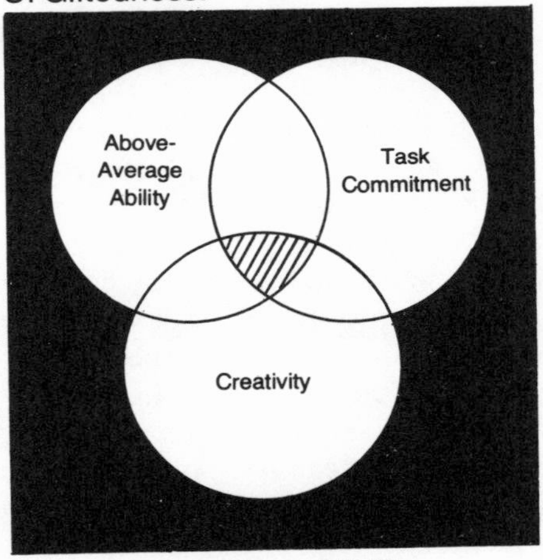

Above-Average General Ability

Above-Average General Ability

Although the influence of intelligence, as traditionally measured, quite obviously varies with areas of achievement, many researchers have found that creative accomplishment is not necessarily a function of measured intelligence. In a review of several research studies dealing with the relationship between academic aptitude tests and professional achievement, M. A. Wallach has concluded that:

> Above intermediate score levels, academic skills assessments are found to show so little criterion validity as to be a questionable basis on which to make consequential decisions about students' futures. What the academic tests do predict are the results a person will obtain on other tests of the same kind (Wallach, 1976).

Wallach goes on to point out that academic test scores at the upper ranges — precisely the score levels that are most often used for selecting persons for entrance into special programs — do not necessarily reflect the potential for creative/productive accomplishment. He suggests that test scores be used to screen out persons who score in the lower ranges and that beyond this point decisions be based on other indicators of potential for superior performance.

Numerous research studies support Wallach's finding that there is little relationship between test scores and school grades on the one hand and real world accomplishments on the other (Parloff et al., 1968; Mednick, 1963; Wallach and Wing, Jr., 1969; Richards, Jr., et al., 1967; Harmon, 1963; Bloom, 1963; Hudson, 1960). In fact, a study dealing with the prediction of various dimensions of achievement among college students, made by J. L. Holland and A. W. Astin, found that

> . . . getting good grades in college has little connection with more remote and more socially relevant kinds of achievement; indeed, in some colleges, the higher the student's grades, the less likely it is that he is a person with creative potential. So it seems desirable to extend our criteria of talented performance (Holland and Astin, 1962).

A study by the American College Testing Program titled "Varieties of Accomplishment After College: Perspectives on the Meaning of Academic Talent" concluded:

> The adult accomplishments were found to be uncorrelated with academic talent, including test scores, high school grades, and college grades. However, the adult accomplishments were related to comparable high school nonacademic (extracurricular) accomplishments. This suggests that there are many kinds of talents related to later success which might be identified and nurtured by educational institutions (Munday and Davis, 1974).

The pervasiveness of this general finding is demonstrated by D. P. Hoyt, who reviewed 46 studies dealing with the relationship between traditional indications of academic success and post-college performance in the fields of business, teaching, engineering, medicine, scientific research, and other areas such as the ministry, journalism, government, and miscellaneous professions (Hoyt, 1965). From this extensive review, Hoyt concluded that traditional indications of academic success have no more than a very modest correlation with various indicators of success in the adult world. He observes, "There is good reason to believe that academic achievement (knowledge) and other types of educational growth and development are relatively independent of each other."

These studies raise some basic questions about the use of tests in making selection decisions. The studies clearly indicate that vast numbers *and* proportions of our most productive persons are *not* those who scored at the ninety-fifth or above percentile on standardized tests, nor were they necessarily straight-A students who discovered early how to play the lesson-learning game. In other words, more creative/productive persons come from below the ninety-fifth percentile than above it, and if such cut-off scores are needed to determine entrance into special programs, we may be guilty of actually discriminating against persons who have the greatest potential for high levels of accomplishment.

Task Commitment

A second cluster of traits that are consistently found in creative/productive persons constitutes a refined or focused form of motivation known as task commitment. Whereas motivation is usually defined in terms of a general energizing process that triggers responses in organisms, task commitment represents energy brought to bear on a particular problem (task) or specific performance area.

The argument for including this nonintellective cluster of traits in a definition of giftedness is nothing short of overwhelming. From popular maxims and autobiographical accounts to hard-core research findings, one of the key ingredients that has characterized the work of gifted persons is the ability to involve oneself totally in a problem or area for an extended period of time.

The legacy of both Sir Francis Galton and Lewis Terman clearly indicates that task commitment is an important part of the making of a gifted person. Although Galton was a strong proponent of the hereditary basis for what he called "natural ability," he nevertheless subscribed strongly to the belief that hard work was part and parcel of giftedness:

> By natural ability I mean those qualities of intellect and disposition which urge and qualify a man to perform acts that lead to reputation. I do not mean capacity without zeal, nor zeal without capacity, nor even a combination of both of them, without an adequate power of doing a great deal of very laborious work. But I mean a nature which, when left to itself, will, urged by an inherent stimulus, climb the path that leads to eminence and has strength to reach the summit — on which, if hindered or thwarted, it will fret and strive until the hindrance is overcome, and it is again free to follow its laboring instinct.[1]

Terman's monumental studies undoubtedly represent the most widely recognized and frequently quoted research on the characteristics of gifted persons. Terman's studies, however, have unintentionally left a mixed legacy, because most persons have dwelt (and continue to dwell) on "early Terman" rather than on the conclusions he reached after several decades of intensive research. Therefore it is important to consider the following conclusion, reached after 30 years of follow-up studies on his initial population:

> ... [A] detailed analysis was made of the 150 most successful and 150 least successful men among the gifted subjects in an attempt to identify some of

60

the nonintellectual factors that affect life success. . . . Since the less successful subjects do not differ to any extent in intelligence as measured by tests, it is clear that notable achievement calls for more than a high order of intelligence.

The results [of the follow-up] indicated that personality factors are extremely important determiners of achievement. . . . The four traits on which [the most and least successful groups] differed most widely were *persistence in the accomplishment of ends, integration toward goals, self-confidence* and *freedom from inferiority feelings*. In the total picture the greatest contrast between the two groups was in all-round emotional and social adjustment and in *drive to achieve* (Terman, 1959). (Emphasis added).

Although Terman never suggested that task commitment should replace intelligence in our conception of giftedness, he did state that "intellect and achievement are far from perfectly correlated."

Several more recent studies support the findings of Galton and Terman and have shown that creative/productive persons are far more task oriented and involved in their work than are people in the general population. Perhaps the best known of these studies is the work of A. Roe and D. W. MacKinnon. Roe conducted an intensive study of the characteristics of 64 eminent scientists and found that *all* of her subjects had a high level of commitment to their work (Roe, 1952). MacKinnon pointed out traits that were important in creative accomplishments: "It is clear that creative architects more often stress their inventiveness, independence, and individuality, their *enthusiasm, determination,* and *industry.*" (MacKinnon, 1965). (Emphasis added).

Extensive reviews of research carried out by J. C. Nicholls (Nicholls, 1972) and H. G. McCurdy (McCurdy, 1960) found patterns of characteristics that were consistently similar to the findings reported by Roe and MacKinnon. Although the researchers cited thus far used different procedures and dealt with a variety of populations, there is a striking similarity in their major conclusions. First, academic ability (as traditionally measured by tests or grade-point averages) showed limited relationships to creative/productive accomplishment. Second, nonintellectual factors, and especially those that relate to task commitment, consistently played an important part in the cluster of traits that characterize highly productive people. Although this second cluster of traits is not as easily and objectively identifiable as are general cognitive abilities, they are nevertheless a major component of giftedness and should therefore be reflected in our definition.

Creativity

The third cluster of traits that characterize gifted persons consists of factors that have usually been lumped together under the general heading of "creativity." As one reviews the literature in this area, it becomes readily apparent that the words "gifted, "genius," and "eminent creators" or "highly creative persons" are used synonymously. In many of the research projects discussed above, the persons ultimately selected for intensive study were in fact recognized *because* of their creative accomplishments. In MacKinnon's study, for example, panels of qualified judges (professors of architecture and editors of major American architectural journals) were asked first to nominate and later to rate an initial pool of nominees, using the following dimensions of creativity: 1) originality of thinking and freshness of approaches to architectural problems, 2) constructive ingenuity, 3) ability to set aside established conventions and procedures when appropriate, and 4) a flair for devising effective and original fulfillments of the major demands of architecture: namely, technology (firmness), visual form (delight), planning (commodity), and human awareness and social purpose (MacKinnon, 1964).

When discussing creativity, it is important to consider the problems researchers have encountered in establishing relationships between scores on creativity tests and other more substantial accomplishments. A major issue that has been raised by several investigators deals with whether or not tests of divergent thinking actually measure "true" creativity. Although some validation studies have reported limited relationships between measures of divergent thinking and creative performance criteria (Torrance, 1969; Shapiro, 1968; Dellas and Gaier, 1970; Guilford, 1964), the research evidence for the predictive validity of such tests has been limited. Unfortunately, very few tests have been validated against real-life criteria of creative accomplishment, and in cases where such studies have been conducted the creativity tests have done poorly (Crockenberg, 1972). Thus, although divergent thinking is indeed a characteristic of highly creative persons, caution should be exercised in the use and interpretation of tests designed to measure this capacity.

Given the inherent limitations of creativity tests, a number of writers have focused attention on alternative methods for assessing creativity. Among others, Nicholls suggests that an analysis of creative products is preferable to the trait-based approach in making predictions about creative potential (Nicholls, op. cit.), and Wallach proposes that student self-reports about creative accomplishment are sufficiently accurate to provide a usable source of data (Wallach, op. cit.).

Although few persons would argue against the importance of including creativity in a definition of giftedness, the conclusions and recommendations discussed above raise the haunting issue of subjectivity in measurement. In view of what the research suggests about the questionable value of more objective measures of divergent thinking perhaps the time has come for persons in all areas of endeavor to develop more careful procedures for evaluating the products of candidates for special programs.

Discussion and Generalizations

The studies reviewed above lend support to a small number of basic generalizations that can be used to develop an operational definition of giftedness. The first is that giftedness consists of an interaction among three clusters of traits — above-average but not necessarily superior general abilities, task commitment, and creativity. Any definition or set of identification procedures that does not give equal attention to all three clusters is simply ignoring the results of the best available research dealing with this topic.

Related to this generalization is the need to make a distinction between traditional indicators of academic proficiency and creative productivity. A sad but true fact is that special programs have favored proficient lesson learners and test takers at the expense of persons who may score somewhat lower on tests but who more than compensate for such scores by having high levels of task commitment and creativity. Research has shown that members of this group ultimately make the most creative/productive contributions to their respective fields of endeavor.

A second generalization is that an operational definition should be applicable to all socially useful performance areas. The one thing that the three clusters discussed above have in common is that each can be brought to bear on a multitude of specific performance areas. As was indicated earlier, the interaction or overlap among the clusters "makes giftedness," but giftedness does not exist in a vacuum. Our definition must, therefore, reflect yet another interaction; but in this case it is the interaction between the overlap of the clusters and any performance area to which the overlap might be applied. This interaction is represented by the large arrow in Figure 2.

A third and final generalization is concerned with the types of information that should be used to identify superior performance in specific areas. Although it is a relatively easy task to include specific performance areas in a definition, developing identification procedures that will enable us to recognize specific areas of superior performance is more difficult. Test developers have thus far devoted most of their energy to producing measures of general ability, and this emphasis is undoubtedly why these tests are relied upon so heavily in identification. However, an operational definition should give direction to needed research and development, especially as these activities relate to instruments and procedures for student selection. A defensible definition can thus become a model that will generate vast amounts of appropriate research in the years ahead.

A Definition of Giftedness

Although no single statement can effectively integrate the many ramifications of the research studies described above, the following definition of giftedness attempts to summarize the major conclusions and generalizations resulting from this review of research:

> Giftedness consists of an interaction among three basic clusters of human traits—these clusters being above-average general abilities, high levels of task commitment, and high levels of creativity. Gifted and talented children are

those possessing or capable of developing this composite set of traits and applying them to any potentially valuable area of human performance. Children who manifest or are capable of developing an interaction among the three clusters require a wide variety of educational opportunities and services that are not ordinarily provided through regular instructional programs.

A graphic representation of this definition is presented in Figure 2. The definition is an operational one because it meets three important criteria. First, it is derived from the best available research studies dealing with characteristics of gifted and talented individuals. Second, it provides guidance for the selection and/or development of instruments and procedures that can be used to design defensible identification systems. And finally, the definition provides direction for programming practices that will capitalize upon the characteristics that bring gifted youngsters to our attention as learners with special needs.

References

Bloom, B. S. Report on creativity research by the examiner's office of the University of Chicago, in C. W. Taylor and F. Barron, eds. *Scientific creativity: Its recognition and development*. New York: John Wiley and Sons, 1963.

Crockenberg, S. B. Creativity tests: A boon or boondoggle for education? *Review of Educational Research*, 1972, **42**, 27-45.

Dellas, M. and E. L. Gaier. Identification of creativity: The individual. *Psychological Bulletin*, 1970, **73**, 55-73.

DuBois, P. H. *A history of psychological testing*. Boston: Allyn & Bacon, 1970.

Guilford, J. P. Some new looks at the nature of creative processes, in M. Frederickson and H. Gilliksen, eds. *Contributions to mathematical psychology*. New York: Holt, Rinehart and Winston, 1964.

Harmon, L. R. The development of a criterion of scientific competence, in C. W. Taylor and F. Barron, eds., op. cit.

Holland, J. L. and A. W. Astin. The prediction of the academic, artistic, scientific, and social achievement of undergraduates of superior scholastic aptitude. *Journal of Educational Psychology*, 1962, **53**, 132, 133.

Hoyt, D. P. *The relationship between college grades and adut achievement: A review of the literature*, research report no. 7. Iowa City, Ia.: American College Testing Program, 1965.

Hudson, L. Degree class and attainment in scientific research. *British Journal of Psychology*, 1960, **51**, 67-73.

MacKinnon, D. W. Personality and the realization of creative potential. *American Psychologist*, 1965, **27**, 717-727.

MacKinnon, D. W. The creativity of architects, in C. W. Taylor, ed. *Widening horizons in creativity*. New York: John Wiley and Sons, 1964, p. 360.

Marland, S. P. *Education of the gifted and talented.* Report to the Congress of the United States by the U.S. Commissioner of Education and Background Papers Submitted to the U. S. Office of Education. Washington, D. C.: U. S. Government Printing Office, 1972. Definition edited for clarity.

McCurdy, H. G. The childhood pattern of genius. *Horizon,* 1960, **2,** 33-38.

Mednick, M. T. Research creativity in psychology graduate students. *Journal of Consulting Psychology,* 1963, **27,** 265, 266.

Munday, L. A. and J. C. Davis. *Varieties of accomplishment after college: Perspectives on the meaning of academic talent,* research report no. 62. Iowa City, Ia.: American College Testing Program, 1974, p. 2.

Nicholls, J. C. Creativity in the person who will never produce anything original and useful: The concept of creativity as a normally distributed trait. *American Psychologist,* 1972, **27,** 717-727.

Nicholls, J. C., op. cit.

Parloff, M. B., et al. Personality characteristics which differentiate creative male adolescents and adults. *Journal of Personality,* 1968, **36,** 528-552.

Richards, J. M., Jr., et al. Prediction of student accomplishment in college. *Journal of Educational Psychology, 1967,* **58,** 343-355.

Roe, A. *The making of a scientist.* New York: Dodd, Mead, 1952.

Shapiro, R. J. Creative research scientists. *Psychologia Africana,* 1968, Supplement No. 4.

Terman, L. M., et al. *Genetic studies of genius: Mental and physical traits of a thousand gifted children.* Stanford, Calif.: Stanford University Press, 1926, p. 43.

Terman, L. M. *Genetic studies of genius: The gifted group at mid-life.* Stanford, Calif.: Stanford University Press, 1959, p. 148.

Torrance, E. P. Prediction of adult creative achievement among high school seniors. *Gifted Child Quarterly,* 1969, **13,** 223-229.

Wallach, M. A. Tests tell us little about talent. *American Scientist,* 1976, **64,** p. 57.

Wallach, M. A. and C. W. Wing, Jr. *The talented students: A validation of the creativity intelligence distinction.* New York: Holt, Rinehart and Winston, 1969.

Wallach, M. A., op. cit.

Witty, P. A. Who are the gifted? in N. B. Henry, ed. *Education of the gifted.* Fifty-seventh Yearbook of the National Society for the Study of Education, Part II. Chicago: University of Chicago Press, 1958, p. 62.

Notes

[1] Francis Galton as quoted in R. S. Albert, Toward a behavioral definition of genius. *American Psychologist,* 1975, **30,** p. 142.

Virgil S. Ward

Basic Concepts

The development of those phases of the total school program which comprise proper education for the gifted demands intelligent thought and skillful development. In this section of the *Manual*, some fundamental concepts which will be needed by all who engage in any part of these endeavors are introduced. The intention is not necessarily to provide definitions in the exact form to which every local school should subscribe, but rather to provide certain educational and psychological concepts from which as a point of departure, each responsible educational group can think through its own needs, problems, policies, and practices. Close consideration of these concepts should aid substantially in the understanding of the various discussions of curriculum and programmatic arrangements in the sections which follow.

Some basic considerations pertaining to the nature of human abilities are presented first; a limited number of generally applicable concepts which pertain both to psychological abilities and to educational provisions designed to bring them to fruition, next; and finally, some general features— "cardinal principles"—which the SRPEG participants observed to characterize the more excellent of the programs observed in the various sections of the nation, and hence to be essential to any serious or ambitious program.

The Nature of Giftedness

The rationale of differential education for the gifted, as has been indicated, involves the belief that identifiable groups of children with high abilities exist for whom different kinds of educational provisions are necessary to equality of educational opportunity. Such groups of children, endowed with various kinds of superior abilities, have been diversely termed "superior and talented," "the able and ambitious," "the academically

Reprinted from *The Gifted Student: A Manual For Program Improvement.* A Report of the Southern Regional Project For Education of the Gifted, 1962, pp. 25-36. By permission of the author and publisher.

talented" and other familiar designations. For convenience, all these may be and are in this *Manual* referred to as "the gifted."

The behavioral sciences recognize certain definable qualities around which subgroups of individuals with superior potential may be categorized with varying degrees of reliability for the purpose of special education. Clearest among these qualities are giftedness in:

1. *General Intelligence,* usually manifest in high I.Q. scores and
2. *Specific Aptitudes* (or talents), as measured by valid tests appropriately designated, or as evidenced through remarkable insights and skills in particular areas of knowledge or human endeavor.

Aptitudes are regarded as specific behavioral efficiencies, usually accompanied by above average general intelligence. These special abilities may be inferred through superior performance in subject areas such as mathematics and foreign languages, in skilled interpersonal relations which make for social leadership, in various forms of artistic expression such as music, dance or painting and in still other particular kinds of behavior.

Within both of these categories of giftedness, general intelligence and specific aptitude, it is practicable to recognize that *degrees* of superiority exist, such that school provisions may be devised respectively to meet the needs of those small numbers singularly exceptional in ability (e.g. one per cent or less), and the broader numbers (e.g. two, five, or ten per cent as variously suggested) still sufficiently above average to justify substantially modified educational procedures. In 1950 the Educational Policies Commission recognized two such levels of intellectual giftedness and identified these in terms of given intelligence quotients. Other organizations and individuals have similarly recognized varying degrees of giftedness in terms of I.Q., specific cutoff points beginning sometimes essentially where the usual demarcation for the upper limit of the "normal" or "average" group occurs. This recognition of levels of variation, of course, applies in substance also to the various aptitudes and to other recognizable clusters of abilities.

What is important to recognize is that any cutoff point on any measured psychological trait is by its nature arbitrary, and that no given demarcation can be defended on grounds of biological or psychological science. The search is for that degree of deviation in behavioral characteristics, comprising a potential for productive learning and thinking, which is so far above average that the graded materials and normal procedures devised for the education of children in the majority are less suited than curricular arrangements that can be deliberately devised to develop the exceptional qualities.

At the present time behavioral scientists are making significant efforts to distinguish other behavioral attributes worthy of special educational attention. Creativity, productive thinking as distinct from reproductive, and divergent thinking as opposed to convergent, are concepts representing attempts to isolate, define, and measure additional significant qualities of mind which relate to giftedness. The development of creativity is now being seen increasingly as a worthy educational objective. As these important behavioral characteristics become sufficiently well established at the levels of behavioral science, educators can and should devote particular thought to their appropriate development.

Finally, it must be recognized that certain aspects of personality, such as motivation, value orientation and cultural background weigh heavily in identifying particular individuals whose present behavioral patterns seem to promise superior performance in the future. Constructive combinations of these aspects of personality in persons of lesser relative ability may lead to higher ultimate attainment. On the other hand, even among youth of high ability-potential, aspects of personality arising from unfortunate experience may combine to hamper present performance, leading to *underachievement* or *emotional instability*. In the case of these gifted children, remediation should be undertaken as an initial phase of differential education in order subsequently to allow fuller operation of the natural potential. What is patently inexcusable is to exclude such children from developed provisions which promise to remove the obstacles to their "self actualization."

Remarkable demonstrations on the part of children in contemporary schools have been noted during the present wave of interest in the problems of the gifted. Reading, self-taught, prior to the age permitting entry into school; successful learning of higher mathematics on the part of elementary school youngsters; brilliant examples of children's insights into social and philosophical issues, and other striking manifestations of remarkable ability have occurred too consistently and too frequently to ignore. Such behavior suggests a potential for learning and thought hitherto undreamed of and defiant of management within the standard patterns and processes of education which serve children of ordinary abilities. Reliable studies indicate further that the prodigious childhood accomplishments tend, on the whole, to be followed in adulthood by similarly constructive behavior through which creative inventions in the arts and sciences occur, and advances in human welfare are made by gifted statesmen and leaders in social thought. These facts and realizations suggest further the absolute urgency that persons in possession of such priceless human assets be identified early and treated with every resource available to the educator.

Specific expressive behaviors which characterize the gifted may be detailed in lists that number into the dozens. These particular behavioral traits, however, derive from a more manageable number of broader psychological variables which serve typically to distinguish the group. The following categories embrace most of the educationally significant behaviors of gifted individuals as they are presently recognized.

Capacity for Learning: Accurate perception of social and natural situations; independent, rapid, efficient learning of fact and principle; fast, meaningful reading, with superior retention and recall.

Power and Sensitivity of Thought: Ready grasp of principles underlying things as they are; sensitivity to inference in fact, consequence of proposition, application of idea; spontaneous elevation of immediate observations to higher planes of abstraction; imagination; meaningful association of ideas; forceful reasoning; original interpretations and conclusions; discriminatory power, quick detection of similarities and differences among things and ideas; able in analysis; synthesis, and organization of elements; critical of situations, self, and other people.

Curiosity and Drive: Mental endurance; tenacity of purpose; stubbornness, sometimes contrarily expressed as reluctance to do as directed; capacity for follow-through with extensive, but meaningful plans; curiosity about things and ideas; intrinsic interest in the challenging and difficult; versatile and vital interests; varied, numerous and penetrating inquiries; boredom with routine and sameness.

From these basic considerations as to the nature of giftedness, the local school may devise serviceable definitions for those groups of youngsters in whose interest they intend to develop specifically applicable school procedures. Starting efforts will perhaps wisely center upon the most clearly known deviant characteristics, i.e., general intellectual superiority, and those for which the clearest educational processes pertain. The identification of groups may be expanded as the program matures to include other kinds of abilities and larger numbers of children. A fair understanding of these concepts on the nature of giftedness will be essential to the establishment of adequate screening and identification procedures in the process of selecting and placing children, and to the broader and more nearly ultimate search for educational provisions exactingly geared to each group distinguishable through deviant characteristics.

A Glossary of Functional Terminology

Terminology can both facilitate and deter progress. The following concepts have been selected for their functional value in thinking through the various problems arising in the accomplishment of a recognizable pattern of provisions for fortunately atypical youth. As with all the "basic concepts" in this section, it is not intended that given school personnel should accept verbatim the definitions offered. The fine arguments necessary for obtaining agreements at such a level of particularity would quite possibly tend rather to impede than to propel the changes integral to a good program. On the other hand, careful study of these deliberated descriptions and explanations on the part of every staff member to be involved in discussions about or responsibilities in the program, should assure some communality of sound understanding around which both thought and action may proceed. Reasoned departures from what is here suggested by way of definitions should be, and quite possibly can be, defensible in terms of more refined insights into educational or psychological processes, or in terms of practical contingencies governing a school's efforts to establish or to improve upon its differential provisions for youth of superior abilities. Such departures should not, however, reflect simple bias of person or of locality.

Ability Grouping: Also sometimes called "segregation." The practice of assembling or deploying students for instructional purposes who are somewhat nearer together in general capacity for learning, or in given specific aptitudes, so that instruction and learning may proceed at a pace and in terms of qualities suited to this (these) capacities. Contrasts with those forms of grouping which utilize chronological age or alphabet as criteria for homogeneity and developmental readiness. May take the form of special classes, special schools, multiple track curricula, etc., and may be arranged for part or for all of the school curriculum. Specific capacities for differing areas of knowledge or skill, with interests related thereto, are recognized as superior criteria for grouping, as opposed to general indices (e.g. composite I.Q.) applied across the range of school activities.

Acceleration: Any administrative practice designed to move the student through school more rapidly than usual. Includes such practices as early admission, grade-skipping, advanced placement, telescoping of grade levels, credit by examination, etc.

Articulation: The sequential arrangement of studies through the total school program so as to avoid undesirable repetition or duplication at various grade levels. Problems of articulation often arise when programs for the gifted are planned to affect given school years but not to encompass the entire graded sequence.

Differential Education (for the gifted): Educational experiences uniquely or predominantly suited to the distinguishing behavioral processes of intellectually superior people and to the adult roles that they typically assume as leaders and innovators. Then successfully arranged to involve the capacities and needs of the gifted, the experience (concepts, studies, activities, courses) by definition is beyond the reach of and not appropriate to the capacities and needs of persons *not* exceptionally endowed with potential for learning and productive or creative behavior.

Enrichment (for the gifted): Practices which are intended to increase the depth or breadth of the gifted student's learning experiences. May include special assignments, independent study, individual projects, small group work, and other adaptations of routine school processes. This purported form of provision for the gifted often in fact merely camouflages donothingness.

Identification: The process of finding those students who meet the criteria of giftedness adopted in a given school or system. Identification should begin as early as possible, should be systematic, i.e., follow a defensible plan, and should be continuous so as to improve the chances of discovering larger numbers of youth qualified for differential education. A variety of techniques exist for screening the pupil population, most of which have some virtue, and no one of which—particularly a single measure of intelligence—is sufficient alone.

Mental Ability: An inclusive term, more properly referred to as "capacity," and including such conceptions as intelligence and aptitude (talent) and related processes such as creativity, productive thinking, divergent thinking, etc.

70

Mental Tests: Devices such as intelligence, aptitude, achievement, and personality tests, or rating scales for various skills, which are designed to provide relatively objective means of assessing or comparing certain of the capacities of characteristics of individuals.

Motivation: The basic psychological process involved in both under- and over-achievement in school. A subtle and complex literature on this aspect of personality exists in the behavioral sciences. As concerns the gifted, *underachievement* is recognized as a critical problem, and is thought of as a failure to perform as well as might be expected from scores on tests of aptitude or intelligence. No agreement exists as to how poorly a student must do, for how long, or in what activities, in order to be called an underachiever. Poor performance by gifted youngsters is not infrequently paralleled by singular out-of-school activities which possess intrinsic appeal to the child.

Program (of special education): A *pattern* of provisions within the total range of school activities which is designed to meet the distinguishable needs and abilities of intellectually superior and talented children. Single or scattered provisions such as advanced placement or early admission to first grade do not alone constitute a *program.*

Ten Cardinal Principles

From a thoughtful review of all that was studied, attended, and observed, certain features which seem to characterize the more excellent programs of education for gifted youngsters appear to be mandatory in an ideal situation. These cardinal tenets, each excellently implemented, will be found altogether only in the rarest and most favored of school systems. On the other hand, unless the more modestly endowed school can show tangible evidence that it has realized as effectively as its circumstances permit each one of these ten disciplines to thought and practice, the chances are good that its claims toward differentiated education for the gifted are merely illusory.

Imaginative local school personnel in systems not yet really "off the ground" in this important respect may sense from a thoughtful perusal of these ten principles many of the particulars which will devolve upon them in developing educational services for supremely educable young people. For those school leaders already having substantially accomplished such special provisions in the total school program, the principles can serve as a broad check-list for systematic re-examination of its endeavors, and for improving those phases of the program revealed through the analysis to be less than what the school is capable of doing.

1. *Particularization of Objectives.* A philosophy of education which a given school might have adopted, and general objectives related thereto, provide a basis for the formulation of more specific realizations concerning

the nature and needs of those deviant groups identified by the school for differential provisions. These statements may take the form of particularized process goals, in order to distinguish them from general objectives of education for all youth. Such explicitly declared objectives should take account (1) of the exceptional abilities of the children intended to be reached—priceless abilities, sloughed off and neglected in the past—which point to potential for learning not yet dreamed of in the typical American school; (2) of the anticipated social roles which these youth characteristically assume as adults—leadership and reconstruction of the culture as distinct from simple participation therein; and (3) of the implications for these young people of the dramatic nature of the world in which they will spin out their lives as cultural frontiersmen—a material world rapidly being made all over by science and technology, and a social world characterized by close, but not necessarily friendly, interrelationships among interest groups of various kinds, and among nations, some of which are only presently emerging as powers on the world scene. Differential education for differentially endowed youth must take exacting account of all these demands in order to be adequate in more than name alone. Such particularized objectives for identifiable segments of the total pupil population are not only harmonious with democratic philosophies of education that are general in scope, but are essential to the fullness of these philosophies.

2. *Staff Training and Responsibility*. The typical school staff can scarcely hope to have within its ranks personnel already knowledgeable and skilled in the various phases of a program of education for the gifted. A wise selection of persons capable of the requisite learnings, and of skill in putting these understandings into practice, is a necessary early step, i.e. selection and then training. Training should be geared to the functions intended. These will cover a variety of needs, including excellence on the part of teachers in the challenging tasks of face-to-face instructional leadership and classroom management, imagination and reasoned thought in the development of curricular materials geared toward the specific task, and administrative ingenuity in leading staff and community through changes in habituated conceptions and established practices. Such staff training should be a bootstrap operation in the hands of committees of local personnel *only* when qualified consultative resources are *not* available. The costs are diverse and substantial when initial errors are made, though these are committed in good faith, and the efforts subsequently necessary for correcting concepts, materials, and actions mis-directed in the beginning are usually greater than what would have been involved in more adequately founded origins.

The time-honored administrative principle of clear designation of responsibility, with commensurate authority, in single persons pertains to this aspect of school practice. According to size and resources, single persons must be designated within the school system as responsible for leading in the hierarchy of functions essential to full-scale endeavor. A single head for system-wide collective efforts, one responsible to the building principal for the efforts of a given school, and further reasonable divisions of functions covering grade levels and subject matter will usually be indicated. Supervisory and guidance personnel must also be made clearly aware of their responsibilities in the special endeavor. In most schools of no greater than average size, it will likely be that these responsibilities are placed in the hands of persons who must continue to carry other duties as well. In any case, the assignment of responsibility is but an idle gesture unless corresponding time and provisions for implementing the required work are established in the process. The more thoroughly each person understands his function, has the requisite personal abilities to carry them out, and the time required for working in essentially uncharted territory, the more nearly adequate will the local program be.

3. *Community Interpretation.* Small and simple adjustments in the routine machinery of school operation will but mock the task at hand. Practices which will break with custom on numerous counts are much more likely to be sensed as necessary by the staff that takes this problem seriously. Ingenuity in interpreting these requisite changes to the community is needed. Forthrightness, perseverance, and patience pay good dividends in this respect, paving the way for active cooperation from resources outside the school setting, and for support by the majority of thoughtful citizens. Especially critical will be the school personnel's ability to obtain support on the part of those parents whose children are not destined to be involved in the highlighted efforts. If differentiated educational provisions for the gifted are shown to parallel provisions for the handicapped, and for groups with already recognized special abilities, as in athletics and music, and if the arguments are clearly made that the established educational program provides for the majority of youngsters according to their needs and capacities, this kind of community support can be developed.

4. *Systematic Pupil Identification.* A differentiated program of education cannot attain appropriate particularity without the tangible identification of persons to be involved in it. Explicit definitions, a knowledgeable utilization of existing psychological instruments, and a judicious involvement of the judgment of personnel closely acquainted with potential candidates for the program are essential to adequate processes of pupil identification. The identification process should begin in the primary grades, and extend continuously throughout the secondary school at least. Children mature and make manifest certain potentials at different times. And, of course, in schools beginning "small", with close and exacting definitions, each expansion in the adapted working conception of giftedness will call for additional screening of larger numbers of children than are expected ultimately to prove needful of the planned curricular processes.

5. *Distinguishable Curricular Experiences.* The demands which govern or delimit all studies and instruction intended to pertain with relative uniqueness to groups of gifted youth have been stated in the above discussion of particularized objectives. Units of the curriculum of the school, instructional patterns such as seminars or independent research projects, and materials devised for system-wide use—all these must involve those higher

powers of mind which bring bright and talented children to attention in the first place, and must be of such nature that they promote the child's natural capacities for judgment, critical analysis, and creative reconstruction of things as they now exist. Unless a school can point to such clearly identifiable provisions, and indicate how these provisions implement and validate the process goals or particularized objectives also on record, it is quite likely that nothing predominantly pertinent to the gifted exists, and that, rather, old merchandise has simply and unfairly been given new tags.

Curricular modifications which are adequate (and more hopefully excellent) for this task are perhaps among the most difficult matters the school staff has ever dealt with. Certain principles to guide these efforts are suggested in Section Five of this *Manual*. Equally mandatory are cautions that in the gradual development of increasingly pertinent processes, no *abusive* practices be allowed to creep in. Bright youngsters are being unwittingly subjected in today's heightened pressures to requirements and expectations some of which unquestionably serve to defeat their intended purpose, rather than to support it. And they are being allowed special courses and related experiences under conditions which connote *punishment* rather than *deserved privileges*. The direct and explicit purposefulness of all extraordinary requirements; the pursuit of unusual courses within the normal school day and week; and the evaluation of work by standards initially acknowledging the student's superior rank—all these must be designed and organically arranged so as to comprise in their totality a constructive and developmental array of experiences, as normal for these deviant youngsters as is the usual school regimen for his fellows in the main stream of organized education. Practices are likely to be inherently wrong if they lead to avoidance on the part of able youngsters and their parents, and if they require work in amount or kind which is not positively attractive in immediate nature and purposeful in ultimate objective.

6. *Flexible Pupil Deployment.* As with curriculum, where simple refinements and moderate rearrangements will not do, so it is with the inevitable placement of bright and talented pupils in instructional groups. Marked departures from traditional practices in administrative arrangements are necessary parallels to sound and forward-looking curricular adaptations. When conceived fundamentally, as the problem should be, a great variety of grouping patterns are feasible for youngsters as they pursue their course through the full range of knowledge provided, the activities conducing toward essential skills, and their progressive attainment of maturity in judgment and power of thought. Indeed, so diverse are the possibilities for variation in day-to-day shifting from group to group, short term reformulation of groups for the attainment of goals close at hand, separation of small numbers for fullest development of excellence in rare talents, and for flexible admission to the grades and movement through the graded structure, that *the only pattern clearly outmoded is the completely heterogeneous grouping of children, in relatively permanent and largely self-contained classes, which proceed by lock-step in a grade-a-year plan* as though this rusty pattern were

a condition of nature inflicted upon the school and its pupil clientele. So great is the distance between schools that lead and those that lag in respect to imaginative administrative practices that known instances exist in which bright children in communities an hour's drive apart endure or enjoy radically different kinds of developmental experience. And so frequent and widespread are schools who have made commendable departures, that the administrator or board member who "does not believe in newer methods" may see within this distance and with his own eyes real and effective differentiated patterns of pupil deployment such as he doesn't believe to exist.

7. *Comprehensiveness and Continuity.* Even in the face of the connotation which the term carries of a *variety* of provisions, numerous "programs" of education for the gifted are comprised of *single* features. Thus early admission to first grade may be practiced in one school system, and aptitude grouping in another, but not both in the same institution. Frequently, too, given provisions worthy of across the board application, are in fact utilized only at selective grade levels, or in selective schools within a system.

Instructional practices and administrative adaptations that are reasoned carefully in terms of reliable knowledge of human abilities and the educative process deserve to be brought to bear upon *every* differentially qualified child in a community, at *every* grade level in his entire school career, in *every* area of academic studies that involve those extremes in learning potential displayed by the identified gifted youngsters. Piecemeal and fragmentary allowances, selectively applied, while probably advantageous in and of themselves, fail in the in-between to provide what is equally necessary by way of properly gauged developmental learnings. Every phase of a total program of differential education for the gifted—identification, guidance, instruction, evaluation—should, therefore apply *comprehensively* across the pupil population and through the subject areas, and continuously (allowing variations on types of processes) through the maturing years of the selected children and the graded structure of the school from the kindergarten through general college.

8. *Progressive Program Development.* The various kinds of special provisions for bright and talented youngsters are not irresponsible devices in the nature of fads and passing fancy. Both careful reasoning and substantial experience lie behind successful practices. In the face of the intricate and highly significant task of developing within the local schools of any given community a full-scale pattern of differentiated educational provisions, it is likely that no school staff can rest satisfied with their present state of program development. A further earmark of excellence in a given program, therefore, is likely to be internal provisions for periodic re-examination of parts and of the whole structure erected to accomplish this function, and for refinement of effort where weaknesses are indicated.

9. *Financial Allocation.* No absolute sums can be indicated as essential to the attainment and maintenance of qualitative differential education for gifted youth. Nor is it necessary that every school system allocate similar amounts for each function within the program. On the other hand, it is

75

simply not realistic to expect that educational provisions which in their nature must be unusual ones, frequently involving extraordinary materials and facilities, can be accomplished within the same framework of allocations that pertained prior to the particular efforts. The usual school budget is characterized by all sorts of differing allocations. The nature of this selective spending reveals the values of the school system and its supporting community. Several activities which favor certain children over others are already heavily financed, and this practice is sanctioned by the community. The belated realization is that it is mandatory to provide differentially for youth of substantially deviant intellectual potential, and this at extraordinary cost proportionate to the economic strength of the system, in order to give these youngsters their fair share of educational opportunity.

In implementation, it is reasonable that any school system, no matter how well endowed, start with immediately clear and apparent outlets for increased funds, and progressively provide dissimilar allocations as the whole range of objectives of the program become more fully materialized. Schools with limited capital must judge where limited funds will do most good. What can no longer be excused is main failure to make selective allocations as demanded by the particular needs and capacities of these groups of deviant youngsters.

10. *Radiation of Excellence.* It is frequently remarked, and validly, that the studied attainment of a sound pattern of education commensurate with the heavily deviant abilities of brighter youth, will in the process lead to general improvements in the whole school program. What is equally true, but not so frequently remarked, is that one is not likely to find a good program for the gifted in other than generally good schools. Enlightened citizens or zealous professional members of the school staff are on sound grounds in pressing this cause to the point where tangible features of the total school program in their community can be identified which pertain with relative uniqueness to the higher degrees of human abilities represented in the concept of giftedness.

Walter B. Barbe

A Study of the Family Background
of the Gifted

Of what influence has heredity and environment been in the development of the gifted child? Specifically, how does the family background of the gifted child differ from that of the child who is average in intelligence? Unfortunately, it is not possible to determine from such a study as this whether heredity or environment played a larger part in the development of the superior intellect of the subject. But by means of such a study, factors in the development of the gifted may be revealed. In a follow-up study of a group of gifted Negro subjects, Jenkins concluded:

> . . . desirable as it would be to know which of these factors (heredity or environment) has been most potent in the development of our subjects, the writer is unable to present any crucial data on the question. The data relative to heredity are meager, and to some extent, superficial; and while the picture of the cultural background is more complete, even here there are intangible factors which elude objective evaluation (1).

The 456 subjects in this study received an I.Q. of 120 or above on the 1917 Form of the Stanford-Binet. These data were taken from the records of the Psychological Clinic of the Cleveland Board of Education. The range of I.Q. is from 120 to 164, with a mean I.Q. of 130.2. The largest number of subjects were in the 125-129 range (37.3 per cent), while almost sixty-two per cent were between 125 and 135. This placed all of the subjects in about the upper ten per cent (2) of the population of the United States at the time they were tested. A large percentage of the group (forty-four per cent) were in the upper one per cent of the population in intellectual ability as measured by this particular test.

Reprinted from *Journal of Educational Psychology*, Vol. 47, No. 5, (May, 1956), pp. 302-309. By permission of the publisher.

All of the subjects were graduates of the Major Work Program of special classes for public school children in Cleveland, Ohio. The data for this study were obtained from information reported on a five-page printed questionnaire which was distributed to the graduates of the program over the last fifteen years. Of those who received the questionnaire, a return of seventy-seven per cent was received.

Racial and Religious Background

It is difficult to determine the racial background of a group of subjects. The question arises just how far back the subject should trace his ancestry. With regard to the ancestry of gifted subjects, Hollingworth states: "So few data have been gathered to show the proportion of gifted children in relation to race, that it is perhaps scarcely worth while to discuss the topic except to say that we are ignorant of the facts. We have, however, a few studies of the proportion of gifted in samplings of the various races found at present in the United States (3, pp. 68-69)."

In a study by Witty (4), the "racial stock included a preponderance of English, Scotch, German, and Jewish ancestors." Ninety-six per cent of the parents were American-born. These findings are similar to those of Terman and Oden: "The reports on racial origin indicate that, in comparison with the general populations of the cities concerned, there is about a one hundred per cent excess of native-born parentage, a probable excess of Scottish parentage and a deficiency of Italian, Portuguese, Mexican, and Negro ancestry (5)."

The racial stock of the subjects in the present study is predominantly German, nearly half (47.6 per cent) of the subjects reported having some degree of German ancestry. The next highest group mentioned, twenty-three per cent, was English. The next most frequent were: Hungarian, 14.7 per cent; Russian, 14.4 per cent; and Polish, 10.2 per cent. Hardly any European country was not at least mentioned.

The fact that the population of Cleveland consists of such a diverse foreign element would tend to make the racial background of the subjects different from the subjects in both Terman and Witty's studies. According to the 1940 Census (6) of the City of Cleveland, the largest foreign-born element, about thirteen per cent, was Polish. Czech, Hungarian and Italian each made up about twelve per cent of the foreign-born population. German, Yugoslavian, English and Russian each represented about seven per cent.

Slightly more than two and one-half per cent of the total sample are Negroes. The percentage of Negroes has risen from less than one per cent in 1938 to nearly five per cent in 1952. According to the census, the per cent of Negroes in Cleveland has risen from eight per cent in 1930 to 9.5 per cent in 1940 (6).

About 11.3 per cent of the group was Catholic, 46.3 Protestant, and 38.8 per cent Jewish. Other groups make up the remaining 3.8 per cent. As Hollingworth reports of New York City (3), children of Catholic parents, many of whom are gifted, are commonly being educated in parochial schools. This explains the rather low percentage of Catholic subjects in Major Work classes. The Jewish group appears to be represented in far greater numbers than its proportional share. This is also true of the gifted in the public schools of New York where Hollingworth reports there is "a marked excess of Jewish parentage (3, p. 70)."

Economic Background

An important phase of a study of the gifted which has not received adequate attention is their socio-economic background. This is difficult to determine and, when done in retrospect, is subject to many errors. The procedure followed in this study was to locate the economic tenth of the census tract in which the subject had lived while he was in public school (7). This gave an indication of the rent and property value of the neighborhood in which the gifted subject had been reared. The results of this phase of the study are presented in Table 1.

The economic tenth from which the greatest number of subjects came was the seventh, while the sixth and seventh economic tenths included more than fifty-eight per cent of the subjects. This indicates that the background of the majority of the subjects in the study may accurately be described as "upper middle-class."

TABLE 1

The Economic Status of 456 Gifted Subjects

Economic Tenths	Per Cent
Highest	1.1
Ninth	7.9
Eighth	10.3
Seventh	37.1
Sixth	21.3
Fifth	11.0
Fourth	5.0
Third	3.5
Second	2.2
Lowest	0.7

Order of Birth and Size of Family

It has long been a popular belief that the gifted child is an only child, or, perhaps, has one sibling. In a study of 253 subjects (8), Goddard reported half as being first-born and three-fourths as being either first- or second-born. Of the first-born, forty-five (about eighteen per cent) were only children.

Hollingworth reported that the gifted child had few siblings. In a study by Cobb and Hollingworth, fifty-seven gifted children averaged less than one sibling each (3). With respect to the order of birth, they found that more than one-half of their subjects were first-born.

In 1940, Terman reported that "the parents of the gifted subjects had produced . . . an average of 3.09 (children) per family." He states that this rate would more than maintain the stock, but "it appears likely that the subjects themselves will not equal the fertility rate of their parents" (5, p. 18).

In the present study two questions were asked to determine the size of the family and the order of birth of the gifted child. About 21.8 per cent of the subjects had no siblings, while 42.6 per cent had only one. Almost twenty per cent had two siblings, and seven per cent three.

About twenty-two per cent of the subjects in this study are only children. This is not as large a number as that found by Cobb and Hollingworth, although their finding that "more than half were first-born" (3, p. 180) is substantiated by the fact that 52.5 per cent of the subjects in this study were first-born. About twenty-nine per cent are second-born, and only 9.3 third-born. The data indicate that in this group the gifted child was the first-born in a family of two children.

Parent or Guardian of Gifted Subjects

Eighty-seven and a half per cent of the gifted subjects were reared by their own parents. The next largest group, 7.2 per cent, were reared by only their mothers. Two per cent were reared by their own mother and a step-father, and 1.5 per cent by their own father and a stepmother. The father or foster parents each reared 0.9 per cent of the total number of subjects.

Witty (9), in studying one hundred gifted children in Kansas, found that most of their parents were American-born. This was not true of the subjects in this study. Slightly less than fifty per cent of the subjects had one or both parents who were foreign-born. This is partially due to the large foreign element in the population of Cleveland.[1] It emphasizes the contribution of the immigrant to the mentally superior groups of the country. Table 2 presents these data.

---

1. About 20 per cent of the population of Cleveland were foreign-born.

TABLE 2
Percentage of Parents of Gifted Subjects
Who Were Born Outside the United States

Both parents U.S.-born	51.3
One parent foreign-born	21.1
Both parents foreign-born	27.5

Even though more rigid government controls have been placed on immigration, no trend is noted which would indicate that fewer of the subjects have parents who are foreign-born.

Education of Parents

Hollingworth states (3) that the educational level of the parents of gifted subjects is far above the average for their generation. "In the majority of the cases where the gifted child has been born since 1915, both parents are graduates of high school, and in far more cases than in the population at large both parents are college graduates (3, p. 180)." Since all of the subjects in the present study were born after 1915, it is interesting to compare Hollingworth's statements with the data obtained for this group.

Of the fathers of the subjects, 38.4 per cent had a grammar school education or less; 33.6 per cent had a high school education; 8.8 per cent trade or business school; and 19.2 per cent had some college. Of the mothers of the subjects, 32.5 per cent had a grammar school education or less; 42.2 per cent had a high school education; 12.3 per cent trade or business school; and 13.0 per cent had some college. The mothers of the gifted subjects on the average appeared to be slightly better educated than the fathers through the high school and business school levels. However, there were more fathers than mothers who attended college.

Marital Status of Parents

Terman reported (5) that until 1922, 5.2 per cent of the parents of his gifted group had been divorced and 1.9 per cent were separated. By 1940, the percentage of divorced and separated parents had risen to 13.9.

The data in the present study are not exactly comparable to the results of Terman's study. The information obtained in this study deals with the marital status of the parents while the subject was in public school. It is perhaps comparable to Terman's 1922 data but is definitely not comparable to his 1940 data.

Eighty-eight per cent of the parents of the subjects were living together while the subject was in public school. About 6.3 per cent were either divorced or separated. This is only slightly higher than the report for Terman's 1922 group and is certainly lower than that of the general population. The remaining five per cent consists of cases where one or both of the parents were deceased.

Occupational Level of Parents of Gifted Subjects

The occupations of the parents were listed according to the U.S. census classification. The *Dictionary of Occupational Titles* (10) was used to classify the occupations into seven distinct groups: professional and managerial; clerical and sales; service; agriculture, fishery, forestry, etc.; skilled; semi-skilled; and unskilled. The subjects were asked the title and description of the father's occupation. It was possible to classify all but a few of the occupations listed. Where descriptions were not given and two classifications were possible, the data were omitted. Classifications of the parent's occupation were made for four hundred and thirty-seven subjects. Three of the remaining nineteen were on government pensions, while the rest gave no response to the question at all. The data are presented in Table 3.

TABLE 3

Occupational Level of Parents of Gifted Subjects

	Per Cent
Professional and managerial	40.3
Clerical and sales	22.4
Service	3.7
Agriculture, fishery, forestry, etc.	0.2
Skilled	21.5
Semi-skilled	8.2
Unskilled	3.7

Hollingworth reports (3) that more than fifty per cent of the children testing above 140 I.Q. have fathers who are professional men or proprietors. The I.Q.'s of the subjects in the present study are not this high, which may partly explain why only about forty per cent of the parents fall into the professional and managerial group. Hollingworth also states (3) that half of the remaining fathers are in semi-professional and clerical occupations. This corresponds to the clerical and sales group of the U.S. Census Bureau, and the data for this group agree with the data in Hollingworth's study.

The fact that over thirty per cent of the parents are in the laboring class, and about forty per cent of these are semi-skilled or unskilled, is noteworthy. It indicates that while the majority of gifted children do come from parents of higher occupational status, the laboring class also contributes a sizeable number.

Summary

In this study data were presented concerning the composition of the group being studied and their family background.

1. The range in I.Q. of the four hundred and fifty-six subjects was from 120 to 164 with a mean I.Q. of 130.2. Almost sixty-two per cent of the group were within the 125-135 range.

2. Slightly less than fifty-two per cent of the subjects are females; slightly more than forty-eight per cent are males.

3. Of the total samples, only 2.6 per cent are Negroes.

4. About thirty-nine per cent of the subjects are Jewish. The Jewish group is represented in far greater numbers than the size of this group in the total population would lead one to expect.

5. The economic tenth of the census tract in which the subjects lived while in public schools was most frequently the sixth and seventh. This would characterize the gifted child as being upper middle-class.

6. The gifted child appears to be either an only child or firstborn in a family of two.

7. Eighty-seven and one-half per cent of the gifted subjects were reared by their own parents.

8. Almost fifty per cent of the subjects had one or both parents who were foreign-born. These data indicate that the group studied is quite unlike other studies of gifted groups. Previously, the gifted child was found to have American parentage. The high percentage of foreign-born in Cleveland (approximately twenty per cent) partially explains these data.

9. The education of the mothers of gifted subjects is slightly higher than that of the fathers, even though more of the fathers went to college.

10. Forty per cent of the parents were in the professional and managerial group, 22.5 per cent in the clerical and sales, and thirty per cent in the laboring class.

The subjects in this study come from about average backgrounds with respect to occupational level, educational level and marital adjustment of their parents. Economically the majority of them come from an upper middle-class group.

References

1. Martin David Jenkins, "A Socio-Psychological Study of Negro Children of Superior Intelligence." Unpublished Doctoral Dissertation. Graduate School, Northwestern University, Evanston, Illinois, p. 53, June, 1935.

2. Merle R. Sumption, *Three Hundred Gifted Children,* p. 6. Yonkers-on-Hudson, New York: World Book Co., 1941.

3. Leta A. Hollingworth, *Gifted Children.* New York: The Macmillan Co. 1926.

4. Paul A. Witty, "A Study of One Hundred Gifted Children." *Bulletin of Education,* University of Kansas, 2:8, February, 1930.

5. Lewis M. Terman and Melita H. Oden, *The Gifted Child Grows Up.* Stanford, California: Stanford University Press, 1947.

6. U. S. Department of Commerce, Bureau of the Census, Sixteenth Census of the United States, 1940, *Population,* 11:712, Part 5, Washington, D. C.: U. S. Government Printing Office, 1943.

7. Howard Whipple Green, *Census Tract Street Index for Cuyahoga County,* fifth edition. Cleveland Health Council, 1951.

8. Henry H. Goddard, *School Training of Gifted Children,* p. 129. Yonkers-on-Hudson, New York: World Book Co., 1928.

9. Paul A. Witty, "A Genetic Study of Fifty Gifted Children," In *Intelligence: Its Nature and Nurture.* Thirty-Ninth Yearbook, Part II, National Society for the Study of Education. Chicago: University of Chicago Press, 1940.

10. Job Analysis and Information Section, Division of Standards and Research, United States Department of Labor, *Dictionary of Occupational Titles, Part I,* second edition. Washington, D. C.: United States Government Printing Office, 1949.

Part II.
Characteristics and Identification of the Gifted and Talented

The concept of giftedness, as of intelligence itself, is today much broader than it was earlier in this century. Early research and especially the classic longitudinal studies of Terman tended to limit the concept of giftedness to high performance on tests of intelligence and academic achievement. Although few would deny that high intelligence and achievement are indeed very important types of superior ability, psychologists and educators in more recent years have asserted that man has a much broader repertoire of highly valuable behaviors. Each of these human behaviors, like intelligence and achievement, exist in the population and in the individual along a continuum, and thus, when we speak of a gifted or superior person, it is relevant to raise the questions, "Gifted in what ways?" or "Superior in what areas of performance?"

The broadened concept of giftedness grew out of a realization that an invaluable amount of human potential was being neglected because intelligence tests failed to measure such important characteristics as originality, leadership ability, foresight, and outstanding performance in nonacademic areas. Furthermore, the use of intelligence tests as the sole criterion for determining giftedness often led to the conclusion that a person is either gifted or not! This limited conception of giftedness failed to take into account the indisputable fact that many people have extremely superior potential in one or two areas, but that the same individuals may be mediocre or even below average in other areas of performance. Unless we view giftedness as a multidimensional set of traits that exist in varying degrees in the individual as well as in the general population, it is quite likely that special educational efforts for the gifted will continue to focus on a relatively restricted number of abilities and a highly restricted portion of the population.

The material selected for Part II of this book reflects much of the thinking and research that has given rise to the broadened conception of giftedness. This section examines a number of cognitive processes that are not ordinarily measured in single factor tests of general intelligence. The article by Guilford is considered by many to be a classic study of the nature and organization of mental abilities. Roe described the attributes of sixty-four eminent scientists in a provocative manner which can only cause the educator concerned with the gifted to rethink many of the preconceived notions about the factors which lead to eminence. MacKinnon's contribution leads the reader into a better understanding of creative talent.

The final articles in Part II deal with the identification and measurement of giftedness and creativity. The Robinson, Roedell and Jackson article stresses the need for early identification and intervention, while the contribution by Treffinger, Renzulli and Fledhusen points out many of the problems in the assessment of creativity. A checklist for rating behavioral characteristics of superior students is presented by Renzulli, Hartman and Callahan. The identification of a specialized talent is dealt with by Ellison, Abe, Fox, Coray and Taylor. Their suggestion of using biographical information in identifying artistic talent is especially noteworthy. Using adaptive behavior and estimated learning potential is suggested by Mercer and Lewis as a means of identifying gifted minority children. The final selection in this section, "The Measurement of Individual Differences in Originality," by Wilson, Guilford and Christensen discusses the problem of developing methods for measuring individual differences in originality.

J. P. Guilford

Three Faces of Intellect

My subject is in the area of human intelligence, in connection with which the names of Terman and Stanford have become known the world over. The Stanford Revision of the Binet intelligence scale has been the standard against which all other instruments for the measurement of intelligence have been compared. The term IQ or intelligence quotient has become a household word in this country. This is illustrated by two brief stories.

> A few years ago, one of my neighbors came home from a PTA meeting, remarking: "That Mrs. So-And-So, thinks she knows so much. She kept talking about the 'intelligence *quota*' of the children, 'intelligence *quota*'; imagine. Why, everybody knows that IQ stands for 'intelligence *quiz*.'"
> The other story comes from a little comic strip in a Los Angeles morning newspaper, called "Junior Grade." In the first picture a little boy meets a little girl, both apparently about the first-grade level. The little girl remarks, "I have a high IQ." The little boy, puzzled, said, "You have a what?" The little girl repeated, "I have a high IQ," then went on her way. The little boy, looking thoughtful, said, "And she looks like such a nice little girl, too."

It is my purpose to speak about the analysis of this thing called human intelligence into its components. I do not believe that either Binet or Terman, if they were still with us, would object to the idea of a searching and detailed study of intelligence, aimed toward a better understanding of its nature. Preceding the development of his intelligence scale, Binet had done much research on different kinds of thinking activities and apparently recognized that intelligence has a number of aspects. It is to the lasting

Reprinted from *American Psychologist*, Vol. 14, No. 8 (August, 1959), pp. 469-479. By permission of the American Psychological Association.

credit of both Binet and Terman that they introduced such a great variety of tasks into their intelligence scales.

Two related events of very recent history make it imperative that we learn all we can regarding the nature of intelligence. I am referring to the advent of the artificial satellites and planets and to the crisis in education that has arisen in part as a consequence. The preservation of our way of life and our future security depend upon our most important national resources: our intellectual abilities and, more particularly, our creative abilities. It is time, then, that we learn all we can about those resources.

Our knowledge of the components of human intelligence has come about mostly within the last 25 years. The major sources of this information in this country have been L. L. Thurstone and his associates, the wartime research of psychologists in the United States Air Forces, and more recently the Aptitudes Project at the University of Southern California, now in its tenth year of research on cognitive and thinking abilities. The results from the Aptitudes Project that have gained perhaps the most attention have pertained to creative-thinking abilities. These are mostly novel findings. But to me, the most significant outcome has been the development of a unified theory of human intellect, which organizes the known, unique or primary intellectual abilities into a single system called the "structure of intellect." It is to this system that I shall devote the major part of my remarks, with very brief mentions of some of the implications for the psychology of thinking and problem solving, for vocational testing, and for education.

The discovery of the components of intelligence has been by means of the experimental application of the method of factor analysis. It is not necessary for you to know anything about the theory or method of factor analysis in order to follow the discussion of the components. I should like to say, however, that factor analysis has no connection with or resemblance to psychoanalysis. A positive statement would be more helpful so I will say that each intellectual component or factor is a unique ability that is needed to do well in a certain class of tasks or tests. As a general principle we find that certain individuals do well in the tests of a certain class, but they may do poorly in the tests of another class. We conclude that a factor has certain properties from the features that the tests of a class have in common. I shall give you very soon a number of examples of tests, each representing a factor.

The Structure of Intellect

Although each factor is sufficiently distinct to be detected by factor analysis, in very recent years it has become apparent that the factors themselves can be classified because they resemble one another in certain ways. One basis of classification is according to the basic kind of process or operation performed. This kind of classification gives us five major groups of intellectual abilities: factors of cognition, memory, convergent thinking, divergent thinking, and evaluation.

Cognition means discovery or rediscovery or recognition. Memory means retention of what is cognized. Two kinds of productive-thinking operations generate new information from known information and remembered information. In divergent-thinking operations we think in different directions, sometimes searching, sometimes seeking variety. In convergent thinking the information leads to one right answer or to a recognized best or conventional answer. In evaluation we reach decisions as to goodness, correctness, suitability, or adequacy of what we know, what we remember, and what we produce in productive thinking.

A second way of classifying the intellectual factors is according to the kind of material or content involved. The factors known thus far involve three kinds of material or content: the content may be figural, symbolic, or semantic. Figural content is concrete material such as is perceived through the senses. It does not represent anything except itself. Visual material has properties such as size, form, color, location, or texture. Things we hear or feel provide other examples of figural material. Symbolic content is composed of letters, digits, and other conventional signs, usually organized in general systems, such as the alphabet or the number system. Semantic content is in the form of verbal meanings or ideas, for which no examples are necessary.

When a certain operation is applied to a certain kind of content, as many as six general kinds of products may be involved. There is enough evidence available to suggest that, regardless of the combinations of operations and content, the same six kinds of products may be found associated. The six kinds of products are: units, classes, relations, systems, transformations, and implications. So far as we have determined from factor analysis, these are the only fundamental kinds of products that we can know. As such, they may serve as basic classes into which one might fit all kinds of information psychologically.

The three kinds of classifications of the factors of intellect can be represented by means of a single solid model, shown in Figure 1. In this model, which we call the "structure of intellect," each dimension represents one of the modes of variation of the factors (2). Along one dimension are found the various kinds of operations, along a second one are the various kinds of products, and along the third are various kinds of content. Along the dimension of content a fourth category has been added, its kind of content being designated as "behavioral." This category has been added on a purely theoretical basis to represent the general area sometimes called "social intelligence." More will be said about this section of the model later.

In order to provide a better basis for understanding the model and a better basis for accepting it as a picture of human intellect, I shall do some exploring of it with you systematically, giving some examples of tests. Each cell in the model calls for a certain kind of ability that can be described in terms of operation, content, and product, for each cell is at the intersection of a unique combination of kinds of operation, content, and product. A test for that ability would have the same three properties. In our exploration of the model, we shall take one vertical layer at a time, beginning with the front

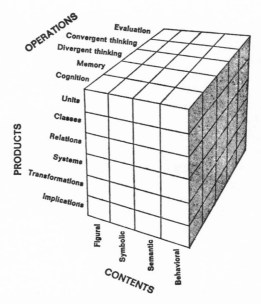

FIG. 1. A Cubical Model Representing the Structure of Intellect

face. The first layer provides us with a matrix of 18 cells (if we ignore the behavioral column for which there are as yet no known factors) each of which should contain a cognitive ability.

THE COGNITIVE ABILITIES.

We know at present the unique abilities that fit logically into 15 of the 18 cells for cognitive abilities. Each row presents a triad of similar abilities, having a single kind of product in common. The factors of the first row are concerned with the knowing of units. A good test of the ability to cognize figural units is the Street Gestalt Completion Test. In this test, the recognition of familiar pictured objects in silhouette form is made difficult for testing purposes by blocking out parts of those objects. There is another factor that is known to involve the perception of auditory figures—in the form of melodies, rhythms, and speech sounds—and still another factor involving kinesthetic forms. The presence of three factors in one cell (they are conceivably distinct abilities, although this has not been tested) suggests that more generally, in the figural column, at least, we should expect to find more than one ability. A fourth dimension pertaining to variations in sense modality may thus apply in connection with figural content. The model could be extended in this manner if the facts call for such an extension.

The ability to cognize symbolic units is measured by tests like the following:

Put vowels in the following blanks to make real words:

P__W__R
M__RV__L
C__RT__N

Rearrange the letters to make real words:

R A C I H
T V O E S
K L C C O

The first of these two tests is called Disemvoweled Words, and the second Scrambled Words.

The ability to cognize semantic units is the well-known factor of verbal comprehension, which is best measured by means of a vocabulary test, with items such as:

GRAVITY means _____
CIRCUS means _____
VIRTUE means _____

From the comparison of these two factors it is obvious that recognizing familiar words as letter structures and knowing what words mean depend upon quite different abilities.

For testing the abilities to know classes of units, we may present the following kinds of items, one with symbolic content and one with semantic content:

Which letter group does not belong?
XECM   PVAA   QXIN   VTRO

Which object does not belong?
clam   tree   oven   rose

A figural test is constructed in a completely parallel form, presenting in each item four figures, three of which have a property in common and the fourth lacking that property.

The three abilities to see relationships are also readily measured by a common kind of test, differing only in terms of content. The well-known analogies test is applicable, two items in symbolic and semantic form being:

JIRE : KIRE : : FORA : KORE   KORA   LIRE   GORA   GIRE
poetry : prose : : dance : music   walk   sing   talk   jump

Such tests usually involve more than the ability to cognize relations, but we are not concerned with this problem at this point.

The three factors for cognizing systems do not at present appear in tests so closely resembling one another as in the case of the examples just given.

There is nevertheless an underlying common core of logical similarity. Ordinary space tests, such as Thurstone's Flags, Figures, and Cards or Part V (Spatial Orientation) of the Guilford-Zimmerman Aptitude Survey (GZAS), serve in the figural column. The system involved is an order or arrangement of objects in space. A system that uses symbolic elements is illustrated by the Letter Triangle Test, a sample item of which is:

$$
\begin{array}{cccc}
 & d & \overline{} & \\
 & & \overline{} & \\
b & & e & \overline{} \\
a & & c & f \quad \underline{\ ?\ } \\
\end{array}
$$

What letter belongs at the place of the question mark?

The ability to understand a semantic system has been known for some time as the factor called general reasoning. One of its most faithful indicators is a test composed of arithmetic-reasoning items. That the phase of understanding only is important for measuring this ability is shown by the fact that such a test works even if the examinee is not asked to give a complete solution; he need only show that he structures the problem properly. For example, an item from the test Necessary Arithmetical Operations simply asks what operations are needed to solve the problem:

A city lot 48 feet wide and 149 feet deep costs $79,432. What is the cost per square foot?

A. add and multiply
B. multiply and divide
C. subtract and divide
D. add and subtract
E. divide and add

Placing the factor of general reasoning in this cell of the structure of intellect gives us some new conceptions of its nature. It should be a broad ability to grasp all kinds of systems that are conceived in terms of verbal concepts, not restricted to the understanding of problems of an arithmetical type.

Transformations are changes of various kinds, including modifications in arrangement, organization, or meaning. In the figural column for the transformations row, we find the factor known as visualization. Common measuring instruments for this factor are the surface-development tests, and an example of a different kind is Part VI (Spatial Visualization) of the GZAS. A test of the ability to make transformations of meaning, for the factor in the semantic column, is called Similarities. The examinee is asked to state several ways in which two objects, such as an apple and an orange, are alike. Only by shifting the meanings of both is the examinee able to give many responses to such an item.

In the set of abilities having to do with the cognition of implications, we find that the individual goes beyond the information given, but not to the extent of what might be called drawing conclusions. We may say that he extrapolates. From the given information he expects or foresees certain consequences, for example. The two factors found in this row of the cognition matrix were first called "foresight" factors. Foresight in connection with figural material can be tested by means of paper-and-pencil mazes. Foresight in connection with ideas, those pertaining to events, for example, is indicated by a test such as Pertinent Questions:

> In planning to open a new hamburger stand in a certain community, what four questions should be considered in deciding upon its location?

The more questions the examinee asks in response to a list of such problems, the more he evidently foresees contingencies.

THE MEMORY ABILITIES.

The area of memory abilities has been explored less than some of the other areas of operation, and only seven of the potential cells of the memory matrix have known factors in them. These cells are restricted to three rows: for units, relations, and systems. The first cell in the memory matrix is now occupied by two factors, parallel to two in the corresponding cognition matrix: visual memory and auditory memory. Memory for series of letters or numbers, as in memory span tests, conforms to the conception of memory for symbolic units. Memory for the ideas in a paragraph conforms to the conception of memory for semantic units.

The formation of associations between units, such as visual forms, syllables, and meaningful words, as in the method of paired associates, would seem to represent three abilities to remember relationships involving three kinds of content. We know of two such abilities, for the symbolic and semantic columns. The memory for known systems is represented by two abilities very recently discovered (1). Remembering the arrangement of objects in space is the nature of an ability in the figural column, and remembering a sequence of events is the nature of a corresponding ability in the semantic column. The differentiation between these two abilities implies that a person may be able to say where he saw an object on a page, but he might not be able to say on which of several pages he saw it after leafing through several pages that included the right one. Considering the blank rows in the memory matrix, we should expect to find abilities also to remember classes, transformations, and implications, as well as units, relations, and systems.

THE DIVERGENT-THINKING ABILITIES.

The unique feature of divergent production is that a *variety* of responses is produced. The product is not completely determined by the given information. This is not to say that divergent thinking does not come into play in the total process of reaching a unique conclusion, for it comes into play wherever there is trial-and-error thinking.

The well-known ability of word fluency is tested by asking the examinee to list words satisfying a specified letter requirement, such as words beginning with the letter "s" or words ending in "-tion." This ability is now regarded as a facility in divergent production of symbolic units. The parallel semantic ability has been known as ideational fluency. A typical test item calls for listing objects that are round and edible. Winston Churchill must have possessed this ability to a high degree. Clement Attlee is reported to have said about him recently that, no matter what problem came up, Churchill always seemed to have about ten ideas. The trouble was, Attlee continued, he did not know which was the good one. The last comment implies some weakness in one or more of the evaluative abilities.

The divergent production of class ideas is believed to be the unique feature of a factor called "spontaneous flexibility." A typical test instructs the examinee to list all the uses he can think of for a common brick, and he is given eight minutes. If his responses are: build a house, build a barn, build a garage, build a school, build a church, build a chimney, build a walk, and build a barbecue, he would earn a fairly high score for ideational fluency but a very low score for spontaneous flexibility, because all these uses fall into the same class. If another person said: make a door stop, make a paper weight, throw it at a dog, make a bookcase, drown a cat, drive a nail, make a red powder, and use for baseball bases, he would also receive a high score for flexibility. He has gone frequently from one class to another.

A current study of unknown but predicted divergent-production abilities includes testing whether there are also figural and symbolic abilities to produce multiple classes. An experimental figural test presents a number of figures that can be classified in groups of three in various ways, each figure being usable in more than one class. An experimental symbolic test presents a few numbers that are also to be classified in multiple ways.

A unique ability involving relations is called "associational fluency." It calls for the production of a variety of things related in a specified way to a given thing. For example, the examinee is asked to list words meaning about the same as "good" or to list words meaning about the opposite of "hard." In these instances the response produced is to complete a relationship, and semantic content is involved. Some of our present experimental tests call for the production of varieties of relations, as such, and involve figural and symbolic content also. For example, given four small digits, in how many ways can they be related in order to produce a sum of eight?

One factor pertaining to the production of systems is known as expressional fluency. The rapid formation of phrases or sentences is the essence of certain tests of this factor. For example, given the initial letters:

with different sentences to be produced, the examinee might write "We can eat nuts" or "Whence came Eve Newton?" In interpreting the factor, we regard the sentence as a symbolic system. By analogy, a figural system would be some kind of organization of lines and other elements, and a

94

semantic system would be in the form of a verbally stated problem or perhaps something as complex as a theory.

In the row of the divergent-production matrix devoted to transformations, we find some very interesting factors. The one called "adaptive flexibility" is now recognized as belonging in the figural column. A faithful test of it has been Match Problems. This is based upon the common game that uses squares, the sides of which are formed by match sticks. The examinee is told to take away a given number of matches to leave a stated number of squares with nothing left over. Nothing is said about the sizes of the squares to be left. If the examinee imposes upon himself the restriction that the squares that he leaves must be of the same size, he will fail. Other odd kinds of solutions are introduced in other items, such as overlapping squares and squares within squares, and so on. In another variation of Match Problems the examinee is told to produce two or more solutions for each problem.

A factor that has been called "originality" is now recognized as adaptive flexibility with semantic material, where there must be a shifting of meanings. The examinee must produce the shifts or changes in meaning and so come up with novel, unusual, clever, or farfetched ideas. The Plot Titles Test presents a short story, the examinee being told to list as many appropriate titles as he can to head the story. One story is about a missionary who has been captured by cannibals in Africa. He is in the pot and about to be boiled when a princess of the tribe obtains a promise for his release if he will become her mate. He refuses and is boiled to death.

In scoring the test, we separate the responses into two categories, clever and nonclever. Examples of nonclever responses are: African Death, Defeat of a Princess, Eaten by Savages, The Princess, The African Missionary, In Darkest Africa, and Boiled by Savages. These titles are appropriate but commonplace. The number of such responses serves as a score for ideational fluency. Examples of clever responses are: Pot's Plot, Potluck Dinner, Stewed Parson, Goil or Boil, A Mate Worse Than Death, He Left a Dish for a Pot, Chaste in Haste, and A Hot Price for Freedom. The number of clever responses given by an examinee is his score for originality, or the divergent production of semantic transformations.

Another test of originality presents a very novel task so that any acceptable response is unusual for the individual. In the Symbol Production Test the examinee is to produce a simple symbol to stand for a noun or a verb in each short sentence, in other words to invent something like pictographic symbols. Still another test of originality asks for writing the "punch lines" for cartoons, a task that almost automatically challenges the examinee to be clever. Thus, quite a variety of tests offer approaches to the measurement of originality, including one or two others that I have not mentioned.

Abilities to produce a variety of implications are assessed by tests calling for elaboration of given information. A figural test of this type provides the examinee with a line or two, to which he is to add other lines to produce an object. The more lines he adds, the greater his score. A semantic test gives the examinee the outlines of a plan to which he is to respond by stating all the details he can think of to make the plan work. A new test we are trying out in the symbolic area presents two simple equations such as $B - C = D$ and $z = A + D$. The examinee is to make as many other equations as he can from this information.

Of the 18 convergent-production abilities expected in the three content columns, 12 are now recognized. In the first row, pertaining to units, we have an ability to name figural properties (forms or colors) and an ability to name abstractions (classes, relations, and so on). It may be that the ability in common to the speed of naming forms and the speed of naming colors is not appropriately placed in the convergent-thinking matrix. One might expect that the thing to be produced in a test of the convergent production of figural units would be in the form of figures rather than words. A better test of such an ability might somehow specify the need for one particular object, the examinee to furnish the object.

A test for the convergent production of classes (Word Grouping) presents a list of 12 words that are to be classified in four, and only four, meaningful groups, no word to appear in more than one group. A parallel test (Figure Concepts Test) presents 20 pictured real objects that are to be grouped in meaningful classes of two or more each.

Convergent production having to do with relationships is represented by three known factors, all involving the "eduction of correlates," as Spearman called it. The given information includes one unit and a stated relation, the examinee to supply the other unit. Analogies tests that call for completion rather than a choice between alternative answers emphasize this kind of ability. With symbolic content such an item might read:

$$\text{pots} \quad \text{stop} \qquad \text{bard} \quad \text{drab} \qquad \text{rats} \quad \underline{?}$$

A semantic item that measures eduction of correlates is:

$$\text{The absence of sound is} \underline{\hspace{2cm}}.$$

Incidentally, the latter item is from a vocabulary-completion test, and its relation to the factor of ability to produce correlates indicates how, by change of form, a vocabulary test may indicate an ability other than that for which vocabulary tests are usually intended, namely, the factor of verbal comprehension.

Only one factor for convergent production of systems is known, and it is in the semantic column. It is measured by a class of tests that may be called ordering tests. The examinee may be presented with a number of events that ordinarily have a best or most logical order, the events being presented in scrambled order. The presentation may be pictorial, as in the Picture Arrangement Test, or verbal. The pictures may be taken from a cartoon strip.

The verbally presented events may be in the form of the various steps needed to plant a new lawn. There are undoubtedly other kinds of systems than temporal order that could be utilized for testing abilities in this row of the convergent-production matrix.

In the way of producing transformations of a unique variety, we have three recognized factors, known as redefinition abilities. In each case, redefinition involves the changing of functions or uses of parts of one unit and giving them new functions or uses in some new unit. For testing the ability of figural redefinition, a task based upon the Gottschaldt figures is suitable. In recognizing the simpler figure within the structure of a more complex figure, certain lines must take on new roles.

In terms of symbolic material, the following sample items will illustrate how groups of letters in given words must be readapted to use in other words. In the test Camouflaged Words, each sentence contains the name of a sport or game:

I did not know that he was ailing.
To beat the Hun, tin goes a long way.

For the factor of semantic redefinition, the Gestalt Transformation Test may be used. A sample item reads:

From which object could you most likely make a needle?
A. a cabbage
B. a splice
C. a steak
D. a paper box
E. a fish

The convergent production of implications means the drawing of fully determined conclusions from given information. The well-known factor of numerical facility belongs in the symbolic column. For the parallel ability in the figural column, we have a test known as Form Reasoning, in which rigorously defined operations with figures are used. For the parallel ability in the semantic column, the factor sometimes called "deduction" probably qualifies. Items of the following type are sometimes used.

Charles is younger than Robert
Charles is older than Frank
Who is older: Robert or Frank?

EVALUATIVE ABILITIES.

The evaluative area has had the least investigation of all the operational categories. In fact, only one systematic analytical study has been devoted to this area. Only eight evaluative abilities are recognized as fitting into the evaluation matrix. But at least five rows have one or more factors each, and

97

also three of the usual columns or content categories. In each case, evaluation involves reaching decisions as to the accuracy, goodness, suitability, or workability of information. In each row, for the particular kind of product of that row, some kind of criterion or standard of judgment is involved.

In the first row, for the evaluation of units, the important decision to be made pertains to the identity of a unit. Is this unit identical with that one? In the figural column we find the factor long known as "perceptual speed." Tests of this factor invariably call for decisions of identity, for example, Part IV (Perceptual Speed) of the GZAS or Thurstone's Identical Forms. I think it has been generally wrongly thought that the ability involved is that of cognition of visual forms. But we have seen that another factor is a more suitable candidate for this definition and for being in the very first cell of cognitive matrix. It is parallel to this evaluative ability but does not require the judgment of identity as one of its properties.

In the symbolic column is an ability to judge identity of symbolic units, in the form of series of letters or numbers or of names of individuals.

Are members of the following pairs identical or not:

825170493 _____ 825176493
dkeltvmpa _____ dkeltvmpa
C. S. Meyerson _____ C. E. Meyerson

Such items are common in tests of clerical aptitude.

There should be a parallel ability to decide whether two ideas are identical or different. Is the idea expressed in this sentence the same as the idea expressed in that one? Do these two proverbs express essentially the same idea? Such tests exist and will be used to test the hypothesis that such an ability can be demonstrated.

No evaluative abilities pertaining to classes have as yet been recognized. The abilities having to do with evaluation where relations are concerned must meet the criterion of logical consistency. Syllogistic-type tests involving letter symbols indicate a different ability than the same type of test involving verbal statements. In the figural column we might expect that tests incorporating geometric reasoning or proof would indicate a parallel ability to sense the soundness of conclusions regarding figural relationships.

The evaluation of systems seems to be concerned with the internal consistency of those systems, so far as we can tell from the knowledge of one such factor. The factor has been called "experiential evaluation," and its representative test presents items asking "What is wrong with this picture?" The things wrong are often internal inconsistencies.

A semantic ability for evaluating transformations is thought to be that known for some time as "judgment." In typical judgment tests, the examinee is asked to tell which of five solutions to a practical problem is most adequate or wise. The solutions frequently involve improvisations, in other words, adaptations of familiar objects to unusual uses. In this way the items present redefinitions to be evaluated.

A factor known first as "sensitivity to problems" has become recognized as an evaluative ability having to do with implications. One test of the factor, the Apparatus Test, asks for two needed improvements with respect to each of several common devices, such as the telephone or the toaster. The Social Institutions Test, a measure of the same factor, asks what things are wrong with each of several institutions, such as tipping or national elections. We may say that defects or deficiencies are implications of an evaluative kind. Another interpretation would be that seeing defects and deficiencies are evaluations of implications to the effect that the various aspects of something are all right (3).

Some Implications of the Structure of Intellect

FOR PSYCHOLOGICAL THEORY.

Although factor analysis as generally employed is best designed to investigate ways in which individuals differ from one another, in other words, to discover traits, the results also tell us much about how individuals are alike. Consequently, information regarding the factors and their interrelationships gives us understanding of functioning individuals. The five kinds of intellectual abilities in terms of operations may be said to represent five ways of functioning. The kinds of intellectual abilities distinguished according to varieties of test content and the kinds of abilities distinguished according to varieties of products suggest a classification of basic forms of information or knowledge. The kind of organism suggested by this way of looking at intellect is that of an agency for dealing with information of various kinds in various ways. The concepts provided by the distinctions among the intellectual abilities and by their classifications may be very useful in our future investigations of learning, memory, problem solving, invention, and decision making, by whatever method we choose to approach those problems.

FOR VOCATIONAL TESTING.

With about 50 intellectual factors already known, we may say that there are at least 50 ways of being intelligent. It has been facetiously suggested that there seem to be a great many more ways of being stupid, unfortunately. The structure of intellect is a theoretical model that predicts as many as 120 distinct abilities, if every cell of the model contains a factor. Already we know that two cells contain two or more factors each, and there probably are actually other cells of this type. Since the model was first conceived, 12 factors predicted by it have found places in it. There is consequently hope of filling many of the other vacancies, and we may eventually end up with more than 120 abilities.

99

The major implication for the assessment of intelligence is that to know an individual's intellectual resources thoroughly we shall need a surprisingly large number of scores. It is expected that many of the factors are intercorrelated, so there is some possibility that by appropriate sampling we shall be able to cover the important abilities with a more limited number of tests. At any rate, a multiple-score approach to the assessment of intelligence is definitely indicated in connection with future vocational operations.

Considering the kinds of abilities classified as to content, we may speak roughly of four kinds of intelligence. The abilities involving the use of figural information may be regarded as "concrete" intelligence. The people who depend most upon these abilities deal with concrete things and their properties. Among these people are mechanics, operators of machines, engineers (in some aspects of their work), artists, and musicians.

In the abilities pertaining to symbolic and semantic content, we have two kinds of "abstract" intelligence. Symbolic abilities should be important in learning to recognize words, to spell, and to operate with numbers. Language and mathematics should depend very much upon them, except that in mathematics some aspects, such as geometry, have strong figural involvement. Semantic intelligence is important for understanding things in terms of verbal concepts and hence is important in all courses where the learning of facts and ideas is essential.

In the hypothesized behavioral column of the structure of intellect, which may be roughly described as "social" intelligence, we have some of the most interesting possibilities. Understanding the behavior of others and of ourselves is largely nonverbal in character. The theory suggests as many as 30 abilities in this area, some having to do with understanding, some with productive thinking about behavior, and some with the evaluation of behavior. The theory also suggests that information regarding behavior is also in the form of the six kinds of products that apply elsewhere in the structure of intellect, including units, relations, systems, and so on. The abilities in the area of social intelligence, whatever they prove to be, will possess considerable importance in connection with all those individuals who deal most with other people: teachers, law officials, social workers, therapists, politicians, statesmen, and leaders of other kinds.

FOR EDUCATION.

The implications for education are numerous, and I have time just to mention a very few. The most fundamental implication is that we might well undergo transformations with respect to our conception of the learner and of the process of learning. Under the prevailing conception, the learner is a kind of stimulus-response device, much on the order of a vending machine. You put in a coin, and something comes out. The machine learns what reaction to put out when a certain coin is put in. If, instead, we think of the learner as an agent for dealing with information, where information is defined very broadly, we have something more analogous to an electronic

100

computor. We feed a computor information; it stores that information; it uses that information for generating new information, either by way of divergent or convergent thinking; and it evaluates its own results. Advantages that a human learner has over a computor include the step of seeking and discovering new information from sources outside itself and the step of programming itself. Perhaps even these steps will be added to computors, if this has not already been done in some cases.

At any rate, this conception of the learner leads us to the idea that learning is discovery of information, not merely the formation of associations, particularly associations in the form of stimulus-response connections. I am aware of the fact that my proposal is rank heresy. But if we are to make significant progress in our understanding of human learning and particularly our understanding of the so-called higher mental processes of thinking, problem solving, and creative thinking, some drastic modifications are due in our theory.

The idea that education is a matter of training the mind or of training the intellect has been rather unpopular, wherever the prevailing psychological doctrines have been followed. In theory, at least, the emphasis has been upon the learning of rather specific habits or skills. If we take our cue from factor theory, however, we recognize that most learning probably has both specific and general aspects or components. The general aspects may be along the lines of the factors of intellect. This is not to say that the individual's status in each factor is entirely determined by learning. We do not know to what extent each factor is determined by heredity and to what extent by learning. The best position for educators to take is that possibly every intellectual factor can be developed in individuals at least to some extent by learning.

If education has the general objective of developing the intellects of students, it can be suggested that each intellectual factor provides a particular goal at which to aim. Defined by a certain combination of content, operation, and product, each goal ability then calls for certain kinds of practice in order to achieve improvement in it. This implies choice of curriculum and the choice or invention of teaching methods that will most likely accomplish the desired results.

Considering the very great variety of abilities revealed by the factorial exploration of intellect, we are in a better position to ask whether any general intellectual skills are now being neglected in education and whether appropriate balances are being observed. It is often observed these days that we have fallen down in the way of producing resourceful, creative graduates. How true this is, in comparison with other times, I do not know. Perhaps the deficit is noticed because the demands for inventiveness are so much greater at this time. At any rate, realization that the more conspicuously creative abilities appear to be concentrated in the divergent-thinking category, and also to some extent in the transformation category, we now ask whether we have been giving these skills appropriate exercise. It is probable that we need a better balance of training in the divergent-thinking area as compared with training in convergent thinking and in critical thinking or evaluation.

The structure of intellect as I have presented it to you may or may not stand the test of time. Even if the general form persists, there are likely to be some modifications. Possibly some different kind of model will be invented. Be that as it may, the fact of a multiplicity of intellectual abilities seems well established.

There are many individuals who long for the good old days of simplicity, when we got along with one unanalyzed intelligence. Simplicity certainly has its appeal. But human nature is exceedingly complex, and we may as well face that fact. The rapidly moving events of the world in which we live have forced upon us the need for knowing human intelligence thoroughly. Humanity's peaceful pursuit of happiness depends upon our control of nature and of our own behavior; and this, in turn, depends upon understanding ourselves, including our intellectual resources.

References

1. Christal, R. E., Factor Analytic Study of Visual Memory. *Psychol. Monogr.*, 1958, **72,** No. 13 (Whole No. 466).

2. Guilford, J. P., The Structure of Intellect. *Psychol. Bull.,* 1956, **53,** 267-293.

3. Guilford, J. P., *Personality.* New York: McGraw-Hill, 1959.

Anne Roe

A Psychologist Examines 64
Eminent Scientists

What elements enter into the making of a scientist? Are there special qualities of personality, mind, intelligence, background or upbringing that mark a person for this calling? Besides the natural interest in these questions, they have a practical importance, because the recruitment of qualified young people into science is a growing problem in our society. Where and how shall we find them?

During the past five years I have been making a study of the attributes of a group of scientists and the reasons why they chose this field of work. The most eminent scientists in the U.S. were selected as subjects, since they are most likely to exemplify the special qualities, if any, that are associated with success in research science. They were selected by panels of experts in each field of science. The study finally settled on a group of 64 eminent men who agreed to participate—20 biologists, 22 physicists and 22 social scientists (psychologists and anthropologists). A high percentage of them are members of the National Academy of Sciences or the American Philosophical Society or both, and among them they have received a staggering number of honorary degrees, prizes and other awards.

Each of the 64 individuals was then examined exhaustively by long personal interviews and tests: his life history, family background, professional and recreational interests, intelligence, achievements, personality, ways of thinking—any information that might have a bearing on the subject's choice of his vocation and his success in it. Each was given an intelligence test and was examined by two of the modern techniques for the study of personality: the Rorschach and the Thematic Apperception Test (TAT). The Rorschach, popularly known as the inkblot test, gives information about such things as the way the subject deals with problems, his manner of approach to them, the extent and efficiency of his use of rational controls, his inner preoccupations, his responsiveness to outside stimuli. The TAT gives information about attitudes toward family and society and self, about expectations and needs and desires, and something about the development of these.

From *Scientific American*, Vol. 187, No. 5 (November, 1952), pp. 21-25. Reprinted with permission. Copyright   1951, 1952 by Scientific American Inc. All rights reserved.

My study was financed during the first four years by grants from the National Institute of Mental Health and is being continued this year under a Guggenheim Fellowship. It has developed a great deal of material, much of which has been published in technical detail in special journals. In this brief article it is possible only to recapitulate the high points.

There is no such thing, of course, as a "typical" scientist. Eminent scientists differ greatly as individuals, and there are well-marked group differences between the biologists and the physicists, and between the natural scientists and the social scientists. Certain common patterns do appear, however, in the group as a whole, and the most convenient way to summarize these generalizations is to try to draw a picture of what might be called the "average" eminent scientist.

He was the first-born child of a middle-class family, the son of a professional man. He is likely to have been a sickly child or have lost a parent at an early age. He has a very high I.Q. and in boyhood began to do a great deal of reading. He tended to feel lonely and "different" and to be shy and aloof from his classmates. He had only a moderate interest in girls and did not begin dating them until college. He married late (at 27), has two children and finds security in family life; his marriage is more stable than the average. Not until his junior or senior year in college did he decide on his vocation as a scientist. What decided him (almost invariably) was a college project in which he had occasion to do some independent research—to find out things for himself. Once he discovered the pleasures of this kind of work, he never turned back. He is completely satisfied with his chosen vocation. (Only one of the 64 eminent scientists—a Nobel prize winner—says he would have preferred to do sometling else: he wanted to be a farmer, but could not make a living at it.) He works hard and devotedly in his laboratory, often seven days a week. He says his work is his life, and he has few recreations, those being restricted to fishing, sailing, walking or some other individualistic activity. The movies bore him. He avoids social affairs and political activity, and religion plays no part in his life or thinking. Better than any other interest or activity, scientific research seems to meet the inner need of his nature.

This generalized picture represents only majority traits; there are, of course, many exceptions to it, not only in individual cases but by groups; the social scientists, for instance, tend to be by no means shy but highly

Field	Age at Time of Study		Average Age at Time of Receiving College Degrees	
	Average	Range	B.A.	Ph.D., Sc.D., M.D.
Biologists	51.2	38-58	21.8	26.0
Physical scientists	44.7	31-56	20.9	24.6
Social scientists	47.7	35-60	21.8	26.8

Average age of the subjects at the time of the study and at the time they received their degrees is given in this table. The upper age limit was set at 60; the lower limit was determined by the eminence of the subjects.

gregarious and social. Let us now consider the differences between groups. I have seperated the physicists into the theorists (12) and the experimentalists (10), because these two groups differ sharply. The biologists (physiologists, botanists, geneticists, biochemists and so on) are sufficiently alike to be grouped together, and so are the social scientists.

No standardized intelligence test was sufficiently difficult for these eminent scientists; hence a special test was constructed by the Educational Testing Service. To provide ratings on particular intellectual factors, the test was divided into three parts: verbal (79 items), spatial (24 items) and mathematical (39). (The mathematical test used was not difficult enough for the physicists, and several of them did not take it.)

While the group as a whole is characterized by very high average intelligence, as would be expected, the range is wide *(see table on page 123)*. Among the biologists, the geneticists and biochemists do relatively better on the nonverbal tests than on the verbal, and the other biologists tend to do relatively better on the verbal. Among the physicists there is some tendency for theorists to do relatively better on the verbal and for the experimentalists to do relatively better on the spatial test. Among the social scientists the experimental psychologists do relatively better on the spatial or mathematical than on the verbal test, and the reverse is true of the other psychologists and anthropologists.

On the TAT the social scientists tended to give much longer stories than the other groups did—verbal fluency is characteristic of them. The biologists were inclined to be much more factual, less interested in feelings and, in general, unwilling to commit themselves. This was true to a lesser extent of the physical scientists. The biologists and physical scientists manifested a quite remarkable independence of parental relations and were without guilt feelings about it, while the social scientists showed many

Field	Visual	Verbal	Imageless	Totals
Biologists	10	4	3	17
Physicists	10	4	4	18
Psychologists and anthropologists	2	11	6	19
Totals	22	19	13	54

Imagery of the scientists was correlated with specialty. The natural scientists were strong in visual imagery; the social scientists in verbal.

Profession of Father	Visual	Verbal	Imageless	Totals
Verbal	5	10	3	18
Non-verbal	8	2	2	12
Totals	13	12	5	30

Imagery of the father's Profession was strongly influential. The numbers on the right side of this table refer to the imagery of the sons.

dependent attitudes, much rebelliousness and considerable helplessness, along with intense concern over interpersonal relations generally. The biologists were the least aggressive (but rather stubborn) and the social scientists the most aggressive. The most striking thing about the TAT results for the total group, however, is the rarity of any indication of the drive for achievement that all of these subjects have actually shown in their lives.

On the Rorschach the social scientists show themselves to be enormously productive and intensely concerned with human beings; the biologists are deeply concerned with form, and rely strongly upon a non-emotional approach to problems; the physicists show a good deal of free anxiety and concern with space and inanimate motion. Again the social scientists, particularly the anthropologists, are the most freely aggressive.

Early in the course of the work it became apparent that there were some differences in habits of thinking, and a special inquiry was instituted along these lines. The data are unsatisfactory from many standpoints—there are no objective tests for such material, and I had to ask many leading questions in order to convey any idea of what I was after. Nevertheless rather definite and meaningful patterns did appear. The biologists and the experimental physicists tend strongly to dependence upon visual imagery in their thinking—images of concrete objects or elaborate diagrams or the like. The theoretical physicists and social scientists tend to verbalization in their thinking—a kind of talking to themselves. All groups report a considerable amount of imageless thinking, particularly at crucial points. Men whose fathers followed talkative occupations (law, ministry, teaching) are more likely to think in words.

The life histories of these 64 men show some general similarities, and there are patterns characterizing some of the subgroups. Geographical factors seem not to be particularly significant, except that only a few came from the South. The economic level was varied, ranging from very poor to well-to-do; among the anthropologists and the theoretical physicists a somewhat higher percentage came from well-to-do homes.

In several respects the scientists' backgrounds differ very much from the population at large. There are no Catholics among this group of eminent scientists; five come from Jewish homes and the rest had Protestant backgrounds. Only three of the 64 now have a serious interest in any church; only a few even maintain church memberships.

Another striking fact is that 53 percent of the scientists were the sons of professional men; not one was the son of an unskilled laborer and only two were sons of skilled workmen. Why do more than half of our leading scientists come from the families of professional men? It seems to me most probable, from more knowledge of the family situations of these men than I can summarize here, that the operative factor is the value placed by these families and their associates on learning—learning for its own sake. Most of the scientists developed intellectual interests at an early age.

Another remarkable finding is how many of them were their parents' first children. This proportion is higher than chance expectancy in all of the

106

	Number	Verbal Test		Spatial Test		Mathematical Test	
		Average	Range	Average	Range	Average	Range
Biologists	19	56.6	28-73	9.4	3-20	6.8	6-27
Experimental physicists	7	46.6	8-71	11.7	3-22		
Theoretical physicists	11	64.2	52-75	13.8	5-19		
Psychologists	14	57.7	23-73	11.3	5-19	15.6	8-27
Anthropologists	8	61.1	43-72	8.2	3-15	9.2	4-13
Total	59	57.7	8-75	10.9	3-22	15.9	4-27
Approximate IQ equivalents		163	121-177	140	123-164	160	128-194

Intelligence test results revealed minor variations among the specialties of the scientists. The theoretical physicists did better in the verbal test; the experimental physicists rated lowest. Both theoretical and experimental physicists did not take the mathematical test because it was not sufficiently difficult. Two anthropologists who took the verbal test did not take the other tests on the ground that they could not do them.

Professions	Biologists 9	Experimental physicists 5	Theoretical physicists 10	Psychologists 7	Anthropologists 3	Totals 34
Research Science	0	1	0	0	0	1
Physician	0	2	1	2	0	5
Lawyer	0	0	1	1	3	5
Engineer	0	0	3	2	0	5
Clergyman	2	0	1	0	0	3
Editor	2	0	0	0	0	2
College teacher	4	0	3	2	0	9
School teacher	0	2	0	0	0	2
School superintendent	1	0	0	0	0	1
Pharmacist	0	0	1	0	0	1
Business	8	1	2	4	5	20
Own business	4	0	2	2	4	12
Clerk, agent, salesman	4	1	0	2	1	8
Farmer	2	4	0	2	0	8
Skilled Labor	1	0	0	1	0	2
Totals	20	10	12	14	8	64
Per cent professional	45	50	84	50	38	53

Occupations of the fathers of the 64 eminent scientists showed a strong bias in favor of the professions. This was especially true of the 12 theoretical physicists, 10 of whose fathers had been professional. The anthropologists were an exception: five out of eight came from business backgrounds. Four of the 10 experimental physicists were the sons of farmers. None of the scientists were the sons of unskilled laborers.

subgroups. Thirty-nine were first born; of the rest five were eldest sons and two who were second born were effectively the eldest because of the early death of the first child. For most of the others there is a considerable difference in age between the subject and the next older brother (averaging five years). It seems probable that all this may point to the most important single factor in the making of a scientist—the need and ability to develop personal independence to a high degree. The independence factor is emphasized by many other findings: the subject's preference for teachers who let them alone, their attitudes toward religion, their attitudes toward personal relations, their satisfaction in a career in which, for the most part, they follow their own interests without direction or interference. It is possible that oldest sons in our culture have a greater amount of independence or more indulgence in the pursuit of their own interests than other children have. On the other hand, there is some psychological evidence that first-born tend to be more dependent, on the average, than other children, and a good case could be made out for a hypothesis that reaction to this overdependence produced the scientists' strong drive to independence.

The early extracurricular interests of these men were varied, but here, too, there are some general patterns. More of the physicists than of the other groups showed early interests directly related to their later occupations, but this seems quite clearly to be due to the common small-boy preoccupation in this country with physical gadgets—radio, Meccano sets and so on. The theoretical physicists were omnivorous readers, the experimentalists much less so. Among the social scientists many went through a stage of considering or even working toward a literary career. Half of the biologists showed some early interest in natural history, but for only five was it of an intense and serious sort, involving keeping field records of birds and flowers, and so on. Many of the biologists did not know during childhood of the possibility of a career in biology. This was even more true of the psychologists and anthropologists, since there are almost no boyhood activities related to professional social science.

It is of considerable interest that over half of these men did not decide upon their vocations until they were juniors or seniors in college. More important, perhaps, than when they decided, is why they decided. It certainly was not just a matter of always following an early bent. From fiddling with gadgets to becoming a physicist may be no great leap, but the attractions of theoretical physics are not so obvious or well known, nor are those of the social sciences or advanced biology. In the stories of the social scientists and of the biologists it becomes clear that the most important factor in the final decision to become a scientist is the discovery of the joys of research. In physics the discovery may come so gradually as not to be noticed as such, but in the other sciences it often came as a revelation of unique moment, and many of these men know just when and how they found it out. A couple of quotations will illustrate this:

"I had no course in biology until my senior year in college. It was a small college and the teacher was about the first on the faculty with a Ph.D. It was about my first contact with the idea that not everything was known, my first contact with research. In that course I think my final decision was really taken. It was mainly that I wanted to do something in the way of research though I didn't know just what, but working out something new."

"One of the professors took a group of us and thought if we wanted to learn about things, the way to do it was to do research. My senior year I carried through some research. That really sent me, that was the thing that trapped me. After that there was no getting out."

That research experience is so often decisive is a fact of very considerable importance for educational practice. The discovery of the possibility of finding things out for oneself usually came through experience in school with a teacher who put the students pretty much on their own.

There are other things in the general process of growing up that may have influenced the choice of career in subtle ways. One fourth of the biologists lost a parent by death or divorce at an early age. This may have tended to shove them to greater independence. Among the theoretical physicists there was a high incidence of serious illness or physical handicaps during childhood, which certainly contributed to the feelings of isolation characteristic of them. Among the social scientists there is an unusually intense concern with personal relationships, which often goes back to family conflicts during clildhood. A relatively large proportion of them seem to have come from homes in which the mother was dominant and the father inadequate in some way. The divorce rate among tle social scientists in this study was remarkably high—41 per cent.

Whereas the characteristic pattern among the biologists and physicists is that of the shy, lonely, over-intellectualized boy, among the social scientists the characteristic picture is very different. They got into social activity and intensive and extensive dating at an early age. They were often presidents of their classes, editors of yearbooks and literary magazines, frequently big shots in college. This contrast between the natural and social scientists was still evident after they grew up. It is true only in general, of course; even among the theoretical physicists there are some ardent party-goers.

The one thing that all of these 64 scientists have in common is their driving absorption in their work. They have worked long hours for many years, frequently with no vacations to speak of, because they would rather be doing their work than anything else.

Donald W. MacKinnon

The Nature and Nurture of Creative Talent

Let me say first how deeply appreciative I am of the honor of having been chosen the Walter Van Dyke Bingham Lecturer for 1962. It has for me especial meaning to be provided this opportunity to honor the memory of a man I respected so much and whose work was such a pioneering contribution to that field of psychology to which I have given most of my energies as a psychologist. I am grateful, too, for this opportunity to express to Mrs. Bingham the gratitude of all psychologists for her generosity in establishing this series of annual lectures on the discovery and development of exceptional abilities and capacities. Our literature has been greatly enriched by the lectures which she has made possible.

I should like also to congratulate Yale University for having been chosen this year as the institution to be honored for its contributions to the study of talent, and to thank all those who have made such pleasant arrangements for this occasion.

There is a story, first told I believe by Mark Twain which, had Dr. Bingham known it, would have been, I am sure, one of his favorites. It is about a man who sought the greatest general who had ever lived. Upon inquiring as to where this individual might be found, he was told that the person he sought had died and gone to Heaven. At the Pearly Gates he informed St. Peter of the purpose of his quest, whereupon St. Peter pointed to a soul nearby. "But that," protested the inquirer, "isn't the greatest of all generals. I knew that person when he lived on earth, and he was only a cobbler." "I know that," replied St. Peter, "but if he had been a general he would have been the greatest of them all."

Dr. Bingham spent his life worrying about cobblers who might have been generals and indeed about all those who fail to become what they are

The Walter Van Dyke Bingham Lecture given at Yale University, New Haven, Connecticut, April 11, 1962.

MacKinnon, Donald W. "The Nature and Nurture of Creative Talent". *American Psychologist*, 17:484-495, 1962.

111

capable of becoming because neither they nor others recognize their potentialities and nourish their realization. Dr. Bingham was one of the first to insist that it is not enough to recognize creative talent after it has come to expression. He reminded us that it is our task as psychologists and as educators either through our insights or through the use of validated predictors to discover talent when it is still potential and to provide that kind of social climate and intellectual environment which will facilitate its development and expression.

Whatever light I shall be able to shed on the nature and nurture of creative talent comes in the main from findings of researches carried on during the last six years in the Institute of Personality Assessment and Research on the Berkeley campus of the University of California, and supported in large part by the Carnegie Corporation of New York.

In undertaking such a study one of our first tasks was to decide what we would consider creativity to be. This was necessary, first, because creativity has been so variously described and defined, and second, because only when we had come to agreement as to how we would conceive creativity would we be in a position to know what kinds of persons we would want to study.

We came easily to agreement that true creativeness fulfills at least three conditions. It involves a response or an idea that is novel or at the very least statistically infrequent. But novelty or originality of thought or action, while a necessary aspect of creativity, is not sufficient. If a response is to lay claim to being a part of the creative process, it must to some extent be adaptive to, or of, reality. It must serve to solve a problem, fit a situation, or accomplish some recognizable goal. And, thirdly, true creativeness involves a sustaining of the original insight, an evaluation and elaboration of it, a developing of it to the full.

Creativity, from this point of view, is a process extended in time and characterized by originality, adaptiveness, and realization. It may be brief, as in a musical improvisation, or it may involve a considerable span of years as was required for Darwin's creation of the theory of evolution.

The acceptance of such a conception of creativity had two important consequences for our researches. It meant that we would not seek to study creativity while it was still potential but only after it had been realized and had found expression in clearly identifiable creative products—buildings designed by architects, mathematical proofs developed by mathematicians, and the published writings of poets and novelists. Our conception of creativity forced us further to reject as indicators or criteria of creativeness the performance of individuals on so-called tests of creativity. While tests of this sort, that require that the subject think, for example, of unusual uses for common objects and the consequences of unusual events, may indeed measure the infrequency or originality of a subject's ideas in response to specific test items, they fail to reveal the extent to which the subject faced with real life problems is likely to come up with solutions that are novel and adaptive and which he will be motivated to apply in all of their ramifications.

Having thus determined that we would limit our researches to the study of persons who had already demonstrated a high level of creative work, we were still confronted with the problem of deciding from which fields of creative endeavor we would seek to recruit our subjects.

The fields which we finally sampled were those of creative writing, architecture, mathematics, industrial research, physical science, and engineering.

If one considers these activities in relation to the distinction often made between artistic and scientific creativity, it may be noted that we have sampled both of these domains as well as overlapping domains of creative striving which require that the practitioner be at one and the same time both artist and scientist.

Artistic creativity, represented in our studies by the work of poets, novelists, and essayists, results in products that are clearly expressions of the creator's inner states, his needs, perceptions, motivations, and the like. In this type of creativity, the creator externalizes something of himself into the public field.

In scientific creativity, the creative product is unrelated to the creator as a person, who in his creative work acts largely as a mediator between externally defined needs and goals. In this kind of creativeness, the creator, represented in our studies by industrial researchers, physical scientists, and engineers, simply operates on some aspect of his environment in such a manner as to produce a novel and appropriate product, but he adds little of himself or of his style as a person to the resultant.

Domains of creative striving in which the practitioner must be both artist and scientist were represented in our researches by mathematicians and architects. Mathematicians contribute to science, yet in a very real sense their important creative efforts are as much as anything else personal cosmologies in which they express themselves as does the artist in his creations. So, too, in architecture, creative products are both an expression of the architect and thus a very personal product, and at the same time an impersonal meeting of the demands of an external problem.

If in reporting the findings of our researches I draw most heavily upon data obtained from our study of architects (MacKinnon, 1962), it is for two reasons. First, it is the study for which, in collaboration with Wallace B. Hall, I have assumed primary responsibility. Second, it is in architects, of all our samples, that we can expect to find what is most generally characteristic of creative persons. Architecture, as a field of creative endeavor, requires that the successful practitioner be both artist and scientist—artist in that his designs must fulfill the demands of "Delight," and scientist in that they must meet the demands of "Firmnesse" and "Commodity," to use the words of Sir Henry Wotton (1624). But surely, one can hardly think that the requirements of effective architecture are limited to these three demands. The successful and effective architect must, with the skill of a juggler, combine, reconcile, and exercise the diverse skills of businessman, lawyer, artist, engineer, and advertising man, as well as those of author and journalist, psychiatrist, educator, and psychologist. In what other profession can one expect better to observe the multifarious expressions of creativity?

It should be clear that any attempt to discover the distinguishing traits of creative persons can succeed only in so far as some group of qualified experts can agree upon who are the more and who are the less creative workers in a given field of endeavor. In our study of architects we began by asking a panel of experts—five professors of architecture, each working independently—to nominate the 40 most creative architects in the United States. All told they supplied us with 86 names instead of the 40 they would have mentioned had there been perfect agreement among them. While 13 of the 86 architects were nominated by all five panel members, and 9 nominated by four, 11 by three, and 13 by two, 40 were individual nominations each proposed by a single panel member.

The agreement among experts is not perfect, yet far greater than one might have expected. Later we asked 11 editors of the major American architectural journals, *Architectual Forum, Architectural Record,* the *Journal of the American Institute of Architects,* and *Progressive Architecture,* to rate the creativity of the 64 of the nominated architects whom we invited to participate in the study. Still later we asked the 40 nominated creative architects who actually accepted our invitation to be studied to rate the creativity of the invited 64 architects, themselves included. Since the editors' ratings of the creativity of the architects correlated +.88 with the architects' own ratings, it is clear that under certain conditions and for certain groups it is possible to obtain remarkable agreement about the relative creativeness of individual members of a profession and thus meet the first requirement for an effective study of creative persons.

A second requirement for the successful establishment of the traits of creative individuals is their willingness to make themselves available for study. Our hope was to win the cooperation of each person whom we invited to participate in the research, but as I have already indicated in the case of the architects, to obtain 40 acceptances, 64 invitations had to be sent out.

The invitation to this group, as to all the creative groups which we have studied, was to come to Berkeley for a weekend of intensive study in the Institute of Personality Assessment and Research. There, in groups of ten, they have been studied by the variety of means which constitute the assessment method—by problem solving experiments; by tests designed to discover what a person does not know or is unable or unwilling to reveal about himself; by tests and questionnaires that permit a person to manifest various aspects of his personality and to express his attitudes, interests, and values; by searching interviews that cover the life history and reveal the present structure of the person; and by specially contrived social situations of a stressful character which call for the subject's best behavior in a socially defined role.

The response of creative persons to the invitation to reveal themselves under such trying circumstances has varied considerably. At the one extreme there have been those who replied in anger at what they perceived to be the audacity of psychologists in presuming to study so ineffable and mysterious a thing as the creative process and so sensitive a being as a creative person. At the other extreme were those who replied courteously and warmheartedly, welcoming the invitation to be studied, and manifesting even an eagerness to contribute to a better understanding of the creative person and the creative process.

Here we were face to face with a problem that plagues us in all our researches: Are those who are willing to be assessed different in important ways from those who refuse? With respect to psychological traits and characteristics we can never know. But with respect to differences in creativeness, if any, between the 40 who accepted and the 24 who declined our invitation, we know that the two groups are indistinguishable. When the nominating panel's ratings of creativity were converted to standard scores and the means for the 24 versus the 40 were compared, they were found to be identical. When the editors' ratings were similarly converted to standard scores, the mean for the nonassessed group was slightly higher (51.9) than for the assessed sample (48.7), but the difference is not statistically significant.

Certainly we cannot claim to have assessed the 40 most creative architects in the country, or the most creative of any of the groups we have studied; but it is clear that we have studied a highly creative group of architects indistinguishable in their creativity from the group of 24 who declined to be studied, and so with the other groups too.

A third requirement for the successful determination of the traits of highly creative persons in any field of endeavor is that the profession be widely sampled beyond those nominated as most creative, for the distinguishing characteristics of the restricted sample might well have nothing to do with their creativeness. Instead they might be traits characterizing all members of the profession whether creative or not, distinguishing the professional group as a whole but in no sense limited or peculiar to its highly creative members. In the case of the architects, to use them once again as an example, two additional samples were recruited for study, both of which matched the highly creative sample (whom I shall now call Architects I) with respect to age and geographic location of practice. The first supplementary sample (Architects II) had had at least two years of work experience and association with one of the originally nominated creative architects. The second additional sample (Architects III) was composed of architects who had never worked with any of the nominated creatives.

By selecting three samples in this manner, we hoped to tap a range of talent sufficiently wide to be fairly representative of the profession as a whole; and we appear to have succeeded. The mean rating of creativity for each of the three groups—the ratings having been made on a nine-point scale by six groups of architects and experts on architecture—was for Architects I, 5.46; for Architects II, 4.25; and for Architects III, 3.54, the differences in mean ratings between each group being statistically highly significant.

So much for method and research design. I turn now to a discussion of the nature of creative talent as it has been revealed to us in our researches.

Persons who are highly creative are inclined to have a good opinion of themselves, as evidenced by the large number of favorable adjectives which they use in self-description and by the relatively high scores they earn on a scale which measures basic acceptance of the self. Indeed, there is here a paradox, for in addition to their favorable self-perceptions the very basic self-acceptance of the more creative persons often permits them to speak more frankly and thus more critically and in unusual ways about themselves. It is clear, too, that the self-images of the more creative differ from the self-images of the less creative. For example, Architects I, in contrast to Architects II and III, more often describe themselves as inventive, determined, independent, individualistic, enthusiastic, and industrious. In striking contrast Architects II and III more often than Architects I describe themselves as responsible, sincere, reliable, dependable, clear thinking, tolerant, and understanding. In short, where creative architects more often stress their inventiveness, independence, and individuality, their enthusiasm, determination, and industry, less creative members of the profession are impressed by their virtue and good character and by their rationality and sympathetic concern for others.

The discrepancies between their descriptions of themselves as they are and as they would ideally be are remarkably alike for all architects regardless of their level of creativeness. All three groups reveal themselves as desiring more personal attractiveness, self-confidence, maturity, and intellectual competence, a higher level of energy, and better social relations. As for differences, however, Architects I would ideally be more sensitive, while both Architects II and III wish for opposites if not incompatibles; they would ideally be more original but at the same time more self-controlled and disciplined.

As for the relation between intelligence and creativity, save for the mathematicians where there is a low positive correlation between intelligence and the level of creativeness, we have found within our creative samples essentially zero relationship between the two variables, and this is not due to a narrow restriction in range of intelligence. Among creative architects who have a mean score of 113 on the Terman Concept Mastery Test (1956), individual scores range widely from 39 to 179, yet scores on this measure of intelligence correlate $-.08$ with rated creativity. Over the whole range of intelligence and creativity there is, of course, a positive relationship between the two variables. No feeble-minded subjects have shown up in any of our creative groups. It is clear, however, that above a certain required minimum level of intelligence which varies from field to field and in some instances may be surprisingly low, being more intelligent does not guarantee a corresponding increase in creativeness. It just is not true that the more intelligent person is necessarily the more creative one.

In view of the often asserted close association of genius with insanity it is also of some interest to inquire into the psychological health of our creative subjects. To this end we can look at their profiles on the Minnesota Multiphasic Personality Inventory (MMPI) (Hathaway & McKinley, 1945), a test originally developed to measure tendencies toward the major psychiatric disturbances that man is heir to: depression, hysteria, paranoia, schizophrenia, and the like. On the eight scales which measure the strength of these dispositions in the person, our creative subjects earn scores which, on the average, are some 5 to 10 points above the general population's average score of 50. It must be noted, however, that elevated scores of this degree on these scales do not have the same meaning for the personality functioning of persons who, like our subjects, are getting along well in their personal lives and professional careers, that they have for hospitalized patients. The manner in which creative subjects describe themselves on this test as well as in the life history psychiatric interview is less suggestive of psychopathology than it is of good intellect, complexity and richness of personality, general lack of defensiveness, and candor in self-description—in other words, an openness to experience and especially to experience of one's inner life. It must also be noted, however, that in the self-reports and in the MMPI profiles of many of our creative subjects, one can find rather clear evidence of psychopathology, but also evidence of adequate control mechanisms, as the success with which they live their productive and creative lives testifies.

However, the most striking aspect of the MMPI profiles of all our male creative groups is an extremely high peak on the *Mf* (femininity) scale. This tendency for creative males to score relatively high on femininity is also demonstrated on the Fe (femininity) scale of the California Psychological Inventory (CPI) (Gough, 1957) and on the masculinity-femininity scale of the Strong Vocational Interest Blank (Strong, 1959). Scores on the latter scale (where high score indicates more masculinity) correlate −.49 with rated creativity.

The evidence is clear: The more creative a person is the more he reveals an openness to his own feelings and emotions, a sensitive intellect and understanding self-awareness, and wide-ranging interests including many which in the American culture are thought of as feminine. In the realm of sexual identification and interests, our creative subjects appear to give more expression to the feminine side of their nature than do less creative persons. In the language of the Swiss psychologist, Carl G. Jung (1956), creative persons are not so completely identified with their masculine *persona* roles as to blind themselves to or to deny expression to the more feminine traits of the *anima*. For some, to be sure, the balance between masculine and feminine traits, interests, and identification, is a precarious one, and for several of our subjects it would appear that their presently achieved reconciliation of these opposites of their nature has been barely effected and only after considerable psychic stress and turmoil.

The perceptiveness of the creative and his openness to richness and complexity of experience is strikingly revealed on the Barron-Welsh Art Scale of the Welsh Figure Preference Test (Welsh, 1959), which presents to the subject a set of 62 abstract line drawings which range from simple and symmetrical figures to complex and asymmetrical ones. In the original study (Barron & Welsh, 1952) which standardized this scale, some 80 painters from New York, San Francisco, New Orleans, Chicago, and Minneapolis showed a marked preference for the complex and asymmetrical, or, as they often referred to them, the vital and dynamic figures. A contrasting sample

117

of nonartists revealed a marked preference for the simple and symmetrical drawings.

All creative groups we have studied have shown a clear preference for the complex and asymmetrical, and in general the more creative a person is the stronger is this preference. Similarly, in our several samples, scores on an Institute scale which measures the preference for perceptual complexity are significantly correlated with creativity. In the sample of architects the correlation is +.48.

Presented with a large selection of one-inch squares of varicolored posterboard and asked to construct within a 30-minute period a pleasing, completely filled-in 8" × 10" mosaic (Hall, 1958), some subjects select the fewest colors possible (one used only one color, all white) while others seek to make order out of the largest possible number, using all of the 22 available colors. And, again citing results from the architects, there is a significant though low positive correlation of +.38 between the number of colors a subject chooses and his creativity as rated by the experts.

If one considers for a moment the meaning of these preferences on the art scale, on the mosaic test, and on the scale that measures preference for perceptual complexity, it is clear that creative persons are especially disposed to admit complexity and even disorder into their perceptions without being made anxious by the resulting chaos. It is not so much that they like disorder per se, but that they prefer the richness of the disordered to the stark barrenness of the simple. They appear to be challenged by disordered multiplicity which arouses in them a strong need which in them is serviced by a superior capacity to achieve the most difficult and far-reaching ordering of the richness they are willing to experience.

The creative person's openness to experience is further revealed on the Myers-Briggs Type Indicator (Myers, 1958), a test based largely upon Carl G. Jung's (1923) theory of psychological functions and types.

Employing the language of the test, though in doing so I oversimplify both it and the theory upon which it is based, one might say that whenever a person uses his mind for any purpose, he performs either an act of perception (he becomes aware of something) or an act of judgment (he comes to a conclusion about something). And most persons tend to show a rather consistent preference for and greater pleasure in one or the other of these, preferring either to perceive or to judge, though every one both perceives and judges.

An habitual preference for the judging attitude may lead to some prejudging and at the very least to the living of a life that is orderly, controlled, and carefully planned. A preference for the perceptive attitude results in a life that is more open to experience both from within and from without, and characterized by flexibility and spontaneity. A judging type places more emphasis upon the control and regulation of experience, while a perceptive type is inclined to be more open and receptive to all experience.

The majority of our creative writers, mathematicians, and architects are perceptive types. Only among research scientists do we find the majority to be judging types, and even in this group it is interesting to note that there is a positive correlation (+.25) between a scientist's preference for perception and his rated creativity as a scientific researcher. For architects, preference for perception correlates +.41 with rated creativity.

The second preference measured by the Type Indicator is for one of two types of perception: sense perception or sensation, which is a direct becoming aware of things by way of the senses versus intuitive perception or intuition, which is an indirect perception of the deeper meanings and possibilities inherent in things and situations. Again, everyone senses and intuits, but preliminary norms for the test suggest that in the United States three out of four persons show a preference for sense perception, concentrating upon immediate sensory experience and centering their attention upon existing facts. The one out of every four who shows a preference for intuitive perception, on the other hand, looks expectantly for a bridge or link between that which is given and present and that which is not yet thought of, focusing habitually upon possibilities.

One would expect creative persons not to be bound to the stimulus and the object but to be ever alert to the as-yet-not-realized. And that is precisely the way they show themselves to be on the Type Indicator. In contrast to an estimated 25% of the general population who are intuitive, 90% of the creative writers, 92% of the mathematicians, 93% of the research scientists, and 100% of the architects are intuitive as measured by this test.

In judging or evaluating experience, according to the underlying Jungian theory of the test, one makes use of thought or of feeling; thinking being a logical process aimed at an impersonal fact-weighing analysis, while feeling is a process of appreciation and evaluation of things that gives them a personal and subjective value. A preference for thinking or for feeling appears to be less related to one's creativity as such than to the type of materials or concepts with which one deals. Of our creative groups, writers prefer feeling, mathematicians, research scientists, and engineers prefer thinking, while architects split fifty-fifty in their preference for one or the other of the two functions.

The final preference in Jungian typology and on the test is the well-known one between introversion and extraversion. Approximately two-thirds of all our creative groups score as introverts, though there is not evidence that introverts as such are more creative than extraverts.

Turning to preferences among interests and values, one would expect the highly creative to be rather different from less creative people, and there is clear evidence that they are.

On the Strong Vocational Interest Blank, which measures the similarity of a person's expressed interests with the known interests of individuals successful in a number of occupations and professions, all of our creative subjects have shown, with only slight variation from group to group, interests similar to those of the psychologist, author-journalist, lawyer, architect, artist, and musician, and interests unlike those of the purchasing agent, office man, banker, farmer, carpenter, veterinarian, and interestingly enough, too, policeman and mortician. Leaving aside any consideration of the specific interests thus revealed we may focus our attention on the inferences that may be drawn from this pattern of scores which suggest that creative persons are relatively uninterested in small details, or in facts for their own sake, and more concerned with their meanings and implications, possessed of considerable cognitive flexibility, verbally skillful, interested in communicating with others and accurate in so doing, intellectually curious, and relatively disinterested in policing either their own impulses and images or those of others.

On the Allport-Vernon-Lindzey Study of Values (1951), a test designed to measure in the individual the relative strength of the six values of men as these values have been conceptualized and described by the German psychologist and educator, Eduard Spranger (1928), namely, the theoretical, economic, esthetic, social, political, and religious values, all of our creative groups have as their highest values the theoretical and the esthetic.

For creative research scientists the theoretical value is the highest, closely followed by the esthetic. For creative architects the highest value is the esthetic, with the theoretical value almost as high. For creative mathematicians, the two values are both high and approximately equally strong.

If, as the authors of the test believe, there is some incompatibility and conflict between the theoretical value with its cognitive and rational concern with truth and the esthetic value with its emotional concern with form and beauty, it would appear that the creative person has the capacity to tolerate the tension that strong opposing values create in him, and in his creative striving he effects some reconciliation of them. For the truly creative person it is not sufficient that problems be solved, there is the further demand that the solutions be elegant. He seeks both truth and beauty.

A summary description of the creative person—especially of the creative architect—as he reveals himself in his profile on the California Psychological Inventory (Gough, 1957) reads as follows:

He is dominant (Do scale); possessed of those qualities and attributes which underlie and lead to the achievement of social status (Cs); poised, spontaneous, and self-confident in personal and social interaction (Sp); though not of an especially sociable or participative temperament (low Sy); intelligent, outspoken, sharp-witted, demanding, aggressive, and self-centered; persuasive and verbally fluent, self-confident and self-assured (Sa); and relatively uninhibited in expressing his worries and complaints (low Wb).

He is relatively free from conventional restraints and inhibitions (low So and Sc), not preoccupied with the impression which he makes on others and thus perhaps capable of great independence and autonomy (low Gi), and relatively ready to recognize and admit self-views that are unusual and unconventional (low Cm).

He is strongly motivated to achieve in situations in which independence in thought and action are called for (Ai). But, unlike his less creative colleagues, he is less inclined to strive for achievement in settings where conforming behavior is expected or required (Ac). In efficiency and steadiness of intellectual effort (Ie), however, he does not differ from his fellow workers.

Finally, he is definitely more psychologically minded (Py), more flexible (Fx), and possessed of more femininity of interests (Fe) than architects in general.

There is one last finding that I wish to present, one that was foreshadowed by a discovery of Dr. Bingham in one of his attempts to study creativity. The subject of his study was Amy Lowell, a close friend of his and Mrs. Bingham's, with whom he discussed at length the birth and growth of her poems, seeking insight into the creative processes of her mind. He also administered to her a word association test and "found that she gave a higher proportion of unique responses than those of any one outside a mental institution" (Bingham, Milicent Todd, 1953, p. 11). We too, administered a word association test to our subjects and found the unusualness of mental associations one of the best predictors of creativity, and especially so when associations given by no more than 1% to 10% of the population, using the Minnesota norms (Russell & Jenkins, 1954), are weighted more heavily than those given by less than 1% of the population. Among architects, for example, this weighted score is for Architects I, 204; Architects II, 128; and Architects III, 114; while for the total sample this measure of unusualness of mental associations correlates +.50 with rated creativity.

And Dr. Bingham, like us, found that there are certain hazards in attempting to study a creative poet. His searchings were rewarded by a poem Amy Lowell later wrote which was first entitled "To the Impudent Psychologist" and published posthumously with the title "To a Gentleman who wanted to see the first drafts of my poems in the interest of psychological research into the workings of the creative mind." We, I must confess, were treated somewhat less kindly by one of our poets who, after assessment, published an article entitled "My Head Gets Tooken Apart" (Rexroth, 1959).

Having described the overall design of our studies, and having presented a selection of our findings which reveal at least some aspects of the nature of creative talent, I turn now, but with considerably less confidence, to the question as to how we can early identify and best encourage the development of creative potential. Our findings concerning the characteristics of highly creative persons are by now reasonably well established, but their implication for the nurture of creative talent are far from clear.

It is one thing to discover the distinguishing characteristics of mature, creative, productive individuals. It is quite another matter to conclude that the traits of creative persons observed several years after school and college characterized these same individuals when they were students. Nor can we be certain that finding these same traits in youngsters today will identify those with creative potential. Only empirical, longitudinal research, which we do not yet have, can settle such issues. Considering, however, the nature of the traits which discriminate creative adults from their non-creative peers, I would venture to guess that most students with creative potential have personality structures congruent with, though possibly less sharply delineated than, those of mature creatives.

Our problem is further complicated by the fact that though our creative subjects have told us about their experiences at home, in school, and in college, and about the forces and persons and situations which, as they see it, nurtured their creativeness, these are, after all, self-reports subject to the misperceptions and self-deceptions of all self-reports. Even if we were to assume that their testimony is essentially accurate we would still have no assurance that the conditions in the home, in school, and society, the qualities of interpersonal relations between instructor and student, and the aspects of the teaching-learning process which would appear to have contributed to creative development a generation ago would facilitate rather than inhibit creativity if these same factors were created in today's quite different world and far different educational climate.

In reporting upon events and situations in the life histories of our subjects which appear to have fostered their creative potential and independent spirit, I shall again restrict myself to architects. One finds in their histories a number of circumstances which, in the early years, could well have provided an opportunity as well as the necessity for developing the secure sense of personal autonomy and zestful commitment to their profession which so markedly characterize them.

What appears most often to have characterized the parents of these future creative architects was an extraordinary respect for the child and confidence in his ability to do what was appropriate. Thus they did not hesitate to grant him rather unusual freedom in exploring his universe and in making decisions for himself—and this early as well as late. The expectation of the parent that the child would act independently but reasonably and responsibly appears to have contributed immensely to the latter's sense of personal autonomy which was to develop to such a marked degree.

The obverse side of this was that there was often a lack of intense closeness with one or both of the parents. Most often this appeared in relation to the father rather than to the mother, but often it characterized the relationship with both parents. There were not strong emotional ties of either a positive or a negative sort between parent and child, but neither was there the type of relationship that fosters overdependency nor the type that results in severe rejection. Thus, if there was a certain distance in the relationship between child and parent, it had a liberating effect so far as the child was concerned. If he lacked something of the emotional closeness which some children experience with their parents, he was also spared that type of psychological exploitation that is so frequently seen in the life histories of clinical patients.

Closely related to this factor of some distance between parent and child were ambiguities in identification with the parents. In place of the more usual clear identification with one parent, there was a tendency for the architects to have identified either with both parents or with neither. It was not that the child's early milieu was a deprived one so far as models for identification and the promotion of ego ideals were concerned. It was rather that the larger familial sphere presented the child with a plentiful supply of diverse and effective models—in addition to the mother and father, grandfathers, uncles, and others who occupied prominent and responsible positions within their community—with whom important identifications could

122

be made. Whatever the emotional interaction between father and son, whether distant, harmonious, or turbulent, the father presented a model of effective and resourceful behavior in an exceptionally demanding career. What is perhaps more significant, though, is the high incidence of distinctly autonomous mothers among families of the creative architects, who led active lives with interests and sometimes careers of their own apart from their husbands'.

Still other factors which would appear to have contributed to the development of the marked personal autonomy of our subjects were the types of discipline and religious training which they received, which suggest that within the family there existed clear standards of conduct and ideas as to what was right and wrong but at the same time an expectation if not requirement of active exploration and internalization of a framework of personal conduct. Discipline was almost always consistent and predictable. In most cases there were rules, family standards, and parental injunctions which were known explicitly by the children and seldom infringed. In nearly half the cases, corporal punishment was not employed and in only a few instances was the punishment harsh or cruel.

As for religious practices, the families of the creative architects showed considerable diversity, but what was most widely emphasized was the development of personal ethical codes rather than formal religious practices. For one-third of the families formal religion was important for one parent or for both, but in two-thirds of the families formal religion was either unimportant or practiced only perfunctorily. For the majority of the families, in which emphasis was placed upon the development of one's own ethical code, it is of interest to inquire into the values that were most stressed. They were most often values related to integrity (e.g., forthrightness, honesty, respect for others), quality (e.g., pride, diligence, joy in work, development of talent), intellectual and cultural endeavor, success and ambition, and being respectable and doing the right thing.

The families of the more creative architects tended to move more frequently, whether within a single community, or from community to community, or even from country to country. This, combined with the fact that the more creative architects as youngsters were given very much more freedom to roam and to explore widely, provided for them an enrichment of experience both cultural and personal which their less creative peers did not have.

But the frequent moving appears also to have resulted frequently in some estrangement of the family from its immediate neighborhood. And it is of interest that in almost every case in which the architect reported that his family differed in its behavior and values from those in the neighborhood, the family was different in showing greater cultural, artistic, and intellectual interests and pursuits.

To what extent this sort of cultural dislocation contributed to the frequently reported experiences of aloneness, shyness, isolation, and solitariness during childhood and adolescence, with little or no dating during adolescence, or to what extent these experiences stemmed from a natural introversion of interests and unusual sensitivity, we cannot say. They were doubtless mutually reinforcing factors in stimulating the young architect's awareness of his own inner life and his growing interest in his artistic skills and his ideational, imaginal, and symbolic processes.

Almost without exception, the creative architects manifested very early considerable interest and skill in drawing and painting. And also, with almost no exception, one or both of the parents were of artistic temperament and considerable skill. Often it was the mother who in the architect's early years fostered his artistic potentialities by her example as well as by her instruction. It is especially interesting to note, however, that while the visual and artistic abilities and interests of the child were encouraged and rewarded, these interests and abilities were, by and large, allowed to develop at their own speed, and this pace varied considerably among the architects. There was not an anxious concern on the part of the parents about the skills and abilities of the child. What is perhaps most significant was the widespread definite lack of strong pressures from the parents toward a particular career. And this was true both for pressures away from architecture as well as for pressures toward architecture by parents who were themselves architects.

The several aspects of the life history which I have described were first noted by Kenneth Craik in the protocols for the highly creative Architects I. Subsequently, in reading the protocols for Architects II and III as well as Architects I, a credit of one point for the presence of each of the factors was assigned and the total for each person taken as a score. The correlation of these life history scores with rated creativity of the architects is $+.36$, significant beyond the .005 level of confidence.

And now I turn finally to a consideration of the implications of the nature of creative talent for the nurturing of it in school and college through the processes of education.

Our findings concerning the relations of intelligence to creativity suggest that we may have overestimated in our educational system the role of intelligence in creative achievement. If our expectation is that a child of a given intelligence will not respond creatively to a task which confronts him, and especially if we make this expectation known to the child, the probability that he will respond creatively is very much reduced. And later on, such a child, now grown older, may find doors closed to him so that he is definitely excluded from certain domains of learning. There is increasing reason to believe that in selecting students for special training of their talent we may have overweighted the role of intelligence either by setting the cutting point for selection on the intellective dimension too high or by assuming that regardless of other factors the student with the higher IQ is the more promising one and should consequently be chosen. Our data suggest, rather, that if a person has the minimum of intelligence required for mastery of a field of knowledge, whether he performs creatively or banally in that field will be crucially determined by nonintellective factors. We would do well

124

then to pay more attention in the future than we have in the past to the nurturing of those nonintellective traits which in our studies have been shown to be intimately associated with creative talent.

There is the openness of the creative person to experience both from within and from without which suggests that whether we be parent or teacher we should use caution in setting limits upon what those whom we are nurturing experience and express.

Discipline and self-control are necessary. They must be learned if one is ever to be truly creative, but it is important that they not be overlearned. Furthermore, there is a time and place for their learning, and having been learned they should be used flexibly, not rigidly or compulsively.

If we consider this specifically with reference to the attitudes of perceiving and judging, everyone must judge as well as perceive. It is not a matter of using one to the exclusion of the other, but a question of how each is used and which is preferred. The danger for one's creative potential is not the judging or evaluating of one's experience but that one prejudges, thus excluding from perception large areas of experience. The danger in all parental instruction, as in all academic instruction, is that new ideas and new possibilities of action are criticized too soon and too often. Training in criticism is obviously important and so widely recognized that I need not plead its case. Rather I would urge that, if we wish to nurture creative potential, an equal emphasis be placed on perceptiveness, discussing with our students as well as with our children, at least upon occasion, the most fantastic of ideas and possibilities. It is the duty of parents to communicate and of professors to profess what they judge to be true, but it is no less their duty by example to encourage in their children and in their students an openness to all ideas and especially to those which most challenge and threaten their own judgments.

The creative person, as we have seen, is not only open to experience, but intuitive about it. We can train students to be accurate in their perceptions, and this, too, is a characteristic of the creative. But can we train them to be intuitive, and if so how?

I would suggest that rote learning, learning of facts for their own sake, repeated drill of material, too much emphasis upon facts unrelated to other facts, and excessive concern with memorizing, can all strengthen and reinforce sense perception. On the other hand, emphasis upon the transfer of training from one subject to another, the searching for common principles in terms of which facts from quite different domains of knowledge can be related, the stressing of analogies, and similes, and metaphors, a seeking for symbolic equivalents of experience in the widest possible number of sensory and imaginal modalities, exercises in imaginative play, training in retreating from the facts in order to see them in larger perspective and in relation to more aspects of the larger context thus achieved—these and still other emphases in learning would, I believe, strengthen the disposition to intuitive perception as well as intuitive thinking.

If the widest possible relationships among facts are to be established, if

125

the structure of knowledge (Bruner, 1960) is to be grasped, it is necessary that the student have a large body of facts which he has learned as well as a large array of reasoning skills which he has mastered. You will see, then, that what I am proposing is not that in teaching one disdain acute and accurate sense perception, but that one use it to build upon, leading the student always to an intuitive understanding of that which he experiences.

The independence of thought and action which our subjects reveal in the assessment setting appears to have long characterized them. It was already manifest in high school, though, according to their reports, tending to increase in college and thereafter.

In college our creative architects earned about a B average. In work and courses which caught their interest they could turn in an A performance, but in courses that failed to strike their imagination, they were quite willing to do no work at all. In general, their attitude in college appears to have been one of profound skepticism. They were unwilling to accept anything on the mere say-so of their instructors. Nothing was to be accepted on faith or because it had behind it the voice of authority. Such matters might be accepted, but only after the student on his own had demonstrated their validity to himself. In a sense, they were rebellious, but they did not run counter to the standards out of sheer rebelliousness. Rather, they were spirited in their disagreement and one gets the impression that they learned most from those who were not easy with them. But clearly many of them were not easy to take. One of the most rebellious, but, as it turned out, one of the most creative, was advised by the Dean of his School to quit because he had no talent; and another, having been failed in his design dissertation which attacked the stylism of the faculty, took his degree in the art department.

These and other data should remind all of us who teach that creative students will not always be to our liking. This will be due not only to their independence in situations in which nonconformity may be seriously disruptive of the work of others, but because, as we have seen, more than most they will be experiencing large quantities of tension produced in them by the richness of their experience and the strong opposites of their nature. In struggling to reconcile these opposites and in striving to achieve creative solutions to the difficult problems which they have set themselves they will often show that psychic turbulence which is so characteristic of the creative person. If, however, we can only recognize the sources of their disturbance, which often enough will result in behavior disturbing to us, we may be in a better position to support and encourage them in their creative striving.

References

Allport, G. W., Vernon, P. E., & Lindzey, G. *Study of values: Manual of directions.* (Rev. ed.) Boston: Houghton Mifflin, 1951.

Barron, F., & Welsh, G. S. Artistic perception as a possible factor in personality style: Its measurement by a figure preference test. *J. Psychol.*, 1952, 33, 199-203.

Bingham, Millicent Todd. Beyond psychology. In, *Homo sapiens auduboniensis: A tribute to Walter Van Dyke Bingham*. New York: National Audubon Society, 1953. Pp. 5-29.

Bruner, J. S. *The process of education*. Cambridge, Mass.: Harvard Univer. Press, 1960.

Gough, H. G. *California Psychological Inventory manual*. Palo Alto, Calif.: Consulting Psychologists Press, 1957.

Hall, W. B. The development of a technique for assessing aesthetic predispositions and its application to a sample of professional research scientists. Paper read at Western Psychological Association, Monterey, California, April 1958.

Hathaway, S. R., & McKinley, J. C. *Minnesota Multiphasic Personality Inventory*. New York: Psychological Corporation, 1945.

Jung, C. G. *Psychological types*. New York: Harcourt, Brace, 1923.

Jung, C. G. *Two essays on analytical psychology*. New York: Meridian, 1956.

MacKinnon, D. W. The personality correlates of creativity: A study of American architects. In G. S. Nielsen (Ed.), *Proceedings of the XIV International Congress of Applied Psychology, Copenhagen 1961*. Vol. 2. Copenhagen: Munksgaard, 1962. Pp. 11-39.

Myers, Isabel B. *Some findings with regard to type and manual for Myers-Briggs Type Indicator, Form E*. Swarthmore, Pa.: Author, 1958.

Rexroth, K. My head gets tooken apart. In, *Bird in the bush: Obvious essays*. New York: New Directions Paperbook, 1959. Pp. 65-74.

Russell, W. A., & Jenkins, J. J. The complete Minnesota norms for responses to 100 words from the Kent-Rosanoff Word Association Test. Technical Report No. 11, 1954, University of Minnesota, Contract N8 onr-66216, Office of Naval Research.

Spranger, E. *Types of men*. (Trans. by Paul J. W. Pigors) Halle (Saale), Germany: Max Niemeyer, 1928.

Strong, E. K., Jr. *Manual for Strong Vocational Interest Blanks for Men and Women, Revised Blanks (Form M and W)*. Palo Alto, Calif.: Consulting Psychologists Press, 1959.

Terman, L. M. *Concept Mastery Test, Form T manual*. New York: Psychological Corporation, 1956.

Welsh, G. S. *Welsh Figure Preference Test: Preliminary manual*. Palo Alto, Calif.: Consulting Psychologists Press, 1959.

Wotton, Henry. *The elements of architecture*. London: John Bill, 1624.

Halbert B. Robinson, Wendy C. Roedell,
and Nancy E. Jackson

Early Identification and Intervention

*T*he information and ideas presented
in this chapter have been generated in the context of the Seattle Project—
a longitudinal study of intellectually advanced children undertaken by the
Child Development Research Group at the University of Washington.
Service activities connected with the study include a preschool program for
some of the project children and a counseling and diagnostic service which
provides families of intellectually advanced children with assessment and
information on school placement.

The strategy followed in the longitudinal study is to identify very
young children through age five who demonstrate extraordinary intellectual
superiority and to monitor the development of each child's individual
pattern of abilities. In brief, children are selected whose development as
measured by standard indices of overall intelligence, spatial reasoning,
reading skill, mathematics skill, and/or memory has proceeded at twice the
average rate. The study also includes children whose documented abilities
are less advanced, but whose behaviors indicate they might be "at risk" for
the development of extraordinary intellectual abilities.

The effects of early educational intervention on the development of
intellectually advanced children are monitored in a preschool program
accommodating thirty-five children. The preschool program attempts to
provide an optimal match between educational programming and each
child's level of competence in various subject areas, and to nurture each
child's intellectual, social, emotional, and physical growth in a supportive
atmosphere.

The Importance of Early Identification

Some might argue that there is no practical reason to expend time and
effort in identifying children who demonstrate advanced intellectual abilities

at an early age. The continuing study of Terman and his colleagues (see chapter 5 in this volume) is often cited as evidence that bright children have few significant problems in growing up. This monumental longitudinal study has suggested that superior intelligence, defined during childhood by performance on a standard intelligence test, is associated with a high degree of academic and professional success, and with a degree of personal and social adjustment which is equal to or better than that of the population at large. A number of smaller scale studies (Barbe, 1956; Breland, 1974; Groth, 1975; Hitchfield, 1973; Kincaid, 1969; Sheldon, 1954) have tended to confirm Terman's findings with, as Getzels and Dillon have noted, "a regularity bordering on redundancy" (Getzels and Dillon, 1973).

There are some questions, however, about the applicability of Terman's findings to the full range of children who might reasonably be defined as gifted (Hughes and Converse, 1962). There is, also, a considerable body of evidence indicating that intellectually advanced children do not develop equally well under all circumstances. This may be particularly true for those who are extraordinarily gifted. In a case study report of children with IQs above 180, Hollingworth has provided convincing evidence that not all extraordinarily bright children do well in life (Hollingworth, 1942). Other case studies report similar findings (McCurdy, 1957). Hollingworth noted that the earlier very superior children are identified, the more favorable is their development.

Early identification and special educational programming have been implicated in the successful careers of remarkably gifted people such as John Locke and Francis Bacon, whose lives have been studied retrospectively by Cox, McCurdy, and others (Cox, 1926; McCurdy, op. cit.). Almost all of these persons were recognized by their families as exceptional, were carefully nurtured within the family, and were given a high degree of adult attention. Many of them were educated entirely within the family setting, at least until entrance into a university. Pressey notes that children who became extraordinary geniuses as adults tended to have been identified very early and "had excellent early opportunities . . . to develop. . . . [They] had the opportunity frequently and continuingly to practice and extend their special ability. . . . [They] had the stimulation of many . . . increasingly strong success experiences—and [their] world acclaimed these successes" (Pressey, 1954).

It is reasonable to hypothesize, then, that early identification of children with exceptional abilities is important. How, though, can we assure that such children are actually identified and helped? Several studies have reported that kindergarten teachers are woefully inaccurate in recognizing those children whose intellectual talents can be confirmed with intelligence tests (Jacobs, 1971; Ryan, 1975). This inaccuracy is particularly disturbing since there is further evidence to suggest that truly superior children who are perceived by their teachers to have only average intelligence decline in intelligence and achievement test performance relative to equally superior children whose abilities are recognized by their teachers (Sutherland and

129

Goldschmid, 1974). Children who are identified as gifted and placed in special programs tend to achieve better. In one study, gifted first-grade students who had been placed in special programs were compared with equally gifted pupils who remained in regular classes. The children in special programs gained an average of two academic years during a single nine-month period, while the gifted children in regular classes gained only the usual one year (Martinson, 1961). Similarly, bright children who have been allowed to enter first grade early learn more during their first year of school than equally bright children who have remained in kindergarten.[1] Superior abilities that are not nurtured will not develop, and the resulting waste is inestimable.

The reasons for identifying intellectually advanced children at an early age are, therefore, eminently practical. Early identification creates the opportunity for early intervention. The parent who is aware of a child's special abilities can plan intelligently for appropriate, challenging educational experiences. The educator who has direct information about a child's advanced abilities can develop programs geared to the child's actual level of competence rather than to a level calibrated on the basis of chronological age alone. Since intellectually advanced children have skills beyond those usual for their age, their educational needs are different—in some instances, radically different—from the needs of their same-age peers. The earlier these needs are identified, the sooner educational programs can be tailored to fit them.

Characteristics of Intellectually Advanced Children

Most of the studies which provide data about gifted children have relied for their operational definition of superior intelligence on a single test score weighted in favor of verbal and abstract reasoning abilities (Getzels and Dillon, op. cit.). This approach to the assessment of intelligence still has both theoretical and practical worth. There are limits, however, to the usefulness of a single test score in estimating a child's intellectual abilities.

Certainly, any screening system that identifies children for educational programming will be more successful if it measures intellectual abilities germane to the program than if it taps irrelevant abilities. It makes little sense to identify a group of children with high scores on a test of vocabulary in order to provide them with a special program in science and mathematics. In addition, differential patterns of mental abilities and skills may reflect individual differences in children's problem-solving styles, which may in turn have direct relevance for curriculum planning and teaching strategies.

Many educators have emphasized that gifted children form a heterogeneous population. Individual case studies also dramatize this point (Hauck and Freehill, 1972). Even when a population of gifted children is defined by an IQ cutoff score, a variety of abilities may be represented. It has long

130

been established that children of varying ages and/or intellectual levels can achieve the same score on a general intelligence test with very different profiles of specific abilities (Achenback, 1970; McNemar, 1972; Thompson and Magaret, 1947; Wechsler, 1958). It is also probable that different children may solve the same problems, and therefore receive identical credit, by utilizing quite different cognitive strategies (Inhelder, 1968; McCall, Hogarty, and Hurlburt, 1972).

The matter of organization of cognitive abilities in young children is of considerable current interest and controversy. A popular view is that "growth during the developmental period proceeds from a relatively unitary system to one with independent parts (Thompson and Grusec, 1970), that is, that progressive differentiation occurs during prenatal, infant, and early childhood growth. Several investigators, however, have been able to uncover separable cognitive dimensions in the test performance of very young children (Hurst, 1960; McCall, Hogarty, and Hurlburt, op. cit.; Meyers et al., 1962; Meyers et al., 1964; McCartin and Meyers, 1966; Stott and Ball, 1965). The distinctiveness of these components and their precise relationship to the factors appearing later in life are unclear. It is possible that such factors may be more easily distinguished in young children who are extremely advanced in particular areas of cognitive functioning. If intellectually advanced children are precocious not only in overall rate of development but also in the differentiation of their abilities, the planning of educational programs may have to be adapted to consider variations in talents and learning styles appearing at very early ages.

The heterogeneity among intellectually advanced children is even more evident, of course, when one considers nonintellectual attributes. While some studies have reported that the average levels of personal and social adjustment, physical health, and the like are slightly higher for gifted children than for the population as a whole, the mean differences favoring the gifted group tend to be small and sometimes disappear when the comparison group is appropriately matched for variables such as social class (Lovell and Shields, 1967; Oden, 1968; Terman et al., 1925; Terman and Oden, 1947; Terman and Oden, 1959). Much more striking than the mean differences is the variability within any gifted group. In fact, intellectually advanced children are about as heterogeneous as any other population on measures other than those directly related to the instruments used to identify them. Statements such as "gifted children are typically larger, healthier, and more socially mature than other children their age" are more misleading than they are helpful.

The heterogeneity of this population in both intellectual and nonintellectual domains has been consistently evident among the children involved in the Seattle project. Young children have been identified who are able to perform extraordinary intellectual feats but who do not necessarily score in the highest ranges on tests of general intelligence. A substantial group of children have been located, for example, who at the age of two or three years were reading at the second-grade level or above. The IQs of these

131

children have ranged from scores in the 120s to above the scale limits as measured by the *Stanford-Binet Intelligence Scale*. One child at the age of three enjoyed drawing detailed and accurate maps of his surroundings, and could copy geometric block designs and trace paths through pencil mazes as quickly and precisely as the average eight-year-old, yet his Stanford-Binet IQ at the time of these accomplishments was a modest 132.

Teachers' impressions of the social abilities of the intellectually advanced children in the preschool of the Seattle project have been collected via the *California Preschool Social Competency* rating scale. In social ability, as in specific intellectual abilities, heterogeneity is the rule. Teacher ratings for intellectually advanced children attending the preschool program have yielded percentile ranks ranging from the 21st percentile to the 98th percentile.

This evidence calls into serious question a prevailing conception of giftedness that might be labeled the "myth of the gifted child." According to this viewpoint, certain individuals possess a general superiority in intellectual potential. This superiority is most reliably indicated by a high IQ. Many theorists, research people, and practitioners have argued that it can also be inferred on the basis of behaviors such as superior leadership, creative talent, and so forth. These diverse talents, while valued in themselves, have also become accepted indices of the "syndrome" entity of giftedness.

There is, however, no such thing as a "typical gifted child." Rather, there are many individual children who demonstrate a variety of surprising skills in both intellective and nonintellective domains. Many two- and three-year-old children can do things one would not normally expect—they can read, they are proficient at arithmetic, they can speak several languages, they can use maps, and so forth. Typically, however, children do not do all of these amazing things equally well, and they differ from one another in personality and style of functioning.

Methods of Identification

There are several points to consider when designing a system for the identification of children of preschool age with advanced intellectual abilities. First, the identification system must include opportunities for children who have extremely advanced abilities to display those skills. Bright children may perform like average children unless they are presented with sufficiently challenging material. Thus, many of the "readiness" tests used to identify children who are not adequately prepared for the typical kindergarten or first-grade program are wholly inadequate for identifying preschool children with advanced abilities. These tests simply do not provide any opportunity for intellectually advanced children to show the extent of what they can do.

Second, an identification system must allow for the inconsistency that often characterizes the performance of young children. If a testing session includes a broad range of tasks, it is more likely that some of the items will both capture the child's interest and elicit the best performance of which the child is capable. A useful maxim is to look for evidence of what the child *can* do, and not be discouraged by what the child cannot, or will not, do.

Finally, experience in the Seattle project has provided ample evidence that even the most comprehensive battery of tests, administered by the most skillful of testers, may not provide a good estimate of a young child's capabilities. For this reason, any identification system should include a detailed parents' report of a child's abilities in addition to the sample of behavior that is collected in a test session.

IDENTIFICATION BY TEST PERFORMANCE

The test battery used to select children for the preschool program in the Seattle project samples a broad spectrum of intellectual and academic skills. Each component of the test battery presents a separate opportunity for children to display the best, most advanced performance of which they are capable. If a child does perform exceptionally well on a test, there can be little doubt about the child's advanced ability. If, however, the child does not score at an advanced level, we do not assume that lack of ability is the problem. Young children's test scores are often depressed by the child's nervousness at being closeted in a strange room with an unfamiliar examiner. Many two- and three-year-olds are more interested in playing their own games with the test materials or conversing with the tester than in solving the particular problems presented by the tests. In evaluating a testing session, one should look for the areas of the child's best performance. Data from the Seattle project suggest that those scores may provide the best information about the child's capabilities. Our identification system does not, then, require that children score consistently at high levels on all test items.

As of 1978, the test battery included the short-form (starred items only) *Stanford-Binet Intelligence Scale*; the Block Design, Mazes and Arithmetic Subtests of the *Wechsler Preschool and Primary Scale of Intelligence* (WPPSI); the Numerical Memory subtest from the *McCarthy Scales of Children's Abilities*; and a brief, informal test of reading. This battery gives estimates of the child's general reasoning ability, spatial-perceptual reasoning ability, arithmetic skill, short-term memory, and reading skill. When a child performs unusually well on the Block Design, Mazes, and/or Arithmetic subtests of the WPPSI, the tester continues into the parallel subtests from the more advanced *Wechsler Intelligence Scale for Children—Revised* (WISC-R). Such flexibility can be very important, for preschool and kindergarten-aged children can score at norms for fifteen- or sixteen-year-olds on the Block Design and Mazes subtests.

This test battery is far from perfect, but it does test the limits of a child's

133

abilities in a broad range of intellectual and academic areas within a single testing session that usually lasts less than one hour. To date, the battery has worked somewhat more effectively with children who are four years old or older than with younger children.

Whenever there is an opportunity for more extensive testing of young children's academic skills, the *Peabody Individual Achievement Test* (PIAT) is administered. This test is easy to give to very young, bright children; many of the children with whom we work score at advanced levels on all areas. Virtually all of our three-year-olds have had reading and mathematics skills at the kindergarten level by the time they have completed a year in the preschool program; reading scores at the fourth-, fifth-, or sixth-grade level have not been uncommon.

Our test battery has been developed to identify children with a diverse array of advanced intellectual and academic skills. An identification program should be tailored to the program it serves. A different test battery might well be more appropriate for a different type of program.

IDENTIFICATION BY PARENT INFORMATION

A single test session provides a limited sample of a child's behavior, which may or may not include some indication of the child's best possible performance. Parents, on the other hand, have an opportunity to observe their child's behavior under a wide variety of conditions. The use of parents' reports as a major source of information is an obvious practical alternative for any project involving intellectually advanced children of preschool-age. Moreover, there is evidence from previous research that parents are reasonably accurate in estimating their children's intellectual abilities—sometimes better, in fact, than kindergarten teachers assigned the same task (Jacobs, op. cit. Ryan, op. cit.). Parents' reports can be even more useful if parents are asked to provide examples of their child's actual behaviors rather than to estimate their child's ability level.

The strategy adopted by the Seattle project has been to use questionnaire and interview formats to obtain information from parents about specific child behaviors chosen from psychometric and theoretical research literature. Theoretical domains of intellectual ability have been translated into particular behaviors that a child might naturally perform at home and that might be easily observed by parents. Parents' responses to questions about their child's current interests and accomplishments have provided a moderately good prediction of how well the child will perform during a testing session. On the other hand, parents' responses to retrospective questions about the age at which their child first began talking or achieved other developmental milestones do not predict test performance and appear to be unrelated to any other measure of the child's current abilities.

While parents' objective responses to specific questions about a child's behavior have provided useful information, equally good prediction of test performance has been obtained from global evaluations of the qualitative

134

information provided by parents. Our questionnaires are designed to encourage parents to provide lengthy anecdotal descriptions of their child's behavior. Parents' comments often provide a vivid picture of a child's behavior which could never be gleaned from a series of yes-no responses. The following are just a few examples of the detailed remarks which parents have provided us:

Does your child easily put together puzzles of over twenty pieces in which the pieces are all part of the same picture?

"Yes (at twenty months). At about age two and a half she had mastered a Springbok forty-eight-piece puzzle, The Three Bears, working entirely by the shape of the pieces, not by the picture. When she was given a Calico Cut puzzle cut with the same stamp, she quickly recognized that the shapes were the same, and put it together" (girl, aged four years, two months at time of report).

Does your child use the word "because" or "cause" even though the child may confuse the meaning of the word?

"Yes. She has been doing this since age three years. For instance, she recently said, 'It is fall, a season of the year, because it is getting ready for winter, because it snows in the winter, because it gets so cold and I wear my heavy coat, because I need to keep warm because I might catch cold.' She frequently talks in paragraphs with all the thoughts connected by 'because' " (girl, aged three years, five months at time of report).

Does your child recognize and name two-digit numbers?

"Yes, he only starts losing track when numbers get into the ten thousands" (boy, aged five years, two months at time of report).

The information that parents provide in response to a questionnaire can be rated by trained judges to yield an overall estimate of the degree of the child's intellectual precocity. In successive years, independent raters were able to reach substantial agreement in judging the data obtained from parents.

We have been encouraged by several years' evidence that evaluations of children based on information from parents consistently show a positive relationship with the child's performance on tests. Our long-term goal, however, is to use parent information, together with test performance, as a predictor of the child's long-range intellectual development. Parent information is based on more extensive samples of a child's behavior than is information from standardized test sessions. For this reason, parent information may ultimately prove to be a better estimate of a very young child's intellectual competence than a test score based on a possibly sub-optimal, and certainly limited, behavior sample. Preliminary findings from our longitudinal follow-up are consistent with this hypothesis. Several of the children who have demonstrated extraordinary test performance at age four earned average test scores at age two. Evaluations of the parent reports obtained when these children were two years of age did, however, predict their later extraordinary test performance.

Goals of Early Intervention

Early intervention programs for intellectually advanced preschool children can serve two general purposes: they can provide guidance and planning aid to parents, and they can provide a supportive educational environment for children.

The counseling and diagnostic service associated with the Seattle project has provided a forum for parents of intellectually advanced children to discuss concerns associated with their children's abilities. A degree of ambivalence is evident in the comments of these parents. They tend to be proud of their child's accomplishments, but are worried about meeting their child's special educational needs, and are frequently uncomfortable about public displays of their child's precocity. A three-year-old who reads the menu in a restaurant can, for example, become the focus of unwanted public attention for the family. Family acquaintances frequently comment that parents must have "pushed" the child into advanced accomplishments. Parents may begin to feel guilty about their child's advanced abilities. Some parents go so far as to attempt to decelerate their child's learning rate by resorting to such measures as hiding advanced schoolbooks. Almost all are concerned that advanced academic abilities will cause difficulty when the child enters public school.

An early intervention program can often confirm for parents that their own estimates of their child's unusual abilities are quite accurate. Parents can be put in contact with families with similar children, and can be assured that intellectual precocity is not the parents' "fault," but is, in fact, a natural occurrence for a good number of children. Early documentation of a child's abilities can also aid parents in planning for their child's education, and may help educators attune school programs to the need for individually tailored programs. Individualization of programs becomes more feasible when information is available that gives a full picture of a child's abilities and interests.

Parents frequently mention that they cannot find enough challenges to keep their intellectually advanced preschoolers occupied at home. A carefully planned educational program can provide supportive nurturance for children's rapidly developing intellectual abilities. Traditionally, preschools have had the general goal of helping children get "ready" for elementary school. Intellectually advanced preschoolers, however, frequently have acquired an impressive array of traditional academic skills before they enter a preschool program. In terms of their intellectual prowess, they have been "ready" for school for a long time.

Most descriptions of educational programs for gifted children assume that these children are somehow "qualitatively different" from other children. In actuality, the behaviors described as qualitatively different are usually behaviors similar to those of children who are older than the child in question. There is currently little, if any, good evidence to support the notion that the thinking of intellectually gifted young children is qualitatively different from the thinking of children who are older than they are. The differences that have been demonstrated seem to be differences in *rate* of intellectual development rather than in *type* of development.

The differences in rate of growth *within* individual children do produce characteristics which are, to say the least, unusual. A three-year-old child who can read at the sixth-grade level but cannot draw a sqaure or a diamond is not an ordinary child; neither is a two-year-old who is not toilet-trained but is learning to multiply and divide. Nonetheless, basic strategies of education do apply to these children.

One of the most widely stated educational truths, agreed upon by educators and psychologists alike, is that the key to successful learning experiences lies in providing an optimal match between the child's skill level and the material presented (Hunt, 1961; Jackson, Robinson, and Dale, 1977). The material should be sufficiently difficult to provide a challenge, but not so difficult that the child cannot relate it to previous learning. Providing such an optimal match for intellectually precocious young children requires a good deal of individual planning because of the unevenness of skills development within individual children. Care must be taken to challenge each child's particular intellectual strengths, while allowing opportunity for the development of less advanced skills. The heterogeneity inherent in any group of intellectually advanced students makes individual planning essential.

To the extent that a child's skill levels are widely disparate, existing program strategies must be modified to provide an appropriate match. A three-year-old child who reads at the fifth-grade level, has the attention span of a five-year-old, and has average small motor skills cannot be treated like a small fifth grader. Neither can the child be treated like an ordinary preschooler. Nonetheless, materials designed to enhance the reading skills of fifth graders can be successfully adapted to meet the attention span and motor skill requirements of such a child and at the same time challenge the child's area of intellectual strength. Too frequently, educational programs are designed to teach at the child's weakest level of ability, rather than being adapted to match all levels appropriately. A child who reads but cannot write will be taught to write, and the reading ignored. Just as a successful identification system focuses on each child's areas of best performance, so too a successful educational program encourages each child's strengths at the same time that it provides help for weaker areas.

In the preschool associated with the Seattle project, allowance has been made for unevenness of skill levels within as well as among children. Advanced material usually presented to older children has been adapted for preschool children whose attention span and reading and writing abilities may not equal their grasp of conceptual material. Intellectual content of such materials may remain at an advanced level, but often the activities are changed to include things to touch and manipulate and to provide alternatives to written responses.

Activities are also planned to provide experiences in group discussion

137

and group decision making. Discussion with peers provides a unique forum for testing ideas, a forum that cannot be duplicated in the usual home environment.

In addition to challenging children's intellectual strengths, the program emphasizes the development of large and small motor skills. This area is particularly important for children whose advanced intellectual abilities frequently outstrip their physical development. Three-year-olds who read at the fourth-grade level but cannot hold a pencil cannot take full advantage of many experiences appropriate to their reading level. The preschool therefore provides many opportunities for children to develop small muscle skills and eye-hand coordination.

The program also contains a strong emphasis on the development of social skills. In many cases, the children's intellectual skills have progressed far beyond their level of social maturity, creating what might be called an "intellectual-social gap." People often become angry at children when their social skills fall short of the expectations generated by their general intellectual maturity. This unevenness in skill level can be particularly difficult for young children who must cope either with being more advanced in intellectual ability than many of their same-age peers, or with being the youngest in a group of older children who are their intellectual peers. Such children need a large repertoire of social skills, a strong self-image, and a realistic appraisal of what their particular intellectual advancement means and does not mean.

The most important characteristic of the Seattle project is individual planning related to the particular strengths and weaknesses evident in each child's pattern of abilities. The educator's task is not, as with compensatory programs, to bring children up to a minimum level of performance. Rather, the task is to provide a match of learning experience with competence level in each subject area, and to facilitate the child's progress at his or her own rate. With such a program of systematic nurturance, it may well be possible to transform early precocity in intellectual achievements into adult intellectual excellence (Roedell and Robinson, 1977).

Directions for Future Research

It seems obvious that the identification and nurturance of exceptional talents should be of the highest priority for our society. Yet, public support for such programs has occurred in sporadic bursts of limited financial, scientific, and philosophical commitment.

Little is known about the long-term implications of various types of intellectual precocity. Would it be possible to identify at an early age those children who might, with proper educational opportunities, become the leading scientists, mathematicians, artists, poets, and social leaders of the future? Retrospective evidence indicates that most individuals who demonstrated intellectual superiority in adulthood were also precocious in some intellective domain in early childhood. Prospective evidence, however, is not available. Many eminent "gifted" adults taught themselves to read at the early age of two or three. We do not know, though, whether all children who learn to read early have the capacity for remarkable intellectual performance in adulthood. Only careful longitudinal research can answer such questions.

Even less information is available concerning the issue of actual differences in thinking and problem-solving strategies between intellectually advanced children and children with average abilities. At present, we have no evidence that would require us to reject a description of the bright child as being mentally equal to the average older child. Yet for good reasons, the doctrine that the thought processes of gifted children are "qualitatively different" persists. Research focused on a process analysis of the thinking strategies of children with differing intellectual talents is needed to clarify this issue. Such information would be of considerable theoretical as well as practical importance.

References

Achenbach, Thomas M. Comparison of Stanford-Binet performance of nonrelated and retarded persons matched for MA and sex. *American Journal of Mental Deficiency,* 1970, **74**, 488–494.

Barbe, Walter. A study of family background of the gifted. *Journal of Educational Psychology,* 1956, **47**, 302–309.

Breland, Hunter M. Birth order, family configuration and verbal achievement. *Child Development,* 1974, **45**, 1011–1019.

Cox, Catherine M. *The early mental traits of three hundred geniuses,* from *Genetic studies of genius,* vol. 2. Stanford, Calif.: Stanford University Press, 1926.

Getzels, Jacob W. and J. T. Dillon. The nature of giftedness and the education of the gifted child, in Robert M. W. Travers, ed. *Second handbook of research on teaching.* Chicago: Rand McNally, 1973, 694.

Getzels, Jacob W. and J. T. Dillon, op. cit.

Groth, Norma J. Mothers of gifted. *Gifted Child Quarterly,* 1975, **19**, 217–222.

Hauck, Barbara B. and Maurice F. Freehill. *The gifted: Case studies.* Dubuque, Iowa: William C. Brown, 1972.

Hitchfield, Elizabeth M. *In search of promise.* London: Longman, 1973.

Hollingworth, Leta. *Children above 180 IQ Stanford-Binet: Origin and development.* Yonkers-on-Hudson, New York: World Book Co., 1942.

Hughes, Herbert F. and Harold D. Converse. Characteristics of the gifted: A case for a sequel to Terman's study. *Exceptional Children,* 1962, 29, 179–183.

Hunt, J. McVicker. *Intelligence and experience.* New York: Ronald Press, 1961.

Hurst, John G. A factor analysis of the Merrill-Palmer with reference to theory and test construction. *Educational and Psychological Measurement,* 1960, **20**, 219–532.

Inhelder, Barbel. *The diagnosis of reasoning in mentally retarded,* 2nd ed., trans. Will B. Stevens. New York: Chandler, 1968.

Jackson, Nancy E., Halbert B. Robinson, and Philip S. Dale. *Cognitive development in young children.* Monterey, Calif.: Brooks/Cole, 1977.

Jacobs, Jon C. Effectiveness of teacher and parent identification of gifted children as a function of school level. *Psychology in the School,* 1971, **8**, 140–142.

Jacobs, Jon C., op. cit.

Kincaid, Donald. A study of highly gifted elementary pupils. *Gifted Child Quarterly,* 1969, **13,** 264–267.

Lovell, K. and J. B. Shields. Some aspects of a study of the gifted child. *British Journal of Educational Psychology,* 1967, **37**, 201–208.

Martinson, Ruth A. *Educational programs for gifted pupils.* Sacramento, Calif.: California State Department of Education, 1961, cited in Sidney P. Marland, Jr. *Education of the gifted and talented,* Report to the Congress of the United States by the U.S. Commissioner of Education. Washington, D.C.: U.S. Government Printing Office, 1972, p. 105.

McCall, Robert B., Pamela S. Hogarty, and Nancy Hurlburt. Transitions in sensorimotor development and the prediction of childhood IQ. *American Psychologist,* 1972, **27**, 728–748.

McCall, Robert B., Pamela S. Hogarty, and Nancy Hurlburt, op. cit.

McCartin, Sister Rose Amata and C. Edward Meyers. An exploration of six semantic factors at first grade. *Multivariate Behavioral Research,* 1966, *I,* 74–94.

McCurdy, Harold. The childhood pattern of genius. *Journal of the Elisha Mitchell Scientific Society,* 1957, **73,** 448–462.

McCurdy, Harold, op. cit.

McNemar, Qinn. *The revision of the Stanford-Binet scale.* Boston: Houghton Mifflin, 1942.

Meyers, C. Edward et al. *Primary abilities at mental age six, monographs of the society for research in child development,* vol. *27*, no. *1,* 1962.

Meyers, C. Edward et al. *Four ability-factor hypotheses at three preliterate levels in normal and retarded children, monographs of the society for research in child development,* vol. **29,** no. **5,** 1964.

Oden, Melita. The fulfillment of promise: Forty-year follow-up of the Terman gifted group. *Genetic psychology monographs,* 1968, *77,* 3–93.

Pressey, Sidney L. Concerning the nature and nurture of genius. *Scientific Monthly,* 1955, **81,** p. 124.

Roedell, Wendy C. and Halbert B. Robinson. *Programming for intellectually advanced preschool children: A program development guide.* Technical report of the Child Development Research Group. Seattle, Wash.: Child Development Research Group, University of Washington, 1977. ERIC ED 151 094.

Ryan, Judith S. Early identification of intellectually superior black children. Doctoral dissertation, University of Michigan, 1975.

Ryan, Judith S., op. cit.

Sheldon, Paul M. The families of highly gifted children. *Marriage and Family Living*, 1954, **16**, 59–60, 67.

Stott, Leland H. and Rachel S. Ball. *Infant and preschool mental tests: Review and evaluation, monographs of the society for research in child development*, vol. *30*, no. *3*, 1965.

Sutherland, Ann and Marcel L. Goldschmid. Negative teacher expectation and change in children with superior intellectual potential. *Child Development*, 1974, **45**, 852–856.

Terman, Lewis M. et al. *Mental and physical traits of a thousand gifted children*, from *Genetic studies of genius*, vol. *1*. Stanford, Calif.: Stanford University Press, 1925.

Terman, Lewis M. and Melita Oden. *The gifted child grows up: Twenty-five years; follow-up of a superior group*, from *Genetic studies of genius*, vol 4. Stanford, Calif.: Stanford University Press, 1947.

Terman, Lewis M. and Melita Oden. *The gifted group at mid-life: Thirty-five years' follow-up of the superior child*, from *Genetic studies of genius*, vol. *5*. Stanford, Calif.: Stanford University Press, 1959.

Thompson, Clare W. and Ann Magaret. Differential test responses of normals and mental defectives. *Journal of Abnormal and Social Psychology*, 1947, **42**, 284–293.

Thompson, William R. and Joan Grusec. Studies of early experience, in Paul H. Mussen, ed. *Carmichael's manual of child psychology*, vol. *1*. New York: John Wiley and Sons, 1970, pp. 565–654.

Wechsler, David. *The measurement and appraisal of adult intelligence*, 4th ed. Baltimore: William and Wilkins, 1958.

Notes

[1] School Board of Broward County, Florida. A study of early entry into first grade, 1973–74. Fort Lauderdale, Fla.: School Board of Broward County, 1974. ERIC ED 122 929.

[2] Pennsylvania Department of Public Instruction. *Mentally gifted children and youth: A guide for parents*. Harrisburg, Pa.: Bureau of Special and Compensatory Education, Pennsylvania Department of Public Instruction, 1973.

Donald J. Treffinger
Joseph S. Renzulli
John F. Feldhusen

Problems in the Assessment of Creative Thinking*

A large number of studies dealing with various aspects of creative thinking have appeared in educational and psychological publications during the last two decades. Evidence of the extent of this interest appears in Razik's (1965) bibliography and this journal's attempts to update it in 1967 and 1968, as well as in recent volumes of *Psychological Abstracts* and *Dissertation Abstracts*. Yet there is a great deal of controversy regarding the nature of the creative process and the strategies that hold maximum promise for accelerating creative production. While such controversy is optimistically viewed as a healthy symptom in any relatively new line of scientific inquiry, our failure to master certain basic problems after nearly twenty years of intensified study has led to a decrease in interest among educational practitioners who at one time were eager to rally round the flag of creativity and to "do something" about this newly discovered (or rediscovered) human ability. Unless researchers can begin to find answers to many unsolved problems, the concept of creativity may be, at best, a catchall. At worst, there exists a very real danger that it could eventually be tossed upon the junk heap of discarded educational fads.

The purpose of this paper is to provide an overview of the major problems and issues that relate to the scientific study of creativity. By isolating the important dimensions of the problem, we hope that some direction may be provided for future research efforts.

Assumptions of This Paper

There are two basic underlying assumptions upon which this paper is based. The first is that certain unique psychological processes, referred to

---

*Based on the authors' presentations in the symposium Assessing Creativity; Progress in Both Directions; at the Annual Meeting of the American Educational Research Association, Minneapolis, March, 1970, Richard E. Ripple, Chairman.

as "creativity," do in fact exist in man's repertoire of behaviors, although in our investigation of those behaviors, we may have merely scratched the surface. The second assumption is that creative process is complex, or multidimensional, in nature.

Problems Treated

In this paper, we will consider two general and interrelated problems and several specific issues within each. The first set of problems involves the *theoretical description* of creative thinking; the second will be referred to as the *criterion problem*.

Theoretical Description of Creative Thinking

The first problem, then, is that there is no single, widely-accepted theory of creativity which can serve to unify and direct our efforts at specifying an adequate assessment procedure. The work of Mednick (1962) and his associates illustrates, perhaps as well as any, the formulation of a theory of creativity from which a particular method of assessment emerges. Yet, for a number of reasons, many researchers have not been attracted to this theory (cf. Jackson and Messick, 1965; Taft and Rossiter, 1963; Cropley, 1966), and it can hardly be described as widely accepted. Other theories, such as those of Rogers (1962) or Kubie (1958), have seldom resulted in the formulation of psychometrically adequate assessment procedures. Guilford's widely-known "structure of intellect" model (1967) does not constitute a theory of creativity *per se*, despite the fact that it has been heuristically or conceptually useful in describing some cognitive abilities which are related to creativity. Even though Guilford (1967) has argued in recent discussions that creative thinking is not merely a matter of divergent production, a comprehensive theory of creativity would necessarily consider in detail the nature and interrelationships of noncognitive components of creative behavior, as well as the cognitive aspects.

Torrance's (1966) tests purport to be broadly eclectic, drawing from the "best" of theory available at the time of their development, but for that very reason—that they lack a unified, comprehensive, theoretical base—difficulties are inevitable. Of course, the variables assessed by the Torrance Tests (fluency, flexibility, originality and elaboration) are all classified in Guilford's "structure of intellect."

The Problems of Measurement

Given the existing array of ideas about creativity, and the absence of "theoretical unity," it is not in the least surprising that there exists a number of tests, all purporting to be measures of "creativity," but differing in a number of ways. Each instrument mirrors the particular set of beliefs and preconceptions of its developer concerning the nature of creativity. Sadly, the theoretical rationale for such tests is often not even sufficient to allow systematic tests of differential predictions.

An outgrowth of this problem, although a major concern in its own right, is that *we do not understand very completely the implications of differences in assessment procedures.* Variations in working time, test atmosphere, and directions given to the examinee, for example, seem to yield different kinds of results and different patterns of intercorrelations between creativity scores and other cognitive or achievement variables. It is quite clear that such changes occur (Wallach and Kogan, 1965; Van Mondfrans, Feldhusen, Treffinger, and Ferris, 1970). What is *not* clear is the reason for those changes, or under what conditions certain results might be predicted.

Van Mondfrans et al. (1970) argued that the matter is much more complex than merely removing the time limits and appearances of a test-like situation. Removing time limits, for example, had no significant effect on pupil performance on verbal tasks. The highest scores on these tasks were obtained under standard "test-like" conditions. On figural tasks, however, removing time limits did influence pupil performance; highest scores were obtained by pupils under "take home" conditions.

Continuing experimental work is needed to understand the problems of test procedures and their implications more completely. Such research would also be more profitable if predictions could be derived from a specific theoretical conception of creativity. In the meantime, a clear implication seems to be that researchers who use "creativity tests" should be extremely careful to report in detail the procedures for test administration, directions, and timing.

Creativity's Relations to Other Abilities

Another very controversial issue, which is related to theoretical problems and has probably prevented educators from achieving some closure in programming for the classroom, is a problem which we will refer to as *dimensionality.* (In measurement terms, the issue is more properly referred to as convergent and discriminant validation; see Campbell and Fiske, 1959.) Simply stated, the dimensionality issue involves the degree to which measures of creativity or divergent thinking are empirically distinguishable from other more traditional measures of cognitive processes such as intelligence and academic achievement. The development of defensible measures of creativity would seem to depend on constructing a series of tasks which share substantial variance with each other, but are at the same time generally independent of other traditional cognitive measures. The concern for this problem is reflected in the disproportionate amount of research that has been devoted to the creativity-intelligence distinction and our inability to arrive upon a generally acceptable operations definition. (Taylor, 1959, for example, has listed over one hundred definitions which have added to the semantic fog that envelops the study of creativity.) A great deal of the concern for the dimensionality issue, and the lack of resolution of this issue, stems from the problem of measurement and the adequacy of currently available tests of creativity and the divergent-thinking processes.

A number of research studies (Ripple and May, 1962; Thorndike, 1963a, 1963b; and Wallach and Kogan, 1965) have cautioned against the uncritical acceptance of the Getzels and Jackson (1962) hypothesis which suggested that creativity and intelligence were unrelated. In a historical perspective upon the measurement of cognitive processes, Ward (1963) called attention to aspects of Binet's and Wechsler's classic definitions of intelligence, parts of which sound surprisingly similar to many present-day definitions of creativity. Others (Guilford, 1967: Wallach, in press) have made a similar case for the relationship between creativity and the classic definitions of problem-solving.

As a result of the lack of a unified, widely-accepted theory of creativity, then, educators have been confronted with several difficulties; establishing a useful operational definition, understanding the implications of differences among tests and test administration procedures, and understanding the relationships of creativity to other human abilities.

The Criterion Problem

The second general problem has been described as the *criterion problem.* What criteria exist against which the validity of creativity tests may be assessed? Although this problem has not generated as much concern as the creativity-intelligence controversy, its interrelatedness to all other aspects of the study of creativity demands that it be given high priority among areas in which research is needed.

Many researchers have tended, on the one hand, to view creativity entirely as a cognitive process or, on the other hand, entirely as a complex set of personality traits. The former have tended to ignore the possibility that there may be an affective component to creativity, and the latter have tended to overlook the importance of underlying cognitive abilities in creative problem-solving. It is most likely, however, that a valid assessment procedure would, of necessity, consider both components. In the meantime, we must be very cautious about our willingness to make inferences about "creativity" from measures which are distinctly cognitive, particularly the divergent-thinking-type tests. This does not imply rejection of the usefulness of tests of divergent thinking. It may be true that some of the critics have been too severe (e.g., Covington, 1968; Wallach, 1968). While divergent-thinking measures certainly do not tell the entire story about creativity, it

145

is quite likely that these measures do assess intellectual abilities which play an important role in creativity. If creativity is viewed as a complex kind of human problem-solving (in which case perhaps the term "creative problem-solving" would be preferable), divergent thinking may be a necessary, although not a sufficient, component.

Teacher and Peer Judgments

There have been many difficulties in identifying acceptable external criteria for the validation of creativity tests. Foremost among them is the difficulty of any attempt to use teacher and peer judgments as a means of identifying creative youngsters. A number of studies which sought to use this approach (Holland, 1959; Wallen and Stevenson, 1960; Rivlin, 1959; Reid, King, and Wickwire, 1959; Torrance, 1966; and Yamamoto, 1964) have shown that when teachers and peers are asked to nominate very creative pupils or those with good imagination or many new ideas and ways of doing things, they usually produce a list of classmates who are the highest achievers or have the highest IQs. Further, there is considerable variability among teachers in the ability to rate pupils against a test criterion, even when specific definitions are provided. Research is needed on the effectiveness of procedures for training teachers or peers to be more effective raters, less influenced by other criteria.

Creativity Profiles

Related attempts to establish external criteria for creativity have been the well-known series of studies that analyzed the characteristics of adults who have made significant contributions to their respective professions (e.g., MacKinnon, 1962; Barron, 1969). While these studies have provided us with excellent profiles and descriptions of the highly creative person, we must be careful not to confuse concurrent validity with predictive validity. MacKinnon (1962) cautioned that it is one thing to discover distinguishing characteristics, but quite another matter to conclude that traits observed several years after school or college truly characterized an individual when he was a student. Nor can we conclude that these same traits in youngsters today will identify individuals with the kind of creative potential that will be valued in tomorrow's world.

Products as Indices of Creativity

Another approach to the criterion problem would be to use products as indices of creative achievement. Thus great discoveries, inventions, works of art, or writings could be used as criteria. In the research by

146

MacKinnon (1962) and Barron (1969), such indices were undoubtedly often used as the basis for judging an individual's significant contribution in a field. Miles (1968) has also attempted to develop tasks for concurrent assessment of an individual's ability to produce a creative object. While seemingly a hopeful approach to the development of criterion measures for validation of creativity tests, this approach through the use of products is beset by reliability problems.

Problem-Solving Tasks

There is also some reason to believe that some of the problems of assessing creative problem-solving relate to the heterogeneity and under-development of the tasks that have been employed. As Davis (1966) and other have pointed out, the literature on problem-solving is very confusing. "Creative problem-solving" tasks have been used in one study and then never used again. Some people have attempted, as Davis did, to categorize or classify problem-solving, but this classification has tended to be rational rather than empirical. Some logical groupings or judgments about tasks may not hold up very well under closer examination; tasks which "on the face" seem to be attractive measures of creative problem-solving may reflect quite different appearances when studied empirically.

There is a great deal to be learned about the assessment of creative problem-solving. It is quite clear that simple measures of fluency, flexibility, and originality are not sufficient. Perhaps substantial effort must be given to finding new, more complex measures. Perhaps as a beginning we must at least look more carefully at the *interactions* among divergent-thinking scores (fluency-flexibility interactions, for example) and between divergent-thinking scores and other abilities; very little use of such combined subscores seems to have been made in the literature.

There are also a number of problems of a very practical nature to solve. How does the researcher know that what *he* considers creative tasks are creative and challenging for the examinee? It may be that the tasks he considers most unusual are boring, unexciting, even trivial, for the most imaginative of our examinees. Perhaps each task that purports to be an assessment of creative problem-solving should be accompanied by a simple rating scale: Have you ever worked on this problem before? Did you solve it? Were you given the solution? What did you think about the problems you have solved here? Were they interesting? Challenging? What did you think of your solutions?" Although many psychologists avoid using the term "introspection," it may be that quite a bit could be learned about measures of creativity by asking subjects to talk about their experiences. Perhaps the adequacy or creative strength of a response, or the extent to which a task captures the subject's attention and stimulates him to think creatively, are important matters, but only capable of being assessed by the subject himself.

147

Measures of Originality

Another dimension of the criterion problem concerns the appropriateness or inappropriateness of our current means for assessing originality. While a few have dissented, almost everyone who has grappled with creativity research appears to be satisfied with the statistical infrequency criterion for measures of originality. At least one researcher (Starkweather, 1964, 1968) has attempted to devise an alternate procedure, involving comparison of a child's response to all of his *own* responses, rather than to the responses of other children. Perhaps our easy acceptance of the statistical infrequency criterion has prevented us from identifying new methods which are useful for measuring this dimension of creative thinking. Ideally one would like a qualitative index with face validity.

An issue of critical importance in solving the problem of assessing creative thinking is concerned with the validity of our measures. Too often, in order to develop tests which are manageable from the psychometric point of view, we have relied on tasks which may have little or no logical relationship to creative behavior as it occurs in the "real world." While there exists a substantial difficulty (identifying adequate criteria against which the test tasks can be validated), the problem warrants our attention. The "creativity" assessed by our tests, after all, should be expected to bear a resemblance to creativity as it is actually manifested among people.

Finally, we should at least acknowledge the existence of a number of other important issues in research on creativity and its assessment: assessing the *relevance* of responses, distinguishing between sensible and bizarre responses, and establishing differential age and sex criteria. Most would agree that these are essentially unresolved problems, and thus appear to be topics that are worthy of the researcher's attention. Occasionally, the study of creativity has been described as a classic case of the blind leading the blind, but researchers in this area may prefer to look upon the situation as somewhat of a challenge, and to keep in mind that in the land of the blind, a one-eyed man can be king!

References

Barron, F. *Creative person and creative process.* New York: Holt, Rinehart, and Winston, 1969.

Campbell, D. T. and Fiske, D. W. Convergent and discriminant validation by the multitrait-multimethod matrix. *Psychological Bulletin,* 1959, **56**, 81–105.

Covington, M. V. New directions in the appraisal of creative thinking. Berkeley, California: University of California, unpublished monograph, 1968.

Cropley, A. J. Creativity and intelligence. *British Journal of Educational Psychology,* 1966, **36**, 259–266.

Davis, G. A. Current status of research and theory in human problem-solving. *Psychological Bulletin,* 1966, **66**, 36–54.

Getzels, J. W. & Jackson, P. W. *Creativity and intelligence: Explorations with gifted students.* New York: Wiley, 1962.

Guilford, J. P. *The nature of human intelligence.* New York; McGraw-Hill, 1967.

Holland, J. L. Some limitations of teacher ratings as predictors of creativity. *Journal of Educational Psychology,* 1959, **50**, 219–223.

Jackson, P. W. & Messick, S. The person, the product, and the response: conceptual problems in the assessment of creativity. *Journal of Personality,* 1965, **33**, 310–329.

Kubie, L. S. *Neurotic distortion of the creative process.* Lawrence: University of Kansas Press, 1958.

MacKinnon, D. W. The nature and nurture of creative talent. *American Psychologist,* 1962, **17**, 484–495.

Mednick, S. A. The associative basis of the creative process. *Psychological Review,* 1962, **69**, 220–232.

Miles, D. T. Development of a test for an experimental research program. Final report, project no. 7–E–037, U.S. Office of Education. July 1968.

Razik, T. *Bibliography of creativity studies and related areas.* Buffalo, New York; Creative Education Foundation, 1965.

Reid, J. B., King, F. J., & Wickwire, P. Cognitive and other personality characteristics of creative children. *Psychological Reports,* 1959, **5**, 729–737.

Ripples, R. E., & May, R. B. Caution in comparing creativity and I.Q. *Psychological Reports,* 1962, **10**, 229–230.

Rivlin, L. G. Creativity and the self-attitudes and sociability of high school students. *Journal of Educational Psychology,* 1959, **50**, 147–152.

Rogers. C. R. Toward a theory of creativity. In Parnes, S. J. & Harding, H. F. (eds.) *A source book for creative thinking.* New York: Scribner's, 1962, 64–72.

Starkweather, E. K. Problems in the measurement of creativity in preschool children. *Journal of Educational Measurement,* 1964, *1*, 109–133.

Starkweather, E. K. Studies of the creative potential of young children. In F. E. Williams (ed.) *Creativity at home and in school,* Saint Paul: Macalester College, 1968, 75–122.

Taft, R. and Rossiter, J. The remote associates test: divergent or convergent thinking? *Psychological Reports,* 1966, **19**, 1313–1314.

Taylor, I. A. The nature of the creative process. In Smith, P. (ed.), *Creativity.* New York: Hastings House, 1959.

Thorndike, R. L. Some methodological issues in the study of creativity. In *Proceedings of the 1962 invitational conference on testing problems.* Princeton, N.J.: Educational Testing Sevice, 1963b.

Torrance, E. P. *Torrance Tests of Creative Thinking: Norms—technical manual.* Princeton, N.J.: Personnel Press, 1966.

Van Mondfrans, A. P., Feldhusen, J. F., Treffinger, D. & Ferris, D.

The effects of instructions and working time on divergent thinking scores. *Psychology in the Schools*, 1970, in press.

Wallach, M. Review of the Torrance Tests of Creative Thinking. *American Educational Research Journal*, 1968, **5**, 272–281.

Wallach, M. A. Creativity and the expression of possibilities. In Graubard, S. R. & Kagan, J. (eds.), *Creativity and Learning*. Boston: Houghton Mifflin, in press.

Wallach, M. A. & Kogan, N. *Modes of thinking in young children: A study of the creativity-intelligence distinction*. New York: Holt, Rinehart and Winston, 1965.

Wallen, N. E. & Stevenson, G. M. Stability and correlates of judged creativity in fifth grade writings. *Journal of Educational Psychology*, 1960, **51**, 273–276.

Ward, V. S. Developing productive thinking: Educational implications. Paper presented at the Second Conference on Productive Thinking, National Education Association, Washington, D.C.: May 2–4, 1963.

Yamamoto, K. Evaluation of some creativity measures in a high school with peer nominations as criteria. *Journal of Psychology*, 1964, **58**, 285–293.

Joseph S. Renzulli
Robert K. Hartman
Carolyn M. Callahan

Teacher Identification of Superior Students

*I*n recent years a number of writers have called attention to a broadened conception of giftedness and the need for a wider range of criteria in the process of identifying gifted, talented, and creative youth (Getzels & Jackson, 1958; Jarecky, 1959; Witty, 1965). Although traditional tests of intelligence and achievement have been the major criteria for screening and selecting superior students, the role of teacher judgment is beginning to play an increasingly important part in efforts to place students in special educational programs that are designed to meet the needs of highly able youngsters (Cutts & Moseley, 1957; Pegnato & Birch, 1959).

In a comprehensive review of the literature dealing with the role of teacher judgment in the identification process, Gallagher (1966) pointed out some of the major weaknesses of teacher ratings. Because of the "frighteningly low level of effectiveness" of unstructured teacher judgment, Gallagher suggested a cautious approach to accepting teacher judgment as a basis for identification and concluded by saying that "most authorities would agree that teachers' opinions definitely need supplementing with more objective rating methods [p. 12]."

The development of the *Scale for Rating Behavioral Characteristics of Superior Students* (SRBCSS)* represents an attempt to provide a more objective and systematic instrument that can be used as an aid in guiding teacher judgment in the identification process. It is not intended to replace existing identification procedures such as measures of intelligence, achievement, and creativity; rather it is offered as a supplementary means that can be used in conjunction with other criteria for identification.

Procedures in the Development of the Scale

Initial "input" for the construction of the SRBCSS was derived from a comprehensive review of the literature dealing with characteristics or traits of superior students. Research studies relating to each of the four dimensions of the instrument were searched and categorized in an effort to isolate observable behavioral characteristics which were supported by common agreement among well known contributors to the literature. For a scale item to be included in the instrument, it was necessary that at least three separate studies had called attention to the importance of a given characteristic. These supportive studies are cited after each item in the scale.

The first experimental edition of the instrument was field tested in a number of school districts offering programs for gifted and talented students. Teachers and counselors completing the scale were asked to provide reactions about the effectiveness and usability of the instrument. Specifically, they were asked to make suggestions relating to clarity of expression, observability of traits, independence of items, and the ability of the instruments to make meaningful discriminations among students on each of the respective scales. This information led to the construction of the present edition, which includes several revisions based on the valuable feedback provided by classroom teachers, counselors, and special program personnel.

A series of studies was conducted to obtain information about the reliability and validity of the SRBCSS. The stability of the instrument (test-retest reliability) and interjudge reliability were established by asking two sets of teachers to rate the same population of students after an interval of 3 months had elapsed. The students were enrolled in fifth and sixth grades and spent a portion of their time each day with the teachers who completed the rating scales.

As can be seen from Table 1, the stability of ratings over time and the consistency of ratings among judges appears to be quite high, and thus these data lend support to the reliability of the instrument.

An attempt was made to determine if the SRBCSS could sufficiently discriminate between groups of children who had been previously classified as "gifted" or "average." The teachers of two special classes for gifted fifth grade students and the teachers of two average fifth grades in the same school were asked to rate each of their students with the SRBCSS. These ratings and test information relating to the intelligence and achievement of

TABLE 1
Stability and Interjudge Reliability Correlations for SRBCSS

Scale	Coefficient of stability (N = 78)	Interjudge reliability (N = 80)
Learning	.88**	.89**
Motivation	.91**	.85**
Creativity	.79**	.91**
Leadership	.77**	.67**

**p < .01

152

TABLE 2
**Means, Standard Deviations, and Analysis of Variance Comparisons
Between Gifted and Average Groups**

Variable	Gifted group (N = 40)		Average group (N = 40)		
	Mean	SD	Mean	SD	F
SRBCSS scales:					
Learning	24.43	6.27	16.00	7.22	41.04**
Motivation	24.43	5.46	17.95	5.50	27.95**
Creativity	25.01	7.64	17.13	4.70	31.43**
Leadership	29.48	5.17	22.33	6.45	29.88**
IQ	136.90	4.73	108.93	9.66	270.55**
Language achievement	53.73	3.37	33.25	6.74	267.30**
Math achievement	43.80	3.93	31.98	7.88	103.41**
Total achievement	47.50	3.37	32.63	6.18	178.53**

**p < 0.01

TABLE 3
**Correlations Between SRBCSS Scales and Standardized Tests of
Intelligence, Achievement, and Creativity**

Variable	Learning (N = 40)	Motivation (N = 40)	Creativity (N = 28)
Intelligence	.61**	.36*	—
Language achievement	.41**	.42**	—
Mathematics achievement	.57**	.60**	—
Total achievement	.46**	.50**	—
Verbal fluency	—	—	.37*
Verbal flexibility	—	—	.44*
Verbal originality	—	—	.48**
Figural fluency	—	—	.28
Figural flexibility	—	—	.29
Figural originality	—	—	.24
Figural elaboration	—	—	.29

*p < .05
**p < .01

the two groups are summarized in Table 2. Comparisons between the two
groups were made by means of a one-way analysis of variance for each
variable, and in every case a significant difference was found between the
gifted and average groups.

A further attempt was made to determine the validity of the SRBCSS
by comparing scores on the Learning and Motivation Scales with scores
from standardized tests of intelligence and achievement and by comparing
scores on the creativity scale with scores from the *Torrance Tests of Creative
Thinking* (TTCT). These data are summarized in Table 3. The Learning
and Motivation Scales correlate fairly well with measures that traditionally
have been used to select students for academically oriented gifted programs.

153

The Creativity Scale compares favorably with the verbal subscores of the TTCT; however, a low nonsignificant relationship was found between this scale and the noverbal subscores of the TTCT. This finding reflects a verbal bias in the Creativity Scale items and suggests that caution should be exercised in using this scale to identify students for programs that emphasize nonverbal creativity.

The Leadership Characteristics Scale was validated by comparing teachers' ratings on the SRBCSS with peer ratings that were obtained through standard sociometric techniques (Hartman, 1969). These groups of students in grades 4, 5, and 6 were asked to rate their classmates on three hypothetical leadership situations involving social, athletic, and intellectual skills. The results of this inquiry are presented in Table 4. The relatively high correlations for fourth and fifth graders indicate that teacher estimates of leadership ability based on the SRBCSS are in close agreement with students' perceptions of the leadership characteristics of their class-mates. The somewhat lower correlations for sixth graders may be due to the fact that youngsters at this grade level tended to restrict their choices to classmates of the same sex.

Each item on the Leadership Characteristics Scale was further evaluated by comparing individual items with total leadership ratings. As shown in Table 5, the positive and generally high correlations for fourth and fifth graders tend to support the internal consistency of the Leadership Scale at these grade levels. Although the correlations for sixth graders are somewhat lower, there is a clear positive relationship between individual items and the total leadership score.

Suggestions for Using the Scale

Teachers can use the SRBCSS most effectively by analyzing students' ratings on each of the four respective scales separately. The four dimensions of the instrument represent relatively different sets of behavioral character-istics, and therefore, no attempt should be made to add the subscores together to form a total score. Students can be rated any time during the

TABLE 4
Correlations Between Sociometric Peer Ratings and SRBCSS Leadership Ratings

Sociometric peer ratings	Grades		
	4 (N = 26)	5 (N = 23)	6 (N = 23)
Social	.80**	.80**	.35*
Athletic	.75**	.82**	.27
Intellectual	.83**	.77**	.29
Total	.83**	.84**	.23

*p < .05
**p < .01

TABLE 5

Correlations Between Total SRBCSS Leadership Ratings and Individual Scale Items

Individual items on SRBCSS leadership scale	Total SRBCSS leadership rating Grades		
	4 (N = 26)	5 (N = 23)	6 (N = 23)
1. Responsibility	.73**	.88**	.48*
2. Self confidence	.87**	.93**	.34
3. Popularity	.83**	.84**	.46*
4. Cooperativeness	.71**	.76**	.30
5. Verbal facility	.73**	.82**	.36*
6. Adaptability	.71**	.83**	.57**
7. Sociability	.64**	.73**	.53**
8. Dominance	.56**	.75**	.33
9. Social participation	.63**	.79**	.57**
10. Athletic ability	.63**	.70**	.61**

*$p < .05$
**$p < .01$

school year; however, the earlier the observations are made, the more use can be made of the results in helping to identify and develop student abilities to the fullest. It is also valuable to obtain ratings from several teachers and counselors who are familiar with a youngster's performance.

Because of variations in student populations, methods of programming for superior students, and the availability of other data that can be used in the screening and identification process, it is impossible to provide the user with a predetermined set of cutoff scores for the scales. The instrument can be used most profitably by computing a mean score on each dimension for the total number of students who are being considered for enrollment in a special program. Those students who deviate markedly upward from the mean should be considered likely candidates for placement in a program or activity that is designed to enhance particular abilities; however, the reader is reminded that the instrument is offered as one means for guiding teacher judgment in the screening and identification process. Whenever possible, it should be used in conjunction with other instruments and techniques as part of a comprehensive system for the identification of superior students.

A guiding principle in using the SRBCSS emphasizes the relationship between a student's subscores and the types of curricular experiences that will be offered in a special program. Every effort should be made to capitalize on an individual's strengths by developing learning experiences that take account of the area or areas in which the student has received high ratings. For example, a student who earns high ratings on the Motivational Characteristics Scale will probably profit most from a program that emphasizes self initiated pursuits and an independent study approach to learning. A student with high scores on the Leadership Characteristics Scale should be given opportunities to organize activities and to assist the teacher and his classmates in developing plans of action for carrying out projects.

In addition to looking at a student's profile of subscores for identification purposes, teachers can derive several useful hints for programming by analyzing student ratings on individual scale items. These items call attention to differences in behavioral characteristics and in most cases suggest the kinds of educational experiences that are most likely to represent the youngster's preferred method or style of learning. Thus, a careful analysis of scale items can assist the teacher in her efforts to develop an individualized program of study for each student.

References

Cutts, N. E., & Moseley, N. *Teaching the bright and the gifted.* Englewood Cliffs, N.J.: Prentice-Hall, 1957.

Gallagher, J. J. *Research summary on gifted child education.* Springfield, Ill.: Superintendent of Public Instruction, State of Illinois, 1966.

Getzels, J. W., & Jackson, P. W. The meaning of "giftedness"—An examination of an expanding concept. *Phi Delta Kappan, 1958,* **40,** 75–77.

Hartman, R. K. Teachers' identification of student. leaders. Unpublished paper, University of Connecticut, 1969. (Mimeo.)

Jarecky, R. K. Identification of the socially gifted. *Exceptional Children, 1959,* **25,** 415–419.

Pegnato, C. W., & Birch, J. W. Locating gifted children in junior high schools: A comparison of methods. *Exceptional Children, 1959,* **25,** 300–304.

Witty, P. A decade of progress in the study of the gifted and creative pupil. In W. B. Barbe (Ed.), *Psychology and education for the gifted.* New York: Appleton-Century-Crofts, 1965, 35–39.

Joseph S. Renzulli
Robert K. Hartman

Scale for Rating Behavioral Characteristics of Superior Students

Name ——————————————— ——————————————— Date ———————————

School ———————————————————————Grade ————— Age —————————————
                                                                          Years   Months

Teacher or person completing this form ————————————————————————

How long have you known this child? ————————————————— Months.

Directions. These scales are designed to obtain teacher estimates of a student's characteristics in the areas of learning, motivation, creativity, and leadership. The items are derived from the research literature dealing with characteristics of gifted and creative persons. It should be pointed out that a considerable amount of individual differences can be found within this population; and therefore, the profiles are likely to vary a great deal. Each item in the scales should be considered separately and should reflect the degree to which you have observed the presence or absence of each characteristic. Since the four dimensions of the instrument represent relatively different sets of behaviors, the scores obtained from the separate scales should *not* be summed to yield a total score. Please read the statements carefully and place an X in the appropriate place according to the following scale of values:

1. If you have *seldom* or *never* observed this characteristic.
2. If you have observed this characteristic *occasionally*.
3. If you have observed this characteristic to a *considerable* degree.
4. If you have observed this characteristic *almost all of the time*.

Space has been provided following each item for your comments.

Scoring. Separate scores for each of the three dimensions may be obtained as follows:

- *Add* the total number of X's in each column to obtain the "Column Total."
- *Multiply* the Column Total by the "Weight" for each column to obtain the "Weighted Column Total."
- *Sum* the Weighted Column Totals across to obtain the "Score" for each dimension of the scale.
- *Enter* the Scores below.

Learning Characteristics .... ——————————
Motivational Characteristics .... ——————————
Creativity Characteristics .... ——————————
Leadership Characteristics .... ——————————

Part I: Learning Characteristics

	1*	2	3	4
1. Has unusually advanced vocabulary for age or grade level; uses terms in a meaningful way; has verbal behavior characterized by "richness" of expression, elaboration, and fluency. (National Education Association, 1960; Terman & Oden, 1947; Witty, 1955)	☐	☐	☐	☐
2. Possesses a large storehouse of information about a variety of topics (beyond the usual interests of youngsters his age). (Ward, 1961; Terman, 1925; Witty, 1958)	☐	☐	☐	☐
3. Has quick mastery and recall of factual information. (Goodhart & Schmidt, 1940; Terman & Oden, 1947; National Education Association, 1960)	☐	☐	☐	☐
4. Has rapid insight into cause-effect relationships; tries to discover the how and why of things; asks many provocative questions (as distinct from informational or factual questions); wants to know what makes things (or people) "tick." (Carroll, 1940; Witty, 1958; Goodhart & Schmidt, 1940)	☐	☐	☐	☐
5. Has a ready grasp of underlying principles and can quickly make valid generalizations about events, people, or things; looks for similarities and differences in events, people, and things. (Bristow, 1951; Carroll, 1940; Ward, 1961)	☐	☐	☐	☐
6. Is a keen and alert observer; usually "sees more" or "gets more" out of a story, film, etc. than others. (Witty, 1958; Carroll, 1940; National Education Association, 1960)	☐	☐	☐	☐
7. Reads a great deal on his own; usually prefers adult level books; does not avoid difficult material; may show a preference for biography, autobiography, encyclopedias, and atlases. (Hollingworth, 1942; Witty, 1958; Terman & Oden, 1947)	☐	☐	☐	☐
8. Tries to understand complicated material by separating it into its respective parts; reasons things out for himself; sees logical and common sense answers. (Freehill, 1961; Ward, 1962; Strang, 1958)	☐	☐	☐	☐
Column Total	☐	☐	☐	☐
Weight	1	2	3	4
Weighted Column Total	☐	☐	☐	☐
Total				☐

---

*1—Seldom or never
2—Occasionally
3—Considerably
4—Almost always

158

Part II: Motivational Characteristics

	1	2	3	4
1. Becomes absorbed and truly involved in certain topics or problems; is persistent in seeking task completion. (It is sometimes difficult to get him to move on to another topic.) (Freehill, 1961; Brandwein, 1955; Strang, 1958)	☐	☐	☐	☐
2. Is easily bored with routine tasks. (Ward, 1962; Terman & Oden, 1947; Ward, 1961)	☐	☐	☐	☐
3. Needs little external motivation to follow through in work that initially excites him. (Carroll, 1940; Ward, 1961; Villars, 1957)	☐	☐	☐	☐
4. Strives toward perfection; is self critical; is not easily satisfied with his own speed or products. (Strang, 1958; Freehill, 1961; Carroll, 1940)	☐	☐	☐	☐
5. Prefers to work independently; requires little direction from teachers. (Torrance, 1965; Gowan & Demos, 1964; Mokovic, 1953)	☐	☐	☐	☐
6. Is interested in many "adult" problems such as religion, politics, sex, race—more than usual for age level. (Witty, 1955; Ward, 1961; Chaffee, 1963)	☐	☐	☐	☐
7. Often is self assertive (sometimes even aggressive); stubborn in his beliefs. (Buhler & Guirl, 1963; Gowan & Demos, 1964; Ward, 1961)	☐	☐	☐	☐
8. Likes to organize and bring structure to things, people, and situations. (Ward, 1961; Gowan & Demos, 1964; Buhler & Guirl, 1963)	☐	☐	☐	☐
9. Is quite concerned with right and wrong, good and bad; often evaluates and passes judgment on events, people, and things. (Getzels & Jackson, 1962; Buhler & Guirl, 1963; Carroll, 1940)	☐	☐	☐	☐
Column Total	☐	☐	☐	☐
Weight	1	2	3	4
Weighted Column Total	☐	☐	☐	☐
Total			☐	

Part III: Creativity Characteristics

	1	2	3	4
1. Displays a great deal of curiosity about many things; is constantly asking questions about anything and everything. (National Education Association, 1960; Goodhart & Schmidt, 1940; Torrance, 1962)	☐	☐	☐	☐
2. Generates a large number of ideas or solutions to problems and questions; often offers unusual ("way out"), unique, clever responses. (Carroll, 1940; Hollingworth, 1942; National Education Association, 1960)	☐	☐	☐	☐

159

3. Is uninhibited in expressions of opinion; is sometimes radical and spirited in disagreement; is tenacious. (Torrance, 1965; Gowan & Demos, 1964; Getzels & Jackson, 1962) ☐ ☐ ☐ ☐

4. Is a high risk taker; is adventurous and speculative. (Getzels & Jackson, 1962; Villars, 1957; Torrance, 1965) ☐ ☐ ☐ ☐

5. Displays a good deal of intellectual playfulness; fantasizes; imagines ("I wonder what would happen if. . . ."); manipulates ideas (i.e., changes, elaborates upon them); is often concerned with adapting, improving, and modifying institutions, objects, and systems. (Rogers, 1959; Gowan & Demos, 1964; Getzels & Jackson, 1962) ☐ ☐ ☐ ☐

6. Displays a keen sense of humor and sees humor in situations that may not appear to be humorous to others. (Torrance, 1962; Gowan & Demos, 1964; Getzels & Jackson, 1962) ☐ ☐ ☐ ☐

7. Is unusually aware of his impulses and more open to the irrational in himself (freer expression of feminine interest for boys, greater than usual amount of independence for girls); shows emotional sensitivity. (Torrance, 1962; Rothney & Coopman, 1958; Gowan & Demos, 1964) ☐ ☐ ☐ ☐

8. Is sensitive to beauty; attends to aesthetic characteristics of things. (Wilson, 1965; Witty, 1958; Villars, 1957) ☐ ☐ ☐ ☐

9. Is nonconforming; accepts disorder; is not interested in details; is individualistic; does not fear being different. (Carroll, 1940; Buhler & Guirl, 1963; Getzels & Jackson, 1962) ☐ ☐ ☐ ☐

Criticizes constructively; is unwilling to accept authoritarian pronouncements without critical examination. (Ward, 1962; Martinson, 1963; Torrance, 1962) ☐ ☐ ☐ ☐

Column Total ☐ ☐ ☐ ☐

Weight 1 2 3 4

Weighted Column Total ☐ ☐ ☐ ☐

Total ▭

Part IV: Leadership Characteristics

	1	2	3	4
1. Carries responsibility well; can be counted on to do what he has promised and usually does it well. (Baldwin, 1932; Bellingrath, 1930; Burks, 1938)	☐	☐	☐	☐
2. Is self confident with children his own age as well as adults; seems comfortable when asked to show his work to the class. (Drake, 1944; Cowley, 1931; Bellingrath, 1930)	☐	☐	☐	☐
3. Seems to be well liked by his classmates. (Bellingrath, 1930; Garrison, 1935; Zeleny, 1939)	☐	☐	☐	☐
4. Is cooperative with teacher and classmates; tends to avoid bickering and is generally easy to get along with. (Dunkerly, 1940; Newcomb, 1943; Fauquier & Gilchrist, 1942)	☐	☐	☐	☐

5. Can express himself well; has good verbal facility and is usually well understood. (Simpson, 1938; Terman, 1904; Burks, 1938) ☐ ☐ ☐ ☐

6. Adapts readily to new situations; is flexible in thought and action and does not seem disturbed when the normal routine is changed. (Eichler, 1934; Flemming, 1935; Caldwell, 1926) ☐ ☐ ☐ ☐

7. Seems to enjoy being around other people; is sociable and prefers not to be alone. (Drake, 1944; Goodenough, 1930; Bonney, 1943) ☐ ☐ ☐ ☐

8. Tends to dominate others when they are around; generally directs the activity in which he is involved. (Richardson & Hanawalt, 1943; Hunter & Jordan, 1939; Bowden, 1926) ☐ ☐ ☐ ☐

9. Participates in most social activities connected with the school; can be counted on to be there if anyone is. (Zeleny, 1939; Link, 1944; Courtenay, 1938) ☐ ☐ ☐ ☐

10. Excels in athletic activities; is well coordinated and enjoys all sorts of athletic games. (Flemming, 1935; Partridge, 1934; Spaulding, 1934) ☐ ☐ ☐ ☐

Column Total ☐ ☐ ☐ ☐

Weight [1] [2] [3] [4]

Weighted Column Total ☐ ☐ ☐ ☐

Total [_____]

References

Baldwin, L. E. A study of factors usually associated with high school male leadership. Unpublished Masters thesis, Ohio State University, 1932.

Bellingrath, G. C. Qualities associated with leadership in extracurricular activities of the high school. *Teachers College Contributions to Education*, 1930, No. 399.

Bonney, M. E. The constancy of sociometric scores and their relationship to teacher judgments of social success and to personality self-ratings. *Sociometry*, 1943, **6**, 409-424.

Bowden, A. O. A study of the personality of student leaders in colleges in the United States. *Journal of Abnormal and Social Psychology*, 1926, **21**, 149–160.

Brandwein, P. *The gifted student as future scientist*. New York: Harcourt Brace, 1955.

Bristow, W. Identifying gifted children. In P. A. Witty (Ed.), *The gifted child*. Boston: Heath, 1951. Pp. 10–19.

Buhler, E. O., & Guirl, E. N. The more able student: Described and rated. In L. D. Crow and A. Crow (Eds.), *Educating the academically able*. New York: David McKay, 1963.

Burks, F. W. Some factors related to social success in college. *Journal of Social Psychology*, 1938, **9**, 125–140.

Caldwell, O. W., & Wellman, B. Characteristics of school leaders. *Journal of Educational Research*, 1926, **14**, 1–15.

Carroll, H. *Genius in the making*. New York: McGraw-Hill, 1940.

Chaffee, E. General policies concerning education of intellectually gifted pupils in Los Angeles. In L. D. Crow and A. Crow (Eds.), *Educating the academically able*. New York: David McKay, 1963.

Courtenay, M. E. Persistence of leadership. *School Review*, 1938, **46**, 97–107.

Cowley, W. H. Traits of face-to-face leaders. *Journal of Abnormal and Social Psychology*, 1931, **26**, 304–313.

Drake, R. M. A study of leadership. *Character and Personality*, 1944, **12**, 285–289.

Dunkerly, M. D. A statistical study of leadership among college women. *Studies in Psychology and Psychiatry*, 1940, **4**, 1–65.

Eichler, G. A. Studies in student leadership. *Penn State College Studies in Education*, 1934, No. 10.

Fauquier, W., & Gilchrist, T. Some aspects of leadership in an institution. *Child Development*, 1942, **13**, 55–64.

Flemming, E. G. A factor analysis of the personality of high school leaders. *Journal of Applied Psychology*, 1935, **19**, 596–605.

Freehill, M. F. *Gifted children: Their psychology and education*. New York: Macmillan, 1961.

Garrison, K. C. A study of some factors related to leadership in high school. *Peabody Journal of Education*, 1935, **11**, 11–17.

Getzels, J. W., & Jackson, P. W. *Creativity and intelligence*. New York: Wiley, 1962.

Goodenough, F. L. Inter-relationships in the behavior of young children. *Child Development*, 1930, **1**, 29–48.

Goodhart, B. F., & Schmidt, S. D. Educational characteristics of superior children. *Baltimore Bulletin of Education,* 1940, **18**, 14–17.

Gowan, J. C., & Demos, G. D. *The education and guidance of the ablest*. Springfield, Ill.: Charles C. Thomas, 1964.

Hollingworth, L. S. *Children above 180 IQ*. Yonkers, N.Y.: World Book, 1942.

Hunter, E. C., & Jordan, A. M. An analysis of qualities associated with leadership among college students. *Journal of Educational Psychology*, 1939, **30**, 497–509.

Link, H. C. The definition of social effectiveness and leadership through measurement. *Educational and Psychological Measurement*, 1944, **4**, 57–67.

Makovic, M. V. The gifted child. In W. F. Jenks (Ed.), *Special education of the exceptional child*. Washington, D.C: Catholic University Press, 1953, Pp. 56–71.

Martinson, R. A. Guidance of the gifted. In L. D. Crow and A. Crow (Eds.), *Educating the academically able*. New York: David McKay, 1963. Pp. 176–182.

National Education Association. *NEA administration: Procedures and school practices for the academically talented student in the secondary school.* Washington, D.C: NEA, 1960.

Newcomb, T. M. *Personality and social change.* New York: Dryden Press, 1943.

Partridge. E. D. Leadership among adolescent boys. *Teachers College Contribution to Education*, 1934, No. 608.

Richardson, H. M. & Hanawalt N. G. Leadership as related to Bernreuter personality measures: I. College leadership in extra curricular activities. *Journal of Social Psychology*, 1943, **17**, 237–249

Rogers, C. R. Toward a theory of creativity. In H. H. Anderson (ed.), *Creativity and its cultivation.* New York: Harper & Brothers, 1959. Pp. 75–76.

Rothney, J. W., & Koopman, N. E. Guidance of the gifted. In N. D. Henry (Ed.), Education for the gifted. *Yearbook of the National Society for the Study of Education*, 1958, **57** (Part II), 346–361.

Simpson, R. H. A study of those who influence and of those who are influenced in discussion. *Teachers College Contributions to Education*, 1938, No. 748.

Spaulding, C. B. Types of junior college leaders. *Sociology and Social Research*, 1934, **18**, 164–168.

Strang, R. The nature of giftedness. In N. D. Henry (Ed.), Education for the gifted. *Yearbook of the National Society for the Study of Education*, 1958, 57 (Part II), 64-86.

Terman, L. M. A preliminary study in the psychology and pedagogy of leadership. Pedagogical Seminary, 1904, **11**, 413–451.

Terman, L. M. (Ed.) Genetic studies of genius. Vol. 1. *Mental and physical traits of a thousand gifted children.* Stanford, Cal.: Stanford University Press, 1925.

Terman, L. M., & Oden, M. H. *The gifted child grows up.* Stanford, Cal.: Stanford University Press, 1947.

Torrance, E. P. *Guiding creative talent.* Englewood Cliffs, N.J.: Prentice-Hall, 1962.

Torrance, E. P. *Rewarding creative behavior.* Englewood Cliffs, N.J.: Prentice-Hall, 1965.

Villars, G. (Ed.), *Educating the gifted in Minnesota schools.* St. Paul, Minn.: Commissioner of Education, State of Minnesota, Department of Education, 1957.

Ward, V. S. *Educating the gifted.* Columbus, Ohio: Charles E. Merrill, 1961.

Ward, V. S. *The gifted student: A manual for regional improvement.* Atlanta: Southern Regional Education Board, 1962.

Wilson, F. T. Some special ability test scores of gifted children. In W. B. Barbe (Ed.), *Psychology and education of gifted.* New York: Appleton-Century-Crofts, 1965. Pp. 103–113.

Witty, P. Gifted children—Our greatest resource. *Nursing Education*, 1955, **47**, 498–500.

Witty, P. Who are the gifted? In N. D. Henry (Ed.), Education for the gifted. *Yearbook of the National Society for the Study of Education*, 1958, **57** (Part II), 41–63.

Zeleny, L. Characteristics of group leaders. *Sociology and Social Research*, 1939, **24**, 140–149.

Robert L. Ellison, Clifford Abe,
David G. Fox, Kevin E. Coray, Calvin W. Taylor

Using Biographical Information In Identifying Artistic Talent

Introduction

Biographical information has been used frequently in the past to predict performances in areas such as management (Laurent, 1970), scientific creativity (Taylor & Ellison, 1967), and less frequently in artistic talent. Such research on artistic talent, for example, could result in improved selection procedures; an examination of these biographical keys built to predict such behavior can provide a profile of the person who is most likely to be gifted and talented in artistic and musical endeavors.

Another perspective and use for biographical information that has been explored recently is to provide information about the kinds and types of artistic and musical activities and experiences to which students have been exposed. This kind of information is valuable to teachers and school administrators as they plan curricula that gives each student opportunities to participate in different types of artistic pursuits. This particular use of biographical information is a valuable supplement, to the more typical use of such information—that of prediction and selection—and provides useful information to those concerned with the development of artistic talent and sensitivity in this society. While students who are talented and gifted in the arts need to be identified, comprehensive programs that allow all students to benefit from such training should also be of high priority.

This article will examine such uses of biographical data in conjunction with other considerations and practices involved, including the criterion problem of defining high level performance in the arts and the validity generalization of the results obtained.

Biographical Information in Predicting Criteria of Artistic Performance

Anastasi (1961) noted that there has been little progress in the development of tests designed to measure aesthetic abilities. Since that time, the

165

identification of artistic talent and the selection and placement of students into special educational programs or schools for the gifted and talented has been the subject of some research, particularly with biographical data (Anastasi & Schaefer, 1969; Ellison, James, Fox, & Taylor, 1971; James, Ellison, Fox, & Taylor, 1974; Schaefer & Anastasi, 1968).

Students are often selected for training programs on the basis of formal and informal procedures which are finalized by the judgment of several "expert" raters in conjunction with general measures, such as GPA and participation in various activities. Such methods may have face validity, but frequently they continue to be used for long periods of time without being evaluated. The present studies looked at the possibility of using biographical characteristics in predicting artistic achievement as part of the selection process. This seemed to be a viable alternative, because of the high predictive validity of biographical information in the past in predicting different kinds of performances (Ellison, James, & Fox, 1970; Taylor & Ellison, 1967).

Relatively little has been done to evaluate the selection methods as to the degree to which the selected students meet the selection criteria or the relevance of the selection criteria to more ultimate criteria, e.g., the extent to which selected students actually become artists, and the relevance of the selection standards for actual artistic achievement as measured by the performance of demonstrated and accepted artists. An evaluation of selection and placement methods would help determine whether those students selected for special programs or schools do, in fact, differ on desired dimensions from those students who are not selected.

Prediction studies necessarily become involved with the criterion problem, which has been the subject of much controversy and debate (Astin, 1964; Brogden & Taylor, 1967; Muthard & Miller, 1966), but little resolution. Criteria should be effective indicators of high levels of performance, while facilitating the development of predictors to be used later as indicators of the desired standards of performance.

The results obtained by Ellison et al. (1971) indicated the feasibility of studies of artistic performance that use common criteria and predictors across different art areas, such as music, dance, theater, and the visual arts. In this study, the relationships among teacher ratings of student sensitivity, motivation, expression of self, and potential and separate criterion measures specifically designed for each artistic area provided evidence that these ratings were pertinent measures of artistic performance within each of the four artistic areas. Furthermore, the criteria were generally predictable across the different samples. This is not to imply that studies within separate art areas or comparisons between areas would not yield higher validities. Additional criterion development and construct validation of art criteria are needed.

Biographical keys used to predict performance are usually built and evaluated on the group from which the sample has been selected. Infrequently, these keys have been used over time and across different samples.

Studies in which this occurs yield information concerning the validity generalization of the biographical keys. The following study investigated three constructs (artistic performance, academic achievement, and leadership) with keys which were built and validated on other samples (Ellison et al., 1971; IBRIC, 1968).

The North Carolina Study[1]

The focus of the study was the selection of students for the Governor's School of North Carolina—the oldest summer residential honors program in the nation, offering advanced training in the arts and academic areas—and the Leadership School which offers advanced leadership training and experience. This study was designed to develop effective predictors of achievement in artistic talent, academic performance, and leadership and to simplify existing selection procedures for the two special schools essentially free of racial bias. Extensive review and screening processes had previously been developed for these two schools, but there was also a perceived need for efficient selection techniques, essentially free from racial bias.

A sample of 1086 North Carolina 11th and 12th grade students was taken principally from four schools—the two specialized schools and two control schools. In addition, other students were nominated by teachers in various North Carolina communities as having exceptional ability in the areas of art and music and were included in the sample.

Form R, a specially developed version of the *Biographical Inventory, (BI)*, was used to collect life history information for predicting academic achievement, leadership ability, and artistic talent. The criteria were delineated by a student being selected for a special program for the gifted and talented or by teacher nominations. Form R is a composite instrument made up of 300 multiple-choice items in which an individual describes himself and his background. The rationale in using such an instrument is very simple—that past behavior, experiences, and self-descriptions can be used as indicators of future performance.

An IQ score—the Otis Mental Ability Score—was included as a traditional predictor of academic achievement. A demographic data form completed by the student's counselor supplied the following information: the student's sex, race, grade level, scaled grade point average, a rating of the student's family income, and the type of community in which the student lived.

The results indicated that the biographical information scores which

The research studies described in this article were supported by grants from the North Carolina State Department of Public Instruction and the Utah State Board of Education.

167

resulted from extensive screening procedures, involving teacher nominations, interviews, and other provisions were extremely effective predictors of criterion group membership. Table 1 gives the validity coefficients for the three BI key scores that were of the most interest in this study—Art and Music, Leadership, and Academic Achievement— against a variety of criterion and control scores.

1. To stimulate his son in the pursuit of partial differential equations a math professor offered to pay him $8 for every equation correctly solved and to fine him $5 for every incorrect solution. At the end of 26 problems, neither owed any money to the other. How many did the boy solve correctly? (Answer at end of article).

Table 1 shows that the cross-validity coefficients for the keys developed in earlier studies against the artistic, leadership, and academic achievement criteria were .65, .58, and .72, respectively. These cross-validities are extremely high and are considerably more effective than the results typically reported for predicting these criteria. Since the keys were constructed on other samples to predict related but different kinds of criteria, the results indicate a considerable degree of validity generalization.

The results also indicate that biographical scores had very low relationships with membership in various ethnic groups. This was in marked contrast to the results obtained with the Otis Mental Ability Score, where minority students had lower scores. The Otis Mental Ability Score also had high validities, but like the BI keys, the obtained validities were somewhat overstated as a function of the sample selection not being random. In random samples, validities more nearly like those obtained in the Ellison et al. (1971) study might be expected, e.g., .50. Also in this study, a pattern of generally low correlations between academic grade point average and artistic criteria was found, also be the expected finding for the Otis score.

The results also pointed out the need for attention and effort that should be devoted to identifying talent among low income groups, as such students have fewer opportunities for selection into the kinds of special

Table 1
Cross-Validity Coefficients for Three A Priori Biographical Keys
Against Criterion and Control Scores

Variable	Artistic Talent Key	Leadership Key	GPA Key
Criterion Scores:			
1. Art and Music	.65*	.25*	.44*
2. Leadership	.52*	.58*	.50*
3. Academic Achievement	.61*	.30*	.72*
Control Scores:			
4. Race	.25*	.02	.11*
5. Sex	−.03	−.07	.02
6. Economic Status	.29*	.13*	.21*

*p < .01

168

programs examined in this study. In general, the conclusions reached through the analysis of the North Carolina data were:

1. Since biographical data have resulted in highly significant validities in identifying the criteria of creativity in art and music, leadership, and academic achievement, further examination and use of the biographical approach is warranted for a wide range of potential applications to help students realize their potential.
2. The Biographical Inventory should be used to help select students for specialized programs within the State of North Carolina. The BI not only contributes to the accuracy of prediction, but also has less racial bias than more traditional measures.
3. Biographical data could help teachers to become aware of the different types of students who have high potential in various specialized areas and of the contribution that they can make in aiding these students to achieve their full potential.

Profile of Artistic Talent Characteristics

An examination of the biographical key and the item statistics for the items within that key provides an insight into the type of person who is most likely to exhibit artistic potential. This information is summarized in Table 2 which presents data on the biographical characteristics associated with high levels of artistic talent.

2 Find the smallest number (x) of persons a boat may carry so that (n) married couples may cross a river in such a way that no woman ever remains in the company of any man unless her husband is present. Also find the least number of passages (y) needed from one bank to the other. Assume that the boat can be rowed by one person only. (Answer at end of article).

The Utah Statewide Assessment Study

The Utah Statewide Educational Assessment was conducted to determine the effectiveness of the educational system in the State of Utah in five different goal areas, among which was the Aesthetic Maturity. These goal areas were designed to provide perspective and direction to staff members of the State Board of Education and all others concerned with education within the state. The Aesthetic Maturity goal area and the general objectives, which provided further definition, then, were designed to provide the setting within which the art and music programs within the state ideally could operate. The Aesthetic Maturity goal area (Utah State Board of Education, 1973) states that:

169

TABLE 2
Examples of Biographical Correlates of Artistic Talent

The person with the following characteristics tended to be identified as having artistic talent

1. Was taking college preparatory courses
2. Intended to obtain a graduate degree
3. Both parents had graduated from college
4. Very responsible and dependable
5. Enjoyed reading literary classics, not novels or mysteries
6. Had no trouble adapting to school rules
7. Had outstanding sensitivity to and awareness of the environment
8. Preferred classical music
9. Was highly competitive, confident and ambitious
10. Stands up for personal beliefs
11. Felt career security less important than advancement potential, personal freedom, or self-expression
12. Preferred a job offering advancement, even at the risk of dismissal
13. Felt that his school lacks adequate facilities
14. Felt that being creative and imaginative is important
15. Preferred to work alone
16. Felt that personal interests have interfered with social life and school work
17. Considered himself outstanding in speed and completion of artistic and academic work
18. Felt he had good knowledge and techniques in his specialty
19. Was willing to discuss problem assignments with teachers
20. Often had a teacher who had taken a strong interest in him
21. Felt that his artistic teachers were outstanding
22. Received adequate recognition for his work from his teachers

An individual's aesthetic maturity is exemplified by an increasing sensitivity in perceiving the environment and acknowledging the human qualities of each individual; by a more satisfying use of one's senses in making aesthetic judgment; by more capably communicating aesthetic insights through the cultural arts; and through a greater harmony with oneself. (p. 16)

The Utah Statewide Educational Assessment (Ellison, Nelson, Abe, Fox & Coray, 1975) was administered to 4,400 5th grade students and 3,357 11th grade students throughout the state. One scale within this assessment was made up of 17 items concerned with *Art and Music Activities*. This scale dealt with participation in artistic endeavors and the attitudes of the student toward art and music. These items were largely developed from the Art and Music key of the North Carolina study, but the score was abbreviated and did not measure the full scope of the North Carolina score. The items included estimates of how often students participate in various kinds of artistic activities, self-ratings of capability in the arts and enjoyment of artistic activities, the value of artistic experiences, number of opportunities for participation in artistic kinds of activities, amount of training received outside of school, etc.

Art Education for March 1976 contains an excellent article by Prof. E. W. Eisner of Stanford "Making the Arts a Reality in the Schools of Tomorrow." Arguing for the primacy of art as a method of inducing creativity prior to verbal creativity he quotes Herbert Read that images

170

must precede articulation in discursive language, and that the image has special advantages in presenting to consciousness new relationships which could come to the verbal mode only after the initial vision or icon had been formed. Education was for Read a process of helping people realize their potential to create forms.

Table 3 shows the correlations of the *Art and Music Activities* scale with selected variables from the Utah Statewide Assessment. Unfortunately, no criterion measures were available for artistic performance, but a number of other measures of interest were included. The art and music achievement scores were specially constructed cognitive achievement measures and are not necessarily an indication of student potential for artistic endeavors. However, they do provide another indicator of student performance and offer another approach for talent identification. The predictive ability of the biographical items is again apparent in the magnitude of the highly significant correlations. It will be noticed that the *Art and Music Activities* scale was considerably more related to the art and music achievement measures than to the mathematics achievement measure.

The results of the Utah study indicated that there was a strong interest in art and music activities for a large percentage of Utah students. For example, 59% of the 5th grade students and 39% of the 11th grade students reported that they spend "quite a bit" or "a lot" of their spare time enjoying some kind of artistic activity (making pictures, studying music, ceramics, etc.). However, the results also indicated that some Utah students had neither become involved in, nor had they derived satisfaction from, different kinds of aesthetic pursuits. To illustrate, 21% of 5th grade students and 46% of the 11th grade students reported that, because of their art experiences in school, either their appreciation for art experiences had not changed considerably or that they avoid most art experiences.

On the total score for the *Art and Music Activities* scale, there were highly significant differences in the average scores obtained per school. These kinds of results provide information to help identify opportunities for improvement that can result in higher levels of student performance.

The influence of socio-economic status (SES) on this area was also very

TABLE 3
Correlations of the Art and Music Activities Scale of the Utah
Statewide Educational Assessment with Selected Variables

Variables	Art and Music Activities	
	5th	11th
Art Achievement	.27*	.38*
Music Achievement	.36*	.43*
Comprehensive Test of Basic Skills (CTBS)		
Mathematics Total Score	.15*	.06*
SES-Total	.27*	.23*

*p < .01

171

apparent and poses both difficulties and potential rewards in helping disadvantaged students realize their potential. The results indicated that a number of small schools in rural areas obtained approximately average scores on the music achievement test, in spite of the impact of low SES.

Some of the conclusions reached in this study included:

1. Utah educators need to review the art and music activities available to the students with the goal of matching activities with the interest level shown.
2. Utah teachers should consider specific strategies, such as additional pre-service and in-service training, innovative programs, allocation of more instructional time, and greater use of curriculum guides to increase the art and music achievement of Utah students.

Conclusions

The conclusions reached through the analyses of the two studies reported would include:

1. The biographical information approach should be used more frequently in identifying gifted students in art, music, leadership, and academic areas. The biographical approach has been superior to the more traditional measures used. The biographical approach does not appear to be racially biased as opposed to the more traditional testing instruments.
2. The characteristics that can be used to identify artists in one geographical area are reliable enough to predict artists in another area using different kinds of artistic criteria. These characteristics do not change drastically and can be studed in the investigation of the creative and talented person. Through the isolation of these characteristics, persons who are more likely to achieve in artistic endeavors can be more easily identified and encouraged to develop their capabilities.
3. Further research is needed which would more thoroughly integrate the evaluation of products and the study of creative individuals on a longitudinal basis to provide reliable and valid information concerning the factors that enter into the creative process. Predictive rather than concurrent validation studies are needed.
4. Although related, quite different subsets of talents and capabilities are needed for achievement in any given artistic area and for achievement in academic subjects. However, the person who was most likely to be an achiever artistically also tended to be a well-rounded individual. Additional independence among these talent areas may emerge from future research, since, for the samples studied, the high achieving academic student was more likely to be chosen for special programs and given more opportunity to exhibit artistic abilities.

References

Anastasi, A. *Psychological testing*. New York: Macmillan, 1961.

Anastasi, A., & Schaefer, C. E. Biographical correlates of artistic and literary creativity in adolescent girls. *Journal of Applied Psychology*, 1969, **53**, 267-273.

Astin, A. W. Criterion-centered research. *Educational and Psychological Measurement*, 1964, **24**, 807-822.

Brogden, H. E., & Taylor, E. K. A theory and classification of criterion bias. In D. A. Payne & R. F. McMorris (eds.), *Educational and psychological measurement*. Waltham, Mass.: Blaisdell, 1967.

Ellison, R. L., James, L. R., & Fox, D. G. *The identification of talent among Negro and white students from biographical data*. Report submitted to the U.S. Office of Education, DHEW. Grant No. OEG-8-9-540033-2026 (058). Project No. 9-H-033. 1970.

Ellison, R. L., James, L. R., Fox, D. G., & Taylor, C. W. *The identification and selection of creative artistic talent by means of biographical information*. Report submitted to the U.S. Office of Education, DHEW. Grant No. OEG-8-9-540215-4004 (010). Project No. 9-0215. 1971.

Ellison, R. L., Nelson, D. E., Abe, C., Fox, D. G., & Coray, K. E. *Utah statewide educational assessment: General report*. Salt Lake City: Utah State Board of Education, 1975.

IBRIC. *ALPHA biographical inventory*. Greensboro: Prediction Press, 1968.

James, L. R., Ellison, R. L., Fox, D. G., & Taylor, C. W. Prediction of artistic performance from biographical data. *Journal of Applied Psychology*, 1974, **59**, 84–86.

Laurent, H. Cross-cultural cross-validation of empirically validated tests. *Journal of Applied Psychology*, 1970, **54**, 417–423.

Muthard, J. E. & Miller, L. A. *The criteria problem in rehabilitation counseling*. Iowa City, Ia.: The University of Iowa, 1966.

Schaefer, C. E., & Anastasi, A. A biographical inventory for identifying creativity in adolescent boys. *Journal of Applied Psychology*, 1968, **52**, 42–48.

Taylor, C. W., & Ellison, R. L. Predictors of scientific performance. *Science*, 1967, **155**, 1075–1079.

Utah State Board of Education. *Goods and general objectives of education in Utah*. Salt Lake City: Author, 1973.

Eighteen states now have full-time consultants for the gifted and talented in their departments of Education. They include: Arizona (Diane Erbert), California (Sieg Efken), Connecticut (Bill Vassar), Florida (Joyce Runyon), Georgia, (Margaret Bynum), Illinois (Jay Stortzum), Kentucky (Chairmian Sperling), Louisiana (Ruth Beck), Minnesota (Lorraine Hertz), Nebraska (Diane Dudley), New York (Roger Ming), North Carolina (Cornelia Tongue), Ohio (George Fichter), Oklahoma (Larry Huff), Pennsylvania (Noretta Bingaman), South Carolina (James Turner), Virginia (Isabelle Rucker), Washington, (Richard Mould).

(Answers to previous problems).
1. 8x-5(26-x) = 0
13x = 130
x = 10

2. EACH VOYAGE INVOLVES THE MOST "restrictive" condition of the three, viz., no woman ever remains in the company of any man unless her husband is present. The least number of couples n in the first is 2 which also equals x and the number of crossings is 5. If n = 3, x = 2, then y = 11. If n = 4 or 5, x = 3 then y = 9, and y = 11, respectively. Happily however for n = 5, x = 4 and y = 2n−1.

Jane R. Mercer
June F. Lewis

Using the System of Multicultural Pluralistic Assessment (SOMPA) to Identify the Gifted Minority Child

Although the System of Multicultural Pluralistic Assessment (SOMPA) (Mercer & Lewis, 1978; Mercer, 1977) was initially developed to prevent the mislabeling of minority children as mentally retarded (Mercer, 1973), the approach may be equally useful in identifying gifted minority children whose potential has been masked by cultural differences between the home and the school.

Three Assessment Models

The SOMPA utilizes three assessment models: the medical model, the social system model, and the pluralistic model. Each model provides a different and important perspective of the child's competencies.

THE MEDICAL MODEL

The medical model is a deficit model that focuses on organic anomalies and pathologies. *Normal* is a residual category consisting of those who show no symptoms of pathology. Distributions of scores for medical model measures have low ceilings and long negative tails. Because of these characteristics, the medical model is not useful in identifying the gifted child.

THE SOCIAL SYSTEM MODEL

The social system model, on the other hand, is useful in identifying the child whose social role performance is outstanding. It derived from the social deviance model of sociology and defines behavior in terms of roles and social system norms. Thus, there are multiple definitions of *normal*. Each role in each social system has its own set of expectations, and

175

different behavior is expected of an individual when he or she is playing different roles. To judge whether a particular set of behaviors is supranormal, normal, or subnormal requires four kinds of information: the system in which the person is functioning, the role he or she is playing in the system at the time the judgment is being made about his or her behavior, the expectations others in the system have for the behavior of persons playing that role, and information on his or her actual behavior. Norms for social systems are determined by political processes within the system. The dominant group in a system establishes the rules that govern behavior for various social roles.

The social system model is multidimensional, with norms for each role in each social system. It is evaluative in that the values of the most powerful groups are enforced. Since definitions of behavior are both role bound and system bound, it is necessary to specify both the role and the system within which the assessment is being made. It is both a deficit and an asset model because both the poor performers and the outstanding performers in various social roles can be identified. Consequently, test scores form a normal distribution. Measures appropriate to this model assess competencies as well as deficits. The validity of a measure is determined by the extent to which scores on the measurement correlate with independent judgments of the person's behavior made by members of the system. In SOMPA,* the Adaptive Behavior Inventory for Children (ABIC) serves as the measure of social role behavior. It provides information about the child's social role performance in the family, in the community, with peers, in nonacademic roles at school, as an earner and consumer, and in self maintenance. The Wechsler Intelligence Scale for Children-Revised (WISC-R; Wechsler, 1974), using standard norms, is also treated as a social system measure in SOMPA because it identifies those who are likely to succeed or fail in the role of student. Thus, the standard WISC-R score is interpreted as a measure of school functioning level (SFL).

Increasing levels of performance on the ABIC are measured by the number of social groups in which the child participates, the number of different roles played in these groups, the extent to which the child demonstrates internal control and independent behavior, and the complexity of his or her role behavior. Role behavior is scored by levels of competency: *latent*, if the child is reported as never demonstrating a particular role competency; *emergent*, if the child performs the role occasionally and/or under the supervision or direction of an adult; *mastered*, if the child regularly demonstrates competency in the role without supervision or adult assistance. High scores indicate the child is experiencing no difficulty in fulfilling social role expectations and may be performing above

---

*SOMPA measures were standardized on 700 Hispanic, 700 Black, and 700 White children attending the California public schools. The samples were chosen to be representative of the public school population of children 5 through 11 years of age in each of those ethnic groups.

the level of expectations appropriate to his or her own age level. We believe that above average levels of competency in social role performance are an area of giftedness that should be identified. Such knowledge would be especially helpful to the educator as a basis for providing academic programming for minority children whose abilities are obscured by socio-cultural differences between home and school.

THE PLURALISTIC MODEL

The pluralistic model is also useful in identifying the gifted minority child (Mercer, 1978). The initial idea for the pluralistic model developed during our earlier studies of the labeling of the mentally retarded in the community (Mercer, 1973). That study clearly indicated that school psychologists were not limiting their interpretations of standardized test scores entirely to predictions about scholastic performance. They evidently believe that the scores on so-called measures of intelligence indicated something about an individual child's learning ability or aptitude in general.

We theorized that it is possible to make inferences about learning potential only *if* certain conditions were met. Those persons whose performances are compared must:

1. Have had similar opportunities to learn the materials and acquire the skills covered in the test.
2. Have been similarly motivated by the significant other persons in their lives to learn this material and acquire these skills.
3. Have had similar experience with taking tests.
4. Have no emotional disturbances or anxieties interfering with test performance.
5. Have no sensorimotor disabilities interfering with prior learning or with their ability to respond in the test situation.

When these factors are held constant, the pluralistic model assumes that the individual who has learned, probably has the most learning potential (Mercer, 1973, Chapter 16). If an individual's sociocultural background influences his or her opportunity to learn, motivation to learn, and test taking experience, we reasoned that controlling for sociocultural background would hold these three factors relatively constant. Those who are emotionally disturbed or physically disabled are detected by other measures.

We have developed four scales to measure sociocultural characteristics: urban acculturation, socioeconomic status, family structure, and family size. In the SOMPA, these four scores, which are measures of the child's sociocultural background, are inserted into multiple regression equations developed for his or her ethnic group by using scores on the WISC-R (Wechsler, 1974) as the dependent variable and the sociocultural scale scores as independent variables. The estimated average score for the sociocultural group to which the child belongs is then calculated. The

177

WISC-R score for a particular child is then compared with the average score for others from precisely the same sociocultural and socioeconomic background. The adjusted WISC-R score is interpreted as the child's estimated learning potential (ELP). In the pluralistic model, *normal* is defined as performance near the average for children who are from similar sociocultural backgrounds. *Supranormal* is defined as performance higher than the average of the child's own sociocultural group.

The pluralistic model, then, is evaluative. It assumes that high potential is better than low potential. It is completely culture bound in that it compares a child's performance with his or her own sociocultural group. It is primarily an "asset" model. The pluralistic model assumes that learning potential is an attribute of the individual and that scholastic potential can exist, unrecognized, because a child's potential is masked by the social and cultural distance between the culture of the home and the culture of the school.

Identifying The Gifted Minority Child

We can identify the child who is gifted in social role performance using the Adaptive Behavior Inventory for Children. In addition, we can identify the child who is gifted in estimated learning potential. This two dimensional procedure yields four possible configurations of scores, as shown in Table 1.

Persons whose performance is represented by cell A of the typology would be those who score very high both in social role performance and in estimated learning potential. Those at cell B are those whose social role performance falls below the gifted level but have an estimated learning potential in the gifted range. Persons at cell C are social role gifted but score below the gifted range in estimated learning potential. Cell D represents those persons who score below the gifted range both in social role performance and in estimated learning potential.

Various cutoff levels could be used for identifying the gifted child depending on the purposes of those making the identification.* For illustrative purposes, we selected those children in the SOMPA samples who achieved a standard score of 80 or higher on any single scale in the ABIC, with no single score lower than 60, and defined them as *social role gifted*. Since the ABIC was standardized to have a mean of 50 and a standard deviation of 15, a score of 80 or above falls in the highest 2.5% of the scores. There were 94 children who met this criterion. Two children

---

*The Educational Policies Commission (1950) suggests that students having IQ scores of 137 and above on a standardized test be identified as highly gifted, and those students having an IQ of 120 to 137 be identified as moderately gifted.

We have arbitrarily selected an IQ score of 130 as the lower limit of giftedness following the criteria of the California Project Talent (Committee on Education of Intellectually Gifted Pupils, 1962). Students with scores at these levels would rank roughly in the upper 2.5% of the total school population.

had a score of 80 or higher on all six ABIC subscales, 4 had high scores on five scales, 6 scored high on four scales, 17 scored high on three scales, 20 scored high on two scales, and the remainder scored high on one scale.

We then selected those children in the SOMPA samples who achieved an estimated learning potential greater than 129. This cutoff also includes only those scores in the highest 2.5%. There were 40 children who met the criterion. Two of the children who met the criterion for estimated learning potential also scored above 80 on one or more ABIC scales and, hence, would be represented by cell A of the typology. The remaining children would be represented either by cell B (if they had high estimated learning potential) or cell C (if they had high social role performance).

We then grouped the children by ethnic group to examine whether the comparative rates of identification were racially and culturally discriminatory. We found that .1% of the White majority group were represented by cell A, 2.8% by cell B, and 3.1% by cell C. We found that .1% of the minority children were represented by cell A, 1.5% by cell B, and 5.1% by cell C. If we add these percentages and define any child who scores in any of the three cells (A, B, or C) as gifted, there are approximately equal percentages of majority and minority children identified as gifted.

Illustrative Cases Of Two Gifted Minority Children

Two children have been selected from the case files to illustrate the usefulness of this approach in uncovering abilities that may be obscured by the cultural distance between home and school.

Belle Madison is a 9 year old Black girl attending the fourth grade in an elementary school located in the inner city of a large metropolitan school district. She lives with her mother and father and three sisters in a five room house. Her father is a painter who provides the sole support for the family. Her mother is not employed outside the home. Her mother and father both grew up in a small town in Mississippi. He completed 9 years of schooling and she completed 8 years. Belle's mother reports that she attends PTA and meetings of church groups a couple times a year but does not participate in any community groups or informal social groups. She also expresses a sense of powerlessness by agreeing that a person's fate is already determined at birth, that one must live for today, and that planning makes a person unhappy since plans hardly ever work out. The urban acculturation of the family background is very low compared with both the Black community and the culture of the school.

Belle's teacher reports that she is interested in schoolwork and eager to learn. She likes to read and takes work home from school. She did a special project for the class on sickle cell anemia in which she presented some drawings that she had done herself. The teacher was so impressed with her work that she referred Belle as possibly gifted.

Belle achieved a verbal score of 111, a performance score of 109, and

179

a full scale score of 111 on the WISC-R when the standard norms were used. Although the scores are above average, they are not high enough to meet the requirements for entrance to a program for the gifted. Pluralistic norms were used and Belle's performance was compared with children from similar sociocultural backgrounds who, presumably, had had similar opportunities to learn the materials in the test. Her estimated learning potential was: verbal 130, performance 128, and full scale 134. The pluralistic model appears to confirm the teacher's assessment of Belle's potential. It places her in the upper 1% of the children in her own sociocultural group.

Roberto Cruz is a 10 year old boy of Hispanic background. He lives with his father and mother, five brothers and sisters, and an aunt and uncle and three cousins in a small, single family dwelling in East Los Angeles. His father provides all of the income for the family by installing ready made cabinets and furniture in mobile homes. Both of Roberto's parents were born and reared in Mexico City. His father completed the third grade and his mother completed the fourth grade in the public schools of that city. They moved to the United States after their marriage. The mother speaks only Spanish. The father has some rudimentary knowledge of English but speaks mainly Spanish. The mother reports that she does not participate in any school, church, community, or informal social groups. She also feels completely powerless in controlling her own fate or planning for the future. Roberto scored well above average on the Adaptive Behavior Inventory and on the Bender-Gestalt test, and there was no evidence of sensorimotor or physical dexterity problems on the Physical Dexterity Tasks in the SOMPA.

Roberto achieved a verbal score of 109 on the WISC-R, a performance score of 107, and a full scale score of 111, using the standard norms for the test. However, when his sociocultural background was taken into account and his score adjusted to compare him only with children from a similar Hispanic background, his estimated learning potential was: verbal 134, performance 120, and full scale 130.

Conclusion

Using adaptive behavior and estimated learning potential to identify gifted minority children is a new approach. There has not yet been sufficient time to explore all the ramifications of this methodology. Our qualitative evaluation of the case reports on children in our files who have been identified as gifted using adaptive behavior and/or estimated learning potential is encouraging. As in the cases of Belle and Roberto, clinical judgment tends to support the numeric conclusions when complete information on the family background of the child is available. During the field test of the SOMPA procedures, the psychological staff of one school district administered all the SOMPA measures to 11 minority children who had

180

been referred as possibly gifted by their teachers. Their full scale WISC-R scores, using the standard norms, ranged from 97 through 130. Their full scale estimated learning potential scores ranged from 99 through 150. Only one minority child would have been identified as gifted using the standard norms and a cutoff of 130. Five minority children would have been identified as gifted using estimated learning potential. Hence, estimated learning potential agreed more closely with teacher estimates than did the standard WISC-R scores. Further experience with these measures will provide more information on their limitations and strengths.

References

Committee on Education of Intellectually Gifted Pupils. *Education of intellectually gifted pupils in Los Angeles city schools*. Los Angeles: Los Angeles Unified School District, May 1962.

Educational Policies Commission. *Education of the gifted*. Washington, D.C.: National Education Association and the American Association of School Administrators, 1950.

Mercer, J. R. *Labeling the mentally retarded: Clinical and social system perspectives on mental retardation*. Berkeley and Los Angeles: University of California Press, 1973.

Mercer, J. R. Identifying the gifted Chicano child. In Joe L. Martinez, Jr. (Ed.), *Chicano psychology*. New York: Academic Press, 1977.

Mercer, J. R. *SOMPA technical manual*. New York: The Psychological Corporation, 1978.

Mercer, J. R., & Lewis, J. F. *Parent interview manual*. New York: The Psychological Corporation, 1977.

Mercer, J. R., & Lewis, J. F. *Student assessment manual*. New York: The Psychological Corporation, 1978.

Wechsler, D. *Wechsler Intelligence Scale for Children-Revised (WISC-R)*. New York: The Psychological Corporation, 1974.

R. C. Wilson
J. P. Guilford
P. R. Christensen

The Measurement of Individual Differences in Originality

One of the most important aspects of creative thinking is originality. This article discusses the problem of developing methods for measuring individual differences in originality. The problem arose in connection with a factor-analytic study of creative thinking conducted at the University of Southern California.

In that investigation various definitions of originality were considered in the light of their implications for measurement. Three definitions and corresponding methods of measuring originality were finally adopted and applied to specially constructed tests. The methods are based upon: (a) uncommonness of responses as measured by weighting the responses of an individual according to the statistical infrequency of those responses in the group as a whole; (b) the production of remote, unusual, or unconventional associations in specially prepared association tests; and (c) cleverness of responses, as evaluated by ratings of degrees of cleverness exhibited in titles suggested for short-story plots.

These three methods permit the operations of measurement of individual differences and, while recasting the definition of originality, they preserve much of the essential meaning usually assigned to the concept. In the following sections, some of the nonmeasurable aspects of originality are pointed out and each of the three proposed methods is discussed in conjunction with a description of tests developed to utilize the method. Since the tests were included in a factor analysis along with other tests of creative thinking, the three methods are evaluated in the light of the loadings of scores from these tests on a factor which has been called originality.

Reprinted from *Psychological Bulletin*, Vol. 50, No. 5 (September, 1953), pp. 362-370. By permission of the senior author and the American Psychological Association.

Definition of Originality

In developing methods for measuring individual differences in originality, the meaning to be assigned to the term *originality* and the operations for measurement must be clearly specified. The term originality has several distinct meanings. We wish to use it as the name for a psychological property, the ability to produce original ideas. What we mean by an original idea will be further specified in relation to each of the proposed methods of measuring originality.

Many writers define an original idea as a "new" idea; that is, an idea that "did not exist before." They are frequently not in agreement, however, in their interpretation of "new," since they use it with different connotations. We shall point out the inadequacy of two of these connotations for the measurement of individual differences in originality.

In one connotation, a "new" idea is an idea that "has never previously been thought of by anyone who has ever lived." In practice, of course, it would be impossible to verify whether or not an idea meets these requirements of newness since one could never examine all the ideas of everyone who ever existed to determine whether the idea has been thought of before. This conception also presents a problem in the case of independent productions of the same idea. Two or more scientists may produce the same idea independently in different parts of the world. One of them may precede the others by a matter of months or weeks, or even hours or minutes. In trying to find creative scientists, we would probably not wish to regard the scientists who produced the idea later as unoriginal merely for having been preceded by someone unknown to them.

On the other hand, we find that "new," while meaning that which did not exist before, is sometimes interpreted, at least by implication, as including all human behavior that is not repetitive. That is, not only poetry, science, and inventions, but dreams, hallucinations, purposive behavior, and all perceptions are regarded as new. They are "new" in the sense that they are never duplicated exactly, even by the individual himself. Such a conception of "new" also fails to be fruitful, since it does not supply us with a basis for differentiating between more original and less original individuals.

For measurement purposes, we have found it useful to regard originality as a continuum. We have further assumed that everyone is original to some degree and that the amount of ability to produce original ideas characteristic of the individual may be inferred from his performance on tests. Rather than define original as "new" or "did not exist before" we have investigated three alternative definitions. We have regarded originality in turn as meaning "uncommon," "remote," and "clever." It was felt that these three definitions include significant aspects of what is commonly meant by the term original. Tests and scoring methods were developed for each of these approaches to originality.

183

The Uncommonness-of-Response Method

Our first approach to the measurement of originality assumes a continuum of uncommonness of response. For this purpose originality is defined operationally as the ability to produce ideas that are statistically infrequent for the population of which the individual is a member. "Population" may here be regarded as any cultural group, professional group, or other aggregation of individuals having significant characteristics in common.

This definition of originality was utilized by constructing completion or open-end tests, which require the examinee to produce responses. The tests were administered to the group of individuals whose relative degrees of originality were to be determined. The responses of all the members of the group were tallied to determine their frequency of occurrence within the group. Weights were assigned to the various responses, the higher weights being given to the statistically more infrequent responses. A score was derived for each individual either by summing the weights assigned to his responses or by counting only the responses having high weights. On the basis of the score thus derived, those individuals with the highest scores were the individuals who had given the most infrequently mentioned responses.

This procedure may be clarified by an example. The items in the Unusual Uses test are six common objects. Each object has a common use, which is stated. The examinee is asked to list six other uses for which the object or parts of the object could serve. For example, given the item "A newspaper," and its common use, "for reading," one might think of the following other uses for a newspaper: (a) to start a fire, (b) to wrap garbage, (c) to swat flies, (d) stuffing to pack boxes, (e) to line drawers or shelves, (f) to make up a kidnap note. The test is given in two separately timed parts of five minutes each. Each part gives the names of three objects and their common use with spaces for listing six other uses per object.

All the responses given by a group of 410 Air Cadets and Student Officers to each object were classified, tallied, and weighted. A system of five weights was used. A weight of 5 was assigned for the (approximately) 1/5 most infrequently mentioned respones, a weight of 4 for the 1/5 next most infrequently mentioned responses, and so on down to a weight of 1 for the 1/5 most frequently mentioned responses. This gave a possible range of scores for each object (six responses) of 0 to 30 and a possible range of scores for the total test (six objects) of 0 to 180. The total scores actually obtained ranged from 5 to 129.

Let us consider the actual frequencies obtained for one of the objects. The 1,767 responses to the object given by the group of 410 Air Cadets and Student Officers were tabulated. One hundred and eighty-two different uses were mentioned. Eighty of these 182 uses were unique in that they were mentioned by only one member of the group. At the other extreme, one of the uses was mentioned by 173 individuals. The three most common uses mentioned, with frequencies of 173, 94, and 90, accounted for 357 responses and were assigned weights of one. The next six most common uses, with frequencies from 89 to 48, were assigned weights of two. Nine uses with frequencies from 45 to 29 received weights of three, 24 uses with frequencies from 23 to 9 received weights of four, and the 139 most uncommon uses, with frequencies from 8 to 1, received weights of five. It should be noted that there were not exactly 1/5 of the total number of responses in each weight category. Because of the way in which the responses distribute themselves it is usually not possible to designate an exactly equal number of responses for each weight. It is possible, however, to achieve a close approximation.

After the weight for each response had been determined for all six objects, each examinee's paper was scored by assigning the appropriate weights to his responses and summing them. By definition, those individuals who tended to produce the most infrequently given ideas were the ones with the highest total scores and were regarded as the most original members of the group. The mean score on the Unusual Uses test was 64.0, its standard deviation was 23.5, and its alternate-forms reliability was .74.

The same procedure was applied to the Quick Responses test and the Figure Concepts test (1). The Quick Responses test is similar to the conventional word-association test. It consists of a list of 50 stimulus words, derived principally from the Kent-Rosanoff list and a more recent list developed by D. P. Wilson (4). The 50 words were read to the examinees at the rate of one every five seconds, the examinee being instructed to respond with the first word that came to mind. Responses of 410 individuals were tabulated for each of the 50 stimulus words. Frequencies of occurrence for each response were determined, weights were assigned, and scores derived in a manner similar to that for the Unusual Uses test. The mean score on the Quick Responses test was 99.8 with the standard deviation of 18.7. The reliability estimate was .81 as computed for odd and even items and corrected for length.

The Figure Concepts test consists of 20 simple pen-and-ink drawings of objects and individuals. Each picture is identified by a letter. The examinee's task is to find qualities or features that are suggested by two or more drawings and to list the features and the letter designations of two drawings which possess them. For example, picture A might be a sketch of a child wearing a hat, picture B might be a sketch of a woman wearing a hat, picture C might be a sketch of young birds in a nest. The examinee might give such responses as "wearing a hat (a, b)"; "young (a, c)"; "family (a, b)"; etc.

All responses for all individuals were tabulated and classified according to frequency of mention. A further breakdown was made for each response mentioned in terms of the combinations of drawings used in identifying the feature. It was noted that while there were 190 possible pairs of drawings available, certain ones were rarely used, while others were used as a source of more than one feature. Weighting of responses was thus based on both the infrequency of the response itself and the infrequency of the drawing combination used as a source of that response.

How this dual classification affected an individual's score may be seen in the situation where two individuals gave the same response (feature name), but cited different combinations of drawings. If one individual's response was derived from a drawing combination that was frequently mentioned by others in connection with that feature, the weight assigned was low. The other individual's response, if derived from a drawing combination infrequently mentioned for that feature, was assigned a high weight.

As with the Unusual Uses test, weights were assigned so that an approximately equal number of all the responses given by the group received each weight. Each examinee's responses were then assigned their appropriate weights and the weights were summed to derive the individual's total score for the test. The mean score on this test was 29.9 with a standard deviation of 12.9. Since the format of this test did not permit the direct computation of a reliability estimate, the communality of the test (.41) found in the factor analysis is offered as an estimate of a lower bound of its reliability.

In the Number Associations test the examinee is given, in turn, four different numbers (digits) and for each is allowed two minutes in which to list as many synonyms, uses, and things associated with the number as he can. For example, for the number 4 he might list coach-and-four, for, fore, foursome, quartet, etc.

The associations listed by the group were tabulated and weights were assigned in a manner similar to that described for the Unusual Uses test. In order to try out a further variation of the uncommonness method, however, the individual's total score was derived in a slightly different manner from that previously described. Instead of summing the weights for all the responses given by the individual, his total score was derived by counting the number of responses with weights of 4 and 5. The mean score for this test was 12.5 with a standard deviation of 3.6 and an alternate-forms reliability of .57.

In the approach described in this section, we have chosen to define original as meaning "uncommon." An original idea or response is one that is uncommon or statistically infrequent, and an individual's degree of originality, as inferred from his scores on the tests described, is characterized by the degree of uncommonness of his responses.*

The Remoteness-of-Association Method

The second approach is in terms of remoteness of association. Originality is here defined as the ability to make remote or indirect associations. To measure originality from this point of view, tests were constructed that required the examinee to make remote associations if he responded at

*The reader may recall that an uncommonness or idiosyncrasy score has previously used in connection with word-association tests in the assessment of abnormalities of behavior in clinical practice, particularly of the schizoid type. The fact that such a score measures an originality factor, as we shall show later, might be regarded as support for the popular idea expressed in the words of Seneca, "There is no great genius without some touch of madness."

all. Remoteness of association was imposed by the task. Three tests of this type were constructed. The degree of originality of an individual, according to this definition, would be manifested in terms of the number of remote associations he made.

The Associations I test presents 25 pairs of words. The associative connection between the two words is not immediately apparent. The examinee's task in each item is to call up a third word that serves as a link between them. For example:

Given:
Indian_____money
Write on the line between these words a word that associates the two.

There are several possible words that could be used such as penny, nickel, copper, and wampum, each of which is related to both Indian and money.

The examinee's score was the number of responses given to the 25 items in four minutes. The mean score for this test was 14.0 with a standard deviation of 4.9. The odd-even reliability estimate was .87, corrected for length.

The Associations II test is similar to the Associations I except that there is more emphasis on the correct response word having two different meanings in its relationship to the two stimulus words. It is also a multiple-choice test in which the examinee must indicate which one of five letters is the first letter of the correct association.

For example:

tree   *a   b   g   m   s*   dog

Which of the five letters is the first letter of a word that is associated with both tree and dog and has a different meaning in relation to each?

The word "bark" is the correct answer. It means the external covering of a tree and it also means the noise made by a dog. It also begins with *b* which is one of the choices, so the examinee circles the letter *b*.

The examinee's score was the number of correct responses given to 25 items in 12 minutes. The mean score was 14.0 with a standard deviation of 3.9. The odd-even reliability estimate was .62, corrected for length.

The Unusual Uses test, previously described, was also regarded as a test requiring the examinee to respond with remote associations. Since the six items composing the test were common objects, each with one well-known use, which was given, the examinee was compelled to utilize remote associations in seeking six additional uses for each object. Both a statistical-infrequency score and a simple-enumeration score were derived for this test. The correlation between these two scores was .94. There is, of course, much spurious overlap of the two scores. In view of the high correlation between the two scores and the similarity of their correlations with other tests in the creative-thinking battery, the simpler score was chosen for inclusion in the factor analysis. The mean for this score on this test was 22.1 with a standard deviation of 6.7 and an alternate-forms reliability of .80.

In the approach described in this section we have chosen to define original as meaning "remote." An original idea or response is "remote" to the extent that the individual is required to bridge an unusually wide gap in making associative responses. An individual's relative originality, as inferred from his scores on these tests, is characterized by the number of remote responses given in a limited time.

Cleverness

According to the third approach, originality is defined as the ability to produce responses that are rated as clever by judges. This definition requires a test that calls forth responses showing variation on a continuum of cleverness. Weights are assigned to an individual's responses in proportion to their degrees of rated cleverness.

The Plot Titles test used to measure this type of originality presents two brief stories. For each story the examinee is allowed three minutes in which to write as many appropriate titles as he can. Although relevancy rather than cleverness is stressed in the instructions, an examination of the responses of the group revealed considerable variation in the ingenuity, cleverness, or striking quality of the titles suggested.

In an attempt to develop a reliable scoring procedure for evaluating cleverness, a sample of 50 individuals was selected from the total group of 410. These 50 individuals averaged approximately six responses for each plot. The approximately 300 titles for each plot were typed on separate slips of paper. Three judges, working independently, sorted the titles into six successive piles on the basis of their judgments of the relative cleverness of the titles. Weights from 0 through 5 were assigned to the titles in the successive piles, with the high weights being assigned to the more clever titles. Agreement among the judges is indicated by the interjudge correlations (of ratings) ranging from .53 to .76. Reliabilities of test scores derived from individual judges ranged from .69 to .77. These reliabilities were computed from the two cleverness scores, one from each story, for each of the 50 individuals. The reliability computed from the composite ratings of the three judges (.76) was not higher than that for the best individual judge. Since the most reliable judge was also the one who agreed best with the other two judges, it was decided to have this one judge do the scoring of the test for all examinees, with one of the other judges serving as a check scorer.

In an effort to simplify scoring, a study was made of total scores derived from the weights 0 through 5. That is, each test paper was scored by the number of responses at each of the cleverness levels of 0, 1, 2, 3, 4, and 5. Intercorrelations among the six scores were computed for the sample of 50 individuals. It was found that scores based on weights 0 and 1 intercorrelated well, and scores based on weights 2, 3, 4, and 5 intercorrelated well.

188

A combination of scores based on weights 0 and 1 had a low correlation with a combination of scores based on weights 2, 3, 4, and 5. It was decided to reduce the scale to two intervals, clever and nonclever. That is, responses receiving weights 0 and 1 would be called nonclever. This greatly reduced the fineness of discrimination required of the scorer. Utilizing the titles already rated as standard, the remainder of the tests were scored on this simple dichotomy. Two scores were recorded for each individual: the number of clever titles and the number of nonclever titles. It was decided to include both scores in the computation of the intercorrelation matrix and to determine, prior to the factor analysis, whether the cleverness and noncleverness scores were sufficiently independent to warrant including both of them in the factor analysis. The correlation between the two scores was $-.031$ and their patterns of intercorrelations with other tests in the battery were quite different; consequently, both scores were included in the factor analysis. The cleverness score (based on weights 2 to 5) emerged with a loading of .55 on the originality factor. The noncleverness scores (weights 0 to 1) had a loading of $-.05$ on this factor and had its highest loading (.59) on a factor identified as ideational fluency. The cleverness score had a loading of .07 on the ideational-fluency factor.

In the approach described in this section, we have chosen to define original as meaning "clever." An original idea or response is one that is rated as clever by judges. An individual's degree of originality, as inferred from this kind of test score, would be characterized by the number of clever responses given in limited time.

Discussion

The seven test scores representing the three scoring methods described were included with 46 other test scores in a battery designed to explore the domain of creative thinking. The test battery was administered to 410 Air Cadets and Student Officers. The scores were intercorrelated and 16 factors were extracted. Orthogonal rotations resulted in 14 readily identifiable factors, a doublet, and a residual. Five of the seven originality test scores emerged with loadings regarded as significant (.30 and above) on one of the factors obtained. Following is a list of the tests, their scoring principles, and their loadings on the factor.

Plot Titles (cleverness)	.55
Quick Responses (uncommonness)	.49
Figure Concepts (uncommonness)	.32
Unusual Uses (remoteness)	.31
Associations I (remoteness)	.30
Number Associations (uncommonness)	.25
Associations II (remoteness)	.09

189

We have tentatively named this factor originality (3). Another test from the creative thinking battery which should be discussed in relation to this factor is the Consequences test. This test requires the examinee to list the consequences of certain unexpected events such as the sudden abolition of all national and local laws. Two scores were derived from this test on the basis of the degree of remoteness of ideas indicated by the individual's responses. The number of remote consequences was counted for one score and the number of immediate or direct consequences for the other. It was hypothesized that the remoteness of ideas represented by the remote-consequences score might refer to something different from the remoteness of ideas required by the originality tests already mentioned. A separate factor of penetration or the ability to see remote consequences in space, in time, or in a causal chain of circumstances was therefore hypothesized. No such factor emerged in the factor analysis. The remote-consequences score of the Consequences test came out with its highest loading (.42) on the originality factor. Evidently, the remoteness of ideas represented by this test score is not different from the remoteness of ideas required by the test scores hypothesized for originality. This finding lends additional support to the generality of the obtained originality factor.

Inasmuch as test scores representing all three methods of measuring originality have significant loadings on this factor, we may have some confidence in its generality. Had test scores of only one method emerged on the factor, we might wonder whether the factor were specific to the particular kind of scoring method.

It should be mentioned that this factor has some appearance of bipolarity since there were a few small negative loadings of other test scores in the battery on this factor. Those test scores with negative loadings are of the kind whose "right" responses are keyed on an arbitrary, conventional basis by the test constructor. The examinee who engages in an unusual line of thought is likely to be penalized for his originality in such tests. In this connection, the essentially zero loading for originality in Associations II (as contrasted with the significant loading in Associations I) is worth mentioning. In this test, too, one "correct" answer is given credit. It may be that the original examinees think of other appropriate responses whose initial letters appear among the alternatives, and for which they receive no credit.

The fact that five of our tests designed to measure originality have in common a single factor is regarded as evidence for the potential fruitfulness of the scoring methods described for the measurement of individual differences in originality. Further work is necessary in refining the tests and in validating them against objective criteria of originality. It is felt that considerable progress has been made toward the development of objectively scored tests of originality, with promise of satisfactory reliability.

As to the relative merits of the three approaches suggested, the uncommonness and cleverness methods have the greatest amount of the originality-factor variance but are the least economical in time and energy required to determine the scores.

In an exploratory study such as this one, expenditure of time and energy in scoring by the less economical methods may be justified in terms of the insights to be gained. In later studies, however, it is desirable to use more economical procedures. The remoteness principle is a more economical procedure, but does not yield factor loadings as high as the less economical cleverness and uncommonness procedures. The next steps will be to revise the remoteness tests in an attempt to increase their originality variance and to seek methods of simplifying further the cleverness and uncommonness scoring procedures without decreasing their originality variance.

References

1. Guilford, J. P., Wilson, R. C., Christensen, P. R., & Lewis, D. J., A Factor-Analytic Study of Creative Thinking, I. Hypotheses and Description of Tests. *Reports from the Psychological Laboratory,* No. 4 Los Angeles: Univer. of Southern California, 1951.

2. Guilford, J. P., Wilson, R. C., & Christensen, P. R., A Factor-Analytic Study of Creative Thinking, II. Administration of Tests and Analysis of Results. *Reports from the Psychological Laboratory,* No. 8 Los Angeles: Univer. of Southern California, 1952.

3. Hargreaves, H. L., The "Faculty" of Imagination. *Brit. J. Psychol. Monogr. Suppl.,* 1927, 3, No. 10.

4. Wilson, D. P., An Extension and Evaluation of Association Word Lists. Unpublished doctor's dissertation. Univer. of Southern California, 1942.

Kenneth Kreitner
Ann W. Engin

Identifying Musical Talent

*T*he past few decades have seen a great variety of definitions for the word "gifted." The definitions are not, of course, always in complete agreement, but most have suggested that giftedness is multidimensional—that it can include not only academic talents but excellence in leadership, the creative and performing arts, and even athletics.

In practice, however, we seem to pay most attention to academics: programs for the gifted have proliferated in science, in mathematics, in language; but the arts seem to be mostly ignored. Why is this? Perhaps school is seen largely as an academic experience, and thus if a school system is to have one program for the gifted, we think it ought to be in an academic area. Perhaps educators believe that scholars and scientists make the greatest contributions to society, and thus should be encouraged first. Perhaps most people concerned with the gifted are themselves more interested in academic subjects than in the arts. Perhaps they are intimidated by the arcane knowledge that music and art teachers seem to have.

Whatever the cause, gifted programs in music are rare, and regrettably so, for such programs are not especially hard to run, and musically talented students certainly stand to gain as much from special attention as do precocious mathematicians.

The Issues

Music education for the gifted has an unusual set of problems. In the first place, the task of programming, a delicate issue in many academic programs, is much easier in music; all we need to do is to match the student with a private teacher and leave the two of them to their own devices. There is no lockstep tradition to fight in music; students can move ahead as fast as they want, and become as good as they can, without anyone shouting, "Elitist!" To set up a program for the musically talented, we need only cooperate with tradition, not change it, as is so often the case in academic subjects. The private teacher-system can be easily adapted into a sort of mentor-student or tutorial arrangement if it is accompanied by a systematic program of identification.

It is here that the problem suddenly becomes very difficult. For it seems to be nearly impossible to identify musical talent with certainty. Music is unique in that it requires specific technical knowledge even to get started; few people ever become musicians without first learning to read music and to play an instrument. But obviously a test of musical talent cannot depend on this technical knowledge, and therefore it cannot require that the student actually make music. Musical talent, then, must be measured not by its products, but by its symptoms, and there seems to be precious little agreement as to what the symptoms really are. The tests on the market differ greatly in their conceptions of talent, and as a result the teacher is faced with the awesome decision of choosing one definition and building an entire program around it. It is often easier to do nothing than to take on this sort of responsibility.

But the stakes here are too high to spend all of our energy brooding about the risks. The way the present system works, the all-important decisions of whether or not to become a musician and, finally, what *kind* of musician, are generally made on the basis of a host of irrelevant factors: chance, sex role pressures, money, myths—anything, it seems, but a knowledge of the student's real aptitudes and inclinations. As a result, we must be losing a great many good musicians, and the misfortune is not only to the students, but to society at large. Any system, however imperfect, is bound to be better than the chaos we have now, and any test is better than no test at all as long as we regard it with all due caution.

The Tests

Musical talent is a complex and mysterious phenomenon. It is probably as hard to define operationally, and as impossible to thoroughly test as intelligence. In fact, the two are measured similarly: the quantity to be measured is broken down to a few components, which are then tested as representative of the whole. But what are the components of musical talent? What do we mean when we say that a certain student is talented? This is one of the most fascinating and perplexing questions in all psychometrics.

For the purposes of this discussion, it is helpful and convenient to break musical talent down into five broad categories. None of these categories can be tested directly, but each contains many smaller, measurable quantities which make up a certain *kind* of information about a student's talent. The five categories are:

1. *Perception*: the ability to distinguish differences in physical quantities (frequency, amplitude, wave form, duration, etc.).

2. *Memory:* the ability to remember these discriminations over time.
3. *Reproduction:* the ability to recreate (by singing, playing an instrument, or whatever) what is remembered.
4. *Taste:* the ability to distinguish good sounds from bad, either by culture's definition or by one's own.
5. *Artistry:* the ability (including creativity) to put one's emotions into music.

A careful examination of these categories will reveal that they form a sort of continuum from the objective to the subjective, from the easy to test to the impossible to test, from the physiological to the mystical. Also, each category is almost a prerequisite for the next—no one can sing a tune who can't tell two notes apart, nor can one be a true artist without being able to distinguish a Bach chorale from the cry of a wounded ape. And because there is such variety in this continuum, it is impossible to construct a test to measure all five quantities perfectly. What the tests generally do is break down musical talent into categories requiring a battery of subtests, usually measuring various aspects of perception, memory, and sometimes taste. These tests and their subtests form the next topic of discussion.

There are at least seventeen tests in print that purport to measure musical talent (Lehman, 1968, pp. 37-56). Of these, six—the Seashore, the Drake, the Wing, the Gaston, the Gordon, and the Bentley—are used most commonly; these represent probably the best tests available. The chart on page 98 shows the subtests and other salient data for these six tests. The chart has been arranged to place subtests that are similar, or at least analogous, opposite one another horizontally, so that it is easy to see where the tests are alike and different.

The Seashore Measures of Musical Talents (Seashore et. al., 1956) is the classic test in its field. Since its first publication in 1919, it has been used by generations of teachers and researchers. The Seashore was the first widely used standardized test of musical talent, and the tests that have followed it have all been in its debt in one degree or another. The six subtests of the Seashore, each comprising 30 to 50 items, all appear on one record.

Pitch:	Pairs of tones are presented, and the subject must tell whether the second tone in each pair is higher or lower than the first; the tones vary in pitch from 17 cycles per second in a 500-cps tone (about a quarter-step) to 2 cps in a 500-cps tone (about .05 of a half-step).
Loudness:	Pairs of tones are presented, and the subject tells if the second is louder or softer; the differences vary from 4.0 dB to .5 dB.
Rhythm:	Pairs of rhythmic patterns are presented, and the subject tells if they are the same or different.
Time:	Pairs of tones are presented, and the subject tells if the second is longer or shorter than the first; differences range from .3 second to .05 second.

194

Test	Seashore Measures of Musical Talents	Drake Musical Aptitude Test	Wing Standardized Tests of Musical Intelligence	Test of Musicality (Gaston)	Musical Aptitude Profile (Gordon)	Measures of Musical Abilities (Bentley)
Date **Time Required** **Ages**	1919/39/56/60 60 minutes Grade 4-16	1934/54/57/65 40-80 minutes Age 8-adult	1939/61 25-35m* or 50-60m Age 8-adult	1942/50/56/57 60 minutes- Grade 4-12	1965 110-150m (3 sess.) Grade 4-12	1966 21-30 minutes Age 7-14
SUBTESTS	Pitch Loudness Rhythm Time Timbre Tonal memory	Rhythm test Memory test	Pitch change* Intensity Rhythmic accent Memory* Chord analysis* Harmony Phrasing	Memory Chord analysis Sight reading Melody completion	Harmony (T) Phrasing (S) Balance (S) Melody (T) Tempo (R) Meter (R) Style (S)	Pitch discrimination Rhythmic memory Tonal memory Chord analysis

*Short form for younger students.

195

Timbre:	Pairs of tones are presented, and the subject tells if they are the same or different in quality.
Tonal Memory:	Pairs of melodic sequences, each containing three to five notes, are presented, and the subject tells which note is different from one to the other.

The 1956 manual for the Seashore reports reliability coefficients ranging from 155 or .85, with a median coefficient of .74. Validity, however, is a more difficult matter. Seashore himself maintained for years that his tests should not be validated against such notoriously inaccurate and unreliable external criteria as teacher ratings; the internal validity, he said, is established, and that is enough. But although this argument may be persuasive to some musicians and psychologists, tests must be selected to fit their educational purpose, and it would be useful to have some idea of how well Seashore scores correlate with musical achievement at various times. Lundin (1953, pp. 206-208) summarizes eleven studies attempting to validate the Seashore against teacher ratings and music grades; validity coefficients range from .27 to .80, with a median coefficient of .17.

The Seashore is a precise and scientific test for measuring some parts of musical perception, discrimination, and memory; but whether or not it measures musical talent is questionable. Its reliance on perception-oriented measures does not fit in with many of the more recent theories of musical talent, and the low validity coefficients found by researchers suggest that its usefulness in the classroom may be limited.

The Drake Musical Aptitude Tests, first published in present form in 1954, combine the 1934 *Drake Musical Memory Test* with a new rhythm test. The two tests appear on opposite sides of a phonograph record. Each section has two forms, each requiring about 20 minutes, which may be given singly or together. On the memory test, the two forms are equivalent; the author recommends giving both forms to musically inexperienced youngsters, and only one form to those with five years or more of musical training. The test consists of twelve melodies, each repeated in several ways; for each repetition the subject tells if the time (rhythm), the notes, or the key has been changed, or if the repetition is the same as the original. On the rhythm test, Form B is more difficult than Form A; the author suggests that only Form B be given to subjects with some musical training, and both forms to unselected groups. On Form A, a metronome clicks several times while a voice counts to four; the clicking then ceases, and the subject counts imagined clicks for a few seconds until the voice says, "Stop." Form B is similar, except that while the subject is counting, another metronome clicks at a different speed as a distractor. The rhythm test, as the author points out, is a test not of rhythmic ability so much as of the ability to keep a steady tempo.

Reliability on the memory test is .91 to .93 for musical subjects and .85 for nonmusical subjects. On Form A of the rhythm test, reliabilities range from .56 to .95, with a median of .86; on Form B, reliabilities range from .69 to .96, with a median of .775. Drake reports low (.02 to .11) correlations between his tests and the Seashore, indicating that the two batteries measure different quantities. Validity coefficients based on teacher ratings range from .32 to .91, with a median of .55, on the memory test; and from .31 to .85, with a median of .58, for the combined forms of the rhythm test.

The chief disadvantage of the Drake is its reliance on two measures—memory and tempo—to the exclusion of other important factors, such as pitch, dynamics, and taste. Despite these limitations, however, its statistics are convincing, and its economy of time and its ease of administration make it a useful tool for the music teacher.

Most of the tests in common use have avoided measures of musical taste, presumably in the interest of pure objectivity. The importance of taste to musical talent cannot be denied, however, and the *Wing Standardized Tests of Musical Intelligence* (Wing, 1960) represent an attempt to measure taste as scientifically as possible. The Wing has seven subtests on a tape recording. For younger children, or as a quick screening device, a shorter form comprising only the pitch change, memory, and chord analysis subtests may be used. The seven subtests of the Wing are as follows:

Chord Analysis: A piano plays a chord (on the tape), and the subject tells how many notes are in the chord.

Pitch Change: The piano plays two chords that are identical except for one note, and the subject tells if that note moved up or down.

Memory: Much like the tonal memory subtest of the Seashore, except that the melodies contain up to ten notes.

Rhythmic Accent, Harmony, Intensity, and Phrasing: In these four tests, passages are played twice, with changes made in the rhythm and accent, the harmonization, the dynamics, and the "punctuation," respectively, and the subject tells which version is better, or if they are the same. (For each of these subtests, great care has been taken to ensure that the worse of the two is definitely worse; if there was room for a difference of opinion among competent musicians on an item, the item was changed or thrown out.)

Reliability on the Wing test is about .90 for older children, and .70 for younger students. Wing computed a validity coefficient of .73 between his test and the *Aliferis Music Achievement Test* (Wing, 1959), and Bentley (Whybrew, 1962, p. 128) found a correlation of .481 between Wing scores and grades earned in courses.

Because the Wing was developed and printed in Great Britain, it is not as widely used in this country as it might be otherwise. Another related problem is the heavy British accent of the voice on the tape, which many American children find distracting and even laughable. This difficulty can be eased by reading the longer instructions aloud instead of playing them on the tape, but still a separate American version, with American norms,

197

would be a great contribution. Even with its slight limitations, the Wing is still for many purposes the most accurate, comprehensive, convenient test available.

The *Test of Musicality* (Gaston, 1957), generally known as the Gaston, is divided into three sections. In the first part, the student answers 18 questions about his or her musical interests, exposure to music, and preferred instrument. The second section appears on a record and consists of four subtests, each comprising five or six items:

Chord Analysis: The piano plays first a note and then a chord, and the student tells whether or not that note is in the chord.

Sight-Reading: A short melody is printed on the answer key; the student compares the printed version with one played by the piano, and then tells if they differ in the notes or the rhythm, or if they are the same.

Melody Completion: The piano plays an incomplete melody, and the student tells if the next note should be above or below the last note played.

Tonal Memory: As in the memory test of the Drake, the piano plays first a melody, then two to six repetitions, and the student tells if the notes or the rhythm are changed from the original, or if the two versions are alike.

The third section of the Gaston consists of a checklist, to be filled in by the teacher, concerning physical as well as other characteristics of the student, such as voice register, instruments played, type of teeth, lip texture, type of fingers, IQ, and general health.

The manual gives split-half reliabilities of .88 to .90 for students of various ages. Gaston also reports a study validating the test against teacher ratings and concludes that the test does indeed measure what it says it measures. The statistics of this study, however, were computed by a peculiar "chi-square r" method which has perplexed many reviewers (Farnsworth, 1959; Whybrew, 1962, p. 126); what inferences can be validly derived from Gaston scores are therefore still questionable.

The *Test of Musicality* is convenient to use and comprehensive in its assessment of different kinds of information. If the Gaston has a failing, it is in the length of its subtests; it is doubtful that a student's skill in chord analysis, for instance, can really be measured accurately by five items. The validity of the Gaston Test, in short, is not entirely certain, and thus it should probably not be used as the sole device for selecting the musically gifted. The Gaston's brevity and broadness, however, might make it a good screening device for use with a more authoritative test such as the Wing or the Gordon.

The *Musical Aptitude Profile* (Gordon, 1965) is the longest, most exhaustive test available for measuring musical talent. It consists of seven subtests, spread over three sessions for a total of 110 to 150 minutes. From these seven subtests the Gordon derives eleven scores: one for each subtest, three subtotals (tonal imagery=melody + harmony; rhythm imagery= tempo + meter; musical sensitivity=phrasing + balance + style), and a total score. Each of the subtests consists of thirty or forty pairs of melodies played by a violin or violin and cello; the two melodies in each pair (the "statement" and the "answer") may be the same or different. For the various subtests, the subject is asked to answer certain questions about each pair of melodies:

Tonal Imagery-Melody:	Is the answer a melodic variation of, or entirely different from, the statement?
Tonal Imagery-Harmony:	Is the lower of the two parts in the answer like, or unlike, that in the statement? (The upper part remains the same.)
Rhythm Imagery-Tempo:	Is the speed of the answer the same as, or different from, that of the statement?
Rhythm Imagery-Meter:	Are the two passages played in the same meter or a different meter?
Musical Sensitivity-Phrasing:	Which of the two melodies is played with better musical expression?
Musical Sensitivity-Balance:	The two passages are the same except for the ending; which ending is more appropriate?
Musical Sensitivity-Style:	The answer is either faster or slower than the statement; which is more appropriate?

As a test becomes longer, its reliability tends to increase (Anastasi, p. 115). The Gordon, therefore, has high reliability coefficients: .66 to .85 for the subtests, .80 to .92 for the three subtotals, and .90 to .96 for the total. Correlations of Gordon scores with teacher estimates range from .19 to .88 for the subtests, from .48 to .85 for the subtotals, and from .64 to .97 for the total.

For thoroughness, precision, and authority, the *Musical Aptitude Profile* is unparalleled. Moreover, the wealth of statistical information presented in the manual makes the Gordon uniquely valuable as a research tool. Its only problem is its epic length, which makes it hard to use as a screening device. No teacher wants to spend three class sessions just checking the aptitudes of the pupils, and relatively few students, particularly at the lower grades, wish to sit through 110 to 150 minutes of music tests. The Gordon, therefore, is often impractical for identifying musically gifted students, but it may be excellent for assessing their strengths and weaknesses after they have been identified.

Bentley's test, *Measures of Musical Abilities* (1966), is unique in its emphasis on younger students; whereas most other tests are standardized down to grade four (the age of selecting a band instrument), the Bentley is designed for subjects of ages seven to fourteen. Its four subtests require

199

only 21 to 30 minutes, making it one of the shortest and most convenient tests available. The subtests include:

Pitch Discrimination: Similar to the pitch test of the Seashore, except that the discriminations are less fine;
Tonal Memory: Similar to its namesake on the Wing;
Rhythmic Memory: Two rhythmic patterns are played, and the subject must tell on what beat they differ, or if they are the same.

Because the Bentley is so short, one might expect relatively low reliability coefficients. Bentley reports a retest reliability of .84 (Lehman, p. 55), but independent research (Rowntree, 1970) has suggested somewhat lower reliability—about .60 Validity of the battery is higher: Bentley gives a correlation of .94 between the test scores and grades in various music courses. Until the reliability is established, however, this validity coefficient must also be suspect. In short, the technical characteristics of the Bentley test are not yet proven. The author, to his credit, gives several cautions in interpreting the results, and presents the standardized scores in the form of five broad categories, instead of the usual percentiles, which would be misleadingly precise.

The Bentley is an especially convenient and practical test, and it is probably the best test available for the elementary music teacher who wants a rough estimate of pupils' relative talents. It should not, however, be used for identifying the gifted. Because it is brief and relatively easy, the Bentley has a low ceiling: the more talented students get perfect scores on the subtests, making their measurements inaccurate (McLeish, 1972). For identifying elementary children for a gifted program, it is probably better to use a more thorough, difficult test, even if it is standardized on older students.

Evaluating the Tests

The six tests just described present a bewildering variety of conceptions and measurements of musical talent. For the teacher who sees the diversity and controversy surrounding the issues, it is easy to be stricken with a paralysis of choice, not knowing which measurements are best and which to sacrifice. But the decision must be made, and the teacher who makes it should be well-informed not only about the tests themselves, but about the criteria that make one better than another.

Herbert Wing, author of the *Wing Standardized Tests of Musical Intelligence*, has presented just such a set of criteria (Wing, 1970, pp. 53–72) for judging measures of musical talent. These guidelines must be approached with some caution, of course, since the author might be expected to show a bias toward his own test; but still they form a thoughtful and thorough set of principles, and they are perhaps the best framework available for appraising the instruments on the market.

1. *They* (the tests) *should be acceptable in their basic principles to musicians.* This is mostly a matter a face and internal validity: is what the test measures a part of musical talent? Obviously, the more subjective tests, such as the Wing and the Gordon, are better in their respect than the physiological tests such as the Seashore, the Drake, the Gaston, and the Bentley, some of which measure sensory discriminations finer than any musician is called upon to make.
2. *They should not be unduly influenced by training and opportunity.* This has long been a matter of debate: will musical training improve the skills being measured? The debate has not been answered completely, but probably the more physiological a test is, the better it is in this respect. The taste-oriented subtests of the Wing and the Gordon are largely culture-bound, and thus more influenced by exposure to the culture; but of course our definition of musical talent is also culture-bound. Clearly, the sight-reading section of the Gaston requires some prior knowledge of elementary music. In all other cases, though, the test constructors have taken care to minimize the effects of training on scores; whether or not they have succeeded is still questionable.
3. *It is preferable that the battery should be comprehensive in its power to assess subjects of widely differing capacity.* In other words, a test should have a low floor and high ceiling. For our purposes (dealing with the gifted), the high ceiling is more important, and the only test deficient here is the Bentley; the rest seem to be difficult enough for nearly any student.
4. *They should cover a sufficiently wide sample of musical talents.* A test of taste necessarily includes many other factors besides the one being measured; on the harmony tests of the Wing and the Gordon, for example, the subject is called upon to use not just harmonic taste but pitch discrimination, memory, and chord analysis as well. In this respect, the more taste-oriented tests do give a broader picture of the student's talent. They are able to do this, however, at the cost of scientific purity; such sensory measures as the Seashore are better able to isolate one quantity and measure it precisely. On the whole, the sensory tests are probably better for certain types of research, and the taste-oriented tests more useful in the classroom.
5. *They should fulfill certain statistical criteria of reliability.* In general, reliability is greater for a total score than for a subtest, and it increases for older pupils. All of the tests described here present complete reliability data, and although some subtests have low coefficients, none of these six tests should be considered seriously unreliable.
6. *They should be suitable for repeated applications to the same subject without any great loss in efficiency.* All of the tests discussed here are good in this respect; most have so many similar questions that it is

nearly impossible to remember the answers for more than a few seconds.

7. *They should give a score which is easily evaluated on a standardized scale.* Again, all the tests fulfill this criterion.

8. *They should be economical in the time required for their application.* This is a problem of balance; if a test is too short, it loses reliability and thoroughness; if it is too long, fatigue becomes a factor, especially in younger children. One hour (Seashore, Drake, Wing, Gaston) seems to be about the standard length; the Bentley is shorter, and the Gordon longer. Each length probably has its place—the shorter ones as screening devices, and the longer ones as profiles.

9. *They should correlate well with an exterior criterion.* This is one of the hardest problems of all because of the difficulty of finding an exterior criterion that is not less reliable than the test being judged. Teacher ratings and school grades (the most frequent criteria) are fallible in academic subjects (Pegnato and Birch, 1959), and even more so in music, where differences in training and opportunity are so critical. A better way to measure validity—criterion-oriented or predictive validity—would be through longitudinal studies to see which tests or subtests are most useful for making certain types of predictions for certain students. Perhaps one test may best predict progress in an individualized musical curriculum in school, and another may be better for predicting outstanding talent in adulthood. Perhaps one test is better for fourth-grade students, and another for ninth-graders. A program to study the validity of the tests of musical talent should use not only the six tests discussed here, but also measures of attitude, motivation, persistence, practice time, and so on. If these measurements were correlated with musical performance at various times in the future, it would be simple to select the combination of measurements that best predicts talent relative to any planned educational program.

10. *They should be of practical use in music education.* All of these tests were designed for use in the classroom, and all have been so used; therefore, it is safe to say that they are all practical for at least some situations.

11. *They should be simple to apply* (i.e. administer). Over the years, the tests are getting better and better in this respect. As recording techniques have improved, the move has been from piano music to crude 78-rpm records to sophisticated tapes and 33-rpm records. All the tests are easy to administer, and most even have the directions on the record, so that the examiner does nothing but pass out papers and work the phonograph.

The problems of identifying musical talent have not been solved, nor have many of the controversies been settled. And when the experts seem so uncertain, it is easy for the consumer to be baffled. From this entire discussion, however, a few points should be clear.

First of all, it seems to be very difficult to test musical talent in primary children. The Bentley, the only test designed for this group, is inadequate for assessing high levels of talent, and the other tests are generally unreliable even for upper-elementary students. It is unclear whether the problem is psychometric or economic—perhaps it really is hard to construct a test for children below the fourth grade, or perhaps there is just not enough demand for such a test. In either case, the increased sophistication of testing techniques and the greater attention being paid to elementary and even preschool gifted programs may lead to more research and publication in this important field. Until then, the primary teacher is forced to improvise with observations, homemade tests, and intuition.

Second, the conflict between the sensory and the taste-oriented tests will probably never be resolved. The Seashore camp asserts that talent can be identified only by finding a few of its components and then measuring them as precisely as possible; the Wing camp accuses sensory tests of being atomistic and short-sighted, and says that musical talent must be measured with real music. Neither view, of course, is entirely right or wrong—they are both matters of perspective. The task of the teacher planning a music program for gifted students is to decide on a perspective for that program, and then choose the test (or combination of tests) that best fits that perspective. It is equally important for that teacher to conduct validation research in his or her own situation, regardless of the amount of validation data from other settings. And we must remember that insofar as a test is objective, it must be incomplete, and insofar as it is subjective, it must necessarily be culture-bound.

Finally, it is clear that tests of musical talent should not be the final authority in selecting musically gifted students. Traditionally, gifted students for academic programs have first been located through grades and teacher nominations, and then been given an individual intelligence test for final selection. It is tempting to follow a similar pattern for music programs. Tempting, but dangerous, because music tests are simply not yet so sophisticated as intelligence tests.

If we think that we can use a music test the way we use an individual IQ test, we are dangerously naive. Certainly the tests are useful—among the most useful tools available—but they are no substitute for a flexible program and a keen ear for talent.

References

Anastasi, A. *Psychological testing* (4th Ed.) New York: Macmillan, 1976.

Bentley, A. *Measures of musical abilities*. London: George G. Harrap & Co., Ltd. (New York: October House), 1966.

Drake, R. M. *Drake musical aptitude tests*. Chicago: Science Research Associates, 1954.

Gaston, E. T. *A test of musicality*. Lawrence, Kansas: Odell's Instrumental Service, 1957.

Gordon, E. *Musical aptitude profile*. Boston: Houghton Mifflin, 1965.

Lehman, P. R. *Tests and measurements in music*. Englewood Cliffs, N.J.: Prentice-Hall, 1968.

Lundin, R. W. *An objective psychology of music*. New York: Ronald Press, 1953.

McLeish, J. Review of Bentley's measures of musical abilities. In O.K. Buros (ed.) *Seventh mental measurements yearbook*. Highland Park, N.J.: Gryphon Press, 1972, p. 524.

Pegnato, C. W., and J. W. Birch. Locating gifted children in junior high schools: a comparison of methods. *Exceptional Children, March, 1959,* **25:7**, 300-304.

Rowntree, J. P. The Bentley "Measures of Musical Abilities"—a critical comparison. *Council for research in music education bulletin*, Fall, 1970, **22**, 25-32.

Seashore, C. E., D. Lewis, and J. G. Seatveit. *Seashore measures of musical talents*. New York: The Psychological Corporation, 1956.

Whybrew, W. E. *Measurement and evaluation in music*. Dubuque, Iowa: Wm. C. Brown Co., 1962.

Wing, H. Review of the Aliferis Music Achievement Test. in O.K. Buros (ed.) *Fifth mental measurements yearbook*. Highland Park, N.J.: Gryphon Press, 1959.

Wing, H. *Wing standardized tests of musical intelligence*. Sheffield, England: Greenup and Thompson, 1960. (Available from National Foundation for Educational Research in England and Wales.)

Wing, H. *Tests of musical ability and appreciation*. Cambridge: University Press, 1970.

Part III.
Developing and
Encouraging Giftedness

With the possible exception of issues related to identification, appropriate procedures for providing educational programs for gifted and talented youth has undoubtedly been the most talked about and written about general topic within this field of special education. The most enduring questions of this field continue to focus upon what are the most effective teaching strategies for superior learners? What kinds of persons should teach the gifted and talented? How should we go about organizing programs for the gifted? Are certain materials more effective than others in teaching the gifted and talented? How should we deal with the personal and social development of gifted individuals? Are there special techniques and approaches for working with underachievers, disadvantaged gifted youngsters, and students who are generally unmotivated by the traditional methods of education?

Part III of this book attempts to deal with many of the questions listed above. In the first section, Program Development, several important concerns about program organization and operation are discussed. Our general approach in selecting material for this section was to look for material that dealt with models of program organization and important features that should be taken into consideration when developing a program for gifted and talented youth. James Gallagher's article is especially insightful because the author has attempted to point out some of the conflicting values that our society holds toward persons of superior ability. Gallagher discusses how the values of a society are reflected in the types of educational programs and services that a society provides for its gifted youth and he cites several examples of the relationships that exist between values on one hand and educational practice on the other. The articles by Barbe, Renzulli and Smith, Treffinger, and Stanley call attention to various models of program organization. Although these articles sometimes appear to be presenting conflicting points of view, the perceptive reader should note that certain of the practices are appropriate for particular situations while others undoubtedly have merit for meeting particular needs in other situations and under varying circumstances.

The second section, Instructional Approaches, focuses primarily upon three major concepts in programming for the gifted and talented. The important role played by the development of gifted youngeters' creative thinking abilities is reflected in the articles by Hughes, Parnes, Gowan, and Sisk. The article by Torrance is also an important contribution to this section because it brings to our attention the great concern that gifted youngsters have with all aspects of futuristics and the problems that face the world in which gifted youngsters will grow up. The article by Renzulli and Smith presents a comprehensive approach for organizing a program for gifted and talented youngsters around an individualization model. This article is related in content and structure to the chapter by these authors that appeared in the previous section.

Section three, Teaching the Gifted and Creative, could easily constitute an entire book in and of itself. The several articles of this section deal with various theoretical points of view about teaching gifted and creative students and several practical suggestions regarding teaching strategies and educational materials. The article by Bishop dealing with characteristics of teachers of the gifted represent an area of research that has long been neglected in special education. It is an important contribution of the literature. However, it also represents the one area in which this field needs to devote a large amount of additional study and research. We hope that by bringing this article to the attention of readers it will stimulate further investigative activity regarding characteristics that contribute to effective teaching for gifted and talented youngsters.

The area of counseling the gifted and talented and dealing with the personal and social development of highly able youth is finally gaining more attention in the literature. The fourth section, Counseling and Personal Development, represents some of the recent contributions in this area and, once again, we hope that the research and commentary included in this section will stimulate additional inquiry related to the important topics of counseling and personal development.

The final section of this book deals with important issues in motivating underdeveloped talent. For far too many years most of the research on gifted and talented individuals dealt with youngsters who generally achieved large measures of success in the "educational game." Articles in this section call attention to the great talent potential that is frequently unidentified and underestimated in our nation's overall school population. The section focuses upon concerns about highly intelligent youngsters who, for one reason or another, drop out of school (physically or psychologically) and thereby have a limited opportunity for realizing their potential. This section also includes an article about the problems faced by gifted women in our society. In many ways the concerns reflected in the final section call attention to the areas where limited research has been done thus far and point the way toward the types of studies that are necessary for overcoming the great talent loss that has resulted from our neglect of minority groups, disadvantaged youngsters, and women. It is hoped that in the years ahead a renewed interest in these groups will result in greater efforts to determine the educational needs, roadblocks, and procedures that can be used to retrieve this unquestionably neglected segment of our general population.

Walter B. Barbe

Homogeneous Grouping for Gifted Children

The need for attention to the education of gifted children has long been recognized. The development of provisions for this, however, has not kept pace with the research findings on the nature and needs of the gifted. To only a limited extent have special provisions been made for them. Acceleration, enrichment and homogeneous grouping are the major types of provisions. Few programs have been based solely upon only one of these. Enrichment has come to be an essential part of any provision for the gifted, while homogeneous grouping is practiced to some extent in every class.

But there are those who believe that formal provisions are necessary if the gifted child is to be adequately provided for. There is much evidence to prove that the gifted child frequently is neglected (1).

Recognizing this need for special attention to gifted children, in 1920 Cleveland, Ohio, began a program of special classes for gifted children. This, known as the Major Work Program, was the beginning of a slow and spasmodic increase in the belief that gifted children can best be provided for in special classes (2).

The program of providing for gifted children in the schools of New York City was started in 1922 by Leta Hollingworth. Even though Public Schools No. 64 and 11 had reported grouping rapid learners shortly before this time, "they did not carry with them the scientific research and evaluation begun by Hollingworth in No. 165 (3)." These classes, known as Special Opportunity Classes, were given partial financial support by the Carnegie Corporation of New York.

In an article in *Ungraded* (4), Hollingworth, Cobb and others stated that the purposes of the program were: "First, the particular children in it must be educated—the class exists for them; but secondly, they must be studied—our knowledge of such children must be increased, for we have, after all, very little information to guide us in differentiating their schooling."

These early classes were entirely of an experimental nature and continued for a period of three years. Two groups of children were selected to

---

Reprinted from *Educational Leadership,* Vol. 13, No. 4 (January, 1956), pp. 225-229. By permission of the copyright © owner, The Association for Supervision and Curriculum Development.

be in the experiment. Group A was formed with children of 150 I.Q. and above, while Group B consisted of children with I.Q.'s between 135 and 154. All of the children were between the ages of 7 ½ and 9 ½ years and were accelerated in their school grade placement.

At the end of the three-year experiment, comparisons were made of achievement of the experimental groups and control groups of children who were of equal intellectual capacity but not in special classes. It was found that there was no great difference in the achievement scores of the segregated and non-segregated groups. In the evaluation, it was concluded that: "The advantages to be hoped for from the homogeneous grouping of gifted children lie not so much in the expectation of greater achievement in the tool subjects of reading, arithmetic and spelling as in an enrichment of scholastic experience (5)."

Hildreth recently reported on another attempt at special schools in New York. In 1940, Hunter College in New York City received authorization from the Board of Education to organize an elementary school for gifted pupils. Children from the ages of 3 to 11 who test above 130 I.Q. and "show other evidence of being mentally gifted and having other favorable traits (6)" are eligible for these classes.

Admission to the school is limited to those children living within a limited area of the Borough of Manhattan who meet the necessary mental and social qualifications. There is no tuition charge. An effort is made to keep the number of boys and girls as nearly equal as possible. Because of the enormous number of applicants, the staff believes that admission on the basis of objective tests is a fair method. An interesting point which Hildreth makes is that "the range [in I.Q.] . . . was around 60 points; the groups were seldom more homogeneous than in other schools except that the minimum rating was not below 130."

In telling of the children in the Hunter program, Hildreth describes them as having attractive personalities and possessing vitality and vivacity.

The parents of the Hunter group are a cross sampling of the population. Their occupations vary from day laborer to business executive. The majority of the parents have had some college, were born in New York, and would be ranked in the high-middle income bracket.

At the present time there are 22 classes for gifted elementary children. In addition to the one regular teacher for each class, there are five full-time special teachers. All of the teachers have the M.A. degree. The physical plant is, in itself, unique. All facilities for which a teacher could ask are available.

The goals of the educational program as outlined by Gertrude Hildreth are:

1. Mental health and adjustment.
2. Health and physical education.
3. Learning to become an economically efficient citizen, both as producer and as consumer.

4. Acquiring skill in social relationships.
5. Learning about one's role as an enlightened and active world citizen.
6. Education for initiative and originality (7).

Oliver (8) reports that an entire school is set aside in Baltimore for gifted junior high school students, while Allentown, Pennsylvania, brings superior students from all over the city to one school for "opportunity classes." A division within a school is described and the Cleveland Major Work Program is mentioned briefly as an example of this type. He mentions the differentiated high school programs in most cities where the college preparatory course, which is essentially for the gifted students, is offered to some, while a commercial curriculum is offered to others.

Colfax School in Pittsburgh, Pennsylvania, operates a partial segregation plan to "provide for better living conditions for its mentally superior children." The entire school, from the third grade on, is on the platoon plan. It is described by Pregler as a "workshop" plan: "The plan provides the maximum opportunity for group acceptance of the individual child, it encourages the pupil to work to capacity, and it makes it possible for superior children to work with and be challenged by their mental peers. Furthermore, it has enabled the school to develop special methods and materials well suited to the teaching of gifted children (9)."

The gifted children at Colfax School are segregated in the skill subjects and mix with their regular home room in the special subjects. Pregler points out that by use of the workshop plan, the gifted child still remains a part of the regular class. When he leaves the regular class, it is just as if a child in the typical school would go to orchestra practice. Actually, it amounts to segregation for half of the day. All of the skill subjects are taught either in the morning or afternoon, and the gifted child leaves his regular group for this period of time.

Baker (10) describes the program in Detroit for mentally superior children. Generally, he says, Detroit has a "mild amount of extra promotion." At the elementary school level, most schools follow the platoon plan of departmentalizing subjects. At the junior high level, the screening of gifted children is done by means of weighted formula. Five points are given for intelligence, four for school achievement, and two for chronological age. Children are then segregated according to the total points which they have. At the high school level, Baker says, the program consists of little more than the customary college preparatory courses.

Interest in provisions for the gifted has been outstanding throughout California. This is perhaps due to Terman's study (11) of gifted California youth.

A program described by Cora Lee Danielson, former supervisor of this work (12) was in operation for over twenty years. Los Angeles no longer has special classes but is attempting to meet the needs of the gifted through various other means.

In considering the merits of special classes, Goddard says that this is the best method by which the school can keep "the child happily employed with work that is educative, both because it is interesting to him and because it challenges his capabilities by calling for his best efforts continually (13)." The Educational Policies Commission says that in its broader sense, enrichment is a policy rather than a plan, and that special classes for the gifted have little justification if they do not provide enrichment. Activities especially appropriate for the gifted involve creative expression, ample opportunity for out-of-school contacts, and a chance for each child to learn more about his fields of special interest and to express his particular talents (14). Witty quotes Schwartz as saying:

> The real purpose of the special class seems to lie in the assignment of tasks which challenge the child's interest and capacity, the enrichment of the curriculum to include a wide variety of experiences which are not possible in a regular class, the opportunity to think and to discuss with other children of equal ability the problems of life within their grasp, the development of initiative and independence of thought, and last, but not least, the realization of responsibility to the community, looking toward the use of their powers for the benefit of mankind (15).

Carroll presents a strong argument for special education of the gifted: ". . . each child must receive the education best suited to his abilities and needs. To force upon all an education planned for average children, regardless of individual intellectual capacity, is to grant special privilege to the central group and to deny to the bright and the dull their rights (16)."

A large number and greater variety of learning experiences can be had by students in a homogeneously superior class, partly because less time is required for routine drill and remedial instruction (17). The enriched curriculum keeps the child's intellectual power active in an environment affording opportunities for association with children who are mentally and physically equal (18).

To the argument that the slower child is stimulated by the bright child, Goddard answered that the slower child is not stimulated but frightened (19). Instead of the special class making the gifted child feel superior, Carroll believes that it is the regular class where this happens and not the special class. He says that in an unselected group the gifted child is constantly made conscious of the fact that he is brighter than his classmates, so that different classes eliminate one of the causes of inflated self-esteem (20). Edith Carlson agrees with this view. She says that the "smugness, feelings of superiority, and other undesirable characteristics are alleviated when bright children are placed in special classes (21)."

Pregler recognizes (22) that there are advantages and disadvantages of each method of providing for the gifted child, but she believes, as do most educators, that it should be determined by what is best for the child. She believes that the partial segregation plan is the best yet devised for the particular situation in which she is located.

In a doctoral dissertation at Columbia University (23), Alice Keliher strongly opposes homogeneous grouping as a provision of caring for the gifted. Her major criticism is that segregation adversely affects society. Throughout her dissertation, however, she is careful to note that segregation, *as it exists today,* is not advisable. The dissertation, written in 1931, was aimed at the idea of complete segregation which was prevalent at that time. Today, in few programs is complete segregation followed. As is true about the Major Work Program, in Cleveland, Ohio, segregation, but not isolation, appears to be the more acceptable method.

Oliver summarizes present day thinking rather well in saying that mere segregation does not assure the gifted child of a better education. The ultimate need of the gifted child is an enriched program, whether it is in a homogeneous or heterogeneous classroom.

In discussing the criticisms of homogeneous grouping, Oliver says:

> There is considerable reason to believe that the alleged shortcomings [of special classes] are not inherent but are a matter of creating a proper environment and of establishing a proper attitude in the gifted, in the other pupils, in the teachers, and especially in the parents (24).

While no definite conclusions can be reached about the best method of providing for the gifted, it is important to recognize that the gifted child is being neglected and is in need of special attention.

References

1. Walter B. Barbe, "Are Gifted Children Being Adequately Provided For?" *Educational Administration and Supervision,* Vol. 40, No. 7 (November 1954), pp. 405-413.

2. Walter B. Barbe and Dorothy Norris, "Special Classes for Gifted Children in Cleveland," *Exceptional Children,* Vol. 21, No.2 (November 1954), pp. 55-57.

3. Grace Loomis, "The Education of the Gifted Child," *Curriculum Bulletin,* No. 97 (December 12, 1951), Eugene, Oregon: School of Education, p.14.

4. Paul Witty, *The Gifted Child* (Boston: D. C. Heath, 1950), p. 55.

5. Howard A. Gray and Leta S. Hollingworth, "The Achievements of Gifted Children Enrolled and Not Enrolled in Special Opportunity Classes," *Journal of Educational Research,* Vol. XXIV (November 1931), p. 261.

6. Gertrude Hildreth, *Education of Gifted Children* (New York: Harper and Brothers, 1952), p. 40.

7. *Ibid.,* pp. 43-46.

8. Albert I. Oliver, "Administrative Problems in Educating the Gifted." *The Nations Schools,* Vol. 48, No. 5 (November 1951), pp. 44-46.

9. Hedwig O. Pregler, "Adjustment Through Partial Segregation," *National Elementary Principal,* Vol. 19 (September 1952), p. 243.

10. Harry J. Baker, "Characteristics of Superior Learners and the Relative Merits of Enrichment and Acceleration for Them." Supplementary Educational Monograph, No. 69. Edited by William S. Gray. Chicago: University of Chicago Press, October 1949, p. 157.

11. Lewis M. Terman and Melita H. Oden, *The Gifted Child Grows Up.* Stanford, California: Stanford University Press, 1947.

12. From personal correspondence with Miss Cora Lee Danielson.

13. Henry H. Goddard, *School Training of Gifted Children.* Yonkers-on-Hudson, New York: World Book Co., 1928, p. 1.

14. Educational Policies Commission, *Education of the Gifted.* National Educational Association of the United States and the American Association of School Administrators. Washington, D.C., 1950, pp. 56-58.

15. Witty, *op. cit.,* p. 189.

16. Herbert Carroll, *Genius in the Making.* New York: McGraw-Hill Book Co., Inc., 1940, p. 253.

17. Educational Policies Commn., *op. cit.,* p. 53.

18. W. J. Osburn and Ben J. Rohan, *Enriching the Curriculum for Gifted Children* (New York: The Macmillan Co., 1931), p.186.

19. Goddard, *op. cit.,* pp. 27-33.

20. Carroll, *op. cit.,* p. 213.

21. Witty, *op. cit.,* p. 188.

22. Pregler, *op. cit.,* p. 242.

23. Alice Keliher, "A Critical Study of Homogeneous Grouping." New York: Columbia University Press, 1931.

24. Oliver, *op. cit.,* p. 44.

Joseph S. Renzulli

Identifying Key Features
in Programs for the Gifted

*I*n recent years renewed attention and effort have been directed toward the development of special programs for gifted and talented students. Evidence of heightened interest in this area is found in the rapidly increasing number of states which have taken legislative action dealing with special provisions for the gifted. In addition to increased support at the state level, a number of communities have developed programs through the use of resources available locally and available under various titles of the Elementary and Secondary Education Act. In view of the renewed interest in this area, it may be useful to call attention to those aspects of differential education for the gifted which are considered to be the keystones of a quality program. Concentration upon a relatively limited number of indispensable program characteristics provides the complicated task of program development with structure and focus, and such an approach may be helpful in avoiding some of the hastily contrived adaptations that characterized the post-Sputnik era—adaptations which, in many cases, suffered an equally hasty demise.

The study reported here was undertaken to identify characteristics considered to be the most necessary for a successful program of differential education for the gifted. The purpose of the study was to isolate through systematic procedures a basic core of key features that could be used for program development and evaluation. The concept of key features represents an essential part of the rationale upon which the study was based. Reflection upon the entire span of characteristics which any educational program might possibly include, from the quality of the classroom teacher to the adequacy of the supplies and materials that a teacher has at her disposal, leads to the conclusion that certain program features and characteristics are extremely more consequential than others. With respect to the whole array of practices and provisions that possess potential, although in varying degrees, to further the objectives of differential education for the gifted, the concept of key features holds that concentration on a minimal number of highly significant features will facilitate both program development and evaluation. This concept also holds that if the more essential

214

features of a program are found to be present and operating excellently, then the probability of less critical features being similarly present is high.

Procedure

The first step in carrying out the study consisted of searching the literature in order to identify the principal aspects of the problem and to locate relevant information and ideas that might prove useful in developing a comprehensive list of features and processes of programs for the gifted. This initial step included a nationwide survey aimed at locating lists of criteria used at state and local levels to evaluate special programs for the gifted.

The second step involved the selection of a panel of 21 expert judges. A larger group of persons who had made substantial contributions to the field of education for the gifted was identified according to a number of specified criteria; then this group was asked to nominate, from among themselves, those persons whom they considered to be the most qualified for judging the adequacy of educational experiences for superior and talented students.

The third procedure consisted of developing a relatively comprehensive list of general features and processes which represented various identifiable dimensions of programs for the gifted. This list was based upon those aspects of differential education which have received considerable and continued emphasis in both the general literature on the gifted and in the literature dealing more specifically with programs and program evaluation. The list was submitted to the panel of judges with the requests that (a) they rank in order of importance those features which they consider to be the most necessary for a worthy program, and (b) they stop ranking when that number of features which would assure a program of high quality had been reached. Thus, it can be seen that isolating the key features of programs for the gifted was based on the judgment of persons who were considered to represent the very best thinking in the field of education for the gifted.

The results of this inquiry were tabulated by means of a pooled frequency rating technique that was based on the popular method of assigning to the most frequently chosen response the rank of number one. In order that the rank numbers used in summing the data correspond to increasing magnitudes of importance, each rank was assigned a rank value. The rank values consisted of a series of numbers which were in the exact reverse order of the ranks. Since the maximum number of program features ranked by any one member of the panel of judges equalled 16, this rank value was assigned to rank one. Accordingly, rank two was assigned a rank value of 15 and so on, down to rank 16 which was assigned a rank value of one. These results are presented in Table 1. The pooled frequency rating of each program feature was expressed in terms of its total rank

215

TABLE 1

Matrix of Frequencies with Which Each of 15 Program Features Were
Ranked in Each of 16 Positions by 21 Selected Judges

	Rank 1	2	3	4	5	6	7	8	9	10	11	12	13	14	15	16	Total rank value
Rank value	16	15	14	13	12	11	10	9	8	7	6	5	4	3	2	1	
Program features																	
The teacher: selection and training	7 (112)	4 (60)	4 (56)	1 (13)	1 (12)	1 (11)	1 (10)										274
The curriculum: purposefully distinctive	3 (48)	4 (60)	6 (74)	1 (13)	2 (24)	1 (11)	1 (10)										240
Student selection procedures		4 (60)	4 (56)	2 (26)	3 (36)	2 (22)	2 (20)										220
A statement of philosophy and objectives	9 (144)	1 (15)	2 (28)	1 (13)					1 (8)								208
Staff orientation	1 (16)	6 (90)	2 (28)	1 (13)	1 (12)	3 (33)			1 (8)								200
A plan of evaluation					4 (48)	4 (44)	2 (20)	1 (9)	1 (8)		1 (6)		1 (4)				139
Administrative responsibility	1 (15)	1 (14)	2 (26)	3 (36)	1 (11)	1 (10)				1 (7)		1 (5)					125
Guidance services				1 (13)	2 (24)	1 (11)	3 (30)	1 (9)	1 (8)								95
Ability grouping and/or acceleration				2 (26)	1 (12)	2 (22)	1 (10)	1 (9)	1 (8)			1 (5)					92
Special equipment and facilities				3 (39)	1 (12)	1 (11)				1 (7)			1 (4)				73
Use of community resources		1 (14)						2 (18)	1 (8)	1 (7)				1 (3)			50
Early admission				1 (13)		1 (11)		1 (9)	1 (8)								41
Community interpretation						1 (11)		3 (27)							1 (2)		40
Supplementary expenditures				1 (13)		1 (11)					1 (6)	1 (5)					35
A program of research				1 (13)					1 (8)					1 (3)		1 (1)	25

Note: The seven write ins, each receiving one vote, and their total rank values, are as follows: Community Support for Quality Education, 10; Morale and Esprit de Corps, 9; Student Assessment and Reassessment, 9; Student Performance, Evaluation, and Reporting, 10; Interpretation to Parents and Selected Students, 9; Small and Flexible Groups, 13; and Pupil Interpretation, 13.

Numbers in parentheses denote the weighted value of each frequency, i.e., the frequency multiplied by its rank value.

value. In addition to the 15 program features included in the original inquiry, Table 1 also contains 7 write-ins submitted by various members of the panel and the total rank value of each. The program features are listed in hierarchical order according to total rank value.

It is readily apparent from Table 1 that the uppermost 7 features of differential programs emerged as a relatively distinguishable group. It should be noted that the remaining features were both good and desirable elements of special programs; however, the ratings of the judges seemed to warrant the assignment of priorities to certain aspects of program development and evaluation. For this reason, the 7 features which achieved the highest collective ratings by the panel of judges were designated as key features. In the sections that follow, brief attention will be given to these important aspects of differential programs.

Discussion

Key feature A: The teacher. Although there is little question that all students should have well qualified teachers, the relatively greater demands made upon teachers by vigorous and imaginative young minds require that special attention be given to the selection and training of teachers for gifted and talented students. A number of statements in the literature in the form of principles (Ward, 1961; Williams, 1958) call attention to this important dimension of special programming and Newland (1962) has provided us with a breakdown of essential qualifications that can serve as guides in teacher selection.

Key feature B: The curriculum. Experiences comprising the curriculum for gifted and talented students should be recognizably different from the general educational program that is geared toward the ability level of average learners. These experiences should be purposefully designed to evoke and develop superior behavioral potentialities in both academic areas and in the fine and performing arts. A systematic and comprehensive program of studies should reach all children identified as gifted at every grade level and in all areas of the curriculum where giftedness is educationally significant. The careful development of distinctive syllabi, methods, and materials will help guard against a fragmentary or "more of the same" conception of differential education. A number of Ward's (1961) theoretical principles of education for the gifted are particularly relevant to curriculum development and can provide valuable guidance in constructing truly differential experiences.

Key feature C: Student selection procedures. The literature on giftedness is replete with information relating to the identification and placement of superior students. This key feature acknowledges the existence of all reliably identifiable types of giftedness and calls for the appropriate and discriminating use of several identifying instruments and processes. Periodic screening to obviate overlooking talent of any kind should be followed by

217

increasingly refined, exacting, and fair appraisal of specific abilities. Identification and placement procedures should be carried out at least once annually, and provisions for succeeding search beyond the initial screening and for transfer into and out of the program should also exist.

Key feature D: A statement of philosophy and objectives. The essential role played by statements of philosophy and objectives in guiding the developing of *all* educational enterprises is well known. Underlying statements of philosophy and objectives should take into account the arguments that support special programs, the broad and specific goals of the program, and the distinction between the objectives of general education and those that have particular relevance to differential education for the gifted. Although there is some possibility of well developed programs existing without written statement about the nature of philosophy and objectives, it seems highly improbable that school systems that have not taken the time to develop such documents will make serious inroads toward the implementation of comprehensive differential programming.

Key feature E: Staff orientation. In order to succeed, any educational venture needs the cooperation and support of those persons who are responsible for its implementation. A sympathetic attitude toward special provisions for the gifted and a basic understanding of the theory and operation of a special program on the part of all staff members are considered to be important elements in helping to realize a program's maximum effectiveness. In most instances, staff members not directly connected with the gifted student program usually participate indirectly by identifying and recommending students for placement. It is therefore necessary that they recognize the nature and needs of potential program participants, are knowledgeable about the available facilities, and are committed to the value of differential qualities of experience.

Key feature F: A plan of evaluation. Within the field of education for the gifted, the need for evidence of program effectiveness is well recognized. But the particularized objectives and relatively unique learning experiences that characterize truly differential programs require the use of objective evaluative schemes that take into account a variety of important program dimensions. One approach to program evaluation developed by Ward and Renzulli (1967) utilized each of the key features here reported as focal points around which a set of evaluative scales were developed. The instrument, entitled Diagnostic and Evaluative Scales for Differential Education for the Gifted, was designed to point out specific areas in which program improvement seems warranted.

Key feature G; Administrative responsibility. A clear designation of administrative responsibility is an essential condition for the most efficient operation of all school programs. Although size and resources of a school system will determine the amount of administrative time that can be allotted to the gifted student program, it is necessary that the person in charge of even the smallest program be given sufficient time and resources to carry out his administrative duties in this area. Already overburdened

218

administrators, supervisors, and teachers who are given the responsibility of a special program as an extra assignment without a corresponding reduction in other duties are likely to approach the task with less than optimal enthusiasm.

Summary and Conclusions

The intent of this study was to isolate those features within programs for gifted that are considered by recognized authorities in the field to be the most essential for a worthy program. The effort was aimed at providing a sound rationale for decision making to persons who are involved in various aspects of programming for the exceptionally able. On the basis of the rankings by the panel of judges, there appears to be justification for designating certain program elements and characteristics as key features in programs for the gifted. Such a designation is considered to be useful in identifying areas in which concentration should be placed in the process of program development and evaluation. The key features isolated in the present study do not pertain to any given pattern or organization, but rather attempt to embrace excellent practices presently operating, either individually or in varying combinations, and practices that can and should be inaugurated in view of the behavioral potential of students who possess identifiably superior abilities.

References

Newland, T.E. Some observations on essential qualifications of teachers of the mentally superior. *Exceptional Children,* 1962, **29,** 111–114.

Ward, V.S. *Educating the gifted: An axiomatic approach.* Columbus, Ohio: Charles E. Merrill, 1961.

Ward, V.S., & Renzulli, J.S. Program evaluation in differential education for the gifted. In The Council for Exceptional Children, *CEC selected convention papers 1967.* Washington, D. C.: CEC, 1967. 36–41.

Williams, C.W. Characteristics and objectives of a program for the gifted. In National Council for the Study of Education, *Education for the gifted.* 57th Yearbook. Chicago: University of Chicago Press, 1958. 147–165.

James J. Gallagher

Needed: A New Partnership
for the Gifted

*T*his paper concentrates on suggestions for new programme adjustments for gifted children. Such suggestions will become understandable only with some background into the American educational ecology. Therefore, a brief review of the effects of that social envelope on American programmes in public schools is in order. Discussions of American higher education are beyond the scope of this paper.

No educational system is understandable apart from the culture it serves. An educational system operates as a mirror of the society it represents. If there are special problems in the educational system, then it is likely that these problems also exist in the society as a whole. It is also probably true that the educational system can deviate only to a small degree from the basic values of the society as a whole, without getting into substantial difficulties.

If one finds students not accepting responsibility for others and thinking only of themselves, then it would be likely that that would be a general characteristic of the larger adult society. If one finds a school system in which only one voice and one authority is permitted, and that intellectual exploration is discouraged beyond certain well-established boundary lines, then it is likely that such restrictions also exist in the larger society. Therefore, the way in which we educate gifted children is inevitably tied to the larger fabric of the society.

Perhaps that is why we pay such particular attention to the visible administrative package in which programmes for the gifted are displayed to the society. We concern ourselves with the form, with the administrative structure, with the nature and shape of the package, rather than the contents of the package, because it is the administrative form that will be seen and reacted to by the significant public in the society.

In the United States we have had prolonged, if not very helpful, discussions about the usefulness of special classes for gifted children versus special stimulation within the regular class, or on such issues as acceleration of gifted students, or on whether open classrooms or team teaching or other such devices are helpful or harmful. We do not often focus on the

220

essential and distinctive interaction between the teacher and the child, distinctive because of the special needs of the gifted and talented youngster.

Each society establishes, informally or formally, areas or boundary lines that tend to shape the manner in which the educational system deals with its general responsibilities, or with the special or unusual issues of education such as the gifted child. Four such parameters in the United States will be noted that seem to be particularly powerful in influencing the nature of the administrative package in which programmes for the gifted child are delivered.

(1) *Egalitarianism.* There is a strong and continuing belief in the need to give all citizens equal treatment and educational opportunity. There is an accompanying determination among American citizens that there shall be no 'special privileges for special people.' There is a healthy suspicion that the wealthy, the powerful, the intellectual élite are probably trying to tip the educational scales in favour of their families and their children. The establishment of special classes or schools for gifted children accordingly is often viewed by the general public as a disguised way of improving the education of the 'ruling class' children at the expense of the other students.

Americans are not opposed to differential education. To the contrary, we speak incessantly about the need to individualise instruction (Lillie, 1975). We have made remarkable strides in providing special education for handicapped citizens. Public money spent on educating handicapped children has increased 300% over the past decade (Gallagher *et al.,* 1974). The society looks with compassion and wishes to support those parents who have children with these special problems, but it still does not allow special programmes for gifted children to be adequately funded.

The same spirit of egalitarianism has caused us to devote a great deal of attention, in the last decade, to finding gifted children from culturally different backgrounds (Torrance, 1974; Gallagher and Kinney, 1974). This interest has caused a broadening of the term 'gifted' to include other talents than the cognitive skills measured by standard IQ tests. We now include creativity, artistic talent, and leadership, in the definition. We have devised special tests and other measures to detect the talents in populations of Blacks, Orientals, Indians, Chicanos and other subgroups of society that do not currently share equally in the advantages of American society. All of this to support the general proposition that fair and equal treatment should be the educational rôle.

(2) *Universal Education.* The United States probably holds more children within its public education system through a longer period of their youth than most other nations. It is the expectation that most students will finish their secondary school programme and, in fact, we call them *dropouts* if they do not.

The consequence of this policy is that many children who ordinarily would have dropped out of the school system, particularly children who have not done well and would otherwise have gone into the world to work, continue in the educational stream. This creates a range of talents and diversity of motivation that must be resolved for effective education to occur in the secondary schools. Much of the pressure for providing special programming for gifted children stems from the manifest impossibility of trying to satisfy simultaneously, within the same learning environment, the needs of children who might have a range in IQ from 70 to 150, and in achievement from the primary grades to college level performance.

(3) *Decentralisation of Educational Decision-making.* Another specific American value involves the tradition within the American society to distrust centralised decision-making. We distrust uncontrolled authority at the federal level and there is a public desire to maintain as much educational decision-making as possible at the local or state level. Although there has been a gradual trend for significant educational decision-making to move from the local to state and federal levels it is always done with great reluctance and reserve.

(4) *The Value of Competition.* There is a long tradition which maintains that there is a great merit in the value of competition in American society. This relates to the economic system of free enterprise with the philosophy that as we compete with one another, we sharpen our skills and make more efficient our business practices. In this way the general public gets the best possible product. The interest in competition extends over into the American passion for sports.

Such a viewpoint can hardly encourage special programmes for the gifted. Support for such programmes is like aiding a powerful opponent who can then more adequately defeat you in life's race.

It has only been recently recognised that we need to stress cooperation as well as competition. We face many complex problems such as energy, pollution, and full-employment and these problems will not be solved in a short term conflict or adversary model, nor by individual competitive efforts, nor even by Presidential proclamation or Congressional legislation. Only a long, hard, cooperative effort of the most talented of our citizens will achieve our long term goals.

STRATEGIES DETERMINED BY SOCIETAL BOUNDARIES

The consequences of these above noted set of values have led to several educational strategies which often seem peculiar to visitors to the United States who are not aware of the effect of the underlying societal values. One consequence stemming from the values noted above is an extraordinarily weak federal effort for education of the gifted, and, in fact, for all levels of education, excluding higher education. The first timid federal legislation designed to pay special attention to the gifted passed only in the last Congressional session, and represents a small effort to stimulate state and local governments to expand their programmes for the gifted.

Many individual states such as California, Illinois, Pennsylvania, North Carolina have had programmes for a decade or more. We must consider that the major federal involvement in public education is only a decade old, and the state and local governments still pay over 93% of the costs of all public education below the college level (Rossmiller *et al.,* 1969).

Another consequence of the underlying value system is a reluctance to engage in long-range planning. The reasons for this reluctance is that 'long-range planning' means some central authority will maintain control over the allocation of resources for an extended period of time. As one of my colleagues once said, 'Whether I am in favour of planning or not depends on whether I am planning for someone else, or whether someone else is planning for me!' The inability to create and maintain long-range plans relates to our separation of powers and a consequent inability to control the necessary resources needed to carry out a plan (Gallagher, 1975).

Finally we see within the educational programmes themselves a strong desire to avoid complete separation of gifted children from the rest of their age mates in the school setting. Such a complete separation in a special school or classroom signals, to some people, an attempt to give a better education to some students at the expense of others. Thus, the most popular administrative device now in use in the US is the *resource room* or *itinerant teacher* approach in which the gifted student spends a part of the academic day with an unselected group, and part of the day with a specially trained teacher assigned to help the gifted and talented. While such resource programmes are expanding, even they are still available to only a very small proportion of gifted students in the US.

SPECIAL EDUCATIONAL PROVISIONS FOR THE GIFTED

With that brief background we might now explore the nature of the special programmes for gifted children that can be created within these administrative boundaries. The research on characteristics of the gifted clearly indicates the general problem (Martinson, 1972). Many of these children are performing three to five grades beyond their age mates and are bored by repetitive and too-easy tasks. Their disenchantment with school and with learning can be profound and troublesome.

In a recent publication, Gallagher (1975) pointed out that there are three major areas where one can modify the existing school programme, in order to meet the needs of exceptional children. The first of these is the *content,* that set of knowledge that one presents to the student. Changes can be made in the nature of the knowledge presented within established subject areas, such as mathematics or history, or in the inclusion of new content areas not always available to other students, such as the development of ethics and value systems.

223

The second area of potential programme change lies in the specific *skills* that one wishes the student to develop. In the case of the gifted, the enhancement of such special skills as the ability to problem-solve and to engage in productive thinking, to be creative, has been a recent US emphasis. This is a recognition of the rapidly changing world we live in and the great need to develop students who are flexible in their thinking skills and their ability to identify problems needing solutions, and in proposing possible solutions.

As Silberman (1970) has put it,

> To be practical, an education should prepare a man for a work that doesn't yet exist and whose nature cannot even be imagined. This can only be done by teaching children how to learn and by giving them the kind of intellectual discipline that will enable them to apply man's accumulated wisdom to new problems.

Much of the work in the last decade in education for the gifted has been on devices to stimulate creative thinking, to produce novel solutions, and to learn the excitement of bringing something new into existence. Much of this in turn has been stimulated by the work of J. P. Guilford (1969) whose model of the *structure of intellect* has been used as the basis for a large number of educational attempts to stimulate youngsters in dimensions of *divergent thinking* that seem related to the creative process. Divergent thinking, the ability to think of many answers and unique solutions to problems, has the virtue of opening up an intellectual area, and allowing for intellectual exploration that is not encouraged by mere factual or tightly structured problems given to the student.

For example, 'What would happen if everyone in the world were born with three fingers and no thumb?' is an example of a question stimulating divergent thinking, encouraging many different answers, stimulating the child's imagination. While such exercises, if kept in isolation, are only intellectual games, divergent thinking can be used with important curricular questions.

Consider the question, 'What would happen if the world's population tripled in the next quarter of a century?' This gives the student free rein to explore a wide variety of dimensions and to begin thinking about issues that need solutions. Since that particular proposition seems to be the best estimate of the United Nations regarding potential population growth in the world, it is appropriate that the best minds of the world should be spending more than a casual amount of time on it and of thinking of all possible solutions.

One of the more popular *skills* to be stimulated for gifted students has been related to the curriculum movement in the physical and social sciences in the 1960's (Martin and Pinck, 1966). It has been labelled the *discovery method*. The virtue of the discovery method is that the students themselves are not told the larger ideas or principles to be discovered, but the materials and experiences are organised by the teacher in such a way that the students will come upon these larger ideas by themselves. This presumably duplicates, in some measure, the scientist's excitement in discovering a new concept or idea, and encourages an activist approach to learning rather than forcing the child to be a passive receptacle of information. Kagan (1965) emphasised four arguments in favour of using the discovery method.

1. Studies of both animals and young children indicate that the more active involvement required of the organism, the greater the likelihood of learning. . . . A major advantage of the discovery strategy is that it creates arousal and as a result, maximal attention.
2. Because the discovery approach requires extra intellectual effort, the value of the task is increased. . . . It is reasonable to assume that activities become valuable to the degree to which effort is expended in their mastering.
3. The inferential or discovery approach is likely to increase the child's expectancy that he is able to solve different problems autonomously. . . .
4. The discovery approach gives the child more latitude and freedom and removes him from the submissive posture ordinarily maintained between teacher and child.

Therefore the basic *skills* that are stimulated in the programmes for the gifted involve extensive attention to the creative process, where the expectation is that something new and original will be produced, and in problem-solving, in which important elements are put together to reach complex answers.

The third major programme element that can be changed to meet the special needs of children is that of the *learning environment* itself. These changes are made to create a facilitating environment which allows for certain instructional goals to be reached that otherwise would not be accomplished. Figure I shows the hierarchy of services for special education arranged according to the amount of special time spent by the student apart from the regular programme. One can note that the change can range from a very minor one such as having a special teacher meet with the gifted a few hours a week, to establishing a special school for the gifted such as the famous Bronx High School of Science or the Julliard School of Music in New York City.

There is currently in American special education a philosophy of the least *restrictive environment* which means the child should be moved out of the regular programmes only to the degree absolutely necessary and to return the child to the regular programme when those special needs have been met. There is some feeling against the use of special schools or special classes for the gifted, if the same results could be obtained through a part-time special class or a class with a resource teacher added, who would work with gifted children for a part of the school day — as does the music teacher or athletic coach.

Leta Hollingworth (1942), a half century ago, posed a question: How shall a democracy educate its most educable? There is no more important question in all American education.' She was right and the question remains, if not untouched, at least unresolved. I would like to focus on one of the three demensions, *content*, as an area most in need of further development. My thesis is that unless special content becomes an integral part of the special programme the emphasis on *skills* and learning *environment* is largely wasted. Furthermore, if the content is properly organised and presented it can be done in any number of environments so that the fuss over programme structure is somewhat spurious.

In the area of *skills* it certainly is appropriate that the gifted child be taught strategies of problem-solving and creativity. However, in the end, they must be creative about *something*! Indeed, the study of creative adults (Barron, 1969) shows that they are sophisticated individuals who have a true passion for a given subject which they often satisfied outside the school setting. They possess personality characteristics to persist in the face of difficulty, and the ego strength to ignore social pressures and criticism that is the essence of the creative person, not necessarily a person who possesses a bag of little cognitive tricks and games.

To spend literally months and years engineering a programme of special classes for the gifted (a change in the *learning environment*) and then pay little attention to what *content* goes into those classes is analogous to the farmer spending months preparing the soil on his farm and then being indifferent to what quality seed he plants there.

In the area of content, the curriculum designed for the gifted student should be different from the average student in its greater stress on advanced conceptualisation and important ideas that cannot be easily grasped by students at similar age but of average or below average ability. The rapid expansion of knowledge in all content fields in recent years has led to an avalanche of new information. Unless school curricula are carefully constructed, and unless strict self-discipline is practised by the teachers, the student can be drowned in a pool of interesting, but distracting, facts and information.

We need to be about the business of trying to synthesise the available information in various content fields into essential principles and ideas, and then designing educational experiences that will help the student grasp these ideas. The rationale for this proposition of teaching the basic ideas of the content field which formed the basis for many of the major curriculum movements in mathematics, science and social science of the 1960's has been most concisely put by Bruner (1960).

> The first is that understanding fundamentals makes a subject more comprehensible. This is true not only in physics and mathematics . . . but equally in the social studies and literature. Once one has grasped the fundamental idea

that a nation must trade to live, then such a presumably special phenomenon as the Triangular Trade of the American Colonies becomes simpler to understand as something more than commerce in molasses, sugar cane, rum and slaves.

The second point relates to human memory. Perhaps the most basic thing that can be said about human memory is that unless detail is placed into a structured pattern, it is rapidly forgotten. A scientist does not try to remember the distances traversed by falling bodies in different gravitational fields. What he carries in memory instead is a formula that permits him to regenerate the details on which the more easily remembered formula is based.

Third, an understanding of fundamental principles and ideas appears to be the main road to adequate transfer of training. To understand something as a specific instance of a more general case is to have learned not only a specific thing but also a model for understanding other things like it that one may encounter (pp. 23-5).

Examples of how such synthesis of important ideas can be done and, in fact, the viability of the approach, has been illustrated by two television series produced by the BBC: the first by Kenneth Clark on *Civilisation* (1970) and the second by Bronowski and the *Ascent of Man* (1973). Each of these series tried to take central ideas and major insights and build a set of illustrative examples, conceptual linkages and consequences around them. Let me read a few brief quotes from the Bronowski series, as examples of major ideas that are well within the grasp of gifted and talented from preadolescence onward.

War, organised war, is not a human instinct. It is a highly planned and cooperative theft. And that form of theft began ten thousand years ago when the harvesters of wheat accumulated a surplus and the nomads rose out of the desert to rob them of what they themselves could not provide.

The architecture of things reveals the structure below the surface, a hidden grain, which, when it is laid bare, makes it possible to take natural formations apart to assemble them in new arrangements. For me this is a step in the ascent of man, in which theoretical science begins.

The different cultures have used fire for the same purposes: to keep warm, to drive off predators, and clear woodland, and to make simple transformations of everyday life, to cook, to dry and harden wood, to heat and split stones. But, of course, the great transformation that helped us make our civilisation goes deeper: it is the use of fire to disclose a wholly new class of materials, the metals.

Easter Island is over a thousand miles from the nearest inhabited island. . . . Distances like that cannot be navigated unless you have a model of the heavens and of star positions by which to find your way. People often ask about Easter Island, how did men come here? They came here by accident: that is not the question. The question is why could they not get off? And they could not get off because they did not have a sense of the movement of the stars by which to find their way.

The horse and the rider have many anatomical features in common. But it is the human creature who rides the horse, and not the other way about. There is no wiring inside the brain that makes us horse riders. Riding a horse is a comparatively recent invention, less than five thousand years old. And yet it has had an immense influence, for instance, on our social structure. Plasticity of human behaviour makes that possible. That is what characterises us in our social institutions, of course, and above all, in our books, because they are the permanent products of the total interest of the human mind.

Can we as educators of gifted students create curriculum materials that circle and orbit around these large powerful ideas? I think the answer is no, not by ourselves. We educators do not have enough depth of content knowledge, in and of ourselves, to create such results. Indeed, one of the clear reasons why educators have been so involved in the *process* of thinking, in creativity and in problem-solving, is that that is the domain in which they have some skill and feel comfortable.

The same confidence and sense of mastery does not apply in fields such as economics, psychology, physics, etc. Ideas of major substance from these fields will not come from teachers or educators but from scholars, so I would suggest a new alliance, a new partnership, of the scholar and the educator that can generate these new products.

For a brief moment of seven or eight years or so there was such a marriage of scholars and teachers, of universities and public schools in the United States to produce a systematic reorganisation of knowledge in mathematics, physical science and social sciences. These projects followed similar structural goals (Goodlad, 1964).

1. To teach the basic structure of the discipline.
2. To have the student approach the subject matter as the specialist approaches it.
3. To introduce ideas as early as possible.

Our current problems can be, and perhaps should be, placed in the boldest of terms. It is too important to allow us to be kind to our own limitations. Let me give one brief example. Can we survive one more generation of economic illiteracies? The attempts to clarify these complex economic issues are few and far between for adults or for children. Senesh (1964) some years ago generated some basic ideas that form the cornerstone of an elementary curriculum in economics.

> All people and all nations are confronted with the conflict between their unlimited wants and limited resources. The degree of conflict may vary but the conflict is always present.
> In all countries, the basic questions to be answered are: What goods and services will be produced? How much of these will be produced? How will they be produced and who will receive the goods and resources?

It takes a knowledgeable professional (like Senesh, Bruner or Bronowski) to talk in such elegantly simple terms, but it takes the creative teacher to bring those ideas to life for young children.

Why can we not merely take the work of the curriculum projects of the Sixties? These were designed for a total curriculum and could not be used without major adaptation. We need material for the resource teacher and

228

the part-time class that fits that mode. We also recognize that we know more now ten years later, and that new knowledge needs to be included too.

The procedure by which this new partnership can be accomplished is not obscure. We know the general outline of what might be needed to accomplish our goal. Let me outline a few of the key steps.

1. Identify key scholars who would participate in their content field.
2. Aid the scholars in obtaining a consensus on major or key concepts in his discipline. The Delphi technique or Delbeque procedure could easily be used (House, 1972).
3. Bring together, in the summer holidays, curriculum teams of teachers and educators to generate curriculum experiences, tasks and materials surrounding these ideas. Some of the scholars could be present to speak on the validity of these efforts.
4. Materials can be field tested in selected programmes for gifted with careful formative evaluation data collected.
5. A second summer can be used to rewrite the materials and then release for dissemination. The training of teachers in the effective use of the materials probably represents the most pertinent use of our limited resources.

We might mention a few barriers that stand in the way of implementing such a 'splendid' idea. It is an American custom to think first of the lack of money as the key barrier to implementing new ideas or programmes. While funds are always a factor, there are other problems as well. They can be expressed in the language of professional status or territorial imperative or 'what are you doing in my garden?' Can the scholars put aside their academic status and mingle with public school teachers without feeling that they are demeaning themselves? Can the educators and teachers who have controlled this small domain of gifted children for many years run the risk of opening up an area to invasion by scholars who just might start taking over the leadership of the movement?

These, plus the natural timidity we all face when interacting with others with different backgrounds from ourselves, are the real barriers. 'Nothing is gained without risk', we tell our gifted children. It is a slogan we need to paste over our bathroom mirrors so that we see it every morning. We all have to decide if the risk is worth the gain. The thesis of this paper is that this risk is worth the manifest strengthening of the content, the heart of a differential educational programme for the gifted.

As Arnold Toynbee said so eloquently:

> The Creator has withheld from Man the shark's teeth, the bird's wings, the elephant's trunk and the hound's or horse's racing feet. The creative power planted in a minority of mankind has to do duty for all the marvellous physical assets that are built into every specimen of Man's nonhuman fellow creatures. If society fails to make the most of this one human asset, or if

perversely sets out to stifle it, then Man is throwing away his birthright of being the lord of creation and is condemning himself to be, instead, the least effective species on the face of this planet.

References

Barron, F. *Creative person and creative process.* New York: Holt, Rinehart and Winston, 1969.

Bronowski, J. *The ascent of man.* Boston: Little Brown, 1973.

Bruner, J. *The process of education.* Cambridge, Mass: Harvard University Press, 1960.

Clark, K. *Civilisation.* New York: Harper & Row, 1970.

Gallagher, J. *Educating the gifted child.* Boston: Allyn & Bacon, 1975.

Gallagher, J., Forsythe, P., Rengelheem, D. & Weintraub, F. Funding patterns and labelling. In Hobbs, N. (Ed.), *Issues in the classification of children. Vol II*, San Francisco: Jossey-Bass Publishers, 1975.

Gallagher, J., & Kinney, L. (Eds.), *Talent delayed—talent denied:* A conference report. Reston, Va.: Foundation for Exceptional Children, 1974.

Goodlad, J. I., *School curriculum reform in the United States.* New York: Fund for the Advancement of Education, 1964.

Gowan, J. *Development of the creative individual.* San Diego, Calif.: Robert Knapp Publishers, 1972.

Guilford, J. P. *The nature of human intelligence.* New York: McGraw Hill, 1972.

Hollingworth, L. *Children above 180 IQ.* New York: World Book, 1942.

House, E. *School evaluation.* Berkeley, California: McCutchon, 1973.

Kagan, J. Personality and the learning process. *Daedelus,* **94**, 553–63, 1965.

Lillie, D. *Early childhood education.* Chicago: Science Research Associates, 1975.

Martin, W. & Pinck, D. (Eds.). *Curriculum improvement and innovation.* Cambridge, Mass.: Bentley, 1966.

Martinson, R. An analysis of problems and priorities: Advocate survey and statistics sources. *Education of the gifted and talented.* Report to the Congress of the United States by the US Commissioner of Education. Washington DC: GPO, 1972.

Reynolds, M. A framework for considering some issues in Special Education. *Exceptional Children,* **28**, 367–70, 1962.

Rossmiller, R. Dimensions of need for educational programmes for exceptional children. In Jolius, R., Alexander, K., & Rossmiller, R. *Dimensions of educational need.* National Education Finance Project. Gainsville, Fla., 1969.

Senesh, L. The organic curriculum: A new experience in economic education. In J. Gallagher (Ed.), *Teaching gifted students: A book of readings.* Boston: Allyn and Bacon, 1965.

Torrance, E. P. Broadening concepts of giftedness in the 70's. In S. Kirk & F. Lord (Eds.), *Exceptional children: Educational resources and perspectives.* Boston: Houghton Mifflin, 1974.

Donald J. Treffinger

Guidelines for Encouraging Independence and Self-Direction Among Gifted Students

Gifted, talented, and creative students are often described as independent in thought and judgment. Consequently, some parents and teachers assume that this means such students will be able to skillfully organize their own efforts, conduct their own learning activities, and behave consistently in a well-organized, self-directed manner. Unfortunately, this assumption is not always warranted. Because a child has the *predisposition* or *potential* for independent, self-directed behavior we cannot infer that he/she already possesses the *skills* necessary for the realization of that potential. Responsible self-direction of learning does not "just happen"; therefore, it is important for gifted, talented, and creative students to have support and well-planned assistance at home and in school in building independence.

Definition of Self-directed Learning

It is important, first of all, to define self-directed learning. This term should not refer to "doing whatever you want to do, whenever you want to do it." Approaches that remove all standards and boundaries may lead to poor quality, lack of motivation and sustained effort, and quick boredom with the tasks at hand. (The cartoon best illustrating this problem portrayed a group of kindergarten students, with one young person asking the teacher, "Do we have to do whatever we want to do again today?")

A more productive definition of independent, self-directed learning might be summarized in the phrase, *"responsible autonomy."* In this approach, we are concerned with helping children learn how to make decisions more effectively concerning all aspects of their learning. In a recent pilot program on self-directed learning at the elementary school

Reprinted from Journal of Creative Behavior, Vol. 12, No. 1 (First quarter, 1978), pp. 14–20.

level, for example, Barton (1976) stated five general goals for self-directed learning:

1. Learning to function more effectively in one's total environment (classroom, school, home, and community) with peers, teachers, parents, and other adults;
2. Learning to make choices and decisions based on self-knowledge of needs and interests;
3. Learning to assume responsibility for choices and decisions by completing all activities at a satisfactory level of achievement and in an acceptable time frame;
4. Learning to define problems and to determine a course of action for their solution;
5. Learning to evaluate one's own work and be able to answer the question, "How well can I do what I want to do?"

Similar goals for self-directed learning for gifted and talented students were presented by Treffinger (1975), and for college students by Treffinger and Johnsen (1973).

We believe, therefore, that responsible autonomy is an *important* goal for teachers and parents of gifted, talented, and creative students. We also believe that this goal can be attained more effectively through *deliberate efforts* by teachers and parents to help students develop the skills of independent, self-directed learning.

Guidelines

The major purpose of this paper, then, is to provide some initial guidelines for parents and teachers. These guidelines are drawn from our pilot programs, and so should be considered tentative; additional research and development activities are now being conducted. The author welcomes correspondence from parents and teachers who are interested in additional information.

1. *Admonitions are inadequate.* It may seem obvious, but many people still don't seem to recognize that *telling* a child to act more independently is not sufficient to help the child *do* it. If such admonitions contribute anything, it may only be that they help focus attention on the question of independence. If the child does not know how to direct his/her own learning, it is unlikely that saying, "Be independent!" will help very much.

2. *Don't assume.* We often get into trouble because we make too many unwarranted assumptions about what children already know or don't know, or about what skills they have or have not mastered. The most basic solution is simply to *find out*, through informal assessment procedures or more formal diagnostic work, just what the student's strengths and skills really are. Parents and teachers frequently complain, for example, that the

gifted child spends too much time with "busywork". However, we cannot always assume that, because a child is bright, all of the "basics" of language, mathematics, or reading will already have been mastered. The child should not have to spend time with useless, repetitive seatwork—*if* indeed it is work that she/he does not need. We should make efforts to *determine* those needs, rather than proceed on assumptions.

3. *Don't smother self-direction by doing for them things they can do (or can learn to do) for themselves.* From the earliest school years teachers and parents trying to help children often do for them many things they could quite readily do themselves. In school, children quickly learn to accept that adults should tell them what to learn, when to learn it, how to go about it, and when it has been completed satisfactorily. At home, parents may be impatient because they can do something for the child more quickly and easily than the child could do it alone. Perhaps, like the reluctant messiah in Richard Bach's *Illusions* (1977), we all need to learn *how* and *when* to say "*I* quit!"

4. *Adults must have or develop an attitude of openness and support for self-directed learning.* Some people are despots and enjoy it. Perhaps they find great satisfaction in their role as parent or teacher because they have the opportunity to direct and control the actions of others. In order to become a facilitator of self-directed, independent learning, however, a different adult role must be learned. You have to be willing to give up your own podium. You have to help the children define tasks for themselves and learn to adjust the difficulty of their goals to reasonable levels. You have to learn how to ask questions (even some for which you don't know the answer). You will learn to find new satisfactions from the children's accomplishments, rather than from your own importance. Our initial work suggests that when the teacher has a receptive attitude, the first step is to learn how to focus on the skills that the children need, and to help them develop those skills. As their behavior changes, however, you must be ready to adapt again: as they begin to behave more independently and creatively, you need to learn new ways to respond. You will not run out of things to do, but you will be doing new things—helping children with their own individual needs, interests, and activities, rather than distributing identical information to every child in the class.

5. *Learn to defer judgment.* It is very difficult for many parents and teachers to learn how and when to suspend or defer judgment in their dealings with children. It seems that it's very "natural" for us to want to tell children what's wrong, to show them their mistakes and direct them clearly toward a better effort. Certainly there is an appropriate time and place for critical review and evaluation. We seem too often unable to discern the appropriate times from the inappropriate, however, and we often behave as if *every* opportunity is an *appropriate* opportunity. Many times, however, excessive, premature, or arbitrary evaluation inhibits curiosity, stifles inquiry, or encourages undue dependency. To encourage self-directed learning involves refraining from continually "pouncing" upon

234

children, reducing our own arbitrary evaluative behavior, and helping children learn how to determine and utilize specific criteria when evaluation is appropriate.

6. *Emphasize the continuity of problems and challenges.* Children can learn to direct their own learning and to identify areas of interest for future investigation more readily when we give them opportunities to *synthesize* or *relate* various topics and problems we study. They can learn that problems and issues can be viewed in many different ways, and that the solution to one problem may become the starting point for formulating many new problems and challenges. This emphasis seems to be much more conducive to independent learning than one in which learning appears to be a matter of mastering an almost infinitely large body of isolated, unrelated facts.

7. *Provide systematic training in problem-solving and the skills of independent research and inquiry.* When we are confronted with a child's curiosity, there is too often the tendency to say, "Go look it up in the encyclopedia." But *how* do you find what you need? Where do you look? Where else beside the encyclopedia might you find useful information? How do you state the question to begin with? Children need systematic training in the methods and techniques of research and problem-solving. Fortunately, there are many effective programs and instructional materials available to assist us in providing these skills systematically. Some examples include the *Guide to Creative Action* (Parnes, Noller & Biondi, 1977), the *Productive Thinking Program* (Covington, Crutchfield, Olton & Davies, 1972), and the *Big Book of Independent Study* (Kaplan, Madsen & Gould, 1976). There have also been several reviews of programs and materials (Feldhusen & Treffinger, 1977; Torrance, 1972; Treffinger, 1977) and surveys of resources and procedures for learning research methodologies in various fields (Renzulli, 1976). Students should learn through active participation, rather than observation, how to assess interests and diagnose needs, develop a plan, locate resources, carry out appropriate activities, present their results, and evaluate their work.

8. *Treat difficult situations at home or school as opportunities to use creative problem-solving techniques, not merely as problems requiring the unilateral wisdom of an adult.* If students are learning how to conduct their own independent projects, and how to use more effectively a variety of methods and techniques for creative problem-solving, they should also have opportunities to use these skills in dealing with *real* problems and challenges. They need to see that these methods do actually help us in determining and implementing solutions to the kinds of problems we face every day. Both teachers and parents can probably identify many common situations, now handled by an adult, that could become the basis for real applications of what is learned by the children. For example, in school, the teacher and students might work together to develop classroom rules and daily procedures; at home, children and parents might work together to solve the problem of keeping rooms clean.

235

9. *Be alert to audiences that are appropriate for sharing children's efforts, or for opportunities to create such audiences.* Involvement in independent, self-directed learning leads students to develop new ideas, new products, or effective solutions to problems, which they are anxious to share with others. Our job is not merely to let them tell *us* about their efforts, or give them a chance to tell the class at "show and tell" time, but to help them find audiences for their efforts that are suitable and interested. Can older children have opportunities to share their efforts with younger ones? Are there community, service, or religious organizations that would be interested in the students' work and participation? Are there special interest clubs or societies in which the student might participate (regardless of age)? Are there places to publish written, artistic, or musical products? Can neighborhood plays or events be planned? Is there a museum or gallery that is interested in children's work? The "gallery" on the refrigerator door may be a beginning as is the bulletin board in the classroom or school corridor, but it is not the final step.

10. *Help students learn how to direct their own learning gradually— don't expect it to happen all at once.* Once a person gets interested in creating a climate for nurturing independent, self-directed learning, it is easy to become impatient, and to want to reach the goal very quickly. Sometimes we seem to say, "Okay, students. Now we want to have a classroom for independent learning. Go ahead!" If we proceed too quickly, we may expect independent behavior that the students cannot yet display. For the students, this can lead to frustration and lack of success in their efforts. For the teacher, it can lead to discouragement and premature rejection of the effort. Too many teachers have said, "I tried that in my room once and it didn't work," without having proceeded carefully and gradually over a sufficient period of time to enable the students to become effective in their efforts. Don't expect miracles from gifted, talented, and creative students, especially with older students who have already participated in several years of strongly teacher-dominated, rigidly-constrained teaching and learning.

We have found that a reasonable approach to the transition toward self-directed learning begins by helping the students learn to make choices from a small set of options (as in selecting from alternatives in learning centers). Next, the students can work together in teacher-learner pairs as they study specific skills selected in cooperative planning with the teacher. Gradually, they begin to work with the teacher to plan together a wider range of learning activities (involving group and individual work, using centers on an individually-planned basis), and, eventually, they can assume considerably greater responsibility for planning and conducting their own learning.[1]

11. *CREATE! Be a model of self-directed learning in your own life.* A teacher is not a person who has finished learning. In order to help your students in their efforts to become more effective in managing and directing their own work, they should have opportunities to know that you too are

a learner. Share with them your own curiosities and interests, and your own efforts to use creative problem-solving and research to deal with problems and challenges. The point is not that they should be interested in what you're interested in (so that you don't *impose* your interests upon them), but that they have opportunities to observe adults who are themselves occupied productively in independent inquiry.

Summary

Independent, self-directed learning is an important goal for educators and parents of gifted, talented, and creative students. It helps students find meaning and value in their learning, and provides an opportunity for creative expression. Through our efforts to encourage self-direction among our students, we can develop educational programs that are more than mere collections of curricula and activities.

We begin to discover what gifted education *is*, most uniquely and most importantly, when we explore ways in which to differentiate instruction, building upon the students' potential for independence in thought, judgment, and creative ability. Teaching or parenting in these ways can be very challenging. We must be prepared for extra hours, extra energy, extra searching and probing. But then, no one ever said that working with gifted, talented, and creative students would be easy.

References

Bach, R. *Illusions: the adventures of a reluctant messiah.* New York: Delacorte, 1977.

Barton, B. L. Toward the development of a self-directed learner. Unpublished Masters Thesis, University of Kansas, Lawrence, September, 1976.

Covington, M., Crutchfield, R., Olton, R. & Davies, L. *The productive thinking program.* Columbus, Oh: Merrill, 1972.

Feldhusen, J. F. & Treffinger, D. J. *Teaching creative thinking and problem-solving.* Dubuque, Ia: Kendall-Hunt, 1977.

Kaplan, S., Madsen, S. & Gould, B. *The big book of independent study.* Pacific Palisades, Ca: Goodyear, 1976.

Parnes, S. J., Noller, R. B. & Biondi, A. M. *Guide to creative action.* New York: Scribners, 1977.

Renzulli, J. S. *The enrichment triad model.* Wethersfield, Ct: Creative Learning Press, 1976.

Torrance, E. P. Can we teach children to think creatively? *Journal of Creative Behavior,* 1972, **6(2)** , 114-143.

Treffinger, D. J. Teaching for self-directed learning: a priority for the gifted and talented. *Gifted Child Quarterly,* 1975, **19**, 46-59.

Treffinger, D. J. Methods, techniques, and educational programs for stimulating creativity: 1975 revision. In Parnes, S. J., Noller, R. B. & Biondi, A. M., *Guide to creative action*. New York: Scribners, 1977, 248-259.

Treffinger, D. J. & Johnsen, E. P. On self-directed learning: when you say hello, do they write it in their notebooks? *Liberal Education*, 1973, **59**, 471-479.

Note

[1] Specific procedures for this transition have been described by Barton, 1976; additional information can be obtained from Dr. Treffinger.

Joseph S. Renzulli
Linda H. Smith

Developing Defensible Programs for the Gifted and Talented*

What is (or should be) different about the types of learning experiences that are advocated for gifted students? Isn't what you are doing for the gifted also good for nearly all youngsters?

Introduction

Unless satisfactory answers to these questions can be provided, programs that serve superior students will be extremely vulnerable to both critics of gifted education and to persons who, though sympathetic with this area, feel such special services are essentially a luxury item that schools can easily get by without. But more importantly, answers are necessary for those who experience pangs of conscience when they can defend programs for gifted youngsters philosophically, but not in terms of day-to-day experiences.

The purpose of this article therefore is threefold. First, some critical questions will be raised about a number of current practices that parade under the banner of special education for the gifted. Second, a rationale will be proposed for special programs that is based upon research studies dealing with the characteristics of gifted and creative persons. The third purpose will be to present a model that can be used as a guide by teachers and administrators in the development of truly defensible programs in this area of special education.

Some Concerns about Current Practices

Far too many programs for the gifted are essentially collections of fun-and-games activities. Children walk into a resource room for the gifted,

---

*This article is a summary by the authors of The Enrichment Triad Model: A Guide for Developing Defensible Programs for the Gifted and Talented, Wethersfield, CT: Creative Learning Press, 1977.

play a game or engage in craft-type activities until their class period is over, and return the next day to pursue some similar type of experience. In questioning teachers about the purpose or objectives of such activities, the reply is almost always that they are "challenging" and "really enjoyable" to the children.

Although gifted students should have an opportunity to participate in a variety of such exploratory experiences and activities, an important part of all programs for the gifted should be the systematic development of the cognitive and affective processes which brought these youngsters to our attention in the first place. Systematic development simply means that professional educators should know and be able to defend the types of processes that are being developed through the activities that gifted children pursue in special programs. While freedom of choice in topic and learning style are important, it is the teacher's responsibility to assist a youngster in developing the skills of inquiry that will make him or her a "first-hand inquirer" in the particular area in which he or she chooses to work.

When gifted youngsters do undertake individual research projects, there is frequently little difference between regular and special programs in the level of quality of inquiry. References consist of the same encyclopedias or library books used in the regular school program. The focus is frequently on the acquisition of knowledge or facts; where differences do exist, it is almost always in terms of freedom of choice, lack of pressure, and the absence of grading. Practices that are limited to this degree of differentiation have raised serious questions about the appropriateness of special programs for the gifted and talented.

Another general area of concern has been a preoccupation with mental processes and an almost complete absence of interest in the structure, methodology, and content of the organized fields of knowledge. In emphasizing mental processes via Bloom's *Taxonomy* and Guilford's *Structure-of-the-Intellect* model, our energies may have been put in the wrong place. While we have attempted to design curriculum that will develop the higher mental processes, it is open for question whether the valid *psychological* concept of mental process has been a useful educational concept so far as curriculum planning is concerned.

This is not to say that we are against process objectives or that these psychological phenomena do not exist and cannot be developed through programming. But it is more than likely that they are things that "just happen" in good learning situations, and the harder we try to force processes into a behavioral objectives type of format, the more artificial and structured the curriculum will become. Our preoccupation with process objectives has in fact caused us to forget that process is the path rather than the goal of learning.

Rationale for Special Programs

If many of the practices currently employed in special programs are not easily defended, what are the types of educational activities that will satisfy the criteria of qualitative differentiation? The answer to this question involves a variety of considerations, perhaps the most important of which is the definiton of giftedness itself. How one defines giftedness is crucial to the ways in which one goes about making provisions for persons in this category of exceptionality.

Research on gifted and creative persons in the adult world has shown that although no single criterion can be used to determine giftedness, persons who have achieved reputations of eminence possess a relatively well-defined cluster of three basic traits. The first of these traits is generally acknowledged to be an above average, though not necessarily exceptional, level of intelligence. In a review of several research studies dealing with the relationship between academic aptitude tests and professional achievement, Wallach (1976) has concluded that:

> Above intermediate score levels, academic skills assessments are found to show so little criterion validity as to be questionable bases on which to make consequential decisions about students' futures. What the academic tests do predict are the results a person will obtain on other tests of the same kind.

An impliction of this conclusion is that entrance into special programs should not be limited only to those students who score in the upper ranges on traditional measures of aptitude. If we accept this conclusion, however, the question is immediately raised—What other criteria should be used for identifying gifted students?

A second and perhaps more influential trait of eminent persons is a high level of task commitment or intrinsic motivation to perform in a particular area. Several studies have shown that accomplished scientists, writers, mathematicians, and architects are far more task-oreinted and involved in their work than are people in the general population (Roe, 1952; McCurdy, 1960; MacKinnon, 1964, 1965; and Helson, 1971). As Roe (1952) suggested in her findings on task commitment:

> The one thing that all of these scientists have in common is their driving absorption in their work. They have worked long hours for many years, frequently with no vacations to speak of, because they would rather be doing their work than anything else.

The third trait that characterizes gifted persons consists of abilities commonly grouped together under the heading of "creativity." Eminence in the adult world is usually regarded as prima-facie evidence that an individual possesses creative ability. In fact, the terms "gifted," "genius," and "eminent" are often used synonymously with the word "creative" when describing persons who have made significant contributions; it is

241

usually the originality, novelty, or uniqueness of a person's contribution that brings him or her to the attention of the public.

The study of eminent persons suggests that an interaction exists among the three basic traits that have been discussed—above average ability, task commitment, and creativity—and it is this interaction rather than any single trait or additive factor that results in superior performance. But in order for these traits to interact and manifest themselves they must have some type of problem with which to deal or a certain arena in which to perform. Thus, any definition of giftedness or formula for eminence in the adult world must take into consideration both the cluster of traits and a particular problem area to which these traits can be applied.

A Program Model

The Enrichment Triad Model represents an attempt to integrate the findings on the characteristics of eminent persons into an overall design for programming for gifted and talented students. As depicted in Figure 1, the Model consists of three interrelated types of enrichment activities. The first two types, General Exploratory Activities and Group Training Activities, are considered to be appropriate for all learners; however, they are also important in the overall enrichment of gifted and talented for at least two reasons. First, they deal with strategies for expanding student interests and developing thinking and feeling processes. Second, and perhaps more importantly, these two types of enrichment represent logical input and support systems for Type III Enrichment, which is considered to be the only type that is appropriate mainly for gifted students. Type III Enrichment, entitled Individual and Small Group Investigations of Real Problems, is the major focus of this model. As suggested in Figure 1, approximately one-half of the time that gifted students spend in enrichment activities should be devoted to these types of experiences.

Type I Enrichment: General Exploratory Experiences. Type I Enrichment consists of those experiences and activities that are designed to bring the learner into touch with the kinds of topics or areas of study in which he or she may have a sincere interest. These experiences should enable youngsters to begin to make their own decisions about the topics that they might like to explore at greater depths and higher levels of involvement. Thus, one of the major objectives of Type I Enrichment is to give both students and teachers some hints about what might be a bona fide Type III Enrichment activity. A second objective of Type I Enrichment situations is to assist teachers in making decisions about the kinds of Type II Enrichment activities that should be selected for particular groups of students.

At least two general guidelines are suggested to help achieve the objectives of Type I Enrichment. First, although a great deal of exploratory freedom must be permitted, students should be made aware that they are expected to pursue exploration activities purposefully, and that after a

FIGURE 1. The enrichment triad model.

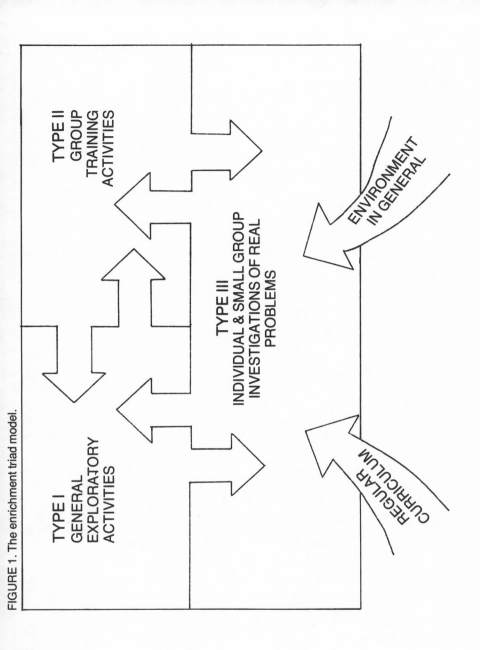

Figure 1. The enrichment triad model.

given period of time has elapsed, each youngster will be responsible for analyzing his or her own experiences and coming up with some alternative suggestions for further study.

The second guideline deals with strategies for developing categorical interest centers in the classroom or resource room. These centers should be stocked with materials that are broadly representative of selected themes or fields of knowledge. The selection of appropriate materials for the interest centers is especially crucial because the objective here is not simply informational, but rather to provoke curiosity about the dynamic nature of a field and an interest in doing further research. Thus, it is essential that the materials in each center include descriptive information about particular fields of knowledge rather than mere collections of the accumulated information in a given field.

Type II Enrichment; Group Training Activities. Type II Enrichment consists of methods, materials, and instructional techniques that are mainly concerned with the development of thinking and feeling processes. Over the years a variety of terms have been used to describe these operations or "powers of the mind." These terms have included critical thinking, problem solving, reflective thinking, inquiry training, divergent thinking, sensitivity training, awareness development, and creative or productive thinking.

Type II Enrichment activities are an important part of a total enrichment model for the gifted and talented for several reasons. First, such activities, if appropriately selected, provide for a range of response options (i.e., they must be open-ended) so that youngsters with superior potential will have an opportunity to escalate their thinking and feeling processes to whatever levels their own natural abilities allow. Giftedness and creativity are in the student's response (not the stimulus materials), and it is what the youngster brings to the learning situation that makes him or her gifted.

Second, Type II Enrichment activities also have the potential for introducing youngsters to more advanced kinds of studies. For example, a student who becomes excited about advertising as a result of doing a creativity training exercise entitled "Let's Write a Slogan" might go on to do very sophisticated work in this area. Thus an interrelationship can be seen between Type II and Type III sections of the model and it is this connection (rather than the creativity training activity per se) that accounts for a truly enriching experience.

Finally, group training activities provide students with the skills and abilities necessaary to solve problems in a variety of areas. Since gifted students are characterized by both a wide range of interests and an investigative attitude, systematic experiences in the thinking and feeling processes are necessary tools for more advanced types of inquiry.

By way of summary, Type II experiences should be carefully selected so that they represent a logical outgrowth of student interests and concerns rather than mere random involvement in whatever happens to be available or whatever the teacher might have a fancy for. Purposefully selected activities can help "tie together" the other two components of the enrichment model but more importantly, by viewing Type II Enrichment as one aspect of a total enrichment model, we can help to avoid the danger of making process-oriented activities the be-all and end-all of a program for the gifted.

Type III Enrichment: Small Group Investigations of Real Problems. Type III Enrichment consists of activities in which the youngster becomes an actual investigator of a real problem or topic by using appropriate methods of inquiry. In order for a student to become an investigator the focus of his or her efforts must shift from consumer-oriented productivity to real-problem-oriented productivity. A very subtle but important distinction exists between these two types of involvement. The student-as-consumer may engage in projects or claim to be "doing research," but such activity frequently consists of writing ritualized reports about conclusions which have been reported by other people. Nowhere in this process does the student use information as raw data.

Real-problem productivity, on the other hand, focuses on the identification and delimitation of problems that are similar in nature to those pursued by authentic researchers or artists in particular fields. Thus, activities that are considered to be bona fide Type III Enrichment experiences should reflect the student's emulation of the professional investigator to such a degree that the student actually becomes a professional himself or herself.

The success of a Type III Enrichment activity is in large part dependent on the degree of task commitment or motivation that the student brings to the investigation. Task commitment is a function of the realness or sincerity of students' interests, and thus, the first major responsibility of the teacher in carrying out Type III activities is to assist students in analyzing their own interests. Several issues should be considered in the identification of student interests. First, many youngsters will have already developed intense interests and commitments to particular topics or areas of study. In such cases our major responsibility is to help them focus their interests and to translate these interests into solvable problems. In addition, several student interests will undoubtedly result from General Exploratory Activities (Type I), Group Training Activities (Type II), the regular curriculum, and the environment in general. These existing or newly developed interests are "Naturals" for Type III Enrichment experiences and should be capitalized upon whenever possible.

One way of obtaining some useful leads for exposing students to relatively new areas of potential involvement is through a community survey that seeks information about both the vocational and avocational interests of parents. Such a survey can also identify persons who might be willing to follow up an exposure activity (i.e., lecture, slide presentation, or visit to their laboratory, studio, or office) with some intensive involvement with individuals or small groups of students. Youngsters can also be helped to examine their present or potential interests through the use of interest inventories.

245

The second responsibility of teachers in developing Type III Enrichment experiences consists of providing students with the tools of inquiry appropriate for the fields of investigation being pursued. In order to do this educators should learn how to teach some general exercises in inquiry training. It is important to keep in mind, however, that exercises in inquiry training are only helpful up to a point. Like "discovery learning," they are highly controlled and can quickly become ends in and of themselves.

General instruction should also be provided in *advanced* library skills. Teachers should familiarize themselves with the existence, nature, and function of the full range of reference materials that are available for in-depth study in most fields. These mateials include such items as indexes, directories, periodicals, source books, dictionaries, specialized encyclopedias, and abstracts.

Perhaps the most important thing that must be learned in order to promote Type III Enrichment is how to identify and locate How-To-Do-It resources. Almost every field of study has such guides and some are written at relatively elementary levels. It is important to analyze all resources in terms of an individual youngster's reading and conceptual level and to serve as a translator whenever a particular concept is beyond the child's level of comprehension. If the teacher cannot serve as a translator, the assistance of a person with specialized training should be sought.

The third and final responsibility of the teacher is concerned with helping students to communicate the results of their investigative work in a realistic and meaningful manner. Creative and productive persons are highly product-oriented and rarely engage in creative work without an audience in mind. Indeed, one of the major characteristics of a real problem (as opposed to a training exercise or presented problem) is that the producer is attempting to inform, to entertain, or to influence a relatively specific but nevertheless real audience.

Developing relatively realistic outlets for student products will require persons involved in the education of the gifted to exercise their own creativity. Assistance in this effort can be sought from creative/productive professionals and with persons from various interest groups. Local organizations, such as historical societies, science clubs, and dramatic groups might be explored as potential audiences, as should children's magazines that routinely include the work of young people.

Identifying appropriate outlets and audiences for student products is a very important part of the management function of teachers. Unless the time is taken to perform this role in an energetic manner, there is little likelihood that Type III Enrichment will achieve a truly qualitative difference from the usual project activities that are popular in most programs.

The extent to which all students can pursue knowledge as a first-hand inquirer or turned-on professional is not yet known. As far as gifted students are concerned, however, the history of human achievement (and indeed, the history of many programs for the gifted) is filled with examples of bright young people who not only emulated the methods of professionals,

246

but who were in fact professionals themselves. Gifted children can unquestionably function in the manner of true inquirers, and for this reason it is recommended that investigations of real problems be the mainstay of programs for the gifted and talented.

References

Helson, R. Woman mathematicians and the creative personality. *Journal of Counseling and Clinical Psychology,* 1971, **36**, 21-220.

MacKinnon, D. W. The creativity of architects. In Taylor, C. W. (ed.), *Widening horizons in creativity.* New York: Wiley, 1964.

MacKinnon, D. W. Personality and the realization of creative potential. *American Psychologist,* 1965, **20**, 273–281.

McCurdy, H. G. The childhood pattern of genius. *Horizon,* 1960, **2**, 33–38.

Roe, A. *The making of a scientist.* New York: Dodd, Mead, 1952.

Wallach, M. A. Tests tell us little about talent. *American Scientist,* 1976, **64**, 57–63.

Julian C. Stanley

Rationale of the Study of Mathematically Precocious Youth (SMPY) During its First Five Years of Promoting Educational Acceleration

*R*esults of the first year of the Study of Mathematically Precocious Youth at The Johns Hopkins University were reported in a book entitled *Mathematical Talent: Discovery, Description, and Development* (Stanley, Keating, and Fox 1974). Findings during the following three years are contained in a larger book entitled *Intellectual Talent: Research and Development* (Keating 1976). In this paper I shall not attempt to summarize the twenty-seven chapters of those two books, but instead shall present the rationale of the study as it has been worked out by me in close collaboration with a number of associates, especially Lynn H. Fox, Daniel P. Keating, Susanne A. Denham, Linda K. Greenstein, William C. George, Cecilia H. Solano, and Sanford J. Cohn. The reader will see how our extreme emphasis on educational acceleration has greatly helped many youths who were *eager* to move ahead academically.

Why Mathematical Reasoning is the Initial Basis for Identification

The Study of Mathematically Precocious Youth (abbreviated SMPY) began informally at The Johns Hopkins University during the summer of 1968 when Doris K. Lidtke, an instructor in computer science, called my attention to a twelve-year-old boy just out of the seventh grade who was

Reprinted from The Gifted and The Creative, A Fifty-Year Perspective, edited by Julian C. Stanley, William C. George, and Cecilia H. Solano. Baltimore: The Johns Hopkins University Press, 1977, pp. 75-112. By permission of the author and publisher.

doing remarkable things in the computer laboratory. It started slowly and without a name.

Emphasis on the mathematical and physical sciences began early, however. Persons often ask us why we chose mathematical reasoning ability rather than something else, or even why we decided to concentrate on one type of talent rather than studying all sorts. We wanted to steer a careful course between excessive specialism and overly broad coverage.

Sharply limited resources made this decision inevitable. Even for the first two years after the study was funded by the Spencer Foundation in 1971 it did not have a single full-time worker, and after that there was just one. During the 1976-77 academic year our entire regular staff consisted of William C. George, the full-timer; Cecilia H. Solano, a fourth-year doctoral student in psychology who worked ten hours per week on the study; Sanford J. Cohn, a second-year doctoral student in psychology who worked twenty hours weekly; me, who devoted to it as much time as being a professor of psychology with unreduced teaching responsibilities permitted; the administrative secretary, Lois Sandhofer; and a part-time secretary, Laura Thommen. Small wonder that we did not also select initially for other talents such as verbal reasoning ability, athletic prowess, musical talent, and leadership potential! No matter how hard we might work (and we do indeed put in long hours), relatively little could be done by us for that varied a group.

In response, however, to persistent inquiries about verbal reasoning ability after SMPY was funded, we encouraged JHU psychology professors Catherine J. Garvey, Robert T. Hogan, and Roger A. Webb to obtain from a philanthropic foundation a five-year grant (1972-77) with which to pioneer in that area. For reports of their work see Hogan et al (1977), Viernstein et al. (1977), McGinn (1976), Viernstein and Hogan (1975), and Webb (1974).

Given that we must specialize, it seemed sensible to choose an ability closely related to major subjects in the academic curricula of public and private schools in the United States. Because we planned to help intellectually talented youths improve their education, it appeared wise to start at as early a grade and age level as the developing of the chosen ability permitted. In order to capitalize on the precocious development of this ability by greatly accelerating school progress in the subject-matter area concerned, it was necessary to choose school subjects much more highly dependent for their mastery on manifest intellectual talent than on chronological age and the associated life experiences. These considerations led to our choosing mathematical reasoning as the ability and the best of the standard courses in mathematics, the mathematical sciences, and the physical sciences as the subjects on which to focus directly. We did not want to develop curricula in mathematics, but instead to help mathematically talented boys and girls use their abilities more effectively in the various academic areas.

We were aided in this choice by more than just armchair considerations.

249

Great precocity in mathematics and the physical sciences is documented by such writers as Harvey C. Lehman (1953), Catharine M. Cox (1926) in the second volume of Terman's *Genetic Studies of Genius* series,[1] Eric Temple Bell (1937), and Edna Kramer (1974). The only clear competitor was musical composition, where the almost unbelievably early accomplishments of Saint-Saëns, Mozart, and Mendelssohn are well known (see Schonberg 1970). This does not articulate well with school curricula, however, nor do we have the knowledge or facilities to nurture young composers. We eliminated chess because it is not an academic discipline.

Two who helped begin the study (Lynn H. Fox and I) had been teachers of high school mathematics, and I of chemistry and general science also. My undergraduate major had been physical science, and much of my graduate and postdoctoral work has been in statistics at three universities. As a Fellow of the American Statistical Association and of the American Association for the Advancement of Science, I felt competent to help students make decisions in the areas of mathematics and science, aided of course by consultation and collaboration with high school and college teachers, supervisors, and administrators.

Also, I had a master's degree in educational and vocational counseling and guidance and much background in evaluation and testing. These proved invaluable.

My interest in intellectually gifted youths began at the University of Georgia during the summer of 1938, after my first year of teaching in high school (see Stanley 1976a, pp. 6-9). It smouldered from then on, coming to the level of publication occasionally (e.g., Stanley 1954a, b; 1958; 1959a, b). Not until 1969, however, did I begin helping intellectually talented youngsters systematically (Stanley 1974, pp. 12-14; 1976a, p. 9).

It is interesting to note here as an aside that the SMPY staff has had little difficulty in planning closely with top-flight mathematicians and scientists, but has met with distrust from some mathematics supervisors and teachers who do not understand how university psychologists could know anything about their subjects. There is an element of defensiveness in this, of course, because we have prodded school personnel to do much more for mathematically highly talented students than is usually done.

Thus we settled upon mathematical reasoning ability developed to a high level at an early age as the basis for initial selection of students to be studied considerably more and helped to develop fast and well in mathematics and related subjects. We did this for logical, empirical, and personal reasons. Somewhat more of our rationale can be gleaned from Stanley (1954a, b; 1958; 1959a, b; 1974; 1976a-f).

We would not have begun this kind of project had we not agreed fully with Thomas Gray ("Elegy Written in a Country Churchyard," 1751, line 53) that

> Full many a gem of purest ray serene
> The dark unfathomed caves of ocean bear;

Full many a flower is born to blush unseen,
And waste its sweetness on the desert air.

Why SAT-M Score is the Initial Criterion

We wanted to find youths who at an early age (mostly twelve or thirteen) were already able to reason extremely well with simple mathematical facts, students who even before taking or completing the first year of algebra would reason mathematically much better than the average male twelfth grader does. We gave applicants for the talent-search contest plenty of practice materials for the forthcoming test so that they would be on essentially the same fotting with respect to opportunity to score well. Because reasoning mathematically involves reasoning with some mathematics, however elementary, this was essential in order to smooth out at least partially their differences in mathematical training and outside-of-school experiences. We did not want scores to depend much on rote knowledge of mathematical concepts or on computational ability, as the usual test of mathematical "aptitude" does, because we surmised that these could be taught readily and quickly to students whose mathematical reasoning ability is splendid. It seemed to us likely that the reasoning test would predict success in later mathematics, at least through advanced calculus and linear algebra, far better than items measuring rote memory and computational speed and accuracy would.

Thus we needed a mathematical reasoning test difficult enough that the average participant in our contest would score on it halfway between a chance score and a perfect score. For example, if there were sixty items and scores were "corrected for chance," we wanted the mean score of our examinees, a highly able group, to be about 30. Also, the test should have enough "ceiling"—be difficult enough for even the ablest entrants into the contest—so that virtually no scores of 60 would occur.

In addition to the considerations of reasoning content and appropriate difficulty, we wanted a professionally prepared, carefully standardized, reliable test for which several well-guarded ("secure") forms existed and for which well-known, meaningful interpretations of scores were available. High scores on the test should command immediate attention and respect at both the high school and college levels, because they could be compared with scores on the same test earned by superior high school seniors.

These considerations led to pilot studies of the mathematical part of the College Entrance Examination Board's Scholastic Aptitude Test (SAT-M).[2] Our first examinee, an obviously brilliant thirteen-year-old eighth grader, scored 669, which was then the 96th percentile of a random sample of male twelfth graders. On the verbal part of SAT, abbreviated SAT-V, he scored 590, the 93rd percentile of the same norm group. The next thirteen-year-old eighth grader on whom we tried the test scored 716 on M and 608 on V. Others scored similarly, some even higher. None scored near the

251

perfect score of 60 right on M or 90 right on V. It seemed likely, then, that SAT-M would be excellent for identifying the level of mathematical reasoning ability we sought among seventh and eighth graders. SAT-V could be used with the high scorers on SAT-M to assess verbal reasoning ability, which seemed likely to be more closely related to speed of thinking and of taking tests than is SAT-M. As has been shown in several publications, especially Stanley, Keating, and Fox (1974) and Keating (1976), for the students we tested SAT-M and SAT-V did indeed prove suitable in both content and difficulty. The mean on each was appropriately between the chance- and the perfect-score levels. The highest scores were never perfect. Only an occasional examinee scored as high as 55 out of 60 on SAT-M. A twelve-year-old did score 58, and a thirteen-year-old scored 59, but these were the extreme exceptions among some 3,000 youths tested.

More importantly, SAT-M and SAT-V proved to have great value for predicting which students would be able to accelerate their mathematical education radically. Of course, motivational factors—especially, willingness to do difficult homework well—proved crucial within the high-scoring group, but without considerable ability of the SAT-M and SAT-V types students could not race ahead successfully in mathematics and related areas.

We have learned that the SAT-M score scale is valid right up to the top-reported score, 800, *if* the criteria themselves have enough "ceiling" for the group. For instance, in the usual eight- or ninth-grade algebra 1 class, variation in this ability would probably make little difference in apparent success of students at SAT-M levels 500, 600, 700, or 800, because all of these exceed the mathematical-reasoning demands of the course. Paying attention and bothering to do homework and tests carefully are probably better determiners of grades among these high-scorers than are differences of the order of even 100 to 300 points. Put a 500-scorer into a fast-paced, homogeneously grouped 700-level algebra III class, however, and he is unlikely to be able to keep up at all. In general, most reports that a test of appropriate difficulty loses its validity at some point short of the top of its score scale are actually commentaries on the lack of ceiling of the criterion, rather than intrinsic dropping off of validity of the predictor. This seems especially true when both the predictor and the criterion variables are ability-test scores.

We realize that a factor analysis of SAT-M scores would show several factors, perhaps somewhat different for our youths than for the usual older examinees (see Pruzek and Coffman 1966). Because the criteria we use are also factorially heterogeneous, however, this is probably at least as much an asset as a liability.

The setting and rules of the mathematics talent searches tended to attract interested, mathematically able students who liked keen competition. The entrants were probably about the upper 1½ percent of their age group in mathematical reasoning ability (i.e., the top 1 in about 67). It would be foolish to administer the SAT-M to twelve-to thirteen-year-old students much less able than that, and even more unwise to test them with SAT-V, because SAT is designed for above-average eleventh and twelfth graders.

SAT-V proved rather difficult for some of the seventh graders who scored extremely high on SAT-M. Verbal reasoning ability seems more closely related to age than mathematical reasoning ability is and also more closely related to the verbal ability of the child's parents and their socioeconomic level. Nevertheless, splendid mathematical reasoners who were seventh or eighth graders seldom scored lower on SAT-V than the average twelfth grader does. For example, in the first mathematics and science talent search the 35 top boys out of the 265 male entrants averaged the 95th percentile of a random sample of high school seniors on M and the 87th on V. Of course, that type of regression (here, .4 of a standard deviation) is to be expected in any group chosen on one variable and then examined on another variable not perfectly correlated with it.

It would be rare, indeed, for a person to have excellent mathematical *reasoning* ability and yet be inferior to average thinkers in verbal *reasoning* ability. SMPY does not seek mere calculating freaks (Barlow 1952). Though its participants are not chosen explicitly for high IQ, virtually none of them have average or below-average IQs.

Most persons who upon entering their teens already reason extremely well mathematically, as indicated by a high score on SAT-M, will not become "pure" mathematicians. Far less than half of them will even major in mathematics as college undergraduates. Instead, most of the boys and some of the girls will specialize in the physical sciences (especially physics), engineering, computer science, mathematical statistics, operations research, economics, and other areas in which a good grasp of mathematics is essential. Some will go into medicine because of the prestige and financial compensation it usually offers, even though few persons holding M.D. degrees can make much use of great talent for mathematics. Medicine and law seem more likely choices for girls than for boys, because even yet the former tend to shy away from mathematics, engineering, and the physical sciences. A large percentage of the boys will probably work toward Ph.D. degrees.

Whenever one uses a test and has a fixed point above which the examinee is considered "successful" and below which he is considered "unsuccessful," the issue of false positives and false negatives arises. Some students will have a good day and equal or exceed the criterion, whereas others will have a bad day and drop below it. On another occasion the former would have failed and the latter have succeeded. SMPY guards against false positives by retesting at a later date with an extremely heavy battery of difficult tests all those persons who attained the criterion—eg., SAT-M score of 640 or more during the second or third talent searches. The initially lucky scorer will be detected easily. Thus, for the retested group positive errors of measurement (see Stanley 1971) are not much of a problem, nor is the inevitably somewhat-less-than-perfect validity of SAT-M itself.

253

There will, however, be some youths inappropriately consigned to the below-640 group. A score of 630 represents only a point or two less, out of the possible 60 points, than a score of 640 does. The 10-point difference between 630 and 640 is only about one third of a standard error of measurement. Obviously, small fluctuations in score at this level will make the difference between being identified as an excellent enough mathematical reasoner to warrant being studied considerably more and helped a great deal and being consigned to the less mathematically brilliant group. This problem is unavoidable, no matter what score criterion is used. The 640 was chosen because it screened in just about as many students (about 7 percent of those who entered the contest) as it was feasible to test further and work with closely. Also, it was only about 20 points below the average SAT-M score as eleventh and twelfth graders of Johns Hopkins's freshmen, an impressive figure indeed for seventh and eighth graders.

There are several justifications for not worrying inordinately about the false negatives:

1. If seventh graders, they were eligible to enter the contest again the next year as eighth graders and were encouraged to do so. This worked, however, only for seventh graders tested in the March 1972 and January 1973 (i.e., the first and second) contests, because the January 1974 contest was the last of the initial series. (The contest resumed, with seventh graders only, in the fall of 1976.)
2. SMPY offered a great deal of help to all contestants who scored 420 or more, and most of them did.
3. It was unlikely that a student who scored as low as 630 would with better luck have exceeded 700, so probably few of the false-negative eighth graders would have been among the very highest scorers.
4. Relatively few students scored in the 610-630 range.
5. Nearly all of the students entering the contests would later, as eleventh graders or earlier, take both the Preliminary SAT and the SAT and recalibrate their levels of mathematical aptitude.
6. The SAT-M scores from the SMPY contest did not "count" anything for school or other purposes. Most such scores made the student look good and gave his parents and teachers evidence with which to argue that special provisions in mathematics for him/her were desirable. For example, 420 on SAT-M exceeds the score earned by approximately 57 percent of male eleventh and twelfth graders. To be that apt three to five years early is impressive.

SMPY Focuses its Efforts

SMPY is developmental and longitudinal but not retrospective. Its staff identifies at the seventh- or eighth-grade level students who are already superior reasoners mathematically and observes their development (while trying to influence it) over the ensuing years. Its staff does not have the time or interest to delve deeply into the "whys" of their precocity. While not wholly without interest to us, questions such as "Is mathematical talent mainly inherited?" are largely outside SMPY's scope. We are concerned mostly with capitalizing on the high-level reasoning ability and the motivation to use it that can be found among youths twelve or thirteen years old. It is already-evident ability we seek, rather than some presumed underlying potential that has not yet become manifest. We leave it to others to study the origins of such ability, the effects of nature and nurture on it during the early years, the failure of mathematical ability to arise in what are otherwise bright children, and the treatment of "underachievers." These are important topics, but strenuous efforts to help the vastly neglected hordes of well-motivated mathematically apt youths who are caught in the interest-killing traps of routine mathematics classrooms leave us little time for them.

We are, however, greatly interested in the nature of mathematical talent as it develops and unfolds, especially from age twelve or so onward. We do care, too, how intellectual prodigies of the past have turned out (e.g., Wiener 1953 and Montour 1976*a*, *b*). Some books that we have found helpful are Bell (1937), Krutetskii (1976), and Skemp (1971). Also, see Fox (1976*c*).

Why Identification Usually Begins at the Junior High School Level

Elementary mathematics is, from the standpoint of the learner, heavily an algorithmic and deductive system, though for those who create it there are usually strong intuitive and aesthetic elements. Unlike understanding philosophy or great novels such as Tolstoy's *War and Peace*, personal experience outside the classroom and maturation closely tied to chronological age are not essential for learning mathematics well. Certain types of reasoning ability necessary for mastering subjects such as high school algebra develop at vastly different ages. A precocious ten-year-old may be superior in this respect to most adults. To him or her, mathematics and related subjects such as computer science may be seen as interesting games, little related to the real world of experience.

A startling example will illustrate this. At age ten one of SMPY's participants made the highest grade in a state college introduction-to-computer-science course, competing with seven of our exceptionally able older students and twelve adults. Before his eleventh birthday he completed at Johns Hopkins most of a second-level computer course on which he earned a final grade of A. At age eleven he earned, by examination, credit for two semesters of the calculus at Johns Hopkins. This is no ordinary boy, of course. His Stanford-Binet IQ at age eight was 190, and he had been in our special fast-mathematics classes for two years. Even he is not the most precocious youth we have discovered.[3] Furthermore, at age twelve to thirteen, when the typical child is in the seventh or eighth grade, there are quite a few students able to forge through all of precalculus mathematics *far* quicker than schools ordinarily permit them to do.

The first year of algebra usually causes serious problems for youths who are among the ablest few percent of their classmates in mathematical reasoning ability. Regardless of how advanced their ability is, seldom are they permitted to take this subject before the eighth or ninth grade. Then, no matter how much algebra I the student can already do or how quickly he or she could learn the material and go on to second-year algebra, the student is usually lockstepped into approximately 180 forty-five- or fifty-minute daily periods throughout the school year. Mathematically highly precocious youths need vastly less exposure to what is for them an extremely easy subject. This is especially true when the student has already had one or more years of "modern" mathematics that may have included much algebra covertly. Several examples from our experience will illustrate the mathematically talented youth's dilemma.

A twelve-year-old seventh grader who scored extremely high in one of SMPY's annual contests asked permission to join his junior high school's eighth-grade algebra I class in February but was refused on the grounds that he already had missed more than half the course. He insisted on being given a standardized test covering the first year of the subject. On this he made a perfect score, 40 right in forty minutes, which is two points above the 99.5th percentile of national norms for ninth-grade students who have been in this type of class all year. Upon seeing this achievement, the teacher agreed with the boy that he was indeed ready to join the class! Instead, he took a college mathematics course that summer and easily earned a final grade of A.

At the end of the sixth grade a student took second-year algebra in summer school without having had first-year algebra; his final grade was A. By the end of the eighth grade he had earned credit by examination for two semesters of college calculus. A year later he had completed third-semester calculus by correspondence from a major university, earning A as his final grade.

A student learned two and one-half years of algebra well by being tutored while in the fifth and sixth grades. He continued, by means of tutoring, with a high-level course in geometry. His tutor in geometry was a sixteen-year-old freshman at Johns Hopkins who enrolled for honors advanced calculus (final grade, A) and other subjects that most nineteen-year-olds would find extremely difficult. He, too, condensed his mathematics radically.

Several girls have accelerated their progress in mathematics considerably, though not as much as the boys discussed above. One of them graduated from high school a year early while being one of the best students in SMPY's second high-level college calculus class.

Many other such examples could be given (e.g., see Stanley 1974, 1976 *a-f*) to show that the usual high school pace in algebra I to III, geometry, trigonometry, analytic geometry, and the calculus is far from optimum for boys and girls who reason extremely well mathematically. Algebra I is a particularly virulent culprit, because being incarcerated in it for a whole year gives the apt student no really appropriate way to behave. He or she can daydream, be excessively meticulous in order to get perfect grades, harass the teacher, show off knowledge arrogantly in the class, or be truant. There is, however, no *suitable* way to while away the class hours when one already knows much of the material and can learn the rest almost instantaneously as it is first presented. Boredom, frustration, and habits of gross inattention are almost sure to result.

We are amazed that even more youths do not sustain obvious academic injury, and we suspect that the damage is greater than it seems. At least, it appears uncomfortably likely that motivation for mathematics may suffer appreciably in all but those few students devoted to the subject. After such snail-pacing in high school precalculus and calculus—often, five and one-half years or more—the number of top minds still excited by mathematics may be few.

The remedy for this unfortunate situation is conceptually simple but seldom employed. It consists of the regular and appropriate use of tests. First, those students with great mathematical reasoning ability are found. Then various tests of achievement in mathematics are administered to them. This enables mathematics teachers to determine what a particular talented student does not yet know and arrange for him or her to learn those points, and those only, fast but well.

Seldom, though, does the teacher of beginning algebra use an achievement test during the first week of class to locate the students who might, with a little individual help, move into second-year algebra right away. Also, not nearly enough use is made of the mathematics scores from the achievement batteries that most schools administer. Those tests are not difficult enough to differentiate adequately among the top several percent of the group, but at least they do single out potentially exceptionally able youths.

In special classes where students are grouped homogeneously according to high mathematical reasoning ability, SMPY has found that first-year algebra can be mastered in from nine to twenty two-hour weekly periods—and, as noted above, some exceptionally able students do not need even that much. Details about this are contained in Fox (1974*a*, 1976*b*) and Stanley (1976*b*). Other precalculus courses and the calculus can also be learned quickly by mathematically apt youths, as George and Denham (1976), George (1976), and Stanley (1976*b*) document rather fully.

To go beyond first-year algebra, youths need certain better-developed mental qualities, especially excellent reasoning ability and Piagetian formal-operations status. SMPY's testing and experience with special instructional programs and the studies by Keating (1975) and Keating and Schaefer (1975) indicate that the intellectually top 1 or 2 percent of students as low

257

as the fifth grade probably already have these abilities well enough developed to learn algebra II and other precalculus courses well. Speed of learning them is dependent on level of ability, quality of instruction and pacing, stimulation by classmates or tutor, and the mysterious ingredient called motivation that makes the student willing (or, ideally, eager) to do a great deal of homework excellently between classes.

For these reasons SMPY conducted its three annual mathematics talent searches among seventh and eighth graders, but also did special work among sixth graders and a few students even younger than that. Students whose mathematical reasoning abilities proved to be superb were encouraged to move fast through the high school mathematics sequence, beginning with algebra I or skipping it and ending *soon* with calculus so well learned that college credit for it could be obtained. Somewhat less able entrants were given less drastic suggestions, but nevertheless encouraged to speed up their progress in mathematics and science. Experience of several years has shown that youths able and eager to move ahead can do so readily if they and their parents are resolute and persistent in their search for suitable ways.

Tentative phsysiological evidence concerning the suitability of the age period twelve to thirteen for accelerating educational progress was suggested rather recently by Epstein (1974*a, b*). He found spurts in both brain development and mental age, one of them at chronological ages ten to twelve. Mental age seemed to grow especially slowly during the years twelve to fourteen and then to spurt again for the final time at fourteen to sixteen. Thus junior high school students (grades seven to nine) may be on a mental plateau. We do not know, however, whether his findings characterize precocious youths, who might spurt at different times than average students do. It seems congruent with our experience to postulate that by age twelve some youths already have great learning potential that seems to accelerate to the point that by age fourteen to sixteen they are fully ready to succeed in a selective college. We have not noticed any tendency for SMPY participants to have merely reached a rather high level of ability early and to remain there. Obviously, though, the developmental curve for a given ability might differ greatly from one person to another, depending on genetically programmed potential, environmental stimulation, and the interaction of these two.

Why Not Conduct a Controlled Experiment?

Because experimentation is a strong force in psychology and in my own background (e.g., Campbell and Stanley 1966; Stanley 1973), we were tempted to set SMPY up as a rigorously controlled experiment. Upon reflection, however, we came to believe that there were cogent reasons for not doing so. Some of those considerations were the following:

258

1. We were rather sure that the smorgasbord of accelerative educational opportunities we planned to offer the "experimental" subjects in the study were much more likely to help than to harm them. Therefore, it would be inadvisable to withhold such opportunities from a portion of the subjects (probably half of them) who in a controlled experiment would be assigned randomly to a "control" group.
2. There were not likely to be enough extremely high scorers to make the numbers in both the experimental and the control group sufficiently large to yield statistically powerful or precise comparisons between groups and subgroups. It seemed more sensible to take the N ablest subjects and mass the experimental efforts on them.
3. The procedures, principles, and techniques that SMPY planned to develop would be disseminated widely by the press and in speeches, letters, articles, books, and newsletters, so withholding knowledge of opportunities from a control group of subjects would be impossible. The control group would be substantially exposed to influences designed only for the experimental group, and that type of contamination would greatly weaken or even nullify the experiment.
4. By not having a control group from which certain presumably beneficial opportunities and information were withheld, it is possible to keep the study completely on an above-board basis, with no need to deceive anyone about anything. This openness is important in gaining the confidence of the students, their parents and teachers, and the general public.
5. Certain comparisons could be made by matching and other quasi-experimental procedures. Fox (1976b) did this in her study of sex differences in mathematical aptitude and achievement, as have other SMPY researchers in trying to determine how well a certain special procedure worked.

SMPY plans to use a completely controlled experimental design in its attempt to increase interest in chemistry among mathematically talented youths, but not to deceive either group about the nature of the study. Members of the control group will get equivalent educational stimulation, though not in chemistry. The staff of SMPY is not at all sure in advance that the chemistry "treatment" will be effective, so it seems reasonable to withhold it from some of the ablest youths (with their knowledge and consent) while giving them the same amount of attention in certain other areas. Of course, despite SMPY's best efforts, this experiment will be contaminated somewhat by knowledge of its nature and by whatever spillover of chemistry influence from the experimental to the control group that may occur, but if the experimental variables are not potent enough to triumph over these, they are probably not of great practical value. Careful attention to the sources of invalidity spelled out by Campbell and Stanley (1966) will help keep the experiment as unbiased as possible. Experimentation with humans in important, relevant "field" situations is seldom as easy or neat as experimentation under laboratory conditions can be. Often, however, it yields more important, albeit perhaps somewhat equivocal, information.

6. A great deal of SMPY's analysis of the results of its programs depends heavily on case-study clinical methods, using all known information about each individual with as much insight as can be mustered on the basis of considerable experience with many mathematically precocious youths (see Hudson 1975). Burt (1975, p. 138) states this point especially clearly:

> With human beings, when the problem is primarily psychological, statistical studies of populations should always be supplemented by case studies of individuals: early histories will often shed further light on the origin and development of this or that peculiarity. Tests should be supplemented by what Binet called the *méthode clinique,* and interpreted by introspective observations, designed to verify the tacit assumption that they really do test what they are intended to assess. After all, each child is a complex and conscious organism, not a mere unit in a statistical sample.

Fortunately, many of SMPY's procedures yield results so different from the usual ones that the effects are obvious. For instance, it is almost preposterous to suggest that if SMPY had not found a certain youth when he was an over-age sixth grader and helped him in many ways to move ahead educationally fast and well he would, nevertheless, have been graduated from a major university at barely seventeen years of age. The youngest recipient of a bachelor's degree in 1971 at Johns Hopkins was nineteen years ten months old (Eisenberg 1977). Two years later, under SMPY's influence, the youngest was seventeen years seven months old, and three months later he had completed a master's degree also. Now seventeen-year-old graudates are frequent. Similar strong observations could be made about most of SMPY's programs, such as the effects of the fast-math classes (Fox 1974*b*; George and Denham 1976; Stanley 1976*b*).

Three Sequential Aspects of SMPY: D³

The first book-length report about SMPY's initial work (Stanley, Keating, and Fox 1974) was entitled *Mathematical Talent: Discovery, Description, and Development.* To emphasize the three D's, we sometimes abbreviate that title, pseudo-mathematically, as MT:D³. Discovery is the identification phase during which the talent is found. Description is the study phase during which the most talented students are tested further and otherwise studied a great deal. This leads to the prime reason for SMPY, the development phase. During it the youths who were found and studied are continually helped, facilitated, and encouraged. Each is offered a

260

smorgasbord of educational possibilities (see Fox 1974*a*, 1976*a;* Stanley 1976*a*) from which to choose whatever combination, including nothing, that best suits the individual. Some splendid mathematical reasoners try almost everything at breakneck speed, whereas others do little special. SMPY offers as much educational and vocational counseling and guidance as its resources permit, both via memoranda and its newsletter—ITYB, the *Intellectually Talented Youth Bulletin*—and individually as requested.

Most studies of intellectually gifted children are heavy on description but light on educational facilitation. From the start the SMPY staff has been determined to intervene strongly on behalf of the able youths it found. Thus discovery and description were seen as necessary steps leading to strong emphasis on accelerating educational development, particularly in mathematics and related subjects.

Why Acceleration Rather Than Enrichment is Stressed

There were both logical and empirical reasons why we chose to emphasize educational acceleration rather than enrichment. Some of them are implied above, such as that mathematically highly apt students can move through the standard mathematics curriculum much faster and better than they usually do. Fears expressed by teachers or parents about their missing important concepts or techniques because of the speed are usually groundless and, indeed, often merely a rationalization for inaction. Such students are likely to doze through the 5 percent they do not know when it is camouflaged by the 95 percent they already know, because under these circumstances there is no incentive for them to be alert. SMPY has evidence (see Fox 1974*b*; George and Denham 1976; Stanley 1976*b*) that students who reason extremely well mathematically learn first-year algebra considerably better in a few two-hour periods with their intellectual peers than they do in regular all-year classes.

There seem to be four main kinds of educational enrichment: busy work, irrelevant academic, cultural, and relevant academic. In our opinion, for reasons to be stated below, only the third (cultural) is well suited to mathematically highly precocious youths; it does not, however, meet their needs in mathematics itself or in the other usual academic subjects.

Busy work is a well-known way for some teachers to keep their brightest students occupied while the class goes on with its regular work. In a common form it consists of having them do a great deal more of the subject in which they are already superb, but at the same level as the class they have surpasssed. One of our eighth graders, whose Stanford-Binet IQ as a kindergartner was 187, was asked by his algebra teacher to work every problem in the book, rather than just the alternate problems that the rest of the class was assigned. He already knew algebra I rather well and therefore needed to work few problems, so he resented this burdensome chore. The busy work proved to be a powerful motivator, however, because after that year he took all of his mathematics at the college level. First, though, during the second semester of the eighth grade and while he was still twelve years old this precocious youth took the regular introductory course in computer science at Johns Hopkins and earned a final grade of A. During the summer, still twelve until July, he took a course in college algebra and trigonometry at Johns Hopkins, earning a B. From then on for two academic years and two more summers he took college mathematics through the calculus and linear algebra and two years of college chemistry, with all A's. At age 15⅙ years he entered Johns Hopkins as a full-time student with 30 percent of the sophomore year completed. During his first year at Hopkins he earned eight A's and one B on difficult courses, majoring in electrical engineering. Thus in a rather perverse sense his teacher had done him a great favor, but without his having been discovered by SMPY, he would probably have been forced to sit a whole year in each of numerous high-school mathematics courses far below his capabilities.

In May 1976 this remarkable young man completed his junior year at Johns Hopkins with an impressive record in both his studies and research. On his sixteenth birthday, July 10, 1975, he had begun work for the summer with General Electric. During the summer of 1976, while still sixteen, he was a full-time researcher at the Bell Telephone Laboratories. He is scheduled to receive a baccalaureate from Johns Hopkins a couple of months before his eighteenth birthday—that is, four years ahead of the usual age-in-grade progression—and continue on to earn a Ph.D. degree in electrical engineering by age twenty or twenty-one. Radical educational acceleration is certainly paying off well for him—academically, professionally, and personally. In March 1977 he was awarded a three-year National Science Foundation graduate fellowship to study electrical engineering at the Massachusetts Institute of Technology.

One of his classmates (who skipped grades seven, nine, ten, twelve, and thirteen) completed his baccalaureate work at Johns Hopkins in December 1976, a few days after his seventeenth birthday, with a major in quantitative studies and considerable work in political science, economics, and astronomy. He plans to start work toward the M.B.A. and Ph.D. in economics at the University of Chicago while still seventeen.

Another of their quite bright classmates received his bachelor's degree in electrical engineering while still 17⅔ years old, and a physics major reached only 18½. Both of these were elected to Phi Beta Kappa, and both won three-year National Science Foundation fellowships.

Irrelevant academic enrichment consists of not determining precisely what types of advanced stimulation the brilliant student needs, such as faster-paced mathematics for the mathematically precocious, but instead offering all high-IQ youths a special academic course such as high-level social studies or essentialy nonacademic work such as games (e.g., chess) or creative training largely divorced from subject matter. Of course, while this may be splendid that year for those whose major interest is touched

262

on, it does not assuage the mental hunger of the mathematically oriented. (See Stanley 1954a, 1958, 1959a.) Also, if the enrichment is academic, special efforts need to be made to alter later courses, or else the enriched students may be more bored than ever in subsequent years.

Cultural enrichment consists of providing certain "cultural" experiences that go beyond the usual school curriculum and therefore do not promote later boredom. Examples are music appreciation, performing arts, and foreign languages such as Latin and Greek (see Mill 1924 and Packe 1954). Early experiences with speaking modern foreign languages and learning about foreign cultures can also fit this pattern and may be a type of stimulation that parents and teachers of high-IQ youths should provide from the early years. These do not, however, meet the specialized academic needs of the intellectually talented.

This may be the place to decry what we at SMPY perceive to be vast overemphasis on the Stanford-Binet or Wechsler-type overall IQ in planning academic experiences for brilliant children. If one takes a group of students who all have exactly the same Stanford-Binet IQ (say, 140), one does not have a group homogeneous with respect to such special abilities as mathematical reasoning. The IQ is a global composite, perhaps the best *single* index of general learning rate. One can, however, earn a certain IQ in a variety of ways, e.g., by being high on memory but much lower on reasoning, or vice versa. *It is illogical and inefficient to group students for instruction in mathematics mainly on the basis of overall mental age or IQ.* Often this is done and then the students who lag behind in the class are accused of not being well motivated, when in fact they simply do not have as high aptitude for learning mathematics as some in the class who have the same IQ. These considerations also apply to other academic subjects, such as history or English literature.

It is difficult to form a group of students really homogeneous for instruction in a given subject even when one uses all the psychometric and other knowledge about them that can be gathered. To rely primarily on the IQ for this purpose, as quite a few city and state programs for the intellectually gifted do, seems to us curious indeed. An obvious corollary is that students should be grouped for instruction separately for each subject and that these groupings should be subject to change from year to year. Probably administrative or political convenience is the cause of undue reliance on a single grouping measure such as IQ. Now that computer scheduling is available, however, this justification for an ineffective process is weakened.

The fourth and last type of enrichment is what we term *relevant academic*. It is likely to be both the best short-term method and one of the worst long-term ones. Suppose, for instance, that an excellent, forward-looking school system provides a splendid modern mathematics curriculum for the upper 10 percent of its students from kindergarten through the seventh grade, and then in the eighth grade these students begin a regular algebra I course. How bored and frustrated they are almost sure to be! It is not educationally or psychologically sound to dump these highly enriched students into the mainstream, and yet that kind of situation often occurs. Only if the kindergarten through twelfth-grade curriculum is considered can this failure of articulation be prevented. Even then, a superb thirteen-year mathematics program without strong provisions for college credit would merely defer the boredom and frustration until the college years.

For the preceding logical reasons we feel strongly that any kind of enrichment except perhaps the cultural sort will, without acceleration, tend to harm the brilliant student. Also, there is excellent support for acceleration in the professional literature. Wiener (1953, 1956), Fefferman (Montour 1976*b*), Bardeen (Young 1972), Wolf (Keating 1976, see index; Montour, 1976*a*), Watson (1968), and others have benefited greatly from it professionally. Norbert Wiener had his baccalaureate at fourteen and his Ph.D. degree at eighteen. Charles Louis Fefferman had his baccalaureate at seventeen and his doctorate at barely twenty; by age twenty-two he was a full professor of mathematics at the University of Chicago. Five years later he was the first winner of the National Academy of Sciences $150,000 Waterman Award.

John Bardeen, twice a Nobel Laureate in physics, completed high school at age fifteen. Merrill Kenneth Wolf, now a prominent neuroanatomist and talented musician, was graduated from Yale University shortly after becoming fourteen years old. James Watson had his Ph.D. degree at age twenty-three and had earned a Nobel prize before he became twenty-five. These examples could go on and on. Counterexamples, such as the ill-fated William James Sidis (Montour 1975, 1977), who was graduated from Harvard College at age sixteen but failed badly thereafter, are rare.

Lehman (1953), a psychologist, teamed up with a specialist in each of various fields to study the ages at which their greatest creative contributions were made by eminent scientists, scholars, and prodigies of other kinds. The typical age at which eminent mathematicians and physical scientists made their most highly rated achievements was lower than the average at which the Ph.D. degree in those fields is awarded in the United States. Many brilliant young men and women are still students when according to logic and history they should be more independent researchers.

Terman and Oden (1947, pp. 264–66) found that the typical member of Terman's gifted group was graduated from high school about a year early. They advocated a moderate amount of acceleration for gifted youths. Hollingworth (1942), who worked with even abler children than the average of Terman's group, recommended considerable acceleration for them.

The University of Chicago's extensive experience with early entrance and fast progress in college during the 1930s showed that this was indeed a feasible approach for certain students. After this program was largely abandoned because of financial and other reasons, the Fund for the Advancement of Education (1953, 1957) set up studies at a number of colleges and universities to admit well-qualified students at the end of the tenth or eleventh grade. These were judged to be markedly successful.

264

Hobson (1963) and Worcester (1956) showed that, when properly arranged, early entrance to public school was beneficial. It seems to me especially unfortunate that their work is not well known to most educational administrators, because its scope, practicality, and clarity make the findings hard to ignore.

The most comprehensive study of educational acceleration was the splendid monograph by Pressey (1949). Anyone who can read it carefully and still oppose such acceleration certainly has the courage of his or her preconvictions. Pressy, Hobson, Worcester, and others reveal that opposition to acceleration is founded on emotionalized prejudices rather than facts. (Also, see Friedenberg 1966.) We do not know of a single careful study of actual accelerants that has shown acceleration not to be beneficial, though armchair articles against it abound (see Daurio 1977).

In SMPY's experience, the eagerness of the brilliant student himself or herself to move ahead rapidly seems crucial. If the youth is reluctant to take a particular accelerative path, such as going into algebra II early without bothering with algebra I, taking a college course, or skipping a grade, probably he or she should not be urged to do so. Unfortunately, many boys and girls are not allowed by their teachers, guidance counselors, principals, or even sometimes their parents to make a calm, rational decision about such matters. They may get so much bad advice that they give up in confusion. Many are simply forbidden to use a particular method of acceleration. It takes an unusually strong-willed youth to buck this adult obfuscation and tyranny.

From its inception SMPY has tried to communicate directly with the youths themselves, rather than through their parents. Reports of the results of the testing competition have gone to them, even including discussion of percentile ranks on national norms and the like. We have also written letters to them in response to their queries or their parents'. In the few instances where we have deviated from this policy—chiefly, with quite young boys and girls who came to our attention by way of their parents rather than through the formal talent search—the youngster's motivation has seemed to suffer. We believe that contacts of the facilitating agency such as SMPY should be mainly through the youth, even though he or she may be only nine or ten years old. After all, a child that age whose Stanford-Binet IQ is 170 or more (and SMPY seldom deals with any that young unless they are that bright) has a mental age of at least fifteen years. He or she will be as able to understand our communications as many parents are. We want the youths to take charge of their own academic planning early and to use their parents and us as means for implementing their own decisions. Some parents object to this approach, of course, because they want to keep their children dependent, but if communication from the beginning is with the student, such friction between SMPY and the parents will not usually be great.

In summary, the SMPY staff believes that offering each splendid mathematical reasoner a varied assortment of accelerative possibilities and

265

letting him or her choose an optimum combination of these to suit the individual's situation is far superior to so-called special academic enrichment. Of course, we would be pleased to see individual courses and curricula improved and special accelerative classes set up by school systems for their intellectually talented students.

Self-Pacing as Inappropriate Neoenrichment, Versus Group Pacing

When we propose accelerative opportunities for mathematically highly talented youths, the school is likely to counter by offering to let them proceed "at their own pace." In practice this usually means still sitting in the too-slow class, such as first-year algebra, while working ahead in the book and perhaps into algebra II. Common sense and observation tell us that this is not likely to work well for most students, no matter how able. Any student that autonomous and well motivated would probably have little use for school. Our model is definitely not self-pacing, whether in the crude way described above or by means of programmed instructional materials, except for an occasional highly unusual student.

We have found that stimulation by one's intellectual peers within a homogeneously grouped class which is fast-paced by the teacher produces astoundingly good results for about half of the students enrolled. Skeptics should read about some of SMPY's fast-mathematics classes: Wolfson I (Fox 1974b; Stanley 1976b); Wolfson II (George and Denham 1976); and McCoart calculus (Stanley 1976b).

Our model is somewhere between the high-ability athletic team that stimulates its members to great achievement against an opposing team, and individual competition such as tennis singles or running the hundred-yard dash. The difference between SMPY's special fast-mathematics classes and athletic events is that the mathematically precocious youths have an opponent against which all of them can win and be stars—namely, national norms on standardized achievement tests. Though they pace each other fast, and students who proceed too slowly may have to leave the group, the SMPY students are not competing directly with one another or with any other team except the anonymous national one.

Programmed instructional materials are almost sure to contain too many steps, and too small ones, for mathematically extremely apt students, who will therefore tend to be bored and frustrated by them. Also, such materials do not usually lend themselves to group-paced stimulation. Most of our precocious youths do not perform well against an abstract standard such as number of chapters or frames completed, just as a track man does not usually run well alone or a tennis player perform his or her best against a weak opponent. Most of our students who have tried self-pacing or correspondence-study courses move far less swiftly and well than they do in special fast-mathematics classes. Therefore, we consider the group-pacing feature essential for most persons (cf. Macken et al. 1976).

Emphasis on Counseling and Tutoring the Individual

All of SMPY's efforts are directed toward helping each youth use his/her mathematical and other abilities best for the ultimate benefit of the person—and, we assume, thereby for society itself. The smorgasbord of accelerative educational possibilities that SMPY develops, tries out, and refines is meant to be adapted flexibly to each student. No one program, in mathematics or other educational areas, could possibly serve many of this highly able group well.

This approach makes the "description" (i.e., the study) phase of SMPY follow crucially from the "discovery" (i.e., identification) phase and lead naturally to the "development" (i.e., facilitation) efforts. Without intensive study of the aptitudes, achievements, interests, values, and attitudes of the youths who scored quite high on SAT-M, appropriate counseling would not be possible. Such study continues, of course, during the entire period that the youths are being helped and followed, but a massive initial assessment program helps begin the counseling process. (See Stanley, Keating, and Fox 1974; Keating 1976).

Part of this studying is done via diagnostic testing and the ensuing specific teaching of just those points not yet known by the student. For example, many seventh- or eighth-grade youths who reason extremely well mathematically can score high on a standardized test of knowledge of first-year high school algebra even though they have not yet studied a school subject entitled "Algebra I." If, for example, such a student can answer correctly thirty out of forty items on Form A of Educational Testing Service's Cooperative Mathematics Algebra I Test in the forty-minute time limit, he has scored better than 89 percent of a random national sample of ninth graders did after studying algebra I for a whole school year. Then the youth is handed back the test booklet, told which ten items he missed, and asked to try them again. If he still misses, say, six items, they are examined carefully and he is helped by a tutor to learn quickly those points that he does not know. After suitable instruction on *just those points* and on any other points in the test about which he was unsure (e.g., items he guessed right), he takes Form B of the test under standard conditions and his success is studied. In this way an able youth can often go on to algebra II within a few hours, rather than wasting nearly all of a long, tedious 180-period school year on algebra I. He already knows most of the material of the first course or can learn almost any not-yet-known point almost instantaneously. This type of diagnostic testing and teaching of superior mathematical reasoners makes so much sense that we cannot understand

267

why it is tried so seldom. SMPY has formalized the procedure into a day-long "algebra tutorial clinic."

As a valuable part of its smorgasbord, SMPY has begun to develop into expert tutors mathematically talented youths who are not much older than the persons they tutor. This one-to-one relationship, modeled on the tutorial system of Oxford and Cambridge universities rather than the remedial tutoring arrangement more common in the United States, is proving to be the fastest and best way to move the typical quite young, mathematically highly apt youth ahead fast and well in mathematics.

For example, a seventh grader who scored 720 on SAT-M was tutored by a brilliant eleventh grader less than two years older than he through algebra I to III and geometry easily on Saturday mornings during eight months of the school year. The tutored youth then entered the ongoing Wolfson II fast-math class that summer and was its best student in trigonometry. He skipped the eighth grade and at barely fourteen years of age received by examination credit for two semesters of college calculus. As a tenth grader he made A's on both calculus III and differential equations. At fifteen he took complex-variable theory in the Johns Hopkins summer session and made a final grade of A. Besides all that, he had completed college courses in oceanography and computer science! After the eleventh grade, two years accelerated, he will enter college with sophomore standing or more at the ancient age of 16½ years. Think how much boredom this extremely able, well-motivated young man would undoubtedly have suffered had his mother not "discovered" SMPY when he was beginning the seventh grade.

Articulation With The Schools

SMPY is not a curriculum-development project. We decided early not to attempt altering the best of the standard school courses and textbooks. That in itself would be a multimillion-dollar project. Fortunately, in the wake of Russia's Sputnik I from 1957 until recently many programs such as SMSG mathematics, BSCS biology, and PSSC physics were carried out on a comprehensive scale by specialists. Elements of these have been incorporated into most high school courses and textbooks. It would be unnecessary and presumptuous of SMPY to engage in curriculum construction.

Thus we work within the better school mathematics curricula, usually in the conventional order of algebra I to II, geometry, college algebra and trigonometry, analytic geometry, and calculus. The special mathematics classes move through these extremely rapidly at a high level of rigor, abstraction, and proof, using standard textbooks. (For calculus a college textbook is used.) Creativity in these courses is promoted by the subject matter itself, the creative skills of the teacher, and the influence of able classmates, rather than by training for so-called creativity itself. We do not deny that such training can probably be useful for some students in certain courses or grades, but for our purposes the direct approach to creative performance in mathematics itself seemed preferable. Actually, until even the brightest students get into mathematics of a least number-theory or advanced-calculus level, much of their learning is algorithmic—how to perform processes and why these processes work. Originating proofs and derivations can be encouraged early, but for quite a while most students will be kept rather busy trying to understand the algorithms and proofs that the instructor and the textbook introduce, rather than devising their own.

A caution is in order here: Before a young student abandons pre-algebra mathematics, including arithmetic, for algebra (which, if he or she is able enough, may be easy), diagnostic testing should be done to discover specifically what this particular student does not yet know about arithmetic concepts and computation so that this material can be taught fast and well on an individual basis. This point has been mentioned earlier in another context; it is especially relevant when, for example, a nine-year-old enters a fast-mathematics class such as the one described by Fox (1974*b*).

Our early rejection of curriculum revision as a goal of SMPY has enabled us to save schools considerable time and money and still not upset their sequences of courses. If, for instance, a student learned all of precalculus mathematics well in one of our special classes while still a seventh or eighth grader, the next stage would simply be finding a high school (or college) calculus course for him or her. Most senior high schools are cooperative about this. The greatest problem occurs in the three-year junior high schools (grades 7 to 9), some of which offer algebra I and II, whereas others offer algebra I and plane geometry. Few provide courses in both algebra I and II and geometry, so the student who completes both years of algebra or algebra I and geometry while a seventh or eighth grader may be left without any mathematics to take for a year or two unless a senior high school is nearby. Some friction between certain junior high schools and SMPY has resulted because of this, but sincere efforts by both parties reduced it.

Our initial purpose was to try out procedures that would augment the usual work of the schools. SMPY was meant to be prototypal, producing exportable principles, techniques, and programs that public and private schools could adopt and adapt for their own uses. We were not going into business as an educational agency except to develop, try out, and improve whatever special procedures mathematically highly gifted youths seemed to need. We did not want to criticize the schools' performance of their usual functions, but merely to offer them ways to meet the highly special needs of a relatively small but extremely important group of their students. This articulation of our methods with theirs was important from the start.

Being aware of the vast and often cumbersome bureaucracy of educational systems, however, we did not want to get enmeshed in prolonged deliberations with supervisory personnel of city and country school systems.

269

We planned to work with the youths themselves, and, through them, with their parents. As noted above, our communications are addressed directly to the students. As we said somewhat facetiously, the students are free to share our memoranda and letters with their parents, who in turn might share them with teachers, counselors, and principals if they wish to do so. Usually, we send an extra copy of each memorandum, to make that easy. We believe that this is the desirable way for us to proceed, because more change can be effected quickly for particular individuals at the child-parent-teacher-counselor-principal level than by trying to institutionalize innovations in a school system. Also, such innovations, even if finally adopted, tend to differ from the original model in what we would consider unfortunate ways. We want to develop our own innovation with minimum demands on the schools and then offer *them* for adoption throughout the country, not just in the Baltimore area.

We departed from this plan with one school system that contacted us early and expressed interest in cooperating. This resulted in many long high-level meetings that took much of our limited time and did not seem productive enough. Supervisory personnel may be quite cautious about proposed innovations, preferring to express their concerns and reservations about them rather than to take positive action. Such talk often serves mainly to delay or fend off the innovation.

This is not to say that school systems cannot be led or forced to change curricular policies. Often they can, especially if a sizable group of determined, well-informed parents whose mathematically highly talented children attend the schools concentrate on attaining specific objectives. Outsiders such as SMPY have far less political leverage, but by working directly with students and their parents they can help initiate pressure for needed policies and programs.

Excellent private schools can often provide well for students who are somewhat above average, e.g., those with IQs of 120 to 140. For youths with IQs much above 140 or so, however, the small size of most private schools and their social nature (usually more intimate than that of public schools) may make them less flexible in dealing with extremely gifted youths than public schools can be. Especially, faculty members of many private schools are even more opposed to educational acceleration than most public school teachers are.

In any event, private schools are not automatic panaceas for the intellectually extremely talented. Parents who expect *any* school to provide optimally for their 160- to 225-IQ child without much help from them simply do not understand the extreme nature of such brightness. In an important sense, an IQ of 160 is the mirror image of an IQ of 40, because both deviate 60 points from the average IQ of people in general. A child with an IQ of 160 is about as bright as a child with an IQ of 40 is dull. Both need much special attention if they are to utilize their respective abilities effectively. A great deal of the thinking and planning for a brilliant child must come from its parents or other interested persons bent on supplementing the efforts of the school.

SMPY is not primarily a service project. It is meant to be prototypal—that is, to develop principles, techniques, and practices that can be used widely to improve the mathematical and other education of youths who reason extremely well mathematically.

Benefits To Students

The benefits to SMPY's participants are numerous. Among them are the following:

1. Increased zest for learning and life, reduced boredom in school, and therefore a better attitude toward education and other activities.
2. Enhanced feelings of self-worth and accomplishment.
3. Reduction of egotism and arrogance. At first this may seem counter-intuitive, but repeatedly we have observed that SMPY students who compete with their intellectual peers in rigorous settings such as special fast-mathematics classes tend to develop more realistic understanding of their ability. These youths learn that, compared with national norms on standardized tests, they are superb, but less spectacular relative to each other. In regular mathematics classes the typical SMPY participant earns such good grades with little effort that the temptation to feel superior is strong. For example, the 190–IQ boy who by age eleven had done so well in two college computer-science courses and on the Advanced Placement Program examination in college calculus seems far less egotistical than he was before entering one of our special precalculus classes at age ten. In the SMPY courses he had to work hard to maintain an average rank, whereas as an accelerated sixth grader he was vastly overqualified for all his regular subjects.
4. Becoming far better prepared educationally than they otherwise would be, especially in mathematics, which is basic to many disciplines.
5. Better preparation for the most selective colleges and improved chance of being admitted to them. For example, in the fall of 1975 four of the students whom SMPY had helped entered Harvard or Radcliffe Colleges, two of them two years early each and one of those as a highly prestigious National Scholar.
6. Getting into college, graduate school, and a profession earlier, thus having more time and energy for creative pursuits.
7. Increased opportunities to explore more specialties and hobbies.
8. More time to explore various careers before marriage.
9. Less cost. Most accelerative procedures save the student and/or the parents money. Even skipping the last year of junior high school and going into senior high school a year early eliminates a year that the

student must be supported at home. Eight credits earned by means of a $32 Advanced Placement Program examination in calculus were worth $1000 of tuition at Johns Hopkins in the fall of 1977, and such costs tend to rise almost every year. Graduating from college in three years rather than four saves about one-fourth of all costs and can lead to paid full-time employment a year earlier than otherwise.

10. Being an unusually well-prepared, advanced entrant to college often brings the student to the attention of professors who help him or her get started on important research early. This, in turn, usually leads to better graduate-school opportunities, including improved financial support there. For example, five of SMPY's six radically accelerated youths who were graduated from college in 1977 at ages fifteen to eighteen won National Science Foundation three-year graduate fellowships.

11. Ultimately, we hope. considerably greater success in life, both professionally and personally.

Benefits To Society

Presumably, whatever helps a sizable group of talented individuals use their abilities better should also benefit the larger society. It is easy to see that a number of the points made above about benefits to SMPY participants themselves fall into this category. Below we shall list a few other, somewhat related gains that society itself can expect from the three D's of SMPY and similar programs.

1. Students superbly prepared to major in the mathematical sciences, physical sciences, quantitative social sciences, and other areas where mathematical talent and keen analytical ability are essential or helpful.

2. More years of professional contribution and effective adulthood.

3. Happier, more effective citizens who will understand better how to educate their own children.

4. Reduced cost of education. The types of policies and activities that SMPY espouses save school systems and colleges money, rather than increasing educational expenditures. When a student who already knows first-year algebra is moved into algebra II, room for another pupil is created in the algebra I class, or the teacher can probably work more effectively with the lesser number because a potential distracter and irritant has been removed. When a student skips an entire school grade, the cost of educating him or her that year is saved. If four and one-half years of precalculus mathematics can be learned in a year, a great saving is likely to ensue. Passing introductory college calculus by examination increases room in the class and enriches the next mathematics course by moving an able, well-motivated student directly into it. Students who go thorugh selective colleges in three years rather than the usual four enable those schools to handle more students.

Of course, it would be naive to assume that special policies and provisions for mathematically highly talented youths do not require any extra efforts. Of course they do, but the more effectively the facilitators of these students work, the greater the savings that can accrue to the school system; above and beyond their salaries and other expenses. Much of the identification, study, and implementation can be done by regular personnel in the mathematics supervisor's office. Even if in a strict cost-accounting sense the mathematically precocious were to cost a little extra, it would be an almost negligible amount relative to the expenditures for other types of special education within most school systems.

An often overlooked factor reducing the cost of working with intellectually gifted youths is the tremendous output that one gets for inputs which take little time. A few instructional minutes spent with a brilliant youth can produce amazing results. This contrasts sharply with the much greater amount of time that one must devote to a slow learner in order to get even moderate gains. Similarly, counseling SMPY participants and their parents by memorandum, telephone, letter or case conference does not usually require a great deal of time but often produces striking changes in their education.

An added advantage is that most intellectually precocious youths have bright parents who can and will read counseling information before asking questions, thereby saving the advisers considerable time.

The two sentences with which I ended the first chapter of the first volume of SMPY's *Studies of Intellectual Precocity* (this is the third) seem appropriate here: "Expensive curricular adjustments are made, quite justifiably, for slow learners. It is past time that fast learners get the much less costly 'special education' they deserve" (Stanley, 1974, p. 19).

Scarce Resources and Elitism

But even after the above points some readers may still feel that any special attention to mathematically highly precocious youths is an unwarranted and unnecessary diversion of scarce special resources. Won't the talented boy or girl get along rather well with the regular resources of the school? Don't elective courses such as algebra I, offered specially in the eighth grade of some school systems, and the considerable array of honors-type subjects in senior high school (calculus being a strong example) take care of the needs of the gifted satisfactorily? Why provide more for those who already have so much? Isn't that elitism and therefore contrary to the American way of life? One could argue endlessly about the philosophical content of these questions. Empirically, however, the answer is clear: Many of the youths in the top few percent of their age mates with respect to mathematical reasoning ability can learn mathematics and related subjects faster and better than the curricula of most schools permit. If held to the age-grade lockstep, a large percentage of them will develop poor work

273

habits and lose interest in the area. Even those who do not would usually benefit from better opportunities.

An example, not highly unusual for SMPY, may serve to illustrate the point that quite a few students lag undesirably far behind their capabilities in the usual school setting. We discovered a certain young man at the end of the summer after he had completed the seventh grade of a public junior high school. Standardized testing showed that without actually having had an algebra course he already had almost perfect knowledge of the first year of that subject. In September he entered our first fast-mathematics class, which had begun in June and had covered algebra I quickly during the summer (see Fox 1974b, Student No. I; Stanley 1976b, app. 7.2). By the next August—that is, in about fifty two-hour Saturday-morning classes— he had completed algebra II and III, geometry, trigonometry, and analytic geometry well. That fall, as a ninth grader, he entered a selective independent school in the Baltimore area. It took considerable effort by us to convince the calculus teacher that he should be allowed in that twelfth-grade subject. As the year wore on he became one of the very best students in the class. At age 14 he took the higher-level (BC) national calculus examination of the Advanced Placement Program and made a grade of 4 (meaning that he was "well qualified" for two semesters of college credit). Only a few of the twelfth graders at that excellent school did as well. While a tenth grader at a public senior high school he took a two-semester course in *advanced* calculus at a state college and made A's. Besides that, he has taken several other college courses and made excellent grades. In the fall of 1976 he entered Johns Hopkins as a sophomore after completing the eleventh grade.

If we had not intervened, it is extremely likely that this boy would have been required to take algebra I (which he did not need) as an eighth grader, algebra II as a ninth grader, and plane geometry as a tenth grader. He could have done splendidly on these with virtually no effort, but probably without any zest, either. From his case and many others one sees that a laissez-faire policy for education of the mathematically talented is misguided and harmful to them. Perhaps "genius will out," but much of the superior talent with which SMPY deals is unlikely to do so if unaided. Valuable time and energy will be squandered in the usual too slowly paced courses.

Relationship to Terman's Longitudinal Study

SMPY owes a heavy debt to Terman's five *Genetic Studies of Genius* volumes and Oden's (1968) monograph. They provided many of the ideas and cautions that undergirded SMPY's initial efforts. It is natural, then, that there should be a number of similarities. Because of the half-century that intervened between the start of Terman's study in 1921 and SMPY's official beginning in 1971, however, it is natural, too, that there should be substantial differences. Some of the similarities, most of which have already been implied in this paper, are the following:

1. Both studies sought approximately the ablest 1 in 200 youths. For some purposes SMPY dipped down to the top 15 in 1,000, and for others went up to the ablest 1 in 1,000 or more. Terman also had special subgroups, though not below IQ 135.
2. Participants in both studies were chosen via standardized tests.
3. Both studies were conducted state-wide, California for Terman and Maryland for SMPY, over a several-year period.
4. Both are longitudinal. Terman's group, born on the average in 1910, is still being followed up. SMPY's first three groups, born as early as 1955 (but chiefly from 1958 to 1961), are meant to be followed until at least the end of this century.
5. Both sexes are involved.
6. No quota was set for representation of any sex or other group.
7. Identification was only the first step. After being found, students were studied extensively.
8. Results of both studies are reported in books, articles, and speeches. Terman's (1925) first book appeared four years after he began. SMPY's first one came out in three (Stanley, Keating, and Fox 1974).
9. Both studies were based in departments of psychology. This may seem somewhat ironic; many of the prime considerations in both belong to the area called educational psychology, which in recent years has involved the gifted all too little. Also, mathematics educators in most universities seem far more interested in curriculum development and textbooks for the average and somewhat-above-average student than for facilitation of the mathematically highly talented. We have detected more interest among some heads of mathematics departments in senior high schools and some college teachers of mathematics.

Certain differences between the studies are indicated above. Others are as follows:

1. SMPY tries to help its participants greatly educationally, rather than just observing their natural progress over the years. We intervene on their behalf vigorously, often, and in varied ways.
2. SMPY's initial screening is by a difficult mathematical reasoning test, rather than an intelligence test. Tests that yield IQs are not used for its later testing, either, though sometimes intelligence-test information is furnished us through the parents. But few of our prime group of about 200 students would have Stanford-Binet IQs much less than 140, and two of them reached 212.
3. We are working rather intensively with about 250 youths, whereas Terman started with more than 1,500. About 1,800 more of SMPY's students are getting considerable counseling and suggestions from us,

275

though. This secondary group represents approximately the upper 1.5 percent of the age group with respect to mathematical aptitude.

4. Nearly all of SMPY's participants entered the difficult test competitions of a mathematical talent search sponsored by SMPY at Johns Hopkins. Thus there is probably a strong volunteering bias that makes our youths somewhat more academically aggressive and self-confident than were quite a few of Terman's. Also, a majority of them are definitely oriented toward academic subjects that involve considerable mathematics.

5. Most of our participants were eleven to thirteen years old and in the seventh or eighth grade when first tested. Terman's ranged across all the school grades.

6. Because of SMPY's initial selection procedure, emphasizing mathematical reasoning ability, most of the high scorers in the contest also score well on other reasoning tests, both nonverbal and verbal.

7. In various ways, including a printed newsletter appearing 10 times per year,[4] we encourage SMPY participants to accelerate their educational progress, particularly in the mathematical and physical sciences. SMPY has devised and tried out many special programs for its students. Terman's study was not meant to be interventional.

Talent Versus Genius

Many persons seem hostile toward intellectually talented youths, perhaps a little less so toward those splendid in mathematics than toward the verbally precocious. This contrasts sharply with their generally favorable attitudes toward prodigies in music and athletics. Friedenberg (1966) and Stanley (1974), among others, have discussed how deep-seated this prejudice is. Expressions such as the following abound in literature back to Shakespeare's time: "Early ripe, early rot"; "So wise so young, they say, do never live long"; "For precocity some great price is always demanded sooner or later in life"; and "Their productions . . . bear the marks of precocity and premature decay" (Stanley 1974, pp. 1–2).

We noted earlier that one disguise for dislike of the intellectually talented is to argue that they need no special help; it is assumed that they will succeed well educationally without it. Another tactic we have noticed is the comparison of a highly able youth with Gauss, Euler, Fermat, Galois, Pascal, Newton, or (especially) Einstein, a sort of *reductio ad absurdum* denigration of talent by asserting that it is not the rarest genius. Terman encountered a great deal of this. Some reviewers criticized him because in his frontier-state sample, identified in a short while, he did not discover someone who later became a worthy successor to the greatest musicians, artists, and writers. [Some insight into problems of defining and predicting genius may be obtained from Albert (1975) and Bell (1937).] Obviously, in the State of Maryland during a three-year period we do not expect to have

276

located or helped to produce a Nobel Laureate, much less a successor to Gauss. To have in the sample someone even of the caliber of Norbert Wiener (1953, 1956) is perhaps more than we can reasonably expect. On his sixteenth birthday, however, one young man already through the sophomore year of college began important research in electrical engineering. Another, at age nineteen, did original research in mathematics. At age seventeen another solved an important problem in computer science. Because SMPY's participants were identified young recently, only nine had been graduated from college by June 1977. Achievements of participants will be studied for at least the next twenty years.

On the other hand, we do believe that SMPY is helping a number of exceptionally able young men and women to go far beyond what they would probably have done without our intervention. That is sufficient for us: strong enhancement of talent, rather than the creation of genius. We might have been able to help a lonely, awkward person such as Wiener use his great talents better at an earlier age, and probably Einstein would have scored quite high in a contest like ours had he deigned to enter it, but those two men are examples of persons who somehow achieved magnificently anyway. If one has already thrown a coin and it has landed with the "head" side up, what is the probability of *that* occurrence? This is a foolish question, of course, but no sillier than reasoning from the success of Einstein and Wiener that great intellectual talent will lead inevitably to success. Those country churchyards chronicled by Thomas Gray hold their share of "mute, inglorious" Wieners and Einsteins as well as of Miltons. We suspect that many classrooms also serve as premature tombs for mathematical talent.

A Strong Bond

SMPY's top 200 participants differ considerably in most personal characteristics except age. Some are tall and others are short. Some are introverted and others are extroverted. Some are much better verbal reasoners than others. Some are males and others are females. In fact, they probably differ at least as much from each other as do youths their age who are only average mathematically. These students have one important thing in common, however: they entered a challenging mathematical-aptitude competition and scored extremely well on a difficult mathematical reasoning test designed to be used with above-average students three to five years older than they. This is a powerful commonality that reminds me of the famous lines from Rudyard Kipling's "The Ballad of East and West":

> Oh, East is East, and West is West, and never the
> twain shall meet,
> Till Earth and Sky stand presently at God's great

Judgment Seat;
But there is neither East nor West, Border, nor
Breed, nor Birth,
When two strong men stand face to face, though
they come from the ends of the earth!

Read Kipling's male-chauvinistic "two strong men" as "mathematically highly precocious youths" and you have a summing up of the rationale for SMPY. We believe that mathematical talent does transcend sex, circumstance, and nationality and mandates special educational treatment of mathematical prodigies with respect to their area(s) of great talent. We consider accelerative procedures crucial because—to paraphrase Robert Browning—"a mathematically precocious youth's reach should exceed his/her grasp, or what's an educational system for?" We at SMPY will continue helping to extend both the reach and the grasp of youths who reason extremely well mathematically.

References

Albert, R. S. 1975. Toward a behavioral definition of genius. *American Psychologist* **30**(**2**): 140–51.

Barlow, F. 1952. *Mental prodigies: An enquiry into the faculties of arithmetical, chess and musical prodigies, famous memorizers, precocious children and the like, with numerous examples of "lightning" calculations and mental magic.* New York: Philosophical Library.

Bell, E. T. 1937. *Men of mathematics.* New York: Simon and Schuster.

Burks, B. S., Jensen, D. W., and Terman, L. M. 1930. The promise of youth: Follow-up studies of a thousand gifted children. *Genetic studies of genius,* vol. III. Stanford, Calif.: Stanford University Press.

Burt, C. L. 1975. *The gifted child.* New York: Wiley.

Campbell, D. T., and Stanley, J. C. 1966 *Experimental and quasi-experimental designs for research.* Chicago: Rand McNally.

Cox, C. M. 1926. The early mental traits of three hundred geniuses. *Genetic studies of genius,* vol. II. Stanford, Calif.: Stanford University Press.

Daurio, S. P. 1977. Educational enrichment versus acceleration: A review of the literature. Baltimore, Md.: Study of Mathematically Precocious Youth, Department of Psychology, The Johns Hopkins University.

Downey, M. T. 1961. *Carl Campbell Brigham: Scientist and educator.* Princeton, N.J.: Educational Testing Service.

Eisenberg, A. R. 1977. Academic acceleration and the relationships between age and gradepoint average. Baltimore, Md.: Study of Mathematically Precocious Youth, Department of Psychology, The Johns Hopkins University.

Epstein, H. T. 1974*a*. Phrenoblysis: Special brain and mind growth periods. I Human brain and skull develpoment. *Developmental Psychobiology.* 7(3): 207–16.

_____ 1974*b*. Phrenoblysis: Special brain and mind growth periods. II. Human mental development. *Developmental Psychobiology* 7(3): 217–24.

Fox, L. H. 1974*a*. Facilitating educational development of mathematically precocious youth. In J. C. Stanley, D. P. Keating, and L. H. Fox (eds.), *Mathematical talent: Discovery, description, and development.* Baltimore, Md.: The Johns Hopkins University Press, 47–69.

_____. 1974*b*. A mathematics program for fostering precocious achievement. In J. C. Stanley, D. P. Keating, and L. H. Fox (eds.), *Mathematical talent: Discovery, description, and development.* Baltimore, Md.: The Johns Hopkins University Press, 101–25.

_____. 1976*a*. Identification and program planning: Models and methods. In D. P. Keating (ed.), *Intellectual talent: Research and development.* Baltimore, Md.: The Johns Hopkins University Press, 32–54.

_____. 1976*b*. Sex differences in mathematical precocity: Bridging the gap. In D. P. Keating (ed.), *Intellectual talent: Research and development.* Baltimore, Md.: The Johns Hopkins University Press, 183–214.

_____. 1976*c*. Women and the career relevance of mathematics and science. *School Science and Mathematics* 76: 347–53.

Friedenberg, E. Z. 1966. The gifted student and his enemies. In E. Z. Friedenberg, *The dignity of youth and other atavisms.* Boston: Beacon Press, pp. 119–35.

Fund for the Advancement of Education of the Ford Foundation. 1953. *Bridging the gap between school and college.* New York: Research Division of the Fund.

_____. 1957. *They went to college early.* New York: Research Division of the Fund.

George, W. C. Accelerating mathematics instruction for the mathematically talented. *Gifted Child Quarterly* 20(3): 246–61.

_____, and Denham, S. A. 1976. Curriculum experimentation for the mathematically talented. In D. P. Keating (ed.), *Intellectual talent: Research and development.* Baltimore, Md.: The Johns Hopkins University Press, 103–31.

Hobson, J. R. 1963. High school performance of underage pupils initially admitted to kindergarten on the basis of physical and psychological examinations. *Educational and Psychological Measurement* 33(1, Spring): 159–70.

Hogan, R., Viernstein, M. C., McGinn, P. V., Daurio, S., and Bohannon, W. 1977. Verbal giftedness and socio-political intelligence: Terman revisited. *Journal of Youth and Adolescence,* 6(2): 107–16.

Hollingworth, L. S. 1942. *Children above 180 IQ, Stanford-Binet: Origin and development.* Yonkers-on-Hudson, N.Y.: World Book.

Hudson, L. 1975. *Human beings: The psychology of human experience.* Garden City, N.Y.: Anchor Press/Doubleday.

Keating, D. P. 1975. Precocious cognitive development at the level of formal operations. *Child Development* 46: 276–80.

—————— (ed.). 1976. *Intellectual talent: Research and development.* Baltimore, Md.: The Johns Hopkins University Press.

——————, and Schaefer, R. A. 1975. Ability and sex differences in the acquisition of formal operations. *Developmental Psychology* 11(4): 531–32.

Kramer, E. A. 1974. *Nature and growth of modern mathematics.* New York, N.Y.: Fawcett World Library (2 vols).

Krutetskii, V. A. 1976. *The psychology of mathematical abilities in schoolchildren.* Chicago: University of Chicago Press.

Lehman, H. C. 1953. *Age and achievement.* Princeton, N.J.: Princeton University Press.

Macken, E., van den Heuvel, R., Suppes, P., and Suppes, T. 1976. *Home-based education: Needs and technological opportunities.* Washington, D.C.: National Institute of Education, U.S. Department of Health, Education, and Welfare, pp. 49–71, "Home-based computer-assisted instruction for gifted students."

McGinn, P. V. 1976. Verbally gifted youth: Selection and description. In D. P. Keating (ed.), *Intellectual talent: Research and development.* Baltimore, Md.: The Johns Hopkins University Press, pp. 160–82.

Mill, J. S. 1924. *Autobiography of John Stuart Mill.* New York: Columbia University Press.

Montour, K. M. 1975. Success vs. tragedy. *ITYB* (Intellectually Talented Youth Bulletin, published by SMPY) 1(9, May 15): 3.

——————. 1976*a.* Merrill Kenneth Wolf: A bachelor's degree at 14. *ITYB* 2(7, Mar. 15): 1–2

——————. 1976*b.* Charles Louis Fefferman: Youngest American full professor? *ITYB* 2(8,Apr. 15): 2.

——————. 1977. William James Sidis, the broken twig. *American Psychologist* 32(4): 265–79.

Oden, M. H. 1968. The fulfillment of promise: 40-year follow-up of the Terman gifted group. *Genetic Psychology Monographs 77* (1st half, Feb.): 3–93.

Packe, M. S. J. 1954. *The life of John Stuart Mill.* New York: Macmillan.

Pressey, S. L. 1949. Educational acceleration: Appraisals and basic problems. *Bureau of Educational Research Monographs No. 31,* The Ohio State University, Columbus, Ohio.

Pruzek, R. M., and Coffman, W. E. 1966. A factor analysis of the mathematical sections of the Scholastic Aptitude Test. *Research Bulletin 66–12,* Educational Testing Service, Princeton, N. J., April.

Schonberg, H. C. 1970. *The lives of the great composers.* New York: W. W. Norton.

Sears, R. R. 1977. Sources of life satisfactions of the Terman gifted men. *American Psychologist* **32(2)**: 119–28.

Skemp, R. R. 1971. *The psychology of learning mathematics.* Baltimore, Md.: Penguin Books.

Stanley, J. C. 1954a. Is the fast learner getting a fair deal in your school? *Wisconsin Journal of Education* **86(10)**: 5–6.

———. 1954b Identification of superior learners in grades ten through fourteen. *Supplementary Educational Monograph No. 81,* University of Chicago, December, pp. 31–34.

———. 1958. Providing for the gifted by means of enrichment of the curriculum. *Bulletin of the Wisconsin Association of Secondary School Principals,* Spring, pp. 5–7.

———. 1959a. Enriching high-school subjects for intellectually gifted students. *School and Society* 87 (2151): 170–71.

———. 1959b Test biases of prospective teachers for identifying gifted children. *School and Society 87* (2151): 175–77.

———. Reliability. 1971. In R. L. Thorndike (ed.), *Educational measurement* (2nd ed.), Washington, D.C.: American Council on Education, pp. 356–442.

———. 1973. Designing psychological experiments. In B. B. Wolman (ed.), *Handbook of general psychology.* Englewood Cliffs, N.J.: Prentice-Hall, pp. 90–106.

———. 1974. Intellectual precocity. In J. C. Stanley, D. P. Keating, and L. H. Fox (eds.), *Mathematical Talent: Discovery, description and development.* Baltimore, Md.: The Johns Hopkins University Press, pp. 1–22.

———. 1976a. Use of tests to discover talent: In D. P. Keating (ed.), *Intellectual talent: Research and Development.* Baltimore, Md.: The Johns Hopkins University Press, pp. 3–22.

———. 1976b. Special fast-math classes taught by college professors to fourth- through twelfth-graders. In D. P. Keating (ed.), *Intellectual talent: research and development.* Baltimore, Md.: The Johns Hopkins University Press, pp. 132–59.

———. 1976c. The student gifted in mathematics and science. *NAASP* (National Association of Secondary School Principals) *Bulletin* 60 (398, Mar.):28-37.

———. 1976d. Test better finder of great math talent than teachers are. *American Psychologist* 31(4, Apr.): 313-14.

———. 1976e. The gift for extreme educational acceleration of intellectually brilliant youths. *Gifted Child Quarterly* 20 (1, Spring): 66-75, 41.

———. 1976f. Concern for intellectually talented youths: How it originated and fluctuated. *Journal of Clinical Child Psychology* **5(3)**: 38–42.

———, Keating, D. P., and Fox, L. H. (eds.). 1974. *Mathematical talent: Discovery, description, and development.* Baltimore, Md.: The Johns Hopkins University Press.

Terman, L. M. 1925. Mental and physical traits of a thousand gifted children. *Genetic studies of genius,* vol. I. Stanford, Calif.: Stanford University Press.

————, and Oden, M. H. 1947. The gifted child grows up. *Genetic studies of genius,* vol. IV. Stanford, Calif.: Stanford University Press.

————. 1959. The gifted group at mid-life: Thirty-five years' follow-up of the superior child. *Genetic studies of genius,* vol. V. Stanford, Calif.: Stanford University Press.

Viernstein, M. C., and Hogan, R. 1975. Parental personality factors and achievement motivation in talented adolescents. *Journal of Youth and Adolescence* **4**(**2**): 183–90.

Viernstein, M. C., McGinn, P.V., and Hogan, R. 1977. The personality correlates of differential verbal and mathematical ability in talented adolescents. *Journal of Youth and Adolescence* **6**(**2**): 169–78.

Watson, J. D. 1968. *The double helix: A personal account of the discovery of the structure of DNA.* New York: Atheneum.

Webb, R. A. 1974. Concrete and formal operations in very bright six- to eleven-year-olds. *Human Development* 17: 292–300.

Wiener, N. 1953. *Ex-prodigy.* Cambridge, Mass.: Massachusetts Institute of Technology Press.

————. 1956. *I am a mathematician.* Cambridge, Mass.: Massachusetts Institute of Technology Press.

Worcester, D. A. 1956. *The education of children of* above-average *mentality.* Lincoln, Nebr.: University of Nebraska Press.

Young, P. 1972. The transistor's coinventor makes history with a super-cold superprize. *National Observer* **11**(**50**): 1, 22.

Additional References, Not Cited

Fox, L. H. 1976. Career education for gifted pre-adolescents. *Gifted Child Quarterly* **20**(**3**): 262–70.

George, W. C. (Chairman). 1977. Negative attitudes and behaviors: Barriers to education of the gifted. *Talents and Gifts* 19(4): 2–15, 21–26. Papers by S. J. Cohn, L. H. Fox, M. C. Pyryt, and C. H. Solano. Discussion by George.

Keating, D. P., and Stanley, J. C. 1972. Extreme measures for the exceptionally gifted in mathematics and science. *Educational Researcher* **1**(**9**): 3–7.

Maeroff, G. I. 1977. The unfavored gifted few. *New York Times Magazine,* Aug. 21, pp. 30–32, 72ff.

Montour, K. M. 1976. Three precocious boys: What happened to them. *Gifted Child Quarterly* **20**(**2**): 173–79.

Stanley, J. C. 1976. Identifying and nurturing the intellectually talented. *Phi Delta Kappan* **58**(**3**): 234–37.

Time. 1977. Smorgasbord for an IQ of 150. **109(23)**: 64. Also see the October 1977 (Vol. 8, No. 7) issue of the *Smithsonian.*

Notes

[1] It is well for the reader to keep in mind the nature of these five volumes, the years in which they appeared, and the fact that their publisher (the Stanford University Press) has kept the whole series in print for more than half a century. References are as follows: Terman (1925), Cox (1926), Burks, Jensen, and Terman (1930), and Terman and Oden (1947, 1959). They have been extended by Oden (1968) and by chapter 3 in this volume. Further analyses of the 1972 follow-up survey are being conducted by Robert R. Sears (1977) and Lee J. Cronbach.

[2] For its history and rationale, see Downey (1961).

[3] Even more psychometrically precocious was the boy of Chinese background who at age ten years one month scored 600 on SAT-V and 680 on SAT-M, and a year later scored 710V and 750M. SMPY's youngest college graduate thus far is Eric Robert Jablow, born 24 March 1962, who received his B.S. degree in mathematics *summa cum laude* from Brooklyn College in June of 1977. In the fall of 1977 he became a doctoral student in mathematics at Princeton University.

[4] It is called *ITYB*, the *Intellectually Talented Youth Bulletin.*

Harold K. Hughes

The Enhancement of Creativity*

There are periods in history when one dominant idea characterizes many facets of intellectual life. In the seventeenth and eighteenth centuries, for example, mechanistic determinism flourished in physics and was reflected notably in philosophy, economics, and music. Possibly man is always in the midst of such periods, but he identifies them more clearly in perspective.

Taxonomists today describe the present scene variously as the second industrial revolution, the paper age, or the age of the anonymous man. Evolutionists speculate that man ceased to develop biologically a million years ago and chose, instead, the route of cultural evolution, a route that has led him through the paradox of his greatest intellectual triumph—the overdemonstration of his personal insignificance—and on to this ultimate tragedy, cosmology's imminent proof of the utter triviality of his species and his world.

At the risk of being declared myopic by taxonomists of the twenty-first century, I suggest that the common thread in these several classifications of the present scene is change, and that the dominant idea of our period in history is creativity.

As a research exercise, the serious study of creativity has long been the province of psychologists. In recent years, however, educators and business managers have culled the creativity literature and encouraged researchers in order, on the one hand, to accelerate discovery and, on the other, to increase profits through the more efficient use of personnel.

For nine years as an Associate of the Creative Science Program at New York University, I have studied scientific creativity in its many aspects and have lately begun to apply some tentative findings to my own teaching. The primary question to myself has been, Is it possible to stimulate the creativity

Hughes, Harold K. "The Enhancement of Creativity." *The Journal of Creative Behavior,* Vol. 3, No. 2, 1969, pp. 73-83.
*The material under this heading is abstracted from published research (see References) by Mooney, 1953; MacKinnon, 1962; Roe, 1953; Eiduson, 1962; Maslow, 1954; Pelz, 1958; Cattell, 1960; Dichter, 1959; Barron, 1958; Coler, 1959; and Drews, 1963.

of undergraduate and graduate students and, if so, will this enhanced creativity carry over into their later professional careers? Currently I have reason to think that the answer to that dual-faceted question is "yes," but I am not yet prepared to specify the boundary conditions between "yes" and "no." Tentatively, my hypothesis is, Scientific creativity in students can be enhanced in a climate and by techniques which can, in part, be created on the basis of a knowledge of those characteristics which distinguish creative from non-creative mature scientists (Terman, 1954). I present no data to support my hypothesis, nor are there any available that I know of. I merely present a series of reasoned and sometimes empirically based suggestions for the kind of ideal climate that may well produce more creative students, particularly scientists.

Naturally, not all future creative scientists have the characteristics which distinguish past or present scientists from their peers, nor would they necessarily benefit from this ideal climate that I propose. Higher education is, however, a group process. We must of necessity make decisions for the benefit of large numbers of students and hope that the flexibility that pervades the proposed climate can at least accommodate most of the exceptions without actually stifling them.

Characteristics

Most creative scientists have good memories in both random and sequential access. A few display remarkable powers. Charles P. Steinmetz, for example, easily memorized the logarithms of the first 100 numbers. Herman P. Mark is reputed to remember the journal, volume, and page number of countless literature references. However, these creative scientists generally prefer to use their storage capacity selectively and decide for themselves what to store. Consequently, they have a low interest in enforced rote memory, seeing little reason to remember formulas which are easy to derive, facts that are readily available in books, or operations that are amenable to simple improvisation.

Creative scientists are particularly open to new experience. Possibly, this characteristic developed because the families of these children moved more often than most. Also, many of the scientists studied had, as children, been left alone for long periods of time during which they had to provide their own entertainment. They have wide interests and long interest spans and are not inclined to feel circumscribed by their environment. They work best when in frequent contact with colleagues having widely different orientations and experience.

The creative scientist works hard and persistently, is independent, antiauthoritarian, and attentive to detail. Apparently, his early home climate created strong drives which were self-controlled and channeled toward constructive and distant goals. Thus, early he experienced delayed satisfaction of desires, as by working a year to get a longed-for bicycle. By attainment of a goal after much persistence, his resolve and creativity were stimulated.

Creative scientists on the average are emotionally cool, aloof, dominant and introspective. Often, as children, they chose to be alone although companionship was available. Nor were they very intimate with their families. Many observed some pathological disturbance at home and so learned to dislike interpersonal conflict. They are more socially concerned than sociable. Just as they enjoy a risk calculated on natural law but not on people, they prefer problems about things to problems that are people-related.

Albert Einstein (1950) illustrates the latter characteristic well when he writes, "My passionate interest in social justice and social responsibility has always stood in curious contrast to a marked lack of desire for direct association with men and women."

Of all the characteristics of a creative scientist, the one which is most related to his public image is his imaginative and unorthodox thinking. Nothing is spared his curiosity. He has neither veneration for the past nor respect for the present. With ideas, though not necessarily in behavior, he is future-oriented and is quite willing to make bold leaps into uncharted territory, guarded principally by intuition. This characteristic may well be a development of an overwhelming interest in reading and particularly in reading science fiction, which a creative scientist is likely to have at some stage in his life.

Likewise, he is not afraid of "way-out" daydreams, for he is confident that he can return to reality at will and appraise his dreams realistically. He is given to advocating changes for good logical but poor personal and political reasons. Being more interested in the goal than in the method of achieving it, he is likely to support his conclusions with vigor. This tendency makes him a disturber of the mental peace, and for the non-flexible teacher who wants to settle into a routine, the creative person creates havoc.

A creative scientist has a high tolerance for ambiguity and discomfort but little for boredom. Indeed, he actively seeks complex, discomforting situations and problems not only for the challenge they present but for aesthetic satisfaction in the elegant solution for which he hopes. Mental effort, then, is to the creative scientist what physical exercise is to an athlete—a chosen activity *and* a necessity. This strong drive almost automatically leads to the next characteristic.

Creative scientists find ways to reduce society's demands on them so that they have time to think. For example, many choose mates who, by competent management of home and children, relieve them of many common living chores. During these "think" periods, they may appear to be loafing. I remember when I was in industry a laboratory director would call me on the phone and say, "Bob has his feet on his desk again." Thus he would badger me about the most creative man in my section.

Creative scientists generally start slowly on a problem, look at many of its facets, and increase their pace as they proceed. Near the climax of success, they work furiously, and at this time observers become aware of the creative person's extraordinary capacity for involvement over extended periods of time. This, too, can be an explanation for the scientist's being so consistently described as an introvert.

The final characteristic of creative scientists that I wish to mention is their sensitivity to approval and disapproval. Although they have a good opinion of themselves, they need recognition and rewards in order to continue producing their best work. Similarly, they tend to learn most from those who are demanding yet fair. A typical creative scientist comes from a home where parental authority, although somewhat impersonal, was consistent, predictable, fair, and psychologically supportive. In general, rebellion was against ideas and seldom took the form of overt misbehavior.

Toward a Total Creative Climate

Taking these eight characteristics into consideration and evaluating the needs inherent to their enhancement, and thus to creativity in general, a restructuring of the overall curriculum in most American colleges would appear to be desirable. Nor is the restructuring so major as to be improbable or even relatively time-consuming. For instance, American colleges commonly request that science students complete the liberal arts requirements in their first two years. This postpones the period of intensive concentration on their major interest and fails to utilize the enthusiasm for study that they bring to the campus. With a more flexible policy, general education courses could be distributed throughout the four years. We could maintain, then, a high level of interest in science for science majors while catering both to the creative person's adaptability and to his need for variety.

In a like vein, a science major should be required to take courses outside his major field—just as I am convinced that other majors should be required to take science courses. As T. S. Eliot has said, "It's a part of education to learn to interest ourselves in subjects for which we have no aptitude."

One, but by no means the only, value in required courses is that they train students in that quality of persistence without which there can be no creativity. Unfortunately, many advisors in the humanities do not share this view and they permit most of their majors to graduate illiterate in the facts and attitudes of science.

On the other hand, we must strike a balance, since, to be creative, an individual must have unprogramed time. Our pattern of required classes, convocations, homework and amusements must be liberalized in order that the student have the necessary opportunity for reflective and creative thinking. As an institution, the college, of course, should make sure that every student, and especially the creative one, is worked hard; yet, in many cases, the individual student can profitably be allowed to choose academically acceptable projects on his own. That is, schools must be rigid enough to force the lazy student to study and flexible enough to let the highly motivated one set his own pace. We need not, for example, be strict with all students about class attendance and deadlines; but we must demand adequate overall performance.

My own department offers credit for undergraduate courses called "Independent Study in Physics" and "Honors in Physics." Our experience with these courses is favorable and good students seem to like them, being able to direct their own theoretical and experimental activities in a wide variety of ways.

Thus, as I said, we have a paradox that needs equalizing: some students won't think unless they are forced to; others cannot exert their best efforts or develop to their full potential under excessive pressure to meet rigid requirements.

This paradox also seeps into the field of finances, in which scholarships and fellowships are needed (and should be provided) for those who are forced to devote a large fraction of each week to earning their support—and yet, a *moderate* level of financial pressure often increases the motivation for high achievement.

In order to resolve the paradoxes totally, of course, we would need a battery of individual-oriented educators supported by an extremely flexible, individual-oriented educational system. This is Educational Utopia. But, given the direction, the goal, we can come closer and closer in our lifetime to the ideal, with, as I see it, little lost and much gained.

In a final word about overall curriculum, the most creative students should be encouraged to change schools after receiving their bachelor's degree. Doctoral candidates thereby experience and benefit from a variety of equipment, emphases and teaching personalities, which is invaluable to their scientific and social maturing.

The college and its faculty should encourage nonclass activities such as attendance at professional meetings and lectures; publication; visits to other institutions, museums and libraries; and (for my particular group of students) a Student Section of the American Institute of Physics. The latter can also serve a social purpose. Whereas many future creative scientists are introverts, others like to be with people and benefit from close technical and social association with their classmates and professors. One graduate student wrote to me, "I find no greater stimulus to hard work and creative thinking than being in constant contact with intelligent, imaginative, critical and hardworking fellow graduate students."

Although we must teach students to expect a hostile or, at best, an indifferent climate from a society that frequently disapproves of creativity, we can easily provide them with lounges and library areas where they can converse with others who would otherwise lead similar lonely intellectual lives.

The teacher who fully understands the creative individual's tendency toward introversion will offer him a friendly, supportive relationship while respecting whatever psychological distance he prefers. In fact, a good instructor has a variety of relationships with his students. To one he is a friend, to another he is a taskmaster. In front of all he holds the carrot of achievement.

I remember one student calling me "a smiling executioner" for allowing him to devote an entire Christmas holiday to a high-gain amplifier which had no chance of working. He deserved the A he received for the course and he thanked me afterward for allowing him to learn so much electronics. Another student, however, complained that I gave him too many reasons why his inventions would not work. I do not pretend that it is easy to find the right way with the right student each time.

To encourage divergent thinking, a creative instructor will maintain an easy willingness to consider any question, any topic, any time. Thus, a good teacher is seen by his students as a "creative observer," according to Eric Barnes (1956), who describes one from a student's viewpoint: "He is perceptive, kind, appreciative, sometimes critical, but always detached. When he is on the sidelines, one's task immediately takes on new meaning and dignity. He finds the order latent in the apparent chaos of your life."

Obviously, to maximize student potential in the sciences or in any field, we must optimize the flexibility and *humaneness* of prospective teachers. They must be educated to be socially conscious, individual-concerned human beings first and educators second. An implication of the "adaptability" characteristic for the educational process is that there should be plenty of variety in course content and meeting formats. We should use audio and visual aids, reports, debates, outside speakers, instructors from other disciplines, visits to industry, and different seating arrangements and room assignments. Changes (particularly in the latter category) should appear logical and occur just often enough to be stimulating but not so often as to be disruptive or obviously capricious. It is perfectly natural, for instance, to have seating in the round for discussion meetings or seminars, since this arrangement is preferred by so many students.

In order to cater to the creative scientist's desire for resolvable disorder we should deal with complex concepts more often than we do now in lecture, laboratory, and homework. Too frequently in physics we simplify the assumptions in a problem in order to simplify the mathematics, but these two levels of difficulty need not be correlated. It is quite possible to devise complex problems without over-elaborating the mathematical tedium in their solution.

The essence of good engineering design is compromise, and problems requiring value-related compromise can be utilized more often. For maximum stimulation, these should cross the conventional boundaries of organized disciplines.

Another exercise in complexity is to devise problems as well as to solve them. Using my field of physics again as an example, one can ask for a pair of 3 by 3 matrices which commute and, therefore, have the same eigenvectors. We might also present a poorly defined situation, asking for a clarification of the problem and a tabulation of data which must be acquired before a solution can be found.

Is it not possible to raise a student's interest in complexity by admitting that much of what we teach him is incomplete and some of it even wrong? Few subjects in our freshmen and sophomore years are not simplified by assumptions: no friction, the absence of natural selection in the Hardy-Weinberg law of gene frequency stability, no chemical impurities present, circular Bohr orbits, etc. Having taught a topic under simplifying assumptions, the instructor might raise a student's creativity by revealing that the full story is really more complex. A good introduction to Heisenberg's uncertainty principle and to Godel's theorem (Nagel & Newman, 1958) is bound to help a science student realize that science is not always simple, or exact, or complete.

Conversely, intelligent simplification of complex situations should be taught as an important part of the creative treatment of scientific problems.

Certain techniques are known to promote divergent thinking. One can be called the "What would happen if. . ." question. John E. Arnold (1956), for example, populated a planet of Arcturus with unusual people for whom his students had to design a variety of products. Recently, I have had success by asking for the effects on the population of Terre Haute of a billion-fold increase in Planck's constant. In my experience, "What would happen if . . ." is a valid device for encouraging thinking and learning.

Puzzles, paradoxes and conundrums are also stimulants to divergent thinking. A story that I found useful concerns a panel truck I was following in my car. The driver stopped just short of a one-lane bridge and so I too had to stop. The driver alighted, seized a long pipe and proceeded to beat the sides of the truck vigorously. Wondering why, I too alighted and asked him what he was doing.

"Well," he said, "see that bridge? It will hold only 5 tons safely and I'm driving a 3-ton truck."

"Then you're all right," I said impatiently. "Go ahead and cross it."

"Oh, no," he replied. "You don't understand. The truck is also loaded with 3 tons of canaries and I'm trying to keep 1 ton of them in flight as I cross the bridge."

The class argued for two days about those canaries.

Another technique for stimulating science majors' creative thinking might well be the assignment of reading that is non-mathematical, reading the area of science fiction, and creative writing in all areas. All reading assignments should contain contradictory material.

At Indiana State University we are considering also a seminar in scientific methods and in the history and philosophy of science to broaden student perspectives after three years of emphasis on unintegrated facts and ideas. One of the reasons for studying the history of science is to allow students to derive emotional support from the past. To learn, for example, that Planck first obtained his equation for black-body radiation by curve-fitting data and only later realized it could have been derived from theoretical principles is to learn that even great men sometimes grope for answers.

Other techniques have proven valid in varying degrees. One of my colleagues is purposely vague about laboratory procedures in his advanced classes and claims that this stimulates the resourcefulness of students. In my thermodynamics class, I have found that I can break the pattern by which a student tends to answer questions in terms of the particular class he is attending: I simply ask a question in thermodynamic terms which really involves subject matter of a prerequisite course, such as mechanics or electricity.

An occasional dramatic stunt is stimulating, as I found out quite by accident. I once informed an elementary physical science class that we were to see a film on scientific methods. Not until the title flashed on the screen did I realize that the film was on superstitions. During the discussion afterward, I pretended to believe in the magic of rabbit's feet and water dowsing. Although most students know an instructor too well for him to deceive them totally, I feel that some of the students present learned as much about scientific method through dramatic use of contrast as they would have had the correct film been run.

Even the testing process can stimulate creativity. If we are to foster and take advantage of the creative person's tendency toward excellent but selective memory, we should give open as well as closed-book tests. The statement of problems in the latter type can include all data and complex formulas needed for their solution. To stimulate reflective thinking, throughout the year I sprinkle tests with problems that contain superfluous, contradictory or incomplete information along with more orthodox questions. A preliminary and admittedly subjective assessment of the value of these questions is that they do, in fact, stimulate students to more creative thinking.

Some tests should have essentially no time or resource limit. Three weeks before a term ends, for example, I distribute the first part of the final examination to some advanced classes. Students may consult any resource except another person. Limited time and extended time (take-home) tests rank students differently. It is not at all clear to me whether either ranking is the superior one. Life places a variety of demands on us and we should, I suspect, prepare students for leisurely problems as well as for urgent ones.

Summary

Mature creative scientists are frequently distinguished from their less creative peers by their good but selective memory, openness to new experience, self-discipline, introversion, divergent thinking, attraction to resolvable disorder, insistence on free time, and need for a supportive climate. It is likely that these characteristics are but superficial manifestations of subconscious drives which produce extraordinary involvement in a problem for an extended period of time.

As a working hypothesis needing much more testing, I propose that these distinguishing characteristics imply that the ideal collegiate climate for the development of future creative scientists includes the following features: a moderate reliance on rote memory (open-book tests are, therefore, com-

291

mon); a variety of teaching methods, materials, topics and out-of-class experiences; formal course requirements in non-science areas; and self-directed education.

The ideal collegiate climate for creativity is supportive but only as personal as the student desires; it encourages divergent thinking about all problems, old and new; it stresses that all life is compromise and few subjects are completely knowable. Since one essence of creativity lies in the simplification of complexity, the ideal collegiate climate presents many complex problems, some of which are unsolvable. The climate is both leisurely and hurried.

The existence of this climate implies a staff capable of its creation, or, in other words, a staff of human beings sensitive to the needs of other human beings.

References

Arnold, John E. The Creative Engineer. *Machine Design,* 3 May 1956, *28,* 119.

Barnes, E. W. *The man who lived twice: The biography of Edward Sheldon.* New York: Scribners, 1956.

Barron, F. The Needs for Order and for Disorder as Motives in Creative Activity. *Second (1957) University of Utah Research Conference on the Identification of Creative Scientific Talent,* Salt Lake City: Univ. of Utah Press, 1958, pp. 119-128.

Cattell, R. B. The Personality and Motivation of the Researcher from Measurements of Contemporaries and from Biography. *Third (1959) University of Utah Research Conference on the Identification of Creative Scientific Talent,* Salt Lake City: Univ. of Utah Press, 1960, pp. 119-131.

Coler, M. A. Creators of environment. *Teaching and learning.* New York: Ethical Culture Schools, 1959. Also, *Chem. & Eng. News,* 15 Aug. 1966, *44,* 72.

Dichter, E. Motivating the Technical Mind. *Industrial Research,* Spring 1959, *1,* 71.

Drews, E. M. Profile of creativity. *Nat. Educ. Assoc. J.,* Jan. 1963, *52,* 26.

Eiduson, B. T. *Scientists: Their psychological world.* New York: Basic Books, 1962.

Einstein, A. Quoted by Lin Yutang in *The wisdom of America,* New York: John Day, 1950, p.453.

MacKinnon, D. W. The Nature and Nurture of Creative Talent. *Amer. Psychol.,* 1962, *17,* 484.

Maslow, A. H. *Motivation and personality.* New York: Harper & Bros., 1954.

Mooney, R. L. *A preliminary listing of indices of creative behavior.* Columbus: Ohio State Univ. Bur. of Educ. Research, 1953.

Nagel, E., & Newman, J. R. *Godel's proof.* New York: New York Univ. Press, 1958.

Pelz, D. C. Social Factors in the Motivation of Engineers and Scientists. *School Sci. & Math.,* June 1958, *58,* 417.

Roe, A. *The making of a scientist.* New York: Dodd, Mead, 1953. Also, *Science,* 1961, *134,* 456.

Smith, R. F. W. The deliberate induction of new ideas. In M. A. Coler, *Essays on creativity in the sciences,* New York: New York Univ. Press, 1963.

Terman, L. M. Scientists and nonscientists in a group of 800 gifted men. *Psychol. Monog.,* 1954, *68 (7),* Whole No. 378.

E. Paul Torrance

Giftedness in
Solving Future Problems

Students currently in differentiated programs for the gifted like to think about the future, and believe that there is much that they can do to change it, and to shape it. However, many are doubtful of the influence their actions will have, and believe that examples from the past are the best guides to the future. As part of the preprogram evaluation of the 1977-78 Future Problem-Solving Program (Torrance, Williams & Torrance, 1977) based at the University of Georgia, we asked gifted students about their attitudes concerning the future and the study of the future. Responses were obtained from 1,729 gifted students from 24 states in grades three through twelve. The results are summarized in Table 1.

The majority of these gifted students indicated that they love to think about the future. This tendency increases, however, from 86 percent in the elementary grades (3 through 6) to 95 percent for the senior high school students (grades 10-12). While only 73 percent of the elementary school students believe that there is much they can do to shape their futures, the percentage rises to 94 among middle school students, and to 97 among senior high schoolers. Responses to this and some of the other items suggest that younger gifted students need help in recognizing that there are

TABLE 1

Attitudes concerning the future of gifted students at the elementary, middle, and senior high school levels.

| | Percentages | | |
Attitude	Elementary (N=876)	Middle (N=650)	Senior (N=203)
I like to think about the future (Agree)	86%	87%	95%
The more I learn about the future the more exciting the future is (Agree)	67%	66%	71%
Nothing we do now will change the future (Disagree)	78%	93%	93%
It is not likely that my actions will influence the future (Disagree)	40%	50%	65%
Examples from the past are the best guides to the future (Disagree)	27%	20%	19%
There is no sense in asking elementary children to discuss alternative futures (Disagree)	75%	76%	80%
Science fiction is not proper for study in school (Disagree)	64%	67%	83%
Students can do little to shape their futures (Disagree)	73%	94%	97%

Reprinted from Journal of Creative Behavior, Vol. 12, No. 2, 1978, pp. 75-86. By permission of the author and publisher.

things that they can do now to influence the future. Forty percent of the elementary school students disagreed with the statement that "it is not likely that my actions will influence the future," as compared to 65 percent of the senior high school students.

Importance of Futurism in Programs for Gifted Children

As suggested by Toffler (1970, 1974), civilization has reached a point at which education should devote a considerable part of the curriculum to helping students enlarge, enrich, and make more accurate their images of the future. While much can be done to help all children, this is especially true in regard to differentiated programs for gifted and talented students.

Perhaps this is one place where we can risk charges of elitism. In his provocative book entitled *The Images of the Future,* Polak (1973) has maintained that throughout history, advances in civilization have been spurred and guided by the future images of its gifted and talented members. In fact, he makes a particular point of the idea that "images of the future are always aristocratic in origin." He argues that the holders of the images of the future that change and improve the world come from a creative minority. The formation of such images, Polak asserts, depends upon awareness of the future that makes possible conscious, voluntary, and responsible choices among alternatives. From his penetrating analyses of images of the future in history, he reaches the following compelling conclusions:

1. There has been a positive image of the future in every instance of the flowering of a culture, and weakened images of the future as a primary factor in the decay of cultures.
2. The potential strength of a culture could be measured by assessing the intensity and energy of its images of the future.

We need to know how gifted and talented students visualize the future. We also need to find out how to help gifted and talented students enrich and enlarge their images of the future, and make them more accurate. Research and development efforts during the past three years have accumulated massive amounts of data, much of which remains unanalyzed. Two projects, the Future Problem-Solving Program (Torrance, Bruch & Torrance, 1976; Torrance, Williams & Torrance, 1977) and a special summer program known as the Career Awareness Component of the Governor's Honors Program (Torrance, Kaufmann, Gibbs & Torrance, 1976), will be presented.

The Future Problem-Solving Program

The Future Problem-Solving Program involves a deliberately interdisciplinary approach to studying and solving future problems, and may be

295

used either as an intramural or combined intramural/interscholastic activity. Several objectives are uniquely fitted to the needs and characteristics of gifted and talented students. These include the development of problem-solving skills, the improvement of teamwork skills, the enlargement and enrichment of images of the future, and the learning of interdisciplinary skills.

Frequently, gifted students lag behind their less gifted peers in problem-solving skills. They are not challenged to solve problems and go beyond learned solutions. Schools reward them for this, and thus reduce the amount of practice they get in solving problems. The acquisition of deliberate, disciplined skills in creative problem solving fits a special need of gifted and talented students.

Similarly, gifted students do not ordinarily excel in teamwork skills. They may do poorly in team sports, and feel so inept that they shun any teamwork activity. Of the 1,729 gifted students responding to our preprogram evaluation, about 30 percent admitted that they were not very good at working on a team to solve problems. Deliberate emphasis has been placed on the teamwork aspect of the Future Problem-Solving Program. Many participants and their parents have praised this highly. One such case is beautifully described by a parent who wrote the following "thank you" note:

> A big thank you for what your future problem-solving idea has done for our son. He has been known as the "lover," not the "fighter," as he watched cloud formations in the baseball outfield or watched an ant negotiate a clover on the football field—totally missing the team effort. But creative thinking is another story and we appreciate your making team cooperation essential to competition. He at last has a sense of having run the good race. . . .

Many gifted students are multitalented, have interests in several different academic disciplines, enjoy thinking of the implications of findings in one discipline upon another, and combine specialties from two or more different disciplines in their careers. At the middle school and secondary school levels, however, subjects are generally taught as separate disciplines, and teachers are irritated if gifted students attempt to do interdisciplinary thinking. Yet the future world of work will require even more of this kind of thinking. Although a program may begin as one in science, it may rapidly become one in psychology, political science, journalism, art, music, anthropology, or engineering.

The early history of the Future Problem-Solving Program was described previously (Torrance, Bruch & Torrance, 1976). Three interscholastic future problem-solving bowls with trophies and other awards for high performing teams have been conducted. During the past two years, year-long programs with practice problems, feedback to teams concerning their practice solutions, and awards of certificates of merit have been held in addition to the bowls at the University of Georgia. Over 300 schools and 6,000 gifted students in 24 different states are involved in the 1977-78 program. In addition there will be system-wide bowls in Des Moines, Iowa; Houston County, Georgia; San Diego, California; Salt Lake City, Utah; and possibly other areas.

The 1977-78 program is operating according to the following schedule:

August: Handbook and Prospectus
September-October: Training of Teams
November-December: Practice Problem 1
January: Practice Problem 2
February: Practice Problem 3
March: Bowl Invitations and Scenario Contest
April: Invitational Bowl for Teams; Open Competition for Individuals

The students and teachers who participated in the 1976-77 program seemed to think that the program did enlarge, enrich, and make more accurate their images of the future. However, a more objective evaluation of the program is needed. Almost all of the participants in the 1977-78 program have indicated a willingness to participate in evaluation. The preprogram evaluation has already provided important baseline information concerning the attitudes of gifted children concerning the future and the study of the future, self-directed learning readiness, future problem-solving skills, and images of the future. The instruments being developed for this purpose will be described and discussed in the final section of this paper.

During the four years in which this program has been sponsored, a definite improvement has been witnessed in the quality of the problem solving submitted by participants. Originally, the program was intended to extend downward to about the fourth of fifth grade. It has been most popular in the fifth, sixth, seventh, and eighth grades. However, a considerable number of third- and fourth-grade students, and one kindergarten class, are now participating. Catherine Rose of Euclid, Ohio, participated in the 1977 Creative Problem-Solving Institute at Buffalo and wanted to try the program with her kindergarten class. The responses submitted by her teams indicate that such an adaptation can be made.

The first practice problem concerned the continuing and increasing problem of providing an adequate supply of drinkable water. The following subproblems were brainstormed by one of Catherine Rose's kindergarten teams (4 children):

What makes the water dirty?
Is much clean drinking water left?
Does a sign saying "No dirtying the water" help?
Is there more clean drinking water somewhere?
What garbage did people throw in the water?
What do factories put in the water that makes it dirty?
Does a sign that says "No polluting" help?
What will get our lake clean?
What will keep our snow from getting dirty when it comes through the air?

297

What makes the rain dirty?
What will keep oil from spilling in our lake?

Their final statement of the problem was: "How might we get more clean drinking water?"

They then brainstormed the following alternative solutions, some fanciful and some realistic:

Have a monkey on roller skates chop a hole in the ice at the North Pole with an ax and carry water to us.
Have Santa Claus take us to the North Pole and we'll get buckets of water.
Santa can bring water to us by sleigh.
Santa can bring everyone presents of water.
Build a road to the North Pole and bring trucks of frozen water.
Have an eagle carry it.
An airplane with tanks of water.
Find more underground water and pipe it up.
Make a well to deep underground water and use pumps.
Go up on your house top and look around for more water . . . mine is the tallest house.
See if other countries can give us some of their water.
Catch rain water.
Break up icebergs and bring them to Euclid in Lake Erie.
Catch the water a whale shoots up.
Bottle water from icebergs and put it in pop machines . . . no, water machines.

Although the problem analysis and the alternative solutions are in terms of the concepts of 5-year-old children, these data indicate that it is possible for children this young to engage in the future problem-solving process. It is clear that statements of problems and proposed solutions have developmental characteristics. However, children can do future thinking at an earlier age than they can think about the past. Even on the Ask-and-Guess Test of the *Torrance Tests of Creative Thinking* (Torrance, 1974a), children are able to produce future consequences at an earlier age than they are able to produce possible causes resulting from past events or conditions.

The Georgia Career Awareness Program for Gifted Students

Since 1964, there has been an annual six-week summer program for gifted and talented high school students in Georgia known as the Governor's Honors Program. Each year, 400 gifted and talented students are selected on the basis of statewide competition for their excellence in the visual arts, the communication arts, foreign languages (French and Spanish), mathematics, music, natural science, and social sciences. Although there have been interdisciplinary seminars, a major part of the program has always focused on the student's area of specialization. In 1976 and 1977, a program was provided for an additonal 200 students with an experimental option known as the Career Awareness Component (Torrance et al., 1976). This program devoted time to the student's area of specialization but in addition offered the following three components which emphasized career education and futurism:

1. scientific and technological implications for 21st century man,
2. western man's social and political culture, and
3. career education.

The first component gave attention to scientific advancements in the medical and health fields, including aging, the have and have-not worlds, medical science, educational problems affecting the masses, business and industry (including human problems), construction, automation, pollution, uses of the environment, criminal detention and penal correction, education of the public through mass media, family life values, and leisure time activities.

The second component emphasized governmental functions and tasks, economics of the free enterprise systems of man, ideas of men and their effects on man's culture, man's environment and how man uses his environment to meet his needs, and man's physical and mental health problems. In this component, a variety of methods was used but realistic simulations were emphasized.

The third component was a career education program which was organized into three units, each encompassing approximately five four-hour sessions. The first unit was concerned with self-awareness and the decision-making process. The second unit provided opportunities to explore specific careers and educational routes to these careers; and the third unit involved a practical study of job survival skills, and concluded with an evaluation of the participant's goals and the goals of the program.

In addition to these three components, there was a very large variety of special interest groups, usually for 5 to 10 students each, and special events and seminars, including student-conducted seminars. Many of these also emphasized the future.

Neither the entire program nor the evidence showing that it did in fact enlarge, enrich, and make more accurate the images of the future of these gifted and talented young people shall be presented. However, some of the methods used in the component on futures study, and one set of very striking and provocative results will be mentioned.

The methodology of the futures and careers components is thoroughly interdisciplinary, and they mesh at many points. This is very important because the jobs of the future for today's gifted students require an interdisciplinary approach. Students were taught to use many of the research methodologies of the futurists and they were also given practice in using such traditonal methods as survey research methods and library research to find out about the future. In fact, some groups almost "went wild" in conducting, summarizing, and publicizing surveys.

A great variety of simulation methods was used. These included game

299

analogs with role playing and the use of some of the production techniques of sociodrama. There were also experiences with metaphorical analogs, mechanical analogs, and mathematical analogs. Considerable use was made of the Delphi technique as a method of consensus attainment. The 100 students in one of the cluster groups directed by Eugene Bledsoe (1977) made future predictions. These were compiled into a master list and subjected to the Delphi technique to establish the characteristics of future communities. The students in groups of 25 then created these future communities.

In order to receive a charter, each of these future communities had to demonstrate how they would deal with each of the following problems to make the community viable:

Government:
1. Establishing parameters for a community to exist.
2. Formation of a government, i.e., council; executive, legislative, judicial, etc.
3. Energy use and control.
4. Other considerations: goods and services, delivery systems, law enforcement, care of the poor, education, health care, fire protection, zoning laws, support of the arts, transportation.

Family:
1. Alternative family lifestyles: single parent, extended low commitment relationships, state as family, group families.
2. Socializing agency: day care centers, schools, church.
3. Care of aged.

Economics:
1. Cash or cashless world.
2. Employment.
3. Inflation

Religion:
1. Organized or personal.
2. Effect of cults on society, e.g., scientology, satanism, etc.
3. Ecumenical movement.
4. Values and changing technology.

Education:
1. Effect of technology, e.g., telecommunications.
2. Competency based education (testing).
3. Financing of education.

In the areas of specialization attention was also given to future problems. For example, students in the Communication Arts area designed a

300

futurist model of a telecommunications system. It was required that this model attempt to solve the following problems:

1. Balance technological communications progress with individual rights of privacy.
2. Balance public interest with financial viability.
3. Thwart political manipulation of the media without restricting free exchange.
4. Provide a robust marketplace of ideas.

In evaluating the 1976 and 1977 programs, both the immediate and long-range influences of the program were assessed. Outcomes of the immediate and first follow-up evaluations of the 1976 program have been prepared for the State Department of Education (Torrance, Kaufmann, Gibbs & Torrance, 1976; Torrance, Kaufmann, Gibbs, Ball & Torrance, 1977).

One group of results is enormously provocative in thinking about the future education of gifted students, and relate directly to Margaret Mead's (1970) observations concerning a striking change that has taken place in today's society. Mead suggests that we have shifted from a "postfigurative" culture, in which the young learn from the old, to one that is "cofigurative," in which both adults and children learn chiefly from their peers. She believes that we are already beginning to shift to the next stage, a "prefigurative" culture in which the old learn from the young. In a prefigurative culture, the future dominates the present, just as in a postfigurative culture the past (tradition) dominates the present. In our evaluations of the 1976 Career Awareness Program, we found interesting evidence of Mead's theories.

Throughout the evaluation of the 1976 program, learninng from peers was rated by 98 percent of the students as the most exciting feature of the program. Only 75 percent rated "exciting, helpful teachers" in this category. In April, 1977, when we conducted the follow-up study, 96 percent reported that they had continued to maintain contacts with their peers from the program. Already they had three reunions, a number unprecedented in the Georgia Governor's Honors Program. In the follow-up we also found that these gifted students had done a great deal of peer teaching. Seventy-four percent reported that they had taught skills learned in the program to their peers or had helped them solve problems or raise consciousness concerning problems; 66 percent of their nominating teachers verified this claim. More striking, however, is the report that 31 percent had taught their teachers or adult leaders some new method or skill, and 25 percent of the nominating teachers verified this. It is hypothesized that this tendency will increase among participants in the 1977 program. This may be facilitated by sending to their schools a self-report detailing their learning, and suggesting how these skills might be used in the schools. Other sources (Torrance, 1973, 1974b), have described work in encouraging disadvantaged and culturally

301

different students to teach their teachers. This may be the only way that teachers can learn some things about the future. As the pace of cultural changes accelerates, people recognize that the younger members of society have absorbed the latest aspects of the culture and are in closer contact than they with the future.

Since the outcomes of the 1976 program have been documented elsewhere (Torrance et al., 1976, 1977) and the outcomes of the 1977 program will be documented in a forthcoming report, only a few global evaluations by participants will be used to illustrate the need for school programs on futurism for gifted students and the promise that such programs offer. The following evaluative comment by a student gifted in the biological sciences is illustrative of many comments which suggest that many gifted students have no exposure to the study of the future in their regular school programs:

> Ideally, the future cluster is a good idea. However, it was a new idea to us and it took a long time to get used to it. We, as students, have been programmed to look at one part of a problem without looking at implications for the future or for other subjects. I strongly urge adoption of a program similar to the future cluster in our high school.

Some students even expressed feelings of inhibition against talking about the future in their own schools. The following comments are illustrative of this phenomenon:

> I think that on a lot of issues about the future I'm going to keep my mouth shut because where I come from, people will think I'm insane if I talk about some of the far out things we've discussed. I wish the rest of the world would treat the future with as much straightforwardness and honesty as we did here at GHP 77.

For many of the gifted students participating in this special statewide program, the entire experience opened up a new future. This was especially true for some of the participants from rural areas lacking in rich contacts with the rest of the world. This is illustrated in the following comment one gifted girl from a rural area appended to her follow-up evaluation of the 1977 program:

> Let me take this opportunity to assure you of this thing: GHP changed my life. I am not the same person as when I left the small town in which I live. I was never quite sure that there was anyone who shared my ideas and intellect in all the world. I had this dismal outlook that for the entirety of my life I would be "gearing down." But GHP was my redemption.
> I met 199 of the most wonderful people in the world. I remain in contact wih as many of them as possible via the U.S. mail. Not once was I referred to as "the girl with the brains." Not once was my dream of being a writer ridiculed and/or shot down. Not once were my fears laughed at, rather they were brought into the open and often worked out.
> I now know of the vast opportunities just waiting for me to grab one and

make it work. And I have, because of GHP, the confidence that I am capable of making such a future opportunity mine!

The Big Challenge

To me the challenge is clear. Programs for gifted children must help them enlarge, enrich, and make more accurate their images of the future. The image of teaching of the future must be one that makes the best use of the best potentialities of teachers, the best potentialities of gifted and talented students, and the best potentialities of mankind.

References

Bledsoe, E. Instructional materials on futurism. Austell, GA: Author, South Cobb High School, 1977.

Mead, M. *Culture and commitment: a study of the generation gap.* New York: Doubleday, Natural History Press, 1970.

Polak, F. L. *The image of the future.* Amsterdam, Holland: Elsevier, 1973.

Toffler, A. *Future shock.* New York: Bantam Books, 1970.

Toffler, A. (ed.) *Learning for tomorrow: the role of the future in education.* New York: Vintage Books, 1974.

Torrance, E. P. What gifted disadvantaged children can teach their teachers. *Gifted Child Quarterly,* 1973, 17: 243–249.

Torrance, E. P. *The Torrance tests of creative thinking: norms-technical manual.* Lexington, MA: Personnel Press, 1974 (a).

Torrance, E. P. Readiness of teachers of gifted to learn from culturally different gifted children. *Gifted Child Quarterly,* 1974, 18: 137–142. (b).

Torrance, E. P., Bruch, C. B. & Torrance, J. P. Interscholastic futuristic creativity problem solving. *Journal of Creative Behavior,* 1976, 10: 117–125.

Torrance, E. P., Kaufmann, F., Gibbs, S. & Torrance, J. P. *Preliminary report: evaluation of the 1976 institute of career development of the Governor's honors program.* Athens, GA: Department of Educational Psychology, University of Georgia, 1976.

Torrance, E. P., Kaufmann, F., Gibbs, S., Ball, O. & Torrance, J. P. *Evaluation of career awareness component, Georgia Governor's honors program: a follow-up study of participants and their high school teachers.* Athens, GA: Department of Educational Psychology, University of Georgia, 1977.

Torrance, E. P., Williams, S. & Torrance, J. P. *Handbook for training future problems solving teams.* Athens, GA: Department of Educational Psychology, University of Georgia, 1977.

Sidney J. Parnes

CPSI: The General System*

A general system might be considered, at the broadest level, as man's interrelationships with the total universe. The world is "coming together" for the general systems theorist, who attempts to describe in an increasingly comprehensive manner his interrelationships with the vast data of the universe. Man gathers this data through the proverbial five senses, as well as, perhaps, with such "sixth" senses as extrasensory perception or clairvoyance.

Bundles of Data

Without debating the question of man's "collective unconscious" that reportedly imprints data from past generations, let us simply consider instincts, such as hunger and sex, as data—whether it be pain, lust, feelings, drives, or anything else we may inherit or learn, *including* all that Jung means by the "collective unconscious." All this might be considered "data" which man's brain computes in directing all of his operations and actions. From the womb to his mother's arms, to crib, to playpen, to school, to work, to career, to family, to death, and perhaps even to the possibility of after-death as the reincarnationists believe—the person accumulates data from *all* personal experience, including "formal education."

The CPSI (Creative Problem-Solving Institute) system acknowledges all of this in a perhaps agnostic way. There isn't a great concern as to where data comes from, where there is or isn't ESP or reincarnation, whether some data comes via genetic coding or by environmental experiences, etc. It is assumed, however, from what we know about the body and brain, that each one's billions of brain cells become the residing places for all of this data, the greatest bulk of which seems quite unrelated to any particular concern of the moment.

It's as though we had within us an almost infinitely deep well of stored-

*Paper prepared for Symposium on Creativity for the 1977 National Convention of the American Association for the Advancement of Science, Denver, Colorado, February 21, 1977. Copyright © Creative Education Foundation, Inc., 1976. Reprinted from Journal of Creative Behavior, Vol. II, No. 1, (First Quarter, 1977), pp. 1-11.

up data from which to draw, while having a constant stream of new data gushing into the well in the form of perceptions of our infinite environment through *all* of the senses.

Bombarding the Brain

What the CPSI system is designed to do is to maximize "teleidoscopically"[1] the interrelationships that we can make among this dazzling, overwhelming array of data the brain holds and gathers, in order to make "new sense" out of it in relation to our present concerns, foci, problems, or challenges. We bombard the brain with novel stimuli in an attempt to accomplish what brain researchers like Coss (1976) is doing in his brain development studies with animals. Repetition of the *same* stimuli tends to bring about "underload"; bombardment with *novel* stimuli causes "overload" and a resultant enriched neural circuitry. In a recent conversation, Coss termed our activities "exercising for insight." Nobel physicist William Shockley once referred to it as "speeding up the hunch mechanism."

Kiefer (1974) explains:

> If creativity or intuition are seen as new associations or correlations of stored sense-data—that is, of recorded arrangements of groups of signs, symbols and images that constitute both memory and imagination[2]—then it could be expected that any mental exercise or practice that tends to dissolve or disrupt fixed associations would be conducive to creativity or intuition.

Griffith (1974) adds:

> The struggle for creative insight in all fields may be regarded as the effort to deautomize the psychic structures that organize cognition and perception. In this sense, deautomization is not a regression but rather an undoing of a pattern in order to permit a new and perhaps more advanced experience.

Land (1973) postulates psychological principles of growth and creativity to be a natural parallel of biological growth processes. As he explains it, nature combines bundles of genetic information into an enormous range of mutations. Environment selects the "fittest" to survive, while the rest die off. The brain, in a parallel process, collects bundles of data and combines them into a variety of alternative patterns, or ideas; however, the brain pretests by judicial processes rather than by trying out each idea in

---

[1]A teleidoscope is somewhat like the more familiar kaleidoscope with one basic difference: while the kaleidoscope makes patterns and new combinations only from what is within it, the teleidoscope gets its structure from within but the raw materials for patterns and colors from the outside, from the changing environment it focuses upon.

[2]The boundary between the experiences designated by these two words is very broad and fuzzy; we often discover that we have imagined what we experienced as remembering, or remembered what we experienced as imagining. The latter accounts for much unconscious plagiarizing.

actuality. Thus there is not the tremendous waste that occurs in the biological realm with its *literal* "survival of the fittest."

Left and Right Hemispheres

Experiences and exercises that are designed to optimize these natural combinative and judicial powers of the brain are used to bombard individuals experiencing CPSI. Current brain research demonstrates that these two powers reside in different hemispheres of the brain. Attempts are made to strengthen both sides. The split-brain research of Bogen (1969, 1972) since the early 60's provides fascinating new understanding of left and right hemispheres of the brain and their relation to creativity. In essence it appears that *integration* of the special abilities of both left and right halves is required for creativity in the sense that we define it; that is for *relevant* originality, or as Alex Osborn put it, "*Applied* Imagination."

Rico (1976) uses the metaphor, "Too many cooks spoil the broth," as an illustration. If you ask a person who has a damaged right hemisphere to interpret that statement, the person will explain very literally, "Too many people in the kitchen will spoil the soup." If you press, the individual will only slightly modify the words, saying perhaps, "Too many chefs working at the stove will ruin the soup," or something similar. The person will not be able to derive broader metaphorical meanings of the statement. Correspondingly, it seems that people *impoverished* in right-hemisphere stimulation may not have the necessary enriched neural circuitry to make many associations beyond those that are literal and conventional, and hence are less apt to make the novel associations required in creativity, creative problem-solving, or invention.

The same notion holds for left-hemisphere, logical, analytical modes of thinking. Damage or impoverishment may cause lack of ability to use logic effectively along with the imagination of the right hemisphere in evaluating, developing, implementing, and gaining acceptance for ideas. Therefore we strive to enrich both sides of the brain by bombarding them with stimuli and exercises that stretch both areas, with a dynamic balance between imagination and judgment.

People vs. Sheep

As humans, we find ourselves at a particular place in a particular point of time. If we were sheep, we might graze there aimlessly for the rest of our lives, satisfying only instinctive biological needs. But we aren't sheep. We are human beings motivated by philosophical, scientific, or religious beliefs that destine us to be more than animals. Hence the brain begins to examine and interrelate data. Questions are posed, many of which seem unanswerable. And then man sets out in quest of the answers.

306

All of us probably recognize the type of mental activity alluded to, which dintinguishes man from sheep. Our CPSI system acknowledges this and deals with this difference *at whatever level of thinking* the participant happens to be—with the purpose of helping each one find more and better alternatives to questions raised explicitly or implicitly (consciously or unconsciously) in one's mind. In addition, we try to help a person broaden his or her perspective to more and more significant questions, that *may* help the individual see lesser questions in a new light.

CPSI Process

The five-step CPSI process involves alternation between imagination and judgment in each of five steps toward creatively handling a situation or meeting an objective: Fact-Finding, Problem-Finding, Idea-Finding, Solution-Finding, and Acceptance-Finding (Parnes et al, 1977). It is only one way of talking about or diagramming the very amorphous process of discovering new and relevant associations among the vast data in our brains toward the resolution of our concerns, problems, and challenges.

I believe that the five steps per se are not as important as the extent to which the imagination is stretched as one alternates throughout the process. We try to help participants react first with imaginative play, then with tempered reality to a new fact, viewpoint, or idea. The openmindedness that we are seeking to instill relies upon how much imagination one first uses in approaching a thought before tempering it with reality. We exercise people in faster and faster, wider and wider imaginative play as a prelude to each judgment they make. As a result of each exercise, the participants can hopefully tolerate a bit more ambiguity in a situation. In the end, they can take more and more factors into consideration *in a given unit of time* while making decisions.

In this regard it is interesting to consider Burger's (1976) discussion of "Haiku, Not Brainstorm" in his thought-provoking essay on the function of the imagination as constrained by the culture. He points out how insights often emerge under culture-countering conditions such as half-sleep, and explains, ". . . under these extremely limited circumstances, a 'romping' mind may indeed be desirable, but for the vast majority of pancultural situations it would be disastrous." CPSI processes help individuals increase their "romping" ability during deliberate stages *between* periods of evaluation, as well as during such nondeliberate stages as half-sleep.

The CPSI system's five-step process is only one possible checklist that may be used to increase the *probability* of the generation and implementation of more and deeper relevant interrelationships of that wealth of data previously discussed. But it is the best way I presently know. Tomorrow there will be even better ways, just as we have evolved the present process

307

over the past quarter-century. One Institute participant, a psychologist, expressed it very closely to my own interpretation:

> ... as I see it, the fundamental message you and your friends have, is not a technique per se, it is a flexible attitude to the environment, to the problems. The techniques are only means to let that attitude come through. I think some of the participants were not aware of that, but I am convinced that they will realize it later, that they will say "aha" and understand it. I believe that the Institute will have long-range effects of that kind.

Thus the general system exemplified by CPSI allows one at any level of development to explore deeply all of the data one is able to derive and handle in one's own computer, toward ever-greater resolutions of hopes, dreams, fantasies, aspirations, goals, problems, challenges, difficulties, and frustrations. The CPSI system attempts to help the individual look at the "universe"—in actuality as well as in the sense of the "universe" of knowledge at one's own individual grasp or disposal—and to deal ever more productively and satisfyingly with this data, be it in a job situation, at home, in school, in family, in spiritual, social or avocational life, or in reaching and expanding a general philosophy of life itself.

Directed Spontaneity

The CPSI system is concerned with *directed* flow or spontaneity, not as some are with flow or spontaneity *alone*. What is meant here is *mutual* direction or control, by *self* and external factors, *mutually*.

Psychotherapist Moreno (1965) put it this way:

> If the spontaneity function is such an important factor for man's world, why is it so poorly developed? The answer may be that man *fears* spontaneity and the uncertainty of it just as his ancestor in the jungle feared fire; he feared fire until he learned how to make it. Man will fear spontaneity until he learns how to unleash it, train and control it. A great deal of man's psycho- and sociopathology can be ascribed to the insufficient development of spontaneity and therefore the inability to mobilize the potential sources of creativity. Spontaneity "training" is therefore the most auspicious skill to be taught to scientists, educators, and therapists in all our institutions of learning and it is their task to teach students or clients how to be more spontaneous without becoming pathological.

In order to have control of flow, we must have some flow to control. Hence we use every means of which we are aware to extend the flow of thoughts surrounding any situation or concern upon which a person is focusing, and then to "direct" that flow toward accomplishment or achievement for the individual of *some purpose* greater than grazing like sheep. This is not to say that grazing like sheep may not be meaningful; only that our stance is that man needs or wants far *more* than merely grazing time. Or perhaps it might be reasonable to conjecture that if one merely continues

308

grazing like sheep, one may become unable to cope with the geometrically increasing rate of change in the world and may find oneself dying like the sheep who run out of grazing land.

Sensitivity to Problems

It might be well to make explicit what is already implicit in the above—that the CPSI system does not operate merely on obvious problems. Instead it stresses and encourages an increasing awareness of data that results in heightened sensitivity to problems, challenges, opportunities, and situations in one's work and life in general.

Thus the CPSI system deals just as heavily with problem *awareness* as with problem-*solving*. Many people seem only to want to know how to deal with a problem that is blatantly standing in their way. They spend most of their time "putting out fires" and very little time structuring their lives so that fires are prevented in the first place. They cope in the sense of "I have to put up with it," instead of coping in the sense of visualizing, dreaming, and foreseeing—then dealing constructively with the vision. They allow themselves to be controlled by their environment rather than being the controllers. One can create the problems, the mysteries, then solve them; or one can act only in the role of a detective, forever solving the mysteries or problems with which someone else confronts him or her.

Moreno (1965) argues:

> The future of man is surrounded with perplexing question marks and tragic conflicts. The process of evolution and natural selection may not allow for harmonization. Man may be at the crossroads. He may be forced to live and survive in two different environments: one, the natural environment in which his freedom as a biological being, the function of the creator, is the most supreme criterion; and the other, a technological automatic, or better said, a conserved and conserving environment in which his freedom and his creative function are restrained and forced to flow between the bedrock of mechanical evolution. Races of men fit for the one may be unfit for the other. The criteria of unfitness are different in both environments. One line of evolution may lead inescapably to societies of men similar to societies of insects, harmonious and 100 percent efficient but unindividualistic. The other line of evolution may lead inescapably to a new race of men who tacitly will follow the direction of their ascendance up to date, modified and enhanced by the triumph over the robot.

Diverse Methods From East and West

The CPSI method introduces many *diverse* methods toward enhancing ascendant man. Eastern philosophies and techniques can teach us "busy" Americans so much about how to relax, meditate, and to *let* the flow happen, *let* the data co-mingle without trying, *let* the connections take place "subconsciously," that is, without consciously being aware.

309

Western philosophy, on the other hand, can teach us procedures like deliberately deferring judgment, brainstorming, checklisting, using morphological analysis, etc., for *making* the data interrelate in new and valuable ways, and for increasing the probability of more and deeper "ahas." We offer countless adaptations and combinations of these processes, both Eastern and Western, each year as we discover, learn, and grow in our ability to help this process take place in individuals and groups.

Experimental Stance

A fundamental philosophy and process of the CPSI system is experimentation. We know many ways, many answers; but we acknowledge without apology that we come nowhere near knowing all the answers. As Ralph Sockman so poetically put it, "The larger the island of knowledge, the greater the shoreline of wonder."

Hence we tend to upset some people, participants and leaders alike, with our extreme tolerance for ambiguity in our environment for discovery, in our alertness to serendipity, in our openness, *along with participants*, to new discoveries. But out of it all, we expect, observe, and have scientific evidence of, a significant change in attitude among participants.

Personal Futuristics

A further way of explaining the CPSI general system is in relation to its stance toward "futuristics" or "futuring." Most futuristics programs with which I am familiar tend to deal with major societal problems and try to extend, project, and predict the future, based on present data, so that society may be better prepared to change and deal with the future. The CPSI system might be considered a *personal* futuristics program for every participant in his or her own life as well as in one's responsibilities toward broader societal questions.

One might say that persons using CPSI concepts in the way they are meant to be used, utilize the vast storehouse and torrent of data referred to earlier not only to retrieve and apply "as is" where appropriate, but also to interrelate and rearrange so as to *create* the future rather than just let it happen. One can drift like the sheep and then fret when it rains and one gets soaked and uncomfortable, or one can wish and dream, "I'd like not to be wet and uncomfortable: how might I make this come about?" With that goal, challenge, aspiration, problem, mess, or objective, one draws *up* and draws *in* data, interrelates it in new ways to form new patterns, and then synthesizes and develops the resultant ideas into creations that satisfy one's objective (tents, houses, umbrellas, etc.). Some develop or are given tents, but then dream bigger dreams and make these come true in the form of houses, or some other form of shelter. As Charles Kettering, engineer-

310

inventor, put it: "Think a bright future—plan for it—and you will have it." Thus one "shocks the future" instead of suffering "future shock."

As one examines the above concept and philosophy, it may be easily seen that everything is relative; that the possibility for planning for the future for each individual is infinite, even though each begins at a different level. This is what makes the CPSI system such an exciting, developmental process for everyone, irrespective of level. One's future—what *will* be—depends a great deal on what each individual *constructs* it to be. It doesn't need to be determined from a crystal ball.

At any particular moment in time (the present) a person can be grazing like sheep—aware only of present and past as it has existed for one—or the person can be "pushing" the future by imaginatively interrelating the data from past and present into scintillating patterns of future possibilities, and then synthesizing and developing these patterns, fantasies, dreams, and wishes into actuality. The future becomes a *new* present and a new *expanded* springboard toward an ever *richer* future—for oneself, one's family, one's group, one's society, one's world, one's universe.

Moral Questions

Note that there are no moral values involved here. The criteria for evaluating what one dreams or creates come from the individual and his perception of society and the world. Thus some very ponderous questions arise as one contemplates this philosophy, just as some awesome questions arise as one begins to contemplate man's new abilities to split the atom, to control genes, or even the child's new abilities to walk when no longer content in the safety of the play pen. But would we deny the child this new discovery because of where it might lead?

An extremely hopeful element to me is derived from research into the effects of the CPSI processes in extensive evaluation studies at State University College at Buffalo (Parnes & Noller, 1973). The most consistently significant change reported by students was their ability to take more factors into consideration in making a decision. This was also confirmed in ability tests from J. P. Guilford's Structure-of-Intellect (1967). My contention is that as you help open people up within the CPSI system to greater awareness of the data in the universe, this is exactly what occurs; they are more likely, as a result, to take more factors, more viewpoints, and the like, into consideration. Thus the criteria one uses to evaluate one's ideas, decisions, and plans are likely, on a probability basis, to be broader and more all-encompassing. The individual is more apt to attain a "deferjudiced stance"[3] that tends to lessen what we term prejudice as well as the opposite extreme of indecisiveness.

---

[3]Ability to take an ever-increasing number of factors into consideration in a given unit of time (see Parnes & Biondi, 1975).

I believe delinquency and most criminality may very well be largely a result of lack of ability to discern enough alternative factors (criteria) in making decisions on one's behavior. In fact, in a study on creativity and delinquency by Kuo (1967), it was found that non-delinquent subjects generally scored higher in measures of creativity than did the delinquent subjects. Often times the "delinquent" may behave as he does because he is not able to, or at least because he *does not* generate new alternatives, but merely *copies* anti-social behavior. Thus his very delinquency may actually be the manifestation of his *lack* of creativity.

Gifted vs. Giftedness

There is much current emphasis, because of recent legislation, on programs for better educating and developing the gifted in our schools. To me, this is an important endeavor for the potential benefit of all society. It is worth pointing out, however, that the CPSI general system approach is effective for the deliberate development of the *giftedness* in *each* individual, at *all* levels. Thus the gifted may be extended greatly, but so may all others at each of their own levels.

Most of our Institute participants tend to be above-average in creativity; their accomplishments seem to indicate this. But, as the research over the past 25 years has shown, there are deliberate procedures that can be used to help stimulate anyone to make increasingly more new and relevant associations, which is the essence of creative bahavior as we define it. For example, two individuals whom I've been fortunate enough to have known well, demonstrated extraordinary, publicly-acknowledged creative productivity over many years. I said to each separately after attendance at our Institute: "You exemplify to me what our Institute is all about; therefore I wonder what you gained from the program." Each responded, in effect: "First of all, I understand for the first time something about *how* I was generating and developing these ideas; before, it was just 'happening.' Thus I am able to do so more deliberately now—on demand. Secondly, I understand something now about helping others to achieve this same rewarding experience of creation. Earlier I only frustrated them with my talent, not knowing how to help them do what I was doing."

Thus educators, managers, parents—people who care about the creative ability in others—can learn to better understand and appreciate their own creative potential, as well as nurture it more fully in individuals and groups for whom they have responsibility. This, to me, is the exciting challenge of our age—to help more and more people in our society to achieve "the delicate balance" of productive creativity.

Conclusion

In summary, it might be well to point out that practitioners like Alex Osborn advocated deferred judgment and brainstorming as ways of tapping

312

the well of data we have and are acquiring, toward rearranging it and interrelating it to productive creativity. Freud and the introspective psychologists said creativity comes from the deep unconscious, and used psychoanalysis to release the flow of related data. The humanistic psychologists emphasize openness of perception, being open to the environment, etc. Behaviorists emphasize "chance" and reinforcement theories.

We do not choose from among these diverse theories; instead we integrate and synthesize them all toward the end of releasing, capturing, harnessing, and directing the greatest *flow* and interrelationship of data toward dealing productively with the concerns, dreams, problems, challenges, wishes, and aspirations of mankind. And as we do this—and the more different ways we talk about it in the different languages and metaphors of the varied systems theorists—the more new insights we get into our own evolving "general system" of viewing our universe.

References

Bogen, J. E. The other side of the brain, part I—dysgraphia and dyscopia following cerebral commissuratomy. *Bulletin of the Los Angeles Neurological Societies*, 1969, 34 *(April)*: 73-105.

Bogen, J. E. The other side of the brain, part II—an appositional mind. *Bulletin of the Los Angeles Neurological Societies,* 1969, 34 *(July)*: 135-162.

Bogen, J. E. & Bogen, G. M. The other side of the brain, part III—the corpus collosum and creativity. *Bulletin of the Los Angeles Neurological Societies*, 1969, 34 *(October)*: 191-220.

Bogen, J.E., DeZure, R., Tenhouten, W. D. et al. The other side of the brain, part IV—the a.p. ratio. *Bulletin of the Los Angeles Neurological Societies*, 1972, 37 *(April)*: 49-61.

Burger, H. G. On the cultural-materialist model of imagination: haiku, not brainstorm. *Current Anthropology*, 1976, 17: 757-758.

Coss, R. G. Constraints on innovation: the role of recognition in the graphic arts. Paper presented at Eighth Western Symposium on Learning: Creative Thinking, October, 1976.

Griffith, F. F. Meditation research: its personal and social significance. In White, J., *Frontiers of consciousness*. New York: Julian Press, 1974.

Guilford, J. P. *The nature of human intelligence*. New York: McGraw-Hill, 1967.

Kiefer, D. Intermeditation notes: reports from inner spaces. In White, J., *Frontiers of consciousness*. New York: Julian Press, 1974.

Kuo, Y. Y. A comparative study of creative thinking between delinquent boys and non-delinquent boys. Doctoral dissertation, University of Maryland, 1967. (University Microfilms, Order No. 67-11, 312.)

Land, G. T. *Grow or die*. New York: Random House, 1973.

Moreno, J. L. The creativity theory of personality: spontaneity, creativity and human potentialities. New York University Bulletin, Arts and Sciences, 1967, LXVI, (4).

Parnes, S. J. & Biondi, A. M. Creative behavior: a delicate balance. *Journal of Creative Behavior,* 1975, **9**(**3**).

Parnes, S. J. & Noller, Ruth B. *Toward supersanity: channeled freedom.* Buffalo: D.O.K. Publishers, 1973.

Parnes, S. J., Noller, Ruth B. & Biondi, A. M. *Guide to creative action.* New York: Scribners, 1977.

Rico, G. L. Metaphor and knowing: analysis, synthesis, rationale. Paper presented at Eighth Western Symposium on Learning: Creative Thinking, October, 1976.

John Curtis Gowan

Some New Thoughts on the Development of Creativity*

One of the most curious characteristics of creativity, and one that generally appears to have escaped critical attention, is the fact that its variability in individuals far exceeds the limits of variability characteristic of other traits and abilities. Wechsler (1974), for example, has conclusively demonstrated that the interpersonal variability of such psychological and physiological measures as height, weight, cranial capacity, grip strength, blood pressure, respiration rate, reaction time, pitch, Snellen acuity, intelligence, mental age, and memory span has a limit of 3/1, where e = 2.818, the basis of the natural logarithm system, and in most cases has a mean of 2.3 or less. Yet comparing the creative productions of a genius such as Einstein, Mozart, or Picasso with those of more ordinary mortals, one finds a ratio of 100/1 or over. Obviously the trait and factor theory of creativity cannot account for all the variance.

It is the thesis of this paper that the remaining variance can best be accounted for by the concept of "psychological openness" akin to the mental health concept of Maslow (1954). Certainly this trait is consonant with Maslow's concepts of high mental health, since it was one of the characteristics he identified in self-actualizing persons.

Both J.P. Guilford (1967) and Alex Osborn (1953) believed that creativity was an outcome of certain problem-solving aspects of intellect; that it could therefore be taught or stimulated; and that it was rational and semantic, consisting essentially of what Hallman has called "connectedness"—that is, the ability, through the use of verbal analogy, to connect (by common ratios or otherwise) elements that heretofore had been viewed as incommensurable or disparate.

If this view is correct, then the obvious way to stimulate creativity in the classroom is to facilitate the child's ability to make such connections via the Williams Cube material, the Meeker method, or by similar curriculum procedures. But while the Structure-of-Intellect and the creative problem-solving methods are certainly useful, it is perhaps time to ask whether we are putting all of our educational eggs in one basket. This is especially pertinent since two other theories as to the genesis of creative ability have gained currency, and each has important educational applications.

The first of these new theories is, of course, Maslow's view that creativity results from mental health. To the extent that this theory is true, we ought to be strengthening the mental health of children, primarily through developmental guidance procedures along lines set down in Blocher (1966) and Bower and Hollister (1968). When the author was director of a summer workshop in creativity for gifted children, this aspect proved to be so important that a full-time counselor accompanied the children to every class (at a 1/25 ratio).

A second theory, in some minds even more important, is that creativity is nothing but psychological openness to preconscious sources. A careful perusal of Ghiselin (1952) will certainly do much to make this theory palatable, and there is considerable other evidence for it besides—in particular, the above-mentioned fact that creative production does not obey the Wechsler law of interpersonal variance less than e. If this is true, then we need to learn how to rub Aladdin's lamp to get the genie to come, and it appears that meditation, reverie, fantasy, and the like are the most promising methods. Outside the Khatena and Torrance *Sounds and Images*, however, there are few facilitations in this area.

But if psychologists are in doubt about which theory of creativity contributes the most variance to the whole, let us turn to an even better set of witnesses—namely, the creative geniuses themselves, in the rare moments when they reveal the workings of the creative process. Consider Mozart:

> The whole, though it be long, stands almost complete and finished in my mind, so that I can survey it . . . at a glance. Nor do I hear in my imagination the parts successively, but I hear them, as it were, all at once. . . . What delight this is I cannot tell! (Vernon, 1970).

And Tchaikowsky:

> The only music capable of moving and touching us is that which flows from the depth of a composer's soul when he is stirred by imagination . . . it takes root with extraordinary force and rapidity, shoots up through the earth, puts forth branches, leaves and finally blossoms. I cannot define the creative process in any other way than by this simile (Vernon, 1970).

And finally Poincaré on his discovery of Fuchsian functions (among the most complicated in higher mathematics). Having labored a long time in vain, he had the following revelation:

> At the moment when I put my foot on the step, the idea came to me, without anything in my former thoughts seeming to have paved the way for it that the transformations I had used to define the Fuchsian functions were identical with those of non-Euclidean geometry. . . . Most striking at first is this

316

appearance of sudden illumination, a manifest sign of long, unconscious prior work ... it is only fruitful if it is on one hand preceded and on the other hand followed by a period of conscious work ... (Vernon, 1970).

What each of these geniuses is doing is confirming the correctness of the Wallas paradigm, which states that preparation and incubation must precede illumination and that verification must follow it. But what is the exact mechanism by which such creative ideas may be induced to occur? It is obvious by the sudden uprush of new ideas which seem to break into consciousness with a shock of recognition that we are here dealing with material that has somehow accumulated at subconscious levels of the mind. Since such ideas are generally not accessible to the ego, but appear to be so under the creative impetus, it is evident that they belong to the preconscious, which has been defined as consisting of just such occasionally accessible material. Moreover, there is a *collective* aspect about the knowledge, as if we were all drilling into a common underground aquifer for well water. Indeed, many great scientific discoveries have had more than one discoverer—Leibniz and Newton in the case of the calculus, and Darwin and Wallace for the theory of evolution.

We theorize that the collective preconscious is best compared to the terminal of a giant computer which is in another realm, outside time and space, and contains an infinity of potentialities; all are real in that realm but only one will eventuate in our dimension. Under conditions of relaxation, meditation, incubation, and the like, messages in the form of images manifest in the printout of that cosmic computer and collator. But with all that random dissociated infinity in the machine, why is it only the creative ideas that are brought through to consciousness?

Poincaré explains the subliminal self's activities as follows:

All the combinations would be formed in consequence of the automatism of the subliminal self, but only the interesting ones would break into consciousness. ... Is it only chance which confers this privilege? ... The privileged unconscious phenomena ... are those which affect most profoundly our emotional sensibility. ... The useful combinations are precisely the most beautiful ... (Ghiselin, 1952).

As the recovery process proceeds from the germ of a creative idea down deep and rises like an expanding bubble through successive layers of consciousness, various individuals become cognizant of the nascent creativity in different modes. Some feel it first prototaxically, like Houseman:

Experience has taught me, when I am shaving of a morning, to keep watch over my thoughts, because, if a line of poetry strays into my memory, my skin bristles so that the razor ceases to act. This particular symptom is accompanied by a shiver down the spine; there is another which consists in a constriction of the throat and a precipitation of water to the eyes; and there is a third which I can only describe by borrowing a phrase from one of Keat's last letters, where he says, speaking of Fanny Brawne, 'everything that

317

reminds me of her goes through me like a spear.' The seat of this sensation is the pit of the stomach (Ghiselin, 1952).

Other feel it parataxically through images and emotions; for example, Einstein:

> Words or language do not seem to play any role in my mechanism of thought. The psychical entities which seem to serve as elements in thought are certain signs and more or less clear images . . . (Ghiselin, 1952).

Wordsworth:

> Poetry is the spontaneous overflow of powerful feelings: it takes its origin from emotion recollected in tranquility (Ghiselin, 1952).

Coleridge, speaking of himself in the third person:

> All the images rose up before him as *things,* with a parallel production of the corresponding expressions, without any sensation of conscious effort (Ghiselin, 1952).

The major question is how to transfer these images/emotions to the alphanumeric syntaxic level, and this analysis is the source of considerable testimony. But the prime secret is relaxation of the conscious mind. Says Kipling:

> When your daemon is in charge, do not try to think consciously. Drift, wait, obey (Ghiselin, 1952).

The reason why it takes higher ability to be verbally creative is that the crossing of the successive discontinuity of psychic layers during the bubble's trip upward to full consciousness requires a complex level of verbal analogy fitting each stage; for one must both see that a proportionate ratio exists below, and also intuit the same ratio in the higher elements which may be semantically very different. This correspondence of a ratio across a semantic chasm from the known to the unknown is the secret of transferring creative affective images to full verbal creativity at the syntaxic level. Amy Lowell says of the poet:

> He must be born with a subconscious factory always working for him or he can never be a poet at all, and he must have knowledge and talent enough to "putty" up his holes. . . . Here is where the conscious training of the poet comes in, for he must fill up what the subconscious has left, and fill it in as much in the key of the rest as possible. Every long poem is sprinkled with these *lacunae.* Let no one undervalue this process of puttying; it is a condition of good poetry (Ghiselin, 1952).

Indeed, Gerard tells us plainly:

> Imagination is more than bringing images into consciousness; this is imagery or at most hallucination. Imagination ... is an action of the mind that produces a new idea or insight. "Out of chaos the imagination frames a thing of beauty. ..." The thing comes unheralded, as a flash, fully formed. ...
>
> Imagination, not reason, creates the novel. It is to social inheritance what mutation is to biological inheritance; it accounts for the arrival of the fittest. Reason or logic applied when judgment indicates that the new is promising acts like natural selection to pan the gold grains from the sand and insure the survival of the fittest.
>
> Imagination supplies the premises and asks questions from which reason grinds out the conclusions ... (Ghiselin, 1952).

Gerard then quotes Dryden as naming "fancy moving the sleeping images of things toward the light ... then chosen or rejected by the judgment," and recalls Coleridge's phrase: "the streamy nature of association, which thinking curbs and rudders." It would be hard to paraphrase the symbiotic relationship between the conscious and preconscious minds in more trenchant manner.

Figure 1 indicates the symbiotic relationship between the conscious mind and the collective preconscious, which produces creative products. On the left the conscious mind has taken over completely, and only convergent production ensues. The part played by the preconscious then, gradually increases and that of the conscious decreases until in the middle of the figure they are both equally present. This represents the acme of creativity. As we move toward the extreme right the preconscious assumes a larger and larger share until eventually it becomes all, and the product is analogous to automatic writing. In the middle of the diagram creative products would be distinguished from one another by the amount of each which they contain. Mathematical and physical discoveries might be toward the left of center, and abstract artistic productions such as "Kubla Khan" or surrealistic paintings would be toward the right.

Because all this "psychological openness" is so much more bizarre and less "respectable" than, say, the Structure-of-Intellect theory with its solid dependence on statistics, it is desirable to reinforce this testimony with other, even more credible witnesses describing even more incredible processes and events.

Recognizing the importance of preconscious inspiration, many creative persons have intuitively derived individual mechanisms for throwing themselves into this mode of knowledge.

Gerald Heard says:

> To have truly original thought the mind must throw off its critical guard, its filtering censor. It must put itself in a state of depersonalization. ... The best researchers when confronting problems and riddles which have defied all solution by ordinary methods, did employ their minds in an unusual way, did put themselves into a state of egoless creativity, which permitted them to have insights so remarkable that by means of these they were able to make their greatest and most original discoveries (Weil, Metsner & Leary, 1971).

Lord Tennyson was accustomed to pass into "an ecstatic state" and had a formula for inducing it. Tennyson says in a letter written in 1794:

> I have had . . . a kind of walking trance . . . when I have been all alone. This has often come upon me through repeating my own name to myself silently, till, all at once out of the intensity and conscious of the individuality, the individuality itself seems to dissolve and fade away into boundless being . . . (Prince, 1963).

Prince (1963) similarly describes the inception of *Uncle Tom's Cabin*, quoting from the biography of Harriet Beecher Stowe:

> Mrs. Stowe was seated in her pew in the college church at Brunswick, during the communion service. . . . Suddenly like the unrolling of a picture scroll, the scene of the death of Uncle Tom seemed to pass before her. . . . She was so affected she could scarcely keep from weeping. . . . That Sunday afternoon she went to her room, locked the door and wrote out, substantially as it appears . . . the chapter called "The Death of Uncle Tom."

But no matter how eminent or noteworthy are writers and authors, creative persons in the sciences carry the most weight of evidence. We are indebted to Krippner (1972) for the following:

> One can cite as well creative dreams of scientists and inventors that gave the solution of a problem analogically or symbolically.

The chemist, Friedrich August Kekule (cited by Koestler, 1964), had a tendency to make theoretical discoveries in hypnagogic reverie states. Kekule wrote:

> I turned my chair to the fire and dozed. Again the atoms were gambolling before my eyes. The smaller groups kept modestly in the background. My mental eye, rendered more acute by visions of this kind, could now distinguish larger structures, of minifold conformations; long rows, sometimes more closely fitted together, all twining and twisting in snakelike motion. But look! What was that? One of the snakes had seized hold of its own tail, and the form whirled mockingly before my eyes. As if by a flash of lightning I awoke.

At this juncture, it is instructive to break into the narrative to ask a searching question: "What did Kekule see?" While you are thinking of the answer, it may be helpful to tell a baseball joke.

Three umpires were arguing about calling balls and strikes. The first said: "I calls 'em as they are."

The second said: "I calls 'em as I sees 'em."

The third said: "They ain't nothin' 'till I calls 'em."

Kekule said that what he saw was a ring. In Krippner's words:

> The dream image of a snake holding its tail in its mouth led Kekule by analogy to his discovery that Benzene has a ringlike structure (usually represented by a hexagon) and to his "closed-chain" or "ring" theory which showed the importance of molecular structure in organic chemistry. The

320

imagery granted Kekule a glimpse into a non-ordinary reality of molecular structure.

Despite what Kekule *concluded* (which was a concept), let us persist in analyzing what Kekule *described*. To do so, please reread his description. In the light of what we know now about molecular structures, the "long rows, sometimes more closely fitted together, all twining and twisting" clearly describes the DNA molecule. Kekule was in the presence of a noncategorical numinous archetype in a nonordinary state of reality—in other words, in the cave of Aladdin. He went in looking for a dollar, and he came out with a dollar. Had he been prepared by prior discipline to look for a thousand dollars he could have found that also. An orchestra can play only the symphonies for which it has the men and instruments. One is reminded of George Kelly's phrase: "One is constrained to experience events in the way one anticipates them."

The numinous archetype presented in hypnagogic dreams and creative reveries is a noncategorical image, and is hence as capable of as many interpretations as there are percipients (e.g., the smile on the *Mona Lisa*). Each participant will interpret the numinous archetype idiosyncratically, in accordance with his level of development (like the seven blind Indians who went to see the elephant). The archetype hence acts as a generating entity, which may produce a number of art forms or alphanumeric scientific statements. Since this nonordinary experience may occur in many persons, the key concept of creativity is to possess the previously prepared matrix of verbal or mathematical analogy which will catch the ephemeral vision and preserve it in concrete form.

In 1969, D. I. Mendeleev went to bed exhausted after struggling to conceptualize a way to categorize the elements based upon their atomic weights (cited by Kedrov, 1957). He reported, "I saw in a dream a table where all the elements fell into place as required. Awakening, I immediately wrote it down on a piece of paper. Only in one place did a correction later seem necessary." In this manner, Mendeleev's Periodic Table of the Elements was created (Krippner, 1972).

We have stated earlier that the collective preconscious seems to be in a realm of nonordinary reality, outside time and space, which of course gives it access to the future. In curious reinforcement of this hypothesis, many creative discoveries have an element of precognition about them. When Kekule saw the whirling forms, he may have glimpsed the DNA molecular structure. When Mendeleev dreamed the atomic order of the elements, he left a hole, where later helium was discovered, and still later his open-ended model had places for all the radioactive and transuranium elements such as plutonium. Again we quote from Krippner (1972):

When Igor Sikorsky was ten years of age, he dreamed of coursing the skies in the softly lit, walnut-paneled cabin of an enormous flying machine. Sikorsky later became an eminent aircraft designer and inventor of the helicopter. Three decades after the dream, he went aboard one of his own four-engine clippers to inspect a job of interior decorating done by Pan American Airways. With a start, he recognized the cabin as identical to the one in his boyhood dream.

Max Planck, the physicist, first spoke of his "constant" when he was twenty-three years of age; however, he did not understand its implications for wave theory until much later. Indeed, he had to convince himself of its correctness; it varied so greatly from the logic of his time that he could not comprehend it when the idea first came to him.

The case of Jonathan Swift (cited by Haefele, 1962), the writer of *Gulliver's Travels* and other novels, combines artistic and scientific creativity. When Gulliver reaches Laputa, the astronomers state that the planet Mars has two moons quite close to the planet. One completed its orbit every ten hours, the other every 21.5 hours. It took astronomers in ordinary reality 150 years to discover that Mars did, indeed, have two moons which completed their orbits around the planet every eight and every 30 hours.

A final instance of the possible association between ESP and creativity concerns *Futility*, a popular novel written by Morgan Robertson in 1898. It described the wreck of a giant ship called the Titan. This ship was considered "unsinkable" by the characters in the novel; it displaced 70,000 tons, was 800 feet long, had 24 lifeboats, and carried 3,000 passengers. Its engines were equipped with three propellers. One night in April, while proceeding at 25 knots, the Titan encountered an iceberg in the fog and sank with great loss of life.

On April 15, 1912, the Titanic was wrecked in a disaster which echoed the events portrayed in the novel 14 years previously. The Titanic displaced 66,000 tons and was 828 feet long. It had three propellers and was proceeding at 23 knots on its maiden voyage, carrying nearly 3,000 passengers. There was great loss of life because the Titanic was equipped with only 20 lifeboats.

If all this sounds wild to you, listen to the most famous aviator of our day, Charles Lindbergh (1969):

> ... I think the great adventures of the future lie—in voyages inconceivable by our 20th century rationality—beyond the solar system, through distant galaxies, possibly through peripheries untouched by time and space. I believe early entrance to this era can be attained by the application of our scientific knowledge not to life's mechanical vehicles but to the essence of life itself: to the infinite and infinitely evolving qualities that have resulted in the awareness, shape and character of man. I believe this application is necessary to the very survival of mankind ... will we discover that only *without* spaceships can we reach the galaxies ... I believe it is through sensing and thinking about such concepts that great adventures of the future will be found.

To conclude this amazing testimony of men of science, we again return to Krippner (1972):

> It can be seen that creative persons in their dreams sometimes appear to experience non-ordinary reality, and at the same time make different types of consolidations. Finding a new reality in a creative dream gives the person a novel slant or direction for consolidating his information, and the consolidation enables him to see the details and structure of the new reality more clearly. In some cases, finding a new reality not only gives the person a new

direction for consolidating his information, but even involves finding additional information to be included in the consolidation.

Perhaps we have labored the point too long, but these concepts are so new and unusual that it is very important to impress them firmly on minds unused to such views. We have long thought of man's brain as a problem-solver; perhaps an even better model would be that of a radio receiver. When the set has been properly assembled through preparation and discipline, the static in the locality has been cleared through relaxation and incubation, and the power is on, then we may hear the faint calls of distant stations—signals which are always in the air, but are only received with the best equipment under the best and clearest operating conditions. Such a simile tells us why high giftedness enhances the creative range and why the easy production of verbal analogies (like the proportion between radio frequency and audio frequency) facilitates high-fidelity reception.

These ideas are so new that all we can do in turning from theory to practice is to sketch some ways in which such views may affect the classroom in the future. It would be a grave error to conclude that we should abandon all that has gone before and delve into divination and the occult; indeed, such a procedure would be disastrous. The Wallas paradigm still holds true and useful. Mental discipline and scholarship are still required for the preparation phase. What we are talking about is more conscious attention to the incubation phase.

Moreover, to look at the end product in highly creative geniuses at their best hardly tells us much about how to induce creativity consciously through educational procedures. What they gained in flashes of creative intuition may come to lesser lights through longer and more painstaking efforts. Inducing creativity in the classroom may not be the same as observing it in the field.

There are, however, some procedures we can begin to make use of. I should like to list a few for you now.

1. We should study creativity directly in high school and university classes. Almost no schools at the present time have courses on this subject. The 21st century will find this lack incomprehensible.
2. We can help young children learn techniques of relaxation and incubation. This does not mean that we should teach them any particular form of meditation, but it might be useful for all children to know what meditation, relaxation, and other types of unstressing are.
3. We should help children practice imagination and imagery during such relaxed periods. The Torrance and Khatena record, *Sounds and Images*, is only one of several devices on the market for this purpose. As a consequence of such periods we should encourage the production of poetry, art, music, etc.
4. As long as the child is in the concrete operations phase, the images will tend to be static and not particularly creative; but when he enters the

323

formal operations phase one can expect and should push for more finished artistic creations, especially in poetic form. Children at this stage should be strongly encouraged to keep a journal and put their poetry and other thoughts into it. The development of the easy ability at this level helps the child to become truly creative in the next stage, and this is where (in upper high school and in lower division college) most gifted children do not make the transition to creative production. I think the most important facilitation which can take place at this time is a seminar type home room where the adolescent can be with others of the same persuasion, for (because of the strong gregarious needs at this stage) nothing does more to inhibit creativity than group sanctions against it in other adolescents.

It might be prudent of us to listen to the last testament of a prophet and sage on educational objectives in a utopia:

> How does he do his thinking, perceiving, and remembering? Is he a visualizer or a non-visualizer? Does his mind work with images or with words, with both at once or with neither? How close to the surface is his story-telling faculty? Does he see the world as Wordsworth and Traherne saw it when they were children? And if so, what can be done to prevent the glory and freshness from fading into the light of common day? Or in more general terms, can we educate children on the conceptual level without killing their capacity for intense non-verbal experience? How can we reconcile analysis with vision? (Huxley, 1962).

Few orthodox teachers will agree with Huxley's tripartite prescription for accomplishing this educational miracle, which consisted of *maithuna* for the psychomotor level, *moksha*-medicine (drugs) for the affective level, and meditation for the cognitive level. But let us remember that Huxley was a visionary, and that many of the predictions in *Brave New World* have come true. Certainly his ideas are worth thinking about, if only to trigger our own.

About 9,000 years ago, prehistoric man was suddenly catapulted into history as the result of an astonishing social discovery. Previous to this, small bands of nomadic tribes had roamed a large hunting area looking for live game and gathering fruits and wild vegetables. Then someone found out that if one domesticated animals and plants, one could have a ready supply of food always at hand in a confined space. Thus was agriculture and civilization born, and man escalated into history, and to the possibility of a far greater population on a given land mass. We are still reaping the benefits of that change, but our continuing ecological crises show us that we are nearing the end of that period. Fortunately we are on the brink of another momentous discovery which will have even greater impact on cultural and personal escalation.

Heretofore we have harvested creativity wild. We have used as creative only those persons who stubbornly remained so despite all efforts of the

324

family, religion, education, and politics to grind it out of them. In the prosecution of this campaign, men and women have been punished, flogged, silenced, imprisoned, tortured, ostracized, and killed. Jesus, Socrates, Huss, Lavosier, Lincoln, Gandhi, Kennedy, and King are good examples. As a result of these misguided efforts, our society produces only a small percentage of its potential of creative individuals (the ones with the most uncooperative dispositions).

If we learn to domesticate creativity—that is, to enhance rather than deny it in our culture—we can increase the number of creative persons in our midst by about fourfold. That would put the number and percent of such individuals over the "critical mass" point. When this level is reached in a culture, as it was in Periclean Athens, the Renaissance, the Aufklarung, the Court of the Sun King, Elizabethan England, and our own Federalist period, there is an escalation of creativity resulting and civilization makes a great leap forward. We can have a golden age of this type such as the world has never seen, and I am convinced that it will occur early in the 21st century. But we must make preparations now, and the society we save will be our own. The alternative is either nuclear war or learning to speak Arabic and bow down four times a day toward Mecca.

In conclusion, if we may be permitted a peep at the future, we see an integrated science of human development and talent. The gestalt we are talking about there is at present at best a shore dimly seen, but it is the coming science of man of the 21st century. A genius is always a forerunner; and the best minds of this age foresee the dawn of that one. All of these branches of humanistic psychology will be welded together in a *structure d'ensemble*, greater than interest in the gifted, greater than interest in creativity, greater, in fact, than anything except the potential of man himself. We may come from dust, but our destiny is in the stars. Thoreau, that rustic seer, prophesized in the last sentence of *Walden*: "That day is yet to dawn, for the sun is only a morning star."

Toynbee tells us that each civilization leaves its monument and its religion. Our monument is on the moon, and the "religion" our culture will bequeath is the coming science of man and his infinite potential. This potential is truly infinite because man may be part animal but he is also part of the noumenon. And as Schroedinger correctly observed in *What Is Life*, "The 'I' that observes the universe is the same 'I' that created it." The present powers of genius are merely the earnest of greater powers to be unfolded. You need not take my word for this. Listen instead to the words of the greatest genius of our age—Albert Einstein:

> A human being is a part of the whole, called by us "Universe"; a part limited in time and space. He experiences himself, his thoughts and feelings as something separated from the rest—a kind of optical delusion of his consciousness. This delusion is a kind of prison for us, restricting us to our personal desires and to affection for a few persons nearest us. Our task must be to free ourselves from this prison by widening our circle of compassion to embrace all living creatures and the whole nature in its beauty. Nobody is

able to achieve this completely, but the striving for such achievement is, in itself, a part of the liberation and a foundation for inner security (cited in Gowan, 1975).

References

Blocher, D. *Developmental counseling*. New York: Ronald Press, 1966.

Bower, E. G. & Hollister, H. G. *Behavioral science frontiers in education*. New York: Wiley, 1968.

Ghiselin, B. (ed.) *The creative process*. New York: New American, 1952.

Gowan, J. C. *Development of the creative individual*. San Diego: Knapp, 1972.

Gowan, J. C. *Trance, art & creativity*. Northridge, CA: Gowan, 1975.

Guilford, J. P. *The nature of human intelligence*. New York: McGraw-Hill, 1967.

Huxley, A. *Island*. New York: Harper, 1962.

Koestler, A. *The act of creation*. New York: Macmillan, 1964.

Krippner, S. The creative person and non-ordinary reality. *The Gifted Child Quarterly*, 1972, 16: 203-228.

Lindbergh, C. A. *A letter from Lindbergh*. New York: Harcourt-Brace, 1969.

Maslow, A. *Motivation and personality*. New York: Harper, 1954.

Osborn, A. *Applied imagination*. New York: Scribners, 1953.

Prince, W. F. *Noted witnesses for psychic occurrences*. Hype Park, NY: University Books, 1963.

Vernon, P. E. *Creativity*. Baltimore: Penguin Books, 1970.

Wechsler, D. *The collected papers of David Wechsler*. New York: Academic Press, 1974.

Weil, G. M., Metsner, R. & Leary, T. *The psychedelic reader*. New York: Citadel Press, 1971.

Dorothy Sisk

The Use of Creative Activities In Leadership Training

*H*ow well do I understand myself? How well do others understand me? Am I able to convey to others what I am thinking, feeling and experiencing? Am I an effective leader? These are questions that plague many individuals who find themselves in leadership or helping positions. A quick survey of the literature will indicate that there are numerous research studies on interpersonal dynamics and theoretical papers and books on the importance of communication. The problem for the individual wishing to experience personal growth in their leadership skills, however, is how to transfer the research and theory into effective practice.

Miller, Nunnally and Wackman (1957) provide a useful framework for looking at relationships which has relevancy for leadership training. A relationship is defined as two people who have a history together and anticipate some kind of future, or two people who have ongoing expectations for each other. Therefore, a relationship could exist between professional colleagues, students and teachers, close friends, parents and children, or husbands and wives.

In their text *Alive and Aware*, Miller et al. describe four relationship states that have relevancy to leadership training, that of Togetherness, Leading/Supporting, Pushing/Resisting, and Apartness.

Togetherness is defined as the state where there is caring, sharing, playing, talking seriously about an issue in the relationship and would include negative aspects such as arguing and fighting. The key feature in the state of togetherness is that both partners are focused on their involvement and their energies are similarly focused on one object or on one another.

The Leading/Supporting state is defined as any activity where one partner assumes the lead in choosing or focusing their energies on some outside interest or activity and the second partner lends support and encouragement.

Reprinted from Gifted Child Quarterly, Vol. XXI, No. 4, (Winter, 1977), pp. 477-486. By permission of the author and publisher.

The Pushing/Resisting state is when one partner endeavors to focus the energy of the second partner in a particular direction or activity. The fourth state of Apartness is when the partners focus their involvement and energy on different things.

These four states can be utilized in moving leaders towards self actualization and effective functioning. In the state of Togetherness, there would be emphasis on knowing and trusting each other and accurately understanding each other. In the more active states of Leading/Supporting and Pushing/Resisting, the emphasis would be on influencing and helping each other, as well as constructively resolving problems and conflicts. And the last state would involve nurturing one's ability to recognize and support the "Apartness," or if you will, the uniqueness of the partner.

The four states build on the concept of the conflict between safety and conflict. As the partners learn about one another and care about one another, they feel safe. As either partner introduces something new or risky, each partner may feel threatened and feel reluctant to take on challenging experiences, thus often limiting their personal creativity. In the stage of Pushing/Resisting if the psychological threat becomes too keen, one partner may remove himself/herself from the situation or the relationship. Maslow (1968) speaks to this conflict of safety and growth as follows:

> Every human being has both sets of forces within him. One set clings to safety and defensiveness out of fear, tending to regress backward, hanging onto the past . . . afraid to take chances, afraid to jeopardize what he already has, afraid of independence, freedom and separateness. The other set of forces impels him forward toward wholeness of Self and uniqueness of Self, toward full functioning of all his capabilities. . . . In the choice between giving up safety or giving up growth, safety will ordinarily win out.

The program for those of us engaged in leadership training is to minimize the dangers and maximize the attractions of learning and personal growth so that our partners, be they colleagues or students, rather than being defensive and self-protective, will choose to be involved and grow.

One method of stimulating growth in leadership training is that of using creative activities. By utilizing the four states of a relationship according to Miller et. al. (1975) and identifying specific interpersonal skills to be developed through creative activities, the dangers involved in a safety/growth conflict can be minimized.

Togetherness State: In this state, the two interpersonal skills of knowing and trusting each other and accurately and unambiguously understanding each other can be emphasized. The following activities will utilize these two skills as objectives.

To know and trust another person means self-disclosing and asking for the support that will be needed in the second state of leading/supporting. In his poem *Revelation*, Robert Frost speaks of the need for support and acceptance and the need to be separate when he states:

328

. . . we make ourselves a place a part
Behind light words that tease and flount . . .

The following activities will call for members to go behind the light words that tease and flount and to simultaneously recognize the necessity for their use in protective behavior.

It's ME and I'm OK

Physical Arrangement: The individuals should be arranged in a circle, comfortably seated with all members facing inward in the circle. The group leader should also be seated in the circle.

Direction: Each member is directed to respond to a question dealing with themselves and the group is requested to defer judgment and accept each response. Questions to be used could be as follows:

When you have spare time, what do you like to do?
If you could spend a half hour with anyone, who would you choose?
When you think of personal strengths, what strength do you admire?
A kaleidoscope of beauty would include what object from your point of view?

Suggestions: It is important that each member be given total attention by the group and this attentiveness should be modeled by the leader. The leader should respond to the questions as a member of the group or relationship. The questions should progress in their complexity and need for self-disclosure. Through listening to one another, group members come to know one another. Through their deferred judgment and acceptance of responses, the members come to trust one another.

Following the first introductory activity, the group can then proceed to a more involving activity such as Constructively Constructing.

Constructively Constructing

Physical Arrangement: The members are casually seated with each member having at their disposal and use the following: a large piece of paper, one colored Kleenex, Scotch Tape, felt pens, different sizes and shapes of construction paper.

Directions: Each member is directed to build something out of the objects that reflect aspects of themselves as individuals. In the past, people have built such objects as skyscapers, trees, and flowers. When the members have had about fifteen minutes to build whatever they wish, they share and explain the various aspects of themselves, utilizing their circle formation, one after another. In this activity, the leader and group may ask questions, respond and provide feedback.

Suggestions: It is important that the leader participate in the activity and model questions and feedback that are supportive. In this activity, the group members begin to test if they are being unambiguously understood and the self-description process begins to involve others.

As Maslow (1968) indicates, growth takes place in little steps and each step forward is made possible by feeling safe and operating out of a safe port. Consequently, the emphasis on feedback should be positive.

Many activities can be designed to supplement the two mentioned above. An activity that is often used is one in which the group members decorate a bag that tells about themselves. Things that they want to openly share are pasted or drawn on the outside and more intimate details that they may not want to share may be pasted, drawn or dropped inside. Collages or self descriptions or characteristics may also be made utilizing magazines and construction paper. A further extension or variation is to pair two people and have them make a collage of who they are to be shared with the group. Throughout this state, the emphasis is on getting to know one another and to build trust. In the second state of Leading/Supporting, the members can be encouraged to develop further interest and support of one another.

Leading/Supporting

In this state, the interpersonal skill of listening and responding will be emphasized to build the support that is needed to encourage one member of the relationship to continue to take risks and to experience support by the other member of the relationship. In the Leading/Supporting state, group members can learn helpful behaviors. As Hunter (1972) states, "Most people do not think of sharing feelings, or of summarizing what has happened . . . or helping the group to continue exploring alternatives. . . ." However, as she quite forcefully emphasizes, people can learn to "try on" new behaviors. In this state, the members will try on listening and responding. The following activity is a progressive exercise in listening and responding.

Physical arrangement: The individuals should be divided into paired groups and sit facing one another.

Directions: At a given signal, one member is to speak extemporaneously on their feelings as an inanimate object, such as a shoe. They are to respond for one minute, while the other member supportively listens. Then the two roles are reversed.

Suggestions: The leader should take part in the activity. This activity should be quickly followed by a small group activity involving four members such as *Creative Quads*.

Creative Quads

Physical Arrangement: The group is divided into small groups of four and a large supply of materials such as cardboard boxes, crayons, paste, glue, magazines and string are available.

Directions: The group should subdivide into two groups of two. Two of the members are to decide on an item that they want to construct and the other two members are to support and help in any way they can to insure success. At the end of 15 minutes, the member who did the construction activity shares with the total group, as to what they've constructed and what the construction means or represents. Following this period, a general discussion should be held concerning the feelings about the supportive member. Did it help? Did you work harder? Was it important to you?

Suggestions: As a leader it is imperative that relevant comments or principles be summarized and reinforced. The following guiding statements of Hunter (1972) are helpful:

> . . . many people actually interfere with the work of the group, without necessarily meaning to do so, by dominating the conversation and preventing others from participating or by attempting to smother controversy which needs to surface and be faced before any workable solutions can be achieved.

This surfacing of controversy is to be capitalized upon in the third stage of Pushing-Resisting and consequently, the leader and group must be aware that it exists in stage two and draw it to the attention of the group, yet still emphasizing support efforts. Upon completion of this activity the groups should proceed to *By Eights*.

By Eights

Physical Arrangement: Eight chairs should be arranged for each group of eight with the chairs facing inward.

Directions: In this activity, one member of the group starts by making a personal statement of a philosophical belief or notion that they hold concerning creativity and its development and the entire group makes supportive statements one by one. At the conclusion of a go-round, the group discusses how it felt to be supported and the recognition that ideas grow as they progress around the circle. Each member receives an opportunity to experience "By Eights."

Suggestion: The emphasis here is to enhance the attractions and minimize the dangers as suggested by Maslow (1968) which will help the person experience growth on an idea that they've been pursuing. It should also be noted that the activities in this state have included discussion, construction and physical activity. This blend should also minimize bore-

331

dom or use of any one learning style that might penalize a given member of the group.

Pushing-Resisting

In this state, the major interpersonal skill is resolving interpersonal conflicts. One of the most creative approaches to interpersonal skill building is that of *Reaching Out* by Johnson (1972). He states the following concerning interpersonal conflict:

> An interpersonal conflict exists whenever an action by one person prevents, obstructs, or interferes with the actions of another person; there can be conflicts between goals, ways of accomplishing the same goal, personal needs, and expectations concerning the behavior of the two individuals.

One of the most successful activities to help a group experience conflict is one called *Nickel Auction* as reported by Johnson (1972).

Nickel Auction

Physical Arrangement: Four volunteers sit in a row.

Directions: One person is designated as auctioneer and given an unlimited supply of nickels. The nickels are supplied by the group members. The auctioneer puts a nickel up for auction and each volunteer bids in turn. Bidding is done in units of 1 cent—fractions are not acceptable. The nickel is sold when three of the four volunteers have decided not to bid in turn. Each time a nickel is put up for auction, the first chance to bid is passed down the line of volunteers. Members observing the auction can communicate by passing notes to the volunteers. At the end of 20 nickels being auctioned, the leader should hold a discussion. Why did they behave as they did? What assumptions had been made? Did they co-operate and thereby facilitate the auction? If so, why?

Suggestions: Following the activity *Nickel Auction*, it is helpful for the leader to guide the discussion into other activities where people have co-operated to facilitate growth and activities where completion has detracted from goal completion.

Another creative activity for the *Pushing-Resisting* state is *Machiavelli*.

Machiavelli

Physical Arrangement: Four members play as a team and sit opposite four other members.

Directions: The four members discuss and decide what they will try

332

and convince the other group to do. They build a strategy and as a group try to achieve that aim. Before the four person team decides on what it is they will try and convince the group to do, they must hold a general round of warm up questions to get to know the group utilizing questions such as: If you could go anywhere, where would you go? When you are happy, what are you doing? If you could be involved in any great movement, what would it be? These questions should be decided on by the group and should elicit as much knowledge concerning the other group as possible. Each member of the four member team decides on which member on the other team that they will exert their influence over. Discussion should follow after one half hour of activity as to how successful the group was and why? How did they feel being prodded or pushed? Did you resist and how?

Suggestion: The emphasis should be on personalizing the experiences and drawing inferences on one's own behavior. The leader participates as a member of a team as this minimizes the group's reluctance to be involved.

Apartness

This state calls to mind Carl Rogers' (1969) qualification for an individual being capable of performing the helping relationship in which Rogers states that one must allow the other to be apart. In this state, the members must encourage apartness and independence. This can be accomplished by the use of *Success Wheels* and the skill to be developed is self-direction with the support skills to be continued as an interpersonal skill.

Success Wheels

Physical Arrangement: The members are seated casually in a large space with each member having a piece of paper, red and black felt tip pens, and Scotch Tape.

Directions: In the middle of your paper draw a circle and put a goal that you want to accomplish in the circle. From that circle draw spokes with other circles noting the methods for accomplishing that goal. When you are finished, place your paper on that wall with your tape and sit quietly till others are finished. When all are finished, each person is to read each individual's paper and add spokes and circles on how they might aid each person in reaching their goal in black and applaud them in red, with comments such as "I like this goal", "Me too", and "Fine!"

Suggestions: This activity is marvelous for a closure in a leadership workshop or session and should not be hurried. It can easily take a full hour and the rapport that is built is quite remarkable.

Another activity that encourages Apartness and goal setting is *Encourage Me To or Commitment Cards*.

Commitment Cards

Physical Arrangement: The members are seated casually and each is given a 4 × 5 card and a pen.

Directions: Think of something you want to do and make a commitment to do it. Outline your strategy on the back of your card. Mill around with your card pinned on your shirt. You may want to state your commitment as Encourage Me to . . . Share the strategies if you desire.

Suggestions: Again this is a good closure activity and should be given ample time for movement and discussion.

The creative activities described herein to build leadership are based on the four factors generally held to be included in creativity, that of fluency, or eliciting many ideas; flexibility in that there are opportunities for shifting ideas and shifting style of activities; originality in that unique ideas are continually rewarded and the dissimilarity of the members of the group encouraged; and lastly that of elaboration or the building on one another's ideas. A creative climate was established in that deferred judgement was utilized as judgement was withheld and a psychologically safe environment was also experienced.

Through taking the framework of Miller et al. 1975 of Togetherness, Leading/Supporting, Pushing-Resisting and Apartness, individuals involved in leadership training can experience creative activities and develop interpersonal skills that will help insure their ability to self actualize and to help others reach their potential. Through experiencing interpersonal skills the leader and group can become primary forces in helping others acquire more effective behaviors through modeling interpersonal skills. As the leader engages in the activities, he or she is modeling effective behavior and helps others "learn by imitation" as they grow together.

References

Hunter, Elizabeth. *Encounter in the classroom.* New York: Holt, Rinehart and Winston, Inc. 1972.

Johnson, David. *Reaching out.* New York: Prentice-Hall, 1972.

Maslow, Abraham. *Toward a psychology of being.* New York: Van Nostrand Reinhold Co. 1968.

Miller, Sherod, Nunnally, Elam and Wackman, Daniel. *Alive and aware: Improving communication in relationships.* Interpersonal Communications Programs, Inc. 1975.

Rogers, Carl. *Freedom to learn.* Columbus, Ohio: Charles E. Merrill Publishing Co., 1969.

Joseph S. Renzulli
Linda H. Smith

A Practical Model for Designing Individualized Educational Programs (IEP) for Gifted and Talented Students

Introduction

The major goals of the IEP model described in this article are twofold. First, we have attempted to provide teachers and administrators with a practical approach for individualization and with the "software" and step-by-step procedures that are necessary for implementing the model. Our second goal is somewhat more abstract but nevertheless equally important. This goal is to provide a valid rationale for special programming that is based on the best knowledge available concerning the characteristics of gifted and creative individuals.

The chart on the opposite page represents several components of the overall IEP model and the ways in which they are interrelated. The top row of the chart deals with three supporting models that are derived from research studies and theories of learning and instruction. The first column focuses on characteristics of gifted and talented students and it is considered to be the keystone of the IEP approach. The second column deals with a learning process model that is based upon the concept of matching students to learning environments. The third column is an enrichment model that attempts to integrate regular curricular experiences with those experiences that are mainly appropriate for gifted students.

The middle row of the chart points out some of the practical matters that should be taken into consideration in developing a program for the gifted and talented. The first column deals with identifying strengths of students from a variety of data sources; the second column deals with the concept of "buying time" so that gifted youngsters can become involved in the higher level experiences that we recommend; and the third column

This Chapter is a summary by the authors of A Guidebook for Developing Individualized Educational Programs (IEP) for Gifted and Talented Students (1979). This Guidebook and accompanying forms are available from Creative Learning Press, P.O. Box 320, Mansfield Center, CT 06250.

INDIVIDUALIZED EDUCATIONAL PROGRAMMING MODEL — — GIFTED/TALENTED

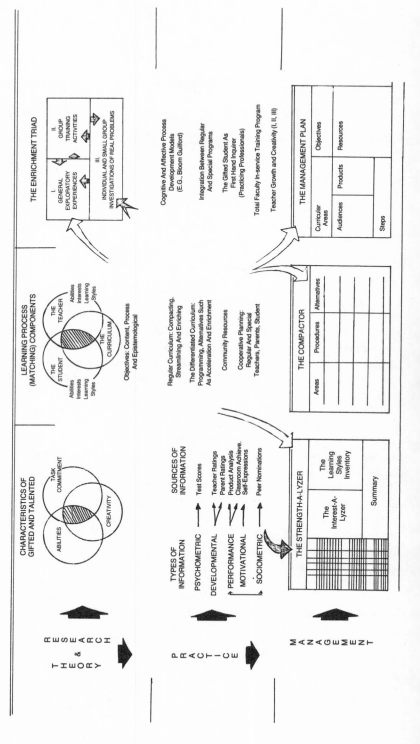

deals with cognitive and affective development, integration with the regular program, total faculty in-service training and how to develop and organize learning experiences that represent *true* differentiation.

The bottom row (Management) deals with a system for organizing and carrying out the theoretical and practical concerns described in the top two rows of the chart. The forms depicted in this row constitute the major components of our IEP approach and represent a step-by-step procedure for translating theory and practice into actual classroom activities. A general description of these forms and the basic principles guiding their use will be provided in the sections which follow. Before proceeding with this description, however, we will point out the major assumptions underlying this IEP approach and delineate the key functions of persons responsible for implementing the model.

Underlying Assumptions of the IEP Model

The first and certainly most unquestionable assumption underlying our IEP approach is that many gifted students are capable of mastering the regular curriculum at a much faster pace and higher level of proficiency than students in the general school population. Although it is important for all students to develop mastery in the basic skill areas necessary for further educational and/or vocational pursuits, it is equally important to provide some alternative means which will allow students with varying ability levels to cover basic material at different rates and in ways which will respect a variety of learning styles.

The second assumption underlying this model is that gifted students should be provided with opportunities to identify and to pursue advanced topics and areas of study that hold special fascination for them. Implementation of our model would thus entail developing specific procedures for allowing gifted students numerous opportunities to (1) explore a wider variety of potential interests, (2) identify general areas of special interest, (3) focus or "frame" problems within these areas, and (4) pursue these self-selected problems in a manner that resembles the *modus operandi* of a first-hand inquirer rather than a passive lesson learner.

The third assumption underlying the model is that the major focus of IEPs for gifted students must be placed on individual strengths rather than weaknesses. Although no one would argue against a diagnostic/remedial approach to IEPs for handicapped children, our main concern with gifted students is *not* to find out what is wrong with them and fix them up! Our primary objective is rather to identify both general and specific *strengths* in higher levels of thinking, creativity and task commitment, and to provide opportunities for developing these strengths in relatively unstructured learning situations.

337

Implementing the IEP Model

The most essential ingredient for implementing our IEP model is careful student advisement. Such advisement might be carried out by classroom or homeroom teachers, guidance counselors, independent study or special program coordinators, department heads, or persons who are specifically designated to advise gifted and talented students. This function might also be performed by a committee composed of combinations of the above persons. Whomever the "advisor" may be, however, his or her major responsibilities consist of the following five functons:

1. Assessing individual students' present levels of scholastic development, individual interests, and learning styles.
2. Reviewing the content of particular courses (or segments of courses) to determine if the student (a) has already mastered basic material, (b) is able to master the material through alternative arrangements, and/or (c) is able to substitute advanced level experiences for regular curricular material.
3. Making arrangements with instructors regarding alternative approaches for covering material in particular courses and arranging for the documentation of information about compacted coverage in the student's file.
4. Assisting students in the development of individual and small group investigations by (a) helping them to identify and focus problems in their individual areas of interest, (b) providing them with methodological and managerial assistance, and (c) helping them to find reasonable outlets and audiences for their work.
5. Monitoring the progress of each pupil and providing periodic feedback to the student, his or her parents, and other teachers who have present and future contact with the student.

Specific responsibilities of the advisor as they relate to each aspect of the IEP model will be discussed in the following sections.

Assessing Student Strengths

The first step in preparing IEPs for gifted students consists of gathering and recording information about abilities, interests and learning styles. Some of this information may be obtained from student's cumulative records of assessment instruments that are routinely administered by the school system. The information might also result from the identification procedures used to screen youngsters for placement in a special program or from instruments that are specifically administered as part of the IEP process. All information should be entered in the appropriate spaces on the *Strength-A-Lyzer* (Figure 1) which is a summary form designed to

INDIVIDUAL EDUCATIONAL PROGRAMMING GUIDE
Strength - A - Lyzer

Prepared by: Joseph Renzulli
Linda H. Smith

NAME _____ AGE _____ TEACHER(S) _____

SCHOOL _____ GRADE _____ PARENT(S) _____

Individual Conference Dates And Persons Participating in Planning Of IEP

ABILITIES

INTELLIGENCE - APTITUDE - CREATIVITY

In the spaces below, enter the results of standardized test scores and circle all scores above the _____ percentile.

Test	Area	Date	Raw Score	Grade Equiv.	% ile

TEACHER RATINGS

In the space below, enter the scores from the Scale for Rating Behavioral Characteristics of Superior Students. Circle unusually high scores.

Scale	Score	Group Mean	Scale	Score	Group Mean
Learning			Musical		
Motivation			Dramatic		
Creativity			Comm.:Precision		
Leadership			Comm.:Expressive		
Artistic			Planning		

END OF YEAR GRADES

Enter final grades for the past two years.

Reading		Art	
Mathematics		Foreign Language	
Language Arts		Other	
Social Studies		Other	
Science			
Music			

☐ Check here if additional assessment information is recorded on the reverse side.

INTERESTS

As a result of student responses to the Interest-A-Lyzer or other interest assessment procedures, indicate the general area(s) in which levels of interest seem to be High, Average and Low.

	H	A	L		H	A	L
Fine Arts/Crafts				Managerial			
Scientific/Technical				Business			
Library/Writing				Historical			
Political/Judicial				Performing Arts			
Mathematical				Other			
Athletic				Other			

SUMMARY AND RECOMMENDED ACTION BASED ON ASSESSMENT INFORMATION

In the space below summarize (1) strengths, interests, and learning styles, (2) areas in which remedial work or additional skill building appears to be warranted, and (3) specific higher mental processes and advanced skills that should be developed.

LEARNING STYLES

Enter the scores from the Learning Styles Inventory in the spaces below. Circle the highest area(s).

Learning Style	Score	Learning Style	Score
Projects		Teaching Games	
Simulation		Independent Study	
Drill and Recitation		Programmed Instruction	
Peer Teaching		Lecture	
Discussion			

Comments regarding informal observations about Learning Styles and relationships between areas of interest and learning styles.

Figure 1. The Strength-A-Lyzer (Actual Size: 11×17)

provide an overview of students' strengths. It should be pointed out that the categories included in this form are merely guides for recording certain types of information. There may be additional types of assessment data which should be included because of the specific objectives of particular programs. In additon, the format of the *Strength-A-Lyzer* should not lead the user to conclude that all assessment information is derived from tests or structured instruments. Informal observations, examples of students' work, peer and parent evaluations, and student self-evaluations are useful sources of informatin about strengths and should be recorded on the reverse side of this form.

ANALYSIS OF ABILITIES

The first section of the *Strength-A-Lyzer* examines information about students' abilities. The results of intelligence, achievement, aptitude and creativity tests should be recorded in the top section of the first block and judgments should be made about the meanings of these scores. Given the fact that all instruments are imperfect devices and that there is no definitive answer to the question "How high is high?", it is important that no single piece of data be used as the basis for final judgments about individualized programming practices. Rather, program personnel should look at the "total picture" for each pupil and base judgments on the degree to which it is felt that a youngster can benefit from one or more programming alternatives and curricular adaptations.

A second source of information about student abilities should be derived from the guided judgment of one or more teachers who are familiar with a child's performance. A number of instruments are available to obtain this information but the one referred to on the *Strength-A-Lyzer* is the *Scales for Rating the Behavioral Characteristics of Superior Students* (SRBCSS, Renzulli, et al., 1976). The SRBCSS consists of ten dimensions, including Learning, Motivation, Creativity, Leadership, Art, Music, Dramatics, Communication (Precision), Communication (Expressiveness), and Planning. Each of these scales is composed of items which were derived from the research literature dealing with characteristics of gifted and talented persons. Teachers are instructed to read the items carefully and to respond in terms of how frequently the cited characteristics are observed in particular students. Once the forms are filled out, a mean score can be computed for each dimension selected for use by program personnel. Those students who deviate markedly upward from the mean and who also have other indicators of exceptionality should be considered prime candidates for programming or activities designed to enhance the particular abilities being assessed.

INTEREST ASSESSMENT

Building educational experiences around student interests is probably one of the most recognizable ways in which special programs for gifted and talented students differ from the regular curriculum. One strategy for helping students examine their present and potential interests is based on an instrument called the *Interest-A-Lyzer* (Renzulli, 1977). This instrument is a thirteen item questionnaire that is designed to assist students in exploring their individual areas of interest. It has been used with students in grades 3–10 and consists of a variety of real and hypothetical situations to which students are asked to respond in terms of the choices they would make (or have made) were they involved in these activities. The major interest area patterns that might emerge from the instrument are as follows:

1. Fine Arts and Crafts
2. Scientific and Technical
3. Creative Writing and Journalism
4. Legal, Political, and Judicial
5. Mathematical
6. Managerial
7. Historical
8. Athletic and Outdoor Related Activities
9. Performing Arts
10. Business
11. Consumer Action and Ecology Related Activities

Four basic guidelines are recommended for interpreting responses to the *Interest-A-Lyzer* or similar interest survey tools. The first step involves small group discussions in which students are asked to share their responses to particular items. During these discussions an effort should be made to discover the general pattern(s) of interest each youngster may have.

The second major step in analyzing responses consists of grouping students together according to similar interest patterns and exploring a wide variety of possible activities that might emerge from such patterns. In certain cases where group projects or whole-class activities are desirable, it is suggested that an area with multifaceted opportunities for creative expression be selected as a vehicle for subsequent activity.

A third step in the follow-up process consists of "feasibility" studies. Certain interests may be outside the realm of possibility because of excessive cost, insufficient time, or the unavailability of needed resource persons or materials. Feasibility studies and discussions about the obstacles and possible consequences of certain areas will help to channel interests within realistic parameters of student activity.

The fourth and perhaps most important step of following up on responses consists of problem focusing. This phase of interest analysis is more complex than the previous ones and entails asking the question: "How does the professional go about choosing and focusing on a topic?" The reader who is interested in an in-depth treatment of this question is referred to *The Enrichment Triad Model: A Guide for Developing Defensible Programs for the Gifted and Talented* (Renzulli, 1977). Suffice it to say at this point that the information and conclusions that result from this four-stage analysis of student interests should be entered on the *Strength-A-Lyzer* in the section entitled "Specific Areas of Interest."

LEARNING STYLES EVALUATION

The final section of the *Strength-A-Lyzer* examines information about students' learning style preferences. Although several definitions of learning style can be found in the educational and psychological literature, the definition we recommend for use in designing individualized educational programs is one which focuses on specific and identifiable learning activities. Our definition considers learning styles to be one or more of the following nine instructional strategies most preferred by individual students as they interact with particular bodies of curricular materials:

1. Projects
2. Drill and Recitation
3. Peer Teaching
4. Discussion
5. Teaching Games
6. Independent Study
7. Programmed Instruction
8. Lecture
9. Simulation

A research-based instrument that was developed to provide information about student attitude toward these nine general modes of instruction is entitled the *Learning Styles Inventory: A Measure of Student Preference for Instructional Techniques* (Renzulli & Smith, 1978). The *Inventory* consists of a series of items which describe various classroom learning experiences. Students are asked to read the items carefully and respond in terms of how pleasant they find participating in each one. They are told that there are no "right" or "wrong" answers and that the information gained from the *Inventory* will be used to help plan future classroom activities.

A teacher version of the *Learning Styles Inventory* accompanies each set of student forms. This form is designed as a tool for teachers to look at the range of instructional strategies used in their own classrooms. The items included on this form parallel those on the student form but in this case, teachers respond in terms of how frequently each activity occurs in the classroom. The profile of instructional styles resulting from this procedure can be compared to individual student preferences and can serve to facilitate a closer match between how teachers instruct and the styles to which students respond most favorably.

All LSI forms are prepared on optical scanning sheets and are scored by computer. Computer analysis results in a variety of classroom reports including:

342

1. Raw scores for individual students on each learning style dimension
2. A quick summary sheet indicating each students' two most preferred and two least preferred learning style dimensions
3. A grouping report which lists students who find each approach in the pleasant and unpleasant range
4. A profile of each student's learning style preferences
5. A class profile of learning style preferences
6. A profile of the teacher's general instructional emphasis

The information derived from these reports should be summarized and entered in the final section of the *Strength-A-Lyzer* form.

Compacting and Streamlining the Regular Curriculum

The second phase of the IEP model is designed to overcome the dilemma between "covering" the regular curriculum and providing enrichment experiences for gifted youngsters. This phase is built around the IEP guide entitled *The Compactor* (Figure 2) which provides a systematic plan for compacting and streamlining the regular curriculum. The basic goals of *The Compactor* are twofold. First, the plan is designed to relieve gifted students of the boredom that often results from unchallenging work in basic skill areas, and at the same time, to *guarantee* the student, his or her parents, and subsequent grade-level teachers that the child has mastered standard competencies necessary for later achievement. The second objective is simply to "buy" the student some time so that he or she can pursue acceleration and enrichment activity.

The Compactor is divided into three major sections. The first section, "Curriculum Areas to be Considered for Compacting," should be pursued after the *Strength-A-Lyzer* has been completed and a comprehensive profile of the child's abilities, interest, and learning styles has been prepared. This profile will assist in providing the assessment information or evidence that suggests a need for compacting in one or more areas of the curriculum. The second section, "Procedures for Compacting Basic Material," will be discussed below as it relates to the material summarized in Column 1 of *The Compactor*.

CURRICULUM AREAS TO BE CONSIDERED FOR COMPACTING AND
PROCEDURES FOR COMPACTING BASIC MATERIAL

The teacher can approach the first column of *The Compactor* in two different ways—by time periods or by topics. The most suitable approach will be determined largely by teacher preferences, the degree of structure that is inherent in certain curricular areas, and the varying degrees of independence that each youngster is capable of handling in the overall individualization effort. The two approaches are directed toward the same

INDIVIDUAL EDUCATIONAL PROGRAMMING GUIDE
The Compactor

Prepared by: Joseph S. Renzulli
Linda H. Smith

NAME _____ AGE _____ TEACHER(S) _____

SCHOOL _____ GRADE _____ PARENT(S) _____

Individual Conference Dates And Persons Participating in Planning Of IEP

CURRICULUM AREAS TO BE CONSIDERED FOR COMPACTING Provide a brief description of basic material to be covered during this marking period and the assessment information or evidence that suggests the need for compacting.	PROCEDURES FOR COMPACTING BASIC MATERIAL Describe activities that will be used to guarantee proficiency in basic curricular areas.	ACCELERATION AND/OR ENRICHMENT ACTIVITIES Describe activities that will be used to provide advanced level learning experiences in each area of the regular curriculum.

☐ Check here if additional information is recorded on the reverse side.

Figure 2. The Compactor (Actual size: 11 × 17)

344

objective, and the methodology for implementing each approach is essentially the same.

The time period approach begins by having the advisor and/or the regular classroom teacher examine each area of the regular curriculum in which a youngster shows a particular strength. Information from the *Strength-A-Lyzer* combined with informal discussion with previous teachers should give a fairly good picture of the degree to which the child is advanced. In cases of extremely advanced ability and in highly sequential subject areas such as mathematics or reading skills, it is conceivable that a compacting plan could be developed for an entire school year. In other cases it may be more advisable to consider marking periods as appropriate time intervals.

The second approach to compacting uses the topic, instructional unit, or coordinated set of basic skill objectives as guides for determining a compacting period. This approach is probably more realistic for gifted students because of the difficulties involved in fitting particular units of study within predetermined time periods. Regardless of which approach is used, however, it is important to monitor the youngster regularly and to insure that the child is maintaining a high level of proficiency in areas that may "show up" on achievement tests or at later grade levels.

The following case study is provided to illustrate how *The Compactor* has been used to "buy time" for a particular gifted student. Brenda is a third grade student who has scored two years above grade level on the reading and language arts sections of a standardized achievement test. She is an avid reader and has recently completed Unit 1 in the *Pathfinder* series and is about to embark upon Unit 2. Brenda's score on the Unit 1 *Criterion Reference Test* was 100 percent and she completed all workbook exercises without making a single error.

Prior to beginning the second unit, Brenda's teacher administered the unit pretest. This instrument assesses the basic skill objectives taught in the unit. The following general areas are covered: decoding, comprehension, language usage, vocabulary, and research and study skills. The fourteen specific objectives related to these general areas are listed in the teacher's edition of the reading text. Figure 3 shows the entry that Brenda's teacher made in the first column of *The Compactor*.

The information in Figure 3 represents (1) the material to be covered in Unit 2 and (2) the evidence that suggests a need for compacting. Since it would be a relatively useless task to rewrite the objectives on the IEP form, the teacher simply referred to the specific pages in the teacher's edition where these objectives are outlined.

Although Brenda has demonstrated almost perfect mastery of the skills in Unit 2, we note in Figure 3 that she has experienced some difficulty in the general area of decoding. The teacher therefore selected some training activities and procedures for checking on subsequent mastery. The teacher's entry for the second column on *The Compactor* (Figure 4) consists of a brief notation of her plan.

CURRICULUM AREAS TO BE CONSIDERED FOR COMPACTING Provide a brief description of basic material to be covered during this marking period and the assessment information or evidence that suggests the need for compacting.

> *Unit 2, Level 14 — Hand Stands. Objectives — see p. 64 in Teacher's Edition (attached). All items on Pretest (attached) correct with exception of questions dealing with grapheme-phoneme correspondence.*

Figure 3. Curriculum Areas to be Considered for Compacting (Sample).

PROCEDURES FOR COMPACTING BASIC MATERIAL Describe activities that will be used to guarantee proficiency in basic curricular areas.

> *Do pg. 23 in Workbook and Skill Reinforcement Master No. 6. Check proficiency by using activity No. 3, pg. 76 in Teacher's Edition and Criterion Reference Test items dealing with decoding (Workbook pg. 133, Nos. 1-4).*

Figure 4. Procedures for Compacting Basic Material (Sample).

This example illustrates only one of numerous ways in which a compacting plan can be notated. Whenever possible, teachers should make use of diagnostic instruments that are available in the basic skill areas, be it reading, language or mathematics. These instruments take the form of pretests, end-of-unit tests, or summary exercises that contain a sampling of the major concepts presented in a designated unit of instruction. Although materials in curricular areas such as science and social studies are not as tightly sequenced as basic skill activities, there is, nevertheless, a general curricular movement toward "management by objectives," and this approach will greatly facilitate both the diagnostic and compacting processes. In cases where such tests or diagnostic instruments are not readily available,

346

the teacher can review the main objectives of a given unit and construct an instrument using related workbook or textbook exercise items.

After having helped a gifted youngster master the regular curriculum in a more economical and efficient manner, the next step in the IEP process is to explore a wide variety of acceleration and/or enrichment alternatives. This will require making some basic decisions about the subject matter "boundaries" within which enrichment activities will fall. If, for example, we have compacted several curriculum units in the area of mathematics, a decision must be made regarding whether the time that has been bought will be devoted to enrichment or acceleration in this particular area of the curriculum. Although practical and organizational concerns may place certain restrictions on enrichment alternatives, the crucial consideration in making decisions about advanced level opportunities should be the interests of the student. Thus, in the situation described above there should be no question whatsoever about an advanced mathematics experience *if* the student is genuinely interested in math. Problems may arise, however, if we "force" the youngster into advanced math when he or she would rather pursue some other topic or area of study.

One of the best ways to facilitate the completion of *The Compactor*'s third column is to develop a list of all available enrichment and acceleration alternatives within a given school district. This list may be modest to begin with but as resources and special services to gifted students expand, the list can serve as an important part of the planning and program development process. In fact, in some cases it may be sufficient to merely report the name of an advanced course into which a youngster has been placed as a result of the IEP process.

Decisions regarding the last column on *The Compactor* will seldom if ever be made with 100 percent certainty. Careful consideration should therefore be given to information assembled on the *Strength-A-Lyzer* form and all acceleration and/or enrichment activities should always be subject to review and modification.

Developing Management Plans for Individual and Small Group Investigations

The third major component of this IEP model is the *Management Plan* (Figure 5) which is designed to guide the development of individual and small group investigations of "real problems." As suggested on this *Plan*, the investigation of real problems is a different type of an experience than the ritualistic reports and projects characteristically assigned in many enrichment programs. In these types of activities, the student emulates the

347

MANAGEMENT PLAN FOR INDIVIDUAL AND SMALL GROUP INVESTIGATIONS

Prepared by: Joseph S. Renzulli
Linda H. Smith

NAME _____ GRADE _____ Beginning Date _____ Estimated
                                                                       Ending Date _____

TEACHER _____ SCHOOL _____ Progress Reports
                                            Due On Following Dates

GENERAL AREA(S) OF STUDY (Check all that apply)

— Language Arts/Humanities — Science   — Personal and Social Development

— Social Studies   — Music   — Other (Specify) _____

— Mathematics   — Art   — Other (Specify) _____

SPECIFIC AREA OF STUDY   Write a brief description of the problem that you plan to investigate. What are the objectives of your investigation? What do you hope to find out?

INTENDED AUDIENCES   Which individuals or groups would be most interested in the findings? List the organized groups (clubs, societies, teams) at the local, regional, state, and national levels. What are the names and addresses of contact persons in these groups? When and where do they meet?

1. _____

2. _____

3. _____

4. _____

5. _____

INTENDED PRODUCT(S) AND OUTLETS   What form(s) will the final product take? How, when, and where will you communicate the results of your investigation to an appropriate audience(s)? What outlet vehicles (journals, conferences, art shows, etc.) are typically used by professionals in this field?

METHODOLOGICAL RESOURCES AND ACTIVITIES   List the names and addresses of persons who might provide assistance in attacking this problem. List the how-to-do-it books that are available in this area of study. List other resources (films, collections, exhibits, etc.) and special equipment (e.g., camera, transit, tape recorder, questionnaire, etc.). Keep a continuous record of all activities that are a part of this investigation.

GETTING STARTED   What are the first steps you should take to begin this investigation? What types of information or data will be needed to solve the problem? If "raw data", how can it be gathered, classified, and presented? If you plan to use already categorized information or data, where is it located and how can you obtain what you need?

A complete description of the model utilizing this form can be found in: *The Enrichment Triad Model: A Guide For Developing Defensible Programs For The Gifted And Talented.* - Creative Learning Press, Inc. P.O. Box 320 Mansfield Center, Ct. 06250

Copyright © 1977 by Creative Learning Press Inc. All rights reserved.

Figure 5. The Management Plan for Individual and Small Group Investigations
(Actual size: 11 × 17)

practicing professional within given fields of endeavor and hopefully becomes a first-hand inquirer him or herself. Although students doing this type of advanced work may draw upon existing knowledge, their purpose in doing so is not simply to rewrite or summarize information that is already known. Rather, their primary goal is to solve an existing problem, to add to present bodies of knowledge, or to create an artistic product that is relatively new to a given field. These contributions, in turn, are shared with well-defined target audiences which can give meaningful and productive feedback to the young scientist, author or artist.

The *Management Plan*, then, attempts to parallel the procedures or "ways of thinking" that are followed by the first-hand inquirer. After the inquirer has identified a general area in which he or she would like to do advanced-level work, the next step is to focus in upon a particular problem within the general area. By using appropriate problem focusing techniques, the student can begin to fill in the material requested in the box entitled "Specific Area of Study." A great deal of careful thought should be given to completing this box because all subsequent activities will reflect the degree of clarity with which the problem is focused and stated.

The two boxes labeled "Intended Audiences" and "Intended Products and Outlets" are designed to help "steer" the student toward thinking about the final form that his or her investigation will take and about the audiences potentially concerned with the results. These boxes are perhaps the key to differentiating between the orientation of normal student reportage and that of first-hand inquiry. While it is neither necessary nor practical for teachers to have the names of all possible audiences and outlets at their fingertips, persons programming for gifted and talented youngsters should be capable of finding out about their existence and availability.

The two larger boxes on the *Management Plan* (i.e., "Getting Started" and "Methodological Resources and Activities") are intended to provide a "running account" of the procedures and resources that will be used throughout the duration of an investigative activity. Both of these boxes should be completed cooperatively by the teacher and student, and modifications should be made as new activities are followed through and as a greater variety of resources are brought to the student's attention.

If completed carefully, the cells on the *Management Plan* will not only guide the student's independent activity but can serve as valuable evaluation data. For example, if one of the objectives of a special program for the gifted is to encourage students to engage in a wider variety of studies or in studies that involve interdisciplinary topics, a simple frequency count or percentage report of the number of areas checked in the "General Areas of Study" box will indicate to some extent whether this particular objective is achieved. And of course the very fact that a student's work has been "good enough" to gain acceptance or recognition by an appropriate audience is itself an indication of quality. For this reason, it is suggested that teachers maintain a continuous record of student articles that have been published,

349

student presentations before various special interest groups, and displays of performances that have resulted from students' investigative activities.

Summary

The purpose of this article was to provide a brief overview of the IEP model that we developed to guide teachers in their efforts to individualize the learning process for gifted and talented students. Three assumptions underlying this model were discussed and a list of five key functions of persons responsible for implementing the model were provided.

The remaining portion of the article was devoted to a description of three management forms that constitute our IEP approach. These forms, entitled the *Strength-A-Lyzer, Compactor,* and *Management Plan for Individual and Small Group Investigations of Real Problems,* represent a step-by-step procedure for translating theoretical principles derived from the research literature into actual classroom learning activities for gifted and talented students.

References

Renzulli, J. S. *The Enrichment Triad Model: A Guide for Developing Defensible Programs for the Gifted and Talented.* Mansfield Center, CT: Creative Learning Press, 1977.

Renzulli, J. S., Smith, L. H., White, A. J., Callahan, C. M. & Hartman, R. K. *Scales for Rating the Behavioral Characteristics of Superior Students.* Mansfield Center, CT: Creative Learning Press, 1976.

Renzulli, J. S. *The Interest-A-Lyzer.* Mansfield Center, CT: Creative Learning Press, 1977.

Renzulli, J. S. & Smith, L. H. *The Learning Styles Inventory: A Measure of Student Preference for Instructional Techniques.* Mansfield Center, CT: Creative Learning Press, 1978.

Renzulli, J. S. & Smith, L. H. *A Guidebook for Developing Individualized Educational Programs (IEP) for Gifted and Talented Students.* Mansfield Center, CT: Creative Learning Press, 1979.

Renzulli, J. S. & Smith, L. H. *The Strength-A-Lyzer.* Mansfield Center, CT: Creative Learning Press, 1978.

Renzulli, J. S. & Smith, L. H. *The Compactor.* Mansfield Center, CT: Creative Learning Press, 1978.

Renzulli, J. S. & Smith, L. H. *Management Plan for Individual and Small Group Investigations of Real Problems.* Mansfield Center, CT: Creative Learning Press, 1977.

Sandra N. Kaplan

The Should Nots and Shoulds of Developing An Appropriate Curriculum for the Gifted

Any discussion concerning an appropriate curriculum for the gifted must address the issues and elements that should as well as those that should not define such a curriculum. Most descriptions of curriculum for the gifted focus on the shoulds of curriculum development because it is assumed that the should nots can be inferred from the shoulds and that the should nots are probably better left unstated. Both of these assumptions are faulty. Recognition of the should nots for developing curriculum for the gifted can underscore the importance of the shoulds that govern the dimensions of such a curriculum. In addition, recognition of the should nots can serve as a reference for determining what an appropriate curriculum for the gifted should be.

An analysis of current curricular practices, a survey of the literature regarding curriculum for the gifted and attention to the types of questions and requests made by educators and parents in school and conference settings design to inform them about curricular issues and elements assist in identifying some generalizations that define what curriculum for the gifted *should not* be.

1. *A curriculum for the gifted should not be exploitative of the gifted learner or the teacher of the gifted.* Often the content area and skills selected for the curriculum are those which preen the student's or the teacher's abilities to the school or community. An example of this is the curriculum designed to develop highly specialized techniques and products necessary to achieve personal status for the student by winning popular accolades or to achieve professional status for the teacher by being acclaimed as the outstanding teacher in the school or district. Learning experiences used as a means toward outcomes that extort or exhibit the learner's or teacher's abilities are sometimes used to illustrate or verify the concept of giftedness and to present evidence of the individual and societal worth of gifted programs. Support for such a curriculum is sometimes based on the idea that it serves to motivate excellence in both teaching and learning. Validation of the appropriateness of this type of curriculum for the gifted is

351

sometimes expressed by the number of scholarships and awards gifted students have obtained as a consequence of the curriculum. However, a curriculum that places emphasis on the learner as the object or product rather than the subject or focus of the curriculum is exploitative of the gifted learner.

Curriculum for the gifted should not be designed to enhance giftedness at the expense of failing the individuals for whom the curriculum was intended. This is not to say that if gifted students are the recipients of honors, they have been victims of an exploitative curriculum. The underlying rationale for deriving learning experiences in an exploitative curriculum is to attain mastery and success that is specified to criteria, such as placement on tests in contests, and/or with peers. The difference between an exploitative and appropriate curriculum for the gifted is dependent on the type of anticipated outcomes or objectives that govern the selection of content, processes, and products to be included in the curriculum. Whereas the outcome for an exploitative curriculum is to gain recognition for ability, the outcome for the appropriate curriculum is to cater to the development of ability.

2. *A curriculum for the gifted should not be designed to disprove the learners' giftedness.* Curriculum decisions that are referenced to expectations of the "ideal" gifted student result in a set of learning experiences that are inappropriately matched the the functional level of the actual gifted learner who will experience the curriculum. In such instances, the incongruity that emerges between the anticipated outcomes of the curriculum and the performance of the learner causes teachers and parents to challenge the learner's giftedness. Awareness of the discrepancy between the curricular expectations and the learner's performance reveal less concern for the curriculum than the learner as a source of the difficulty. Seldom is the curriculum reexamined to verify its appropriateness for the gifted learner. Subsequently it is assumed that faulty identification procedures and the student's lack of ability become the factors responsible for the student's unsuccessful learning endeavors. In essence, the curriculum that is founded on an unrealistic understanding of the definition of giftedness and perceptions of what the gifted need and can do becomes a tool to disprove the child's giftedness.

3. *An appropriate curriculum for the gifted should not become a vehicle for the popular or current educational trends that do not seem to fit into other types of curricula.* Oftentimes the determinants of a curriculum for the gifted are the most current educational areas of emphasis rather than the needs and interests of the gifted learners. To some, the curriculum for the gifted is a catch-all for those topics, skills and products that educators do not see as being relevant to other types of learners. For example, it is often perceived that gifted students have already mastered the regular curriculum and therefore, have time to become involved in the current educational trends. The inclusion or reservation of the most current or popular educational concerns for the gifted is also believed by some to

earmark the differences that differentiate the curriculum for the gifted. However, an appropriate curriculum for the gifted analyzes and incorporates current educational trends into the curriculum as they relate to the purposes held for the curriculum and the identified needs, interests, and abilities of the gifted student.

4. *An appropriate curriculum for the gifted should not represent or stress a single point of view regarding the means for educating the gifted.* In an attempt to define and develop curriculum for the gifted, educators have been eager to accept possible theories and models to achieve this end. The ambiguity about what constitutes an appropriate curriculum for the gifted and the variety of alternatives available to those defining curriculum for the gifted has resulted in some educators selecting or aligning themselves with a single philosophical or technical model. Some curriculum developers chose to match their curriculum to a particular philosophy or model rather than to select elements from various philosophies and models and integrate them into a curriculum appropriate to their gifted population.

To some degree the polarization of curriculum developers into a "camp" is related to the need to accommodate the gifted without sufficient knowledge or time to do so. In addition, educators often seek to sell rather than explain their theories and models by using past successes as the basis for suggesting total rather than selective adoption. The theories and models selected to formulate an appropriate curriculum for the gifted should be derived from an acceptable set of predetermined and specific objectives. In this way, theories and models become the *means* to the ends (the objectives) of the curriculum rather than the ends. Development of an appropriate curriculum is dependent on learner suitability; it is not dependent on the popularity of given theories or models.

5. *An appropriate curriculum for the gifted should not be based on a series of content-free nonrelated activities.* In order to formulate a curriculum for the gifted, educators often select exposure activities rather than learning experiences. Whereas exposure activities usually introduce a skill in a one-shot game-oriented manner that is independent of specific or relevant content, learning experiences introduce skills in a content-related manner that extends or reinforces these skills with continuity over a period of time. Exposure activities are basically a series of disjointed tasks that students seem to enjoy, but do not seem to make a significant impact on learning. An illustration of the differences between an exposure activity and a learning experience can be noted in the difference between having a student do page 14 of a critical thinking workbook one day and Exercise B on problem solving the next day versus integrating critical thinking and problem solving skills into a particular unit of study. A curriculum for the gifted that simply exposes student to a variety of activities disregards the principles of learning and arouses suspicion about the intent of curriculum for these learners.

6. *An appropriate curriculum for the gifted should not assume that*

353

teaching is not necessary and that the gifted can be self-taught. The concept that the gifted do not need to be taught because they can learn on their own has been translated into curricular designs that emphasize self-teaching. Such curricula presupposes that the gifted have already mastered the prerequisites needed for successful learning, that the allocation of time and materials is all that is needed to facilitate learning, and that the gifted have unilateral abilities that enable them to learn anything at anytime. While some educators rationalize the self-taught curriculum because they lack funding for staff appointments to teach the gifted and while others postulate that a self-taught curriculum reinforces the development of independence or self-directedness, the fact remains that a self-taught curriculum can facilitate personal failure as well as cognitive and/or affective growth. Basically, self-taught curriculum frees educators from their responsibility to the gifted and robs the gifted of their right and need to be taught. An appropriate curriculum for the gifted balances teachers and student-directed learning experience according to the anticipated outcomes of the curriculum and an awareness of learner need relative to the attainment of these outcomes.

The formation of an appropriate curriculum for the gifted is predicted on certain elements and issues. These must be considered as the basis for arriving at a philosophy and an organizational framework for defining what the curriculum for the gifted *should be.*

1. *An appropriate curriculum for the gifted should be derived from an understanding of the differences that characterize the gifted learners from other types of learners, the differences found among gifted learners, and the relationship of these differences to the purposes for educating the gifted.* When the curriculum is determined by responses from how-to questions rather than why questions posed by those responsible to design curriculum, extraneous and expeditious criteria govern curricular decisions. The result is a curriculum that is more reflective of teacher needs as opposed to student needs. However, unless the developers of curriculum are encouraged to ask why questions *prior* to or in *conjunction* with how-to questions, relevance and substantiation of the curriculum's appropriateness for the gifted could be ignored. Teachers should be able to explain *why* a particular experience has been selected for the gifted as well as being able to know how to make the experience available to the learner. Why the curriculum is appropriate for the gifted forms the rationale or guidelines for framing and determining an appropriate curriculum for the gifted.

The curriculum development flow-chart provides a structure for deriving curriculum from an understanding of the gifted learner. Beginning with a delineation of the characteristics of the gifted population, implications for the teaching/learning process are defined and subsequently translated into the specific content, process, and product elements for the curriculum. These elements are then integrated into a set of objectives or learning experiences that comprise the curriculum. It is at this point that responses to how-to questions are appropriately regarded. This flow-chart places prime importance on clarifying the why for a curriculum before attending to the what's and how-to's.

2. *An appropriate curriculum for the gifted is a comprehensive set of learning experiences that mutually reinforce specified content, process, and product elements selected to attain the goals underlying education for the gifted.* The development of the learning experiences that comprise a curriculum for the gifted is contingent on a predetermined and specific definition of content (concepts, generalizations, theories), process (skills), and products (expressive outcomes). The organization of the learning experiences should be related to a topic, theme, issue, or problem that serve as the framework to give unity and structure to the total curriculum. A curriculum that is founded on these factors should:

—integrate content, process and product to form a set of learning experiences directed toward identified ends.

—provide multiple and varied opportunities to introduce, reinforce and/or extend the specified content, process, and product of the curriculum into learning experiences that encourage mastery and transfer of these elements to a variety of learning situations.

—determines the criteria for the selection of materials and activities to augment the curriculum.

Perhaps the most crucial step in developing curriculum for the gifted is to specify content, process and product elements so they are appropriate for the gifted:

Content—Introduction of the more abstract and/or complex concepts, generalizations or theories that are an extension of, an addition to, or a replacement for the regular curriculum.

Process— Reinforcement of basic or rudimentary skills and the introduction of creative, critical, problem-solving, and logic skills and research skills.

Product—Introduction of methods, techniques, and media to present or exhibit learned content and process and/or the means and the procedures that encourage new ways to reconceptualize or structure what is to be or has been learned.

After delineating the content, process, and product elements for the curriculum, the curriculum developer must integrate the knowledge to be assimilated (content) with the skills (process) and a mode of expression (product) into a set of learning experiences.

3. *An appropriate curriculum for the gifted introduces and reinforces the content, process, and product elements of the curriculum as they relate to other subject areas for different purposes and varied times.* The expectation that the gifted learner will or can transfer and/or integrate learning from one curricular area to another curricular area without provisions for such action included as part of each curriculum is erroneous. Teachers' remarks that express displeasure about the gifted learner's inability to evidence proficiency in content, process or product elements from one curriculum to

another curriculum is often the result of the curriculum and not the fault of the learner.

Unless coordination and articulation between curricula for the gifted are considered to be an important part of the curriculum development process, the gifted learner should not be expected to transfer and integrate learnings from one curriculum to another. Too often, those designated with the responsibility to formulate the curriculum for the gifted do so in isolation from the regular curriculum or in isolation from other curriculum developers. Consequently, gifted students are not given opportunities to practice or apply learnings in a variety of subject areas. In such situations, students also fail to see the relevance of what has been learned in the curriculum designed for them. Lack of communication about the content, process, and product elements of a curriculum for the gifted that can be integrated with other types of curricula exonorates teachers from a commitment to reinforce these elements in their curricula. This is especially true when a curriculum for the gifted has been developed for pull-out or honors programs.

4. *An appropriate curriculum for the gifted emphasizes the importance of principles of learning and incorporates them into the planning and development of the learning experiences that comprise the curriculum.* While it is accepted that learning is dependent on principles of learning (such as readiness, motivation, appropriate practice, transfer and feedback), these principles are often ignored in the development of curriculum for and in the teaching of gifted students. Some feel that the characteristics of giftedness transcends the need to attend to these principles for the gifted learner. For example, some believe that since the gifted are those who have multiple interests and exhibit curiosity, it is unnecessary to motivate these learners. Unfortunately, the gifted learner is *expected* to be able and willing to participate in the curriculum designed for the gifted without need for prior instruction or concern for personal interests, needs, or abilities. An analysis of each learning experience that identifies the present status of the gifted learner in relationship to the principles of learning could serve to modify the task so it more adequately defines the teaching/learning process for the gifted.

Defining and developing curriculum for the gifted is not an easy task. It is confounded by the proliferation of ideas and materials about what an appropriate curriculum for the gifted should be and the number of protagonists and antagonists of gifted education that willingly proclaim what curriculum for these students should not be. Therefore, it is incumbent on the curriculum developer to assess the shoulds and should nots related to curriculum for the gifted in order to arrive at a philosophy that can be used to derive an appropriate curriculum for these students.

TABLE 1

CURRICULUM DEVELOPMENT FLOW CHART

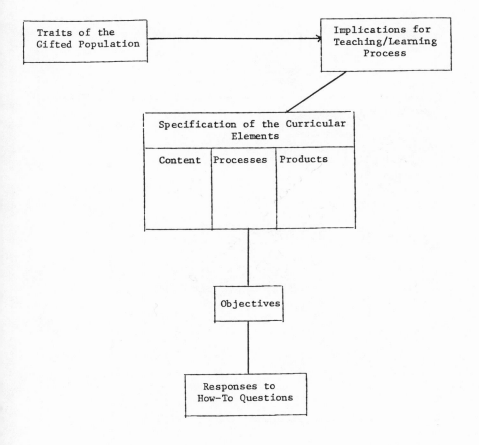

CURRICULUM ACTIVITIES GRID

Issue/Problem/Theme: EXPLORATION

Strategy: CRITICAL THINKING

PROCESSES/SKILLS

	DIFFEREN-TIATE FACT FROM FICTION	JUSTIFY OR NEGATE AN ASSUMPTION	EVALUATE WITH ESTABLISHED CRITERIA		
CHARACTERIS-TICS OF THE "EXPLORER" IN DIFFERENT DISCIPLINES	DIFFERENTIATE THE TRUE FROM STEREOTYPICAL CHARACTERISTICS OF AN EXPLORER IN A PARTICULAR CONTENT AREA, BY WRITING A PERSONAL PROFILE OF THE EXPLORER.				MURAL
THE EFFECT OF AN EXPLORATION ON SOCIETY					MULTI-MEDIA ORAL REPORT
CULTURAL, POLITICAL, ECONOMIC REASONS FOR EXPLORING		DEVELOP A SET OF ASSUMPTIONS ABOUT WHY A PARTICULAR EXPLORATION TOOK PLACE AND JUSTIFY OR NEGATE THESE ASSUMPTIONS WITH RESEARCH. PRESENT YOUR FINDINGS IN A MULTI-MEDIA ORAL REPORT			PERSONAL PROFILE

DELINEATION OF CONTENT

DELINEATION OF PRODUCTS

358

Donald J. Treffinger
John Curtis Gowan

An Updated Representative List of Methods and Educational Programs for Stimulating Creativity*

*T*his list of methods and programs has been developed for two major purposes: first, to serve as a source of references for further study of particular methods and programs; and second, as an indication of the relationship of a wide variety of methods and programs to the common goals of creative development and expression. Many of the items described first appeared in the *Creative Behavior Guidebook* by Sidney J. Parnes, published by Charles Scribner's Sons.

No attempt has been made to provide detailed explanations of any of the methods or programs. Nor is the list intended to be completely comprehensive or critical; certainly, we have not uncovered every possible resource which might have been included. Neither is every item which has been included of equal quality or importance. This compilation attempts to provide merely a representative listing of the great range of available methods, resources, and programs.

1. Affective Domain

Stimulation of the feelings and emotions of persons, to improve or enhance sensitivity to feelings, environments, and responses of others, as well as to develop values and release creative potential.

> Borton, T. *Reach, Touch, and Teach.* New York: McGraw-Hill, 1970.
> Brown, G. I. *Human Teaching for Human Learning.* New York: Viking, 1971.

Treffinger, Donald J. and Gowan, John Curtis "An Updated Representative List of Methods and Educational Programs for Stimulating Creativity." *The Journal of Creative Behavior*, Vol. 5, No. 2, Second Quarter, 1971, pp. 127-139.

*An updated version of an article which appeared in the "Creative Behavior Guidebook" by Sidney J. Parnes, published by Charles Scribner's Sons.

Casebeer, R. L. *Project Prometheus: Education for the Technetronic Age.* (1968). Jackson County Schools, 1133 South Riverside, Medford, Oregon, 97501.

Greenberg, H. M. *Teaching With Feeling.* New York: Macmillan, 1969.

Gunther, B. *Sense Relaxation.* New York: Collier, 1968.

Johnson, J. L. & Seagull, A. A. "Form and function in the affective training of teachers." *Phi Delta Kappan,* 1968, 50, 166.

Krathwohl, D. R., Bloom, B. S. & Masia, B. B. *Taxonomy of Educational Objectives, Handbook II: The Affective Domain.* New York: David McKay, 1964.

Mager, R. F. *Developing Attitude Toward Learning.* Palo Alto, California: Fearon, 1968.

Neill, A. S. *Summerhill: a Radical Approach to Child Rearing.* New York: Hart Publishing, 1960.

Rogers, C. R. *On Becoming a Person.* Boston: Houghton-Mifflin, 1961.

Rogers, C. R. *Freedom to Learn.* Columbus: Merrill, 1969.

Shaftel, F. *Role Playing for Social Values.* Englewood Cliffs: Prentice-Hall, 1967.

Spolin, V. *Improvisation for the Theater.* Evanston, Illinois: Northwestern University Press, 1967.

Weinstein, G. & Fantini, M. D. *Toward Humanistic Education: a Curriculum of Affect.* New York: Praeger, 1970.

2. Attribute Listing

Emphasizes the detailed observation of each particular characteristic or quality of an item or situation. Attempts are then made to profitably change the characteristic or to relate it to a different item. See: Crawford, R. P. *Direct Creativity* (with attribute listing). Wells, Vermont: Fraser, 1964.

3. Awareness Development

A program to increase the individual's sensitivity to what is going on within himself and how he relates to the here and now. See: Perls, F. S., Hefferline, R. F. & Goodman, P. *Gestalt Therapy.* New York: Julian Press, 1951.

4. Biographical Film Program

An educational program of ten documentary biographical films and a flexible textbook. It provides filmed contact with exemplary personalities and opportunity to draw from students' own inner resources in expressing themselves. Designed for college-bound students. See: Drews, E. M. & Knowlton, D. "The being and becoming series for college-bound students". *Audiovisual Instruction,* 1963 (January), 8, 29-32.

5. Bionics

A technique which seeks discovery in nature of ideas which are related to the solution of man's problems. For example, attributes of the eye of a beetle have suggested new types of groundspeed indicators for aircraft. See: "Bionics". *J. Creative Behavior,* 1968, 1, 52-57.

6. Brainstorming

Promotes rapid and unfettered associations in group discussions through deferment-of-judgment. See: Osborn, A. F. *Applied Imagination.* New York: Scribners, 1963.

7. Candid Camera Films

The Cornell Candid Camera Collection, which includes films originally made for and used by the television program, has many delightful short films which illustrate principles of creative problem solving and effective (as well as not-so-effective) thinking. Write for further information and catalog to: Du Art Film Laboratories, Du Art Film Building, 245 West 55th Street, New York, New York 10019.

8. Checklists

Focuses one's attention on a logical list of diverse categories to which the problem could conceivably relate. See: Osborn, A. F. *Applied Imagination.* New York: Scribners, 1963.
(See also Think Products).

9. Classroom Teaching and Creativity

Many articles and books have been addressed to the classroom teacher, providing ideas for encouraging creativity in the classroom. The following bibliography summarizes some useful resources:

Burton, W. H., Kimball, R. B. & Wing, R. I. *Education for effective thinking.* New York: Appleton-Century-Crofts, 1960. (pp. 323-6, 342-3 in partic.)
Carlson, R. K. "Emergence of creative personality." *Childhood Education,* 1960, 36, 402-404.

Cole, H. P. "Process curricula and creative development." *Journal of Creative Behavior,* 1969, 3, 243-259.

Givens, P. R. "Identifying and encouraging creative processes." *Journal of Higher Education,* 1962, 33, 295-301.

Hallman, R. J. "Techniques of creative teaching." *Journal of Creative Behavior,* 1967, 1, 325-330.

Hughes, H. K. "The enchancement of creativity." *Journal of Creative Behavior,* 1969, 3, 73-83.

Hutchinson, W. L. "Creative and productiive thinking in the classroom." *Journal of Creative Behavior,* 1967, 1, 419-427.

Kranyik, R. D. & Wagner, R. A. "Creativity and the elementary school teacher." *Elementary School Journal,* 1965, 66, 2-9.

Rusch, R. R., Denny, D. & Ives, S. "Fostering creativity in the sixth grade." *Elementary School Journal,* 1965, 65, 262-268.

Smith, J. A. *Setting conditions for creative teaching in the elementary school.* Boston: Allyn and Bacon, 1966. (Also: several companion paperbacks dealing with specific subject areas.)

Strang, R. "Creativity in the elementary school classroom." *NEA Journal,* 1961, 50, 20-22.

Taylor, C. W. & Harding, H. F. "Questioning and creating a model for curriculum reform." *Journal of Creative Behavior,* 1967, 1, 22-33.

Torrance, E. P. *Guiding creative talent.* Englewood Cliffs: Prentice Hall, 1962.

Torrance, E. P. *Rewarding Creative Behavior.* Englewood Cliffs: Prentice Hall, 1965.

Torrance, E. P. "Developing creativity through school experiences." In Parnes, S. J. and H. Harding (Eds.) *A Source Book For Creative Thinking.* New York: Scribners, 1962, pp. 31-47.

Torrance, E. P. *Encouraging Creativity in the Classroom.* Dubuque, Iowa: William C. Brown, 1970.

Torrance, E. P. & Myers, R. *Creative Learning and Teaching.* New York: Dutton, 1970.

Wodtke, K. & Wallen, N. "Teacher classroom control, pupil creativity, and pupil classroom behavior." *Journal of Experimental Education,* 1965, 34, 59-65.

10. Collective Notebook

Participants record their thoughts about a problem several times daily, then review the list, selecting the most promising ideas for further investigation. See: Haefele, J. W. *Creative Innovation.* New York: Reinhold, 1962.

11. Creative Analysis

A program of exercises designed to increase the college student's facility in discovering relationships within the knowledge he possesses, and thereby in creating new knowledge. Emphasizes words as tools of the mind and the thought process. See: Upton, A. & Samson, R., *Creative Analysis.* New York: Dutton, 1964.

12. Creative Instructions

Emphasizes how instructions are given (problem presented, etc.) as a key determinant in stimulating individual or group production of creative responses. See unpublished doctoral dissertation (67-15607), Colgrove, Melba, Annetta. "Stimulating Creative Problem Solving Performance Innovative Set". University of Michigan, 1967.

13. Creative Thinking Workbook

A program for adults and college-level students; many exercises suitable for high school students. The exercises are designed to remove internal governors and to provide practice in stretching the imagination problem-finding and problem-solving. Problems are included on product design and on presenting ideas. Can be self-instructional. Available from: W. O. Uraneck, 56 Turning Mill Road, Lexington, Massachusetts 02173 (1963).

14. Curriculum — General

Many recent developments in curriculum and instruction have been concerned with providing opportunities for creative growth. In this section, and the next five, several representative publications are listed in a variety of curriculum areas. (See also Affective Domain.)

Franco, J. M. *Project Beacon.* Public Schools, Rochester, New York 14608. (Concerned with the development of ego strength in primary grades.)

Gibson, J. S. *The Intergroup Relations Curriculum.* Medford, Massachusetts: Tufts University Press.

Jaynes, R. & Woodbridge, B. *Bowman Early Childhood Series.* Glendale, California: Bowman Publishing, 1969. (Designed to help develop positive self-awareness and identity, awareness of self as a person, ability to relate to others.)

Kreese, F. H. *Match Projects.* Boston: American Science and Engineering, Inc., 20 Overland Street. (Materials and activities across many areas, for grades 4-6+).

Massialas, B. G. & Zevin, J. *Creative Encounters in the Classroom.* New York: Wiley, 1967.

For anthologies dealing with educational and curricular implications of creativity studies:

Gowan, J. C., Demos, G. D. & Torrance, E. P. (Eds.) *Creativity: its Educational Implications.* New York: Wiley, 1967.

Davis, G. A. & Scott, J. A. (Eds.) *Training Creative Thinking.* New York: Holt, Rinehart, and Winston, 1971.

Treffinger, D. J. (Ed.) *Readings on Creativity in Education.* To be published by Prentice-Hall, Inc.

15. Curriculum—Mathematics

Davis, R. B. *The Madison Project.* Reading, Massachusetts: Addison Wesley. Five different curricula; grades 2-8.

Matthews, G. *Nuffield Mathematics Project.* New York: Wiley. A British program for ages 5-13.

Werntz, J. H. *MINNEMAST Project.* For grades K-6; write: 720 Washington Avenue SE, Minneapolis, Minnesota 55414.

16. Curriculum—Preprimary

Dunn, L. M. *Peabody Language Development Kit.* American Guidance Publishers, Circle Pines, Minnesota 55014.

Frostig, M. *Frostig Visual Perception Program.* Chicago: Follett.

Stendler, C. *Early Childhood Curriculum: a Piaget Approach.* Boston: American Science and Engineering.

For research on creativity among preprimary children, contact Professor Elizabeth Starkweather, Oklahoma State University, Stillwater, Oklahoma.

17. Curriculum—Reading, Literature, Language Arts

Clymer, T. et al. *Reading 360.* Boston: Ginn and Company, 1969. An innovative series, in which E. Paul Torrance served as creativity consultant.

Medeiros, V. *The Voices of Man Literature Series.* Reading, Massachusetts: Addison-Wesley. High school literature series for disadvantaged students.

Moffet, J. *A Student Centered Language Arts Curriculum.* (Volume 1: K-6; Volume 2: K-13). Boston: Houghton Mifflin, 1968.

18. Curriculum—Science

Brown, R. R. *Elementary Science Study.* (K-6). Manchester, Missouri: Webster Division, McGraw-Hill.

Karplus, R. & Thier, H. D. *Science Curriculum Improvement Study.* (K-6). Chicago: Rand-McNally.

LaSalle, D. Write for information concerning an independent science center. *Talcott Mountain Science Center,* Montevideo Road, Avon, Connecticut 06001.

Mayor, J. *Science: a Process Approach.* (K-6). New York: Xerox Corporation.

Washton, N. S. *Teaching Science Creatively.* Philadelphia: W. B. Saunders, 1967.

Anderson, R. D., DeVito, A., Dyrli, O. E., Kellogg, M., Kochendorfer, L. & Weigand, J. *Developing Childrens' Thinking Through Science.* Englewood Cliffs: Prentice-Hall, 1970.

19. Curriculum—Social Studies

Bruner, J. S. *Man: a Course of Study.* Curriculum Development Associates, 1211 Connecticut Ave., NW, Washington, D. C. 20036.

Edcom Systems. *Space, Time, and Life.* (Grades 4-6). EDCOM Systems, 145 Witherspoon Road, Princeton, N. J. 08540.

Educational Research Council of America. *Concepts and Inquiry.* (Gr. K-8). Boston: Allyn and Bacon.

Lippitt, R. *Social Science Laboratory Units.* (Gr. 4-6). Chicago: Science Research Associates.

Muessig, R. *Discussion Pictures for Beginning Social Studies.* New York: Harper and Row, 1967.

Taba, H. & Durkin, M. *Taba Social Studies Curriculum.* (Gr. 1-8). Reading, Mass.: Addison-Wesley Co.

20. Delphi Technique

Polling procedure resembling an absentee "brainstorming" effort used to generate alternative futures for a particular topic or series of topics. See: Helmer, Olaf. SOCIAL TECHNOLOGY Basic, 1966. For additional references, contact Book Service, World Future Society, P.O. Box 19285, Twentieth Street Station, Washington, D.C., 20036.

21. Developmental Stage Analysis of Creativity

See: Gowan, J. C. *The Development of the Creative Individual.* (1971). Robert Knapp Pub., Box 7234, San Diego, California, 92107.

22. Experimental Psychology Techniques

Caron, A. J. "A test of Maltzman's theory of originality training." *Journal of Verbal Learning and Verbal Behavior,* 1963, 1, 436-442.

Duncan, C. P. "Attempts to influence performance on an insight problem." *Psychological Reports,* 1961, 9, 35-42.

Gallup, H. F. "Originality in free and controlled association responses." *Psychological Reports,* 1963, 13, 923-929.

Maltzman, I. "On the training of originality." *Psychological Review.* 1960, 67, 229-242.

Maltzman, I., Belloni, Marigold, & Fishbein, M. "Experimental studies of associational variables in originality." *Psychological Monographs,* 1964, 78, 3. (Whole #580).

Maltzman, I., Brooks, L., Bogartz, W. & Summers, S. "The facilitation of problem-solving by prior exposure to uncommon responses." *Journal of Experimental Psychology,* 1958, 56, 339-406.

Maltzman, I., Bogartz, W. & Breger, L. "A procedure for increasing word association originality and its transfer effects." *Journal of Experimental Psychology,* 1958, 56, 392-398.

Maltzman, I. & Gallup, H. F. "Comments on 'originality' in free and controlled association responses." *Psychological Reports,* 1964, 14, 573-574.

Maltzman, I., Simon, S., Raskin, P. & Licht, L. "Experimental studies in the training of originality." *Psychological Monographs,* 1960, 74(6). Whole #493.

23. Forced Relationship Techniques

Specific types of exercises designed to derive new combinations of items and thoughts. See: Whiting, C. S. *Creative Thinking.* New York: Reinhold, 1958. (See also Management of Intelligence; Racking)

24. Futuristics

Predicting the future, with projections for five, ten, and fifty year periods. Write: Carl Gregory, California State College, School of Business, Long Beach, California 90801. Also contact: World Future Society, P.O. Box 19285, 20th St. Station, Washington D.C. 20036.

25. General Semantics

Approaches which help the individual to discover multiple meanings or relationships in words and expressions. See: Hayakawa, S. I. *Language in Thought and Action.* New York: Harcourt, Brace and World, Inc., 1964. For continuing current information, see ETC.: *a Review of General Semantics,* a quarterly journal with editorial offices at San Francisco State College, San Francisco, California 94132. (Business office: 540 Powell Street, San Francisco, California 94108.) See: True, S. R. "A Study of the Relation of General Semantics and Creativity." *Dissertation Abstracts,* 1964, 25 (4), 2390.

(Note: a conference on Creativity and General Semantics was held in conjunction with the 17th Annual Creative Problem-Solving Institute, in June 1971.)

26. Incident Process

A problem-solving approach (and/or training program) developed at the college and adult level. It stresses multiple viewpoints and a wide search for

366

problem-elements; applies many methods similar to the older Job Relations Training program. See: Pigors, P. W. & Pigors, F. C. *Case Method in Human Relations: the Incident Process.* New York: McGraw-Hill, 1961.

27. Kepner-Tregoe Method

An approach (or training program) that emphasizes "what a man *does* with information," i.e., how he interrelates facts in analyzing problems and making decisions. Developed at adult level. See: Kepner, C. H. & Tregoe, B. B. *The Rational Manager.* New York: McGraw-Hill, 1965.

28. Management of Intelligence

A number of techniques for creative problem-solving, including negative ideation, 7 × 7 technique,, and others, are included in: Carl E. Gregory. *The Management of Intelligence: Scientific Problem Solving and Creativity.* New York: McGraw-Hill, 1967.

29. Morphology (or Morphological Analysis)

A system involving the methodical interrelating of all elements of a problem in order to discover new approaches to a solution. See: Allen, M. S. *Morphological Creativity.* Englewood Cliffs, N. J.: Prentice-Hall, 1962.

30. Problem-Solving Training

A program on problem-solving skills for high-IQ first graders. Consists of units called "games." Presented by the teacher as a programmed script for individual instruction (one child at a time). See: Anderson, R. C. "Can First Graders Learn an Advanced Problem-Solving Skill?". *Journal of Educational Psychology,* 1965, 56(6), 283-294.

31. Process Education Resources

A survey of materials and resources which can be utilized in process education: Seferian, A., & Cole, H. P. *Encounters In Thinking: a Compendium of*

Curricula for Process Education. Buffalo, New York: Creative Education Foundation, (Occasional Paper #6).

32. Productive Thinking Program

A self-instructional program for the upper elementary grades. It attempts to help children improve their creative problem-solving ability. To be published, in an expanded version, by Charles E. Merrill, Inc., of Columbus, Ohio. Considerable research has been conducted in which the original version of the *Productive Thinking Program* was used; much of this research is reviewed in: Treffinger, D. J. & Ripple, R. E. "Programmed instruction in creative problem-solving." *Educational Leadership,* 1971, 28, 667-675. Other published reports include:

Covington, M. V. "Some experimental evidence on teaching for creative understanding." *The Reading Teacher,* 1967 (Feb.), 390-396.

Covington, M. V. & Crutchfield, R. S. "Facilitation of creative problem-solving." *Programmed Instruction,* 1965, 4, 3-5, 10.

Crutchfield, R. S. "Creative thinking in children: its teaching and testing." In: H. Brim, R. Crutchfield and W. Holtzman (Eds.) *Intelligence: Perspectives 1965.* New York: Harcourt, Brace, and World, 1966 (pp. 33-64.)

Crutchfield, R. S. "Instructing the individual in creativity." In: Educational Testing Service's *Individualizing Instruction* (Princeton, 1965); also in Mooney and Razik's *Explorations in Creativity* (1967), pp. 196-206.

Crutchfield, R. S. & Covington, M. V. "Programmed instruction and creativity." *Programmed Instruction,* 1965, 4, 1-2, 8-10.

Evans, D., Ripple, R. E. & Treffinger, D. J. "Programmed instruction and productive thinking: a preliminary report of a cross-national comparison." In: Dunn, W. R. & Holyroyd, C., (Eds.) *Aspects of Educational Technology.* London: Methuen, 1968 (115-120).

Olton, R. M. "A self-instructional program for the development of productive thinking in fifth- and sixth-grade children." In: F. E. Williams (Ed.) *First Seminar on Productive Thinking in Education.* St. Paul, Minnesota: Macalester College, 1966, 53-60.

Olton, R. M. "A self-instructional program for developing productive thinking skills in fifth- and sixth-grade children." *Journal of Creative Behavior,* 1969, 3, 16-25.

Olton, R. M. & Crutchfield, R. S. "Developing the skills of productive thinking." In: Mussen, P., Langer, J. & Covington, M. (Eds.) *New directions in developmental psychology.* New York: Holt, Rinehart, and Winston, 1969.

Olton, R. M., Wardrop, J., Covington, M., Goodwin, W., Crutchfield, R., Klausmeier, H. & Ronda, T. "The development of productive thinking skills in fifth-grade children." Technical Report #34. Madison: University of Wisconsin Rand D Center for Cognitive Learning, 1967.

Ripple, R. E. & Dacey, J. S. "The facilitation of problem-solving and verbal creativity by exposure to programed instruction." *Psychology in the Schools,* 1967, 4, 240-245.

Treffinger, D. J. & Ripple, R. E. *The effects of programed instruction in productive thinking on verbal creativity and problem-solving among elementary school children.* Ithaca, New York: Cornell University, 1968. Final Report of USOE Research Project OEG-0-8-080002-0220-010.

Treffinger, D. J. & Ripple, R. E. "The effects of programed instruction in productive thinking on verbal creativity and problem-solving among pupils in grades four through seven." *Irish Journal of Education,* 1970, 4, 47-59.

Treffinger, D. J. & Ripple, R. E. "Developing creative problem-solving abilities and related attitudes through programed instruction." *Journal of Creative Behavior,* 1969, 3, 105-110.

Wardrop, J. L., Olton, R., Goodwin, W., Covington, M., Klausmeier, H., Crutchfield, R. & Ronda, T. "The development of productive thinking skills in fifth-grade children." *Journal of Experimental Education,* 1969, 37, 67-77.

33. Psychodramatic Approaches

These include a variety of techniques such as role playing and role reversal. In psychodrama the attempt is made to bring into focus all elements of an individual's problem; whereas in sociodrama the emphasis is on shared problems of group members. Elements of these techniques have been used in various types of educational settings and training programs. See: Moreno, J. L., *Who Shall Survive?,* New York: Beacon House, 1953. For current reading, see the quarterly journal *Group Psychotherapy* by the same publisher.

34. Purdue Creativity Training Program

The *Purdue Creativity Training Program* consists of 28 audio tapes and accompanying printed exercises, for the development of creative thinking and problem-solving abilities among elementary school pupils. For further information, write: John F. Feldhusen or Donald J. Treffinger, Educational Psychology Section, Purdue University, South Campus Courts G, Lafayette, Indiana 47907. Published descriptions and research reports include:

Bahlke, S. J. *A study of the enhancement of creative abilities in elementary school children.* Unpublished master's thesis, Purdue University, 1967.

Bahlke, S. J. *Componential evaluation of creativity instructional materials.* Unpublished doctoral thesis, Purdue University, 1969.

Feldhusen, J. F., Bahlke, S. J. & Treffinger, D. J. "Teaching creative thinking." *Elementary School Journal,* 1969, 70, 48-53.

Feldhusen, J. F., Treffinger, D. J. & Bahlke, S. J. "Developing creative thinking: the Purdue Creativity Program." *Journal of Creative Behavior,* 1970, 4, 85-90.

Robinson, W. L. T. *Taped-creativity-series versus conventional teaching and learning.* Unpublished master's thesis, Atlanta University, 1969.

WBAA. *Creative Thinking: the American Pioneers.* (A manual for teachers). West Lafayette, Indiana: Purdue University, 1966.

35. Racking Techniques

(also 7×7 technique and other forcing techniques)
See: Gregory, C. E. *Management of Intelligence: Scientific Problem-Solving & Creativity.* New York: McGraw-Hill, 1967.

36. Self-Enhancing Education

Emphasis on basic principles of creative problem-solving, including education for setting as well as solving one's own problems. See: Randolph, Norma & Howe, W. A. *Self-Enhancing Education, a Program to Motivate Learners.* Sanford Press, Sanford Office, 200 California Avenue, Palo Alto, California, 1967.

37. Self-Instructional Course in Applied Imagination

Programmed set of 28 self-instructional booklets. For complete curriculum No. 015677 or microfiche of report EDO-10382 write to ERIC Document Report Service, 4936 Fairmont Ave., Bethesda, Maryland 20014.

38. Sensitivity ("T Group")

A training program designed to help a person gain insight into himself and his functioning in a group. It attempts to increase the person's openness to ideas and viewpoints. See: Bradford, Leland P., Gibb, Jack R. & Benne, K. (eds.). *T Group Theory and Laboratory Method.* New York: Wiley, 1964. (See Affective Domain)

39. Structure of Intellect

A model devised by J. P. Guilford giving organization to the various factors of intellect, and arranging them into three grand dimensions: contents, operations, and products.
See: Guilford, J. P. *The Nature of Human Intelligence:* New York: McGraw-Hill Co., 1967.
Guilford, J. P. *Intelligence, Creativity, and Their Educational Implications.* San Diego: Knapp, 1968.

40. Synectics (or Operational Creativity)

A training program which stresses the practical use of analogy and metaphor in problem-solving. The Synectics mechanisms "force new ideas and associations up for conscious consideration rather than waiting for them to arise fortuitously." Developed at adult level. See: Gordon, W. J. *Synectics: the Development of Creative Capacity.* New York: Harper Bros. 1961.

41. Theoretical Issues

The question, "Can creativity be developed?" has interested many scholars, and the literature, both supportive and critical, contains many stimulating papers. Among them are:

Anderson, H. H. "Creativity and education." *College and University Bulletin,* 1961, 13.

Ausubel, D. P. "Fostering creativity in the school." *Proceedings of the Centennial Symposium, "How Children Learn."* Toronto, Ontario, Canada: Phi Delta Kappa and O.I.S.E., 1967, 37-49.

Ausubel, D. P. *Educational psychology: a cognitive view.* New York: Holt, Rinehart and Winston, 1968. (Ch. 16, particularly pp. 549-555, 559-562.)

Ausubel, D. P. & Robinson, F. *School learning.* New York: Holt, Rinehart and Winston, 1969. (Ch. 17, partic. 523-540, 543-4).

Danziger, K. "Fostering creativity in the school: social psychological aspects." *Proceedings of the Centennial Symposium, "How Children Learn."* Toronto: Phi Delta Kappa and O.I.S.E., 1967, 50-59.

deMille, R. "The creativity boom." *Teachers College Record,* 1963, 54, 199+.

Gagne, R. M. *The conditions of learning.* New York: Holt, Rinehart, Winston, 1965. (partic. pp. 166-170.)

Getzels, J. W. "Creativity thinking, problem-solving, and instruction." In NSSE Yearbook, *Theories of learning and instruction.* 1964, 240-267.

Guilford, J. P. "Factors that aid and hinder creativity." *Teachers College Record,* 1962, 63, 391.

Hallman, R. J. "Can creativity be taught?" *Educational Theory,* 1964, 14, 15+.

Parnes, S. J. "Can creativity be increased?" In Parnes and Harding. *A source book for creative thinking.* New York: Charles Scribner's Sons, 1962, pp. 151-168.

Parnes, S. J. *Creative potential and the educational experience.* Buffalo: Creative Education Foundation, 1967. (Occasional Paper #2.)

Taylor, C. W. & Williams, F. E. (Eds.) *Instructional Media and Creativity.* New York: Wiley, 1966.

Taylor, C. W. & Williams, F. E. (Eds.) *Instructionnal Media and Creativity.* New York: Wiley, 1966.

White, W. F. *Psychosocial principles applied to classroom teaching.* New York: McGraw-Hill, 1969, (Ch. 7, particularly pp. 136ff.)

42. Think Products

A series of materials for teachers and industry to stimulate creative performance. Included is a series of TNT materials for teachers (techniques and tips) and a little magazine called "The Creative Thinker". Available from Think Products, 1209 Robin Hood Circle, Towson, Md. 21204.

43. Thinking Creatively

Gary A. Davis, Department of Educational Psychology, University of Wisconsin, Madison, Wisconsin, has been active in research on the development of creative thinking abilities, and in constructing instructional programs and materials as well. He has also published with Joseph A. Scott, an anthology entitled, "Training Creative Thinking". New York: Holt, Rinehart, and Winston, 1971. Related articles and materials include:

> Davis, G. A. "Training creativity in adolescents: a discussion of strategy." *Journal of Creative Behavior,* 1969, 3, 95-104.
> Davis, G. A. & Houtman, S. E. *Thinking creatively: a guide to training imagination.* Madison: University of Wisconsin Res. and Devel. Center for Cognitive Learning, 1968.
> Davis, G. A., Houtman, S., Warren, T. & Roweton, W. "A program for training creative thinking: I. Preliminary Field Test." Madison: University of Wisconsin, Res. and Devel. Center for Cognitive Learning, 1969.
> Davis, G. A. & Manske, M. "An instructional method of increasing originality." *Psychonomic Science,* 1966, 6, 73-74.
> Davis, G. A. & Roweton, W. "Using idea checklists with college students: overcoming resistance." *Journal of Psychology,* 1968, 70, 221-226.
> Manske, M. & Davis, G. "Effects of simple instructional biases upon performance on the Unusual Uses Tests." *Journal of General Psychology,* 1968, 79, 25-33.

44. Torrance's Materials

E. Paul Torrance, Professor of Educational Psychology at the University of Georgia, Athens, Georgia, has developed with colleagues several sets of instructional materials for fostering creative thinking among elementary school children. His *Ideabooks* series, with Robert Myers, includes "Can You Imagine?", "For Those Who Wonder," "Invitations To Thinking and Doing," "Invitations To Speaking and Writing Creatively," and "Plots, Puzzles, and Ploys." The *Imagicraft* series, with B. F. Cunnington, includes recorded exercises, based on biographical sketches of famous people and the "Sounds and Images" exercises. Most are intended for elementary school children, but contain imaginative exercises which might readily be used with adolescents and adults with minor modifications. For information, write

Ginn and Company, Waltham, Massachusetts 02154. The *Torrance Tests of Creative Thinking* are published by the Personnel Press, Princeton, New Jersey.

See also:

Britton, R. J. *A study of creativity in selected sixth-grade groups.* Unpublished doctoral thesis, University of Virginia, 1967.

Torrance, E. P. & Gupta, R. "Development and evaluation of recorded programed experiences in creative thinking in the fourth grade." Minneapolis: University of Minnesota, Bureau of Educational Research, 1964.

Torrance, E. P. "Priming creative thinking in the primary grades." *Elementary School Journal,* 1961, 62, 34-41.

(See also Classroom Teaching and Creativity above.)

45. Value Engineering (or Value Analysis, Value Innovation, Value Management, Etc.)

Training programs applying general principles of creative problem-solving to group efforts toward reducing costs or optimizing value. Adult level. See: Miles, L. D., *Techniques of Value Analysis and Engineering.* New York: McGraw-Hill, 1961; also Value Engineering Handbook, H111, U. S. Department of Defense, March 29, 1963 (U. S. Government Printing Office, Washington, D. C.). For current information, conference reports, bibliographies, etc., write Society of American Value Engineers, Windy Hill, Suite E-9, 1741 Rosewell Street, Smyrna, Georgia 30080.

46. Wff'n Proof

A symbolic logic game designed to increase one's ability to discover new relationships in a logical manner. Portions applicable at elementary level, proceeding through adult levels. Available from author, L. E. Allen (*WFF'N PROOF, The Game of Modern Logic*), P.O. Box 71, New Haven, Connecticut 06501.

47. Williams' Model

Frank E. Williams, Portland State College, Portland, Oregon, has developed an approach for helping teachers integrate the teaching of cognitive and affective skills with the presentation of subject matter. Recent published reports include:

373

Williams, F. E. "Fostering classroom creativity." *Cal. Teachers Assn. Journal,* March 1961.

Williams, F. E. "The search for the creative teacher." *Cal. Teachers Assn. Journal,* January 1964, 60, 14-16.

Williams, F. E. "Perspective of a model for developing productive-creative behaviors in the classroom." In: Williams, F. E. (Ed.) *First Seminar on Productive Thinking in Education.* St. Paul: Macalester College, 1966, 108-116.

Williams, F. E. "Training children to be creative may have little effect on original classroom performance, unless. . ." *Cal. Journal of Ed. Research,* 1966, 17.

Williams, F. E. "Models for encouraging creativity in the classroom by integrating cognitive-affective behaviors." *Educational Technology,* 1969, 9, 7-13.

Williams, F. E. *Classroom Ideas For Encouraging Thinking and Feeling.* Buffalo, New York: D. O. K. Publishers, 711 East Delevan Avenue, Buffalo, N.Y. 14215.

Williams, F. E. *Media For Developing Creative Thinking in Young Children.* Buffalo, New York: Creative Education Foundation, 1968 (Occasional Paper #3).

48. *Work Simplification*

An industrial training program that applies some of the general principles of creative problem-solving to the simplification of operations or procedures. Provides opportunity for personnel to use their mental resources in helping improve organizational operations, using simple industrial engineering principles. ("Job Methods Training," as well as other similarly named programs of World War II and thereafter, applied the basic concepts of this program.) See: Goodwin, H. F. "Work Simplification" (a documentary series of articles). *Factory Management and Maintenance,* July 1958. Briefer but more recent information may be obtained from Work Simplification Conferences, P.O. Box 30, Lake Placid, New York 12947 and from an article on Work Simplification by Auren Uris in the September 1965 issue of *Factory.*

49. *Young Thinker (1964)*

For children between 5-10 years of age. A series of more than 50 projects and exercises which can be used by the individual or by groups. These have been used in the home and in schools. Available from W. O. Uraneck, 56 Turning Mill Road, Lexington, Massachusetts 02173.

Robert A. Goodale

Methods for Encouraging Creativity in the Classroom

"*T*eaching for creativity" has become a modern pedagogical fad, but, unfortunately, few educationists have taken the time to dig into the research literature to determine exactly what it means to "teach for creativity." The link between creativity and art, music, and dancing has made teaching for creativity synonymous in some instances with increased emphasis on art education and the banishment of "color books," and in other instances with encouraging students to simply "do whatever you'd like to do." Yet the research on creativity suggests that there is far more to the encouragement of creativity than the simple introduction of new books, audio-visual aids, or computer consoles. In an effort to relate this research to the process of encouraging creativity, I would like to spell out several specific ways in which teachers may encourage creativity in the classroom.

Such as it is, the research on creativity to date suggests that more important than the *types of materials* used to promote creativity is the *personality development of the learner*. All psychological studies conducted so far on creative people have concurred in their reporting of an admixture of certain "desirable" and "undesirable" traits in creative people as contrasted with noncreative people. Drevdahl and Cattell (1958) and Cattell (1963) found that writers, artists, and eminent researchers were significantly more intelligent, adventurous, sensitive, self-sufficient, and emotionally stable than the general population. At the same time these creative groups were also seen to be more socially withdrawn, dominant, aloof, nonconformist, bohemian and radical than the general population. Barron (1957) differentiated the 25 most original from the 25 least original of 100 Air Force captains and found the high scorers to be intelligent, widely informed, concerned with basic problems, clever and imaginative, socially effective, personally dominant, verbally fluent, and possessed of initiative. The low scorers were seen as conforming, rigid and stereotyped, uninsightful, commonplace, apathetic, and dull. Rees and Goldman (1961) separated 68 university students into high, middle, and low creative groups on the basis of honors and

Goodale, Robert A. "Methods for Encouraging Creativity in the Classroom." *Journal of Creative Behavior,* Vol. 4, No. 2, Spring, 1970, pp. 91-102.

375

prizes won in their fields. Personality traits were assessed by use of the Guilford-Zimmerman Temperament Survey and the Minnesota Multiphasic Personality Inventory. The initial division into three groups produced no significant differences, but when the high creativity group was further subdivided into high-high and low-high groups, the high-high group was seen as more impulsive, more aggressive, more domineering, and more ascendant than their "bridesmaid" counterparts. Personality adjustment or maladjustment was compared by Rees and Goldman for all three groups, and there was no indication that creativity was related to maladjustment.

Personality Variables Among the Highly Intelligent

The work by Getzels and Jackson (1962), for all its methodological limitations, did serve to point out the wide differences in goals and behaviors between "Highly Intelligent" and "Highly Creative" students. The high creative group was less concerned with conventional vocational goals (teacher, doctor, engineer) and more interested in so-called off-beat vocations (inventor, artist, disc jockey). Neither were they overly concerned with whether or not they possessed the character traits admired by teachers or parents. These highly creative students were more self-reliant and independent, and despite the fact that they scored significantly lower (127) in mean IQ scores than their brighter classmates (150), they attained the same degree of academic achievement as the high intelligence group.

Since the Getzels and Jackson study it has become fashionable to point out that the highly intelligent person is not necessarily the most creative, and later investigations concerned with college grade-point averages have tended to bear this out (Harmon, 1963; Taylor, Smith & Ghiselin, 1963). However, in the haste for those on the short end of the standard intelligence scale to grab at this sign of redemption, they have frequently overlooked the fact that although measured intelligence is not a sufficient condition for high level creative output, it does show up again and again as being a necessary ingredient (Guilford, 1967). Terman's group of 800 men (Terman, 1954) with IQ's above 140 would certainly be tagged as creative by any criterion based on products or eminence. At the average age of 40 this group had published 67 books; 1400 scientific, technical, and professional articles; 200 short stories, novelettes, and plays; 236 miscellaneous articles; and more than 150 patents. Of 112 scientists in the group of 800, 42 were listed in the 1949 edition of *American Men of Science*. In addition, the group produced countless newspaper stories, radio and TV scripts, and secret documents not included in the above count. Surely this record far surpasses the productivity of any 800 men randomly selected from the general population.

What makes Terman's study more relevant for our discussion on the personality correlates of creative people is his further investigation into

376

what he called his A group and his C group. Terman noticed that not all in his group of 800 men had contributed equally, and so he selected from this group the 150 rated highest for success and the 150 rated lowest for success. Success was defined as the extent to which an individual had made use of his superior intellectual ability. The A group was composed of the individuals achieving highest success, the C group those achieving the lowest amount of success. Neither group differed significantly in average IQ, and all were intelligent enough so that lack of intelligence was not a limiting factor in the attainment of success (all had IQ's of 140 or above). What Terman found was that personality and motivational factors prevented the C group from fulfilling their early promise. The C group was rated as non-persistent in striving toward goal achievement (quitters); they showed no "spark" or drive; they lacked self-confidence, and were immobilized by feelings of inferiority. Checking back through his earlier records, Terman found as early as 1922, 18 years before it even occurred to him to separate out the A and C groups from the 800 men, that the A group was then recognized by their raters as significantly superior to the C group in self-confidence, perseverance, and desire to excel. Thus the debilitating personality factors recognized as far back as their high school and college days apparently prevented members of the C group from contributing their expected share of creative products.

Implications for the Teacher

The implications of these studies on the personality correlates of creative people suggests that a major step in encouraging creativity in the classroom is the support of activities which increase the student's self-confidence and persistence, and the toleration by teachers of student behaviors currently seen as "unpleasant." The quiet, well-behaved, bright student may be ideal from the teacher's point of view, since her crammed schedule requires smooth-running efficiency if all topics are to be adequately covered, and the creative child is more apt to want to ask questions or voice his own opinions, thus slowing down the machinery. Sometimes, too, the opinion the creative voices is a negative reaction to teacher-imposed tasks; a reaction which may quickly earn him the title of "troublemaker" from anxious, dogmatic, and authoritarian teachers. The curiosity of the creative child is such that he is more apt to "fool around" with lab materials and attempt things not outlined in the lab manual. Also, because he is less concerned with social conformity, he is more prone toward bohemian dress, and less motivated to gain the highest marks in the class.

The toleration of "unpleasant" (non-teacher-oriented) behaviors does not mean, of course, that teachers must give free license to all behaviors. A necessary amount of social responsibility is always associated with freedom. The young child allowed to get up from his seat and roam around the room when his seat work is completed is not at liberty to disrupt the reading group, nor is the college student who prefers to rephrase the exam question to be rewarded for shoddy work. The important point is that the child or student not be penalized for being different or for exhibiting his independence and curiosity. In most cases what is needed is a reshaping of the traditional classroom so that materials and facilities are arranged in ways that make it convenient for students to move from task to task, rather than in ways that make it easy and convenient for teachers to exercise complete and unyielding control.

Focusing on personality variables suggests that the teacher should be aware of her own personality. No teacher intends to squelch creativity, yet it is obvious that some do. The rigid and compulsive teacher is intolerant of deviations from the lesson plan and penalizes the student who passes his work in late. ("They need to learn to get their work done on time!") Thus, deadlines become more important than quality. The self-conscious teacher, unsure of her ability to control the class, dares not allow students to wander around the room or talk quietly among themselves for fear of precipitating chaos. The narcissistic teacher cannot bear the thought that students may sometimes think of better projects or solutions than she can, and the self-effacing teacher distrusts her own ability to experiment with new methods or materials because she doubts that she can implement them well and fears the ridicule which may accompany failure. Creative behavior is not apt to occur in an environment where creative activity is not encouraged. The teacher who demands that students abide by her wishes on matters that are not really important to social responsibility or intellectual skill can hardly be viewed as encouraging independent thinking.

As the purveyor of rewards and punishments for social and intellectual skills, the teacher stands in an advantageous position for encouraging creativity, curiosity, independence, and self-reliance. When the child shows some independent thinking the teacher can praise him, and when the child shows signs that his personal interests are not being satisfied by a proposed assignment, she can modify the assignment enough for that one child or any others, to include his interests. For example, if the child is interested in the sea and the assignment is on Colonial history, the teacher could suggest that the child write or report about the *Mayflower;* or if the assignment is about the first Thanksgiving, teacher might suggest that the child write about the wisdom of using fish as a fertilizer to grow corn.

The student can be made leader of a group project if he shows the requisite skills, or he can be made a one-man committee if he prefers to work alone. Reinforcement and feedback are powerful influences in shaping behavior, and if creative effort is to be encouraged then the teacher should be alert to see that every effort in the direction of creativity, curiosity, independence, and self-reliance is rewarded. Notes on the margins of college papers are every bit as good as the gold stars given in kindergarten. Papers should be graded as much for new ideas and generalization to other areas as for spelling, neatness, and factual content. Many graduate schools claim that their theses are graded on the former, when, as a matter of fact, they are graded mainly on the latter.

Strategies for Creativity

If a response that is reinforced tends to be emitted again, then the first task for the teacher who wants to encourage creativity in the classroom is to get the student to emit a creative response so that it can be rewarded. This is not so difficult as it sounds, and it may not even require any new materials or texts, although such products are commercially available. What it does require is a change in how topics are taught or how questions about the topic are asked. Frank Williams has formulated an excellent approach to the problem in his enumeration of teaching strategies which encourage creative thinking (Williams, 1968). He lists 23 different strategies such as teaching by paradox (How can we explain poverty in the midst of plenty?), by analogy (Airplane cargo doors designed like the opening of a clam shell), by using examples of deficiencies (What are some things that man does not know?), by making allowances for thinking about possibles and making guesses; teaching the skill for change of things rather than adjustment to things; presenting unsolved social issues or scientific problems and asking the student to go off into his own areas of information to seek solutions; teaching about rigidities, fixations, and habit; showing how failures, mistakes, and accidents have led to the development of worthwhile things; studying creative individuals; etc. Massialas & Zevin (1967) also demonstrate how creative behaviors can be encouraged in the teaching of any subject through the use of open-ended discussions and problem solving. In one instance high school students were asked to interpret a textbook writer's prediction that the continued influx of non-Western immigrants into Israel would soon result in a shift of Israel's foreign policy. In another instance, students in a geography course were asked to select from a map a site for a large city and to defend their choice. A third example was that of students given ten haiku poems and asked to determine where the poems came from. Each task prompted a great deal of discussion in which opportunity arose again and again for students to be rewarded by both teachers and peers for opening up a new line of discussion.

For some years now, in a college course on the psychology of creativity, I have had great success with take-home examinations involving questions that as yet have no hard and fast answers. For example: What is a creative toy? How much conformity is necessary for society's safety? Has the concept of creativity been distorted or diminished by extending it to scientists, engineers, teachers, sales clerks, and plumbers? Are humor and creativity related? Why is J. P. Guilford seen as about to have a great impact on American education during the next 50 years?

Notice that with all of the preceding strategies no major change in curriculum content is required. Rather, what has changed is the opportunity for the student to offer his own ideas and evaluations, and to be rewarded for

379

them. There is usually no single, correct answer, and the students accomplish all the usual goals of the curriculum as they are forced to give reasons for their choices or opinions. The nice part of this approach is that it fits in well with those intellectual factors believed to be part and parcel of the creative process as outlined by Guilford (1967); viz.: a variety of solutions (divergent production); changes or modifications of existing ideas (transformations); and sensitivity to the fact that things can often be made better than they are (sensitivity to problems).

Establishing Confidence

A major move to increase creative production by increasing the learner's feelings of self-worth and self-esteem has recently been outlined by Randolph & Howe (1966) in *Self-Enhancing Education*. They describe an experimental elementary school program in California where children set their own behavior limits and expectations, establish the rules for their own self-management, increase their self-esteem by being seen by their teachers and peers as worthy, and also by valuing themselves as a unique resource. Of all the recent approaches to encouraging creativity in the classroom, this one seems to me to be far and away the best solution, since it calls for a change in the teacher from an authority figure to a "helping person," a change in the classroom environment from competition to mutual support, and a change in the learner's self-concept that leads him from fearing failure to contributing what he can.

John Holt (1964) has suggested that something like 40% of our children fail in school, and if we were to raise our academic standards as some would have us do, then the figure would increase substantially. While Holt confronts us dramatically with *how* children fail in school, he is not so sure *why* they do. The answer lies in Randolph & Howe's *Self-Enhancing Education*. While schools have been busily evaluating achievement and potential in the three R's, the large majority of less skilled learners have been quietly lowering their self-esteem, self-confidence, and perseverance. If schools are really interested in encouraging creativity, and salvaging the 40% who fail, then they are going to have to develop ways to give back these children's self-confidence and feelings of personal worth. Jonathan Kozol's (1967) *Death at an Early Age* describes too well what happens to young children at a time in their development when they do not have the emotional or intellectual defenses to cope with rigid teachers and a non-supportive environment. Somewhere along the line schools are going to have to move in the direction of educating students for full humanness if we sincerely value adventurous students.

Some Teacher Aids

For those teachers who feel they must have tangible evidence that they are teaching for creativity, or a few props to help them get started, there are a number of workbooks available. Myers & Torrance (1964, 1965, 1966a,

380

1966b) have recently published a set of workbooks for elementary and secondary school children containing materials designed to encourage new ideas and to inhibit rigidity. These workbooks include open-ended questions such as: What kinds of fads might be beneficial to people? Would you rather be a frog, a deer, or on the moon? Why? What would happen if it was against the law to sing? When is the sky? What do the following have in common: a watch, a wagon, and an airplane? How many different ways can a ball be used? Other tasks include a few simple lines in which the child adds more lines to complete the drawing of a figure suggested by his own imagination, and invitations to write some silly stories. Myers & Torrance report that children are highly motivated to complete the exercises in the workbooks because they are "fun." No doubt one of the reasons children find such exercises interesting is because they deal more with experiences the child has been a part of and of which he can draw on from personal experience rather than what can be remembered from a study unit. More traditional curriculum content can also be approached the same way, as we saw with Massialas & Zevin, but it usually requires much more nose-grinding in order for the child to build up resources of knowledge to draw on.

Allyn & Bacon has brought out a whole series of instructive texts designed to stimulate creative teaching in a variety of subjects (Piltz & Sund, 1968; Smith, 1966, 1967a, 1967b, 1967c, 1967d; Westcott & Smith, 1967). The books describe a number of projects and ideas to stimulate creative thinking. The really nice part about the books is that the authors are fully aware of all the personality, environmental, and creative process variables brought to light so far by research on creativity, and they use the information to bring about the kinds of conditions that stimulate creative thinking in the classroom.

William Uraneck has published a couple of workbooks based largely on the factor of divergent thinking (1965, 1967). Most of the tasks revolve around giving ten or a dozen ideas: List 10 uses for a man's old belt; List 10 different birthday presents to give to a relative or a pet; What are some things you would do if you were small as a mouse? Again, the tasks draw a great deal on non-academic experiences.

My own feelings about the workbooks just described and other similar materials is that they are great for teachers who want to get started encouraging creativity and need some ideas. Presumably, such teachers will soon move on and develop their own ideas. As Smith himself says,

. . . You will violate the very concept of creativity if you try to use [these books] as cookbooks. Copying in any form is a contradiction of the creative act. Creativeness follows no set pattern, but comes from the innermost being of each individual. This is not to say that you should not try the ideas from these books in your own classroom. Do so by all means! But every time you use an idea, ask yourself, 'What ideas do I as a creative person have that fit my particular group,' or 'What ideas do my children as creative people have that I could use to develop that creative ability?' [Smith, 1966. p.xiii]

The danger of such workbooks on creativity is that teachers who have no understanding of the creative person or the creative process will use them in rigid and authoritarian ways and thus continue to destroy the very thing they think they are encouraging. Fortunately, the Allyn & Bacon series includes a great deal of material on the creative person, the creative process and the creative environment in each book so that the teacher who uses them also learns a great deal about creativity in the process. The Myers & Torrance series also includes a teacher's manual with each type of workbook to help the unsophisticated teacher learn something about the entire concept of creativity and how the exercises in the workbooks are designed to stimulate it.

Encouraging the Process

A less dramatic but no less important way of encouraging creativity is not to interfere with the creative process. All creative people report a period of incubation in which different alternatives are mulled over and over again prior to solution of a problem (Ghiselin, 1952). During such activity the person wishes to be left alone; not to be disturbed. It is not an uncommon experience for teachers to catch their pupils "daydreaming" now and then, and also not uncommonly the teacher asks the child if he has nothing to do. The implication is, of course, that children are not only supposed to be busy, they are supposed to look busy—which they do not show while thinking, although they may be very busy indeed. Teachers could be a little more tolerant of "daydreaming" and related behaviors when the child is obviously lost in his thinking. That is not to suggest that teacher is never to interrupt the process for, again, the child must meet his responsibilities, too. Neither is it to suggest encouragement of schizophrenic withdrawal. But there are occasions when teachers could respect the child's wish to stop and just "think" for a while, even if he may not be thinking about schoolwork.

Traditional exams disembowel the creative process completely, since they are usually strong on memory processes only and offer little opportunity for divergent production or evaluation. Little wonder that so many teachers complain that students do not think, when, as a matter of fact teachers do not ask the kinds of questions that require thinking, or give the student time to do so if he does have the opportunity. Many deadlines on term papers and other such projects are established for the teacher's convenience and not the student's.

Another method of encouraging creativity is to institute a program of breadth into the curriculum. One cannot help but get distressed at the fact that every year from grades 6-12, children are required to learn the parts of speech, but these same children are never given any instruction in anthropology, archeology, geology, philosophy, bird watching, or the history of Kenya. The same plays by Shakespeare are read by the same English classes year after year all over the U.S., but few students get a chance to read Chekhov, Gandhi, Darwin, or Marx. Mednick, in his paper

382

on the associative basis of the creative process makes the following statement: "It would be predicted that the greater the concentration of associative strength in a small number of stereotyped associative responses the less probable it is that the individual will attain the creative solution" [1962, p. 223]. Breadth of experience has long been recognized as advantageous to creative insight (Bartlett, 1958; Birch, 1945; Hebb, 1949; Hymovitch, 1952; Osborn, 1953), yet every year teachers teach the exact same materials to a new group of students, and by graduation nearly all students have been exposed to nearly all the same things. It's a wonder that such a homogeneous group *ever* comes up with any new ideas. A little heterogeneity might generate more. Good school systems and colleges have recognized this principle for a long time and have looked for teachers and students from widely different backgrounds and geographic origins.

As a final way of encouraging creativity, educational systems might consider the administration of creativity tests, despite their present shortcomings. Although test interpreters and teachers still tend to abuse the purposes for which the tests are intended—guidelines only, tests are here to stay. They do offer objective measurement and predictive utility, and since it appears that some people will misinterpret test results despite all warnings to the contrary, one way of partially overcoming the problem would be to make creativity test scores available along with IQ and achievement scores. Such an additional measure may at least serve to suggest to the teacher that intellectual ability (as presently measured) is not *the* single most important quality that a student can possess, and that a child's imaginative processes need to be cultivated along with his reasoning and memory processes.

References

Barron, F. Originality in relation to personality and intellect. *J. of Pers.,* 1957, *25,* 730-742.

Bartlett, F. *Thinking.* N.Y.: Basic Books, 1958.

Birch, H. G. The relation of previous experience to insightful problem-solving. *J. of Comp. & Physiol. Psychol.,* 1945, *38,* 367-383.

Cattell, R. B. The personality and motivation of the researcher from measurements of contemporaries and from biography. In C. W. Taylor & F. Barron (Eds.), *Scientific creativity: Its recognition and development.* N.Y.: Wiley, 1963. Pp. 119-131.

Drevdahl, J. E., & Cattell, R. B. Personality and creativity in artists and writers. *J. of Clin. Psychol.,* 1958, *14,* 107-111.

Getzels, J. W., & Jackson, P. W. *Creativity and intelligence.* N.Y.: Wiley, 1962.

Ghiselin, B. (Ed.) *The creative process.* N.Y.: Mentor Books, 1952.

Guilford, J. P. *The nature of human intelligence.* N.Y.: McGraw-Hill, 1967.

Harmon, L. R. The development of a criterion of scientific competence. In C. W. Taylor & F. Barron (Eds.), *Scientific creativity: Its recognition and development.* N.Y.: Wiley, 1963. Pp. 44-52.

Hebb, D. O. *The organization of behavior.* N.Y.: Wiley, 1949.

Holt, J. *How children fail.* N.Y.: Delta, 1964.

Hymovitch, B. The effects of experimental variations on problem solving in the rat. *J. of Comp. & Physiol. Psychol.,* 1952, *45,* 313-321.

Kozol, J. *Death at an early age.* Boston: Houghton Mifflin, 1967.

Massialas, B. G., & Zevin, J. *Creative encounters in the classroom.* N.Y.: Wiley, 1967.

Mednick, S. A. The associative basis of the creative process. *Psychol. Rev.,* 1962, *69,* 220-232.

Myers, R. E., & Torrance, E. P. *Invitations to thinking and doing.* Boston: Ginn, 1964.

Myers, R. E., & Torrance, E. P. *Can you imagine?* Boston: Ginn, 1965.

Myers, R. E., & Torrance, E. P. *For those who wonder.* Boston: Ginn, 1966a.

Myers, R. E., & Torrance, E. P. *Plots, puzzles, and ploys.* Boston: Ginn, 1966b.

Osborn, A. F. *Applied imagination.* N.Y.: Scribners, 1953.

Piltz, A., & Sund, R. *Creative teaching of science in the elementary school.* Boston: Allyn & Bacon, 1968.

Randolph, N., & Howe, W. *Self-enhancing education.* Palo Alto, Calif.: Stanford Press, 1966.

Rees, M., & Goldman, M. Some relationships between creativity and personality. *J. of Gen. Psychol.,* 1961, *65,* 145-161.

Smith, J. A. *Setting conditions for creative teaching in the elementary school.* Boston: Allyn & Bacon, 1966.

Smith, J. A. *Creative teaching of reading and literature in the elementary school.* Boston: Allyn & Bacon, 1967a.

Smith, J. A. *Creative teaching of the language arts in the elementary school.* Boston: Allyn & Bacon, 1967b.

Smith, J. A. *Creative teaching of the creative arts in the elementary school.* Boston: Allyn & Bacon, 1967c.

Smith, J. A. *Creative teaching of the social studies in the elementary school.* Boston: Allyn & Bacon, 1967d.

Taylor, C. W., Smith, W. R., & Ghiselin, B. The creative and other contributions of one sample of research scientists. In C. W. Taylor & F. Barron (Eds.), *Scientifiic creativity: Its recognition and development.* N.Y.: Wiley, 1963. Pp. 53-76.

Terman, L. M. The discovery and encouragement of exceptional talent. *Amer. Psychol.,* 1954, *9,* 221-230.

Uraneck, W. O. *The young thinker.* Lexington, Mass.: Author, 1965.

Uraneck, W. O. *Creative thinking workbook.* (Rev. ed.) Lexington, Mass.: Author, 1967.

Westcott, A. M., & Smith, J. A. *Creative teaching of mathematics in the elementary school.* Boston: Allyn & Bacon, 1967.

Williams, F. E. Perspective of a model for developing productive creative behaviors in the classroom. Unpublished manuscript, Macalester College, 1968.

John F. Feldhusen
Donald J. Treffinger

The Role of Instructional Material
in Teaching Creative Thinking

*I*n 1974 we received a grant from the National Institute of Education to conduct a dissemination project on the teaching of creative thinking and problem solving. Specifically the purposes of the project were as follows:

1. Conduct a field study of teachers' perceptions of their problems and needs in teaching creativity and problem solving.
2. Review the published material for teaching creativity and problem solving.
3. Review the research on teaching creativity and problem solving.
4. Prepare a report for teachers offering guidance and directions in this area.
5. Design, conduct and evaluate a workshop for teachers on creativity and problem solving.

Our efforts were to focus on the needs of teachers in schools which enrolled large numbers of minority students and students from economically disadvantaged families.

As an approach to the first purpose we interviewed and gave questionnaires to 408 elementary teachers in five cities: Indianapolis, Atlanta, Kansas City, Los Angeles, and Lafayette, Indiana. The results were reported in an article in *Psychological Reports* (1975). Briefly they showed that teachers knew very little about special methods or materials for teaching creative thinking and problem solving; that they would be willing to devote more teaching time to this area; and that they would prefer to do the teaching of creative thinking or problem solving in connection with regular instruction in language arts, social studies, math, or science. They were quite divided in their opinions concerning the question, "Do minority and disadvantaged students need special methods and materials?"

For the second purpose we sifted through countless journals, bibliographic sources, and catalogs to identify the published material which might have some value in teaching creativity and problem solving. Then we ordered sets of all hopeful material and examined them carefully, using these guidelines:

1. There should be a defensible theoretical rationale for the material in relation to the goal of teaching creativity and/or problem solving.
2. Research or evaluation evidence for its effectiveness would be desirable.
3. Good teaching strategies should be suggested.
4. The material should be attractive and motivating for children.
5. It should be conveniently usable in the typical classroom. Out of the vast collection of materials we received, we succeeded in identifying a basic set of about sixty very fine sets of published material.

We conducted a review of published research and ERIC reports in fulfillment of the third purpose. This was a relatively discouraging activity from one point of view, but encouraging from another. Very few of the published materials have undergone any systematic research or evaluation. A few, however, have been extensively researched such as the *Productive Thinking Program* (Covington, Crutchfield, Davies & Olton, 1972), the *Purdue Creative Thinking Program* (Feldhusen, Treffinger & Bahlke, 1970), or *Thinking Creatively* (Davis, 1973). The results of research with these and a few other published and unpublished sets were highly positive. Thus it seemed safe to conclude that, even without extensive formal research or evaluation, reasonably well-designed materials which were based on a sound rationale should be effective in teaching creative thinking and problem solving.

The fourth purpose was to prepare a report for teachers offering guidance and direction in teaching creativity and problem solving. That has been accomplished in the form of a book which will be published by Kendall-Hunt Publishing Company (Feldhusen & Treffinger, 1977). The book includes chapters on the special needs of minority and disadvantaged students, methods for encouraging creativity and problem solving, reviews of published material, and suggestions for initiating a classroom project. Preliminary evaluations of the materials in workshops and university courses have been favorable.

The fifth purpose of the project was to design, conduct, and evaluate a workshop program for teachers on creative thinking and problem solving. Our workshop provides a flexible plan which can be presented in as little as two hours or expanded to a day or even a week. It features a set of slides which introduces key concepts and methods for teaching creativity and problem solving, teacher participation throughout the workshop, a slide show review of published materials, and a "shopping tour", with our book in hand, through an extensive display of the actual published materials. The workshop has been conducted in a number of cities throughout the United States. Formal evaluations have indicated that the teacher-participants learn a great deal from the program, and find it stimulating and enjoyable. A recent article in the *Journal of Creative*

Behavior (Feldhusen & Treffinger, 1976) described the workshop and reported the evaluation results.

Using Instructional Packages and Individualizing Instruction in Creativity and Problem Solving

Instruction in creative thinking and problem solving has long been characterized by group or total class activities in which the teacher leads, talks, or displays her creative abilities while most students remain passive or even inattentive to the instruction. Only in individualized, carefully planned, participatory activities are students able to exercise their own creative and problem solving abilities. High quality instructional materials always involve a *small* amount of exposition, directions, or didactic instruction and a *large* amount of carefully planned practice and reinforceable activity.

Some teachers are very actively involved in developing individualized or self-instructional learning packages for their students. These packages may utilize books, films, filmstrips, activities, or worksheets from a variety of published sources, or they may depend upon teacher-created materials. These projects are named in a variety of ways: Learning Centers, Learning Stations, modules or mini-courses, Learning Packages, and many others. While they are quite useful in teaching basic subject matter, it is also important to recognize that they can be used to teach creativity and problem solving.

The teacher can do this in several ways. First of all, published material for teaching creativity and problem solving can be incorporated into packages which are being used. Second, if the package utilizes material previously developed by the teacher, or other published material specifically concerned only with the subject matter, a variety of specific methods and techniques can be used to develop supplementary creativity and problem solving activities and exercises for the students. Finally, the teacher can develop her own instructional package to teach creativity and problem solving.

Guidelines for Teacher-Planned Projects

We have developed several general guidelines to assist teachers who plan to develop their own instructional packages. These are: *(1) Know the basic components of an instructional package.*

Two models for the design of instruction are presented. These models of instruction deal primarily with the organization and planning involved in the production of instructional material packages.

The first model we offer is the basic model of instruction pioneered by Glaser (1962).

There are four aspects to this model: planning instructional objectives, assessing entering behavior, planning and implementing teaching activities, and assessing how much has been learned. We use this model as a general guide or orienter, recognizing its somewhat offensive technological orientation.

Once these basic parts of an instructional model are understood, the actual structure of instructional materials can be examined. One widely used form is the Learning Activity Package (LAP). A LAP is a totally individualized mode of instruction. It provides for students' individual and differential rates and styles of learning, and for the different ability levels of the students. A LAP provides a working outline that tells the student what he is expected to accomplish, presents materials and activities that will help meet objectives, and provides for self-testing and evaluation of achievement. These are the basic components of a Learning Activity Package:

1. An introductory overview to orient and motivate students.
2. Objectives stated informally and at students' levels.
3. Self-Tests or Inventories. For creativity objectives these may often take the form of self-ratings, checklists, etc.
4. Learning materials and activities. These may be in many and varied forms. Listed below are just a few examples of kinds of materials and activities that may be used.
   (A) Optional or taped lectures.
   (B) Information sheets.
   (C) Resources and guidance in using resources.
   (D) Experimentation.
   (E) Media (filmstrips, video-tape, films and film loops, slides and transparencies).
   (F) Discussion sessions, simulated activities, and other small group activities.
5. Evaluation of student learning.

(2) The second major guideline is to develop goals or objectives.

Many advocates of behavioral objectives insist that teachers begin work in developing a unit of instruction by writing the objectives. A better way to begin is by preparing a subject matter or content outline. The outline will not be used as a lecture guide, but will be used to develop objectives which focus on specific abilities to be taught through the topics in the content outline.

In a social studies class, the teacher might, for example, develop a content or subject matter outline as follows:

The Family:
(A) Types of family structure.
(B) The economics of family life.
(C) Families and politics.

(D) Evolution and family structure.

(E) Current trends in family life.

Under each of these headings the teacher would also be likely to identify subtopics to be taught.

After the general content outline has been prepared, the creative thinking and problem solving skills to be developed should be identified. This can be accomplished with a charting procedure which we have developed for writing objectives (Feldhusen & Treffinger, 1971; Treffinger, Hohn, Feldhusen, Bleakeley & Huber, 1976).

You begin the process by drawing a chart on a large sheet of paper. Enter the content outline at the left side of the page, from top to bottom leaving two inches or so at the top for column headings. Next, horizontally across the top of the page, enter the thinking skill or processes to be included. As a suggestion, consider these categories for the levels of thinking skills: (1) information-comprehension; (2) creative thinking; (3) synthesis skills; and (4) problem solving. Level 1 is probably self explanatory. Level 2 includes the divergent thinking operations of fluency, flexibility, originality, and elaboration. Level 3 refers to synthesis projects in which students research a topic and prepare a report or product. Level 4 refers to all types of problem sensing and solving activities.

Now we can examine each box in the chart. We ask, "Will this instructional package attempt to teach the learner this part of the content, using this thinking skill?" Not every topic in the content outline will necessarily have to be included under *every* thinking skill, of course. We make a small check in each box we plan to incorporate into the package. Our decision is based on a judgement of the potential of developing a particular thinking skill through that topic.

Next we must examine each of the boxes which have been checked, one at a time. If a box is checked, the package should include some activity for the student to learn using that particular thinking process or skill. Thus, for each such box, there should be one or more instructional objectives.

For example, for the first topic, the information-comprehension box might be checked. That means that the student will use this package to learn some basic ideas about types of families. Here is an illustrative objective: To be able to identify and describe several different basic types of families. For the topic "Families and politics" creativity was checked. Here is an illustrative objective: Think of several unusual ways families might become involved in politics. For the topic "Evolution of the family" synthesis skills was checked. Here is an illustrative objective: Prepare a report, using library resources, concerning the structure of families in several primitive cultures. For the topic "Economics of the family," problem solving was checked. An illustrative objective: Using maps and library resources, try to determine why Eskimo villages are located as they are. Many more objectives would probably be written for this unit. The first level, information-comprehension, is usually checked for each topic and thus there is an objective at that level for each topic.

390

The result of this analysis will be a set of objectives in which the content *and* the thinking skills are planned. Note that this is merely a planning device; it does not impose any sequence in which the student will study the material, but merely maps out in a systematic way the content and thinking skills that will be developed in the package.

(3) The third major guideline is to search for and select creativity instructional materials, methods, and tasks to achieve the objectives.

In developing an instructional packet, it is not necessary that every part of the packet be originally prepared for that purpose. Existing published resources can be used very effectively. Thus, it is desirable to search for useful resources *before* actually beginning planning procedures and specific student learning activities. Books, articles, worksheets, problem sets, and exercises can all be used or adapted to relate to the planned objectives. There may also be published self-instructional programs, tapes, films, slides, filmstrips, models, demonstration kits, and other supplementary material that will be useful and save the time and expense of developing new materials. Some of these resources may be incorporated into the packet with only minimum change; others may require modifications, excerpting, and the development of study guides to tell students how to use them.

Another step that is useful to take before actually beginning to design specific learning activities for a package is to review methods and techniques for teaching creativity and problem solving. These techniques should provide useful ideas for designing learning activities for individuals, small groups, or large groups. Another source of good ideas to review before starting to play learning activities are tasks that have been used frequently in creativity research and training studies to foster students' creative thinking abilities.

(4) The fourth guideline then is to assemble the learning activity package and evaluate it.

Careful thought should be given to the actual procedures for using the package in the classroom. What materials will each student receive? How will they be distributed or made available in learning centers, files, or student folders? What kinds of products will be called for, and how will the student be expected to demonstrate completion of the activities for any of the objectives?

In general, as we develop the package, we should try to include a variety of activities, so that students may use different skills during a unit of study and complete several different kinds of products. Providing a variety of experiences, along with a blend of individual and group work, will help sustain the students' curiosity and interest. When testing is necessary, we can often arrange for it to be done individually.

The plan for learning activities should be checked very carefully, to determine the amount of time various activities may require, the adequacy of resources and supplies, and to plan any sequence that will be important for the student to observe.

Time requirements for any activity may vary considerably among students, of course. However, we can make a general assessment of the total amount of instructional time that may be required, on the average. Then we consider how long it will take the fastest and slowest students to complete various activities, using best estimates on the basis of their previous efforts. Some thought should be given as to how to accommodate students' differing time requirements. Should some activities be required of every student, regardless of how long they will take? Are there some activities that might be omitted for slower students or added for faster ones? Are there some objectives (and corresponding activities) that may be reserved as "optional work" for students who progress more rapidly? Are there alternative packages or assignments (or opportunities for free reading, recreation, or relaxation) that should be planned in relation to individual pacing of the learning experiences? (Feldhusen, Rand & Crowe, 1975).

The plans for resources should also be checked carefully. If equipment is needed, will it be available when needed? Will individual students be able to obtain it? Will they know how to use it? If books, articles, or other material are incorporated into the packet, will there be sufficient copies available for the number of students who may need it at the same time?

If the package seems to be successful, the next step might be to have other teachers examine it and try it in their classrooms. Will it work when the teacher's biases, enthusiasm, and guidance are removed and neutral teachers give it to new groups of students? Packages which survive this level of evaluation can become useful instructional materials in the school for a number of years.

Conclusions

Developing an instructional package is a valuable experience for the teacher. In addition to having some new instructional material to use in the classroom, the teacher will learn much about students' learning processes. Of course, the kind of planning activities described in these steps, and the amount of time required to complete them may seem to place a great demand on the teacner's energy. However, we have found that teachers who have learned to employ a systematic approach to instructional planning have found it to be a valuable tool. Often teachers will find that time spent in planning instruction pays its dividends later, in increased classroom efficiency and greater satisfaction.

We are also optimistic that with the wealth of excellent published material for teaching creativity and problem solving which is now on the market and with guidance, teachers can develop greatly improved instruction in this area for all students. However, we are also of the opinion that these materials and methods can be unusually valuable in meeting the

392

needs of gifted and highly creative students. In two publications we have inventoried the characteristics of gifted students (Feldhusen, 1963; Feldhusen, Elias & Treffinger, 1969) and have especially argued that they can profit more than other students from self-instructional materials and procedures. Now, after conducting our review, we are also convinced that these gifted and creative students can profit immeasurably from the power of these methods and materials to develop thinking abilities and problem solving skills. Above all else, gifted and creative students have tremendous potential for intellectual and artistic development and these methods and materials can help them reach that potential.

References

Covington, M.J., Crutchfield, R.S., Davies, L.B. & Olton, R.M. *The productive thinking program*. Columbus, Ohio; Charles E. Merrill, 1972.

Davis, G.A. *Psychology of problem solving*. New York: Basic Books, 1973, pages 133–149.

Feldhusen, J.F. Programming and the talented pupil. *The Clearing House*, 1963, **38**, 151–154.

Feldhusen, J.F., Rand, D.R. & Crowe, M.B. Designing open and individualized instruction at the elementary level. *Educational Technology*, 1975, **15**, 17–21.

Feldhusen, J.F. & Treffinger, D.J. Psychological background and rationale for instructional design. *Educational Technology*, 1971, **11**, 1–4.

Feldhusen, J.F. & Treffinger, D.J. Teachers' attitudes and practices in teaching creativity and problem solving to economically disadvantaged and minority children. *Psychological Reports*, 1975, **37**, 1161–1162.

Feldhusen, J.F. & Treffinger, D.J. Design and evaluation of a workshop on creativity and problem solving for teachers. *Journal of Creative Behavior*, 1976, **10**, 12–14.

Feldhusen, J.F. & Treffinger, D.J. *Teaching creative thinking and problem solving*. Dubuque: Kendall/Hunt, 1977.

Feldhusen, J.F. & Treffinger, D.J. and Bahlke, S.J. Developing creative thinking. *The Journal of Creative Behavior*, 1970, **4**, 85–90.

Feldhusen, J.F., Treffinger, D.J. & Elias, R.M. The right kind of programmed instruction for the gifted. *Journal of the National Society for Performance and Instruction*, 1969, **8**, 6–11.

Glaser, R. Psychology and instructional technology. In R. Glaser (Ed.) *Training research and education*. Pittsburgh: University of Pittsburgh Press, 1962, pages 1–30.

Treffinger, D.J., Hohn, R.L., Feldhusen, J.F., Bleakley, J. & Huber, J. *Handbook for individualized instructional design*. Lawrence, Kansas: Unpublished technical report, October, 1976.

Carolyn M. Callahan
and Joseph S. Renzulli

The Effectiveness of a Creativity Training Program in The Language Arts

Introduction

Research has shown that almost all children have the potential to think creatively and that creative production can be improved by providing youngsters with learning experience that encourages them to use their imaginations. Studies by Tisdal (1962), Cawley and Chase, (1967), and Rouse (1965) have found that children of all ability levels, including mentally retarded youngsters, are capable of creative thinking.

A major problem that has hampered efforts to promote creative thinking in the classroom has been the shortage of validated curriculum materials in this area. The purpose of this article is to describe a systematic creativity program and to report the results of field studies that were conducted to determine the effectiveness of the program.

The *New Directions in Creativity*[1] program consists of three volumes: Mark 1, Mark 2, and Mark 3. Each volume contains twenty-four types of creativity training activities[2] (prepared on duplicating masters) and teacher's guides that include suggestions for individualized instruction and follow-up programming. Two activity sheets, containing one or more exercises apiece, are provided for each type of activity; and each type is classified according to the kinds of information involved in the exercises and the ways that information is organized. This classification scheme is based on Guilford's (1967) model of the structure of human abilities (See Figure 1). The program is designed to develop each of the following general creative thinking abilities:

---

[1]The New Directions in Creativity program is copyrighted by Harper and Row, Publishers, 1973.

[2]Activities 1, 4, 5, 7 were selected on the basis of previous investigations using this test and conversations with E. Paul Torrance, which indicated these activities to be the most valid in the Verbal form of the test.

1. *Fluency*—The ability to generate a ready flow of ideas, possibilities, consequences, and objects.
2. *Flexibility*—The ability to use many different approaches or strategies in solving a problem; the willingness to change direction and modify given information.
3. *Originality*—The ability to produce clever, unique, and unusual responses.
4. *Elaboration*—The ability to expand, develop, particularize, and embellish one's ideas, stories, and illustrations.

The following specific skills in creative thinking are utilized: brainstorming, forced relationships, multiple viewpoints, techniques, categorization, planning, imagery, fantasy, and modification techniques. The program is also designed to develop skills in language arts such as phonology, morphology, syntax, semantics, and rhetoric. Since there are no "right" or "wrong" answers to any of the exercises, students are given an opportunity to develop their skills in peer and self-evaluation.

Although *New Directions in Creativity* was designed for upper-elementary age youngsters, the open-ended nature of the exercises has provided an opportunity to develop truly nongraded activities. Each student is able to respond in terms of his own background and experience *without* the fear of being judged to be wrong.

Design of Field Study on The New Directions in Creativity Program

Initial research on the effectiveness of the *New Directions in Creativity* program was carried out using a pilot edition of the activities. Of necessity, only the immediate, short-term effects of the program on a limited population were examined. The focus of the investigation were 660 sixth grade students in 22 rural, suburban, and urban schools. Assignment of classrooms to experimental and control groups was random.

Following a posttest only control group design, the teachers of the experimental S's were asked to use the program for 2½ hours per week for eight weeks as part of their language arts program. Control group subjects continued regular classroom activities. At the end of the eight week experimental period all subjects were administered the *Torrance Tests of Creative Thinking* —Verbal Form A (modified[1]) and Figural Form B. A questionnaire was designed to assess students' perceptions of the activities, the teachers' presentations, and discussions about responses to the activities. Teachers of the experimental S's were asked to complete a questionnaire devised to assess their opinion of the program as a whole, the teacher's manual, and the activity sheets.

The intact nature of the classrooms involved in this study necessitated the adoption of a partial hierarchical design with classrooms nested within treatment and class rank (high, middle, or low) crossing classrooms and treatment. This determination to include class rank as a factor in the analysis was based on the hypothesis that children who rank in the top, middle, and bottom of their class (according to IQ) receive differential treatment and rewards from their teachers, and that this different treatment might have an effect on their performance. Analyses of variance with sums of squares appropriately adjusted for the design were carried out for each subscore of the TTCT. Questionnaire data were tallied and summarized.

Results of Analyses Of Torrance Test Scores

The most emphatic outcomes of the analyses of variance were the findings with regard to classrooms within treatment. This main effect proved to be significant at the .01 level for all subscores of the TTCT.* This finding extends the notion that the classroom teacher and the interaction of that teacher with a given group of students may well be the single most influential variable in the learning situation in creative as well as cognitive areas of study. The overwhelming amount of variation between classrooms within treatment resulted in non-significant differences between treatment groups, even though the experimental group achieved higher mean scores on six of the seven subscores of the TTCT. This finding would suggest that the *New Directions in Creativity* program may have an overall positive effect on creative thinking, but that this effect is modified by the teacher and classroom setting. Teachers for this study were randomly assigned to experimental and control groups and therefore some measure of classroom effect could logically be attributed to attitudes toward the value of such materials.

Class rank did not have a significant effect on scores of the TTCT, and there were no treatment by class rank interactions. These findings suggest either that the "Pygmalion effect" did not carry over generally to this area of study or that the goals of self-evaluation and peer evaluation outlined in the *New Directions* program were attained. Teacher and student questionnaire data tend to support the latter hypothesis. Significant interactions of class rank with classroom within treatment, however, do suggest again that individual teachers and their judgments have a significant effect on the learning environment.

Teacher Reactions

Inherent to the success of any curricular program is the willingness on the part of a teacher to use the program. The teachers who participated in

---

*For tables, write authors.

this study were randomly assigned to experimental or control groups. Their evaluations of the program were obtained by means of a questionnaire designed to examine specifically reactions to the teacher's manual, the activities themselves, and the discussions as well as general feelings. The results of the questionnaire are presented in Table 4.*

The Teacher's Manual. General opinion of the Teacher's Manual was very good. Nearly three-quarters of the teachers who responded rated the manual as excellent or good, and 64 percent indicated that it was easily read and understood. Those who found some parts vague or confusing indicated that the confusion arose over a need to have more direction in the sequencing of activities. Specific parts of the manual, the introductory lesson and the lesson plans, were also favorably evaluated. The introductory lesson was considered a success by 86 percent of the teachers, and the lesson plans were considered realistic and helpful by 64 percent of the teachers.

Discussions. One of the goals of the *New Directions* program was the development of student self-evaluation skills through class discussions about responses on the creativity exercises. According to teacher opinion, this goal appears to have been achieved in a large number of cases. Almost the entire group expressed the opinion that the children learned to be self-evaluators of their own work and their peer's work to a great extent or at least somewhat, and no one judged that the goal had not been achieved at all. All of the teachers responding to Question II—2 expressed the opinion that the children did benefit from follow-up discussions in general, but like the children in their classes, they generally felt that discussions were not necessary for all activities.

General. Teacher opinion regarding grade-level appropriateness of the activities was unanimous with all teachers indicating that these exercises were indeed suitable for sixth graders. This result was in accord with student opinion about the difficulty of the activities. A majority of the teachers also felt that children of all ability levels benefitted equally from the activities and sixty percent of the respondents expressed the opinion that 50-100 percent of below average children would benefit from such a program.

The crucial items on this questionnaire were numbers 4 and 5 of Section III. These questions were aimed at teacher judgements about changes in their students. Of 28 teachers responding to the questionnaire, 32 percent indicated that they felt that pupils in their class had greatly improved their creative thinking abilities, and 49 percent indicate that their pupils had improved their creative abilities to some degree. Only 8 percent expressed the opinion that there had been little change, and no one indicated an absence of change. Nearly one-half of the teachers noted some carry over to other subjects, and only 8 percent saw no transfer effects.

---

*For this table of results, write authors.

Almost one-quarter of the teachers did not respond to this item, but of those responding, 65 percent noted transfer to other subjects.*

When asked to summarize their feelings about the *New Directions* program, teachers' responses included such favorable comments as:

We all enjoyed the activities, and as a teacher I had the opportunity to see some of my slower pupils really "blossom."

We enjoyed it thoroughly.

I would love this set of activities again to use throughout the year.

After working with the *New Directions* program the children seemed to come up with a greater variety of ideas for projects in science and social studies. The stories, poems, etc. seemed to show much more imagination. The children seemed to be more interested in creative writing, unusual projects, etc.

They (the children) seemed to learn to appreciate the creative abilities of others.

(The children) made social progress, gave each other *constructive* criticism, learned standards of evaluation, became freer and more creative.

As time went on, they began to use their imaginations more, or to trust it more.

Stories written in language arts improved greatly by many of the slow pupils.

Slower children who are almost always non-participants were eager to express themselves.

Student's Reactions

Enjoyment factor. It is clear from the results of the survey of students that the objective of providing activities which are enjoyable was achieved. As indicated by the responses to Question 1 on Table 5,* 90 percent of the students would include the same number or more creativity exercises if they were to teach sixth grade. (Forty-eight percent would include more creativity exercises; 32 percent would include the same number.) In addition, 66 percent of the students would vote to continue working on this type of activity in the future, and only 14 percent would not vote to continue (Question 2). Further evidence of enjoyment of the activities is demonstrated in the responses to Questions 3, 9, and 13. Creativity exercises were the favorite classroom activity for 56 percent of the students. Seventy-two percent of the children indicated they would like to work on the activity more than once a week with only 10 percent not choosing to work on the activities at all. The creativity activities were judged to be more fun than working on other subjects for 61 percent of the respondents, and only 14 percent found them boring.

---

*For Table 5, write authors.

Discussions. Examination of responses to Questions 4 and 5 reveals that the discussions about responses to creativity activities were generally considered beneficial. However, this judgment was qualified by a majority of respondents (53 percent) who indicated that these discussions were sometimes valuable, but only helpful for some activities.

Self-perception of creative abilities. In addition to the changes measured by the standardized tests of creative thinking, changes in self-perception of general thinking abilities and of creative abilities in particular were also hypothesized. This hypothesis is supported on the self-report level by Questions 10, 11, 12, and 15. More than three-fourths of the students felt that their thinking abilities had improved as a result of working on creativity activities. The same proportion of students indicated that they enjoyed using their mind more than they did before working on the activity sheets. Further, 72 percent of the students judged that they were thinking in different ways while working on these activities, and 65 percent perceived themselves as more creative than they used to be (with only 2 percent judging themselves to be not creative at all). Although 66 percent of the respondents felt that the creativity program had helped them think of solutions to problems, only 32 percent saw the program as an aide in finding *many* solutions to problems (Question 7). Thus, the self-perception of problem-solving abilities of the children seems to have improved, but divergent problem-solving abilities (i.e., the ability to find many solutions to a given problem) had not become a self-assigned characteristic of the majority of the students.

Classroom atmosphere. The teacher's manual instructed the teachers to provide an atmosphere where unusual and impractical ideas were accepted and peer evaluation was given at the same importance as teacher evaluation. The students indicated on Question 6 that 92 percent of them judged that all ideas were, in fact, accepted by their teachers, and 49 percent of them saw the teacher as an aide in formulation of evaluation judgments rather than as the final determiner of evaluations. The classroom atmosphere was also judged by the number of students participating in discussion (Question 8). Sixty-one percent of students assessed the classroom situation to be one in which everyone tried to contribute to the discussions. Only 10 percent perceived a situation where the teacher did most of the talking.

Level of difficulty. Seventy-six percent of the students found activities to be of an appropriate difficulty level, and only ´ percent found them to be too hard (Question 14).

References

Cawley, J. F., & Chase, D. V. *Productive thinking in retarded and non-retarded children.* Washington, D.C: U.S. Department of Health, Education, and Welfare, Office of Education Project No. 5-8106-2-12-1, 1967.

Guilford, J. P. *The nature of human intelligence.* New York: McGraw-Hill, 1967.

Rouse, S. T. Effects of a training program on the productive thinking of educable mental retardates. *American Journal of Mental Deficiency,* **69,** 1965, 666-73.

Tisdall, W. J. Productive thinking in retarded children. *Exceptional Children,* **29,** 1962, 36-41.

Frank E. Williams

Models for Encouraging Creativity in the Classroom

*R*ecognizing and meeting the intellectual as well as emotional needs of children, which both lead toward uncovering their creative potential, have become respectable goals or purposes of education. As Dr. Donald W. MacKinnon (1969) reports, the characteristics of the creative process and person are distinguished, most generally, by two fundamental sets of traits, one intellective and the other attitudinal or motivational. This article will discuss a theoretical rationale for several cognitive-affective models for which a new model has been designed for use by the classroom teacher concerned about encouraging creativity through thinking and feeling behaviors among young children.

Cognitive Domain

The first set of traits, but certainly not first in importance for being or becoming creative, requires a breadth and depth of knowledge and a set of thinking skills for recording, retaining, and processing one's cognized information. Such skills or multidimensional talents commonly go under the name of the cognitive domain and consist of a pupil's logical and rational concerns with what is—algorithmic truths. These are in almost every school's statements of behavioral objectives. Within this set of broad purposes or goals of education, classroom teaching emphasizes academic excellence, subject-matter mastery, and the learning of someone else's information. These are played for real with a great deal of time and effort spent on them by the classroom teacher and regarded as fair game in measuring and assessing a child's intellectual growth.

Most models of the cognitive domain are in the form of a taxonomy consisting of a sequential classification of from low- to high-order thinking processes. However, those mental processes such as hypothesizing, syn-

From Frank E. Williams, "Models for Encouraging Creativity in the Classroom," Educational Technology Magazine, 456 Sylvan Ave., Englewood Cliffs, N.J. 07632, December 1969.

401

thesizing, inventing, associating, transforming, relating, designing, translating, or combining have been used synonymously by many to define the creative process; yet they are only found within the higher stages or levels of these taxonomy models.

For example, Piaget's (Flavell, 1963) stage theory of intellectual development places those mental abilities (italicized terms) which define and describe the creative process in the formal operations stage, as can be seen appearing at the top level of this taxonomy. Even in Bloom's *Taxonomy of Educational Objectives* (1956), the processes of synthesis are the most predominant ingredients of creativity and likewise appear as higher level thought processes at the fifth step of this model.

Those who have developed taxonomy models advocate that later operations are built upon earlier ones, and that intellectual development follows an ordered sequence. They say a child is incapable of learning these higher level thought processes before earlier ones are mastered. Here is where we get into trouble when teachers want to encourage a young child's creative potential, because these models indicate that creative thinking consists of higher mental processes which may not develop much before middle childhood. Yet, all primary grade teachers are aware of how free and open every young child is to be imaginative, inventive, flexible, and perceptive *at his or her own intellectual level*. That is to say, surely the young child may not be able to break new boundaries, at least in any sophisticated degree, by creating new concepts in the physical sciences; but he or she may be highly original and imaginative in dealing with their own discoveries and uses of already existing scientific concepts. Hence, there are some questions raised by classroom teachers when they attempt to apply taxonomical models of cognition for curriculum development or for planning learning experiences which encourage those thinking processes associated with a child's creative potential.

Affective Domain

Another set of traits equally important for being or becoming creative is that broad area of aesthetic concerns for feeling, beauty, and form. These make up another important area of educational objectives which deal with attitudes, values, dispositions, and motivations of the pupil *to want to* do something with information, data, and knowledge which has been cognized. Such feeling processes include a pupil's inward openness to his own hunches, nudges, guesses, emotions, and intuitive feelings about facts which he has become sensitive to and is curious about. These personal-motivational factors may be most crucial and make the real difference for the pupil to be willing to appreciate either their own or others' creative productions. These are processes which cause the pupil to operate as much by feeling as by logic because he is able and willing to deal with fantasy, imagination, and emotion in terms of things that might be—heuristics. This is the insightful person who has the courage to be a bold risk-taker by venturing past the edges of the familiar; who is curious about other possibilities and alternatives rather than dealing with absolutes and permanencies; who uses his imagination to reach beyond artificial or limited boundaries; and who is willing to delve into the complexities of intricate problems, situations, or ideas just to see where they will take him. Here we are talking about experiences within an educational program that legitimize feelings, offered by teachers who have empathy for intuition and guessing rather than always expecting the child to know. The affective domain has likewise been presented by Krathwohl (Krathwohl et al., 1964) as a taxonomical model.

Most teachers would agree that thinking processes really cannot operate without feeling processes. Even as Krathwohl states, "nearly all cognitive behaviors have an affective component." One involves the other, and they cannot be separated. It is possible to attain feeling goals by cognitive means; and also to attain thinking goals by affective behaviors. The better the pupil feels about some fact or piece of data the more curious he becomes, at the conscious level, to want to dig in and learn more about it. And vice versa, the more he knows about a subject or area of knowledge, the better he appreciates and values it. Closely related to a pupil's need for knowledge and information is his preference for an internal set of values and personality dispositions which are nonintellective and comprise the affective domain. I would argue very strongly that a combination of both domains, cognitive and affective, is what makes for *effective* human development and the fully-functioning, creative individual.

Piaget (1967) writes,

> There is a close parallel between the development of affectivity and that of the intellectual functions, since these are two indissociable aspects of every action. In all behavior the motive and energizing dynamisms reveal affectivity, while the techniques and adjustment of the means employed constitute the cognitive sensorimotor or rational aspect. There is never a purely intellectual action, and numerous emotions, interests, values, impressions of harmony, etc. intervene, for example, in the solving of a mathematical problem. Likewise, there is never a purely affective act, e.g., love presupposes comprehension. Alway and everywhere, in object-related behavior as well as in interpersonal behavior, both elements are involved because the one presupposes the other.

Even though professional educators have for a long time talked about motivating the pupil and building positive self-concepts, attitudes, and values, classroom practices for dealing systematically with the promotion of affective behaviors are usually infrequent, and if they do occur many teachers really cannot explain what happened or evaluate affective behavioral changes within pupils. There is a new trend for programs which humanize education, but when measurement or assessment is called for the usual cognitive instruments are used; i.e., convergent thinking such as IQ, achievement, or subject-matter recall tests. And it should be pointed out

403

that so-called creativity tests, even though their instructions ask the pupil to use his imagination and be curious, are scored solely on four divergent production factors which are cognitive. These are fluent thinking, flexible thinking, elaborate thinking, and original thinking, all identified and operationally defined by Guilford's work and his Structure of Intellect Model (1967). There are no direct measures of affective processes derived from current creative thinking tests which have been used predominantly by researchers and teachers to assess children's creative potential.

Relationship Between the Cognitive and Affective Domains

Attempts to bridge cognitive thinking with affective feeling pupil behaviors or processes have so far been relatively sparse. Michaelis' (Michaelis, Grossman, & Scott, 1967) book for elementary school teachers discusses evaluating pupil progress in the substantive areas of the curriculum by taxonomical categories across both cognitive and affective domains according to level of increasing complexity. This book attempts to blend the various stages of the cognitive domain to comparable stages in the affective domain by subject area.

Albert Eiss and Mary Harbeck (1969) have published a book which discusses scientific behavioral objectives in the affective domain. Within this book Dr. Eiss presents and discusses an instructional systems model consisting of a closed, feedback loop which relates psychomotor-affective-cognitive domains together. Williams' (1968) Model for Implementing Cognitive Affective Behaviors in the Classroom attempts to bridge four specific intellective traits with four attitudinal or temperament traits among elementary school pupils.

Figure 4 indicates a hierarchical order, interrelated schema between cognitive and affective domain models. Even though this schema is one attempt to bridge the two domains, it still lacks definitive application when early grade teachers want to foster creativity because both models are taxonomies with placement of those processes which comprise this human phenomena at higher levels. There are some differing viewpoints among cognitive theorists concerning such categories arranged according to level of increasing complexity, with each category dependent on the preceding ones. Bruner (1960), for instance, has for some time stressed the importance of guiding students to discover how knowledge at any level is related, and indicates that *appropriate method or strategy* to bring this about may be most important. Piaget (Ginsberg & Opper, 1969) likewise indicates that it is possible to accelerate some types of learning by suitable environmental stimuli, and suitable methods may expedite processes of intellectual development. There are some who claim creative processes may only appear later in the life of the child because before this time he lacks an appropriate cognitive structure in order to make new associations which are novel or

404

unique. Others say that by appropriate teaching strategies, learning conditions, and a multitude of different opportunities in a lush environment, any normal child can be creative at his own particular level of creativeness. Thus, different theories about how cognitive and affective processes develop among young children do exist.

What may be one method of alleviating these discrepant viewpoints is a different kind of system or model other than a taxonomy. Such a system has been utilized by Dr. J. P. Guilford for his Structure of Intellect Model of cognitive abilities. By means of a three-dimensional, cubical model, he adopted a morphological approach to conceptualize intellectual abilities.

A morphology is a way of considering form and structure as an interrelated whole, and differs from taxonomy in that there is no hierarchical order implied. One very simple example of a morphology is that of forming a chemical compound. When you put two or more chemical elements together, i.e., sodium and chlorine, the relationship of both form a new chemical compound—salt. According to Guilford's model, up to five mental operations may be performed upon four types of content to produce six kinds of products resulting in 120 ($5 \times 4 \times 6$) possible kinds of intellectual acts.

As Mary Meeker (1969) in her new book states, "The order [of abilities] is strictly conventional; that is, no priority—logical or psychological, developmental or hierarchical—is intended either within or between the categories of classification." The model, then, implies an interrelated classification of human abilities, many of which contribute to intellectual creativity.

But since Guilford's Structure of Intellect Model was never intended to be used for curriculum planning or for classroom teachers, and it does not include any affective factors, another model or adaptation of existing models was needed. Such a model or morphological structure has been designed by Williams (1966a; 1968) as a modification of Guilford's model for the purpose of implementing certain thinking and feeling processes directly related to creativity in the classroom. Figure 6 shows this three-dimensional cube, much the same as Guilford's cubical model, with each dimension made relevant to an ongoing elementary school program. The structure characterizes an interrelationship between one or more strategies employed by the teacher (Dimension 2), across the various subject-matter areas of the curriculum (Dimension 1) in order to elicit a set of four cognitive and four affective pupil behaviors (Dimension 3). What the teacher does or the media she or he uses is strategy, but how the pupil thinks or feels is process; and both are related to subject-matter content.

Dimension 1 lists subject-matter areas of a conventional elementary school curriculum. However, it is felt it may be possible to substitute subjects from any other grade level, including high school and college, in this dimension.

Dimension 2 initially listed twenty-three styles or strategies in a prototype model which teachers can employ in their classroom teaching.

Upon extensive field testing of the model this list of strategies had been reduced to eighteen, which avoided a great deal of overlap between some strategies.

These have been devised empirically from studies of how all good teachers operated implicitly in the classroom. Teaching styles or strategies become a means, through subject-matter content, toward an end for fostering eight thinking and feeling pupil behaviors. As one considers these eighteen teaching strategies which can be appropriately applied across all subject-matter areas a vast number of combinations for learning become apparent.

Dimension 3 consists of eight processes deduced from theoretical studies of how children think and feel divergently. These divergent production factors are certainly most crucial when encouraging a child's creative potential but have received less attention or have been commonly ignored in the traditional curriculum and classroom. Hence, this dimension of the model is intended to focus upon those cognitive and affective processes that undoubtedly are most vital yet have been seriously neglected or at most treated randomly in school classrooms. These pupil behaviors become goals or objectives within themselves, and are regarded as ends to be achieved in classroom teaching.

The model is an applied yet complex structure, based upon theoretical constructs, interrelating a repertoire of eighteen ways for a teacher to cause pupils to think and feel creatively across the substantive areas of the curriculum. Assuming that the teacher is able to install it across the six subject-matter areas shown, the model indicates there are 864 ($8 \times 6 \times 18$) possible interrelated combinations for classroom teaching!

It has been used as a working structure for curriculum planning and as an instructional system to improve teacher competencies through inservice training at project schools across the country. An accompanying training program integrated across the model has been designed to show teachers how it is possible to encourage the eight creative processes directly through subject matter content rather than indirectly or in isolation of the regular school program.

Use of the model has likewise been focused upon classifying instructional media, such as books and films and teachers' developments and field tested lesson ideas designed for use in primary and elementary education (see Williams, 1968; 1970). It is currently being used as a classification system for some of the more recent kits and instructional programs which have concentrated upon a process approach to learning, particularly those relevant to promoting divergent production behaviors in young children. Some of these include the Science Improvement Curriculum Study, the AAAS—Science, a Process Approach Program, the EDC— Man, a Course of Study, the Reading 360 Program, the Peabody Language Development Kits, the Taba Social Studies Program, and several of the Inquiry Approach Programs. The model is also being adopted by one state department of education program for gifted and talented youth by changing the content

406

dimension, since such children are in need and capable of handling different subject areas other than the regularly established curriculum.

This model, unlike the others discussed herein, is essentially directed toward and has utility for both pre-service and in-service education programs. It can be used to develop more competent teachers, requiring no radical change in curriculum materials or content. Teachers can be trained to adapt their normal curriculum to the promotion of these important cognitive affective behaviors among pupils. The model itself specifies terminal behaviors or competencies for which both the pupil and the teacher may aspire. As an interaction model, it specifies performance objectives for both teacher and pupil related to the subject-matter curriculum. In spite of recent emphasis on the necessity for integrating cognitive with affective processes, the gap between what is known about the nature and development of thinking-feeling processes and how this is translated into instructional practices is still enormously wide. This model may serve to somewhat narrow this gap, at least within the area of divergent production.

References

Bloom, Benjamin S. (Ed.). *Taxonomy of Educational Objectives, Handbook I: Cognitive Domain.* New York: David McKay Co., Inc., 1956.

Bruner, Jerome S. *The Process of Education.* Cambridge, Mass.: Harvard University Press, 1960.

Eiss, Albert F., and Harbeck, Mary Blatt. *Behavioral Objectives in the Affective Domain.* Washington, D.C.: National Science Supervisors Association, 1969.

Flavell, John H. *The Developmental Psychology of Jean Piaget.* Princeton, N.J.: D. Van Nostrand Co., Inc., 1963.

Ginsberg, Herbert, and Opper, Sylvia. *Piaget's Theory of Intellectual Development.* Englewood Cliffs, N.J.: Prentice-Hall, Inc., 1969.

Guilford, J. P. *The Nature of Human Intelligence.* New York: McGraw-Hill Book Co., 1967.

Krathwohl, David R.; Bloom, Benjamin S.; and Masia, Bertram B. *Taxonomy of Educational Objectives, Handbook II: Affective Domain.* New York: David McKay Co., Inc., 1964.

MacKinnon, Donald W. "The Courage to Be: Realizing Creative Potential." In Louis J. Rubin (Ed.), *Life Skills in School and Society,* A.S.C.D. Yearbook. Washington, D.C.: National Education Association, Association for Supervision and Curriculum Development, 1969.

Meeker, Mary Nacol. *The Structure of Intellect.* Columbus, Ohio: Charles E. Merrill Books, Inc., 1969.

Michaelis, John U.; Grossman, Ruth H.; and Scott, Lloyd F. *New Designs for the Elementary School Curriculum.* New York: McGraw-Hill Book Co., 1967.

407

Jean Piaget. *Six Psychological Studies.* New York: Random House, Inc., 1967.

Williams, Frank E. (Ed.). *Seminar on Productive Thinking in Education.* Creativity Project, Macalester College, St. Paul, Minn., 1966(a).

Williams, Frank E. "Creativity in the Substantive Fields." Revised paper from a chapter in "Perspectives of a Model for Developing Productive Creative Behaviors in the Classroom." In Frank E. Williams (Ed.), *Seminar on Productive Thinking in Education.* Creativity Project, Macalester College, St. Paul, Minn., 1966(b).

Williams, Frank E. *Classroom Ideas for Encouraging Thinking and Feeling.* Buffalo, N.Y.: D.O.K. Publishers, Inc., 771 E. Delavan Ave., Buffalo, 14215, 1970.

Williams, Frank E. "Creativity—An Innovation in the Classroom." In Mary Jane Aschner and Charles E. Bish (Eds.), *Productive Thinking in Education.* Wassington, D.C.: The National Education Association, 1968.

Walter B. Barbe
Edward C. Frierson

Teaching the Gifted—
A New Frame of Reference

Concern for the gifted in the twentieth century may be traced through three distinct periods. Beginning with the work of Lewis Terman and Leta Hollingworth, emphasis was primarily upon the identification of individuals with superior mental abilities in an attempt to discover those characteristics which were unique to these individuals. Although Terman and Hollingworth considered the implications of their findings for education, their major contributions were to dispel false preconceived ideas and to arouse widespread interest in gifted children.

Terman and Oden's twenty-five-year follow-up study in 1947 clearly indicated that in addition to identification there was a need for specific educational programs for the gifted. The Educational Policies Commission and the American Association for Gifted Children followed Terman and Oden's report with publications that laid the groundwork for special educational planning. Interest in providing for gifted children became of national concern with the unexpected launching of man's first earth satellite.

Through these three stages educators have been primarily concerned with developing identification procedures and administrative provisions for the gifted. Extensive programming, which is the characteristic of the current stage, has brought with it the need for the development of teaching techniques designed specifically for the gifted.

There is a belated awareness today that teaching the gifted does not mean merely exposure to more work or the expectation of completing the same work in a shorter period of time. Administrative provisions have been successful in many situations, but except in the case of individual teachers there has been no consideration of the possibility that the learning pattern followed by the gifted child is different from that of the average child.

If this is true, the teacher of the gifted must not be satisfied only to teach more, or more rapidly, but must teach differently.

Reprinted from the April, 1962, issue of Education by permission of the Bobbs-Merrill Co., Inc., Indianapolis, Indiana.

Product or Process?

Traditionally the teacher has been concerned with the product of learning rather than the process, the possession of knowledge rather than the projection of knowledge. Emphasis upon end-results fostered a teaching approach which called for the presentation of subject matter in a logical progression. Usually this meant simple to complex, concrete to abstract, cause to effect, singular to plural, and whenever possible in chronological order.

It is a credit to gifted students that they have been able to adjust themselves to this pattern of teaching. Underachievement might be only an indication of some gifted students' inability to fit themselves satisfactorily into this pattern of learning.

The process-oriented teacher, as opposed to the product-oriented teacher, is concerned with how gifted students learn, rather than how the material is learned by most students. Emphasis upon the learning patterns of the gifted fosters a teaching approach which calls for the introduction of material at the exploratory level.

The exploratory level is the point toward which the product-oriented teacher is working, but it is the beginning point of the process-oriented teacher. The exact point of the exploratory level can be defined by the process-oriented teacher no more clearly than the point at which the product-oriented teacher can say with assurance that the child "understands."

Different Roles for Teachers

The role of the teacher in the product-oriented concept of teaching necessitates (1) mastery of the material to be taught in the course, (2) experience in teaching the subject in order that emphasis can be put on those areas which have proved to be difficult, (3) pre-planning to avoid confusion or interruption of the thought processes of the students, (4) sequential presentation of material, and (5) quantitative measurement of how much was learned. Since the average student needs this structure in order to retain the vast amount of information to which he is being exposed, he learns best under the leadership of such a teacher.

The product-oriented classroom requires a teacher who is a leader-participant. This teacher must be able either to answer students' questions or direct them to the answer.

The product-oriented teacher is primarily concerned with how much and how rapidly each child has learned. Therefore her effectiveness is measured in terms of how much progress the students have made on an achievement test.

The role of the teacher in the process-oriented concept of teaching is different. It necessitates (1) mastery of a teaching approach that introduces

410

students to material at the exploratory level, (2) experience which manifests itself in the continuing pursuit of knowledge, (3) pre-planning to insure presentation of materials at the exploratory level, (4) intentional interruption of the "lock-step" sequential development of ideas, and (5) teacher involvement in the learning process to the extent that there is an awareness of individual students' involvement.

The process-oriented approach requires a teacher who is a learner-participant. She must involve herself skillfully in the learning process itself, teaching by example the pursuit of knowledge. The absence of predetermined goals allows her to use her experience of the learning process to involve the students in the process. The evaluation of the involvement of the student becomes not only the function of the teacher-participant, but also the function of the student himself.

Direction of Learning

As has been pointed out, in the product-oriented pattern of teaching, the direction of learning is the same for all students, In process-oriented teaching for the gifted direction is determined by each student for himself. The material is presented at the exploratory level, but the direction which the learning process takes is then determined by the student and not the teacher. Some students may work in the direction of established facts, while others may work toward the discovery of novel solutions or applications.

Creativity about which there is so much concern today, can result from either product-oriented or process-oriented teaching. Since process-oriented teaching encourages individual direction, however, creative pursuits are more likely in this type of teaching. The very absence of rigidity in teaching will encourage creativity.

Existence of "Content Bounds"

In both product-oriented and process-oriented teaching there are "content bounds." In product-oriented teaching these bounds evolve from resources the teacher has at her disposal. They may be bounds or limitations imposed by textbooks, library facilities, curriculum guides, school policies, the teacher's educational background, or any number of other things which might be called teachers' resources.

In process-oriented teaching the bounds are also present, but they evolve not from predetermined teachers' resources but instead from students' resources. The age of the students, their experiences both real and vicarious, their interests, and a variety of other individual student characteristics establish these bounds. The important point is that the bounds are

411

determined by characteristics of the students, not of the teacher or the school.

Summary

It must be recognized that teaching gifted children effectively requires a different concept of teaching. This results in a different perspective and role as well as different teaching techniques and evaluative emphases. The differences in emphasis of these two types of teaching, product-oriented teaching and process-oriented teaching, can best be demonstrated as follows.

Joan B. Nelson and Donald L. Cleland

The Role of the Teacher of Gifted and Creative Children

*I*n all educational programs, the teacher
is the key to effective learning. This fact has been shown repeatedly in
studies of the value of various methods of teaching reading to primary
grade children. In Chapter 2 of this monograph, studies are discussed
which make it clear that the way the teacher proceeds is more important
than the materials or the specific methods utilized. It is the teacher who
sets the environment which inspires or destroys self-confidence, encourages
or suppresses interests, develops or neglects abilities, fosters or banishes
creativity, stimulates or discourages critical thinking, and facilitates or
frustrates achievement.

Implicit in the consideration of the role of the teacher of gifted and
creative children is the assumption that this role differs in some substantive
way from the role of the teacher in general. Are there specific traits which
characterize the successful teacher of the gifted? Does the role require
deviance in intellectual aptitude and creativity similar to gifted children
themselves? Are there knowledges, understandings, methods, techniques,
and materials which are unique to effective teaching of the gifted?

There has been little research indicating characteristics that identify
successful teachers of the gifted. Indeed, there is little research to indicate
those traits which differentiate between good and poor teachers in general.
The attributes most frequently cited as appropriate for teachers of the
gifted are the same attributes as those desirable for any good teacher. Lists
of desirable traits usually include good health and stamina, knowledge of
content field, broad background of information in related fields, a knowledge of the psychology of learning, familiarity with varied teaching
methods, patience, creativity, flexibility, and a supportive attitude. Case
studies have suggested rather clearly the importance of the teacher's ability
to employ child-study techniques to determine the nature and needs of
gifted children. Studies have revealed also the value of proficiency on the

Nelson, Joan B. and Cleland, Donald L. "The Role of the Teacher of Gifted
and Creative Children." In: Witty, Paul A. (Ed.) Reading for the Gifted and
Creative Student. Newark, Delaware: International Reading Association, 1971.

413

part of the teacher in using children's literature to satisfy interests and needs. Surely, the teacher of gifted children should possess the aforementioned characteristics and should be acquainted with the particular needs and interests of the gifted.

The special problems associated with the teaching of the gifted are often basically the problems of dealing with individual differences in children. The apparent differences in teaching roles may be based upon the unique characteristics that the gifted child brings to the learning situation and the way that the teacher reacts and responds to these characteristics. If one subscribes to the philosophy of education which recognizes individual differences and seeks to develop each child's unique capabilities and talents to that child's full potential, there can be no doubt that teacher's roles must vary acccording to the attributes of the students they teach.

What are the implications of this philosophy for the teacher of gifted children? What should be the components of a reading program for the gifted?

Implications for the Teacher

The teacher must possess an understanding of self. The learning of children is influenced not only by what teachers do but also by what they are. It would be foolish to assume that a person can understand the needs, feelings, and behaviors of others if he does not understand himself. In dealing with students, the good teacher is constantly evaluating his own feelings, perceptions, motivations, and abilities.

Even the decision to work with gifted children must be based on the teacher's awareness of his own strengths and limitations. Gifted children progress most satisfactorily under teachers of superior intelligence who have a broad, general knowledge as well as a thorough mastery of subject area. To meet the demands put upon them, teachers must know subjects and their sources. It is very difficult to "fake it" with gifted students. Their superior reasoning ability and questioning attitude are apt to cause the faker some very uncomfortable moments. A simple, "I don't know; let's find out," creates greater respect and trust between student and teacher than any attempt to deceive. A persistent gap, however, between student need for information and guidance and teacher ability to present or direct students to significant data can be discouraging. Only the teacher who knows his limitations can make an intelligent assessment of his ability to work with the gifted.

Teachers must also examine their feelings about gifted children. The inquisitiveness and questioning attitude typical of gifted children can be a constant source of irritation for an authoritarian teacher. Explanations which are accepted by most children may be questioned or rejected by gifted children. If a teacher shows resentment at a challenging question, he

414

may destroy incipient curiosity. The teacher who is open to new ideas and experiences expands the dimensions of student interests.

The teacher must possess an understanding of giftedness. Giftedness has been defined in various ways. Some educators define it in terms of intellectual capacity; others, as consistently outstanding performance in one or more areas of endeavor. Some educators believe that the gifted child may be identified by a constellation of factors which includes intelligence, creativity, drive, perseverance, and performance.

It is extremely important that the verbally gifted child's ability be recognized early in his school career to insure a learning program that challenges him. Though we rarely hear of gifted children failing in school work, many do fail to develop more than a small measure of their potential for learning because of pressure to conformity in undifferentiated programs. Since it is the teacher who comes in personal contact with all the children, it is he who is most likely to identify the gifted children in his charge. For this reason it is vital that every teacher know the characteristics of gifted children.

Although there is no entirely adequate composite of traits for the gifted child, there are several compilations which provide a basis for the teacher in the identification of gifted children. Included are the following items which apply primarily to the verbally gifted:

*Better health, social adjustment, and physical endowment
*Longer attention span
*Larger vocabulary
*Greater fluency of ideas
*Greater intellectual curiosity
*More rapid and efficient learning
*Greater ability to generalize and form concepts
*Greater insight into problems
*More curiosity and interest in intellectual tasks
*Earlier reading attainment (sometimes before school entrance)
*Wider range of interests

Teachers should be aware also of certain traits and behaviors which characterize highly creative children:

*Less concern with convention and authority
*More independence in judgment and thinking
*Keener sense of humor
*Less concern with order and organization
*A more temperamental nature

Once the gifted child is identified, the teacher must provide a learning environment appropriate to the development of the child's outstanding

415

ability to conceptualize, generalize, create, initiate, relate, organize, and imagine.

The teacher should be a facilitator of learning rather than a director of learning. A function of education is to prepare the student for lifelong learning. Every child has an innate curiosity which expands and renews itself in the act of learning. Who has not marveled at the boundless energy and enthusiasm of the bright preschool child as he looks, listens, tastes, smells, and touches everything in sight to satisfy his curiosity? He is open to each new experience and learns from each that which is relevant to his needs. His learning is self-initiated, self-sustaining, and self-satisfying. The act of learning is, in itself, both the result and cause of his increasing curiosity. It is only when the child comes to school that his natural desire to learn is blunted by the imposition of an undifferentiated learning program and a rigid curriculum. Teachers who believe that they must control what a child does, learns, and feels, overlook the built-in drive for learning which resides in each child. If this natural drive is thwarted by the school, the curiosity dies and apathy takes its place. It is only then that external motivation and reward systems are necessary to arouse interest.

The bright child—with his heightened curiosity, wide range of interests, and insight into problems—is particularly thwarted by rigid curriculum requirements. The following suggestions, while appropriate for all children, are vital to the enhancement of lifelong learning habits for gifted children.

1. Build learning experiences around the child's natural curiosity by dealing with problems relevant to his own needs, purposes, and interests.

2. Allow the student to engage in the organization and planning of learning activities.

3. Provide real-life experiences that call for the active participation of the child, and then stress the skills necessary for that participation.

4. Act as a resource for learning rather than as a dispenser of information; resist temptation to impose knowledge upon a child before he is ready for it.

5. Keep programs flexible enough to encourage exploration and invention.

6. Encourage and reward initiative, inquisitiveness, originality, and a questioning attitude.

7. Allow a child to make his own mistakes and to accept the consequences (as long as the consequences are not dangerous).

One may wonder about the difference between direction and facilitation of learning. It is perhaps a difference in orientation as well as in behavior. Imagine the director standing in front of children and imposing his purposes, desires, and needs upon them; the facilitator stands behind the children and guides them in the realization of their own purposes, desires, and needs. The director imposes assignments, sets requirements, and evaluates outcomes; the facilitator supports the students' self-initiated learning and self-determined goals and provides feedback for self-evaluation.

The teacher must provide challenge rather than pressure. The role of the facilitator of learning implies acceptance of the principle that children should be challenged rather than pressured. Because of his initiative and perseverance, the gifted child is particularly receptive to a challenging situation. He enjoys pitting his abilities and experiences against a task that has meaning for him. He doesn't want easy answers. He may even resent being told how to do something because it deprives him of the chance to figure it out for himself. The bright child is far more willing than his less-gifted peer to strike out on his own to explore the difficult and the unknown. He has experienced the exhilaration of accomplishment. This remark is not to suggest that less bright children cannot experience the same exhilaration. The fact is that persistent failure in school makes the less talented child afraid to try. The gifted child is not "turned off" quite so easily.

By the same token, a gifted and creative child is impatient with routine or repetitive assignments. Pressure will not suffice to inspire a child when the teacher views education as the coverage of a body of knowledge. Challenge, on the other hand, gives the child the opportunity to gain confidence in his own powers to think, analyze, organize, and act. The teacher's wise use of questions that ask not only *what* and *when* but *why, how, for what reason, with what intent,* and *to what purpose* aids in challenging a bright student to the kind of thinking that provides the building blocks for speculative theory and philosophy. Assuming that the challenge is appropriate to the child's maturity and experience, it gives him a chance to explore the extent of his powers and to know himself.

The teacher must be as concerned with the process of learning as with the product. In spite of recognition given to an educational philosophy that stresses *learning how to learn*, many teachers act as if education consists of the mastery of a body of knowledge. To make matters worse, educational progress is measured largely through the use of standardized achievement tests which emphasize the acquisition of skills and the memorization of facts. This narrow view of learning is highly undesirable since the abilities involved in recall and application of learned facts are low in the hierarchy of intellectual processes. Much more important to the individual in lifelong learning are the thought processes such as comprehending, analyzing, synthesizing, organizing, and evaluating.

The gifted child is often shortchanged in a system that sees the learner as the passive receiver of knowledge. The gifted child's superior learning ability allows him to score well on most standardized achievement tests, making it appear as though he is doing very well when, in fact, he is failing to develop more than a small fraction of his potential. Emphasis on the following kinds of activities will aid the teacher of gifted children in stressing the importance of the processes of learning rather than the product:

*Problem solving (emphasizing the process rather than the solution)
*Classifying and categorizing

417

*Comparing and contrasting
*Making judgments according to criteria
*Using resources (dictionaries, encyclopedias, libraries)
*Conducting research projects
*Discussing and debating
*Taking part in class meetings involving group process
*Planning future activities
*Evaluating experiences

In Chapter 3, there are descriptions of programs which have successfully emphasized these processes.

Knowledge of things as they are now becomes obsolete in this world of rapid and inevitable change. The only secure knowledge is the understanding of the processes involved in learning and the ability to apply these processes to new and constantly changing experiences.

The teacher must provide feedback rather than judgment. To become independent and self-reliant adults, children must learn early to evaluate their own learning experiences and achievements. Gifted students are ready for self-assessment and self-evaluation from the time they enter school. It is the job of the teacher to provide feedback information and a behavior model, but the seat of evaluation should be within the child. He should be encouraged to evaluate his own work not in terms of grades and norms but in terms of his own needs, purposes, and goals. Extrinsic evaluation of the child's efforts should be subordinate to intrinsic evaluation. This statement does not mean that the teacher may not evaluate the child's progress and achievement to learn his strengths and weaknesses as a basis for helping him to improve. It does mean, however, that the teacher should refrain from imposing his judgment on the child. Instead of red-penciling and grading a child's composition, the teacher might write a note and point out where the child failed to communicate because of spelling, mechanical, or organizational errors. This approach represents the difference between feedback and judgment.

The teacher must provide alternate learning strategies. One of the most important things a child can learn is that usually there is more than one way to accomplish an objective or attain a goal. There may be several solutions to a problem, several ways of categorizing objects, or several points of view in a discussion. All too often teachers insist that a learning goal be attained in a specified way. Creative children may be quick to point out different strategies which lead to the same outcome. The direct path to a goal may not be the most interesting. Children should be allowed to explore different pathways and even to pause along the way if their interest is captured by a more relevant goal.

For the gifted child who is less creative, alternative learning strategies should be pointed out and demonstrated by the teacher. Creativity is fostered in an atmosphere which provides freedom to experiment. Strategies that are being employed successfully in schools are indicated in Chapter 3.

418

The teacher must provide a classroom climate which promotes self-esteem and offers safety for creative and cognitive risk-taking. Every child has the right to feel safe to try out novel procedures and to explore new ideas in the classroom (5). The fearful child may consume so much energy in compensating for his repressions and anxieties that he has little energy left to apply to productive and joyful learning. Many creative children are blocked in freedom of expression through fear of criticism, of not pleasing the teacher, of failing, of not being liked, of making mistakes, of being wrong, of not meeting parents' expectations, or by other repressive influences and pressures. New ideas and other forms of divergent response must be welcomed in the classroom which fosters creativity.

Teachers can combat fear by creating a classroom atmosphere in which each child has a sense of belonging, a feeling of self-worth, and a sense of value in his individuality. How is such an atmosphere created? Some suggestions follow:

*The teacher is supportive and accepting.
*Coercion is not used to manipulate children (i.e. threats about grades, loss of approval, loss of prestige, or banishment).
*The teacher recognizes, accepts, and values individual differences.
*The teacher provides differentiated learning experiences.
*Each child shares in planning his own work and the work of the group.
*The teacher provides enough structure for the child to feel secure but not enough to limit or stifle creative response.
*The teacher accepts and empathizes with strong feelings.
*The teacher recognizes his own limitations.
*The teacher values creativity and welcomes new ideas.

Gifted and creative children are willing to take risks in a warm supportive climate. They will risk the exploration of a new field; they will experiment with different learning techniques; they will share cherished ideas; they will define difficult problems; they will reveal their feelings; they will make mistakes and discover that they can learn from their mistakes; and finally, they will not fear to be themselves.

Implications for the Reading Program

Reading programs for gifted children will deviate in methods, materials, and content utilized; but certain features, such as the following, will be recognized as necessary components of a program for the gifted.

Early assessment of intellectual, perceptual, and reading abilities is vital. Many gifted children learn to read before they come to school. This

419

accomplishment is not necessarily the result of formal instruction but rather of a combination of high interest, extraordinary discrimination, and generalizing abilities. Gifted children often discover phonic elements on their own and use context and picture clues readily.

Children who learn to read early may be considered problems when they enter school. Placed with other children in a readiness program or the first preprimer, these gifted children may become bored, restless, and disruptive. Worse, they may withdraw into fantasy to escape the boredom, lose their eagerness to read, and become disillusioned with school in general.

A combination of intelligence and readiness tests, along with careful teacher observation and skill checklists, will give a fair indication of the child's level of competency. The ultimate test is, of course, whether the child can and does read and comprehend written materials.

*Evaluating materials in terms of worth and relevancy to purpose
*Understanding the use of connotation, figures of speech, plot, setting, and characterization in reading selections
*Appreciating the motives, intents, and feelings of the author and/or characters in a selection
*Selecting a reading technique and speed appropriate to the difficulty of the material and the purpose for reading it

The reading program should extend interest in reading. The importance of adequate reading skills instruction for the gifted cannot be overstated, but reading is much more than just knowing how to read. The ultimate goal of reading instruction is to establish permanent interest in reading.

An abundance of reading material is required. The voracious reading appetite of the gifted child makes it necessary to provide not only a wide range of materials in terms of variety of subject matter but also material in which in-depth study may be undertaken according to the interests of the student.

It is not enough, however, to provide interesting reading material. Even eager readers need help in choosing books to broaden and enrich their interests as well as to satisfy them. The teacher should become skilled in using child-study techniques, such as an interest inventory, in order to ascertain interests and employ them in the guidance of reading. Combining reading with social experience through the use of group projects, play writing and production, creative dramatics, discussion of favorite books, debate of a social issue, and sharing of creative writing broadens reading interest and enriches social relations.

We must be sure that our gifted youth are being provided with the best possible reading instruction not only to develop skill in reading but to nurture a love of learning that guarantees that their education will continue as long as there are good books to read.

References

Barbe, Walter B. (Ed.). *Psychology and Education of the Gifted: Selected Readings.* New York: Appleton-Century-Crofts, 1965.

French, Joseph L. (Ed.). *Educating the Gifted.* New York: Holt, Rinehart and Winston, 1960. (Revised, 1964.)

Gallagher, James J. (Ed.). *Teaching Gifted Students: A Book of Readings.* Boston: Allyn and Bacon, 1965.

Smith, James A. *Creative Teaching of Reading and Literature in the Elementary School.* Boston: Allyn and Bacon, 1967.

Torrance, E. Paul. *Rewarding Creative Behavior.* Englewood Cliffs, New Jersey: Prentice-Hall, 1965.

Wittich, M. L. "Innovations in Reading Instruction: For Beginners," in Helen M. Robinson (Ed.), *Innovation and Change in Reading Instruction,* Sixty-seventh Yearbook of the National Society for the Study of Education, Part II. Chicago: University of Chicago Press, 1968.

Witty, Paul A. "Who are the Gifted?" *Education for the Gifted,* Fifty-seventh Yearbook of the National Society for the Study of Education, Part II. Chicago: University of Chicago Press, 1958.

Witty, Paul A., Alma M. Freeland, and Edith H. Grotberg. *The Teaching of Reading.* Boston: D.C. Heath, 1966.

Witty, Paul A. *Helping the Gifted Child.* Chicago: Science Research Associates, 1952. (Revised with Edith H. Grotberg, 1970).

William E. Bishop

Characteristics of Teachers Judged Successful By Intellectually Gifted, High Achieving High School Students

The purpose of this study was to analyze selected characteristics of high school teachers who were identified as successful by intellectually gifted, high achieving students and to discover what differentiates these teachers from teachers not so identified. More specifically, the study was concerned with personal and social traits and behaviors, professional attitudes and educational viewpoints, and classroom behavior patterns of effective teachers of gifted high school students.

Data for this investigation were obtained from three groups of teachers from throughout the State of Georgia. One study group included 109 teachers who were selected by one or more gifted students as his "most successful" high school teacher. The students who selected the teachers were high school seniors who had participated in the First Governor's Honors Program in Georgia. Another study group included ninety-seven teachers who were selected at random from a list of teachers who had formerly taught students in the First Governor's Honors Program but who had not been selected by any of these students as his "most successful" teacher. The group of 109 identified teachers is called the Identified Group; the group of ninety-seven "non-selected" teachers is called the Validity Sample.

The third study group included thirty teachers in the Identified Group who were selected for intensive study, including a personal interview. This group was called the Interview Sample. The Interview Sample was a stratified random sample of the total number of identified teachers.

Every teacher in the study completed a copy of the Teacher Characteristics Schedule which provided estimates of the teacher's classroom behavior, attitudes, educational viewpoints, verbal ability, and emotional adjustment. A response analysis of the T.C.S. items provided additional data

Bishop, William E. "Characteristics of Teachers Judged Successful by Intellectually Gifted, High Achieving High School Students." Unpublished Doctoral dissertation, Indiana Central College, Indiana (Last chapter of dissertation).

relative to the personal and professional status of teachers in the different study groups.

Questionnaires were completed by the students who selected the teachers for this study. These questionnaires provided extensive data relative to the identified teachers.

In addition to information obtained from the T.C.S. and the student questionnaires, data on the Interview Sample were collected from the following sources:

1) Personal interview with each teacher
2) Wechsler Adult Intelligence Scale (verbal section)
3) Edwards Personal Preference Schedule
4) College transcripts

The data obtained from these sources provided the bases for the major findings of this study. The major findings of the study are summarized in the following section.

Summary of Major Study Findings

Major study findings are presented within the framework of the specific questions listed in the Statement of the Problem. The first question was stated as follows:

What are the unique personal and social traits and behaviors which characterize high school teachers who are identified as successful by intellectually gifted, high achieving students?

It has been proposed that "teachers of the gifted should be deviant with respect to those qualities common to the gifted group." . . . Several findings of this study lend empirical support to the validity of this proposal. One of the areas where this is best demonstrated is the intellectual level and interests of the identified teachers.

INTELLIGENCE LEVEL OF IDENTIFIED TEACHERS.

Several findings suggest the intellectual superiority of teachers identified as successful by gifted high school students. The most cogent is the mean score earned on the Wechsler Adult Intelligence Scale (W.A.I.S.) which was given to teachers in the Interview Sample. Their mean score of 128 on the W.A.I.S. places them 1.87 standard deviations above the mean or in the upper 3 percent relative to the general adult population. While giftedness is generally conceded to be a broader concept than can be represented by a single I.Q. it is recognized that those who score in the upper 3 percent on an individually administered test of intelligence evidence mental superiority.

Additional evidence of the superior mental ability of the identified teachers is revealed by their mean score on Characteristic 1 on the Teacher

Characteristics Schedule. This score is purported to estimate the respondent's verbal ability (comprehension). The mean score of teachers in the Identified Group was significantly higher than the mean score of teachers in the Validity Sample on this T.C.S. dimension.

TEACHER INTERESTS AND ACTIVITIES

Several significant differences between the Identified Group and the Validity Sample are revealed in the intellectual nature of the personal interests and activities they pursue. These data suggest a total life pattern of the identified teachers which is dissimilar to other teachers. This is perhaps best demonstrated in their literary interests. A significantly higher percent of the Identified Group than the Validity Sample follow what they call a literary hobby. Their higher literary interest is evidenced in several ways. A significantly higher percent belong to a book purchasing club. A significantly larger number frequently read collections of poems, essays, stories, and so forth. The same is true relative to the reading of biographies. A larger proportion of the Identified Group indicate that they frequently read fiction, read book reviews in newspapers or magazines, and prefer *Harper's Magazine* to *Saturday Evening Post, Popular Mechanics,* or *Redbook.*

Teachers in the Identified Group also indicate a higher level of cultural interest and involvement. A significantly higher proportion state that they attend concerts, exhibits, and the like when the opportunities are available. A higher percent have visited an art gallery or museum within the past year and a significantly greater number have bought some painting or art work within the past year.

The desire for intellectual growth is cited as a reason for choosing teaching as a career by a significantly greater number of the identified teachers. Continued evidence of this desire may be reflected in the higher incidence of teachers in the Identified Group who have taken a college course within the past two years.

ACHIEVEMENT LEVEL OF TEACHERS.

It has been suggested that gifted students have much to gain from teachers who manifest high intelligence and characteristics positively correlated with superior intellect. . . . High achievement tends to be positively correlated with high intelligence. Several data obtained in this study indicate that the identified teachers are characterized by a high achievement level.

A strong need to achieve on the part of the successful teachers is reflected in their mean score on the Achievement scale of the Edwards Personal Preference Schedule. Edwards defines Achievement as "the need to do one's best, to be successful, to accomplish tasks requiring skill and effort . . . to do a difficult job well . . . to be able to do things better than

424

others.". ... In six of seven comparisons with normative and parametric data, the Interview Sample shows a higher mean score on Achievement. In three comparisons the mean score on Achievement is significantly higher.

Evidence of high achievement is also reflected in the past scholastic performance of teachers in the Interview Sample. These teachers earned a mean grade-point average at the undergraduate level of 2.95 in professional education courses and 3.14 in courses in their major teaching area, based on a 4.00 system. At the graduate level, they earned a mean grade point average of 3.30 in professional education courses and 3.48 in the teaching area preparation. Over seventy percent of the teachers in the Identified Group indicate that they were "good" or "outstanding" students while in college.

Less direct data relative to the identified teachers' high achievement level are provided by other study findings. Ninety-three percent of the identified teachers indicate that they chose teaching as a career because they enjoyed past satisfactory experience in school work. A significantly greater number of teachers in the Identified Group were advised by former teachers that they would be good teachers. While the teacher-advisor may have had numerous and varied reasons for his advice, it seems unlikely that the suggestion would have been proposed to a low achiever.

Student descriptions of the selected teachers included repeated testimony to the achievement level of the teachers. A thorough command of their subject matter and a patent desire to increase their own knowledge and understanding were frequently noted by the students.

Several other personal traits and behaviors of teachers were considered in this study. On several variables there were no significant differences between teachers identified as successful by gifted students and teachers not so identified. These included such variables as sex, marital status, type of undergraduate institution attended, highest degrees held, course work preparation, and extent of association with professional organizations.

Two personal variables on which teachers in the two groups did differ were age and length of teaching experience. These differences were not great, however, and could not be tested for statistical significance. The median age of teachers in the Identified Group is in the forty to forty-five age range. The median age of teachers in the Validity Sample is in the forty-five to forty-nine age range. The median length of teaching experience for the two groups is between ten to fourteen years and fifteen to nineteen years respectively.

The use of student evaluations as a research procedure in studies on teaching effectiveness has been criticized because students will choose a teacher who is "young, genial, and entertaining, while the serious, more experienced individual . . . is rarely popular." This criticism of student evaluations for research purposes does not seem justified relative to the present study. Less than 2 percent of the selected teachers are in the twenty to twenty-four age range while more than 8 percent are in the sixty or over category. Fewer than 3 percent of these teachers have less than three years' teaching experience while nearly 30 percent have twenty or more years experience. It is true, however, that the students preferred teachers who are slightly younger and less experienced than their teaching colleagues.

Professional Attitudes
and Educational Viewpoints

The second question posed in the Statement of the Problem was:

What professional attitudes and educational viewpoints characterize these teachers (those identified as successful by gifted students)?

Data relative to this question were collected from several sources and are discussed in this section.

Two of the teacher characteristics estimated by the T.C.S. which relate to professional attitude and philosophy are Characteristic R (favorable versus unfavorable attitudes toward pupils) and Characteristic B (learning-centered "traditional" versus student-centered "permissive' educational viewpoints). The Identified Group scored significantly lower than the Validity Sample on Characteristic R. This result indicates that teachers in the Identified Group have more favorable attitudes toward students.

The results of the E.P.P.S. administration lend additional support to the conclusion that identified teachers are characterized by sensitivity to others which is probably reflected in a student-centered approach to teaching. Mean scores on five E.P.P.S. variables are especially suggestive of this attitude.

The E.P.P.S. variable on which the Interview Sample scored most consistently and significantly higher than comparison groups was Intraception. Edwards defines Intraception as follows:

To analyze one's motives and feelings, to observe others, to understand how others feel about problems, to put one's self in another's place, to judge people by why they do things rather than by what they do, to analyze the behavior of others, to analyze the motives of others, to predict how others will act.

An E.P.P.S. variable on which both male and female teachers in this study scored lower than all comparison groups was Autonomy. In five cases the difference was statistically significant. Autonomy has been defined as the need "to act without regard to the opinion of others." . . . An E.P.P.S. variable on which female teachers in the study scored significantly lower than the three groups with which they were compared was Exhibition, which has been defined as the need "to talk cleverly for the sake of impressing others, to be the center of attention. . . .

Male teachers in the Interview Sample scored significantly lower than three of the four groups with which they were compared on two E.P.P.S.

426

variables, Succorance and Aggression. Succorance reflects a self-centered interest in the need "to gain encouragement and sympathy from others when one is depressed or hurt." Aggression has been defined as "the need to show anger and criticize others openly." . . . This profile of E.P.P.S. results suggests that the teachers in this study are not overly concerned with themselves. They seem to be sensitive to the feelings and needs of others; e.g., their students. The teachers' favorable attitudes toward students also manifests itself specifically in relation to gifted students. All teachers in the study were asked to indicate what type of class they would prefer to teach. A significantly higher percent of the Identified Group than the Validity Sample stated that they would prefer to teach a class of exceptionally bright students rather than a class of average students, a class of slow and retarded students, or a class of children of widely varying ability. Nearly three-fourths of the Identified Group stated this preference. Not one of them stated that he would prefer to teach a class of slow or retarded students. Favorable attitudes toward gifted students were further evidenced in the teacher interviews with the Interview Sample. Every teacher in the sample expressed his support for special educational attention to the gifted, though the specific proposals for meeting the need varied widely.

Teacher Classroom Behavior

The third specific question listed in the Statement of the Problem was stated as follows:

What are the patterns of classroom behavior of teachers who are judged effective by gifted students? How do these teachers perceive their teaching role and responsibility and how do they assess their success in this regard?

This section presents conclusions based on study findings relative to this question.

Three of the dimensions estimated by the T.C.S. relate to teacher classroom behavior. On two of those three variables, the identified teachers differed significantly from the teachers not so identified. The Identified Group scored significantly higher on Characteristic Y, which provides an estimate of the respondent's responsible, businesslike, systematic versus evading, unplanned, slipshod classroom behavior. They also scored significantly higher than the Validity Sample on Characteristic Z which purports to measure the teacher's stimulating, imaginative versus dull, routine teacher classroom behavior.

It was noted in the previous section that teachers in the Identified Group also scored significantly higher on T.C.S. Characteristics B and R. These scores reflect favorable attitudes toward students and student-centered educational viewpoints.

The estimates of teacher classroom behaviors of the identified teachers

427

indicated by T.C.S. results are supported by other study findings. Testimony of the identified teachers' stimulating and imaginative classroom behavior was provided by the student questionnaire responses. The most frequent reason the students mentioned for having selected the teachers for the study was the teacher's stimulating, motivational, and inspirational qualities. The teacher's ability to present his subject in a meaningful and effective way and his success in increasing or instilling student interest in the subject were also frequently listed. The teacher's enthusiasm for this subject and for teaching were often cited by the students. One student described what he called his teacher's "contagious enthusiasm." Another noted that her teacher stimulates the willing and unwilling to accomplish on their own.

Additional evidence in this regard is provided by the teachers' self-descriptions. Teachers are asked to indicate characteristics which they feel are most descriptive of themselves. A significantly higher proportion of the Identified Group than the Validity Sample stated that enthusiasm is a strong trait in their own make-up.

Student comments also lend support to the findings that the identified teachers have a favorable attitude toward and interest in their students. The teacher's personal interest in his students was the fifth most frequently given reason stated by students for selecting a teacher.

Further evidence of identified teachers' permissive (student-centered) educational viewpoints was provided by their own expressions of opinion. A significantly *smaller* proportion of those in the Identified Group than in the Validity Sample stated that they believe that attentiveness of students is a more important indication of a good class than willingness of students to try and to volunteer, students who are well prepared, or courtesy of students. A larger proportion of the identified teachers indicated that willingness of the students to try and to volunteer is a better indication of a good class than the other three factors mentioned above. The greater emphasis of the Identified Group on student activity and participation than on student attentiveness, which implies a passive student response, indicates a more student-centered philosophy. A larger proportion of the Identified Group indicated their belief that a severe and aloof manner is a more important failing in a teacher than inability to maintain a systematic or orderly approach or inadequate mastery of subject.

It should not be concluded from this finding and related findings reported above that the identified teachers de-emphasized the importance of subject matter. The majority of the identified teachers indicated their belief that inadequate mastery of subject matter is a more important teacher failing than inability to maintain a systematic and orderly approach or a severe and aloof manner. A larger proportion of the Identified Group than the Validity Sample also stated that they believe it is more important for a teacher to extend subject-matter knowledge rather than to keep up to date on educational theories or to take part in community activities.

Several other study findings indicate that teachers who are judged successful by gifted students emphasize the importance of subject matter.

428

The students often cited the teacher's interest in and command of his particular discipline as their major reason for choosing him as their most effective teacher. The teacher's success in transmitting this interest in a particular subject to the students was also noted by many students.

ROLE PERCEPTION.

Interviews with the teachers in the Interview Sample provided data relative to the teachers' classroom behavior as they perceive it. These data provided additional support to the major conclusions suggested above.

The majority of teachers interviewed stated that they believe their major role is one of motivating students to want to study, learn, and think independently. They frequently noted their responsibility to instill an interest in and appreciation for their particular subject as well as for learning in general. Very few, however, see their major role as imparting a specific body of knowledge. They emphasize the importance of demonstrating personal interest in each student.

Their descriptions of personal incidents which they feel represent effective and ineffective classroom behavior reflected this philosophical position. Effectiveness was usually defined in terms of methodological and/or motivational success experiences and ineffectiveness was represented by lack of success in these areas.

Conclusions of Study

The conclusions which are suggested by the major study findings can be summarized as follows:

1. Teachers who are judged effective by intellectually gifted, high achieving students do not differ with respect to teachers not so identified relative to such variables as sex, marital status, type of undergraduate institution attended, highest degree held, course work preparation, and extent of association with professional organizations.

2. Successful teachers of gifted students tend to be mature, experienced teachers.

3. Teachers who are successful with mentally superior students are mentally superior themselves. They stand in the upper 3 percent relative to the general adult population and significantly higher than their teaching colleagues.

4. The effective teachers tend to pursue avocational interests which are "intellectual" in nature. They have a significantly greater interest than their teaching colleagues in literature, in the arts and cultural life of their community.

5. The identified teachers are characterized by high achievement needs—they attempt to do their best and to succeed. This is reflected in past scholastic achievement as well as present teaching success.

429

6. A significantly greater number of the identified teachers decided to become teachers because of a desire for intellectual growth and because they were advised by a teacher that they would be a good teacher.

7. Effective teachers have more favorable attitudes toward students than other teachers. They take a personal interest in their students and are sensitive to the students' motives and behaviors; they attempt to see things from the students' point of view and to understand how they feel.

8. Effective teachers tend to be more student-centered in their teaching approach. They encourage students to participate in class activities and they take students' opinions into consideration.

9. Effective teachers are more systematic, orderly, and businesslike in their classroom approach.

10. Teachers who are effective with gifted students are more stimulating and imaginative in the classroom than their teaching colleagues. They are well-grounded in and enthusiastic about their particular subject and about teaching. They define their success in terms of how well they motivate their students to want to study, to learn, and to think independently. They are able to instill interest in and appreciation for their subject in their students.

11. Teachers identified as effective by gifted students support special educational provisions for gifted students. A significantly greater percent of them would prefer to teach a class of exceptionally bright students than would their fellow teachers.

In summary, these conclusions indicate that there are unique personal and social traits, professional attitudes, and educational viewpoints and classroom behavior patterns which characterize successful high school teachers of intellectually gifted high achieving students.

Implications

The major findings of this study and the conclusions proposed above suggest several implications for educational planning and programming. It behooves those who have the responsibility for the pre-service education, placement and/or guidance of teachers to base their policies and decisions on the most reliable information available.

Assuming that the identified teachers in this study can serve as a prototype, the conclusions listed above are suggestive of factors which might guide the decision-making processes of those charged with the important responsibilities of educating, selecting, and guiding teachers of gifted high school students. More specifically the following implications of this study are suggested.

1. School administrators should give careful consideration to the proper selection and placement of teachers for gifted students. Teachers placed with special classes of bright students should possess those qualities which are common to the gifted group. They should also have a special interest in working with these students. The findings of this study indicate

that a large percentage of teachers do not prefer to teach classes of gifted students while most of the teachers who are successful with these students state a definite preference for teaching students of exceptional ability.

A recent report of the National Commission on Teacher Education and Professional Standards notes that misassignment ranks fifth among the twelve most important factors which educators cite as limiting the quality of education. One of the violations mentioned in the report is the teachers' "lack of ability to understand particular groups of students."[10] The majority of misassignments is reported in grades ten through twelve.

Teachers are sometimes assigned to classes of gifted students on the basis of seniority. Another common practice is to assign high school teachers to several different types of classes (i.e., slow, average, gifted) on the pretext that such an assignment adds variety to a teacher's work schedule and effects a form of "distributive justice." Both of these practices undoubtedly result in misassignment of teachers for gifted students. While gifted students may continue to learn "in spite of" and not "because of" the teacher, the results of this study indicate that there are special qualities which characterize teachers who are successful with these students. Attempts should be made to identify those teachers who will provide the optimum educational experience for students of exceptional ability and teaching assignments made on this basis.

2. The special qualities and interests which characterize teachers who are successful with gifted students suggest the need for identifying pre-service as well as in-service teachers to work with these students. The problem of attracting able young people into the teaching profession has received considerable attention in recent years. The report of the Commission on Teacher Education and Professional Standards calls this the number one problem limiting the quality of education today.[11]

If teacher education institutions were to develop special courses or programs at the undergraduate and graduate levels which would specifically prepare able young people to teach high school students, more superior college students might be attracted to the teaching profession.

3. Special preparatory programs for teaching gifted students should result in special certification in this area. The unique nature and needs of gifted students call for the recognition of educational personnel who possess those personal qualities and professional competencies which will guarantee that gifted students receive the optimum educational experience which they deserve and the democratic ideal demands.

References

Virgil Ward, *Educating the Gifted: An Axiomatic Approach* (Columbus, Ohio: Charles E. Merrill Books, 1961), p. 115.

Ibid., p. 116.

Alan L. Edwards, *Edwards Personal Preference Schedule Manual* (New York: The Psychological Corporation, 1959),p. 11.

J. E. Morsh and E. W. Wilder, *Identifying the Effective Instructor: Review of Quantitative Studies* (San Antonio, Texas: U.S.A.F. Personnel Training Research Center, 1955), p. 61.

Alan L. Edwards, *E.P.P.S. Manual*, p. 11.

E. G. Guba, P. W. Jackson, and C. E. Bidwell, "Occupational Choice and the Teaching Career," *Educational Research Bulletin*, XXXVIII (January 14, 1959), p.3.

Ibid., p. 3.

Ibid., p. 3.

Ibid., p.4.

National Education Association, National Commission on Teacher Education and Professional Standards. *The Assignment and Misassignment of American Teachers: A Summary of the Complete Report.* (Washington, D.C.: The Commission, 1965).

Ibid.

E. Paul Torrance

Creative Teaching Makes a Difference

*A*few years ago, it was commonly thought that creativity, scientific discovery, the production of new ideas, inventions, and the like had to be left to chance. Indeed many people still think so. With today's accumulated knowledge, however, I do not see how any reasonable, well-informed person can still hold this view. The amazing record of inventions, scientific discoveries, and other creative achievements amassed through deliberate methods of creative problem-solving should convince even the most stubborn skeptic. Both laboratory and field experiments involving these deliberate methods of improving the level of creative behavior have also been rather convincing. In my own classes and seminars I have consistently found that these deliberate methods can be taught from the primary grades through the graduate school with the effect that students improve their ability to develop original and useful solutions to problems. The evidence is strong that creativity does not have to be left to chance.

I have similarly maintained that the development of the creative thinking abilities does not have to be left to chance. Here I find myself in a distinct minority. Indeed, some educators believe that it would be extremely dangerous to educate children to be creative while they are still children. They argue that the emphasis must be on obedience, conformity, discipline, and fundamentals like the three R's. One educator sought to clinch his argument by saying, "A child has to know the three R's in order to do anything! Isn't it enough that the schools teach him to read, write and figure? Let him dash off on his own errands later; let him specialize in college!" Such a statement, of course, reflects a gross misunderstanding of the nature of creative thinking. The development of the creative thinking abilities is at the very heart of the achievement of even the most fundamental educational objectives, even the acquisition of the three R's. It is certainly not a matter of specialization.

Torrance, E. Paul. "Creative Teaching Makes a Difference." In Gowan, Demos, and Torrance. Creativity: Its Educational Implications. New York: John Wiley and Sons, 1967.
*The Florence S. Dunlap Memorial Lecture, Ontario Council for Exceptional Children, Point Credit, Ontario, Canada, October 30, 1964.

For years, students of creative development have observed that five-year olds lose much of their curiosity and excitement about learning, that nine-year olds become greatly concerned about conformity to peer pressures and give up many of their creative activities, that the beginning junior highs show a new kind of concern for conformity to behavioral norms with the consequences that their thinking becomes more obvious, commonplace, and safe. In 1930, Andrews published data to document the drops at about age five. Even earlier, the drops at about ages nine and thirteen had been documented and have been further supported in the Minnesota Studies of Creative Thinking (1962).

Those who have commented on the drops in creative thinking ability and creative behavior in general have almost always assumed that these were purely developmental phenomena. (For example, Wilt (1959) observed that creativity may all but take a holiday at about age nine or ten and returns only for a few after the crisis has passed. She concludes that about all that can be done is to keep open the gates for its return. Rarely, however, has anyone taken a contrary stand. One of these rare individuals, Susan Nichols Pulsifer (1960), has taken such a stand concerning the abandonment of creativity at about age five. She maintains that it is not a natural development change but is due to the sharp man-made change which confronts the five-year old and impels him by its rules and regulations.)

If our research at the University of Minnesota has contributed anything to thinking about this problem, it has come from my unwillingness to accept the assumption that the severe drops in measured creative thinking ability are purely developmental phenomena that must be accepted as unchangeable. As we entered into our longitudinal studies, it seemed obvious to me that many children needlessly sacrificed their creativity, especially in the fourth grade, and that many of them did not recover as they continued through school. It also seemed to me that many of our problems of school drop outs, delinquency, and mental illness have their roots in the same forces that cause these drops.

It will certainly take a great deal more research than we now have before very many people will be convinced about this matter. Personally, I consider the accumulated evidence rather convincing. One of the first positive bits of evidence came from my experiences in studying the creative development of two fourth-grade classes taught by teachers who are highly successful in establishing creative relationships with their pupils and who give them many opportunities to acquire information and skills in creative ways. There was no fourth-grade slump in these classes, either in measured creative thinking abilities or in participation in creative activities.

A somewhat more convincing line of evidence has come from our studies of the development of the creative thinking abilities in different cultures. As we have obtained results from the administration of our tests of creative thinking in diverse cultures, we have found that the developmental curve takes on a different shape in each culture and that the

434

characteristics of the developmental curve can be explained in terms of the way the culture treats curiosity and creative needs.

For purposes of illustration, let us examine the developmental curve for non-verbal originality in the United States, Western Samoa, Australia, Germany, India, and in United States Negroes. There are no drops in the developmental curve for Samoan subjects. The level of originality begins in the first grade at the lowest level of any of the cultures studied but the growth is continuous from year to year. The second greatest continuity in development is shown by the U.S. Negro sample, although some of the specific cultural groups in India show curves almost identical to those of the Samoan subjects. Through the fourth grade, German and Australian children seem to show about the same level and pattern of development. Pressures towards standardization and conformity apparently occur quite early and continue for the Australian child but not for the German child. The overall pattern of growth among the children in India is much the same as in the United States, especially in the mission schools and public schools.

What are some of the things which make a difference? This is the search in which my staff and I have engaged for the past five years. We have studied the development of the creative thinking abilities in a variety of schools in the United States and in other countries. We have tried to discover what are the factors in nature and society which influence this development. We have conducted both laboratory-type experiments and field experiments in an attempt to see what effect certain changes in teaching procedures will have. We have tried to create various kinds of instructional materials which will have built into them many of the principles which have been discovered through this research.

These and other experiences have left me with the firm conviction that teaching can indeed make a difference insofar as creative development is concerned. Methods, materials, attitudes, relationships with pupils, and other aspects of teaching have been shown to make a difference. Yesterday I stated that I believe creative needs and abilities are universal enough to make creative ways of learning useful for all children, though not an exclusive way of learning for any children. Yet I am convinced that some children who do not learn in other ways will learn if permitted or encouraged to learn in creative ways. In others words, for these children learning in creative ways truly *makes the difference!*

When Does Creative Learning Occur?

You may be asking, "How can I tell that creative learning is taking place?" I do not believe this is difficult. This summer I asked 200 students in my class in "Creative Ways of Teaching" to list within a five-minute period all of the signs they could think of to tell whether creative learning is taking place. When I analyzed their lists, I found that altogether they had listed 230 different signs I would accept as valid indicators that creative learning is occurring in a classroom or other learning situation. Since a person can be creative in an infinite number of ways, it is not surprising that a list of 230 signs was produced within a five-minute period. You might be interested in some of these signs. I have them arranged alphabetically, so let us examine the A, B, C's of creative learning, remembering that there are also D. E. F's and so on.

Absorption—there is absorbed listening, absorbed watching, absorbed thinking, or absorbed doing—sometimes irritating but searching for the truth

Achievement—there is a feeling of moving forward towards goals, getting things done

Acceptance—of individual differences in preferred ways of learning, differences in learning rates, faults, etc.

Admission—of errors, mistakes, and failures

Alert—listening and observation, intense awareness of the environment

Aloneness respected—there are times when the best learning can be done outside of the group but with purpose

Animation—there is movement, aliveness and spirit in whatever is done

Analogizing—there is play with various kinds of analogies as ways of stating and solving problems

Arguments—differences are permitted and used to correct mistaken ideas and find more creative productive solutions

Art media—are used to develop and elaborate ideas and to give them concreteness

Atmosphere—is tingling with excitement and communication of ideas

Behavior problems rare
Bells frequently unheard or unnoticed
Bodily involvement in writing, speaking, thinking, etc.
Boldness of ideas, drawings, stories, etc.
Brainstorming possible
Bulletin boards contain pupils' ideas
Bursting out to complete the teacher's sentence or to communicate some new idea or discovery
Busy hum of activity

Change of pace and approaches to learning or problem-solving
Challenging of ideas
Charged atmosphere
Changes in plans to permit one thing to lead to another
Checking many sources of information and ideas
Choice making
Close observations possible
Colorful, bold art work
Communication of ideas and feelings

Comparisons and contrasts are made

Community used

Combination activities cutting across the curriculum

Composing own songs

Consideration of apparently unrelated ideas and showing relationships

Concentration on work, not easily distracted

Conflicting ideas leading to new ideas

Continuation of activities after the bell

Continuity of activities, one thing leading to another

Control freedom

Curiosity evident in questions, experimenting, manipulating, and reading to find out.

What Difference Does Creative Teaching Make?

Even from this partial list of signs of creative learning, logical reasoning would lead us to expect that changes will occur in the lives of the children who participate in such learning. In our experimental work we have usually been concerned about some effect of creative teaching on classes, schools, or school systems. From these studies, we know that creative teaching seems to result in increased creative growth as measured by changes in performance on tests of creative thinking ability, creative writing, and the like; increased participation in creative activities on one's own; increased liking for school; and changed career aspirations. These experiments do not tell us what differences creative teaching makes in individual lives over extended periods of time.

To obtain some exploratory data to develop some clues about this matter, I asked my California students to recall instances in which they had allowed or encouraged children, young people, or adults to express themselves creatively and then observed that the experience made a difference in achievement and behavior. These students included teachers, administrators, and school psychologists at all levels of education from nursery school to college and adult education. Of the 165 students present when this request was made, 135 or 82 per cent were able to recall such instances.

Only a few of these respondents denied that creative teaching can make a difference. In these rare instances the denial seems to stem from the mistaken notion that all changes in behavior and achievement are of a developmental nature and independent of teacher influence. For example, one teacher wrote as follows:

> Right now, I can't really remember any particular child whom I've encouraged and where there has been a noticeable change. I have always felt that any change at the end of kindergarten year was due mainly to the natural development growth for the five-year old . . .

437

This attitude is encountered frequently among teachers and developmental psychologists who have accepted the view that developmental processes are set, genetically determined, and unchangeable. I believe that this view results from a misinterpretation of developmental studies. These studies describe the developmental processes which occur when children experience only what the environment happens to provide. Recent studies are showing that the developmental processes can be quite different when children experience guided, planned experiences designed to lead to certain kinds of development.

Let us examine some of the changes mentioned most frequently by the 135 students who responded to my request to recall an incident in which creative teaching had made a difference:

From non-readers to average or superior readers
From vandalism, destructiveness, and lack of school achievement to constructive behavior and improved achievement
From emotionally disturbed and unproductive behavior to productive behavior and even outstanding school achievement
From estrangement and lack of communication to good contact with reality and sensitive communication with others
From social isolation and rejection to social acceptance and productive group membership
From fighting and hostility to improved speech skills and lack of hostility
From bitter, hostile sarcasm to kindly, courteous, thoughtful behavior
From apathy and dislike of school to enthusiasm about learning
From lack of self-confidence and self-expression to adequate self-confidence and creative expression
From mediocrity of achievement among gifted pupils to outstanding performance
From diagnoses of mental retardation to diagnoses of normal or superior mental functioning
From a troublesome student to outstanding job performance

I was interested to note that some of these experienced teachers indicated that it was only a knowledge that teaching can make a difference that sustains them in their teaching roles.

Let us examine now a few examples which illustrate some of the different kinds of changes attributed to creative teaching.

FROM NON-READER TO READER

The most frequently mentioned type to change mentioned by the 135 respondents is from non-reader to reader, usually accompanied by improved behavior and achievement in general. Some of these changes occur in the primary grades, while others do not occur until the intermediate grades or the junior high school years. The following anecdote describes the occurrence of such a change during the second grade:

438

In second grade we do lots of creative writing and I usually type the children's stories and let them illustrate them. John, a dreamy lad, artistic, sloppy, and a very slow reader, disturbed me by never getting more than a sentence or so written. Usually that was lost in the crumpled welter in his desk by the time the next chance to work on it came around. John was a "poor listener" and took offense over nothing. He often cried because he thought he was being slighted. (The sociogram showed him not so much rejected as ignored.)

One day I let him dictate to me and I typed his story as he talked. He wanted to tell the story of the *Spider*—from a TV horror story. I was tempted to censor this, but fortunately kept my mouth shut. John's story was long. It was a problem to take the time to do it all, but I did, while the class carried on. His choice of words, sentence structure, use of suspense, etc. were very vivid, imaginative, mature. When I read the story to the class, the reaction was one of wild enthusiasm. John was starry-eyed. He learned to read the story, did many more, and learned to read other things. His behavior improved and he made friends.

FROM DESTRUCTIVE BEHAVIOR TO CONSTRUCTIVE BEHAVIOR

Destructive behavior on the part of a child or adolescent is especially disturbing to teachers, classmates, and administrative and custodial personnel. Students describing the consequences of creative teaching indicate that destructive behavior can be transformed into positive, creative energy and generally constructive behavior. The following is an account of one such instance:

"The principal, the janitor, the teachers all worked on the problem of John, the vandal. He was reported as being the culprit of many a weekend shambles at our school, but no one could prove anything. He couldn't stay still very long; his iron muscles seemed to need to move every minute; he was as strong, at 12 years, as most grown men. He was almost a permanent fixture in the office because of undesirable behavior. He was skilled, a *natural*, in things mechanical. He liked to boss and was often swaggering and bully-like in his playground behavior. The consensus as a result of brainstorming, was that John did not feel he belonged. The problem was how to make him feel he *did* belong.

"He was appointed by the Student Council (in which he could never be an officer, because of their strict code of grades and behavior) to be a chairman of the Lunchroom Committee. He organized a team of boys; they spent half their noon recess cleaning, moving tables, helping the janitor. He began to notice the litter which collected in certain windy corners of the schoolyard. His 'gang' cleaned it up. He helped park cars for Back-to-School Night. One woman ran her car into a deep ditch, when she did not wait for John to show her the way. The way he directed her, telling her how to cramp the wheels and when was a marvel. She would have had to have a tow-away, except for his know-how. He had organized the entire parking area without a hitch, where the drivers followed his directions, and all this done as well as an adult could have done it.

"Happily, as John became 'part' of the school, the vandalism became less and less. Reports came to us that he threatened (and coming from this

439

boy that was no mean threat) others who tried to destroy school property. Happily, he began to take an interest in school work. His father told us that John had at last said, 'I like school.' He said John had learned to read things around the house, in the neighborhood, at the store, and on trips for the first time in his life. His art work (racing cars, car engines, and antique cars) was excellent. We all hope some of this progress will continue when he leaves us this fall to go to junior high school."

FROM TROUBLE MAKER TO STAR LEARNER AND TEACHER

In the case of John, ability for verbal learning is perhaps limited although his capacity for art, mechanics, and leadership may be outstanding. Thus, the development of his potentialities might make a direction quite different from that reported for David, a younger learner:

"David had been a problem in kindergarten. He knew it and acted it out in the first and second grades. He had thoroughly convinced everyone he was a problem by the time he entered my third grade.

"A thatch of yellow hair, crystal clear blue eyes—as he walked along the path to school all he needed was a fishing pole over his shoulder to be the perfect Huckleberry Finn! He intrigued me and interested me beyond words— there must be a key to David, and I must try to find it.

"I set the stage in every possible way so he would do a few things at least that we could praise—this was a shock to him and he didn't know quite what to do with praise! . . . By Christmas time we had arrived at the point of mutual respect for one another.

"At Christmas in our room we take a trip around the world and explore the Christmas customs of the children in our countries. This year we had decided to go by plane. We had a representative from the airlines as a guest speaker—telling about tickets, traveling by plane, and showing some slides of various countries.

"The day came when each child was to make his ticket for the country he wished to visit. I was surprised as I watched David— usually he was one of the last ones to start, but this time he was well on his way immediately. As I "toured" the room, I noticed David's ticket would be for Sweden. This surprised me as he had brought many things from Mexico in for Sharing Time, and I had rather thought his ticket would be for Mexico. The 'Captain' for the trip arranged for his 'passenger' list by countries. David was the only one for Sweden. This seemed to please him, and as time passed we were all amazed at the responsibility he assumed in finding things to present about 'his country.'

"We found that he had chosen this country because his favorite grandmother had come from Sweden. . . . He found it necessary to write five or six letters to her for various items of information. I was surprised at the neatness and the care with which he did the job—would that he had done many of his other papers in like manner!

"He wrote some wonderful factual stories about Sweden. His Swedish

440

fairy tales were really something! He often found expression at the easal—and such vivid colors.

"The day when the class were his 'guests' in Sweden he told of the customs and even taught us a game the Swedish children play. He also taught us to make little 'goodie' baskets they hang on their Christmas trees.

"Our children come to school by bus, but the two weeks before Christmas David walked nearly every morning because he wanted to get there early so he could get extra painting or writing done. As he was telling me goodbye on the last day of school before the holidays, he said, 'Gee, Miss T., this is the neatest Christmas I've ever had—I feel like I've almost been to Sweden.'

"I had found my 'key' to David. He needed to find out things and tell them—sometimes do a bit of embroidery on them—sometimes do a bit of dreaming and make-believe on them. He liked his real world much better too.

"This did change David—he no longer needed to be the 'bad boy'—he adjusted to the praise and found it 'fun' (as he said) to write stories, draw pictures, etc. of his 'secret world.' He was so busy doing this he didn't have time to revert to the 'old' David."

FROM ESTRANGEMENT AND RETARDATION
TO ADJUSTMENT AND ACHIEVEMENT

A number of the anecdotes related by the respondents involved children who seemed to be estranged and out of contact with reality and regarded as mentally retarded. The following account of Jamie at the time he was in the fifth grade falls into this category:

"Jamie lived on another planet. He seemed to feel no need to relate to the world around him. As he entered the fifth grade, the children thought of him as a 'dumb kid.' In a flexible individual reading program I was able to let him skip around in the book as the spirit moved him and report in the way he was able through drawings. He completed one fourth grade and two fifth grade readers during the year and I feel he is ready to face my sixth grade reading material.

"At the same time in a 'slow' math class he was exposed to an imaginative teacher. By allowing him to use his interest in motors to develop a math project he was able to show a real flair for teaching others and his classmates discovered that Jamie had brains!"

What Made the Difference?

The incidents I have just reported provide many provocative ideas about what makes a difference. In some ways, the teacher provided a responsive environment—one which involved a sensitive and alert kind of guidance and direction, the creation of an atmosphere of receptive listening,

441

responding to children and young people as they are or might become rather than as they have been told that they are, fighting off ridicule and criticism, and making their efforts to learn worthwhile.

Now, I would like to give you a list of the factors mentioned most frequently by my students in "Creative Ways of Teaching."

Recognizing some heretofore unrecognized and unused potential

Respecting a child's need to work alone

Inhibiting the censorship role long enough for a creative response to occur

Allowing or encouraging a child to go ahead and achieve success in an area and in a way possible for him

Permitting the curriculum to be different for different pupils

Giving concrete embodiment to the creative ideas of children

Giving a chance to make a contribution to the welfare of the group

Encouraging or permitting self-initiated projects

Reducing pressure, providing a relatively non-punitive environment

Approval in one area to provide courage to try in others

Voicing the beauty of individual differences

Respecting the potential of low achievers

Enthusiasm of the teacher

Support of the teacher against peer pressures to conformity

Placing an unproductive child in contact with a productive, creative child

Using fantasy ability to establish contacts with reality

Capitalizing upon hobby and special interests and enthusiasms

Tolerance of complexity and disorder, at least for a period

Involvement

Not being afraid of bodily contact with children

Communicating that the teacher is "for" rather than "against" the child

Permitting Children to Work Alone and in Their in Their Own Way

In learning and in doing creative work, many people are unable to function very well in a group. They seem to need to "march to a different drumbeat" and to work at their own pace. Much in established ways of teaching creates a set which makes this difficult. Even beginning teachers find it possible, however, to permit such divergency. The following story of Mark's report on Latin America illustrates this point and suggests a number of other ideas as well:

"Last year was my first year of teaching. I had a student, Mark, whom I immediately recognized as an extremely creative student, and someone for whom I had an enormous respect.

"The study of Latin America is a required part of our social studies

442

curriculum for the sixth grade. I followed every step of what I had been taught in 'Teaching Social Studies in the Elementary School' . . . letting the class decide what you need to learn about a people and a country to understand them and their needs, and then a secretary wrote the names of the various Latin American countries on the board, so that the children could select the country's committee they would like to be on to prepare written reports. We decided that the major countries would need more on a committee . . . Ecuador came up, and two people volunteered and were given that country to research and do a project on. After all of the countries had been spoken for, I noticed that Mark had not made a choice.

"Talking with him, I learned that he had wanted Ecuador, as he had been reading Darwin's journals and was fascinated by the Galapagos Islands, but he hadn't wanted to work with anyone, so hadn't held up his hand. Well, I said that was all right, and that he could make up a separate report on the Galapagos Islands, which he agreed to do.

"Three weeks later, Mark had not begun his report, in the sense that he had nothing on paper. He was just too busy reading books, interviewing anthropologists at the University of California, and thinking. I tried very hard to help him get something on paper, but when I saw that he just was too interested in Darwin's discoveries and their implications and the evidence of it that remains to this day on the Islands, I decided Mark's assignment would be changed to an oral report. He reacted very favorably to this, delivering a magnificent account of what kind of person Darwin was, an account of the voyage of the *Beagle*, and then delivered a very instructive lecture on the various forms of a single species as they appear on the different islands, drawing pictures of the variants on the chalkboard, complete with describing the differing environment a different island would offer and asking the other students in the class to guess what variant they would imagine would result!

"Mark got such a good feeling out of this experience, I was able, when the next report came up, to talk with him in terms of being able to operate in more than one manner and thus be prepared to be flexible and able to choose—put it to him in terms of baseball; that a player might be a right-hander but it would be to his advantage to also learn to bat left-handed so that he could be a switch-hitter—that he decided he would prepare a written report, which he did—a very good one, and in on time and beautifully done, even as far as presentation—right down to the bibliography.

"The point is, I think, that in honoring his involvement at a particular time in research, he learned to respect me enough to consider the advantages when the next report came around of knowing how to prepare and get in on time a written report."

If we examine the teacher's report of this episode closely, we find several factors involved. It is likely that one of the more salient factors contributing to the success of the teacher in working with Mark was her willingness to change or bend her planned sequence of experiences to permit Mark to function in such a way to achieve his potentialities. He was able to function in terms of his abilities and interests, without actually upsetting the curriculum or the classroom organization. We find, however, that the teacher had already recognized Mark's creative potential and that she had an enormous respect for him. She recognized that she would be a bucking a strong force to divert him at this time from his interest in the Galapagos Islands; furthermore, she saw how he might be able to contribute meaningfully to the curriculum for the entire class. She had not counted upon his absorption being so great that he could not find time to write his report. She remained open and flexible, however, and saw that he might contribute most by giving an oral report, a challenge which he met with unexpected skill. Having achieved success and having achieved respect for his teacher, he was then ready to learn some of the more conforming ways of behaving in the educational environment. In fact, he was even able to include a very proper bibliography documenting his report, He has learned adaptive and constructive ways of behaving which will doubtless stand him in good stead throughout his educational career.

A Concluding Suggestion

My final suggestion is one created by J. H. Mohrman, one of my students, at the end of the course on "Creative Ways of Teaching." I shall present it to you just as he presented it to me—A Checklist for Creative Teaching:

"There is a story, common in the Navy and Merchant Marine, of the young third mate who had a great admiration for the Master of the ship in which he sailed. He was, however, puzzled about one of the Captain's habits. Quite occasionally while they were at sea, the Captain would take a dog-eared piece of paper from his pocket and study it intently for a few minutes. Following this ritual, the Captain was his usual picture of calm, self-assurance. Although he was never able to learn what was written on the paper, the Third Mate felt that it must contain the ultimate secret of the Captain's success as a seafarer. On one voyage the Captain died while they were at sea, and the Third Mate was given the task of inventorying and packing the Captain's belongings. He was in a high state of excitement as he went about this task knowing that, at last, he would discover the secret written on the slip of paper which the Captain had guarded so jealously. With trembling fingers, the Third Mate removed the paper from the Captain's jacket pocket and opened it to find this "secret" written inside: 'Starboard is Right—Port is Left.'

"We are all somewhat like the Sea Captain, and occasionally need some simple reminder of the elementary principles that we all 'know perfectly well.' For many reasons; partly because we all need a crutch for our courage from time to time, and a stiffner for our resolve, or perhaps more likely, simply a reminder of our good intentions, I have prepared a

444

checklist to keep handy in my desk drawer to remind myself frequently of at least some aspects of the creative process. We all tend to be creatures of habit and to have our judgment beclouded by our ingrained prejudices and predelictions, particularly with regard to what the 'good' pupil or the 'good' classroom is like. Because of the many possibilities for conflict with our own personalities and the creative personality, or some aspect of the classroom where creative learning is taking place, I hope that this simple 'Starboard is Right—Port is Left' type of list will keep us closer to the creative course."

Don't be too "threatened" by the exceptional child—or the unexpected response.

Pay attention to the "atmosphere" of the room.

Don't be too concerned about a higher noise level—if it's a "busy hum."

Remember the creative need to communicate—maybe the whisper is all right.

Don't be blinded by "intelligence" test scores—they don't tell the *whole* story.

Don't be afraid to wander off your teaching schedule—stay flexible.

Encourage divergent ideas—too many of the "right" ideas are stifling.

Be accepting and forgiving of the "mistakes."

Remember, the "obnoxious" child may simply be escaping from the tedium of your class.

Don't let your pride get in the way of your teaching.

Different kinds of children learn in different ways.

Let them "test their limits."

Don't let the pressure for "evaluation" get the upper hand.

Give them a chance to "warm-up" to producing ideas.

Respect the privacy of their responses (especially the less successful ones).

Criticism is killing—use it carefully and in small doses.

How about those "Provocative Questions?"

Don't forget to define the problem.

Don't be afraid to try something different.

"This list could, of course, be added to indefinitely—and I intend to. Also these items won't 'translate' properly for everyone, but it's at least a start, and it will have served its purpose if it helps only me."

I would urge you to create your own list to fit yourself. Each teacher's way of teaching must ultimately be his own unique invention. I wish for you the very greatest success in perfecting your own invention—your way of teaching.

References

Pulsifer, Susan Nicholas. *Children Are Poets*. Cambridge, Mass.: Dresser, Chapman—Grimes, Inc., 1963.

Torrance, E. P. *Guiding Creative Talent*. Englewood Cliffs, N. J.: Prentice-Hall, Inc., 1962.

Wilt, Miriam E. *Creativity in the Elementary School*. New York: Appleton-Century-Crofts, 1959.

Annotated Bibliography

Bedmar, R. L. and Parker, C. A. "The Creative Development and Growth of Exceptional College Students." *Journal of Educational Research* 59: 133-136, Nov. 1965.

Guilford tests administered to 90 students in an honors program at Brigham Young University revealed no significant relationship or growth during three years.

Eberle, R. F. *Experimentation in the Teaching of the Creative Thinking Processes*. Edwardsville Junior High School, Edwardsville, Illinois, June 1965.

A research report which combines a search of the literature with a local study. Following a review of the literature the author reports that "aspects of creative thinking are learnable, and as such can be taught." Significant gains may take place in short periods and these are accompanied by personality changes. In the local study of 7 out of 16 cases significant differences on pre- and post-tests were obtained.

Lincoln, J. W. "Developing a Creativeness in People" (pp. 269-75) in Parnes, S. R., and Harding, H. F. *A Source Book for Creative Thinking*. New York: Charles Scribner's Sons, 1962.

The "Gordon technique" of synectics and its applications to operational creativity is discussed.

Maltzman, I. "On the Training of Originality." *Psychological Review* 67: 229–42; 1960.

Reviews his work on training originality which he believes can be accomplished.

Mednick, Martha "Research Creativity in Psychology Graduate Students" *Journal of Consulting Psychology* 27:265-6, 1963.

The validity of the RAT (Remote Associates Test) was investigated by comparing ratings given individuals on a research creativity check list with the RAT. The correlation was .55 supporting the use of this test as a selection device for creativity.

Mednick, Martha, Sarnoff and Edward. "Incubation of Creative Performance and Specific Associate Priming." *Journal of Abnormal and Social Psychology* 69:84-88, July, 1964.

An investigation of the effect of associative priming on incubation of creative performance found that high scorers on the RAT (Remote Associates Test) performed better than low scorers and that the effect of specific priming was greater than no priming. Time relationship had no effect. Results support an associative interpretation of incubation.

Taylor, D. U., and others. "Does Group Participation When Using Brainstorming Facilitate or Inhibit Creative Thinking?" *Travail Humain* 24:1-20; 1961.

In attempting to test high pressure creation of new ideas, 96 Yale students were tested singly and in groups of 4. There were significantly more ideas produced in groups, although 4 persons produced slightly less than twice the number produced by persons working alone.

Torrance, E. P. "Factors Affecting Creative Thinking in Children: An Interim Report." *Merrill-Palmer Quarterly* 7:171-8O; 1961.

Discusses psychological factors affecting the creative thinking of young children.

Yee, G. F. *The Influences of Problem-Solving Instruction and Personal-Social Adjustment upon Creativity Test Scores of Twelfth Grade Students.* Unp. Ed. D. thesis, Pennsylvania State University, 1964. (*Disseration Abstracts* 26:916, 1965.)

High-ability students showed significant increase in creativity scores after problem-solving instruction as compared with matched controls. Low-ability students did not. Creative high-ability students have greater sense of personal worth, and fewer anti-social tendencies than counterparts; creative low-ability students also differ in the same way from their less creative counterparts. There was no significant difference, however, in adjustment among high-ability students varying in creativity or in low-ability students varying in creativity.

Ronald T. Zaffrann

Gifted and Talented Students: Implications for School Counselors

*T*he purpose of this article is to present three guidance functions involved with gifted and talented students: the counseling function; the consulting function; the research and evaluation function. These functions are usually performed by school counselors. However, many other people play a significant intervention role with the gifted, for example, parents, teachers, administrators, peers, and community members. In a way, these people serve as "counselors." So while the terms "guidance" or "counseling" are usually applied to school personnel, they can, in general, apply to these other helpers as well.

I will focus on these guidance functions for two reasons: (1) to present in general the major issues under each guidance function; and (2) to offer practical, tested suggestions and activities (Colangelo & Zaffrann, 1975; Pulvino, Colangelo & Zaffrann, 1976; Sanborn, Pulvino & Wunderlin, 1971).

The Counseling Function

School counselors typically deal with a variety of concerns of gifted youngsters. These concerns are divided into the following areas: educational; career/vocational; social; personal. Zaffrann, Colangelo, and Gowan (1977) have discussed these major areas in detail. For the purposes of this article, therefore, each counseling area will only be outlined or introduced.

Zaffran, Ronald J. "Gifted and Talented Students: Implications for School Counselors." Roeper Review, Vol. 1, No. 2, (December, 1978) pp. 9-13. By permission of the publisher, Roeper Review, 2190 N. Woodward, Bloomfield Hills, MI 48013.

One of the most prevalent myths about gifted and talented students is that they have no handicaps in the area of academics. Yet they often need remedial work in several areas, each of which can be emphasized during the elementary and middle as well as the high school years.

Study Skills. Since many gifted students have never been forced to study very diligently, they often do not know how to study or how to learn. Units on note-taking, summarizing, studying for exams, reviewing, memorizing, and reading for fun are often necessary.

Reading. Gifted youngsters may get good grades and do well on exams, yet not be able to read very well. In fact, it may be a remedial problem for some merely to read at grade level.

Testing. Most gifted students are "tested to death" for a variety of reasons (selection and screening for special programs; college entrance; scholarships; research and program development). On these tests—as well as on classroom examinations—these youngsters may need assistance regarding preparation, attitudes, and test-taking skills.

CAREER/VOCATIONAL CONCERNS

Although a variety of career guidance models have been offered (Ginsberg, 1957; Perrone, 1976; Walz et al., 1974), counselors must focus on specific *issues* relating to career guidance of gifted youngsters. Sanborn (1974) identified 3 such critical issues.

Multipotentiality. Since gifted students are often proficient in several academic areas, it is difficult to choose only one or two areas for potential careers. School counselors must invest more energy and time with individual gifted students to help them choose among the number of realistic career opportunities available to them.

Expectations. Well-meaning parents, teachers, and relatives often present special career dilemmas for gifted youngsters because of their own expectations. On the one hand, many parents expect their high ability children to enroll in the most prestigious colleges, to win the highest awards, to enter status careers. This can easily bring about unwarranted pressure and frustration. On the other hand, some parents ignore or disbelieve the unique characteristics and abilities of their gifted children, and expect them to enter the family business or continue working on the farm, but certainly not to go on for specialized training or advanced college work.

Gifted women. Like most young women, gifted and talented girls must face the dilemma of choosing between a career and a family—or arranging for both simultaneously. The pressures and expectations from others (parents, friends, future mates) require counselors to sensitively apply a family approach to assist gifted women in making career decisions.

The research on gifted abounds with references to the unique personal and social needs of gifted that require the counselor's attention (Goldberg, 1965; Gowan and Demos, 1964; Keating, 1976; Newland, 1976; Sanborn, 1974).

Since the term "gifted" is often defined in terms of being removed from the norm, it is not surprising that problems of isolation, boredom, nonconformity, and resentment are associated with the gifted. These students are often in situations that do not meet their social, emotional, or intellectual needs.

"Peerness" is essentially a term that refers to mental age rather than chronological age (Newland, 1976). A lack of peers contributes to a lack of communication. Yet gifted students need to communicate with others who have similar needs, interests, and abilities. Lack of communication is a basis for social "maladjustment" (Newland, 1976).

PERSONAL CONCERNS

In one-to-one and group counseling contacts, school counselors offer gifted students an opportunity to share their personal concerns. However, it can be difficult or uncomfortable for some youngsters to express these private matters. Since gifted students are usually skilled in writing, personal essays and journals can be used by counselors as a means of student self-exploration, as a "jumping-off-point" for counseling interviews, and as a reference point for follow-up sessions. Examples of structured guideline essay questions are included in Figure 1, and unstructured, open-ended, and direct exploration questions in Figure 2.

By having students write about these areas and by using these essays and journals as stimuli for personal sharing or counseling interviews, school counselors can help gifted and talented youngsters in the powerful, complex process of emotional development and the sensitive, painful search for personal beliefs and values.

The Consulting Function

A current contention in the helping professions is that graduate students and practicing counselors should be trained in consultation as well as counseling skills (Personnel and Guidance Journal, 1978). It has been suggested that counselors should serve as consultants *with school personnel* (Dinkmeyer, 1967; Mackey & Hassier, 1966; Pancrazio, 1971); *with parents and families* (Christensen, 1972; McWhirter & Kincaid, 1974); *with students* (Ciaverella, 1970; Dustin & Burden, 1972; Kramer, 1972); *and regarding intervention strategies for change* (Aubrey, 1972; Carlson, 1972; Cook, 1972; Margulies, 1971; Schmuck et al., 1972).

A variety of consultation models have been offered elsewhere (Baer, 1970; Blocher, 1975; Brokes, 1975; Christensen, 1972; Cohen, 1975; Dinkmeyer, 1971; Gallesich, 1972; McGehearty, 1968; Tharp, 1975; Werner, 1972). It is not the purpose of this section to discuss the formation or testing of consultation models, nor to critique them. Rather, suggestions will be offered as to how school counselors can use the consulting function—with teachers, administrators, and parents—in their work with gifted youngsters.

CONSULTING WITH TEACHERS

Classroom teachers continue to have the most contact with gifted students. Counselors would do well, then, to consult with (i.e., to learn from) these teachers about what these students are like, how they learn, what their interests, goals, abilities, values are. In this way, counselors can learn from the experience and knowledge of teachers. On the other hand, teachers may need the assistance of counselors to learn some of the special characteristics and needs of gifted and to set up learning environments which stimulate and challenge them; which allow them to work at their own pace; which give them the opportunity to set up their own goals and methods for classes; which allow them a role in evaluation and grading; in short, which help them to assume more responsibility for their own education. In Figure 3 for example, an independent study contract is presented, describing previous courses that generally relate to the topic at hand; objectives of the independent study project; plan of action to attain the objectives; and an evaluation system. In Figure 4, individualized and group programs for gifted youngsters are listed.

It is recommended here that counselors use these and related ideas when consulting with teachers about projects and programs for their gifted students.

CONSULTING WITH ADMINISTRATORS

It is striking that, when administrators were asked about gifted education, over 50% responded that they had no gifted students in their schools (Goldberg, 1965)! As with teachers, administrators may need to be informed about the existence, characteristics and needs of gifted youngsters. Counselors should play a major role in this "awareness" phase. Counselors can then help to convince administrators that special projects or programs should be tried for these youngsters with "exceptional educational needs." Administrators may need to examine a variety of programs and ideas which can be incorporated into their system. Figure 5 contains a list of inexpensive provisions for gifted in some Wisconsin schools. Counselors, using the consulting function, can help administrators to test out such provisions for their gifted and talented students.

Parents are often unaware of the special needs of their gifted children. They have expectations of their own regarding the futures of their children, and may unknowingly apply subtle pressures and frustrations upon them. For these reasons, parent discussion groups—begun as "awareness" sessions—are helpful and informative for parents.

But there is another side to this coin. Parents themselves have much to offer in the way of information about their children; perceptions about their children's needs, goals, abilities, values, interests, shortcomings, ways in which their children can contribute to the lives of other students and school personnel. Counselors can use the consulting function for both of these purposes: to *help* parents understand, appreciate, and cultivate their children's unique gifts and talents, and to *learn* from parents by sharing perceptions, feelings, frustrations, joys, and failures. Figure 6 contains a sample parent conference form. Some of the topics often covered in such parent interviews are the student's work and study habits; use of leisure time; church and community activities; employment; career choice; school activities. Interview notes also help to insure frequent follow-ups for continued, open communication with parents.

The Research and Evaluation Function

The research and evaluation function is typically the most disorganized, unsystematic, and limited part of a school counselor's role. This is most often due to the misconception that good research and evaluation must be a very involved process; be time-consuming; be laden with statistical manipulations and educational jargon; appear intricate, sophisticated, and unreadable. While these assumptions are (too) often believed, it simply does not have to be this way. Goldman (1978) presents practical research methods for counselors in field settings—methods which are concrete, succinct, precise, and functional—all in an understandable way. For the purposes of this section, two examples of research and evaluation will be offered: program evaluation and accountability, and longitudinal case studies.

PROGRAM EVALUATION AND ACCOUNTABILITY

Although the terms "program evaluation" and "accountability" have become overused and trite, they are nevertheless necessary educational processes. School personnel can help to build a stronger case for funding counseling positions for work with gifted and others (or for keeping such positions, if they already exist) by initiating and conscientiously carrying out such an evaluation of their guidance functions and of their gifted programs. Figure 7 includes an accountability model (Pulvina & Sanborn, 1972) which can be used by counselors in schools to evaluate their gifted programs. The procedural steps are (1) dialogue with the public, or needs assessment phase (assess the needs of gifted youngsters and the needs of teachers, administrators, parents; this can be done by the counselor in discussions with these various groups); (2) joint development of measureable objectives (these various groups decide, with the counselor, what they want to accomplish in their gifted programs and how they will know if they have indeed accomplished it); (3) counseling/teaching process (variety of counseling and teaching methods used to meet the needs of gifted and their helpers); (4) evaluation of the *product* (were the objectives listed in phase 2 actually met?) and of the *process* (were the methods described in phase 3 really effective, helpful, appropriate?); (5) communication of results (sharing the findings with the original needs assessment group in phase 1).

Counselors who would diligently use such an evaluation or accountability model to examine their gifted programs would help to guarantee the continued funding of such programs; the continued success and improvement of such programs; the continued existence and success of their jobs.

LONGITUDINAL CASE STUDIES

Essentially, the best way to get to know what gifted students are like or what they really need is not to talk to parents, teachers, administrators, or peers, but to talk with the students themselves. By putting together information gained from counseling interviews, from personal essays and other personal documents, as well as from conferences with significant others, a rich, detailed picture of these students can be started. If continued over a period of time (i.e., a longitudinal case study), this picture may actually begin to resemble the complex, intricate person who has been focused upon all along!

Such an approach to gifted students seems to rest on at least three assumptions: that each of these youngsters is *unique* (contrary to our occasional lip-service to this concept, we continue to refer to these students as a homogeneous group—"the gifted," "the talented," etc.); that each of these youngsters is extremely *complex* (and so it will actually take a longitudinal study to learn all the things there are to know about this one person); and that *generalizations* are too often feeble, ill-founded, and essentially meaningless (the goal is to consider *each* gifted youngster, not *all* gifted youngsters as a whole).

Helpful resources exist on the methods and procedures of conducting good longitudinal case studies (Rothney, 1968; Sanborn, 1977). Counselors could easily adapt these suggestions to find out how to better meet the exceptional educational needs of these youngsters.

453

Conclusion

There are, of course, many special areas of need regarding the education of gifted, for example, identification and selection; creativity; culturally different and disadvantaged; career concerns; gifted women; parent involvement; programming; professional training. Colangelo and Zaffrann (1978) have addressed each of these areas—both from theoretical and practical viewpoints—and have provided resources and references for the practitioner.

The aim of this article was simply to introduce and outline three guidance functions involving gifted youngsters. It is hoped that school counselors take the responsibility to initiate and carry out these functions in providing for the education of gifted and talented students.

References

Aubrey, R. F. Power bases: the consultant's vehicle for change. *Elementary School Guidance and Counseling*, 1972, *7*, 90-97.

Baer, D. M. The consultation process model as an irrational state of affairs. *Psychology in the Schools*, 1970, *7*, 341-344.

Barbe, W. B. *Psychology and education of the gifted.* New York: Appleton-Century-Crofts, 1965.

Blocher, D. H. A systematic eclectic approach to consultation. In Clyde Parker (Ed.), *Psychological consultation: Helping teachers meet special needs.* Minneapolis: Leadership Training Institute/Special Education, University of Minnesota. 1975.

Brokes, A. A process model of consultation. In Clyde Parker (Ed.), *Psychological consultation: Helping teachers meet special needs.* Minneapolis: Leadership Training Institute/Special Education, University of Minnesota, 1975.

Carlson, J. Consulting: Facilitating school change. *Elementary School Guidance and Counseling.* 1972, *7*, 83-88.6.

Christensen, O. C. Family education: A model for consultation. *Elementary School Guidance and Counseling*, 1972, *7*, 121-126.

Ciaverella, M. A. The counselor as a mental health consultant. *School Counselor*, 1970, *18*, 121-125.

Cohen, R. Co-professional collaboration. In Clyde Parker (Ed.), *Psychological consultation: Helping teachers meet special needs.* Minneapolis: Leadership Training Institute/Special Education, University of Minnesota, 1975.

Colangelo, N. & Zaffrann, R. T. *Counseling the gifted student.* Madison: University of Wisconsin, Research and Guidance Laboratory, 1975.

Colangelo, N. & Zaffrann, R. T. *Counseling the gifted today.* Dubuque, Iowa; Kendall/Hunt Publishing Co., 1978, (In progress).

Cook, D. R. The change agent counselor: A conceptual context, *School Counselor*, 1972, *20*, 9-15.

Dinkmeyer, D. The counselor as consultant: Rationale and procedures. *Elementary School Guidance and Counseling*, 1967, *3*, 146-151.

Dinkmeyer, D. A developmental model for counseling-consulting. *Elementary School Guidance and Counseling*, 1971, *6*, 81-85.

Dustin, R., & Burden, C. The counselor as a behavioral consultant. *Elementary School Guidance and Counseling*, 1972, *7*, 14-19.

Gallesch, J. A systems model of mental health consultation. *Psychology in the Schools*, 1972, *9*, 13-15.

Ginsberg, E., & others. *Occupational choice: An approach to a general theory*. New York: Columbia University Press, 1951.

Goldberg, M. L. *Research on the talented*. New York: Bureau of Publication, Teachers College, Columbia University, 1965.

Goldman, L. *Research methods for counselors: Practical approaches in field settings*. New York: John Wiley and Sons, 1978.

Gowan, J. C., & Demos, G. D. *The education and guidance of the ablest*. Springfield, Ill.: C. C. Thomas, 1964.

Gowan, J., & Groth, N. The development of vocational choice in gifted children. In J. Gowan (Ed.), *The development of the creative individual*. San Diego: R. Knapp, 1972.

Keating, D. P. (Ed.). *Intellectual talent: Research and development*. Baltimore: Johns Hopkins University Press, 1976.

Kramer, H. Counselors and consulting: Using values in consultation. *Journal of College Student Personnel*, 1972, *13*, 534-537.

Mackey, R. A., & Hassier, F. R. Group consultation with school personnel. *Mental Hygiene*, 1966, *50*, 416-420.

Margulies, N. Implementing organizational change through an internal consulting team. *Training and Development Journal*, 1971, *25*, 26-33.

McGehearty, J. The case for consultation. *Personnel and Guidance Journal*, 1968, *47*, 247-262.

McWhirter, J. & Kincaid, M. Family group consultation: Adjunct to a parent program. *Journal of Family Counseling*, 1974, *2*, 45-48.

Newland, T. E. *The gifted in socio-educational perspective*. Englewood Cliffs, N.J.: Prentice-Hall, 1976.

Pancrazio, J. J. The school counselor as a human relations consultant. *School Counselor*, 1971, *19*, 81-87.

Parker, C. (Ed.). *Psychological consultation: Helping teachers meet special needs*. Minneapolis: Leadership Training Institute/Special Education, University of Minnesota, 1975.

Perrone, P. *Career development model*. Unpublished manuscript, University of Wisconsin-Madison, 1976.

Personnel and Guidance Journal, 1978, *56*(6), 320-383. (Entire issue: Consultation 1 . . . Definition-models-programs.)

Personnel and Guidance Journal, 1978, *56*(7), 394-448. (Entire issue: Consultation 11 . . . Dimensions-training-bibliography.)

455

Principles, objectives and curricula in the education of mentally gifted minors. California State Department of Education, 1971.

Pulvino, C., Colangelo, N., & Zaffrann, R.T. *Laboratory counseling programs: Counseling and program development for gifted.* Madison, Wisconsin: Research and Guidance Laboratory, 1976.

Pulvino, C. J., & Sanborn, M. P. Feedback and accountability. *Personnel and Guidance Journal.* 1972, *51*, 15-20.

Rothney, J. W. M. *Methods of studying the individual child: The psychological case study.* Xerox Corporation, 1968.

Sanborn, M. P., Pulvino, C. J., & Wunderlin, R. F. *Research reports superior students in Wisconsin high schools.* Madison; Research and Guidance Laboratory for Superior Students. University of Wisconsin, 1971.

Sanborn, M. P. Career development problems of gifted and talented students. In K. B. Hoyt, & J. R. Hebeler (Eds.). *Career education for gifted and talented students.* Salt Lake City, Utah; Olympus Publishing Co., 1974.

Sanborn, M. P. Longitudinal research: Studies in a development framework. In L. Goldman (Ed.), *Research methods for counselors: Practical approaches in field settings.* New York: John Wiley & Sons, 1978.

Schmuck, R. A. Runkel, P. J., Saturen, S. L. Martell, R. J., & Durr, C. B. *Handbook of organization development in schools.* Palo Alto: National Press Books, 1972.

Tharp, R. The triadic model of consultation. In Clyde Parker (Ed.), *Psychological consultation: Helping teachers meet special needs.* Minneapolis: Leadership Training Institute/Special Education, University of Minnesota, 1975.

Walz, G. R., Smith, R. L., & Benjamin, L. A. *Comprehensive view of career development.* Washington, D.C.: APGA Press, 1974.

Werner, J. A. developmental consulting model for rural elementary schools. *Viewpoints*, 1972, *48*, 73-96.

Jerome H. Morton, Ph.D.
Edward A. Workman, Ed.D.

Insights: Assisting Intellectually Gifted Students with Emotional Difficulties

Our experiences in providing services to intellectually gifted young people who are experiencing observable emotional or behavior problems has led us to several conclusions.

First, the child must be perceived as part of a larger ecological system. Within that system we usually find three main subsystems. The family structure and how members of that unit perceive or interpret the actions of the young person is one subsystem. A second subsystem is the school environment including other students as well as the teachers and staff. The other subsystem lies within the target child and is expressed in the ways in which he/she interprets his/her own inner environment. The continuous dialogue the person seems to maintain within him/herself produces interpretations that carry over into the interpersonal interaction of the home or school situation.

A second conclusion we have reached is that any intervention strategy we attempt has to take into account the three-dimensional aspect of the environmental factors. While one can focus the intervention approach on one dimension, usually the student's internal environment, the other aspects cannot be ignored. In some cases it is better to address the problems of the related school or home situation. But again, all the factors must be considered if reasonable success is to be achieved.

Another conclusion we have reached is that the key starting point is one that focuses on behavior the young person wishes to change or control more effectively within him/herself. In brief, the gifted student needs to feel he/she has gained greater self-control. That control is translated into a greater realization of the student's own potentials and leads to generalizations into other aspects of the student's life.

Finally, we find a behaviorally oriented psychological approach to be appropriate in providing a successful framework for intervention activ-

Morton, Jerome H., and Workman, Edward A. "Insights: Assisting Intellectually Gifted Students with Emotional Difficulties," Roeper Review, Vol. 1, No. 2 (December 1978), pp. 16-18. Reprinted by permission of the publisher, Roeper Review, 2190 Woodward, Bloomfield Hills, MI 48013.

ities. This is not to deny the value of philosophical dialogues with the gifted youth, but rather to establish a consistency in overall approach.

This article will explore our conclusions in greater depth and provide some examples of the actual intervention process we are currently employing.

Conclusion 1

The intellectually gifted child with emotional or behavioral difficulties must be viewed in terms of an ecological system beyond her inner self. More specifically the home and school environment must be understood along with the inner world of the person.

Although the three environments interact, each individual in the various systems maintains her own interpretation of each interaction. Individual interpretations of the same event may differ widely from one another. For example, the mother of a three year old gifted child may know that in first grade children learn to print letters. When the gifted child starts asking for help in "making" letters, the parent refuses, telling the child to draw pictures like other three year olds. However, the gifted child's inherent drive to learn, do, and acquire more skills pushes her to experiment on her own in making letters. When the child actually enters first grade, the child makes the assumption that she can print letters. In fact, she can print most of the letters; however, she has developed some bad habits such as "going outside the lines." When the teacher tries to correct the child, the child resents it because she already "knows" and wants to learn something new. In this example we see faulty assumptions made by a parent and a gifted child that lead to a problem within the school environment. In this case all three individuals involved were operating from worthwhile intentions. Yet the failure to understand the other dimension led to conflict. While this example can be criticized for its simplicity, it does demonstrate how much more complex situations evolve. What is of particular interest in this example is that the faulty assumptions are based upon good intentions. Very frequently we find this to be the case in the complex situations we encounter.

What makes intellectually gifted childrens' situation so unique is the whole series of faulty assumptions made about them by their parents, their educators, and themselves. We know the intellectually gifted think more rapidly than the rest of the population. They seek out information on a wide variety of topics and investigate interest areas to a far greater depth than the general population. The rapidity of thought, accumulation of information, the quest to know are innate urges that cannot be denied, only twisted or bent. While we acknowledge these assumptions when we deal with specific gifted individuals, the tendency is to forget the special qualities. Too often, with the best of intentions, we choose to fall back on our experiences with nongifted children, and unintentionally force specific

458

children who are gifted to fit into our predetermined role. The "we" referred to are the parents, the educators, the children. Prevention of serious emotional disturbances within gifted children lies in increasing the awareness of parents, educators, and the gifted children as to the uniqueness possessed by the gifted and addressing their needs appropriately.

Conclusion 2

Any intervention strategy we attempt has to take into account the three dimensional aspect of the environmental factors. As we observed in the example used in the first conclusion, the parent, the educator, and the gifted child had distinct perceptual sets about the conflict situation. In truth, each of the points of view is valid when observed in isolation. An effective solution that satisfies everyone cannot be found without looking at the whole picture. Far too many times we've heard teachers accuse intervention specialists (counselors, school psychologists, teachers of the gifted, etc.) of siding with the child against the teacher. While we can criticize the teacher for not seeing the situation from the child's point of view, we often find that the solution proposed by the intervention specialist did not take into account the teacher's perspective. If it did, the criticism would not have been made. As stated before, we find that "good intentions" abound. What has been lacking is the consideration of all environmental factors. An example of these points can be found in the following situation.

John[1] was a gifted junior high school student who was extremely anxious and withdrawn in the presence of other students. With the approval of his elderly adoptive parents and his teachers, a counseling program designed to decrease his internal anxiety and to teach him to interact positively with his peers was implemented.[2] In this situation the entire system in which the child functions was involved; however, simply involving all the subsystems was not enough.

On the initial problem, the need for better interaction with peers, the program was highly successful. John was having effective interactions with boys his own age. For the first time in his life, he had made several friends at school and engaged in such social activities as going to the movies and having friends over to spend the night.

The success, however, allowed an equally critical problem to surface. The more John interacted with his new friends, the greater became his conflicts with his parents. The parents, who had adopted John as an only

---

[1]The examples used are composites of our experiences and are not meant to be presented as actual case studies of specific persons.

[2]This program focused on teaching John to eliminate his internal anxiety reactions in peer settings. This was done by teaching him to 1) engage in calm-inducing internal reactions in the presence of previously anxiety-provoking events, and 2) make self-statements which focused upon feelings of mastery and confidence rather than self-criticism.

child late in their lives, felt that he wanted to have "hippies running in and out of (their) house continuously." Their definition of "hippies" included anyone with hair that extended beyond the upper portion of the ear and listened to rock music. Their perceptual set of what "normal" teenagers were like was not accurate. As a subsystem of John's environment, they have a reality under which they function that has to be addressed as a separate unit before their effective assistance can be incorporated in assisting John. Clearly, their concept of normal teenagers played a role in John's withdrawn behavior long before any intervention strategies were devised. Neither John, his parents, nor the intervention specialists were initially aware of the underlying impact the parents' attitude played in this situation.

Once the underlying conflict between the two environmental factors was identified, John and his parents were brought together and assisted in better understanding the situation and in developing more appropriate communication skills.

While the initial intervention point focused on John, if we had ignored the concept of reality the parents held, independent of John, we would not have successfully assisted this gifted person.

Conclusion 3

In order to be more effective in bringing about behavioral changes that will continue, the initial entrance point of intervention needs to focus on behavior the young person wishes to change or have greater control over. Far too often our experience has shown that the behaviors the child wishes to change are not the same or lack the same priority as those desired by parents and educators. If a gifted student is not clearly motivated to change, the strategies will frequently be unsuccessful. The student's motivation for change is usually accompanied by an understanding of the necessity for change in a given situation. If the student does not wish change to take place, she often becomes actively engaged in defeating the strategies implemented. Unfortunately, the intellectually gifted child is particularly well equipped to thwart efforts to assist her. It is nice to acknowledge that once such a child becomes constructively committed to changing, progress is excellent. We have learned to take the approach of (1) assisting the student in determining which behaviors should be changed in order for maximum success and minimum failure to occur in a given situation, and (2) assisting the student in implementing a behavior change program for the desired behavior improvements. This approach ensures that the student will be motivated to change since the behaviors targeted for change were selected by the student. It also allows the student to take responsibility for his/her own actions. We believe that this results in breaking down power struggles between gifted children with behavior problems and others in their environment. The breaking of those power struggles results in a clearer perception by the student of a reciprocal relationship between herself and the environment. No longer is the environment viewed as being in constant opposition to the student. Instead, the environment is viewed as an important resource to draw upon. In turn, the gifted student tends to be much more flexible and creatively constructive in dealing with the world.

Conclusion 4

Our fourth conclusion is that a behaviorally oriented approach has much to offer a psychological services program for gifted students. Factors that make such an approach highly desirable include (1) its use of behavior change procedures which are empirically validated; (2) the requirement that behavior change goals be clearly specified; and (3) the focus on how the individual influences and is influenced by the environment.

Two behavioral approaches have been used in our program with highly positive results: behavioral self management (Workman and Hector, 1978; Williams and Long, 1975), and environmental restructuring (Williams and Anandam, 1973). The behavioral self management approach involves teaching a student to change his/her own behavior through the use of self-administered behavior change techniques. For example, our previously mentioned student, John, learned to change his own behavior by (1) recording his own internal and overt behaviors in social situations himself, and (2) carrying out, on his own, various techniques (e.g., self-administered relaxation) designed to reduce his internal anxiety and make him more comfortable in social situations.

Environmental restructuring involves changing some aspects of a student's surroundings in order to facilitate the change of some aspect of the student's behavior. For example, we can train a student's teacher or parent to praise her verbally for interacting positively with other students if verbal praise from these individuals is valued. In most cases, we have combined behavioral self management and environmental restructuring procedures. The nature of the emotional problems of the gifted are so interwoven among the individual's internal environment and the external environment (people at home or school) that a dual approach is usually necessary.

It would be misleading to leave the reader with the impression that our behavioral intervention approach excludes other strategies. Our approach reflects the framework within which we analyze the problems and develop strategies to remediate the problems. Often we engage in group discussions or counseling sessions that incorporate techniques developed by the encounter group movement, Parent Effectiveness Training, or Gestalt Therapy. We choose to interpret the emotional needs of gifted students and the effectiveness of the strategies used to meet those needs in behaviorally oriented psychological terms. Behavioral psychological concepts effectively

461

and efficiently organize our efforts to assist the students. In short, it helps us achieve success. It helps the gifted student.

Summary

Throughout this article we have tried to stress the need to consider the gifted child in terms of the total environment. If one is to successfully assist a gifted child with an emotional problem, all of the human beings involved must be considered as part of the problem and part of the solution. Each person involved, including the gifted child, has his/her own interpretations of events and statements made by others. Whether or not the interpretation is factually correct is irrelevant. if the individual thinks the interpretation is correct, he/she will act on that interpretation. Thus we must know the interpretations or "perceptual sets" that people carry into their interactions if we are to successfully bring about change. In turn, the entrance point in initiating change must rest with the targeted person, the gifted student, and that person must want a change to take place before ultimate success can be achieved. A behaviorally oriented approach has provided us with a structure in which to analyze, interpret, and remediate the numerous variables involved.

References

Williams, R., and Anandam, K. *Cooperative Classroom Management.* Charles E. Merrill, 1973.

Williams, R., and Long, J. *Toward a Self-Managed Life Style.* Houghton-Mifflin, 1975.

Workman, E., and Hector, M. Behavioral Self-Control in Classroom Settings: A Review of the Literature. *Journal of School Psychology*, 1978, *16*, 227-236.

Marvin J. Fine

Facilitating Parent-Child Relationships for Creativity

Most persons would agree on the importance of early home experiences in affecting the development of attitudes and values in the child; it has also been long believed and demonstrated that the stimulative affects of the home will either nurture or inhibit the child's intellectual and creative potential (Skodak & Skeels, 1949; Skeels, 1966; Gallagher, 1964; Havighurst, 1964; and Oden, 1968) aside from whatever the genetic contribution to a person's intellectual makeup. The intention of this paper is to contribute a viewpoint and some relevant ideas to the parenting of gifted and creative children. Since much of the literature and concepts cited applied to both groups, and also because the two groups are indeed similar in many respects, a clear distinction will not be maintained in this paper between "gifted" and "creative" children.

Parent-Child Relationships

The literature on gifted and creative children has a history of concern with parent-child relationships. A number of articles have been written by parents describing their home experiences and often their frustrations with school personnel (Burns, 1974; Ostrom, 1973). Chronic concerns of individual parents and of parent organizations are (a) how do we get the schools to be more responsive to the needs of our children and (b) what can we as parents do to facilitate the development of giftedness and creativity in our children? An article by Malone (1975) further defined the expressed needs of parents by reporting the results of a parent survey.

> Expressed needs of the parents were more counseling and a knowledge of teaching methods. Counseling was being requested in the areas of discipline, developing strengths, guiding sensitivity, and determining the rights of parents. Teaching methodology was requested so that parents could fill areas

Reprinted from Gifted Child Quarterly, Vol. XXI, No. 4 (Winter 1977), pp. 487-500. By permission of the author and publisher.

463

in which they felt the schools were not succeeding. The parents recognized that children have different kinds of learning styles and hoped to provide facilities and a proper atmosphere in their homes so that their children could develop individual styles of learning (p. 225).

Parents of gifted children are not only vociferous on behalf of their children but as a group are quite perceptive (Ciha et al, 1974), and themselves accomplished (Groth, 1975). There seems to be a great deal of rapport between parents and "experts" who write and speak to the needs of the gifted. A number of supportive and sympathetic articles have been published with parents as the target audience. The *Gifted Child Quarterly* has a section entitled "Parent Perspective," which typically features inform- ative and sympathetic articles, for example those by Gensley (1971; 1973). Also of note is an article by Isaacs (1971) on some of the problems gifted children encounter with well intentioned persons, Khatena's (1974) talk to parents about the creatively gifted, Malone's (1976) concise set of directives to parents on how to facilitate their children's involvement in the arts, and Parnes' (1968) chapter on a model for the parental encouragement of their children's creative potential.

The literature on gifted and creative children has also addressed itself to aspects of family structure and affectional ties. Groth (1974) reported on how the affective needs of adult gifted were related to their recollection of the emotional responses of their parents. She stated that ". . . parents of the same sex as that of their gifted children might exert more impact on the needs development of their children than would parents of the opposite sex" (p. 286). In an earlier article, Groth (1971) reported "men derived their inspiration to achieve primarily from their warm mothers—the opposite-sexed parent. Achieving women needed the warm support of both the opposite-sexed and the same-sexed parent" (p. 259). Gowan (1965; 1971) has also discussed in detail the importance of affectional ties with the opposite-sexed parent as a condition for the generating or releasing of creativity in the child.

The importance of family interaction patterns was further underscored by Dewing's (1970) review of the literature on family influences and creativity. She reported "The most important factors seem to be non- authoritarian discipline, diverse and relatively intellectual interests, and a parent-child relationship which is not overly dependent" (p. 403).

Children Who Are Not "Making It"

Our understanding of the complexities of nurturing creative and gifted children can be enhanced through the study of such children who are not "making it." However, before focusing on these children it should be reiterated that gifted children as a group do very well in personal and social development and in their productive integration into society (Terman &

464

Oden, 1947; Halpin, Payne & Elliot, 1975). It would be spurious, however, to treat the successes and mental health of the gifted population as a fait accompli. Such a posture would ignore the children who outrightly are experiencing personal, social, or achievement difficulties, and also those who seem on the surface to be succeeding, but are doing so at some great personal expense that will show up later.

Studies of gifted underachieving children have revealed a number of correlates. Once again as with many other problems, boys predominate over girls (Gallagher, 1964; Shaw, 1959; Cutts & Moseley, 1957). A number of articles have looked to the schooling experiences of the child as causally related to underachievement (Drews, 1961; French, 1959; Zilli, 1971). Negative schooling experiences include a variety of considerations beginning with the school's lack of recognition, acceptance, and appropriate planning for the gifted child. Also, the perception of some gifted children that in order to "get along" they have to deny their brightness has been long touted as an in-school factor depressing the functioning of the gifted child.

More general motivational considerations have also been identified (Bish, 1963; Sumption & Luecking, 1960; French, 1959; Newman, Dember & Krug, 1973; and Zilli, 1971). Due to family, cultural, or peer influences, the child's achievement capabilities may center on non-academic areas. Academic accomplishment per se may not be as reinforcing or gratifying for the child as other areas such as mechanical, social, or athletic endeavors. There also may be important personality factors contributing to the underachievement. Many underachieving children are of low self esteem or may be acting out anger and rebellion through their poor achievement pattern. Some understanding of how "underachieving" obtains secondary psychological gains for the child, comes from observing the consternation and excessive efforts by teachers and parents to motivate and energize the recalcitrant child.

It is also understandable how excessively high expectations from important persons in the child's life may discourage the child and lead him to disbelieving what others believe about his talents and capabilities. The parental response to the perception of high ability may also include in extreme cases not only demands for constant high performance, but an external structuring of the child's time and friendships. Some loss of personal autonomy and sense of self are likely to follow in a child so managed. More common among underachievers than parents with excessive expectations, are parents who have low expectations and who do not adequately encourage and support their gifted child (Cutts & Mosely, 1957; Drews, 1961; Oden, 1968). Brookover's position on the importance of significant others in the child's determination of what is appropriate for himself (Brookover & Erikson, 1975), and the well-known literature on expectancy effects (Rosenthal, 1968) underscore the importance of appropriate teacher and parental expectations.

465

An important descriptive study of gifted underachievers was reported by Newman, Dember, and Krug (1973) and was extremely rich in observations of developmental, psychodynamic, and family variables. The fifteen subjects, all boys, were seen as extremely verbally fluent with depressed performance skills. The study depicted how marital unhappiness and personal frustrations by the mothers encouraged excessive emotional investments in their verbally precocious sons. The motor or performance behaviors were not responded to as actively as the child's verbalizations, which further encouraged the child to develop and use his language facility. The quality of thinking behind the language display was more limited, with the child often developing a pattern of superficial intellectualization and "hop-scotching" shifting from one topic to another. The mothers would ignore this and "adultize" their conversations with their children.

Newman, Dember, and Krug described in detail the ways in which the child's ego development could become problematic. This included difficulties with separation-individuation which contributed toward the seemingly intellectually advanced child being perceived by others as immature. Problems of self esteem were predictable as were peer socialization difficulties, attention difficulties, and the presence of passive-aggressive dynamics. This study not only depicted the genesis of the child's idiosyncratic ways of viewing self and other, but how the child via his brightness and verbal skills acted out, manipulated, and supported his maladaptive pattern. Also described were the insidious ways that the child's negativism can interfere with the development of actual capabilities. The authors summarized this phenomena as follows:

I can, but I won't

I won't, so I don't

I don't, so I can't

I can't, but I'll say I won't.

Teachers, initially taken by the high verbal skills, rich imagination, and often high reading ability, soon discover they have "a tiger by the tail."

> The boys' capacity to charm and entertain adults, and to tantalize them with glimmers of verbal "giftedness," be it for "knowledge" in class or rich "fantasies" in the office, evoke enthusiasm and delight early in the adult-child relationship. However, disappointment, frustration, and counterhostility soon follow as a frequent countertransference sequence. (p. 121)

Given this review of some of the dynamics and characteristics of underachievement in gifted children, it is apparent that the underachievement and related personal difficulties are likely to remain long term characteristics of the individual. This statement, supported by studies (Barrett, 1957; Shaw & McCuen, 1960), may be disconcerting to teachers or parents who prefer to believe that "someday something will catch his interest and then he'll produce."

466

Parenting Gifted Children: A Frame of Reference

Considering the literature that argues how successful most gifted children turn out, a set of directives to parents on how to raise their children may seem uncalled for and even pretentious. But there is evidence, as reviewed, that parents of gifted and creative children are very concerned, are seeking guidance or at least more information as to their parenting task, and also that parent-child relationships can be problematic. Furthermore, this writer's experience with bright and inventive children who have personal problems, is that once they funnel their intellectual capabilities into distorting their experiences via rationalizaton, intellectualization, and elaborate projections, that they are very difficult to assist and that parents may have to settle in for the "long haul." Accordingly the best solution for gifted children with problems is for the problem not to have happened in the first place.

The ensuing discussion will attempt to say something about how parents can facilitate their child's healthy development and avoid supporting the development of pathological processes. While some of the comments may appear specific to the gifted or creative, what is being shared are simply ideas on effective parenting that are applicable in any family.

An Idealization of the Person

A good starting point is to consider the child as we might idealize him to be at some stage in his development. Not everyone would agree of course on what the "finished product" should look like. Some parents value "assertiveness" and some might emphasize "being responsible"; other parents might want a child who has "compassion and caring for others" while yet other parents might take the position that they only want their child to "be happy" or "able to decide for himself as to what he wants to be." A study by Bochtold (1974) reported that the most desirable characteristics that parents wanted for their children were, "sense of humor," "self confident," "considerate of others," "health," "courageous in convictions," "independent in thinking," "a self starter," "self sufficient," "a sense of beauty," "curiosity," "affection," "independent in judgment," "sincere," and "receptive to ideas of others." Only four of those characteristics, however, were among the characteristics of the creative personality as described by Torrance (1963): "Independence in thinking and judgment," "curiosity," and "courageous in convictions."

In the revealing book, *Cradles of Eminence* (Goertzel & Goertzel, 1962), we are given the picture of many high achieving, creative individuals as being driven and perfectionistic, chronically dissatisfied with their achievements, and incessantly striving for the next discovery or the more perfect product. Something in common to many of these eminent persons, were strong willed and authoritarian parents. It was speculated that the child had to become equally strong willed in order to survive. We might also speculate as to those who did not survive that style of parenting.

The view being espoused in this paper is that the ideal gifted or creative child is not different from the ideal child; they share similar characterological, personality, and behavioral characteristics. The following itemization of these characteristics is derived from the writings of Rogers (1969), Hamachek (1971), and Maslow (1962), among others.

This idealized person, whom we will refer to as "fully functioning," has a positive concept of self and other, has a sense of humor, can see more than one side to a situation, is aware of his thoughts and feelings, has a capacity for close relationships, can be assertive on his own behalf, and accepts responsibility for his own behavior. Another way of describing this idealization is to say that the person is free to think, to feel, to relate with others, to be himself, and to succeed. The person is an aware chooser and is not prohibited by inner conflicts, fears, or pathological needs. As a correlate of these characteristics, the person's intellectual and creative capacities are likely to emerge. His perceptions are likely to be broad and rich rather than narrow and stimulus bound; accordingly the person will be aware of the possibilities of situations and may respond in original rather than stereotyped fashion.

This description was referred to as an idealization, and is not likely to ever be fully achieved by anyone. Growing up in a family and cultural context extracts a psychological price, and most people spend a lifetime working progressively toward actualization and fulfilling their potential. These last statements were not meant to be pessimistic, only the simple recognition that each of us is involved in a lifetime developmental process. This introduces a final and very real consideration into this characterization of the "way people ought to be," which is that they be growth oriented. Without their original growth orientation permitted to remain and flourish as an aspect of self, the other identified characteristics will not fully develop.

So What's A Parent To Do?

Many curriculum guides and parent "handouts" tout the gifted child as the "leader of tomorrow" and emphasize the careful nurturing of the child's giftedness. It is suspected that a number of teachers of the gifted might be in awe of their task. A reasonable analogy is how the servant of the young prince would feel, knowing that someday this child will grow up to be the king, and that he has a responsibility to influence the young prince so he will be a just and noble king.

This paper hopes to establish a reasonable perspective on the parenting of gifted and creative children (after all, they "tinkle" in their diapers too). Not every gifted child, whatever his potential, *has* to grow up to be a

468

"world-beater" and a molder of the destiny of mankind. From this writer's viewpoint it will be sufficient if a gifted child grows up feeling good about himself, is productive and competent in his work and personal relationships, and able to enjoy a full, rich life. Also, the concept of multiple causality is a good one for parents and educators to keep in mind. There is a tendency to focus on one event or variable as if it would account by itself for the success or failure of the parenting process. For example a parent might believe that "reinforcing the child's interest" is the *key* to nurturing the child's giftedness. This idea of encouraging a child is valuable but it would be simplistic to conclude least of all to prove that this factor alone is the main contribution to the full development of the child. There are numerous inputs from family and community that affect the child as they intermesh with the child's own developmental processes. The reader should keep this in mind, since the review of parenting concepts will be presented in point form and without any intent of inferring a ranking of priorities. These ideas derive from several sources including humanistic considerations, communication models, developmental theory, and the literature on family process.

1. *Recognize the child for "being" as well as for "doing."* Children need to know they have worth for who they are, not just for what they can do. With gifted children some parents may excessively respond to the child's accomplishments, leaving the child with the sense that he must perform to please his parents. The child needs and deserves strokes or recognition unconditionally, just because he's there and he is loved for himself. Parental approval can be a strong and useful reinforcer of attitudes and behavior patterns, and should be used appropriately. When self esteem or a sense of well being becomes associated in the child mainly with accomplishment, then problems can arise. The child might become excessively driven to perform or conversely he may rebel as in the instance of some underachieving children.

2. *Precocious development does not equal maturity.* Some gifted children are quite precocious in specific areas of development such as language or motor. Just because a child for example can walk at 8 months, does not mean he has the maturity of judgment to know where to go. It will be helpful to the child for parents to stay in touch with the many facets of development, to realize that the child may develop unevenly, and that the child still needs a parent in the parenting role.

3. *Individuation—the goal of life.* This title may sound somewhat grand or dramatic, but it seems valid to state that becoming one's person, achieving a sense of autonomy, being able to see one's self as a complete entity, are long term goals of living. Contrast this with the state of healthy symbiosis of the infant who cannot survive alone early in life and is unaware of his separateness from parent figures. Assisting children toward individuation is an important parenting task. Pushing a child into independence usually backfires as does a parent attempting to hold a child back from the appropriate development of independence. Health guidance

469

involves a balance of prohibitions and permissions, and some risk taking by the parents within the boundaries of good judgment.

4. *Caring and protection promote internal caring and protection.* As children begin to explore their environments they need a caring and protecting parent to guide and monitor their experiences. Children can learn about what hurts without becoming injured. Parents who care and protect children appropriately, help that child to internalize the belief that he is valuable and that he needs to protect himself. Some children seem to ricochet from one disaster to another, almost courting annihilation. We might speculate as to how those children feel about themselves and what they expect for themselves. Persons who value themselves and believe themselves to be worthwhile don't knowingly take foolish risks or put themselves into situations where physical or psychological hurt are likely to occur. The game of "kick me" is played chronically by individuals with negative self concepts and the putdowns or rebuffs they provoke only confirm their belief as to "how it's going to be for me."

5. *Other people count too!* The egocentricity of the young child is acted out in an "I want what I want when I want it" pattern. Parents taken by their child's precocity or having difficulty with their own self regard may offer the child too much freedom to act out his will on others. An important aspect of getting along in this world is the capacity to empathize with the other person; that is, to see things from the other person's viewpoint. Tied in with this is the importance of respecting the rights of others. Children who are excessively catered to and whose demanding behaviors are tolerated or even nurtured by parents in the name perhaps of "encouraging the child to express his feelings and wants," are not very likely to develop positive regard for others. The term "social contract" has been used to describe the point when a child does accept that others have rights and that it will be appropriate at different times for the rights of others to take precedent over the child's preferences.

6. *When is it "good enough?"* At what degree of accomplishment can the parent indicate satisfaction with the child's performance? An old standard is the child who comes home and proudly shows Mom a paper on which he got 98 out of 100. The mother's critical response is "so who got the other two points?" Parents in the name of high standards can be excessively critical and possibly discourage the child who knows he can never please Mom or Dad. Just as problematic is the child who internalizes this "critical parent" and is never satisfied with his own effort.

The obvious challenge for the parent is to be supportive and accepting of the child's efforts, to set realistic expectations, and to know when to back off and let the child be the judge of satisfaction with his efforts. Stroking or giving a positive reaction to the child for being involved and attempting tasks may also be overlooked if the focus is always on the "super product." Additionally, parents may overgeneralize the child's capabilities in one area to other areas of activity where the child is less than gifted.

7. *Will the real child please stand up.* An anecdote described by Danial Boorstin (1962) involves a woman looking at an infant and remarking "what a pretty child." The mother replies, "if you think she's pretty, you should see her pictures." Some parents are so taken by their child's giftedness as to lose sight of the real child. They manufacture an image out of their projections and then relate to their projection rather than the real child. Earlier, mention was made of how some children with precocious language development are seen as very mature by their parents. The parents project the image of a mature child and relate to the child in an "adultized" fashion, losing sight of the shallow thinking behind the big words and long sentences. A vicious circle occurs when the child attempts to adapt to the parent's projection, thereby losing touch with his own feelings and needs.

8. *Me parent—You child!* In healthy families there are clear generation boundaries. Mom and dad have certain prerogratives and authority that come with their maturity and responsibility in the child rearing area. Bright children have their ideas about how things should be in the family or how certain issues should be resolved. A family with a democratic orientation encourages the sharing of opinions and views by all its members; this is healthy. What is not healthy is when the child is permitted to assume parenting functions involving important decisions regarding the family's welfare. Again there is a fine line here between valuing involvement of the children in decision making and determining when the parents need to exercise their authority.

It would be equally disruptive of a healthy family pattern if the parents encroach on the lives of their children. An example of this would be Dad insisting on going along to play ball with his teenage son, as if he were "one of the guys," or Mom relating as a sister to her daughter.

9. *You can't tell the players without a program.* Problems in the marital relationship can affect family dynamics and negatively affect the children. The parent conflict can be acted out openly or in covert fashion. For example, Mom and Dad might make incompatible demands of the child. Mom insists that Billy study and excell academically while Dad instructs him to have fun, socialize, and not to spend all of his time studying. Since the parents do not communicate with each other the child is left in a no-win bind.

Another negative pattern involves one parent in collusion with the child. For example Dad leaves specific chore instructions for Sally. Later in the day Mom lets procrastinating Sally go out with her friends and ignore Dad's instructions. That night Mom rationalizes Sally's behavior which sets Sally and Mom up against Dad and teaches Sally some things about manipulating people, redefining situations, and how to "divide and conquer."

10. *Effective communication really does effect communication.* Communication, defined simply as the sending and receiving of messages, is at the heart of relationships and can either facilitate or hinder family dynamics and individual growth. Some effective communication patterns include; (a)

471

being willing to listen to each other. This means paying attention to both the thoughts and feelings of the other person; (b) avoiding responses that shut off, put down, or inappropriately solutionize; (c) being willing to think through alternatives including the consequences of different options; (d) owning your thoughts and feelings. This often gets expressed by the use of "I" such as "I want to tell you how I feel," rather than the use of blaming "you" as in "you make me feel . . . ;" (e) being aware of what issues are negotiable and what issues are not and letting the children know in a straight way. Otherwise the discussion is phony since the parent has an established position; and (f) being explicit rather than assuming that others are able to "read your mind." Disagreements that include phrases such as "but I thought you knew what I wanted . . . ," suggest that a limited or distorted communication pattern existed.

Conclusions

The parenting of gifted and creative children for the most part involves similar issues and challenges to the parenting of any child. The description presented in this paper of the fully functioning person is considered to be valid for all children. However, the "special" status of gifted and creative children in terms of their contemporary behaviors and presumed future potentials, can pull different responses from parents.

As many parents will testify, it can be exciting and enjoyable being part of their child's growth process. Many parents would also agree that being a part of their child's growth process facilitated their own personal growth.

A number of the ideas presented revolved around the question of how emotionally involved and directing parents should be as contrasted with their being more unqualifyingly accepting and encouraging of the child. There is a need for parents to be very self aware regarding their personal investments in the child and also to maintain an accurate and balanced perception of the child as a total and growing person. Gifted and creative children need parents for emotional support and encouragement, for value and behavioral guidance, and to set realistic limits; it is appropriate and important that parents of gifted and creative children in fact do fulfill a parenting "contract" with their children.

References

Bachtold, L. The creative personality and the ideal pupil revisited. *The Journal of Creative Behavior*, 1974, *8*, 47-54.

Bish, C. Underachievement of gifted students, in L. Crow and A. Crow, *Educating the academically able*. New York: David McKay, 1963.

Boorstin, D. *The image*, New York: Atheneum, 1962.

Brookover, W., and Erickson, E. *Sociology of education.* Homewood, Ill.: Dorsey Press, 1975.

Burns, D. Letter from a parent. *National Elementary Principal,* 1972, *51,* 32-36.

Ciha, T., Harris, R., and Hoffman, C. Parents as identifiers of giftedness, ignored but accurate. *The Gifted Child Quarterly,* 1974, *18,* 191-195.

Cutts, N., and Mosely, N. *Teaching the bright and gifted.* Englewood Cliffs, N.J.: Prentice Hall, Inc., 1957.

Dewing, K. Family influences on creativity: A review and discussion. *The Journal of Special Education,* 1970, *4,* 399-404.

Drews, E. (Ed.) Guidance for the academically talented student. Report of a Conference Sponsored Jointly by the American Personnel and Guidance Association and the National Education Association, Washington, D.C., 1961.

French, J. *Educating the gifted: A book of readings.* New York: Holt, Rinehart & Winston, 1959.

Gallagher, J. *Teaching the gifted child.* Boston: Allyn and Bacon, 1964.

Gensley, J. The bored child. *The Gifted Child Quarterly,* 1971, *15,* 60-61.

Gensley, J. The pre-school gifted child. *The Gifted Child Quarterly,* 1973, *17,* 219-220.

Goertzel, V., and Goertzel, M.G. *Cradles of emminence.* Boston: Little, Brown, 1962.

Gowan, J. What makes a gifted child creative. *Gifted Child Quarterly,* 1965, *9,* 3-6.

Gowan, J. Why some children become creative. *The Gifted Child Quarterly,* 1971, *15,* 13-18.

Groth, N. Differences in parental environment needed for degree achievement for gifted men and women. *The Gifted Child Quarterly,* 1971, *15,* 256-261.

Groth, N. Mothers of gifted. *The Gifted Child Quarterly,* 1975, *19,* 259.

Groth, N. The relationship of the affective needs of a sample of intellectually gifted adults to their age, sex, and perceptions of emotional warmth to their parents. *Dissertation Abstracts,* 1974, *35,* 286.

Halpin, B., Payne, D., and Elliot, C. Life history antecedents of current personality traits of gifted adolescents. *Measurement and Evaluation in Guidance,* 1975, 8, 29-36.

Hamachek, D. *Encounters with the self.* New York: Holt, Rinehart, and Winston, 1971.

Havighurst, R. Conditions productive of superior children. In W. Fullager, H. Lewis, and C. Cumber (Eds.), *Readings for educational psychology.* New York: Thomas Y. Crowell, 1964.

Isaacs, A. Being gifted is a bed of roses, with the thorns included. *The Gifted Child Quarterly,* 1971, *15,* 54-56.

Khatena J. Parents and the creatively gifted. *The Gifted Child Quarterly*, 1974, *18*, 202-209.

Malone, C. Education for parents of the gifted. *The Gifted Child Quarterly*, 1975, *19*.

Malone, C. Parents as facilitators of talent in the arts. *The Gifted Child Quarterly*, 1976, *20*, 447-450.

Maslow, A. *Toward a psychology of being*. New York: D. Van Nostrand Co., 1962.

Newman, J. Dember, D., and Krug, O. "He can but he won't." *Psychoanalytic Study of the Child*, 1973, *28*, 83-129.

Oden, M. The fulfillment of promise: 40 year follow-up of the Terman gifted group. *Genetic Psychology Monograph*, 1968, *77*, 3-93.

Ostrom, G. The self-concept of gifted children grows through freedom of choice, freedom of movement and freedom to do what is right. *The Gifted Child Quarterly*, 1973, *17*, 285-287.

Parnes, S. A suggested model for parents' use in developing the child's creative potential. In F. Williams (Ed.) *Creativity at home and in the school*. St. Paul, Minn.: Macalester Creativity Project, 1968, 245-249.

Rogers, C. *Freedom to learn*. Columbus, Ohio: Charles E. Merrill, 1969.

Rosenthal, R., and Jacobson, L. *Pygmalion in the classroom*. New York: Holt, Rinehart and Winston, 1968.

Shaw, M. Definition and identification of academic underachievers, in J. French (Ed.), *Educating the gifted: A book of readings*, New York: Holt, Rinehart and Winston, 1959.

Shaw, M. and McCuen, J. The onset of academic underachievement in bright children. *Journal of Educational Psychology*, 1960, *51*, 103-108.

Skeels, H. Adult status of children with contrasting early life experiences. *Monographs of the Society for Research in Child Development*, 1966, *31*, 1-66.

Skodak, M., and Skeels, H. A final follow-up study of one hundred adopted children. *Journal of Genetic Psychology*, 1949, *75*, 85-125.

Sumption, M., and Luecking, E. *Education of the gifted*. New York: Ronald Press Co., 1960.

Terman, L. and Oden, M. *The gifted child grows up*. Stanford: Stanford University Press, 1947.

Torrance, E. The creative potential and the ideal pupil. *Teachers College Record*, 1963, *65*, 220-226.

Zilli, M. Reasons why the gifted adolescent underachieves and some of the implications of guidance and counseling to this problem. *The Gifted Child Quarterly*, 1971, *15*, 279-292.

474

Philip A. Perrone
Charles J. Pulvino

New Directions in the Guidance of the Gifted and Talented

Introduction

While efforts to identify gifted children have been made since the start of the century, (Baker, 1907; Whipple, 1924; Terman and others, 1925; Bentley 1937; Sumpton, Norris and Terman, 1950; Witty, 1951; and Terman, 1954) efforts to guide them did not originate until the fifties, (Strang, 1952; Barbe, 1954; Barbour, 1954; Buchwald, 1954; Gowan, 1955; Neuber, 1957; Conant, 1959; Gowan, 1960; NEA, 1961).

Despite these attempts it was not until 1958 when Congress reacted to "Sputnik" with passage of the National Defense Education Act that federal emphasis was directed toward this population of students. Legislation was provided to prepare counselors who could better identify and guide gifted and talented high school students. Schools were funded to develop programs which could effectively channel gifted and talented youth into the sciences and engineering. History shows that to a large degree the program was successful. The United States put the first man on the moon, took close-up pictures of Mars, and successfully completed interplanetary soil sampling.

Although the program was successful it does not appear that defining gifted and talented as high achieving science and mathematics students resulted in either a comprehensive definition of gifted and talented nor in a comprehensive program for identifying, educating, and guiding the gifted and talented students. The educational pendulum apparently is taking shorter swings because the needs of gifted and talented pupils are coming to the fore once again—and the concern is broader than in 1958. It appears today the concern is for the individual as well as society. Moreover much of the present support comes from parties directly involved with gifted students, their parents, and school personnel.

The Research and Guidance Laboratory at the University of Wisconsin

Reprinted from Gifted Child Quarterly, Vol. XXI, No. 3, (Fall, 1977), pp. 326-335. By Permission of the author and publisher.

has been studying and guiding and following the development of superior high school students since the Sputnik era in 1958. Although we have been interested in individual high school students and their later accomplishments, at this time we want to broaden our scope and thus find it necessary to develop a comprehensive definition of gifted and talented and differentiated guidance for them. In this regard it seems useful to utilize the Office of Education's definitions of talented and gifted. A talented student is defined in terms of performing in the highest 15% among a peer population in both measures of cognitive development and measures of performance or achievement. A gifted student is defined in terms of performing in the highest 3% among a peer population in measures of cognitive development and measures of performance or achievement (U.S. Senate Subcommittee Report, 1972).

Rationale

In developing the present framework we have been attracted by the writings of many people. Gowan (1974) has described a developmental stage theory associating Erikson's life stages (affective component) with Piaget's cognitive developmental stages. Gowan links affective and cognitive components to three attentional modes (the world, the self, and interpersonal relations) in infancy-childhood, adolescence, and adulthood. A table representing this linkage follows.

Information in Table 1 fails to adequately represent the complexity and interrelatedness of the various components. It is our belief that the affective dimension provides the necessary conditions for cognitive devel-

Erikson—Piaget—Gowan Stage Development

	Infancy-Childhood Affective-Cognitive	Youth-Adolescence Affective-Cognitive	Adult Effective-Cognitive
THE WORLD	TRUST— SENSORIMOTOR (perception emerges)	INDUSTRY— CONCRETE OPERATIONS	ENERATIVITY— PSYCHEDELIA
THE SELF	IDENTITY—FORMAL OPERATIONS (Child can formulate hypotheses and think logically)	GO INTEGRITY— ILLUMINATON	
RELATING TO OTHERS	INITIATIVE— INTUITIVE (Child can imagine incomplete connection between precept and conceptualization)	INTIMACY— CREATIVITY (Child is able to create concepts)	

*this transition point we hypothesize that the individual has achieved field independence.

476

opment and that at higher levels of cognitive development all previous affective conditions must be present. If this hypothesis is correct, educational emphasis would have to be on establishing and maintaining a positive affective environment, without which cognitive development would not occur. It is our contention that further research is needed to investigate the relationship between the affective and cognitive domains. Also, research regarding the latter stages of affective and cognitive development is sparse compared to the research generated regarding the first five stages. It appears that understanding the creative process is linked to knowing more about these latter stages of Piaget's and Samples' hierarchies (see Figure 1).

Ornstein (1972) sheds additional light on the hemispheric function of

FIGURE 1

LEFT HEMISPHERE FUNCTION RATIONAL MIND
(Piaget)

RIGHT HEMISPHERE FUNCTON METAPHORIC MIND
(Samples)

Formal Operations Stage
(12 years of age) Ability to think in ways that result in problems being solved without direct experience with the qualities involved. Its hallmark is abstract deduction.

Concrete Operations
(7 to 12 years of age) Beginning to translate experience preferentially into generalizations that can be approached mentally without experience.

Pre-Operational Stage
(18 months to 7 years) Cannot translate experience into abstrct representation or symbolism. Discriminates between modes of sensory input but shows little preferences toward abstraction.

Sensory-Motor Stage
(Birth to 18 months) Treats all experience without preference of input. So involved with senses and sensory experience that abstractions are of little importance.

Inventive Mode
The mind uses existing knowledge to create objects and processes that have never existed. There is a total synergic combination of external and/or internal qualities with no link to precedent. *All metaphoric and rational modes may contribute.*

Integrative Mode
Personal analogy, becoming, something, total immersion; e.g., becoming a ball-feeling, sensing the way a ball rolls, bounces, etc.

Comparative Mode
Direct analogy such as "a city is like a heart, one pulse beat in the morning when corpuscles (traffic) flow in and another pulse beat at night when corpuscles (traffic) flow out."

Symbolic Mode
Substitution of symbols for natural realities, e.g., I-90 for a four-lane road running from Chicago to Minneapolis.

Adapted from Samples (1975), indicating the hierarchical functions of the left hemisphere as described by piaget and proposed metaphorical functions of the right hemisphere posited by Samples.

the brain. He suggests that "although each hemisphere shares the potential for many functions, and both sides participate in most activities, in the normal person the two hemispheres tend to specialize" (p. 51). Ornstein's statement can be pictorially represented by a Venn diagram in which the logical (left) hemisphere circle overlaps the metamorphic (right) hemisphere circle and this overlap portion indicates that potential for generalized function, and the non-overlapped, the potential for specialization.

In this conceptualization the left hemisphere is involved with analytic, logical thinking and the right hemisphere is holistic in nature and is primarily responsible for intuition, feelings, space orientation, and diffuse processing of information. Whereas the left hemisphere processes information linearly, the right processes information holistically. The two "halves" have the specialized potential for approaching problems from two quite different perspectives. It is in this potential that they are functionally complementary. At the highest level of mental functioning the shaded area represents the "Inventive Mode" described by Samples.

Another perspective regarding the rational mind and metaphoric need is suggested by Rollo May (1977). May describes two types of learning humans experience. One type is determinism where one acquires new facts, new data, new habits, and new behavior patterns which can be viewed as having a logical or left hemispheric origin. The second type is freedom which is based upon assumption of transference, resistence, and other functions of the unconscious which is metaphoric or right hemispheric based.

Field Dependence-Field Independence

Thinking in terms of the brain's specialized halves has led us to examine other human behaviors frequently characterized as dichotomous. The works of Witkin (1977) has been most enlightening and has led to a variety of suggestions including:

1. Field-independent persons are more likely to be aware of their own needs, feelings, and attributes which they experience as distinct from those of others. This distinction in effect provides an internal frame of reference to which the person may adhere in dealing with others.
2. Field-independent persons show significantly more non-verbal behaviors (such as arm crossing, leg crossing, absence of forward leaning). . . . interpreted as reflecting a need to gain psychological distance from others.
3. Field-dependent persons are likely to be attentive to and make use of prevailing social frames of reference.
4. Field-dependent persons . . . take greater account of external social referents in defining their attitudes and feelings . . . particularly under conditions of ambiguity.

478

5. A relatively field-independent person is likely to overcome the organization of the field, or to restructure it, when presented with a field of having a dominant organization, whereas the relatively field-dependent person tends to adhere to the organization of the field as given.
6. Field-independent people attempt to use an hypothesis-testing approach and field-dependent persons a spectator approach to concept attainment.

Our questions at this point are whether field dependence-independence is a direct function of hemispheric specialization. If it is, can we assess field dependence-independence by measuring hemispheric functioning? What are the educational implications if this relationship exists?

Convergent-Divergent Thought

Investigation of convergent-divergent thought processes follows closely on the examination of hemispheric specialization and field dependence-field independence theory. Combining these two lines of inquiry leads us to the following:

Convergent thinking is illustrative of rational thinking in that there is formed (learned) associations between external stimuli (ES) and responses (R). Learning appropriate generalizations and discriminations are essential in being judged logical. The correctness and appropriateness of responses are determined (externally) by others.

Within social parameters the individual should learn to become less dependent, less externally evaluated and more independent, and self-evaluative. We make the same differentiation Samples (1975) makes regarding the meaning of stimulation and motivation. Stimulation is external or extrinsic and is provided by the culture. Motivation is instrinsic, born inside, calling itself to action. You cannot determine whether behavior is stimulated or motivated without knowing the individual's thought processes including the reasons for his/her behavior. An appropriate learning environment provides the individual stimulation, support, and reinforcement which in turn should produce a relatively secure, intellectually curious individual who eventually can be motivated, self-reinforcing, and self-evaluating.

At the highest levels of divergent thinking the individual should be able to respond to external stimuli with appropriate learned responses or respond with a newly created response. Individuals can also create stimuli (internally created stimuli) to which they can respond. Responses may be evaluated externally and internally and these evaluations may frequently be in conflict. It is being suggested that convergent thinking capability is necessary but not sufficient for higher levels of divergent thought and that the highest levels of divergent thought *encompass the highest levels of convergent thought and high levels of metaphoric thought.* In effect this corresponds with the Inventive Mode listed at the top of Samples' hierarchy.

479

This hypothesis is consistent with the research of Getzels and Jackson (1962), DeBono (1971), Johnson (1972), Olson (1977), and Crockenberg (1972).

The work of Getzels and Jackson (1962), Torrance (1962), and more recently Wallach and Kogan (1965) make a strong case for focusing on the attributes/characteristics of convergent and divergent thinking as the key to enhancing the ultimate development of gifted and talented persons. Research and analysis research on the relationship of divergent and convergent thinking by Wallach and Kogan provides a convincing argument that although convergent and divergent thinking are related at lower levels they appear to be unrelated at higher levels.

Educational Considerations

Our present system of characterizing gifted or talented persons as being *either* high convergent *or* high divergent thinkers may reflect more upon the nature of learning environments (home, school, and community) and their impact (reinforcements) on individual personality development than be indicative of fundamental differences among persons.

May (1977) sheds some light on this issue in his discussion of anxiety that accompanies freedom or creativity. He suggests that there is no insight without some anxiety and that anxiety is a primary reason people reject freedom. Anxiety occurs because insight consists of two possibilities—of failure or of success. The sense of failure can explain why people block off most original ideas before they reach consciousness, repressing ideas that are counter to views of esteemed others. May concludes that courage is necessary to accept constructive anxiety and that individuals in a supportive environment need less courage to be creative. Positive reinforcers in home, school, and community may allow an individual to be creative by effectively reducing fear of failure.

To more adequately determine the impact of home, school, and community, to better understand creative anxiety, and, ultimately, to be able to understand differences between individuals we must assess how individual students incode and decode stimuli. To help us we have turned to the work of Grinder and Bandler (1975, 1976) whose research indicates that the language individuals use is indicative of how they process data from their world. They hypothesize that of the data processed through the five sensory input channels, the three major input channels are vision, audition, and kinesthetic and that the remaining two channels—smell and taste—are apparently little used as ways of gaining information about the world.

Grinder and Bandler believe that individuals gain meaning from their experiences and store them for future use by creating a map or model of their experiences which are called *representational systems*. Individuals store their experiences directly in a representational system most closely associ-

480

ated with sensory input channels. For each individual, there are more or less highly developed, or preferred, representational systems which parallel the visionary, auditory, and kinesthetic input channels.

In addition, an individual may have preferred short and long term storage systems and preferred retrieval systems which correspond to their primary mode for obtaining data. Little is known about how these systems operate, either individually or collectively. What may shed light on the underlying organizational structure of these systems, however, is the theoretical work being accomplished with split-brain research. Samples' (1975) work described earlier suggests that development of visual metaphoric, symbolic thinking (a right hemisphere function) occurs readily in some cultures and that individuals from those cultures are frequently able to create extensive "maps" of their world which are extremely rich in detail, formationally accurate, and readily retrievable. Individuals in the Anglo American culture, by contrast, apparently have difficulty in utilizing visual metaphoric, symbolic processes and experience greater success in sharing their representation of the world with symbolic images such as the written word, a left hemispheric function.

Conclusion

What is suggested by the research of Samples (1975), Ornstein (1972), and Sperry (1974) is that different cultures educate their youth in a differential manner, some focusing on left hemispheric functioning, others on right hemispheric functioning. Given this belief it is important to assess educational influences of majority and minority cultures to determine which activities, customs, beliefs, influences, etc., lead to development of one hemisphere or the other. Secondly, it is our assumption that development of diverse potential in both hemispheres of the brain is preferable to development of one hemisphere only. Therefore, it is important to assess an individual's cognitive style, representational systems, and consequent learning preferences so that educational offerings can be designed and implemented which will enhance the person's strength while ameliorating his/her weaknesses. More productivity from both hemispheres is the desired outcome. May (1977) emphasizes this point with his statement that without determinism (convergent thinking), and the predictability that goes with it, we have *anarchy*. Without freedom (divergent thinking), and the exuberance that goes with it, we have *apathy* (p. 9).

Another desired outcome of educating gifted and talented pupils is creativeness. Creativity has traditionally been viewed as a process which is determined to exist by its products. You cannot equate product and process. It appears to us to be more fruitful to research the necessary conditions for creativeness which are represented by field-independence and high convergent and divergent intelligence which we believe are produced by affective support and cognitive stimulation.

481

As more becomes known through our research and the research of others, we will modify assumptions presented in this paper. Educational procedures that result should lead to better educated gifted and talented youth, a society that better utilizes the talents of all its citizens, and an end to crisis programming such as that which was ushered in by Sputnik.

References

Baker, J. H. *American problems.* Longman, Green & Co., New York: 1907.

Barbe, W.B. Differentiated guidance for the gifted. *Education* 74:306 11, Jan. 1954.

Bentley, J.E. *Superior children,* W.W. Norton & Co., Inc., New York: 1937

Barbour, E. Counseling gifted h.s. students. *California J. Secondary Education* 29:476–79, Dec. 1954.

Buchwald, Leona, The counselor's role in identifying and guiding the superior child: *Baltimore Bulletin of Education,* 31:16–17, June 1954.

Conant, J.B. The identification and education of the academically talented. *NEA Conference Report,* Washington, D.C. 1958.

Crockenberg, S.B. Creativity tests: A boon or boondoggle for education? *Review of Educational Research,* Vol. 42, No. 1, 1972, 27–45.

DeBono, E. *The use of lateral thinking.* Toronto: Holt Publishing Co., 1971.

Garrett, S.V. Putting our whole brain to use: A fresh look at the creative process. *Journal of Creative Behavior,* 1976, 10, 239–249.

Getzels, J.W., & Jackson, P.W. *Creativity and intelligence.* New York: John Wiley & Sons, Inc., 1962.

Gowan, J.C. *Development of the psychedelic individual.* Buffalo, N.Y.: Creative Education Foundation, S.U.C., 1974.

Gowan, J.C. The gifted underachiever—a problem for everyone. *Exceptional Children* 21:7:247–9, 1955.

Gowan, J.C. The organization of guidance for the able. *Personnel & Guidance J.* 39:4:275–79, Dec. 1960.

Grinder, J., & Bandler, R. *The structure of magic,* Vol. I. Palo Alto, Calif.: Science and Behavior Books, Inc., 1975.

Grinder, J., & Bandler, R. *The structure of magic,* Vol. II. Palo Alto, Calif.: Science and Behavior Books, Inc., 1976.

Johnson, D.M. *Systematic introduction to the psychology of thinking.* New York: Harper, 1972.

A. Harry Passow

The Gifted
and the Disadvantaged

*M*ore than 15 years have elapsed since the inception of what has been called the "third wave of interest in the gifted." Fewer than a half dozen years have passed since such terms as *disadvantaged* and *deprived* were added to the educational lexicon. For some persons, the two populations—both lacking uniform, widely accepted definition—represent opposite ends of a continuum of talent potential. For others, both groups represent different aspects of the same problem of talent development. Certainly, one stimulus for the present concern for the education of the disadvantaged is the firm belief that children from low-income, ethnic, and racial minority groups represent the nation's largest unmined source of talent. Aside from the humanitarian aspects of overcoming poverty and discrimination, aside from the moral values in providing equal opportunity for all, the nation's welfare and survival depend on its success in identifying and nurturing talents of many kinds wherever they may be found.

Schemes for encouraging talent development among the disadvantaged tend to follow many of the patterns employed by planners of programs for the gifted a few years ago and, as might be expected, even commit some of the same errors. Many of the issues raised regarding programs for the gifted are now paraphrased to apply plans for the disadvantaged. Ironically, concern for the disadvantaged has triggered opposition to what had become established and accepted practices for the gifted. Most notably, special provisions for the gifted and particularly special groupings have become a prime target for attack on the basis of alleged "discrimination against the disadvantaged." Identification procedures, especially those involving standardized intelligence tests, have been condemned as being discriminatory against the poor and culturally different.

Stripped of polemics, the hard-nut question is basically one of how to

Passow, Harry A. "The Gifted and the Disadvantaged." *The National Elementary Principal*, Vol. LI, No. 5, Feb., 1972, pp. 24-31.

provide for the wide range of individual differences found in any school population. Having known for some time that identical experiences are not the same as equal opportunities, educational program planners continue to be concerned with the problems of individualization and differentiation of instruction. With respect to both the gifted and the disadvantaged, the perennial questions persist: What sorts of education will best educate? What constitutes adequate and appropriate education for all?

In a position paper prepared for the 1960 White House Conference on Children and Youth, seven problem areas in the education of the gifted and talented were identified as most pressing:

1. Improvements of means for measuring the multidimensions of high level ability, thus sharpening the identification of the talented.

2. Improvement of procedures for locating the potential underachiever at an early stage to prevent negative attitudes, learning patterns, and self-concepts from forming and choking his capabilities.

3. Recruitment, education, and retention of talented individuals in the teaching profession—in instruction, counseling, supervisory, and administrative positions.

4. Development of means for keeping abreast of new knowledge and revision of instruction to include these new insights and understandings.

5. Development and appraisal of instructional techniques, materials, and resources that will yield deeper learnings for the gifted.

6. Development of means for measuring deeper learnings that are untapped by the conventional achievement tests of today.

7. Increased understanding of the kinds of learning experiences that will nourish a love of learning; foster independence in thinking; feed the desire to experiment, to test, and to venture forth; and create a built-in standard of excellence in performance.

Miriam Goldberg's paper on the gifted, delivered at the 1965 White House Conference on Education, examined several issues that she felt needed clarification, since "the directions in which they are resolved may well determine the future of special provisions for the talented." The issues were listed under such headings as: The Climate for Talent Development, Current Oppositions to Special Programs, Expanded Conceptions of Talent, Increasing the Talent Pool—Womanpower and the Disadvantaged, and Administrative Arrangements for the Talented.

These five issues paralleled those identified five years earlier, even though programs for the gifted mushroomed throughout the country in the intervening years—spurred in part by Sputnik. To the 1960 conference, the major needs seemed to be for research and experimentation "to understand better the phenomenon of giftedness and its development, to assess the value of specific educational procedures and practices, to appraise proposals and plans, and to use available resources more effectively." These continue to be major needs in the area of the gifted, although there are now available research findings and operational experience that might be synthesized, interpreted, and applied to improved program planning. However, such issues

484

as racial isolation, student power, and community control were hardly considered at a time when most research on ability grouping, for instance, did not consider race or social class as significant variables.

Many innovations that were sharply debated a decade ago—even the need for special provisions for the gifted—have now become more or less institutionalized. A concern with nurturing creativity, productive thinking, and inquiry has become more focused as enthusiasm for novelty alone has been replaced with more tempered insights into the nature of these phenomena. True, there is still no adequate theory of talent development that might provide a framework for program planning, nor are we yet able to adequately define what constitutes "enrichment for the gifted." We have expanded our notions of giftedness and its multifaceted nature so that new assessment procedures have been developed to supplement or, in some instances, replace traditional techniques. Much of the so-called curriculum revolution, while not necessarily aimed at the intellectually gifted student, has since been found to be most appropriate for this population, since such programs deal with content and processes calling for the higher abstractions and conceptual abilities that are components of giftedness. Significant as such curricular changes have been, they tend not to contribute to integrated, articulated, sequential programs for the gifted, except in those few instances where some attempts have been made to attain such an end.

There have been curricular changes during the past decade that have opened alternatives for the gifted. Some of these can be described as *vertical,* moving courses or units down so that students have contact with material at an earlier age or in less time than is normal; some are *horizontal* changes, providing for greater depth and breadth than is usual; some are *reorganizational,* redesigning the curriculum content itself; and some may be called *augmentation,* introducing experiences that have not been part of the curriculum earlier. Seminars on standard and esoteric subjects have become part of school programs. Independent study has flourished. Extended school weeks and years have been provided for the gifted. Secondary schools and colleges have shared programs and resources, including staff. The Advanced Placement Program, featuring college-level work in high schools, has involved thousands of students in hundreds of schools.The National Merit Scholarship Program, with its related projects, has become part of an annual nationwide talent search. Early admissions to college have become standard across the nation.

Thus, in the area of the gifted and the talented, "new" and "promising" developments appear to be consolidations of what has been learned from the research and experience of the past dozen or so years. For example, there was a period during which the gifted underachiever was the target of much study, a great deal of research being supported by federal and state funds. The findings of such studies shed light on the relationships between motivational and personality variables, environmental conditions, and the instructional program as these factors affected the development of intellectual potential. However, our progress in moving from analysis and diagnosis to intervention and program has been painfully slow. We have, consequently, applied little of this research to the broader concerns with achievement, especially for the disadvantaged, probably because the populations studied have tended to be primarily the middle-class gifted.

Efforts to identify and nurture "creativity" provided considerable excitement and intense effort for a period, but the crest of that commitment passed quickly. We still do not understand the nature and causes of the so-called morning glories (individuals whose giftedness appears early but soon wanes or disappears) or the late bloomers (persons whose talents emerge somewhat late) or how these phenomena should influence identification or instructional and counseling procedures. We still profess concern for developing nonacademic talents (such as musical, artistic, mechanical, social, and dramatic), but we have given relatively scant attention to what kinds of provisions are appropriate and essential. The problems of adequate programs for highly gifted individuals—those with unusually rare genius—have been generally ignored on the tacit assumption that such talent will eventually come out anyway. Finally, we have hardly tackled, let alone resolved, the many issues regarding development of talent in its social context.

The problem of talent development continues to be one of devising educational opportunities that will unlock potential of all kinds to the fullest, programs that will be concerned with values, attitudes, self-concepts, and commitment to continued growth, not just the acquisition of knowledge and intellectual development. The research and development efforts of the late fifties and early sixties—many of them encouraged and supported by federal and state governments—helped broaden definitions of talent and helped us to understand that giftedness is multifaceted. Expanded notions of giftedness and its many-faceted nature suggest that, as David McClelland once observed, "talent potential may be fairly widespread, a characteristic which can be transformed into actually talented performance by various sorts of the right kinds of education." The drive for "quality education" and for "equal educational opportunity" represent, in some ways, a press to test the hypothesis. As students from impoverished backgrounds and from racial and ethnic minorities have "achieved" when provided with appropriate educational opportunities, they have demonstrated that "the right kinds of education" can indeed transform potential into "actually talented performance."*

The disappearance from the educational scene of some programs for the gifted, however, indicates our continued tendency to discard the baby with the bath-water. No program or provision for the gifted is so sacred that continuous assessment and evaluation is no longer needed. And, as education programs become inevitably intertwined with social and political processes within the school and the community at large, such educational processes must be continually examined in terms of overall effects.

*McClelland, David C., and others, editors. *Talent and Society.* New York: Van Nostrand Reinhold Co., 1958.

Ability grouping, for example, was viewed, along with acceleration and enrichment, as "a means of providing for the gifted." All three terms took on a variety of forms, of course, in different contexts and at different levels. When ability grouping in certain school situations led to a tracking system that segregated white, middle-class students from poor, nonwhite students, leading the former into college bound programs and the latter into dead-end terminal programs, clearly such provisions no longer contributed to full talent development. In abandoning grouping provisions, all too often schools failed to provide for curriculum differentiation, for appropriate teaching and learning strategies, for instructional resources—for all of the kinds of educational opportunities that grouping was originally intended to facilitate. Consequently, the gifted—white and nonwhite, middle and lower class—were deprived of appropriate educational opportunities.

The needs of gifted and talented chidren are, in a sense, the same as those of other children, differing in degree and quality. All children "need" opportunities to develop their individual talents, and the gifted and talented students are no exception. Such talented individuals come from all races, socioeconomic groups, geographic locales, and environments. To the extent that educational programs discriminate, sort out, and stifle talent development, they cannot be tolerated, no matter what political power is brought to maintain them.

The recently published report of the U.S. Office of Education survey of programs and provisions for the gifted (pursuant to Public Law 91-230, Section 806) uses language reminiscent of the 1950's, such as "the widespread neglect of gifted and talented children." In the sense of the school's inability or unwillingness to provide for the particular needs of the gifted, this neglect is even more intense and widespread among the disadvantaged and minority groups. These students are caught in a vortex of educational and environmental forces that mitigate against their being identified and having their talents nurtured.

In schools that are *de facto* segregated (as are many inner-city schools), where low achievement is widespread, teachers and administrators have low expectations, the curriculum is sterile and irrelevant, resources are limited, and individual diagnosis absent, the potentially gifted child may very likely be lost. Differing school milieus and predominant value systems affect general scholastic performance and individual attainment. Giftedness and talent always have a social referent—those abilities that are identified and developed are those that are valued by the society—and the child in a depressed area who is potentially gifted may be doubly disadvantaged, for he lives in an environment that may be hostile or apathetic to his particular abilities. In some instances, outstanding scholastic achievement is perceived as "The Man's Game" and not to be pursued by the poor and the nonwhite lest they be coopted.

In schools where desegregation has taken place, integration may not have occurred, and the minority group students are often a minority. The schools from which they have come are frequently perceived as inferior, the

487

levels of past performance lower, and potentials for outstanding performance limited. All too often the result has been a resegregation through grouping and tracking procedures that relegate the blacks, the poor, and the non-English speaking to the "slower" or "nonacademic" programs, where they are provided with an education that is basically inferior in quality. Since such procedures tend to be "class actions," in that all members of the minority group are treated as if homogeneity existed, the gifted and the talented among them are particularly vulnerable and suffer as a result of such discrimination. Furthermore, the social conditions in the classroom and the school, the nature of acceptance or rejection and the minority group student's perception of these interactions, the peer values—all affect the pupil's achievement motivation and the extent to which he will manifest and develop his giftedness. When students are black, red, or brown, are different culturally from the majority group, are non-English speaking or have "nonstandard" dialects, those who are gifted or talented among them may be particularly disadvantaged because of discriminatory practices.

The gifted and talented among disadvantaged and minority groups pose a particular challenge and opportunity for educators. To begin to meet this challenge, educators must examine their own expectations regarding this untapped talent pool: To what extent have the biases of educators contributed to the limited development of gifted minority group youth? The fact that some unusually gifted black or Chicanos or Puerto Ricans have emerged and demonstrated outstanding ability does not change the urgent need for planners and researchers to attend to the special problems within this more general area of concern. More specifically, attention will have to be given to the following dimensions of the problem:

Identification. Procedures used to locate gifted and talented individuals, given all the problems that exist with the population in general, are even more problematic in identifying the gifted among the disadvantaged. Some educators have argued for discarding existing instruments and procedures and developing "culture fair" tests. Others, questioning the possibilities of such bias-free instruments and techniques, propose that the focus be on the interpretation of the data so as to take into account the disadvantaged background of the child. Still others urge that efforts emphasize the creation of settings that will encourage self-identification of the gifted through outstanding performance. Identification procedures that stress a search for talent rather than simply screen out and bar participation in programs for the gifted are crucial for minority group youth. As a start, such procedures should be more, rather than less, inclusive.

Development of programs. Experience of the past several decades has clearly indicated the need for differentiated opportunities for the gifted to develop their special abilities while, at the same time, they are given opportunities to develop certain general skills and abilities by interacting with students of less and greater potential. No single uniform program has emerged. However, educators need to turn their attention to the special problems of program development in educational and social settings where the disadvan-

488

aged are found. To recognize the nature of such problems would be a step forward at this point. The success of some mini- and prep schools in ghetto areas suggests one approach worth further exploration. By attending to the affective as well as cognitive development of students and by creating a climate for achievement, such schools seem to be providing another chance for able pupils who have been missed or turned off by the more traditional programs. Programs that provide opportunities for students to teach fellow pupils or for service in various community agencies can extend the possibilities for developing potentials. Education is not limited to the place we call school. Support is needed for encouragement of various opportunities for talent development in nonconventional settings, involving non-traditional personnel.

Development of staff. By creating the conditions for learning and by serving as the gatekeepers for programs and services, school staffs are critical in talent development. Staff development is needed in terms of altering expectations with respect to the identification and nurturing of talent among the disadvantaged. Coupled with attitudinal changes must come new teaching strategies and ways of using learning resources, in school and community.

Enrichment of the learning environment. For a variety of reasons, inner-city schools may be able to provide only limited resources for talent development. However, they are situated in urban centers, and the resources for learning are extremely rich. The entire community, not the classroom alone, must become the locus for learning. Not only will this extend opportunities for learning but it could, at the same time, alter the climate for learning—the attitudes toward unusual talents and their development.

Development of strategies for bilingual and multicultural education. The barriers to optimum development of the gifted among minority group students may include both the fact that the language of instruction differs from the child's mother tongue and the existence of discontinuities between the culture of the school and that of the home and neighborhood. If talent potential is to be realized, better strategies must be found for recognizing language needs and the potential richness of cultural differences.

Development of appropriate guidance and other ancillary services. In addition to the special guidance needs—personal and educational—of all gifted students, there are particular problems that may be encountered by the gifted minority group student. These may range from help with affective matters, such as peer and family attitudes toward the gifted child's "difference," to assistance in recognizing and selecting from the options available to him. Higher education opportunities, for example, have been expanded considerably in the last decade or so, and the gifted minority group student and his family may not be fully aware of the possibilities or the means for taking advantage of them.

Development of financial resources. Poor and minority group students need financial assistance to be able to develop their special abilities. While there has been increased support for minority group youth in the realm of higher education scholarships and stipends, it has not been sufficient. By

489

continuing to study, the poor child is unable to contribute to support of the family in any way, aside from answering his own intellectual needs. What is required are expanded opportunities to serve and to work as a means of earning some income, which will have a beneficial effect on both the talented individual and his family.

There is ample evidence that schools have failed to come to grips with the problems of identifying and developing giftedness and talent among various racial and ethnic minorities and children of the poor. When federal and state agencies, through appropriations for research and program development, encouraged and enlargement of opportunities for the gifted, there was a renaissance of interest and activity. The minority group gifted profited from that revived concern, but only to a limited extent.

In recent years, many school systems have misinterpreted the long overdue concern for the education of poor and minority group students as meaning that programs for the disadvantaged must take precedence over provisions for the gifted. What is needed now is a clear affirmation by educators and communities that they are concerned with the development of talent potential of all kinds, wherever such special abilities may be found. The issue is not one of providing for the gifted (meaning only white, middle-class, suburban children) or the disadvantaged (meaning only poor, nonwhite, ghetto dwellers). Gifted and talented individuals are found in all groups. There is no need or justification for depriving some students of opportunities at the expense of others. Nor is there any basis for not providing the disadvantaged gifted student with special opportunities that are essentially compensatory in nature.

What is needed is a real commitment to developing the total range of abilities and talents—including the unusually able and gifted. Such commitment would be manifested in the kinds of programs funded, the areas of research and development supported, the varieties of training programs underwritten, and so on. Unfortunately, too many educators and lay persons are unwilling to concede that there really are individual differences, that such differences should help determine the nature of appropriate education that must be provided, and that identical experiences do not make for equal opportunities. Certainly, in the last two decades we have acquired sufficient research data and program development experience to be able to provide the kinds of flexibility, openness, personnel, and material support to nurture individual talents more effectively than we are presently doing.

Talent is not the prerogative of any racial or ethnic group, any social class, or any residential area. It may lie untapped in some situations under some conditions, but no population has either a monopoly on or an absence of talents. Nor will depriving the gifted and talented pupil of opportunities to develop and use his gifts result in upgrading the attainments of his less able peers. Such misguided and meaningless egalitarianism contributes to the development of no one in particular. Obviously, with broadened insights into the natue of giftedness, some traditional identification procedures, college preparatory programs, and rewards systems are no longer valid. With he years of research and experience now behind us, we should view educational opportunities and engagement differently, based on modified values; and we should be more sensitive to the sociopolitical context in which learning takes place and programs function.

It was the civil rights movement and the war on poverty that underscored the failure of our schools to provide adequate educational opportunities for large numbers of our poor and disadvantaged groups. The U.S. Commissioner of Education has announced that he will become a "visible advocate for increased attention" to the gifted and talented. All educators must become advocates for increased, appropriate attention to the gifted, especially those among the disadvantaged and minorities, where discrimination and neglect have resulted in an even greater loss of talent development.

Joseph L. French

The Highly Intelligent Dropout

*I*n recent years many people have assumed that all students of above average intellectual ability not only graduate from high school, but go on to college. Such an assumption is incorrect. Recent studies indicate that eight to 11 per cent of high school dropouts have IQ's of 110 or above. In a comprehensive study of Pennsylvania youth in 1964-65 we found more than 800 high ability dropouts. Nearly 500 had IQ's of 120 and above and 80 had IQ's of 130 or more. These figures are impressive when it is recognized that Pennsylvania has one of the lowest dropout rates in the country.

Some frequently mentioned correlates of school withdrawal were not substantiated in the findings of this study of dropouts with IQ's of 110 and above. Noticeably absent from the dropout data are indications of frequent school transfers, early part time employment, unemployment upon leaving school, generally low parental education, and lower parental employment status. What is noticed is that dropouts differ from "persisters" (students of the same age, IQ, neighborhood, and sex who were still in school) in such areas as personality, interests, educational skills, and family orientation toward school processes.

The male dropouts, when compared with the persisters, were found to be more frank, uninhibited, and happy-go-lucky. Although they tended to be easy going, their actions were marked with deliberateness. The male dropouts were more assertive, independent, unconventional, and rebellious than the persisters. Their overall response pattern, however, would suggest that they fell within normal limits with regard to their mental health.

The girls dropping out of school for reasons other than marriage were very similar to the boys. However, two-thirds of the female dropouts in this study were pregnant, married, and/or planning to marry when they withdrew.

The girls who withdrew because of pregnancy and/or marriage were far less socially oriented than the persisters; they were less prone to seek social recognition. These girls could be described as tending to be shy and retiring. Their personality pattern would indicate reason to suspect proneness to poor social adjustment in junior and senior high school.

Seldom did dropouts express attitudes which were opposite to those of

ersisters. The differences found were generally a matter of degree. Both the
male dropouts and persisters, for example, believed that their parents considered school to be important; the dropouts were not as implicit however.
Male dropouts did not demonstrate a truly negative attitude toward the
schools. They did point to a number of areas which they found to be difficult to accept. They often expressed concern that schools are not preparing
students for the "real" world. There also appeared to be an emotional gap
between the male dropouts and their teachers. The dropouts were not inclined to describe their teachers as being well prepared, knowledgeable with
regard to subject matter, or concerned about the feelings and needs of the
students. "Favoritism" was a problem listed by a number of dropouts.
Dropouts tended to complain about the strong forces within the schools to
conform. More than did the persisters, they expressed the importance of be-
ng able to be an individual.

The attitudes of the unmarried female dropouts were similar to those of
the boys. They also expressed the notion that school training did not meet
their needs as related to their vocational or professional goals. Although
these girls also appeared to be estranged from their teachers, there was little
reference made to unfair treatment or favoritism.

The married female dropouts were more similar to persisters than to unmarried female dropouts in their attitudes. They did not appear to feel as if
teachers were partial in their treatment of students nor were they unhappy
with their courses. They did, more so than the persisters or unmarried
female dropouts, feel as if their parents weren't satisfied with the school setting.

Elizabeth V. Swenson

Teacher-Assessment of Creative Behavior in Disadvantaged Children

*C*reativity is currently an aspect of cognitive functioning of particular interest in assessing giftedness in disadvantaged children (Johnson, 1976 and Bruch, 1975). It is an especially attractive alternative to the concept of intelligence which, irrespective of its method of measurement, is fraught with overtones of cultural bias. Attempts to construct culture-fair IQ tests have been somewhat successful (Renzulli, 1973), and, furthermore, serve to reinforce a deficit model of cognitive development. Creativity, on the other hand, represents a more positive approach, an area of ability in which disadvantaged youngsters might have a fair chance of excelling. Several articles (Solomon, 1974, and Torrance, 1971) have cited evidence to indicate that at least one measure of creativity, the figural forms of the Torrance Test of Creative Thinking, is fair to all socio-economic classes of children.

On an intuitive level, "creative" seems to be an appropriate description of many disadvantaged children. Houston (1973), in a study of story-repeating ability, concluded that poor test performance by disadvantaged children was actually a result of their creative thinking ability. Indeed, it may be that deprived youngsters, having to make do with the commonplace type of play objects and activities available to them might be encouraged to use their imaginations at an early age and more frequently than their more advantaged counterparts. Only such inner resources, it would seem, could account for the urban slum child's apparent adjustment to a deprived and often hostile environment. Typical of this point of view are these words of Edmund Gordon (1968): "These youngsters show ingeniousness and resourcefulness in pursuing self-selected goals and in coping with very difficult and complex conditions of life (p. 390)."

Although several instruments exist for the purpose of assessing creative thinking, often children are labelled "creative" without resort to a standardized test. Usually for expediency, but also because of his/her frequent interaction with students, a teacher is the one who most often

Reprinted from Gifted Child Quarterly, Vol. XXII, No. 3, (Fall 1978), pp. 338-343. By permission of the author and publisher.

494

elects creatively-talented children or casually remarks that a youngster is quite creative". On what criteria would such a seemingly off-the-cuff ssessment be based?

To answer this question, the present investigation attempted to lefine creativity in terms of specific observable behaviors believed by lementary school teachers of the disadvantaged to indicate creativity in he classroom setting. Thirty-six teachers in a predominantly lower and vorking class urban school system were selected by random sampling, tratified according to grade level, to indicate three specific things a child le/she would call "creative" in his/her classroom does differently from a ion-creative child. From those responses obtained, the items retained met he following criteria:

1. A specific, overt, countable behavior (as opposed to an inference of emotion, e.g.: "*feels* happy when . . .")
2. Possession of face validity.
3. Omission of the word "creativity and its derivatives.
4. Listing by teachers of at least two different grade levels.

The remaining behavior statements, numbering twenty-five, were compiled in random order into the following list:

1. Repeats activities so that he/she can do them differently.
2. Invents imaginative lies.
3. Shows that he/she sees hidden meanings, cause and effect relationships that are not obvious.
4. Writes and illustrates stories without being asked to do so as an assignment.
5. Utilizes free-time by making up games or making something from paper and material scraps as opposed to more structured activities.
6. Finds many answers to a situational question.
7. Lets his/her imagination "run" when writing a story; sees more possibilities.
8. Finds activities for spare-time work with little or no additional help.
9. Decorates the border of his/her paper when doing an assignment.
10. Doesn't copy other children's ideas in art.
11. Builds and constructs things using unusual materials; uses ordinary materials in different ways.
12. Interrelates his/her experiences and draws on them with ease in discussions.
13. Doesn't let classroom events go unnoticed; questions them.
14. Accomplishes things on his/her own without help.
15. Writes poems and stories in his/her spare time.
16. Asks unusual questions during class discussions.
17. Makes up his/her own ideas when the class does a project together.
18. Suggests to the teacher alternate ways of doing an activity.

495

19. Is willing to risk friendship to express his/her feelings or thoughts.
20. Enthusiastic about new activities in music and art.
21. Goes beyond what is required in class assignments; makes his/her work "fancier."
22. Comes up with fresh, original comments or an unusual correct answer when there is more than one correct answer.
23. Finds new ways to get attention.
24. Tries original ways to get out of work he/she doesn't want to do.
25. Takes the initiative when he/she wants to know something; reads or asks questions without prompting.

Inspection of the teacher-generated list of creative behaviors in disadvantaged children indicates heavy emphasis on originality in class work art, and anti-social behavior. Additional traits evident in more than one item are curiosity, independence, and the ability to keep oneself productively occupied with a minimum amount of external stimulation.

Compilation of the creative behavior list into a check list or rating scale should enable the selection of the creative disadvantaged child to be based on specific objective classroom behaviors. Student selection is relatively easy, involving observations rather than tedious test scoring. Furthermore it is based precisely on what teachers use as criteria anyway when they are asked to select their most creative children.

Rating 90 disadvantaged children (equally divided among fourth, fifth, and sixth grade males and females) on the creative behaviors in terms of a frequency of occurrence category (almost never, sometimes, and usually) yielded some interesting results. The correlation of the behavior list with composite reading and arithmetic scores on the Stanford Achievement Test was +39 (p < .001). This corresponds to findings of Holland (1959) and others reported by Wallach (1970) that teacher ratings of a diversity of personal qualities often correlates highly with measures of a student's intelligence. This correlation, however, was considerably higher for females (+.49) than males (+.29) indicating that teachers might view creativity as a general indicant of mature, achievement-oriented behavior in females but not in male students. Current teachers rating thirty-two pupils two years later yielded a reliability coefficient of +.31 (p < .05). Despite two years of maturation and a different rater, the creative behaviors appear to be relatively consistent.

The correlation between ratings on the creative behavior scale and the figural form of the Torrance Test of Creative Thinking (Torrance, 1974), however, was not significantly greater than zero (+.08). In other words, knowledge of the teacher rating score explains less than 1% of the variance in the composite Torrance creativity scores. This absence of a linear relationship can be explained by noting that the rating scale items were obviously not designed to assess creativity by the same definition as that used by the Torrance Tests, but creativity as defined by teachers who, as Torrance (1966) has noted, determine most placements in special programs or the creatively gifted. If one considers the Torrance Test scores as a criterion, these results serve to extend Gear's (1976) conclusion to creativity, that teachers leave something to be desired as predictors of intelligence test performance.

Rating scale items generated by teachers of the disadvantaged bear a remarkable resemblance to lists of qualities of "gifted" children (Renzulli and Hartman, 1971). This again points out the blurring of the distinction between "gifted" and "creatively gifted" disadvantaged children in the eyes of their teachers. In a typical list of characteristics of superior students, Renzulli and Hartman also included such items as insight into causal relationships, lack of need for external motivation, independent work, and the ability to understand more than the obvious in a situation.

A multifaceted view of creativity would include some behavioral correlates of creativity closely related to intellective aptitude. In evaluating creative behavior with respect to a population of disadvantaged children, specific classroom behaviors and their significance to the teacher both need to be considered.

References

Bruch, Catherine B. Assessment of Creativity in Culturally Different Children. *The Gifted Child Quarterly*, 1975, 19, 164-174.

Gear, Gayle Haywood. Accuracy of Teacher Judgment in Indentifying Intellectually Gifted Children: A Review of the Literature. *The Gifted Child Quarterly*, 1976, 20, 478-489.

Gordon, Edmund W. Programs of Compensatory Education. In Deutsch, Martin, Katz, Irwin, and Jensen, Arthur R. (Eds.), *Social Class, Race, and Psychological Development*. New York: Holt, Rinehart, and Winston, 1968.

Holland John L. Some Limitations of Teacher Ratings as Predictors of Creativity. *Journal of Educational Psychology*, 1959, 50, 219-223.

Houston, Susan H. Black English. *Psychology Today*, 1973, 6(10), 45-48.

Johnson, Roger A. Teacher and Student Perception of Student Creativity. *The Gifted Child Quarterly*, 1976, 20, 164-167.

Carolyn M. Callahan

The Gifted Girl: An Anomaly?

*I*n recent years increasing attention has been directed toward the needs of special subgroups of the population of students considered gifted and talented. This emphasis on the culturally different gifted child, the gifted-handicapped child, the very young gifted child, and the gifted girl has been predicated on the assumption that there are unique characteristics of the individuals in these categories that warrant the consideration of alternative means of identification and program planning if the full spectrum of gifted and talented children are to be served. That is, it has been assumed that the students in these subgroups differ from the average students in more ways than other gifted students, or that they differ from other gifted students in some way. In order to appropriately serve these special groups, it is important that those unique characteristics be clearly identified and be related to programmatic or curricular alternatives.

On the one hand, to assume that the gifted girl is significantly different from "other gifted students" causes somewhat of a problem since we would expect that about 50% of all gifted children are female. However, an examination of the literature on gifted adults clearly indicates that in spite of the approximately equal numbers of male and female gifted children, an overwhelming number of adults who are identified as gifted and creative are male.[1] For example, Terman's follow-up studies of the children whom he identified as gifted focus predominantly on the achievements of the male subjects.[2] *Cradles of Eminence,* a study of 400 eminent personalities includes mention of only 52 women;[3] and only 78 of the persons named in *300 Eminent Personalities,* a study of contemporary prominent individuals, are female.[4] It would thus seem that the young gifted female does not realize her potential to the same degree as the gifted male. Therefore, we conclude that there must be factors, either in innate ability, environment, personality, or some combination of these, which impact on gifted females in a different or unique way. The next logical step becomes the identification of those factors which differentiate the male gifted individual from the female gifted individual and to plan programs

Reprinted by permission of the publisher, Roeper Review, 2190 Woodward, Bloomfield Hills, MI 48013.

which minimize negative influences on the ultimate productivity of gifted
women.

Intellectual Abilities and Achievements

Even though gifted girls tend to earn higher grades in school and the
prevailing stereotype of females includes superior performance in English,
foreign languages and the arts, the adult productivity of males is superior
in all fields. Men write more novels and more poetry, produce more works
of art, earn more degrees, and make more contributions in all professional
fields—not just those related to math and science. Are the stereotypes
untrue or do females not realize their potential? Are the stereotypes of
male superiority in mathematics and science well-founded?

One would logically first look to differences in innate ability between
the sexes to account for the differential achievements of the two groups
and to judge the stereotypic images of males and females. Unfortunately,
there is little literature which specifically considers differences in gifted
male and females and we must often generalize from the characteristics of
the general population.

The comprehensive review of sex differences by Maccoby and Jacklin
includes the following set of conclusions about differences in intellectual
abilities:

1. There does not appear to be any difference in *how* the two sexes learn.
   That is, there is great similarity in the basic intellectual processes of
   perception, learning, and memory.
2. Up to age 10 or 11 girls and boys do equally well on measures of verbal
   performance.
3. After age 11, girls frequently outscore boys on tests of verbal performance by .1 to .5 standard deviations. It is important to note that this
   difference exists on tests requiring more than simple tasks such as
   spelling. The differences are also noted on measures of comprehension
   of complex text, measures of understanding of logical relations expressed
   in verbal terms, and some measures of verbal creativity.
4. There do not seem to be any differences in measures of quantitative
   ability until about age 9–13 when boys begin to do better. These
   differences still favor boys when the number of mathematics courses
   completed is equal.
5. Differences in quantitative ability seem to be accompanied by differences
   in science achievement.
6. On tests of spatial ability, an advantage for boys appears at the
   beginning of adolescence and increases through high school.
7. No difference is found in the problem-solving tasks of response inhibition or problem restructuring.
8. No differences are found on tests of concept mastery and reasoning and

499

measures of nonverbal creativity. Girls are superior on measures of verbal creativity after age 7.[5]

In summary, it would appear that, in general, males and females do not differ significantly in innate abilities. Older boys seem constantly superior to girls on the variables of visual-spatial ability, mathematics achievement, and science achievement, but only after the onset of adolescence. The specific literature on gifted children tends to support the findings related to visual-spatial ability and mathematics achievement,[6] but there is much conflicting evidence about other intellectual abilities.[7] At this point, the results of studies of sex difference in the general population and among gifted students offer little evidence that innate intellectual abilities account for the overwhelming dominance of males among those identified as gifted as adults.

Cognitive Styles

The areas of intellectual ability in which there have been noticeably and consistent differences between males and females is in visual-spatial ability, mathematics achievement, and science achievement—areas very closely related in process and content. One interpretation of the origins of the relationship between mathematics and visual-spatial abilities includes a consideration of cognitive styles and environmental influences on these styles. Maccoby and Jacklin suggest that visual-spatial ability appears to be closely connected to field independence on visual tasks and field independence is positively related to cultural conditions which allow one to be more assertive and less restricted. Because girls are not encouraged to be assertive and are restricted in play and exploration of their environment, they are at a disadvantage in developing field independence and, thus, visual-spatial abilities and mathematical abilities. Another cognitive style which has been linked to mathematics and visual-spatial ability is the global/analytic dimension of perception. It has been suggested that girls learn a more global style of problem solving, while boys learn analytic approaches and thus become more skilled at quantitative tasks. (Fox, op. cit.) This global approach to processing information is attributed to a tendency for parents to overprotect and discourage independent problem solving among females.

Personality, Interests and Values

Although differences between boys and girls in one presumably innate intellectual ability (visual-spatial) have been used to explain differences in particular intellectual achievements (in mathematics), many more of the

500

xplanations offered for the differences between males and females in ntellectual ability and achievement are based on differences in personality and the interactions among personality, the environment, and cognitive variables. In many instances, environmental and cultural influences on the development of personality characteristics are integral parts of the hypothesis examined in exploring reasons for the failure of females to actualize their potential. Therefore, such influences will be discussed in conjunction with descriptions of the personality characteristics of the gifted and talented female.

One aspect of the literature relevant to the personality traits of gifted women is derived from male/female comparisons in characteristics considered to be associated with success. As previously mentioned, one must be cautious in generalizing from the general population to the gifted; however, these studies provide some useful clues for understanding the gifted female. Other studies comparing the successful female to less successful peers add considerable information about the personality characteristics of the successful, talented female.

One personality characteristic which has been considered often as an influence on the success of women is achievement motivation. In the analysis presented in *The Psychology of Sex Differences,* Maccoby and Jacklin concluded that there is no demonstrated difference by sex among school age children in achievement motivation, although males show more arousal of this motivation under directly competitive conditions.[10] No direct comparisons of gifted male and female students is available, but studies which compare more accomplished gifted females to their less successful peers do seem to indicate that achievement motivation has a differential effect on achievement among gifted women. For example, a group of high ability college women identified as "achievers" scored significantly higher than their underachieving peers on the Achievement via Conformity and Achievement via Independence scales of the *California Psychological Inventory* (CPI).[11] On the *Adjective Check List* these groups responded similarly with the achieving group checking conscientious, capable, and industrious significantly more often than the underachieving group, and the underachieving group checking lazy, leisurely, dreamy, and easy-going more often. In a similar study of academically gifted women college students, *MMPI* scores of those who completed their programs were compared with scores of those who had not completed their programs. Those who had completed their programs were characterized as more persevering and as having more achievement motivation than those who did not complete their programs.[12] The "fear of success" variable investigated initially by Matina Horner seems closely related to achievement motivation and particularly relevant to this discussion. Data collected via a projective situational instrument suggest that women may develop a "fear of success motive" which acts to inhibit achievement motivation.[13] This phenomenon may account for the lowered arousal of achievement motivation for females in competitive situations. The origins of the "fear of

501

success" are not clear; however, it appears that many young girls and women have been enculturated to the extent that they fear that they will be rejected socially or be considered unfeminine if they appear to be too bright or too competent. It is postulated that the motive to avoid success is greatest for those women of high ability and the conflicts between achievement motivation and fear of success may create anxiety which reduces the likelihood that these women will pursue success.[14] High levels of anxiety may also be detrimental to learning and creativity. It thus appears that achievement motivation must be strong with a concomitant absence of motives to avoid success in order for women to seek actualization of their potential.

Another personality variable which may have an impact on the relative achievement of females is locus of control. Maccoby and Jacklin report that throughout the elementary and high school years both sexes are likely to believe that they can determine their own destinies. Yet, during college, men exhibit greater internal locus of control and greater confidence in their ability to succeed at school-related tasks.[15] Studies of gifted achieving college women would indicate that relative to gifted peers who have been as successful, they had greater self-confidence, good ego strength, greater rebellious independence, and greater rejection of outside influence.[16] Gifted and creative girls also score significantly higher on measures of such traits than do their normal peers.[17] One might hypothesize from the data presented above that gifted women must be encouraged to develop a strong locus of control and gain confidence in their own ability to control their fates if maximum potential is to be realized.

The interests and values of gifted women have been used as indicators of motivation to succeed in given academic pursuits. The assumptions that academic and professional success is predicated on interest as well as ability is supported by findings that intellectually gifted women are more successful in completing degrees if they demonstrate interests characteristic of professional or academic careers.[18] Even though gifted females do seem to exhibit scores which are significantly greater in masculine areas than normal peers, these same girls also score high on feminine interests, thus presenting potential conflicts in interests when making career choices.[19]

Environmental Factors Impinging on the Success of the Gifted Female

Underlying the problems of achievement and motivation of gifted and talented females lie hypotheses yet to be tested and perhaps untestable in the experimental tradition. As in all questions focusing on the relative impact of heredity and environment, it is impossible to completely control the hereditary and environmental factors influencing the development of males and females. Yet, there are certain factors within the environment which would seem logically to have an impact on the development of girls

502

and young women. Until cultural or environmental factors are altered considerably to neutralize the potential effects, there will be no way of assessing how great that impact is.

It has been hypothesized that one of the reasons that females do not attain higher levels of success is a lack of motivation to seek careers in certain professions. Traditionally, school programs fail to provide examples of females who have succeeded and have been rewarded for achievement in professions not typically judged female. Even in the English classroom where it would seem that there is ample opportunity to explore the lives and writings of both men and women, it is common practice to choose books that boys will enjoy with the rationale that girls will usually read anything assigned anyway.[20] Thus, literature written by men and about men predominates. Further, textbooks, beginning with the reading primers, have portrayed females as wives and mothers, weaker sisters, and dependent and helpless minor characters.[21] Standardized educational achievement test batteries also contribute to the general bias presented in classrooms through both content bias (a greater number of male nouns and pronouns—excluding generic nouns and pronouns) and sex-role stereotyping.[22] All females have, of course, been influenced by these pervasive biases in texts, tests, and other instructional materials, but it is perhaps the gifted female who has been stunted the most because her potential was the greatest for fulfilling a wide variety of roles and careers. Hopefully, greater emphasis in the general curriculum on nontraditional role possibilities and greater acceptance of female achievement in a variety of careers will affect the gifted girl in positive ways.

Other, more subtle barriers to the achievement of gifted and talented females may be found in the literature on discrimination against women. Two others which will be noted here are test bias and reinforcement of inappropriate behavior. Ironically, even behaviors which earn gifted females good grades in school may act against them in competitive professional situations. Walberg, for example, found girls in physics classes to be more conforming, dependent, and docile; Gallagher, Aschner, and Jenne found girls to express themselves less often while boys were eight times as likely to quarrel with teachers in biology classes.[23] These same females are rewarded with high grades and are, therefore, likely to interpret their in-class behaviors as contributing to high grades and, thus, appropriate for success. Test bias has been offered as one explanation for differences in measured achievement in mathematics and science. Walberg noted that on a physics test which had predominantly visual-spatial items boys did better while on a physics test that had primarily verbal items, girls did better. Another study indicated that women improved their mathematical performance (even on abstract reasoning problems) if problems are worded so as to involve feminine tasks rather than masculine tasks even though the solution to the problem requires exactly the same process.[24] Potential discrimination in other areas of testing has not been explored, but must not be discounted.

Administrative and Curricular Programming for the Gifted and Talented Female

The literature and research on the appropriateness of models for administrative adaptations in programs for the gifted and talented have generally failed to consider systematically the differential effects of those models on males and females.[25] The conclusions of most reviews of the literature on the effects of various administrative options such as enrichment, acceleration (including early admission), homogeneous ability grouping, and independent study include statements which favor acceleration as a preferred alternative based on research findings regarding the impact of such programs. However, the potential for varied effects that these types of programs might have on the intellectual, social, or emotional adjustment of males or females as subgroups of gifted children is not noted.[26] This lack of consideration of sex as a relevant variable may be a result of an assumption that the learning characteristics of gifted students are generalizable to both sexes, and, therefore, that a given administrative change would be equally beneficial or nonbeneficial to all gifted and talented children. Whether this assumption has been made in these studies, or whether nonsignificant sex differences were simply not noted, cannot be known. The lack of attention to sex as a relevant variable in studying the efficacy of various programs for the gifted lends further credence to the statement of Passow that "no single adaptation has yet proven to be *the* conclusive method for providing adequately for all kinds and degrees of giftedness"[27] and the conclusion of Passow, et al., that research has not clearly suggested "for whom and under what circumstances one kind of plan is more desirable than another."[28]

Recent research on mathematically talented young women (Study of Mathematically Precocious Youth—SMPY) would suggest that perhaps there is a great need to attend to the differing effects that certain strategies for dealing with the gifted may have on young adolescent women and men.[29] Although these studies have focused primarily on programs that are accelerative in nature and include only mathematically precocious children, the findings would appear to suggest that closer attention must be paid to the possibility that young gifted girls may self-select themselves out of potentially valuable educational experiences simply because the structure of the program is unattractive to females. Fox, in assessing the attitudes of mathematically gifted seventh and eight grade boys and girls, found that girls had significantly less favorable attitudes than boys toward acceleration for themselves. Further, these same girls felt that their parents would not approve of acceleration.[30] These findings were supported by earlier observations that gifted girls in the SMPY appeared to be more fearful than boys of being rejected by peers if they participated in programs which included academic acceleration and that fear of failure among adolescent girls seems to inhibit them from taking part in new and different academic activities. It was also noted that there was no correlation between willing-less to participate in accelerative type programs and actual ability level.[31] Even when gifted adolescent females are offered the option of taking part in a subject-matter acceleration program in mathematics which simply involves being in accelerated classes in one specific subject area, girls are less likely to take part in these activities.[32]

Fox has suggested that willingness to participate in subject-matter acceleration may be a function of a sex-by-subject-area interaction.[33] In fact, it may be a three-way interaction of sex, age, and subject area. The suggestion that sex and subject matter interact is based on the observation that greater numbers of boys elect to take optional mathematics courses, that few girls expressed an interest in participating in the SMPY program at Johns Hopkins, and that data from the Advanced Placement Program show that participation by females in nonmathematical or nonscience related programs is far greater than participation in the mathematics and science programs. Males also outnumber females in mathematics and science advanced placement programs. That age may also be an interacting variable influencing the receptivity of females to accelerative programs is suggested by the studies of children who enter school early. In most of these studies girls have outnumbered boys, and yet the programs have been highly successful with positive intellectual and social adjustments.[34] It would seem that if girls become actively involved in accelerative programs at an age where social pressures are minimal and are not forced to be separated from established peer groups in adolescence, the chances of positive and greater involvement are increased. Quite obviously, these observations are based largely on observations of female reactions to mathematics and must be cautiously interpreted. Fear of social rejection may not be as big a factor in accelerative programs in language arts or art or music. The literature gives us no evidence that similar feelings might influence these areas. Further research in comparing the differential effects of acceleration on boys and girls in other subject or talent areas is needed. Furthermore, these studies do not investigate the achievement of students, but rather their willingness to participate and their attitudes toward the program.

The research on other administrative program possibilities does not allow one to draw any conclusions about their sociological or affective effects on gifted or talented females. Flesher and Pressey did not find early admission to college to inhibit the academic success of females,[35] however little data is available regarding the willingness of gifted females to participate in such programs.[36] Enrichment programs as a general class of programs have not been systematically studied to yield evidence of their effects on females, nor have mentor programs, internship programs, or independent study programs. Further research on all of these programs is needed before any firm conclusions can be drawn about the gifted student and interactions of age, subject area, type of program, and sex.

Other variables also seem to be influential in the willingness of young adolescent girls to take part in accelerative mathematics classes. If those classes take place during the regular school day, females are more likely to attend than if those classes are held on Saturday. Girls are also more likely to achieve on a par with boys if the classes are predominantly female and taught by women.[37] These differences reflected here are quite likely to be a result of cultural biases. The identity with other gifted females in the classroom probably serves to make the gifted girl feel much less "different" or "abnormal." Certainly, math and science classes would seem to be the most likely classes to be impacted by these variables since they are the areas which are generally regarded as part of the male domain.

In planning for other types of classes or programs, however, these observations made about math and science may provide some useful guidelines for consideration. For example, are the most effective mentor relationships based on a consideration of the sex of the mentor? Are the gifted females in internships where there are more females in nonprofessional subordinate roles than in leadership or professional roles? What impact does this have on her goals? Answers to these questions are not known at this time and may depend on many cultural factors which may or may not change over the next ten years. As Fox has suggested, the purpose of these observations is not to guide in the construction of gifted programs which will reinforce existing stereotypes, but rather to guide in the construction of programs which will attend to the existing values, needs, and interests of females and work to broaden those values, needs, and interests within nonthreatening structures.[38]

The curriculum itself must, of course, be considered in the planning of programs for gifted females. Several suggestions relating to the differences noted in abilities and personality are given below:

1. Provide activities which require females to practice visual-spatial problem-solving from a young age.
2. Provide role models of gifted women engaging in successful problem-solving activities.
3. Provide activities which teach gifted girls the impact they can have on their own destinies, i.e., help them develop an internal locus of control.
4. Provide opportunities for gifted females to interact with successful, attractive, feminine role models in a variety of professions.
5. Provide activities which encourage women to establish their own personal goals.
6. Set equivalent standards and criteria for reinforcement for males and females.

In conjunction with providing for the academic and social need of the gifted females as discussed previously, it is important to consider the counseling needs of this group. The more obvious components of a satisfactory counseling program for gifted females include exposure to a wide variety of career options, provision of models of women in varied careers and professions, consideration of alternative learning programs

506

which allow the girl to develop intellectually while not sacrificing social development, and encouragement of career aspirations which may be nontraditional. However, there are more subtle components of a counseling program which may have a significant impact on the gifted female. One of these elements of many counseling programs which has the potential for biasing the choices of females is the testing of interests. Many interest inventories contain considerable test bias and restrict the range of career options for women. Interest inventories which have not been sex-balanced (constructed to provide item pools which reflect activities and experiences equally familiar and attractive to males and females) may tend to have a negative, limiting effect on the career choices of young women and discourage by omission interests which might have been viable career options. Achievement or aptitude tests should also be examined for potential stereotyping through the role models presented or possible discrimination as a result of types of problems presented.

Other counseling activities such as academic program planning should not be neglected in considering the needs of gifted and talented women. There is some evidence that counselors have not always been supportive of programs which could be beneficial to this group.[39]

One final area in which counselors may have an impact in encouraging gifted and talented women is through family advising, teacher contacts, and individual counseling. Encouragement from parents, female role models, teachers, and peers have been shown to be factors influencing creative women mathematicians and women who have achieved doctorates.[40] The counselor should be prepared to advise parents of gifted children of their role in encouraging their daughters to pursue development of their talents, to seek out and provide contacts with appropriate female role models, and to encourage teachers to view all students as equally competent, regardless of sex and subject area. In short, counselors should attempt to provide opportunities for the gifted and talented female to see a wide variety of options for career and lifestyle and encourage her choices regardless of the sex-role stereotyping of those choices. Through the efforts of all of those around the gifted and talented female, perhaps the barriers to the success and achievements can be broken down. Certainly, society stands to gain from the contribution of this largely untapped resource.

References

[1]Galton, Francis. *Hereditary Genius* (London: Macmillan, 1869); James M. Cattell, "A Statistical Study of American Men of Science," *Science*, 24 (1906), 732–42; *The Creative Process*, ed., Brewster Ghiselin (New York: Mentor, 1952); Anne Roe, *The Making of a Scientist* (New York: Dodd, Mead, 1952); Terman, Lewis and Oden, Melita, *Genetic Study of Genius*, Vol. 5. *The Gifted Group at Mid-Life* (Stanford, CA: Stanford University Press, 1959); Barron, Frank. *Creativity and Psychological Health* (Princeton,

NJ: Van Nostrand, 1963); MacKinnon, Donald N. "The Study of Creative Persons: A Method and Some Results," in *Creativity and Learning,* ed. J. Kagan (Boston: Beacon Press, 1967) pp. 20–35.

[2]Terman, Lewis M. et al. *Genetic Studies of Genius:* Vol. I–V (Stanford, CA: Stanford University Press, 1925, 1926, 1930, 1947, 1959).

[3]Goertzel, Victor and Goertzel, Mildred G. *Cradles of Eminence* (Boston: Little, Brown, 1962).

[4]Goertzel, Victor, Goertzel, Mildred G., and Goertzel, Ted G. *300 Eminence Personalities* (San Francisco: Jossey-Bass, 1978).

[5]Maccoby, Eleanor E. and Jacklin, Carol. *The Psychology of Sex Differences* (Stanford, CA: Stanford University Press, 1974), p. 68.

[6]Fox, Lynn H. "Sex Differences: Implications for Program Planning for the Academically Gifted." Paper presented at the Lewis M. Terman Memorial Symposium on Intellectual Talent, Baltimore, MD, November, 1975, p. 3.

[7]Terman, op. cit.; Hitchfield, E. M. *In Search of Promise* (London: Longman Group Limited, 1973); McGinn, Peter V. "Verbally Gifted Youth: Selection and Description," in Intellectual Talent: *Research and Development,* ed. Daniel P. Keating (Baltimore, MD: The Johns Hopkins University Press, 1976), pp. 160–182.

[8]Maccoby and Jacklin, op. cit., p. 133; Maccoby, Eleanor E. "Women's Intellect," in the *Potential of Women,* ed. Farber, S. M. and Wilson, R. H. L. (New York: McGraw-Hill Book Company, 1963) pp. 24–39.

[9]Fox, op. cit., pp. 5–6.

[10]Maccoby and Jacklin, op. cit.

[11]Norfleet, Mary Ann Warburton. "Personality Characteristics of Achieving and Underachieving High Ability Senior Women," *Personal and Guidance Journal* 46 (1968), 976–980.

[12]Faunce, Patricia S. "Personality Characteristics and Vocational Interests Related to the College Persistence of Academically Gifted Women," *Journal of Counseling Psychology* 15 (1968), 31–40.

[13]Horner, Matina S. "Femininity and Successful Achievement: Basic Inconsistency," in *Feminine Personality and Conflict,* eds. J. M. Bardwick, et al. (Belmont, CA: Brooks Cole Publishing Company, 1970), pp. 45–74.

[14]Horner, Matina S. "Toward an Understanding of Achievement-Related Conflicts in Women," *Journal of Social Issues* 28 (1972), 157–175.

[15]Maccoby and Jacklin, op. cit., p. 350.

[16]Faunce, op. cit.; Helson, Ravenna. "Women Mathematicians and the Creative Personality," *Journal of Consulting and Clinical Psychology* 36 (1971), 210–220; Norfleet, op. cit.

[17]Schaefer, Charles E. "A Psychological Study of 10 Exceptionally Creative Adolescent Girls," *Exceptional Children* 36 (1970) 431–441; Werner, Emmy E. and Backtold, Louise M. "Personality Factors of Gifted Boys and Girls in Middle Childhood and Adolescence," *Psychology in the Schools* 2 (1969), 177–182.

[18]Schaefer, op. cit.

[19]Fox, Lynn H. "Identification and Program Planning: Models and Methods," in *Intellectual Talent: Research and Development*, ed. Daniel P. Keating (Baltimore, MD: The Johns Hopkins University Press, 1976) 32–54.

[20]Rutherford, Millicent. "Reinforced Concrete," *English Journal* 63 (1974), 25–33.

[21]B. U'Ren, Marjorie. "The Image of Women in Textbooks," *Women in a Sexist Society*, ed. Vivian Gornick and Barbara K. Moran (New York: Signet, 1972) 318–328.

[22]Tittle, Carol K., McCarthy, Karen, and Stickler, Janet Faggen. *Women in Educational Testing* (Princeton, NJ: Educational Testing Service, 1974).

[23]Walberg, Herbert J. "Physics, Femininity and Creativity," *Developmental Psychology* 1 (1969) 47–54; James J. Gallagher, Mary Jane Aschner, and William Jenne, *Thinking of Gifted Children in Classroom Interaction*, Council for Exceptional Children Research Monograph B5. (Arlington, VA: Council for Exceptional Children, 1967).

[24]Walberg, op. cit.; G. A. Milton, "Sex Differences in Problem Solving as a Function of Role Appropriateness of the Problem Content," *Psychological Reports* 5 (1959), 705–708.

[25]Ward, Virgil S. "Program Organization and Implementation," in *Psychology and Education of the Gifted*, ed. W. S. Barbe (New York: Appleton-Century Crofts, 1965), pp. 382–389; Pressey, Sidney L. "A New Look at 'Acceleration,' " in *Psychology and Education of the Gifted*, ed. W. S. Barbe (New York: Appleton-Century-Crofts, 1965) pp. 413–448; Birch, Jack W. "Early School Achievement for Mentally Advanced Children," *Exceptional Children* 21 (1954), 84–87; Sklarsky, Judie B. and Baxter, Merle R. "Science Study with a Community Accent," *Elementary School Journal* 61 (1961), 301–307; Ryder, Virginia P. "A Docent Program in Science for Gifted Elementary Pupils," *Exceptional Children* 38 (1972), 629–631.

[26]Witty, Paul A. and Wilkins, Leroy W. "The Status of Acceleration on Grade Skipping as an Administrative Practice," in *Psychology and Education of the Gifted*, ed. W. S. Barbe (New York: Appleton-Century-Crofts, 1965), pp. 390–413; Gallagher, James J. *Teaching the Gifted Child* 2nd ed. (Boston: Allyn and Bacon, 1975); Gallagher, James J. *Research Summary on Gifted Education* (Springfield, IL: Office of the Superintendent of Public Instruction, 1966).

[27]Passow, Harry A. "Enrichment of Education for the Gifted," in *Education for the Gifted*, Fifty-Seventh Yearbook of the National Society for the Study of Education, Part II (Chicago: University of Chicago Press, 1958), p. 201.

[28]Passow, A. Harry. et al., *Planning for Talented Youth*, (New York: Bureau of Publications, Teacher's College, Columbia University, 1958), p. 35.

[29]Fox, Lynn H. "Sex Differences: Implications for Program Planning for the Academically Gifted." Paper presented at the Lewis M. Terman

Memorial Symposium on Intellectual Talent, Baltimore, MD, November, 1975, p. 3.

[30]Fox, Lynn H. "Career Interests in Mathematical Acceleration for Girls." Paper presented at the 1975 Annual Meeting of the American Psychological Association. Chicago, IL. (August, 1975).

[31]Fox, Lynn H. "Facilitating the Educational Development of Mathematically Precocious Youth," in J. C. Stanley, D. P. Keating, and L. H. Fox (eds), *Mathematical Talent: Discovery, Description, and Development* (Baltimore, MD: The Johns Hopkins University Press, 1974) pp. 47–69.

[32]Fox, Lynn H. "Sex Differences: Implications for Program Planning for the Academically Gifted," op. cit.

[33]Ibid.

[34]Worchester, Dean A. *The Education of Children of Above-Average Mentality* (Lincoln, NE: University of Nebraska Press, 1956); Joseph L. Braga, "Early Admission as Evidence," *Elementary School Journal* 72 (1972), 35–46; Reynolds, Maynard, Buck, John, and Tuseth, A. "Review of Research on Early Admission," in *Early Admission for Mentally Advanced Children,* ed. M. Reynolds (Reston, VA: Council for Exceptional Children, 1962); Witty and Wilkins, op. cit.

[35]Flesher, M. and Pressey, Sidney L. "War-Time Accelerates Ten Years After," *Journal of Educational Psychology* 46 (1955), 228–238.

[36]Fox, op. cit.

[37]Flesher and Pressey, op. cit.

[38]Fox, op. cit.

[39]Hanson, Gary R. and Rayman, Jack. "Validity of Sex-Balanced Interest Inventories." Paper presented at the annual meeting of the American Educational Research Association, San Francisco, CA (April, 1976).

[40]Helson, Ravenna, "Generality of Sex Differences in Creative Style," *Journal of Personality* 36 (1968), pp. 33–48; Helen S. Astin, *The Woman Doctorate in America* (New York: Russell Sage Foundation, 1969); Casserly, Pauline L. "An Assessment of Factors Affecting Female Participation in Advanced Placement Programs in Mathematics, Chemistry, and Physics." Report of National Science Foundation Grant, GY-11325 (1975).

Index

514